GOVERNING KNOWLEDGE COMMONS

Governing Knowledge Commons

Edited by
Brett M. Frischmann
Michael J. Madison
Katherine J. Strandburg

OXFORD
UNIVERSITY PRESS

Oxford University Press is a department of the University of Oxford. It furthers the University's objective of excellence in research, scholarship, and education by publishing worldwide.

Oxford   New York
Auckland   Cape Town   Dar es Salaam   Hong Kong   Karachi   Kuala Lumpur   Madrid   Melbourne
Mexico City   Nairobi   New Delhi   Shanghai   Taipei   Toronto

With offices in

Argentina   Austria   Brazil   Chile   Czech Republic   France   Greece   Guatemala   Hungary
Italy   Japan   Poland   Portugal   Singapore   South Korea   Switzerland   Thailand
Turkey   Ukraine   Vietnam

Oxford is a registered trademark of Oxford University Press in the UK and certain other countries.

Published in the United States of America by
Oxford University Press
198 Madison Avenue, New York, NY 10016

Library of Congress Cataloging-in-Publication Data

Governing knowledge commons / edited by Brett M. Frischmann, Michael J. Madison, Katherine J. Strandburg.
    pages cm.
    Includes bibliographical references and index.
    ISBN 978-0-19-997203-6 (hardback : alk. paper)
    ISBN 978-0-19-022582-7 (paperback : alk. paper)
1. Information commons. 2. Knowledge management. 3. Information networks. 4. Communities. I. Frischmann, Brett M., editor of compilation. II. Madison, Michael J., 1961- editor of compilation. III. Strandburg, Katherine Jo, 1957- editor of compilation.
    ZA3270.G68 2014
    001—dc23

                                                                            2014004258

9 8 7 6 5 4 3 2 1

Printed in the United States of America on acid-free paper

Note to Readers

This publication is designed to provide accurate and authoritative information in regard to the subject matter covered. It is based upon sources believed to be accurate and reliable and is intended to be current as of the time it was written. It is sold with the understanding that the publisher is not engaged in rendering legal, accounting, or other professional services. If legal advice or other expert assistance is required, the services of a competent professional person should be sought. Also, to confirm that the information has not been affected or changed by recent developments, traditional legal research techniques should be used, including checking primary sources where appropriate.

*(Based on the Declaration of Principles jointly adopted by a Committee of the
American Bar Association and a Committee of Publishers and Associations.)*

About the Editors

Brett M. Frischmann is Professor of Law and Director of the Intellectual Property and Information Law Program at Benjamin N. Cardozo School of Law, Yeshiva University. He is the author of *Infrastructure: The Social Value of Shared Resources* (Oxford, 2012), which won the 2013 PROSE Book Award for the best book in law and legal studies. He is co-author of *Cyberlaw: Problems of Policy and Jurisprudence in the Information Age* (4th edition, 2011).

Michael J. Madison is Professor of Law and Faculty Director of the Innovation Practice Institute at the University of Pittsburgh. He teaches and writes about information law, intellectual property law, contracts and commercial law, and property law. He is co-author of *The Law of Intellectual Property* (4th edition, 2013).

Katherine J. Strandburg is Alfred B. Engelberg Professor of Law and a Faculty Director of the Engelberg Center on Innovation Law and Policy at New York University. She studies intellectual property law, especially at its intersections with user and commons-based innovation, and information privacy law. She also regularly authors amicus briefs on these topics.

Contents

Introduction

Brett M. Frischmann, Michael J. Madison, and Katherine J. Strandburg*

> The economics of the new commons is still in its infancy. It is too soon to be confident about its hypotheses. But it may yet prove a useful way of thinking about problems, such as managing the internet, intellectual property or international pollution, on which policymakers need all the help they can get.[1]

This book seeks to contribute to evidence-based policy making about innovation and creative production. Critics rightly complain that anecdote, ideology, wishful thinking, and brute political influence, more than empirical understanding, often drive intellectual property policy making. We are concerned that recent enthusiasm about knowledge commons approaches (which we share) may be open to the same critique. Rather than embracing knowledge commons indiscriminately, policy making should be based on more evidence and deeper understanding of what makes them tick.

We embrace the analogy between the cultural environment and the natural environment (Boyle 2008; Frischmann 2007) in order to explore the proposition that just as natural resources often are governed by commons, rather than being managed as either public or private property, the production and sharing of knowledge often is sustained by commons governance. Scholars of the natural environment have developed successful methods for

---

* Brett M. Frischmann is Professor of Law and Director of the Intellectual Property and Information Law Program at the Benjamin N. Cardozo School of Law, Yeshiva University, New York, New York, USA. Michael J. Madison is Professor of Law and Faculty Director of the Innovation Practice Institute at the University of Pittsburgh School of Law, Pittsburgh, Pennsylvania, USA. Katherine J. Strandburg is the Alfred B. Engelberg Professor of Law and a Faculty Director of the Engelberg Center for Innovation Law and Policy at the New York University School of Law, New York, New York, USA. Each is also a member of the Affiliated Faculty of the Vincent and Elinor Ostrom Workshop in Political Theory and Policy Analysis.

1 *Commons Sense*, THE ECONOMIST (July 31, 2008), at 76, http://www.economist.com/node/11848182.

studying commons arrangements systematically and in detail. We borrow from them and propose a framework for studying knowledge commons that begins with the Institutional Analysis and Development (IAD) framework developed and used by Elinor Ostrom and others and adapts it to the unique attributes of knowledge and information.

This book describes the framework, in Chapter 1 and then includes case studies, reactions, and comments from a group of interdisciplinary researchers. The purpose of this book is to begin the careful, detailed exploration of how knowledge commons function, the place they occupy in the cultural environment, the specific benefits they offer, the costs and risks they create, and their relationships to other institutional structures. Eleven case studies of knowledge commons are the heart of the book. The case study authors come from many different research traditions. The cases vary across a broad range of cultural and scientific domains and historical and contemporary practice. This volume brings these studies together as an initial demonstration of the value of studying knowledge commons carefully, in a comparative fashion, in order to develop evidence of the details of their purposes and operations. We hope that in time, empirical study of knowledge commons will show that, properly understood, they may be harnessed and even designed for broad public benefit Our concluding chapter highlights the framework's success in bringing forward commonalities and differences between knowledge commons, while recognizing that producing generalizable understanding will require many more studies.

As law professors, we undertook this project initially out of interest in the functioning of systems of intellectual property rights—patent, copyright, and related bodies of law. Whether we look at the economics of the global knowledge economy or at the potential for collaboration and innovation unleashed by the computer and network revolutions of the last thirty years, the impulse to examine innovation institutions and behaviors is immediate. Wikipedia is a fascinating thing. The questions that it raises include not only "why do people contribute to Wikipedia?" but also "in cultural, economic, and legal terms, how does Wikipedia function today and how will it evolve in the future?" Linux is a widely used and commercially successful example of an open source computer program. Why have it and other open source programs succeeded, institutionally and organizationally? Why have some open source computer programs not thrived? Similarly broad questions can and should be directed to collaborative enterprises in science, technology, the arts, government, and beyond.

Traditionally, when intellectual property law scholarship examined institutions for promoting innovation and creativity, it divided the world into two, default perspectives: innovation systems organized around markets, supported by intellectual property rights directed to exclusivity and ownership, and innovation systems organized around governments, which intervene in markets (or avoid markets) in various ways to sponsor and subsidize innovation. A third approach, commons-based *sharing* of knowledge and information resources to produce innovation and creativity, is increasingly acknowledged and celebrated, as suggested by the article in *The Economist* magazine quoted above. But writing about the commons approach is often conceptual or political, using the idea of commons as a rhetorical device to oppose the expansion of intellectual property protection (Boyle 2008; Hyde 2010). Empirical study of norm- and custom-based innovation communities often is developed in opposition to (and therefore in reliance on) market-based presumptions of the need for exclusivity, substituting norm-based exclusivity for legal-defined intellectual property (Raustiala & Sprigman 2012).

One of our goals here is to stake out knowledge commons as an independent, affirmative means for producing innovation and creativity and an important domain for research. In our view, commons are neither wholly independent of nor opposed to markets based on exclusive rights (whether formal or informal), nor are they subordinate to them.

As noted, our approach is inspired by the pathbreaking research of the late Elinor Ostrom, who was awarded the Nobel Prize in Economic Sciences in 2009 for her lifetime of research into the functioning of commons governance, especially in the natural resources context. Ostrom was far from the first scholar to examine resource systems and governance using tools of comparative institutional analysis. But her work and that of her collaborators and successors highlighted commons as an object of study in a way that no scholar had done before. Ostrom also approached the topic with an extraordinary humility and disciplinary generosity, recognizing that understanding this complex area could only be achieved through the contributions of researchers from many fields, aligned via shared methods. Her impact was magnified by her emphasis on a shared research framework accessible to and usable by numerous disciplines. We have tried to extend both the spirit and style of Ostrom's work to our own.

Toward the end of Ostrom's career, she and her colleagues recognized the emerging importance of knowledge commons as an area for sustained research and began to apply the IAD framework to them (Ostrom & Hess 2007; Hess 2012). In 2010 we developed a research framework specifically tailored to the properties that distinguish knowledge and information from natural resources (Madison, Frischmann, & Strandburg 2010). That framework, with some elaborations and clarifications, follows this introduction as Chapter 1 of this book.

The balance of the book is organized as follows.

Chapter 1 lays out our research framework in detail, including its origins in Ostrom's work on commons, the background assumptions of scholarship on intellectual property rights and theories, and the template for organizing research inquiries in particular case studies. It explains in more detail what we mean by knowledge commons, why knowledge commons deserve systematic study, and why we were motivated to write this book. Chapter 1 provides a thorough explanation of our proposed framework that we hope will encourage and enable others to use and improve upon it in their own studies of knowledge commons.

Chapters 2 and 3 situate the study of knowledge commons within a broader context. In Chapter 2, Dan Cole relates the knowledge commons project to Elinor Ostrom's work on natural resource commons, illustrating points of continuity and points of distinction.

Cole offers encouragement and caution to scholars seeking to use Ostrom's work as a starting point for studying knowledge commons. He encourages those seeking "conceptual, analytical, and methodological guidance," arguing that Ostrom's work can provide a foundation for "improv[ing] understanding of information and information flows under alternative institutional arrangements," "diagnos[ing] problems in existing institutional arrangements," and even "predict[ing] outcomes under alternative institutional arrangements." He cautions, however, that those looking to Ostrom's work for normative guidance as to the proper structure of intellectual property law are "bound to be disappointed (or dishonest)" for two reasons: First, Ostrom's work teaches that there are "no panaceas." Second, researchers necessarily choose metrics for assessing commons outcomes. Whereas long-run sustainability is a widely accepted goal for natural resource commons, Cole suggests that outcome metrics for knowledge commons are likely to be much more contested.

In Chapter 3, Yochai Benkler provides a conceptual map for understanding the range of different types of commons that are important to society and deserve systematic study. He argues that there are important differences between the institutional arrangements studied by Ostrom and colleagues, in which a "defined set of claimants" share resources in a self-governing arrangement, and public domain or open access commons, which provide "freedom-to-operate under symmetric constraints, available to an open, or undefined, class of users." Benkler reminds us that knowledge commons arrangements are layered on top of and dependent upon substantial resource sets governed either as public domain commons or through private property arrangements.

Chapters 4, 5, and 6 apply the knowledge commons research framework to commons arrangements for scientific research, where tradition and custom teach that formal intellectual property rights are particularly unlikely to play key roles in institutional governance, but where the knowledge commons research framework nonetheless reveals meaningful structure and governance of knowledge sharing. In Chapter 4, Jorge Contreras targets the genomics research collaborative that constituted the Human Genome Project. Geertrui Van Overwalle follows that chapter with a comment that notes the global context of research on genomic commons, illustrating that commons in general have important international and comparative dimensions. In Chapter 5, Katherine Strandburg, Brett Frischmann, and Can Cui delve into a network of medical researchers and patient advocacy groups titled the Rare Diseases Clinical Research Network, and the related Urea Cycle Disorders Consortium. In Chapter 6, Michael Madison describes a citizen science project, called Galaxy Zoo, that pairs professional astronomers with amateurs.

Chapters 7 and 8 involve commons cases situated in the context of information and communications technologies (sometimes abbreviated ICTs). In Chapter 7, Charles Schweik presents the results of a comparative analysis of open source software development communities. In Chapter 8, Mayo Fuster Morell reports a study of online creation communities (OCCs) such as the photosharing site, Flickr, used for sharing creative content supplied by individuals.

Chapters 9, 10, and 11 involve commons cases that highlight the role of commons governance as it intersects with or overlaps with other governance institutions directed to knowledge production. In Chapter 9, Sonali Shah and Cyrus Mody describe entrepreneurship, and particularly entrepreneurship by technology users, using the knowledge commons perspective and borrowing examples from such diverse domains as windsurfing and probe microscopy. In Chapter 10, Peter Meyer reviews the history of the development of the fixed-wing airplane as an industrial invention, and its associated industries, as the product of open innovation communities that operated in the shadow of patent law. In Chapter 11, Laura Murray describes the history of newspapers with specific attention to historical norms that balanced proprietary control and sharing in journalism.

Chapters 12, 13, and 14 push the knowledge commons research framework in directions that illustrate its utility in contexts far from those the term immediately brings to mind. In Chapter 12, S. Tina Piper studies the history collaborative invention communities in the Canadian military. In Chapter 13, David Fagundes delves into the world of roller derby, an amateur sporting community that is governed almost entirely by informal norms. In Chapter 14, Brigham Daniels subjects the U.S. Congress to study as a case of commons governance in its production of legislation.

As the conclusion to this book points out in greater detail, the first and perhaps most important takeaway from this book is borrowed from a line sometimes attributed to Mark Twain. Asked if he believed in infant baptism, Twain allegedly replied, "Believe it? I've seen it done!" And so with the study of knowledge commons. An impressive collection of extremely thoughtful scholars has dissected a broad range of cases of commons in ways that usefully illuminate the workings of each case and, even more important, set the stage for continued comparative analysis of their results. The power and future of commons lies not just in the politics and rhetoric of commons but also in empirical understanding of when and how knowledge commons governance works—and when it doesn't.

We conclude this introduction by pointing out that our collaboration in producing this work, and in collaborating with the other contributors, is itself best described as a knowledge commons. None of this research would be possible without extraordinary sharing of time, expertise, interest, and ideas. The future of this project depends on continuing that collaboration and expanding it. We hope that reading it inspires you to consider giving our framework a try and encourage you to reach out to us with your ideas and insights for follow-on work.

Acknowledgments

The collaboration that underlies this book began in conversations among the editors about cultural commons and knowledge commons in 2006 and 2007. It took root with the publication of Madison, Frischmann, & Strandburg (2010) and with responses to that article from a group of generous scholars (Ostrom 2010; Merges 2010; Gordon 2010; Solum 2010; Macey 2010; Eggertson 2010). It continued in September 2011 as a number of researchers from around the world gathered at the Engelberg Center for Innovation Law and Policy at New York University School of Law for a workshop titled "Convening Cultural Commons." Many of the chapters in this volume were shared in early form in that setting. As editors of this volume and participants in an emerging global enterprise for the study of knowledge commons, we are grateful for the openness with which the work has been received so far and look forward to more and continuing discussion of this important topic.

Professor Strandburg acknowledges the generous support of the Filomen D'Agostino and Max E. Greenberg Research Fund.

References

James Boyle, The Public Domain: Enclosing the Commons of the Mind (Yale University Press 2008)

Commons Sense, The Economist (July 31, 2008), at 76, http://www.economist.com/node/11848182.

Thráinn Eggertsson, *Response: Mapping Social Technologies in the Cultural Commons*, 95 Cornell L. Rev. 711 (2010).

Brett M. Frischmann, *Cultural Environmentalism and the Wealth of Networks*, 74 U. Chi. L. Rev. 1083 (2007).

Wendy J. Gordon, *Response: Discipline and Nourish: On Constructing Commons*, 95 Cornell L. Rev. 733 (2010).

Charlotte Hess, *Constructing a New Research Agenda for Cultural Commons*, in Cultural Commons: A New Perspective on the Production and Evolution of Cultures 19 (Enrico Bertacchini et al. eds., Edward Elgar Publishing 2012).

Lewis Hyde, Common as Air: Revolution, Art, and Ownership (Farrar, Straus and Giroux 2010).

Gregg P. Macey, *Response: Cooperative Institutions in Cultural Commons*, 95 Cornell L. Rev. 757 (2010).

Michael J. Madison, Brett M. Frischmann, & Katherine J. Strandburg, *Constructing Commons in the Cultural Environment*, 95 Cornell L. Rev. 657 (2010).

Robert P. Merges, *Response: Individual Creators in the Cultural Commons*, 95 Cornell L. Rev. 793 (2010).

Elinor Ostrom, *Response: The Institutional Analysis and Development Framework and the Commons*, 95 Cornell L. Rev. 807 (2010).

Elinor Ostrom & Charlotte Hess, *A Framework for Analyzing the Knowledge Commons*, in Understanding Knowledge as a Commons: From Theory to Practice (Charlotte Hess & Elinor Ostrom eds., MIT Press 2007).

Kal Raustiala & Christopher Sprigman, The Knockoff Economy: How Imitation Sparks Innovation (Oxford University Press 2012).

Lawrence B. Solum, *Response: Questioning Cultural Commons*, 95 Cornell L. Rev. 817 (2010).

1 Governing Knowledge Commons

Brett M. Frischmann, Michael J. Madison, and
Katherine J. Strandburg*

I. Introduction

This chapter sets out the knowledge commons framework that forms the foundation for
the case study chapters that follow (Madison, Frischmann, & Strandburg 2010a). The
framework builds on the Institutional Analysis and Development (IAD) approach pioneered by Elinor Ostrom and her collaborators for studying commons arrangements in
the natural environment (Ostrom 1990). By "knowledge commons" we refer broadly to
commons arrangements for overcoming various social dilemmas associated with sharing
and producing information, innovation, and creative works (Ostrom & Hess 2006).[1] This

---

* Brett M. Frischmann is Professor of Law and Director of the Intellectual Property and Information Law
Program at the Benjamin N. Cardozo School of Law, Yeshiva University, New York, New York, USA. Michael
J. Madison is Professor of Law and Faculty Director of the Innovation Practice Institute at the University of
Pittsburgh School of Law, Pittsburgh, Pennsylvania, USA. Katherine J. Strandburg is the Alfred B. Engelberg
Professor of Law and a Faculty Director of the Engelberg Center for Innovation Law and Policy at the New York
University School of Law, New York, New York, USA. Each is also a member of the Affiliated Faculty of the
Vincent and Elinor Ostrom Workshop in Political Theory and Policy Analysis.
[1] In the paper on which this chapter is based (Madison, Frischmann, & Strandburg 2010a), we referred to these
as *cultural commons*, which we treat as equivalent to knowledge commons, and as *constructed cultural commons*.
Cultural commons has been used recently by some other commons scholars (Enrico Bertacchini et al. 2012; Hess
2012). Our approach is inclusive of theirs but perhaps broader. The term "constructed" refers to the idea, which
we address in more detail below, that the resources in knowledge commons are built by human agency, rather
than found somehow in nature.

book includes case studies of a number of knowledge commons arrangements involving the creation and sharing of a diverse array of knowledge resources, such as scientific data, open source software, news resources for journalism, technological innovations, online knowledge resources such as Wikipedia, congressional legislation, and information used by roller derby participants. Some further examples of the types of arrangements we have in mind are patent pools (such as the Manufacturers Aircraft Association), the Associated Press, certain jamband communities, medieval guilds, and modern research universities. These examples are illustrative and far from exhaustive.

The systematic approach to case study design and analysis provided by the knowledge commons framework is intended not only to structure individual case studies in a useful and productive way but also to make it possible eventually to produce generalizable results. By comparing and aggregating case studies performed according to the knowledge commons framework, it should be possible to inventory the structural similarities and differences between commons in different industries, disciplines, and knowledge domains and to shed light on the underlying contextual reasons for the differences. This structured inquiry will provide a basis for developing theories to explain the emergence, form, and stability of the observed variety of knowledge commons and, eventually, for designing models to explicate and inform institutional design. In addition, an improved understanding of knowledge commons is critical for obtaining a more complete perspective on intellectual property (IP) doctrine and its interactions with other legal and social mechanisms for governing creativity and innovation.

WHAT DO WE MEAN BY KNOWLEDGE COMMONS?

"Knowledge commons" is shorthand. It refers to an approach (commons) to governing the management or production of a particular type of resource (knowledge).

Commons refers to a form of community management or governance. It applies to resources, and involves a group or community of people, but commons does not denote the resources, the community, a place, or a thing. Commons is the institutional arrangement of these elements. "The basic characteristic that distinguishes commons from noncommons is institutionalized sharing of resources among members of a community" (Madison, Frischmann, & Strandburg 2010b: 841). Critically, commons governance is used by a wide variety of communities to manage many different types of resources. Commons governance confronts various obstacles to sustainable sharing and cooperation. Some of those obstacles derive from the nature of the resources and others derive from other factors, such as the nature of the community or external influences. Communities can and often do overcome obstacles through constructed as well as emergent commons.

Knowledge refers to a broad set of intellectual and cultural resources. In prior work, we used the term "cultural environment" to invoke the various cultural, intellectual, scientific, and social resources (and resource systems) that we inherit, use, experience, interact with, change, and pass on to future generations. We used this terminology to convey the broad range of resources we had in mind but have since realized that some readers found it confusing. Here we use the term "knowledge." We emphasize that we cast a wide net and that we group information, science, knowledge, creative works, data, and so on together.

Knowledge commons is thus shorthand for the institutionalized community governance of the sharing and, in some cases, creation, of information, science, knowledge, data, and other types of intellectual and cultural resources.

Some initial illustrations of knowledge commons suggest the variety of institutional arrangements we believe may be usefully studied using the framework described here.

Intellectual property pools. A patent pool is an agreement by two or more patent holders to aggregate and share their patents by cross-licensing (Shapiro 2000). The patents in question typically relate to complementary technologies, where one holder's exercise of patent rights "blocks" a different holder's exercise of related rights. Pooled patents are typically available to all members of the pool and are available to nonmembers on standard licensing terms. A well-known example of an early patent pool in the United States is the Manufacturers Aircraft Association (MAA), which formed in 1917 and encompassed nearly all American aircraft manufacturers. The Wright Company and Curtiss Company held major patents on aircraft technology, but Wright and Curtiss did not hold all relevant patents, and for any given manufacturer, the cost of licensing a single needed patent from a competitor might have made manufacturing an airplane prohibitively expensive. During World War I, the U.S. government needed airplanes at reasonable costs and in a short time. As a result, the government facilitated the implementation of the MAA, a private corporation. The MAA entered into an agreement with airplane manufacturers, through which the manufacturers pooled their patents and their potential claims for exploitation of the patents by rivals and agreed to cross-licensing of the patents to one another on what was, essentially, a royalty-free basis (Dykman 1964; Merges 1996: 1343–46). Largely because of this functioning commons of patented inventions, airplanes were built.

Open source software. The Linux operating system, an alternative to Windows and Mac OS (the Macintosh operating system), was produced and is still maintained by a collaborative of individual programmers, many of whom are volunteers (some are employed in firms, some of which produce and/or support commercial versions of the Linux software). The Linux collaborative is linked loosely by communications technologies, by members' voluntary allegiance to the project, and by the terms of an open source license. Unlike proprietary computer programs, which are distributed to users in object code or executable format only, open source programs such as Linux are made available in source code form so that members of the community may modify their copies and, under the terms of the governing license, publish their modifications for use by others. Members of the community may also volunteer their modifications for inclusion in the standard Linux code base. Each member of the Linux community may use material in the Linux commons and may contribute material back to the Linux commons. Each individual member of the community contributes code to the accumulated archive of the Linux kernel, which is the core of the operating system. The rules governing the use of open source material and contributions to the open source commons are partly formal and partly informal. Formally, the software is governed by copyright law, and its use is managed by the terms of the General Public License. Informally, the integrity of Linux as an identifiable and stable program depends on a thin hierarchy of informal authority, which extends from Linus Torvalds at the top to the body of individual developers at the bottom. The result is an exemplary version of a successful open source software program: a complete, complex, and successful industrial product that is built and maintained not by a traditional, hierarchical, industrial firm, but by a loose-knit community (Kelty 2008; Schweik & English 2012).

Wikipedia. This free, online encyclopedia is widely read and cited. It resembles an open source software project in many respects. Volunteer authors create and edit Wikipedia entries; anyone with Internet access can read and use the contents of Wikipedia. Wikipedia is not the product of unregulated, potentially chaotic, openness. A governance structure exists among "Wikipedians" that modulates the openness of the project and operates as a kind of law (Hoffman & Mehra 2009). For example, not all additions and edits to Wikipedia are automatically added to the site. Moreover, a Creative Commons Attribution-ShareAlike license, the copyright license that governs the contents of Wikipedia, restricts the use of the contents of the site.[2] Wikipedia also has a dispute-resolution system that plays an important role in sustaining the commons. The site is open, but with limits.

The Associated Press. For more than a century, the Associated Press (AP) has been the leading American wire service for newspapers (Reporters of the Associated Press 2007). It offers a compelling example of a knowledge commons that is not grounded in formal IP rights. As factual material, the news itself cannot be copyrighted (though there is an important but narrow "hot news misappropriation" tort rule (Gordon 2009: 2421–23)). Local newspapers could not afford to cover all of the stories that their readers wanted to read, yet the ease with which news stories can be appropriated served as a disincentive to invest in reporting—a classic free-rider dilemma. The solution was a not-for-profit cooperative, owned by the participant news organizations, which partnered originally with Western Union (Shmanske 1986). Cooperative members could both upload material that they originated locally to the wire service and download material that other members produced from the wire service. Local papers were able to carry AP reports on national and international news that they otherwise could not have afforded to produce. Without discounting allegations that the AP's content was biased politically and that it behaved

---

[2] See Wikipedia: Licensing update, at http://en.wikipedia.org/wiki/Wikipedia:Licensing_update.

monopolistically, considerations that highlight the need to view commons with a critical eye, the AP itself operated as a structured commons managed by its members.

Jamband fan communities. Musical groups known as jambands "jam," or improvise heavily, during live performances. Beginning with fans of the best-known jamband, the Grateful Dead, jamband fan communities have long been encouraged by the artists themselves to produce and share their own concert recordings. These recordings initially were shared via physical media and now are shared using online archives (organized via the website and organization etree.org). The bands encourage this sharing, provided that the fans comply with informal rules that are set by the bands and honored and policed by the fan communities themselves (Schultz 2006). For example, as Schultz describes in his detailed case study of the jamband phenomenon, fan communities generally undertake not to interfere with commercial exploitation of the bands' own concert recordings (Schultz 2006, 675–76). Commons governance of jamband recordings is structured not merely by fan expectations that norms will be honored but also by file sharing and archiving technologies that reinforce the commercial/noncommercial distinction, by intermediary institutions that host jamband archives, and by the bands, which cooperate with and nurture their fan communities (Schultz 2006: 679–80).

At first glance, these examples may appear to be disparate and unrelated. Yet we believe that a systematic, comprehensive, and theoretically informed research framework offers significant potential to produce generalizable insights into these commons phenomena. Comparative institutional investigation of knowledge commons is relevant to our understanding of social ordering and institutional governance generally. It should also produce insights important to intellectual property law. The conventional view of intellectual property is that resource production and consumption are (and ought to be) characterized primarily by entitlements to individual resource units, held individually and allocated via market mechanisms (Merges 1996: 4–7). To the extent that those market mechanisms are inadequate to optimize the welfare of society, or, in other words, in the event of market failure, government intervention may be appropriate. Intellectual property rights traditionally are justified on precisely this basis (Lemley 2005: 1073). Creative works and new inventions are characterized as public goods, whose intangibility prevents their originators from excluding potential users and thus recouping their investments via sales (Lemley 2005: 1050–55). Copyright and patent laws create artificial but legally sanctioned forms of exclusion, restoring a measure of market control to creators and innovators. Where propertization is insufficient, government subsidy is seen as the primary alternative. Communal and collectivist institutions, particularly those that blend informal normative structures with formal governance rules, are generally regarded as exceptional and dependent upon preexisting property entitlements (Rose 2008: 432–28).

The research framework that we describe below offers a method for assessing the validity of this property-focused narrative. We anticipate that study of a large number of cases using the framework, ranging broadly across different knowledge and cultural contexts, is likely to demonstrate that successful knowledge production and management occurs within a wide variety of formal and informal institutional arrangements. We suspect that the logical and normative priority assigned to proprietary rights and government intervention will turn out to be misplaced.

II. The Backdrop: Intellectual Property, Free Riding, Commons, and the Need for Empirical Study of Knowledge Commons

This part begins with a brief discussion of the free-rider allegory that provides the traditional foundation for intellectual property law and theory. It describes the limitations of the free-rider paradigm and of intellectual property as a panacean approach to knowledge production. It then notes the rise of community production as an alternative model for knowledge production and expresses concern that, in some circles, community production may be emerging as an alternative panacean approach. It argues that policy and theory aimed at resolving the complex issue of how best to produce and manage intellectual resources should be grounded in a more detailed and nuanced empirical understanding.

A. FUNCTIONALIST INTELLECTUAL PROPERTY THEORY AND ITS LIMITS

Intellectual property law scholarship typically has viewed invention, creative expression, innovation, and related or subsidiary activities (such as research and development) as a special set of practices for which extra encouragement is warranted. Despite considerable variation and nuance, these activities all can be understood to present the same core problem. The "outputs" from these activities—whether described as information, expression, invention, innovation, research, ideas, or otherwise—are public goods. They are naturally nonrivalrous or nondepletable, meaning that consumption of the good does not deplete the amount available to other users, and nonexcludable, meaning that knowledge outputs are not naturally defined by boundaries that permit cheap exclusion of users (Frischmann 2012: 24–30, 261–68; Frischmann & Lemley 2007: 272–273; Cornes & Sandler 1996: 40–43). As a result, the production of such resources faces a well-known supply-side problem, common to public goods. The inability to (cheaply) exclude competitors and nonpaying consumers (often called "free riders") presents a risk to investors. This risk is perceivable ex ante (prior to production of the good) and thus may lead to undersupply. Essentially, in the absence of some institutional solution, there would be a significant underinvestment in (some types of) intellectual resources because of the risk that competitors would appropriate their value (Frischmann 2009a: 2156).

The extent of the free-rider problem in a given instance will depend on the costs of exclusion and boundary setting. But even if low-cost exclusion of free riders is feasible, the nonrivalry of intellectual resources means that markets still will tend to undersupply them. While exclusion enhances incentives to create some intellectual resources, it simultaneously limits their availability (Frischmann 2012: 261–68). An additional layer of complexity emerges when we look beyond intellectual resources as isolated "goods" and consider their importance as inputs, outputs, and continuous constituents of complex intellectual, cultural, economic, and social processes and systems (Frischmann 2012: 268–75; Benkler 2006: 37). The conventional approach to intellectual property collapses this complexity into a linear conception of trade-offs or balancing between "upstream" and "downstream" creators.

At its core, the free-rider allegory illustrates the social dilemma associated with a standard externality problem—each individual free rider rationally maximizes his or her private welfare without accounting for external costs. In this context, the social costs encompass the risk to investment and resulting underproduction of public goods over time. The model easily can be mapped onto the classic collective action problem, in which unconstrained consumption appears unsustainable, producing the so-called "tragedy of the commons."

In remarkable parallelism with the history of the tragedy of the commons allegory and its role in environmental circles, many analysts of knowledge production issues simply assume the free-rider allegory describes a normal rather than exceptional problem. Also, in remarkable parallelism, a binary solution set, comparable to the standard set of solutions in physical resource production settings, seems to follow naturally: To avoid tragedy, society must turn to production subsidized by government or to markets enabled by property rights, specifically intellectual property rights. Both approaches rely on collective action through government, but they differ substantially in terms of the manner in which resource allocation decisions are made (Frischmann 2013). Government subsidization deals with the underproduction problem head on. Government allocates funds to selected research activities that yield intellectual resources, which can, in principle, be shared openly and freely within the "public domain."[3] Intellectual property rights, such as patents and copyrights, address the underproduction problem by enabling markets to function more effectively in supplying intellectual resources. Intellectual property rights lower the costs of exclusion, enable transactions, and mitigate the risks to investment posed by free riders. Yet, for a variety of reasons that are beyond the scope of this introduction, both solutions are incomplete and entail a host of significant problems.

The free-rider allegory heavily influences the framing and perception of the institutional arrangement of the cultural environment, by dividing it into two conceptual domains. First, there is the domain of intellectual property, in which producers of creative and innovative things employ proprietary rights sanctioned by law to control development, distribution, and exploitation of intellectual resources. IP law constructs and assigns these exclusive rights and encourages their exploitation through market exchange.

---

[3] For various reasons that are beyond the scope of this discussion, government-subsidized knowledge resources are not always contributed to the public domain.

Private rights and private market exchange serve to limit, by law, the natural shareability of knowledge and innovation. The intellectual property perspective assumes that producers would abandon their efforts to produce, develop, and/or disseminate knowledge goods for fear of free riding by competitors or consumers.

Second, there is the public domain, a vast collection of openly accessible knowledge resources. The purpose of maintaining a public domain is to permit any and all comers to appropriate its resources freely and to use them to create or innovate anew. For some resources, the benefits of overcoming the free-rider problem are outweighed by the social value of permitting the resources to serve as the foundation for new creations and innovations or otherwise to be used in ways that are socially beneficial, such as when fair uses of copyrighted expression support public capabilities associated with education or political participation. Some resources enter the public domain as the result of direct or indirect provisioning by government using a combination of grants to researchers; tax credits or subsidies to researchers and enterprises that employ them; prizes; and production and distribution of knowledge and innovation by the government itself, either by organizing research enterprises or by purchasing and distributing private research. Other resources occupy the public domain because of limitations to existing intellectual property systems (for example, due to express exclusion from the system as uncopyrightable ideas[4] or unpatentable laws or products of nature,[5] or to expiration of rights.[6]) These limitations attempt to balance free-rider concerns against the social costs of awarding exclusive rights to nonrivalrous resources. Sometimes resources effectively belong to the public domain despite being legally subject to intellectual property rights because those rights are not enforced (for example, because potential owners dedicate their resources to the public or because exclusion is practically impossible).

This conventional two-part framing is woefully inadequate as a descriptive matter. The traditional free-rider allegory provides little insight into determining how and whether particular intellectual resources should be, or are, supplied to the public domain. Essentially, both the allegory and the institutional framing to which it relates are caricatures—oversimplified accounts that roughly describe some cultural practices and productive activities but leave much too much out of frame, unexamined, and unaccounted for. Frischmann (2013) recently suggested that

> we should ask two foundational sets of questions: First, how well does the free
> rider allegory describe reality? Is it a useful theory for making predictions about

---

[4] See, e.g., 17 U.S.C. §§ 102, 107 (2012) (providing for limits on the scope of copyrightable subject matter and for the fair use defense).

[5] See, e.g., 35 U.S.C. §§ 101, 102, 103 (2012) (providing for limits on the scope of patentable subject matter); Diamond v. Chakrabarty, 447 U.S. 303, 309 (1980) (noting that the laws of nature, physical phenomena, and abstract ideas are not patentable).

[6] See U.S. Const. Art. I, § 8, cl. 8 ("limited times"); 17 U.S.C. § 302 (2012) (establishing the duration of a copyright); 35 U.S.C. § 154(a)(2) (2012) (establishing the duration of a patent).

real-world behavior of individuals? Does it describe a normal or exceptional situation? Does it provide a useful basis for choosing or designing regulatory solutions? Second, does the binary choice between government subsidization and intellectual property-enabled markets reflect the full range of options? Are there alternative institutions and/or means for collective action?

In many circumstances, the free-rider allegory does not provide an adequate description of reality. Moreover, even where there are free-rider concerns, the binary choice between IP and government subsidy completely misses the possibility for alternative institutional solutions.

First, reality is considerably more complex than the free-rider allegory suggests. There are many situations in which free riding does not undermine incentives to produce knowledge resources. Whether that is the case depends on contextual factors such as the type of investment required and the type of intellectual resources created. Many intellectual resources plainly are not subject to this concern; people produce them regularly without regard for misappropriation (Frischmann 2012). Often, people innovate because their expected private benefits exceed their fixed costs, regardless of whether or not others free ride. Benefits conferred on "free riders" may be irrelevant to these kinds of incentives or even may add to them (Amabile 1996; Baron & Shane 2007; Frey 2008; Lakhani & Wolf 2005; Tirole & Lerner 2002; Stock et al. 2013; von Hippel 2005).

Participation can be fun, intellectually stimulating, educational or service-oriented, among other things (Benkler 2006; Quiggin & Hunter 2008; Loren 2008; Tushnet 2009; Zimmerman 2011; Schweik & English 2012). Participation may not be effortless or free; it may require substantial investment. Regardless, the private value derived from participation may be sufficient, and external benefits conferred to others that use or consume the output (i.e., the intellectual resource) may be irrelevant to incentives to invest. Similarly, in many situations, people create, invent, and innovate because the anticipated returns from their own uses of the results are sufficient to justify the investment. A rich literature on user innovation demonstrates how many significant innovations result from users seeking to solve their own particular problems, needs, or curiosities (von Hippel 2005; Strandburg 2009: 871–88). People often engage in such activities without disabling concern over free riding and without reliance on government subsidies.

The point should be clear. Free riding does not necessarily reduce incentives to invest and does not inevitably lead to a social dilemma. Reality is considerably more complex than the free-rider allegory suggests, and there is no good reason for systematically marginalizing the many situations in which free riding does not reduce incentives to invest. Such myopia is inexcusable. Indeed, a myopic focus on the free-rider issue may distract researchers and policy makers from other social dilemmas that may be more important in some contexts. For example, some intellectual resources may be exploited in secrecy, as is recognized by trade secrecy laws and by patent law's disclosure requirements. Such resources do not suffer from free-rider problems, but from a different set of social dilemmas related to the social costs of secrecy. Another example arises in the user innovation context. Intrinsic or user motivations for innovation sufficient to overcome free-rider concerns, may not incentivize investments in codifying and disclosing those innovations for the benefit of society and in disseminating embodiments of those innovations for others' use (Strandburg 2010). While user innovators often disclose their innovations to other users because they can benefit when other users critique or improve upon them (Franke & Shah 2003; Harhoff et al. 2003), recent studies show that many user innovators do not invest in disclosure and dissemination, again posing social dilemmas unrelated to the dominant free-rider allegory (Gault & von Hippel 2009; von Hippel & Demonaco 2013). We discuss various examples of other social dilemmas throughout this book.

Second, as is our focus here, the traditional binary of IP rights and government subsidy misses out on a wide variety of alternative institutions for solving social dilemmas involved in the production and management of knowledge resources, including free-rider problems (Merges 1996; Reichman & Uhlir 2003; Raustiala & Sprigman 2012). Unfortunately, comparative institutional analysis is limited in this area (Rai 1999; Frischmann 2000; Newell et al. 2008; Sarnoff 2013), as is more systematic analysis of interdependencies among various institutions.

We must emphasize how much contemporary analysis of the law and public policy of knowledge production rests on the traditional account of the basic public goods problem and binary set of solutions. That account shapes—if not determines—the set of baseline premises that undergird the legal and social institutions that structure the cultural environment and shape normative outcomes. Although our undertaking is emphatically positive and descriptive, we strongly believe that significant normative implications should eventually flow from a better understanding of knowledge commons. The bottom line is that the free-rider allegory and associated binary solution set rarely describe shared resource settings in a sufficiently complete manner to qualify as a useful theory for making predictions or prescribing solutions. Much more is needed.

B. THE NEED FOR SYSTEMATIC EMPIRICAL STUDY OF KNOWLEDGE COMMONS

Much of the debate in IP law has pitted proponents of privatization as a means of incentivizing production of intellectual goods against proponents of a widely available public domain upon which cultural goods can be built. That discussion has often devolved into a disagreement over the relative importance of upstream incentives and downstream access for generating ideas and creative expression. As technology facilitates an increasingly extensive, varied landscape of social and cooperative projects that enable creativity and innovation, a third perspective has emerged. Books, articles, and scholarly discussion of such projects increasingly extol community production as a solution to the free-rider problems of cultural production (Benkler 2006).

Recognizing the importance of community production, but concerned that the amorphous idea of "openness" might become the new one-size-fits-all panacean approach in rivalry with privatization and public subsidy, scholars have pointed out that many of the most interesting and important aspects of the information environment exist in the area between these extremes. The information environment is riddled with complex combinations of private intellectual property rights, contracts, and social norms that are partly open and partly closed, usable by members and sometimes by the public at large, though not always on a purely "free" basis. Examples of these knowledge commons—sometimes called "semicommons" (Smith 2000)—include such diverse institutions as public lending libraries, research universities, trade and craft organizations, and repositories of biological information. Default rules of intellectual property may be combined with licenses and contracts, with social norms and with cultural and other institutional forms to construct these knowledge commons, which depend on—but are built alongside and on top of—basic forms of knowledge and culture. Knowledge commons arrangements often are characterized by what Frischmann and Lemley term "spillovers": social benefits that flow from uses and reuses of information resources and sustain the dynamic character of the information environment (Frischmann & Lemley 2007: 268–71). Legal limitations on intellectual property rights support the possibility of constructing commons governance arrangements that allow resources to be used in ways that generate spillovers (Madison 2005a: 409).

Our knowledge commons framework emerges from our belief that the production and management of knowledge and information resources is an inherently social phenomenon, taking place over a wide range of scales and within a complex, overlapping variety of formal and informal institutional structures (Madison 2005b). Certainly, social production of cultural goods has become more salient and more economically important as a result of globalization and of the communications revolution symbolized by the Internet. Scholars are beginning to grapple with the realization that legal facilitation of innovation and creative production is not and cannot be confined to a simple set of property rules to incentivize individual innovative and creative efforts. Sustaining innovation and creativity is a matter of governance, using legal and other tools. The question for public policy, law, and legal theory becomes how best to use those tools to encourage the growth and persistence of creative, sustainable, and equitable cultural environments.

If commons are truly common, then they should be given a central place as research subjects, rather than either marginalized by conventional, overly simple private rights/ public domain dualism or uncritically extolled. The increasing salience of the community production alternative should motivate us to explore the details of the landscape of knowledge and information production systematically from an institutional standpoint and to identify where, when, and how knowledge governance regimes work to society's benefit.

III. The Institutional Analysis and Development Framework

A. MOTIVATION FOR A FRAMEWORK APPROACH IN THE NATURAL RESOURCE CONTEXT

A group of scholars of commons regimes in the natural environment, spearheaded by the late Elinor Ostrom and her collaborators, have for decades been studying commons in the natural resource environment (Ostrom 2007). Examples of natural resources systems governed as commons include lobster fisheries, grazing pastures, forests, and irrigation systems (Ostrom 1990: 58–88; Acheson 2003). For each of these resources, previous scholars had diagnosed a similar underlying problem, often called, following Hardin (1968), a "tragedy of the commons" (Rose 2008: 411). Given a pool of rivalrous resources that is presumptively open to all comers, such as a meadow for grazing sheep, and absent a mechanism for coordinating the actions of resource users (the owners of the sheep), the resources are likely to be overconsumed and under-replenished. If resource users act rationally and independently in pursuit of their own self-interest, without regard for the costs imposed on other users, the pool eventually will be destroyed. This "tragedy of the commons" illustrates a standard externality problem that manifests a failure of collective action. The "tragedy of the commons" story often is coupled with an assumption that tragedy can be avoided only by one of a binary set of choices: exclusionary property rights allocated via markets (Demsetz 1967: 348) and government intervention and regulation (Cornes & Sandler 1996: 72–78). The work of commons scholars in the natural resource arena demonstrated the fallacy in this binary perspective by grounding theory in in-depth empirical study of the ways in which people actually organize and govern their use of common-pool resources.

Ostrom's approach to governance of natural resources broke with convention by recognizing the importance of institutions intermediate between private property and the state in solving problems of collective action. These intermediate institutions, sometimes called "limited commons" or "semicommons," are collective, locally organized, means for governing and making productive and sustainable use of shareable, but depletable, resources such as fish, water, and trees (Ostrom 1990: 88–90). The empirical research of Ostrom and other scholars demonstrates that solutions to these resource-sharing problems are various and highly contextual, and may be formal or informal. Such common-pool resources, or resource systems, often exist in complex institutional settings in which smaller commons are "nested" within larger ones, so that researchers must explore these institutions at different scales or levels of detail (Ostrom 2005: 58–62). Standard theoretic models, whether or not grounded in the presumption that a tragedy of the commons is present, can therefore be only the beginning of a much more complex analysis. The temptation to seek out regulatory panaceas based on universal models, whether through private property, state action, or even notions of community, must be resisted in favor of a more nuanced approach (Ostrom 2007). That approach begins with a research framework, guided by multiple theoretical possibilities and openness to considering the different variables that might affect outcomes. Only later, in light of the aggregation and analysis of data, does it become possible and meaningful to generalize and eventually to construct testable models.

As Ostrom explains, frameworks, theories, and models have different roles to play:

> The development and use of a general framework helps to identify the elements (and the relationships among these elements) that one needs to consider for institutional analysis. Frameworks...provide the most general set of variables that should be used to analyze all types of settings relevant for the framework....They attempt to identify the universal elements that any relevant theory would need to include....
>
> The development and use of theories enable the analyst to specify which components of a framework are relevant for certain kinds of questions and to make broad working assumptions about these elements. Thus, theories focus on parts of a framework and make specific assumptions that are necessary for an analyst to diagnose a phenomenon, explain its processes, and predict outcomes....Microeconomic theory, game theory, transaction cost theory, social choice theory, public choice, constitutional and covenantal theory, and theories of public goods and common-pool resources are all compatible with the IAD framework....
>
> One needs a common framework and family of theories in order to address questions of reforms and transitions. Particular models then help the analyst to deduce specific predictions about likely outcomes of highly simplified structures. Models are useful in policy analysis when they are well-tailored to the particular problem at hand. Models are used inappropriately when applied to the study of problematic situations that do not closely fit the assumptions of the model....(Ostrom 2005: 28–29)

B. THE INSTITUTIONAL ANALYSIS AND DEVELOPMENT FRAMEWORK

The Institutional Analysis and Development (IAD) framework was developed and used to structure a common set of research questions to apply across these diverse contexts. It has been successful in coming to some conclusions about the significance and interactions of various factors in facilitating effective management of natural resources (Ostrom 2007: 15181–82). Based on the information obtained by applying their framework to structured case studies, these researchers developed theories and models for particular commons situations, designed experiments to test those theories, and used statistical methods to look for regularities across cases. Based on this empirical work, Ostrom advanced a set of design principles for successful natural resource commons.

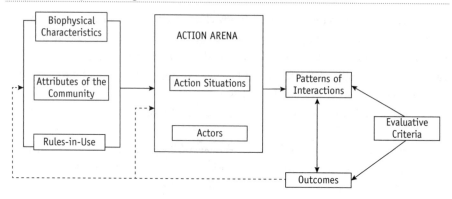

FIGURE 1.1 The Institutional Analysis and Development Framework.

The IAD framework for natural resource commons is illustrated in Figure 1.1

On the left are represented a group of variables that are "exogenous" with respect to a particular set of interactions taking place in an "action arena" (Ostrom 2005: 13). The IAD framework identifies the important variables for analyzing the way that community members interact in a particular situation as biophysical characteristics, attributes of the community, and "rules-in-use." In the case of the lobster fishery, for example, these attributes might include the relevant biological characteristics of lobsters, such as the rates at which they age and reproduce; attributes of the community of fishermen, such as the proximity in which they live to others, the existence of familial relationships, and the skill sets needed for lobster fishing; and the rules—which are the net result of whatever informal and formal rules nominally apply to a particular situation—that actually govern the way that fishermen (and any other relevant actors) interact with one another and with the resource in various situations that arise (Ostrom 2007: 15184–85). The central portion of the figure identifies the variables that define the "action arena." An action arena "refers to the social space where participants with diverse preferences interact, exchange goods and services, solve problems, dominate one another, or fight (among the many things that individuals do in action arenas)" (Ostrom 2005: 14)—in other words, the place at which the exogenous variables combine in particular instances, leading over time to observed patterns of interactions and outcomes. A particular action arena involves specific action situations and specific actors, along with those actors' identities and roles. At the far right of the figure are the patterns of interactions, outcomes, and evaluative criteria that determine how the variables that are exogenous in a particular interaction may eventually respond and change.

The "tragedy of the commons" allegory makes assumptions about the biophysical characteristics (depletable), community (independent, self-interested rational actors), and "rules-in-use" (every fisherman for himself) that apply in the action arena of fishing for lobsters. It also assumes that independent fishermen are the only actors in the action arena and that the collective action problem posed by the "tragedy of the commons" is the only type of social dilemma involved in the situation. Under those assumptions, the outcome that ensues is scarcity, depletion, and, eventually collapse. Viewing the "tragedy of the commons" story through the lens of the IAD framework illuminates its empirical shortcomings. Lobsters are not purely depletable. They can, as a biological matter, reproduce and replenish the resource. The community does not consist of entirely independent actors. Fishermen and their communities have more complicated relationships, which permit them to cooperate, at least in some respects. The "rules-in-use" in the lobster fishery are more complex than "every fisherman for himself." As a result, the interactions in the lobster fishing action arena can produce very different outcomes than the tragedy of the commons story would predict. A successful commons governance regime may, however, require the community to resolve a nested set of social dilemmas over and above the basic collective action problem.

As a methodological matter, structuring a case study according to the IAD framework, involves asking specific questions about each of the sets of variables identified in Figure 1.1, which assist the researcher in drilling down into the facts of a particular case (Ostrom 2005: 13–14). Questions about the biophysical characteristics, attributes of the community, and rules-in-use, for example, include the following:

- What boundaries define the shared resource pool? What is the source of supply and sustainability of the resource units? Under what conditions may resource units be appropriated from the pool?
- How does the population monitor and enforce rules regarding contribution and appropriation? What sorts of sanctions are available, and what sanctions are actually used? What conflict resolution mechanisms are in place?
- If the community relies on other populations in some respects, or if the population delegates some functions to subsidiary populations, what is the character of these relationships?
- In all instances, to what extent are these attributes inscribed in formal institutions of the state? To what extent are they inscribed in other formal, legal institutions, and to what extent are they inscribed in social norms or other social or cultural structures?

Employing the IAD framework to investigate a number of different real-world cases illuminated the diversity of possible combinations of exogenous variables that determine what actually happens in particular instances and, hence, the outcomes that result. The rules governing lobster fishing contribute to the activity's long-term sustainability, for example, but the patterns of interaction actually observed depend on the richness of the particular environment for lobsters, the degree to which rules are actually enforced, seasonal factors such as weather, and interaction with outside influences such as pollution and the state of the larger economy. Understanding the observed success or failure of a commons enterprise such as a lobster fishery may require accounting for all of these factors, even though it may turn out that outcomes are relatively impervious to some of them.

The IAD framework thus allows researchers to move beyond the overly general assumptions of the "tragedy of the commons" story to investigate how resources actually are governed, structuring the empirical inquiry so that comparisons between cases are possible, while avoiding unwarranted assumptions related to particular theories or models.

IV. Developing a Framework for the Study of Knowledge Commons

A. LEARNING FROM AND ADAPTING THE INSTITUTIONAL ANALYSIS AND DEVELOPMENT FRAMEWORK

The IAD framework has proven fruitful in the natural resources context (The Economist 2008). We argue that the lessons learned by these scholars of natural resource commons caution against an overly simplistic view of community knowledge production and management. The devil is in the details. The nested, multi-tiered character of productive and sustainable knowledge and information systems and the diversity of attributes that contribute to successful governance regimes are key to understanding knowledge commons as mechanisms for knowledge production, collection, curation, and distribution in the context of modern information and IP law regimes. We therefore propose that Ostrom's approach to the systematized study of natural resource commons be adapted to study knowledge commons in the cultural environment. We use the "cultural environment" metaphor advisedly, following the work of Boyle (Boyle 1997: 108–12). The environmental metaphor for information law and policy—focusing on knowledge and information resources rather than physical or natural resources—offers an illuminating and useful starting point for this project.

Ostrom and her colleagues have taken preliminary steps toward understanding how the IAD framework might be used to investigate certain knowledge commons. Ostrom and Hess have analyzed the management of digital collections of existing knowledge resources, an admirable first step that signals the need for and plausibility of extending the IAD framework to the cultural environment (Ostrom & Hess 2007).

The environmental metaphor has its limitations, however. We argue that the IAD framework must be modified and extended to account adequately for the wide variety of knowledge commons. Unlike commons in the natural resource environment, knowledge commons arrangements usually must create a governance structure within which participants not only share existing resources but also engage in producing those resources and, indeed, in determining their character. In fact, knowledge commons members often come together for the very purpose of creating particular kinds of knowledge resources. The relevant community is determined not by geographical proximity to an existing resource, but by some connection—perhaps of interest or of expertise—to the knowledge resources to be created. These characteristics of knowledge commons suggest that neatly separating the attributes of the managed resources from the attributes and rules-in-use of the community that produces and uses them is impossible.

Just as the simple tragedy of the commons allegory is insufficient to specify the social dilemmas that must be overcome by a natural resource commons, the simple free-rider allegory is only one of the possible social dilemmas that are likely to confront a knowledge commons. Indeed, the characteristics of knowledge commons just described suggest that a more complex set of social dilemmas is likely to arise in the knowledge context. Here we give several illustrations of this point.

First, like the natural resource commons that Ostrom studied, knowledge commons not only allocate resource consumption opportunities but also must cope with challenges in coordinating and combining resources. In knowledge and information contexts, solutions to a range of coordination challenges are fundamental. Those who create, invent or innovate, and participate in similar intellectually driven, productive activities necessarily borrow from and share with others. It is impossible to divest oneself of that to which one has been exposed. Inevitably, the intellectual products of past and contemporary "producers" (creators, inventors, innovators, thinkers, and the like) serve as inputs into later productive activities. Producers necessarily borrow and share—and not in any fixed or small number of ways.

Second, the nonrivalrous and nonexcludable knowledge resources that make up the cultural environment are not naturally defined by boundaries that permit exclusion of users. Boundaries are built rather than found. They come from at least two sources. Intangible knowledge resources often are embodied in tangible product forms, which create boundaries. Additionally, law and other social practices may create boundaries around the intangible resources themselves, as, for example, in the case of the "claims" of a patent. The creation of boundaries is partly within and partly outside of the control of the members of a knowledge commons community and generates a series of social dilemmas to be resolved.

Third, knowledge and information resources must be created (or at least identified as knowledge and information resources) before they can be shared. Therefore, knowledge commons must manage coordination, combination, and competition issues relating both to resource production and to resource use within and potentially beyond the commons participants. The public goods character of knowledge resources necessitates consideration not only of dynamics internal to a commons community but also of relationships between commons and other, related institutions. Knowledge commons must confront questions of openness that may generate additional social dilemmas (Madison, Frischmann, & Strandburg 2009: 368–69.)

Fourth, the nonrivalry of knowledge and information resources often rides on top of various rivalrous inputs (such as time or money) and may provide a foundation for various rivalrous outputs (such as money or fame). Knowledge commons must confront the social dilemmas associated with obtaining and distributing these rivalrous resources.

Finally, understanding a knowledge commons may require researchers to engage with the particular narratives of the community, which may be grounded in storytelling, metaphor, history, and analogy. The property scholar Carol Rose emphasizes the role of narratives, especially of origin stories, in explaining features of property regimes that are not determinable strictly on theoretical or functional grounds, particularly if one assumes that everyone begins from a position of rational self-interest (Rose 1994: 35–42). The stories that are told about knowledge commons, and by those who participate in them, are instructive with respect to understanding the construction, consumption, and coordination of knowledge resources. Particular histories, stories, and self-understandings may be important in constructing the social dilemmas that arise and in determining why a particular knowledge commons approaches them in a particular way.

Given the broad range of possible social dilemmas that may arise, a research framework can help researchers to develop, apply, and ultimately choose among an equally broad set of different relevant theories. Not only law but also economics, sociology, and history each may have much to offer in the future when interpreting case studies on knowledge commons. There is no reason now to limit the disciplinary conversation to only one of those fields—or to preempt future conversations about knowledge commons from blending them. For example, club theory, which distinguishes sharply between community members and outsiders, may be helpful in understanding the dynamics of patent pools but poorly suited to understanding Wikipedia, which is quite open in terms of membership, contributions, and participation in various aspects of the project. Patent pools manage shared resources in a fashion that is much less focused than Wikipedia on sustaining joint production. Consequently, club theory is not likely to be particularly helpful for a researcher studying Wikipedia. Other theories of cooperation might be better suited to the task. A research framework such as ours aims to systematize the investigation, facilitate a more rigorous evaluation by matching and testing of theories and models with observed phenomena, and, most generally, enable learning over time. We do not, for example, advocate adopting a strict definition in the first place that answers the question "what is a commons?" (Madison, Frischmann, & Strandburg 2010b: 840–42). Nor do we adopt strict boundaries on the set of potentially relevant resources. The IAD framework in the natural resource domain was intended to be an inclusive method for conducting case-based research and collecting and comparing cases. By design, the IAD framework remains a work in progress, which is one of its strengths. We follow that tradition in proposing a framework for knowledge commons research. We designed our IAD-based framework based on our intuitions regarding the challenges and opportunities posed by governance institutions that *feature* shared resources, but we expect that it will be developed and honed as it is used.

B. SPECIFYING A FRAMEWORK FOR STUDYING KNOWLEDGE COMMONS

We illustrate our proposed framework for knowledge commons with the flow chart in Figure 1.2, which reflects the iterative and constructed character of the commons community, its knowledge or information resources, and its governing "rules-in-use." Figure 1.2 is based on the IAD flow chart reproduced in Figure 1.1 (Ostrom 2005: 15), but it differs

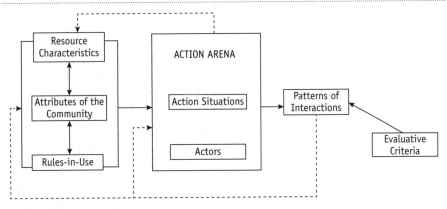

FIGURE 1.2 The Knowledge Commons Framework.

in some key respects. Because of the more complex relationships among resources, participants, and governance structures in knowledge commons, relevant attributes may not divide as neatly into categories as they do when one is describing a pool of natural resources. Thus, in the left-most part of the chart, we place new emphasis on the interactions among and constructed or manufactured nature of the knowledge and information resources themselves, as indicated by the arrows between them. We also illustrate the way in which interactions in the action arena, by creating intellectual resources, can feed directly back into the characteristics of the resources being managed by a knowledge commons.

Figure 1.2 also collapses a distinction made in the original IAD framework between "patterns of interactions" that follow from the action arena, and outcomes that follow from the patterns of interaction. We argue that the patterns of interactions generated by the formal and informal rules systems of a knowledge commons are often inseparable from the outcomes it produces. How people interact with rules, resources, and each other, in other words, is itself an outcome that is inextricably linked with and determinative of the form and content of the knowledge or informational output of the commons. In an open source software project, for example, the existence and operation of the open source development collaborative, the identity of the dynamic thing called the open source software program, and the existence and operation of the relevant open source software license and other governance mechanisms are constitutive of one another.[7]

With this general modified framework in mind, we now describe our proposed framework for empirical study of particular constructed cultural commons. Building on the high-level categories reflected in Figure 1.2, we now elucidate the categories of questions that should guide any specific investigation in more detail. The box, "Knowledge Commons Framework and Representative Research Questions," below, provides an

---

[7] See Jacobsen v. Katzer, 535 F.3d 1373, 1381–82 (Fed. Cir. 2008) (concluding that violations of an open source software license can be remedied by injunction, in order to preserve the productive character of the open source community).

overview of the framework for reference. During the course of a case study, the proposed framework of questions described below and in the box is used in two ways. First, it is used as a guide in planning interviews with relevant actors. Second, it is used as a framework for organizing and analyzing the information gained from interviews, review of relevant documents and related materials, and so forth. Though we describe the various "buckets" of questions in the framework sequentially, in practice the inquiry is likely to be iterative. Learning more about goals and objectives is likely to result in the identification of additional shared resources, understanding the makeup of the community will lead to new questions about general governance, and so forth. Moreover, we anticipate that the framework itself will evolve and be honed through use. Indeed, the questions in the box and the discussion below already reflect some reorganization and fine-tuning of the framework as presented in our original work (Madison, Frischmann, & Strandburg 2010a) in response to our experience with the case studies in this book, as discussed in more detail in the concluding chapter.

KNOWLEDGE COMMONS FRAMEWORK AND REPRESENTATIVE RESEARCH QUESTIONS

Background Environment
- What is the background context (legal, cultural, etc.) of this particular commons?
- What is the "default" status of the resources involved in the commons (patented, copyrighted, open, or other)?

Attributes
Resources
- What resources are pooled and how are they created or obtained?
- What are the characteristics of the resources? Are they rival or nonrival, tangible or intangible? Is there shared infrastructure?
- What technologies and skills are needed to create, obtain, maintain, and use the resources?

Community Members
- Who are the community members and what are their roles?
- What are the degree and nature of openness with respect to each type of community member and the general public?

Goals and Objectives
- What are the goals and objectives of the commons and its members, including obstacles or dilemmas to be overcome?
- What are the history and narrative of the commons?

Governance

- What are the relevant action arenas and how do they relate to the goals and objective of the commons and the relationships among various types of participants and with the general public?
- What are the governance mechanisms (e.g., membership rules, resource contribution or extraction standards and requirements, conflict resolution mechanisms, sanctions for rule violation)?
- Who are the decision makers and how are they selected?
- What are the institutions and technological infrastructures that structure and govern decision making?
- What informal norms govern the commons?
- How do nonmembers interact with the commons? What institutions govern those interactions?
- What legal structures (e.g., intellectual property, subsidies, contract, licensing, tax, antitrust) apply?

Patterns and Outcomes

- What benefits are delivered to members and to others (e.g., innovations and creative output, production, sharing, and dissemination to a broader audience, and social interactions that emerge from the commons)?
- What costs and risks are associated with the commons, including any negative externalities?

1. The Background Environment: An Initial Conundrum

When seeking to apply the IAD approach to knowledge commons, we immediately confront a conceptual challenge. Ostrom's inquiry begins by asking questions about the "biophysical characteristics" of the relevant resources. This inquiry takes as given a natural environment and natural resources that are to be shared and managed. In describing a knowledge commons, we must take a step back before describing the relevant characteristics of the shared resources to ask how we should define the environmental or contextual backdrop against which the knowledge commons operates. There is no clean way to separate a particular knowledge commons from its "natural" cultural background, because cultural activity is always grounded not only in the natural environment but also in human social interaction, the human-made material environment, laws, histories, practices, traditions, and social norms. Although there may not be one "natural" background environment for knowledge commons, it is nonetheless important, in investigating a knowledge commons, to understand the cultural environment within which it is nested. The inquiry into the characteristics of its shared resources, community, and governance institutions must be framed in relation to that background environment. An appropriate description of the background environment will lead to a more concise and useful description of the knowledge commons under investigation and a better understanding of the sources and significance of the social, political, and economic aspects of knowledge commons.

We identify two canonical "default" background environments for knowledge commons: a cultural environment without intellectual property rights, on the one hand, and an intellectual-property-based cultural environment on the other hand. In many cases, the background cultural environment for a particular knowledge commons will combine elements from these default regimes.

a. The Default "Natural" Cultural Environment

Despite the expansive scope of IP rights, a significant range of activities, practices, and intellectual resources remain outside the intended scope of IP regimes. This "natural" cultural environment includes cultural resources (including broad traditions, practices, disciplines, and concepts, as well as more specific artifacts and items of knowledge) that are excluded from IP regimes on subject matter grounds, material as to which IP protection has expired, and material that is excepted from IP coverage in certain circumstances (for example, via rules of fair use or fair dealing). Much of this natural cultural environment is in the public domain, and hence accessible and usable by anyone without the permission of anyone else, though the "natural" environment also includes the possibility for secrecy with respect to some resources.

When knowledge commons are constructed in arenas where IP rights do not apply, the most appropriate choice of background environment against which to describe them is a "natural" cultural environment unmediated by rights of exclusion or other regulation. The "natural" cultural environment also may be a useful baseline for investigating some knowledge commons where intellectual property protection is available for the relevant resources, but plays a marginal role. For example, the Associated Press was constructed initially as a means of managing the sharing of an intellectual resource (news) that was not protected by the standard forms of IP law (the First Amendment to the U.S. Constitution generally precludes copyright protection for facts). The AP was the plaintiff in the leading case that established an intellectual-property-like, but very limited, "hot news" doctrine barring a very specific type of misappropriation of factual information.[8] Despite the existence of these limited IP-like rights, the AP knowledge commons is probably most concisely and clearly described in terms of its differences from the IP-free "natural" cultural environment.

For some resources, the "natural" cultural environment also includes the possibility of secrecy. A background culture of secrecy may provide the most useful default backdrop for describing some knowledge commons involving such resources. The norms of sharing access to magic tricks within the community of magicians, for example, arise in an environment of strong background norms of secrecy (Loshin 2008).

---

[8] See International News Service v. Associated Press, 248 U.S. 215 (1918).

b. The Default Proprietary Environments

The two principal regimes of IP law—patent and copyright law—are the most salient alternatives to the "natural" environmental baseline described above. Patent rules vary somewhat from country to country, but generally time-limited patent rights are granted to the developers of an "invention" in some field of technology or human endeavor after an appropriate government agency examines a patent application (Nard, Madison, & McKenna 2013: 19–27). Patents are available for a wide range of subject matter, but certain types of subject matter, such as natural phenomena and abstract ideas, are not eligible for patent protection. A patent applicant must demonstrate to the satisfaction of the patent examiner that the invention claimed in the application is new (or "novel," in the language of patent law) in that no one has invented it before; it is useful; it is nonobvious (in the language of American patent law) or possesses an "inventive step" (in most European systems), such that the invention represents a sufficiently great technical advance over the existing art; and it is adequately described in the application for the benefit of future adopters and adapters of the technology. The holder of a valid patent possesses a statutory right to exclude all others from using, producing, or selling the invention, subject to extremely limited exceptions for experimentation and research on the subject matter of the patent. Notably, however, patent rights expire after a relatively short term, typically twenty years. The invention covered by the patent then passes into the public domain. An example of a knowledge commons for which a patented environment serves as an appropriate baseline is a patent pool.

Copyright law departs from the "natural environment" norm for the cultural environment in similar ways, and for similar reasons, but applies to artistic and creative cultural expression rather than to technological invention. Like patent laws, copyright statutes vary in their details from country to country yet generally embody a set of core principles. The author of an "original" or creative work is granted a statutory entitlement to exclude others from reproducing, adapting, performing or disseminating that work to the public (Nard, Madison, & McKenna 2013: 435–39). By comparison to patent doctrine, copyright doctrine generally incorporates a relatively broad range of exceptions and exclusions. It generally excludes subject matter that is functional rather than expressive (and therefore the subject of patent law) or that is too broad or abstract to be identified clearly as the specific product of a specific author. Even when a work is covered by copyright, the author's exclusive rights are generally subject to exceptions for uses that are deemed "fair use" in the United States or "fair dealing" in the United Kingdom, Canada, and some other countries, and to a range of other statutory exceptions, exclusions, and compulsory licenses. As with patents, expiration of the copyright delivers the covered material to the public domain. In general the term of copyright lasts far longer than the term of patent—the life of the author plus fifty years, in most countries, and the life of the author plus seventy years in the United States and European Union countries. Examples of knowledge commons for which copyright is an appropriate baseline are open source computer software under the General Public License (GPL) and open access repositories for academic publishing.

2. The Basic Attributes of the Knowledge Commons

The next step after choosing an appropriate characterization of the "natural" environment in which a particular knowledge commons resides is to identify and describe its basic attributes, which include its resources, participants, and goals and objectives. For each of these attributes, this section suggests a "basket" of questions to be asked during a case study. The resource characteristics and makeup of the community of a knowledge commons are generally co-determined with its goals and objectives and dependent upon its historical narrative. These are critical subjects of inquiry. In addition to baskets of questions directly aimed at describing the resources and community, the inquiry into basic attributes includes baskets of questions relating to goals and objectives, history, and narrative.

a. Resources

After choosing an appropriate baseline environment, the next step in investigating a knowledge commons is to identify the set of resources being pooled and the relevant community of actors. The resources being pooled in a given knowledge commons might appear to be obvious, such as patents in a patent pool, news items for a news service, or recordings for a database of music. But we caution against focusing too reflexively on the most obvious resources. For example, members of a patent pool might share other knowledge resources, such as pricing information, tacit knowledge about future research, or past failures. Often, it will take some consideration to identify the most salient description of the relevant resources. What resources are pooled and shared in an open source software community? Ideas? Computer code? Coding expertise? Debugging opportunities?

In many contexts, multiple types of resources might be shared within a knowledge commons. The dynamic character of intellectual and knowledge resources means that shared resources may not be fully independent of one another both in the sense that the value of one shared resource may depend on its relationship to other shared resources, and in the sense that any shared resource may arise from or be developed from a different shared resource. The multiple contributions to a single open source software project demonstrate both features. The durability of shared resources also must be considered. Patents and copyrights expire; tangible objects, in which patented inventions and copyrighted works of authorship often are embodied, may wear out or be consumed.

Our framework aims to be inclusive and aware of the variety of resources collected in knowledge commons. We avoid a focus solely on intellectual property assets or even on knowledge resources. Though its focus is on knowledge, a knowledge commons also may use, produce, and manage various rival resources. To understand the governance and effectiveness of a knowledge commons arrangement, it may be very important to study how these rival resources are managed.

b. Community

Community members may be clearly and relatively simply identified—as they are in a patent pool—or the constitution of the community may be more complex. Does the open source software community consist of programmers alone? Does it include users of the code? People who submit comments or assist with debugging? Entrepreneurs who initiate meetings and dialogue or organize the community? People who develop, disseminate, and manage the relevant licenses? Those who monitor compliance with license terms? People who develop tools, host websites, and otherwise support the community? A single answer is not necessarily appropriate; each of these constituencies and their specific roles should be described (Schweik & English 2012).

c. Goals and Objectives

The goals and objectives of a knowledge commons often are critical to defining the resources it creates and shares, its membership, and the action arenas in which its members interact. Goals and objectives also are closely related to the social dilemmas that the commons must resolve. The goals and objectives of a natural resource commons often are evident from the common-pool resource itself and are defined by the problem of depletability or rivalrousness (e.g., removing lobsters from a fishery results in fewer lobsters for everyone else) and the risk that a common-pool resource will be exhausted by uncoordinated self-interested activity (e.g., unmanaged harvesting may jeopardize the sustainability of the lobster population).

Some knowledge commons have emerged and evolved over long periods of time and been influenced by large-scale historical, social, and/or economic forces that cannot be parceled neatly into an answer to the question, "what problem was being solved?" Contemporary research universities are, in one sense, examples of that phenomenon (Madison, Frischmann, & Strandburg 2009). Commons are not always built; sometimes they emerge. Indeed, as discussed below, we believe that an inquiry into the history and narrative of a knowledge commons is always important to understanding it. Nonetheless, we believe it is usually sensible to speak of knowledge commons governance regimes as having particular goals and objectives. Moreover, often, knowledge commons are purpose-built.

While the particular goals and objectives of a knowledge commons will usually be closely related to the specific resources and community involved, the goals and objectives of a knowledge commons often will be tied to solving various problems and social dilemmas. Problems often addressed by knowledge commons include the production of intellectual goods to be shared, the overcoming of transaction costs leading to bargaining breakdown among different actors interested in exploiting the shared intellectual resource, the production of commonly useful platforms for further creativity, and so forth (Merges 1996: 1295–1301, 2005: 1514–19).

Some knowledge commons deploy IP rights to solve collective action, coordination, or transactions cost problems that exist apart from IP rights and perhaps would not be solvable without these rights (e.g., IP might be essential to facilitating collective action). Open source software projects, mediated by formal free and open source licenses and by informal communal structures for determining what code becomes part of the "authorized" code base, are examples of this type. Standard-setting enterprises also fit into this category, as do joint ventures for scientific research and development. These knowledge commons depend on each member's possessing certain intellectual property interests as a facilitator of participation.

Other knowledge commons are created, at least in part, to solve collective action, coordination, or transactions cost problems that exist only because of IP rights (Heller 1998: 625). In some of these cases, commons governance offers a defense against potential privatization of commonly useful shared resources and the possibility that an individual IP rights owner would "hold up" the enterprise as a whole. Examples of such arrangements might include "open source" commons constructed for basic biological building blocks such as the Single Nucleotide Polymorphism (SNP) consortium (Morgan 2003) or the publicly available databases of genomic sequences that are part of the Human Genome Project (Kumar & Rai 2007). Formal licenses and related agreements assure that participants become part of what amounts to a mutual nonaggression pact that is necessary precisely because of the possibility that intellectual resources may be propertized. So long as the resource is part of a commons institution, it can be shared among commons members, and neither commons members nor outsiders are able to appropriate that resource, patent it, and then assert a patent claim against a commons member. Within commons, research proceeds more or less as it otherwise would, according to informal disciplinary norms and free of (or at least, less burdened by) undue anxiety about propertization and potential holdup.

A knowledge commons may also have the goal of mediating among communities with different default norms. Technology transfer institutions, which enable universities and other nonprofit research enterprises to deliver information resources (such as the technical knowledge described in patent specifications) to the private market, are examples of this type of commons (Jones & Strandburg 2010: 13–17). The cultural environment inside the university is typically characterized by information sharing not governed by IP rights, even if IP rights are present as matters of form (Walsh et al. 2007: 1199–1200). Markets outside the university are governed largely by IP rights. Technology transfer institutions may constitute an institutional pool or commons that mediates these two regimes (Auerswald & Branscomb 2003: 79–80). Similarly, open source projects have developed "boundary organizations" to mediate their relations with commercial firms (O'Mahony & Bechky 2008).

Knowledge commons may also have less socially salutary goals. Most obvious is the case of members colluding to restrict competition (some believe that the Associated Press, for example, falls into this category (Baird 2005)). The inquiry into goals and objects should be sensitive to the possibility of such goals and objectives. But by requiring as an initial matter that knowledge commons operate via sharing of intellectual resources, we distinguish knowledge commons from cartels as such, which op. sharing price and output information and which pose significant and obvious anticompetitive behavior without offsetting welfare benefits (Viscusi et al. 2005: 116–32). The functional purpose of cartels differs from the purpose of the knowledge arrangements noted above; that is, cartels are not designed to create an open environment within which resources may be shared and productively used by members or to sustain individual members. The line between commons and cartels may be difficult to draw, however. Antitrust regulators have long faced the challenge of identifying illegitimate cartels disguised as legitimate patent pools and other knowledge-sharing institutions (Hovencamp 2012: §§ 30.4, 34.2).

These examples of the types of goals and objectives that may motivate the construction of knowledge commons arrangements are illustrative rather than exhaustive. Moreover, it may be the case—and may even likely be the case—that the motivations for any particular knowledge commons arise from a variety of considerations.

d. History and Narrative

All of the basic attributes of a knowledge commons—resources, community, and goals and objectives—often depend significantly on its narratives of creation and operation and on its history. Those narratives depend in turn on a variety of linguistic resources: the vocabulary and syntax that participants and observers use in describing the regime are keys to unlocking its origins, its operation, and even its future. The very phrase "patent pool," for example, has come to signify a specific set of legal expectations and criticisms. If one says "patent pool," an informed commentator thinks immediately of a self-governing arrangement and various antitrust considerations, rather than intellectual property problems and solutions, much less knowledge sharing.

Explicitly giving attention to history and narrative also encourages attention to evolutionary processes and avoidance of an overly static perspective. Looking at history can help answer the question of how the commons came to have its particular members, goals and objectives, and resources. History also reflects how a knowledge commons has changed and adapted over time and gives some basis for anticipating problems it may encounter in the future. Changes in a knowledge commons' narrative over time, or conflicts embedded within the narrative, can illustrate debates over purpose, which can illuminate the normative foundations of a commons and highlight points of conflict.

History and narrative also emphasize the importance of contextual details that are ignored or marginalized in an overly rationalist account of institutional design. They may provide information about individuals and their relationships to relevant institutions. They also are likely to be useful in uncovering details concerning the influence of power, position, politics, and personalities in a particular knowledge commons that may be swept under the rug in a more taxonomic approach to describing the basic attributes of a knowledge commons.

3. Governance and Rules-in-Use

The governance of a knowledge commons can, and should, be investigated from a several angles. First, the governance of a knowledge commons is often reflected in its approach to openness, with respect both to resources and community. Second, the governance of a knowledge commons often is reflected in general governance structures, some of which arise from the background environment and some of which are specific to the particular knowledge commons. Third, the governance of a knowledge commons is reflected in specific rules and norms that apply to particular action arenas. These different perspectives on governance overlap to some degree, and all are relevant to describing the "rules-in-use" that apply to particular action situations.

a. Degrees of Openness and the Character of Control

The nonrivalrousness of knowledge resources often means that the community has a wide range of choice about the degree to which use of the resources and participation in the community is open to all comers or confined to some. These choices about the degree of openness are matters of governance, but are influenced by and co-determine the community's goals and objectives, its membership, and the characteristics of its resources.

Commons regimes are defined both by the degree of openness and control that they exhibit with respect to contributors, users, and resources and by the assignment of control, or custody, of the power to administer access. The rules-in-use of knowledge commons will reflect and delineate the degree of openness, particularly with respect to use of the resources by outsiders who do not contribute to resource creation. The inquiry into openness is often less relevant to natural resource commons arrangements, so we highlight it here. Natural resource commons generally are finite, depletable in consumption, often congested (such that overuse reduces the value of the remaining resources), and subject to tragic overconsumption, even taking into account differences in the depletability and renewability of different natural resource pools (Frischmann 2008: 166–68). Consequently, it is often necessary to limit access to a common-pool resource to members of a defined community, often geographically determined. The boundaries of the community sharing a resource tend to be coextensive with the boundaries of commons self-governance (Ostrom 1990: 61–88). In many cases, a natural resource commons is open to members and closed to everyone else, and that is the end of the story.

Knowledge and information resources, by contrast, are not subject to the same constraints and are naturally shareable without a risk of congestion or overconsumption. Rarely does "too much information" diminish the value of individual items of information (Karjala 2006). It is entirely possible and desirable for a community to produce and/or manage a cluster of cultural goods that is accessible to outsiders. Frischmann refers to this as "leveraging" the "nonrivalry" of intellectual resources (Frischmann 2009b: 810). One of the measures of the social benefit of knowledge commons may be the degree to which it disseminates its products to a wider audience.

I. OPENNESS AS APPLIED TO RESOURCES. What do we mean by openness? Little ambiguity exists in most everyday contexts (e.g., an open door), but openness can be a confusing term when used to describe a knowledge or information resource. Openness, as we use it here, describes the capacity to relate to a resource by accessing and using it. In other words, the openness of a resource corresponds to the extent to which there are barriers to possession or use. Openness varies according to the costs of surmounting barriers (in terms of money, conditions, or other restrictions) to exploitation. Openness in this sense may encompass joint or shared access to and use of the resource (West 2007).

Barriers to possession or use of a resource may be natural or constructed. A resource may be open naturally because its characteristics prevent it from being possessed, owned, or controlled by anyone (consider, for example, the ocean). A resource also may be open as the result of social construction. That is, laws or rules may prohibit ownership or ensure a certain degree of openness. For example, copyright law grants protection over creative expression but excludes protection for ideas in order to maintain open access and the possibility of use. Patent law does likewise with respect to abstract ideas. Openness also may arise through social norms and customs among owners and users and through institutional design.

Openness and the vesting of control over openness are related. In part, both concepts may simply reflect choices regarding how best to manage resources. In the context of intellectual property pools, for example, management of the pooled resources may be vested in a central institution created specifically for that purpose, or it may be decentralized and vested in the hands of individual IP rights holders. Openness and the sources of control also reflect power and its distribution among potential possessors and users. Openness may be measured by the degree of control that is exercised by one person or group over the terms of access and use of a specific resource by others. Openness relies on social institutions; it is a relational variable that describes the structure of relationships among potential resource users.

II. OPENNESS AS APPLIED TO A COMMUNITY. As a resource or set of resources may have an open character, so may a community. As with resources, the degree of openness of a community is defined partly in functional terms, by natural and constructed attributes that define membership in the community, and partly in terms of power and other bases for relations among participants. (Accordingly, we focus much less on whether some social context is or is not a "community" according to predefined criteria and much more on the functional characteristics of that context.) As with openness applied to resources, openness with regard to a community describes an individual's capacity to relate to that community as a contributor, manager, or user of resources that make up the knowledge commons. Openness describes the extent to which there are criteria for or barriers to membership or participation in the creation or innovation processes that a knowledge commons is intended to support. Openness also describes the extent to which a particular community is accessible to and interconnected with related contexts, institutions, and social practices.

The degree of openness of a knowledge commons with respect to community has an internal dimension as well as an external one, as it reflects the degree to which participants in the commons collaborate with one another or otherwise share human capital as well as (or rather than) resources. For example, the participants in an intellectual property pool may specify rules regarding how resources are contributed to and withdrawn from the pool. The General Public License for open source computer programs specifies that membership in the community defined by users of the program is open to anyone. Anyone may add to, use, or redistribute the licensed program. Redistributors, however, must abide by the license term that they make the full source code of the program accessible to further users of the program. Moreover, in most open source software projects, only certain contributions are accepted into "official" versions of the code (Kelty 2008: 27–31). Although use and modification of the code for personal use are open to anyone, the ability to contribute to the shared resource is regulated.

In describing and assessing the degrees of openness and control that characterize knowledge commons, one should bear in mind more than just the conventional producer perspective by which information and knowledge shareability problems often are analyzed. Hardin's "tragedy of the commons" is typically understood as challenging markets and governments to offer ways to supply resources in the face of cooperation and competition problems (Ostrom 2008). In analyzing openness with respect to resources and communities, it is likewise tempting to limit the analysis to openness with respect to actual and potential resource producers.

The cumulative and aggregative character of knowledge is fundamental to human culture. Producers of knowledge and culture resources therefore are simultaneously users and consumers. It is important to consider whether and how the degree of openness of a knowledge commons accommodates the interests of users, as matters of both function and relation. In particular, a knowledge commons in the cultural environment may function as infrastructure, a platform, or collection of resources that serves as a foundation for further creation or innovation (Frischmann 2012). In the cultural environment, the tragedy of the commons that Hardin described may appear not as an undersupply of a resource prompted by overconsumption but instead as an undersupply prompted by the failure of the private market to aggregate user or consumer preferences for certain fundamental or "infrastructural" resources. This situation occurs, for example, in the context of basic research conducted within and across universities (Strandburg 2005: 97–99). The Internet itself constitutes a knowledge commons in a sense (as well as a collection of commons), and it is likely better characterized as an infrastructural resource that solves certain problems of consumption rather than as a resource that addresses problems of production.

b. General Governance Structures

The general governance structures for a knowledge commons may include both exogenous elements arising from the background cultural environment and formal or informal leadership or decision-making structures specific to the knowledge commons. Here we identify several relevant clusters of variables that will be important to explore to gain an understanding of the general governance structure of a knowledge commons:

- entitlement structures and resource provisions;
- institutional setting (including markets and related firm and collective structures, social structures that accommodate the roles and interests of individual actors in the commons, and boundary organizations or mechanisms mediating the knowledge commons' interactions with external markets, the public domain, and other institutions);
- legal structures (including intellectual property rules, subsidies, contract and licensing law, antitrust provisions); and
- governance mechanisms of the commons (membership rules, resource contribution or extraction standards and requirements, conflict resolution mechanisms, sanctions for rule violation).

I. ENTITLEMENT STRUCTURES AND RESOURCE PROVISIONS. This cluster of questions is intended to address the boundaries around the resources themselves and to analyze how those boundaries are socially constructed, by law, technology, tradition, custom, or practice. Complicating the initial set of questions concerning what resources are contributed and subject to the commons arrangement, this part of the inquiry aims to understand how the resources are delineated, contributed, and made part of the commons.

The "natural" information environment contains an abundance of raw information resources, including inherited and experienced knowledge. Those resources often are transformed into information "things" (such as works of authorship, patented inventions, and commercial "trade secrets") and therefore into resources in the common pool via some cultural construct, such as the default copyright or patent law systems, via some other institution, such as a publishing industry producing books, films, or songs, or via some combination of these and other institutions, such as cultural practices or norms—including, to be clear, the agency of individual actors. Understanding a knowledge commons therefore requires understanding the mechanisms by which resources are provisioned to the commons, whether via legal entitlements or otherwise, and the nature of entitlements to use and consume those resources while they are part of that commons.

As with some natural resource pools that (when suitably managed) are self-sustaining and thus supply their own resources, in the cultural context commons resources may be inputs to the generation of additional resources. The follow-on invention is an obvious example. An essential attribute of the governance of a knowledge commons, therefore, is the way in which it allocates resources as they are produced dynamically. In a patent pool, for example, the patents themselves are resources constructed via rights of exclusion offered by patent law. As pool members develop follow-on inventions based on the pooled resources, the agreement by which the pool is constituted may obligate members to contribute patents covering those inventions to the pool. (Such grantbacks may raise antitrust concerns,[9] which highlight the complexities of assessing the successes of commons governance as a knowledge and information management strategy.)

Boundaries in an information environment are likewise more obviously culturally constructed than their counterparts in the field of natural resources. Oceans, lakes, and rivers have beds and shores; forests yield to fields. Boundary maintenance is an important part of commons management in natural resources, but the maintenance question often has a reference point in naturally occurring boundaries. In the information environment, all boundaries ultimately depend on social and cultural constructs, that is, on what law or society recognizes as boundaries of relevant things and resources (Madison 2003). Accordingly, this cluster of questions is intended to help flesh out the connections between the construction of commons resources and their location—what we might call "nestedness"—in broader social and cultural systems.

II. INSTITUTIONAL SETTING. Knowledge commons are functional entities; they often serve participants in markets, industries, and firms. In such cases, it is important to understand the identities and roles of those institutions and how their functions relate to the pool and its members. The Manufacturers Aircraft Association, an example of an early, well-known patent pool, was organized in large part to facilitate the production of aircraft for military use during World War I. A full account of the MAA as a knowledge commons would need to explore not only the relationships among the members of the MAA but also the relationship between the MAA and the United States government.

The institutional and social setting of a knowledge commons also may include related collectivist enterprises. Each member of a pool may be part of a network structure that extends to related collectives, firms, individuals, groups, and social structures, including professional disciplines and social norms (Strandburg et al. 2006: 1301). For example, research scientists may be organized formally into pools or commons structures within formal institutions, such as universities, including schools, institutes, and departments. The shared discipline of a particular group of scientists will cross formal institutional boundaries and may be embedded in its own formal institutions. A scientist's functional network may include members of his or her own technical art and related arts along with researchers in different arts who share a related but distinct set of social norms related

---

[9] See U.S. Dep't of Justice & Fed. Trade Comm'n, Antitrust Guidelines for the Licensing of Intellectual Property § 5.6 (1995), http://www.usdoj.gov/atr/public/guidelines/0558.pdf.

to sharing of information and knowledge. Networks in not-for-profit or educational research settings also will overlap to a degree with related networks in commercial environments. For example, researchers in university science departments will be interested in sharing information resources with researchers in corporate research-and-development groups (Strandburg 2009, 2010). A knowledge commons may bridge gaps created by the edges of formal institutional structures. Moreover, knowledge commons also may be situated in nonhierarchical and distributed institutional settings, in which participants are only loosely connected and sometimes are connected only by their participation in a particular project (Benkler 2006: 59–90).

III. LEGAL STRUCTURES THAT AFFECT THE COMMONS. Although industry, market, and networked institutional structures are essential reference points for many knowledge commons, positive law and direct government involvement with a particular commons may likewise be keys to understanding it. We distinguish between law that creates and enforces the entitlements that sustain information works, on the one hand, and law that is specifically addressed to knowledge commons themselves, on the other hand. In some circumstances, law can reinforce and sustain knowledge commons that are determined by legislators or judges to be welfare-enhancing. For example, market conditions or technologies might be such that some kind of information collective would be useful, but fear of prosecution under antitrust law or relevant IP law may be a barrier to the emergence of the pool. In such a case, a safe harbor for knowledge sharing of a sort may emerge, either via legislation or judicial decision. An exemption or more deferential treatment from antitrust scrutiny for parties engaged in a form of concerted activity, or intended to engage in concerted activity, might be adopted (Hovencamp 2012: § 36).

Legal rules may create subsidies or safe harbors for knowledge commons in ways other than by relieving at-risk parties from potential liability. For example, income-tax regimes may permit (or limit) the deduction of research expenses by firms, nonprofit enterprises, and/or research collectives. In the U.S. patent statute, the section that bars patenting inventions that are "obvious" in light of prior art in the relevant technical field formerly excluded prior art from consideration if the patent applicant and the producer of the relevant prior art were part of a common "joint research agreement."[10] Laws designed for one purpose also may effectively promote collaborations or collectives in ways not intended by their drafters. Such rules may become part of the constitution of a knowledge commons, even if they were not designed to do so. For example, Jessica Litman explains the persistence of a legal regime subsidizing jukeboxes in American copyright law along similar lines (Litman 2002: 351–53). A compulsory

---

[10] 35 U.S.C. § 103(c)(2) (2012). As part of the America Invents Act of 2012, applicable to patents that issue based on applications filed after March 16, 2013, that section was rewritten, and its provisions relocated to the section that requires that patentable inventions be novel. See 35 U.S.C. § 102(c)(2) (2012).

license permitting owners of coin-operated record players to use copyrighted American music without authorization was initially incorporated into the copyright statute to prevent copyright holders from monopolizing adjacent markets for performances. Over time, the rationale for the subsidy became less significant, but the statute was retained because a new entity emerged to support its continued existence—companies that manufactured and distributed jukeboxes. The compulsory license enabled a form of sharing of recorded music that was mandated by law rather than by consent of the individual rights owners.

IV. ENDOGENOUS GOVERNANCE MECHANISMS. Understanding the governance mechanisms particular to a given knowledge commons is at the heart of the analysis. In Ostrom's work, the degree of self-governance is an important characteristic of a resource pool (Ostrom 1990: 29–55). Membership in natural resource commons often entails rights not only to contribute to and extract from the pool but also to participate in governance processes for adopting and modifying the relevant rules of participation. Endogenous governance mechanisms may include formal or informal leadership roles, general approaches to decision making, conflict resolution procedures, technological platforms for communication and other general purposes, and so forth.

The inquiry into the governance mechanisms of a knowledge commons overlaps to some extent with the inquiry into its openness. The focus shifts, however, from access to shared resources to participation in decision making about how the resources will be produced and managed. Who decides who may be a member of the commons and what does membership entail? How are resource contribution and extraction monitored and, if necessary, limited? What sanctions and dispute resolution mechanisms are provided for dealing with conflict or misconduct? To what extent do the self-governance mechanisms of the commons rely on or incorporate formal legal mechanisms, and to what extent do they rely on or incorporate other, nonlegal institutions, technologies, or social structures?

For example, in the context of the General Public License for open source computer programs, commons membership is defined in part by the terms of the license and in part by use of the program, which, according to the terms of the license, constitutes assent to its terms.[11] Violation of the terms of the open source license, for example by distributing a copy of a program without including a copy of the program's source code, purports to terminate membership in the open source community automatically, by operation of law. Enforcement of the license regime typically is not pursued by individual contributors to the open source commons. Instead, the Free Software Foundation, a freestanding nonprofit entity dedicated to advocacy on behalf of "free" software and accompanying

---

[11] See Free Software Foundation, GNU General Public License, http://www.gnu.org/licenses/gpl.html, § 9.

open source license terms undertakes responsibility for enforcement (Free Software Foundation 2013).

Effective enforcement of the rules-in-use of a commons depends on the availability of means to monitor members' compliance with those rules. Before the emergence of the Internet, research on self-governing communities emphasized the size of the community and the distances between its members as key variables in the effectiveness of a monitoring system. Accordingly, conventional wisdom expected that informally governed groups would be relatively rare and believed that success would require modest size and relative homogeneity of interest. As Benkler (2006: 29–127) and Cohen (2006: 37–43) each argue, networking technology offers not only expanded potential for community development and resource aggregation but also the potential for increased monitoring and enforcement. (As the next section makes clear, that is not automatically a good thing, but it can help explain commons functioning.) Examination of a pool should include assessment of whether and how it is embedded in network technologies that perform or facilitate governance functions.

Research on natural resource commons also emphasizes that effective self-governance typically requires formal access to public sanctioning and/or enforcement mechanisms. Without the threat of seizure or attachment or injunction, community-based or purely norm-based mechanisms may lack sufficient bite to sustain the commons. In the context of knowledge commons, it is not yet clear when and whether it is important for commons governance to be backed up by legal enforcement. Indeed, many social norms–based governance regimes have been identified and studied (Raustiala & Sprigman 2012). In the open source computer software area, for example, courts only recently have begun to consider the enforceability of the licenses. For the most part, breaches are handled by informal norms.

c. Rules and Norms for Particular Action Arenas

A given knowledge commons may involve a number of different types of interactions among members or "action arenas." Often, these action arenas will be closely related to the community's goals and objectives. Over and above the exogenous and internal general governance mechanisms of a knowledge commons, the rules-in-use of a particular action arena may be determined by rules or norms specific to that arena. It will probably be important to analyze how the basic attributes of a knowledge commons play out in a number of its action arenas to get a full understanding of how that commons functions.

4. Patterns and Outcomes Emanating from a Particular Action Arena

Finally, the analysis of a knowledge commons should include an inquiry into its patterns of interactions and outcomes. The outcomes of a knowledge commons typically will take two forms, which in a particular case often will be inextricably linked. With respect to knowledge and information resources, a knowledge commons usually will produce some intellectual or knowledge-related (or material) output. Thus, the MAA enabled the production of airplanes. The Linux open source project supports the Linux computer program. Wikipedia produces Wikipedia.org. The AP enables the production of newspapers and other news resources.

In addition, the social patterns that emerge from the construction and governance of a knowledge commons may themselves constitute ongoing, constantly refreshed commons outcomes. Many of the companies that were parties to the original MAA agreement combined via merger and acquisition by 1929 to form the Curtiss-Wright Corporation, which is still a significant defense contractor today (Patillo 1998:80–81). The Linux project and Wikipedia are notable not only for their production of complex industrial-scale products but also for their production of networks of contributors, distributed broadly in space and time, for whom participation in the commons is an important and meaningful individual and social practice (Benkler 2006: 65–74). The AP and other wire services have cultivated and retained identities as distinct and productive enterprises despite the fact that much of what they publish is created by their members. The jamband community is a recognized community that defines itself partly via its practices of archiving and sharing jamband performances.

The inquiry into outcomes should focus explicitly on any costs or harms associated with the commons as well as on its benefits. Knowledge commons should be assessed in light both of whether and how they serve their self-identified goals and objectives and of any collateral consequences. The patterns and outcomes bucket of questions should aim both to identify the outcomes of the commons under study and to describe relevant criteria for evaluating those outcomes. Often, the evaluation of outcomes will begin with the identified goals and objectives of the community. The community may change its goals over time, and specific action areas may lead to the development of more fine-grained objectives that provide further basis for evaluation. Moreover, interactions with non-members may provide additional outcomes to evaluate.

Since the eventual goal of this research is to extract generalizable knowledge that will be useful for policy makers, the evaluation of outcomes raises difficult and important issues about how to derive metrics that will permit comparative institutional analysis. The evaluation of success is explicitly normative; for example, one can ask about whether a community met its internal goals and objectives or about its overall impact on the welfare of society. Comparing knowledge commons arrangements to one another requires comparable outcome metrics. For similarly situated communities with similar objectives, it may be relatively straightforward to develop appropriate metrics on a case-by-case basis. If one wants to compare differently situated communities with different objectives, the task is harder. Devising metrics that allow one to compare knowledge commons to other institutions for producing innovation and creativity may be even more difficult. The design of outcome metrics, which is a general challenge to comparative institutional analysis, is a subject for further research.

a. Solutions and Benefits

We have noted that knowledge commons in the cultural environment emerge or are created for a variety of reasons: as solutions to collective action or other transactions cost problems unrelated to legal intellectual property, as solutions to problems that arise from the nature of intellectual property entitlements, as solutions to boundary-spanning dilemmas, and as reactions to "infrastructure"-type problems stemming from the market's inability to aggregate individual demand for standards or platform resources—the inverse of the standard tragedy-of-the-commons diagnosis. The pool of potential knowledge commons cases is, therefore, quite broad, and the range of possible solutions and benefits they produce is likewise broad.

For any specific knowledge commons, the inquiry into solutions and benefits should address not only the problems that the commons appears to be designed to solve and precisely how and whether it solves those problems but also whether the commons succeeds in generating and sustaining spillovers and contributing to a dynamic cultural environment more broadly. Quantifying or otherwise documenting the latter type of outcome may be particularly difficult, because the benefits of spillovers often accrue not only to direct consumers of the creative output of the commons, but to other members of society. As a result, assessments of success may, of necessity, take comparative rather than absolute form. Indeed, both the original IAD framework and our adaptation are intended for comparative institutional analysis. What kinds of comparisons might be relevant and useful as benchmarks in the knowledge commons setting? Researchers might ask about the respects in which commons governance helps to achieve outcomes (whether in terms of resources or community or both) different than (if not necessarily better than, in all cases) the outcomes achieved by attempts to solve those problems using other institutional regimes, such as private rights allocated in markets, or government regulation.

b. Costs and Risks Associated with a Cultural Commons

A knowledge commons approach often may involve a trade-off between the benefits anticipated from the commons, such as the dynamic welfare enhancements expected from open sharing, and the costs and risks associated with cooperation between those who might otherwise compete to provide knowledge resources in a market setting. In conventional law-and-economics terms, these costs and risks are fairly well understood. Importantly, they are in many instances better understood and easier to describe and quantify than the dynamic benefits that knowledge commons may supply. For example, institutions that enable firms to share access to pooled information resources may also facilitate cooperation along lines that may be anticompetitive and therefore socially harmful: agreements to raise and fix costs and agreements to reduce output. Knowledge commons also involve administrative costs associated with constructing, monitoring, and enforcing compliance with the rules of the pool. Here again the analysis is comparative. Both costs and benefits associated with producing particular information resources must be compared to the costs and benefits associated with producing the same kind of information resources by IP-based market transactions, government subsidy, or some alternative system.

V. Conclusion

Applying an environmental metaphor pioneered by earlier intellectual property law scholars, we analogize information and knowledge resources in the cultural environment to physical resources in the natural environment. We identify a set of knowledge commons, or pools of information resources, that serve functions in the cultural environment similar to the functions provided by common-pool resources in the natural environment. These knowledge commons serve as alternatives to purely private rights of exclusion and to government intervention in solving a variety of underproduction and overconsumption problems associated with an unmanaged or "natural" resource. Although knowledge commons exist for a variety of purposes, we hypothesize that they are often welfare-enhancing, because they solve the problems associated with producing nonrival information resources, while promoting knowledge distribution and valuable information spillovers.

We argue that understanding the origins and operation of knowledge commons requires case studies aimed at empirical assessment of a variety of attributes whose role and importance cannot be specified in advance based on simple models or our current understanding. Borrowing from Ostrom's Institutional Analysis and Development framework, we suggest a framework that should guide case studies of knowledge commons in exploring the ways in which information resources and resource commons are structured by default rules of exclusion, and the ways in which members of these pools manage participation in the collection, production, preservation, and extraction of information resources.

We offer the framework described in this chapter as a template for ongoing case study investigations of knowledge commons across a broad variety of domains. The case studies collected in this volume represent a small step in that direction. We hypothesize (and expect) that approaching the study of knowledge commons as an integrated field of research will elevate collective, intermediate solutions to a place of significance in accounts of property regimes and diminish skepticism about the range of situations that are amenable to collectively governed, "open" approaches to knowledge production. Case studies will also call attention to the designed character of both the cultural and the legal environments in which knowledge and information policy problems reside. Like Ostrom's studies of natural resource commons, systematic analyses of knowledge commons across a wide range of collected case studies are likely to lead us to doubt panacea prescriptions drawn from overly simplistic models. Understanding how knowledge commons work should enable better design of knowledge-producing and knowledge-distributing institutions generally.

The existing scholarly literature reports various case study investigations of creative institutions grounded in social norms (Schultz 2006), transactions cost economics (Merges 1996), and even history and anthropology (Kelty 2008), all of which may be profitably aggregated and recast as examples of knowledge commons. One step in that direction is our application of the framework to analyze universities as cultural commons (Madison, Frischmann, & Strandburg 2009). Collecting and reconstructing this literature using the clusters of questions listed above will, in our estimation, yield new insights into the emergence and effective functioning of knowledge commons. Going forward, and beginning with the cases included in this volume, we anticipate developing an inventory of new commons case studies. We also hope other scholars will consider using this framework as part of their own work. Over time, we hope that the results of further case studies will yield not only better descriptive information regarding knowledge commons but also refinements to the knowledge commons framework and to the above clusters of questions. In a real sense, the study of commons is itself a knowledge commons, and our own three-part collaboration is a nested commons within the scholarly community that studies commons.

Acknowledgments

Professor Strandburg acknowledges the generous support of the Filomen D'Agostino and Max E. Greenberg Research Fund.

References

James M. Acheson, Capturing the Commons: Devising Institutions to Manage the Maine Lobster Industry (University Press of New England 2003).

Teresa M. Amabile, Creativity in Context (Westview Press 1996).

Philip E. Auerswald & Lewis M. Branscomb, *Start-ups and Spin-offs: Collective Entrepreneurship Between Invention and Innovation*, in The Emergence of Entrepreneurship Policy: Governance, Start-ups, and Growth in the U.S. Knowledge Economy 61 (David M. Hart ed., Cambridge University Press 2003).

Douglas G. Baird, *The Story of INS v. AP: Property, Natural Monopoly, and the Uneasy Legacy of Concocted Controversy*, in Intellectual Property Stories 9 (Jane C. Ginsburg & Rochelle Cooper Dreyfuss eds., Foundation Press 2005).

Robert A. Baron & Scott A. Shane, Entrepreneurship: A Process Perspective (Cengage Learning 2007).

Yochai Benkler, The Wealth of Networks: How Social Production Transforms Markets and Freedom (Yale University Press 2006).

Enrico Bertacchini et al. eds., Cultural Commons: A New Perspective on the Production and Evolution of Cultures (Edward Elgar Publishing 2012).

James Boyle, *A Politics of Intellectual Property: Environmentalism for the Net?*, 47 Duke L.J. 87 (1997).

Julie E. Cohen, *Pervasively Distributed Copyright Enforcement*, 95 GEORGETOWN L.J. 1 (2006).

RICHARD CORNES & TODD SANDLER, THE THEORY OF EXTERNALITIES, PUBLIC GOODS, AND CLUB GOODS (2d ed., Cambridge University Press 1996).

Harold Demsetz, *Toward a Theory of Property Rights*, 57 AM. ECONOMIC REV. 347 (1967).

Harry T. Dykman, *Patent Licensing Within the Manufacturer's Aircraft Association (MAA)*, 46 J. PATENT OFFICE SOCIETY 646 (1964).

Nikolaus Franke & Sonali Shah, *How Communities Support Innovative Activities: A Exploration of Assistance and Sharing among End-Users*, 32 RESEARCH POLICY 157 (2003).

Free Software Foundation, *What Is Free Software and Why Is It So Important for Society?*, http://www.fsf.org/about/what-is-free-software (accessed June 16, 2013).

Bruno S. Frey, *What Values Should Count in the Arts? The Tension between Economic Effects and Cultural Value, in* BEYOND PRICE. VALUE IN CULTURE, ECONOMICS AND THE ARTS (Michael Hutter & David Throsby eds., Cambridge University Press 2008).

Brett M. Frischmann, *Innovation and Institutions: Rethinking the Economics of U.S. Science and Technology Policy*, 24 VERMONT. L. REV. 347 (2000).

Brett M. Frischmann, *Environmental Infrastructure*, 35 ECOLOGY L.Q. 151 (2008).

Brett M. Frischmann, *The Pull of Patents*, 77 FORDHAM L. REV. 2143 (2009a).

Brett Frischmann, *Spillovers Theory and Its Conceptual Boundaries*, 51 WILLIAM & MARY L. REV. 801 (2009b).

Brett M. Frischmann & Mark A. Lemley, *Spillovers*, 107 COLUMBIA L. REV. 257 (2007).

BRETT M. FRISCHMANN, INFRASTRUCTURE: THE SOCIAL VALUE OF SHARED RESOURCES (Oxford University Press 2012).

Brett M. Frischmann, *Two Enduring Lessons from Elinor Ostrom*, 9 J. OF INSTITUTIONAL ECONOMICS 387 (2013).

Fred Gault & Eric A. von Hippel, *The Prevalence of User Innovation and Free Innovation Transfers: Implications for Statistical Indicators and Innovation Policy* (MIT Sloan School of Management Working Paper 2009), http://evhippel.files.wordpress.com/2013/08/fred-and-eric-ssrn-2009.pdf.

Wendy J. Gordon, *Harmless Use: Gleaning from Fields of Copyrighted Works*, 77 FORDHAM L. REV. 2411 (2009).

Garrett Hardin, *The Tragedy of the Commons*, 162 SCIENCE 1243 (1968).

Dietmar Harhoff, Joachim Henkel & Eric von Hippel, *Profiting from Voluntary Information Spillovers: How Users Benefits by Freely Revealing Their Innovations*, 32 RESEARCH POLICY 1753 (2003).

Michael A. Heller, *The Tragedy of the Anticommons: Property in the Transition from Marx to Markets*, 111 HARVARD L. REV. 621 (1998).

Charlotte Hess, *Constructing a New Research Agenda for Cultural Commons, in* CULTURAL COMMONS: A NEW PERSPECTIVE ON THE PRODUCTION AND EVOLUTION OF CULTURES (Enrico Bertacchini et al. eds., Edward Elgar Publishing 2012).

David A. Hoffman & Salil K. Mehra, *Wikitruth Through Wikiorder*, 59 EMORY L.J. 151 (2009).

HERBERT HOVENKAMP ET AL., IP AND ANTITRUST: AN ANALYSIS OF ANTITRUST PRINCIPLES APPLIED TO INTELLECTUAL PROPERTY LAW (Aspen Publishers 2012).

Patrick L. Jones & Katherine J. Strandburg, *Technology Transfer and an Information View of Universities: A Conceptual Framework for Academic Freedom, Intellectual Property, Technology Transfer and the University Mission* (Feb. 22, 2010) (unpublished manuscript, on file with authors).

Dennis S. Karjala, *Congestion Externalities and Extended Copyright Protection*, 94 GEORGETOWN L.J. 1065 (2006).

CHRISTOPHER M. KELTY, TWO BITS: THE CULTURAL SIGNIFICANCE OF FREE SOFTWARE (Duke University Press 2008).

Sapna Kumar & Arti Rai, *Synthetic Biology: The Intellectual Property Puzzle*, 85 TEXAS L. REV. 1745 (2007).

Karim R. Lakhani & Robert G. Wolf, *Why Hackers Do What They Do: Understanding Motivation and Effort in Free/Open Source Software Projects*, in PERSPECTIVES ON FREE AND OPEN SOURCE SOFTWARE (J. Feller et al. eds., MIT Press 2005).

Mark A. Lemley, *Property, Intellectual Property, and Free Riding*, 83 TEXAS L. REV. 1031 (2005).

Jessica Litman, *War Stories*, 20 CARDOZO ARTS & ENT. L.J. 337 (2002).

Lydia Pallas Loren, *The Pope's Copyright? Aligning Incentives with Reality by Using Creative Motivation to Shape Copyright Protection*, 69 LOUISIANA. L. REV. 1, 11 (2008).

Jacob Loshin, *Secrets Revealed: How Magicians Protect Intellectual Property Without Law*, in LAW AND MAGIC: A COLLECTION OF ESSAYS (Christine A. Corcos ed., Carolina Academic Press 2008).

Michael J. Madison, *Rights of Access and the Shape of the Internet*, 44 BOSTON COLLEGE L. REV. 433 (2003).

Michael J. Madison, *Rewriting Fair Use and the Future of Copyright Reform*, 23 CARDOZO ARTS & ENT. L.J. 391 (2005a).

Michael J. Madison, *Law as Design: Objects, Concepts, and Digital Things*, 56 CASE WESTERN. RESERVE L. REV. 381 (2005b).

Michael J. Madison, Brett M. Frischmann, & Katherine J. Strandburg, *The University as Constructed Cultural Commons*, 30 WASHINGTON UNIVERSITY J. LAW & POLICY 365 (2009).

Michael J. Madison, Brett M. Frischmann, & Katherine J. Strandburg, *Constructing Commons in the Cultural Environment*, 95 CORNELL L. REV. 657 (2010a).

Michael J. Madison, Brett M. Frischmann, & Katherine J. Strandburg, *Reply: The Complexity of Commons*, 95 CORNELL L. REV. 839 (2010b).

Robert P. Merges, *Contracting into Liability Rules: Intellectual Property Rights and Collective Rights Organizations*, 84 CALIFORNIA L. REV. 1293 (1996).

Robert P. Merges, *A Transactional View of Property Rights*, 20 BERKELEY TECH. L.J. 1477 (2005).

Michael Morgan, *New Paradigms in Industry: The Single Nucleotide Polymorphism Consortium*, in THE ROLE OF SCIENTIFIC AND TECHNICAL DATA AND INFORMATION IN THE PUBLIC DOMAIN: PROCEEDINGS OF A SYMPOSIUM 194 (Julie M. Esanu & Paul F. Uhlir eds., National Academies Press 2003).

CRAIG ALLEN NARD, MICHAEL J. MADISON, & MARK MCKENNA, THE LAW OF INTELLECTUAL PROPERTY (4th ed., Aspen Publishers 2013).

Richard Newell, Arti Rai, Jerome Reichman, & Jonathan B. Wiener, *Intellectual Property and Alternatives: Strategies for Green Innovation* (Chatham House Energy, Environment and Development Programme Paper No. 08/03, December 2008).

Siobhán O'Mahony & Beth A. Bechky, *Boundary Organizations: Enabling Collaboration Among Unexpected Allies*, 53 ADMINISTRATIVE SCIENCE Q. 422 (2008).

ELINOR Ostrom, GOVERNING THE COMMONS: THE EVOLUTION OF INSTITUTIONS FOR COLLECTIVE ACTION (Cambridge University Press 1990).

ELINOR Ostrom, UNDERSTANDING INSTITUTIONAL DIVERSITY (Princeton University Press 2005).

Elinor Ostrom & Charlotte Hess, *A Framework for Analyzing the Knowledge Commons, in* UNDERSTANDING KNOWLEDGE AS A COMMONS: FROM THEORY TO PRACTICE 41 (Charlotte Hess & Elinor Ostrom eds., MIT Press 2006).

Elinor Ostrom, *Tragedy of the Commons, in* THE NEW PALGRAVE DICTIONARY OF ECONOMICS (Steven N. Durlauf & Lawrence E. Blume eds., 2d ed. 2008), http://www.dictionaryofeconomics.com/article?id=pde2008_T000193.

Elinor Ostrom et al., *Going Beyond Panaceas*, 104 PROCEEDINGS OF THE NATIONAL ACADEMY OF SCIENCE U.S. 15176 (2007).

DONALD M. PATTILLO, PUSHING THE ENVELOPE: THE AMERICAN AIRCRAFT INDUSTRY (University of Michigan Press 1998).

John Quiggin & Dan Hunter, *Money Ruins Everything*, 30 HASTINGS COMM. & ENT. L.J. 203 (2008).

Arti K. Rai, *Intellectual Property Rights in Biotechnology: Addressing New Technology*, 34 WAKE FOREST L. REV. 827 (1999).

KAL RAUSTIALA & CHRISTOPHER SPRIGMAN, THE KNOCKOFF ECONOMY: HOW IMITATION SPARKS INNOVATION (Oxford University Press 2012).

J. H. Reichman & Paul F. Uhlir, *A Contractually Reconstructed Research Commons for Scientific Data in a Highly Protectionist Intellectual Property Environment*, 66 LAW & CONTEMP. PROBS. 315 (2003).

REPORTERS OF THE ASSOCIATED PRESS, BREAKING NEWS: HOW THE ASSOCIATED PRESS HAS COVERED WAR, PEACE, AND EVERYTHING ELSE (Princeton Architectural Press 2007).

CAROL M. ROSE, PROPERTY AND PERSUASION: ESSAYS ON THE HISTORY, THEORY, AND RHETORIC OF OWNERSHIP (Westview Press 1994).

Carol M. Rose, *Big Roads, Big Rights: Varieties of Public Infrastructure and Their Impact on Environmental Resources*, 50 ARIZONA L. REV. 409 (2008).

Joshua D. Sarnoff, *Government Choices in Innovation Funding (with Reference to Climate Change)*, 62 EMORY L.J. 1087 (2013).

Mark F. Schultz, *Fear and Norms and Rock & Roll: What Jambands Can Teach Us About Persuading People to Obey Copyright Law*, 21 BERKELEY TECH. L.J. 651 (2006).

CHARLES M. SCHWEIK & ROBERT C. ENGLISH, INTERNET SUCCESS: A STUDY OF OPEN-SOURCE SOFTWARE COMMONS (MIT Press 2012).

Carl Shapiro, *Navigating the Patent Thicket: Cross Licenses, Patent Pools, and Standard Setting, in* 1 INNOVATION POLICY AND THE ECONOMY 119 (Adam B. Jaffe et al. eds., NBER 2000).

Stephen Shmanske, *News as a Public Good: Cooperative Ownership, Price Commitments, and the Success of the Associated Press*, 60 BUSINESS HISTORY REV. 55 (1986).

Henry E. Smith, *Semicommon Property Rights and Scattering in the Open Fields*, 29 J. LEGAL STUDIES 131 (2000).

Ruth Maria Stock, Pedro Oliveira, & Eric A. Von Hippel, *Impacts of Hedonic and Utilitarian User Motives on the Innovativeness of User-Developed Solutions* (MIT Sloan School of Management Working Paper 2013), http://ssrn.com/abstract=2260436.

Katherine J. Strandburg, *Curiosity-Driven Research and University Technology Transfer, in* 16 UNIVERSITY ENTREPRENEURSHIP AND TECHNOLOGY TRANSFER: PROCESS, DESIGN, AND INTELLECTUAL PROPERTY 93 (JAI Press 2005).

Katherine J. Strandburg et al., *Law and the Science of Networks: An Overview and an Application to the "Patent Explosion,"* 21 BERKELEY TECH. L.J. 1293 (2006).

Katherine J. Strandburg, *User Innovator Community Norms: At the Boundary Between Academic and Industry Research*, 77 FORDHAM L. REV. 2237 (2009).

Katherine J. Strandburg, *Norms and the Sharing of Research Materials and Tacit Knowledge*, *in* WORKING WITHIN THE BOUNDARIES OF INTELLECTUAL PROPERTY (Rochelle C. Dreyfuss et al. eds., Oxford University Press 2010).

Jean Tirole & Josh Lerner, *Some Simple Economics of Open Source*, 50 J. INDUSTRIAL ECONOMICS 197 (2002)

Rebecca Tushnet, *Economies of Desire: Fair Use and Marketplace Assumptions*, 51 WILLIAM & MARY L. REV. 513 (2009).

W. KIP VISCUSI ET AL., ECONOMICS OF REGULATION AND ANTITRUST (4th ed. MIT Press 2005).

ERIC VON HIPPEL, DEMOCRATIZING INNOVATION (MIT Press 2005).

Eric von Hippel & Harold Demonaco, *Market Failure in Diffusion of User Innovations: The Case of "Off-Label" Innovations by Medical Clinicians*, (MIT Sloan School of Management Working Paper 2013), http://ssrn.com/abstract=2275562.

John P. Walsh et al., *Where Excludability Matters: Material Versus Intellectual Property in Academic Biomedical Research*, 36 RESEARCH POLICY 1184 (2007).

Joel West, *Seeking Open Infrastructure: Contrasting Open Standards, Open Source and Open Innovation*, 12 FIRST MONDAY no. 6 (June 4, 2007), http://firstmonday.org/htbin/cgiwrap/bin/ojs/index.php/fm/article/view/1913/1795.

Diane Leenheer Zimmerman, *Copyrights as Incentives: Did We Just Imagine That?*, 12 THEORETICAL INQUIRIES L. 29 (2011).

2 Learning from Lin: Lessons and Cautions from the Natural Commons for the Knowledge Commons
Daniel H. Cole*

I. Introduction

Legal scholars who write about information and intellectual property (IP), especially those concerned with drawing appropriate boundaries between private and public domains, understandably have been mining the voluminous writings of the late Elinor ("Lin") Ostrom for valuable lessons. Ostrom spent a lifetime studying the wide variety of property regimes used anywhere in the world for governing common-pool resources, primarily (but not exclusively) in the natural world (E. Ostrom 2010a, 2010c). Later in her career, Ostrom contributed applications of her frameworks, theories, and models to what she called the "knowledge commons." (Hess & E. Ostrom 2007). She recognized the knowledge commons as a separate realm from the natural commons, which would not admit simple transfer of lessons learned from her earlier work, but required systematic study of its own resources, actors, institutions, action situations, and so forth. Each chapter in this book contributes to that systematic study.

* Daniel H. Cole is Professor of Law and of Public and Environmental Affairs at Indiana University, Bloomington, Indiana, USA. He is also a member of the Affiliated Faculty of the Vincent and Elinor Ostrom Workshop in Political Theory and Policy Analysis. He is author or editor of seven books, including most recently *Property in Land and Other Resources* (Lincoln Institute of Land Policy 2012), which he co-edited with Elinor Ostrom.

This chapter offers guidance to IP scholars who are seeking to adapt, analogize to, or otherwise use Ostrom's work to inform their own research. The main lessons are two: (1) those looking for *normative* guidance from Ostrom as to the proper structure of IP law are bound to be disappointed (or dishonest); but (2) those looking for conceptual, analytical, and methodological guidance will find it in Ostrom's Institutional Analysis and Development (IAD) framework, which can (a) improve IP scholars' understanding of information and information flows under alternative institutional arrangements;[1] (b) diagnose problems (or dilemmas) in existing institutional arrangements; and (c) in select cases predict outcomes under alternative institutional arrangements. Even then, normative implications will remain scarce (to nonexistent), and all predictions will be contingent and contestable. No panacea solutions to social dilemmas relating to information will be discovered (Frischmann 2013).

Even analytical lessons from Ostrom's work for IP scholars will be limited, as Madison, Frischmann, & Strandburg (2010) have observed, by an important distinction between natural common-pool resources and information or knowledge commons, which too often goes unremarked: they are very different kinds of goods, implying different governance mechanisms. Suffice it to say, at this point, that for natural common-pool resources "open access" is nearly always a problem requiring an institutional remedy, whereas in information commons it is a viable (though not necessarily preferable) institutional means of achieving social goals.

II. IP Scholars Seeking Normative Support from Ostrom's Work Will Not Find It

Legal scholarship, including in the field of intellectual property (IP), is overwhelmingly normative. Scholars argue about what sets of rules *should* apply, and who should apply them, to interactions among individuals in society. In IP, nearly all of the biggest questions are normative: What constitutional limits should apply to copyright terms? What should be the scope of private ownership under copyright and patent laws? How best to resolve the tension between creating incentives to innovate, for example, by providing exclusive property rights, and facilitating market competition for the benefit of consumers? What should be the scope of "fair use"? How best to prevent the proliferation of IP

---

[1] By "institutional arrangement," I mean sets of rules implemented through some organizational structure. I generally follow Douglass North's definition of an "institution" as a human-devised rule—whether a formal legal rule or an informal social norm—for structuring social interactions (North 1990: 3). For North, organizations are not institutions, but amalgams of actors. Elinor Ostrom defined "institutions" variously, but not inconsistently, in her works (see Cole 2013: 390-391). Moreover, as Ostrom points out, her own definitions were consistent with North's understanding of the distinctions between "institutions" and "organizations" (see E. Ostrom 2005: 179). However, in Ostrom's analytical framework, it might sometimes at least be more useful to consider organizations as "action arenas" rather than as actors. For more on "action arenas" as part of Ostrom's analytical framework, see infra.

rights from creating tangled webs that perversely impede further innovations? Which, if any, innovations that contribute to the stock of useful knowledge fall immediately into the "knowledge commons"? Which should *never* do so?

That IP law is dominated by such normative issues is not surprising. After all, laws *are* (or embody) norms.[2] Few other academic disciplines are so heavily normative in focus as legal studies. Most social-scientific disciplines, and scholars within those disciplines, tend to be more analytical than normative in their approaches and methods.[3]

Elinor Ostrom's work provides a veritable model of social-scientific analysis. She focused on constructing empirically informed frameworks, theories, and models that were (1) conceptually clear; (2) thickly descriptive (embracing complexity); (2) diagnostic; (3) analytically rigorous; and (4) integrative of configural interactions among explanatory factors, suggesting patterns of social interactions and their social-ecological consequences—as with the "design principles" from *Governing the Commons* (E. Ostrom 1990). The integration of explanatory factors might sometimes allow for (tentative) predictions about the (relative) success or failure of similar institutional applications in similar social-ecological circumstances. But rarely, if ever, will a reader of her work come across an expressly normative argument (unless one considers to be "normative" her frequent arguments about the importance of conceptual clarity and interdisciplinary cooperation using multiple methods).

Throughout much of her work, Ostrom evinced one substantive normative commitment to the principle of self-governance, as reflected in the "polycentric approach" pioneered by her husband, the political theorist Vincent Ostrom (V. Ostrom 1999; V. Ostrom, Tiebout, & Warren 1961; E. Ostrom 2009a, 2009b, 2010b, 2010c, 2010d, 2012). That approach embodies a normative principle of subsidiarity according to which governance is a "coresponsibility" of units at central (or national), regional (subnational), and local levels (see *Decentralization: A Sampling of Omissions*). But even that commitment to polycentrism was contingent, context-specific, and focused on matching the scale of governance to the scale of operations appropriate for the particular production or provision problem under investigation. For example, in her early studies of municipal versus neighborhood policing in Indianapolis, Indiana, Ostrom hypothesized that smaller police departments would function more effectively (according to a variable of criteria) than would highly consolidated, metropolitan police departments. But her empirical research revealed that medium-size police departments overall outperformed both smaller (neighborhood) and larger (municipal-level) units (E. Ostrom, Parks, &

---

[2] More specifically, they are the *formal* "rules of the game," which, together with informal social norms, structure social interactions (see North 1990: 3).

[3] The recent rise of empirical legal scholarship and other applications of social-scientific methodologies to law have reduced, but not eliminated, the dominance of normative legal scholarship. On the rise of empirical legal scholarship, see, e.g., Heise (2002). On more general applications of social-scientific methodologies to law, see, e.g., Lempert & Sanders (1986); Monahan & Walker (2009); Baird, Gertner, & Picker (1998).

Whitaker 1978).[4] Thus, polycentricism itself was not immune to Ostrom's oft-repeated injunction that there are no institutional panaceas for resolving complex social dilemmas (E. Ostrom 2007).

Aside from her strong (but contingent) commitment to polycentricism, the relevance of which is unclear in the context of the information or knowledge commons, the goal of Ostrom's work never was to promote specific social outcomes. Though she is sometimes portrayed as an "advocate" for local self-governance using common-property regimes, she really was only a proponent of the *idea* that such governance systems are *sometimes* successful according to some evaluative criterion, such as sustainability of the resource base over time. As such, she argued that scholars should not summarily exclude, as Garrett Hardin (1968) did, common-property regimes from comparative analyses of alternative institutional solutions to social-ecological dilemmas.[5] Ostrom did not believe local self-governance was *the* answer to resource overuse problems any more than public ownership/regulation or private ownership/markets (E. Ostrom, Janssen, & Anderies 2007; Frischmann 2012). Again, there are no panaceas—no universal, first-best, institutional solutions to inevitably complex social dilemmas (E. Ostrom 2011–2012; Acheson 2011).

That Elinor Ostrom, like many other social scientists, elevated analytical and methodological considerations over normative arguments creates an insuperable problem for legal scholars who would appropriate her frameworks, theories, and models to further their own normative policy preferences, whether in natural resources law or IP law. It just won't work. No one can point to anything in any of Ostrom's voluminous writings that would support arguments that, for example, IP rights should be more restricted than they are at present or the scope of "fair use" should be broader (or narrower).[6] Ostrom might (or might not) have agreed personally with those normative assertions, but nothing in her work on local common-property regimes, including the "design principles" she derived in *Governing the Commons*, supports normative conclusions.

That might seem odd, given that Ostrom's famous IAD framework, which predated *Governing the Commons*, has a box devoted to "Evaluative Criteria." The purpose of that box was to adjudge, as people inevitably do, social and ecological outcomes of social interactions in which actors, holding designated positions, behave strategically but in general accordance with "rules-in-use."[7] It would seem that any such evaluative criteria must

---

[4] More generally, Ostrom and her co-authors found little empirical support for conventional presumptions of constant economies of scale in provision of public services. They found both economies of scale and diseconomies of scale, depending on the types of public services being provided and the circumstances (e.g., community attributes) in which they were being provided.

[5] On comparative institutional analysis, see, e.g., Cole (2013); Komesar (1994); Aoki (2001).

[6] One arguable exception is mentioned in Section 6 below, where I claim that Ostrom (and co-author Charlotte Hess) simply (perhaps "casually" would be a better word) erred in implying that open-access information repositories invariably are a "positive" outcome of collective action and proprietary information systems with gated access invariably are a "negative" outcome. If anything, this example is so exceptional that it proves the rule that Ostrom was exceedingly reluctant to make or support sweeping normative generalizations.

[7] The IAD framework is set out in much more detail, infra.

themselves be normative or at least imply normative consequences. Tellingly, Ostrom herself paid scant attention to the "Evaluative Criteria" box in her IAD framework, but recognized that the box might be populated by various (not necessarily consistent) criteria. For example, she referred to alternative evaluative criteria, including (1) economic efficiency, (2) fiscal equivalence, (3) redistributional equity, (4) accountability, (5) conformance to values of local actors, and (6) sustainability, and noted the need to make trade-offs among evaluative criteria (E. Ostrom 2011). Ostrom's decision to avoid committing to a specific evaluative criterion or set of criteria was quite intentional. Her goal was to provide a framework for analysis consistent with a wide variety of theories and models, which might embody varying normative commitments. Indeed, she contended that her IAD framework was congenial to microeconomic theory, game theory, transaction cost theory, social cost theory, public choice, and constitutional and covenantal theory, along with theories of public goods and common-pool resources (E. Ostrom 2005: 28; Madison, Frischmann, & Strandburg 2010). Such a diversity of theories could only be compatible with the IAD framework if the framework itself was not tilted to favor one or more of them to the detriment of others. Moreover, as recognized by the editors of this book and incorporated into their adapted version of the IAD framework, Evaluative Criteria often are, or can be, based on the relevant community's explicit (and sometimes implicit) objectives.

The most that can be said is that, in a social-ecological systems context, Ostrom *assumed* that more robust and resilient resource-management regimes tended to be more successful (perhaps by definition) and, therefore, better. From that point, we might legitimately argue that the "design principles" from *Governing the Commons* were informed by an implicit normative commitment to long-run sustainability of social-ecological systems—hardly a controversial policy goal in the context of natural resources. Indeed, the widespread agreement about that implicit normative goal of sustainability, among diverse scholars with varying normative commitments, may have enabled Ostrom to pay less attention to "evaluative criteria" than would have been necessary in the absence of such consensus.

III. What IP Scholars *Can* Learn from Ostrom: Conceptual, Analytical, and Methodological Lessons

Setting normative considerations to one side, Ostrom's work has a great deal to offer IP scholars seeking to understand and diagnose IP problems, and possibly (just possibly) to predict outcomes from interactions under alternative IP arrangements. Indeed, unlike many of her fellow political scientists who have fallen in love with abstract models and statistical analyses for their own sakes, Ostrom was never satisfied if her research did not yield policy-relevant insights. Indeed, she possessed a unique ability to simultaneously combine scientific rigor with policy relevance. But she always was more interested in *informing* policy, than pushing it in one direction or another.

In the remainder of this chapter, I will suggest that Ostrom's work offers (at least) two useful and applicable *analytical* and *methodological* lessons for IP scholars, including (1) the importance of conceptual clarity, particularly in distinguishing between resource attributes, institutions, and actors; and (2) the IAD framework (or some variant of it) for understanding social interactions structured in substantial part by IP rights.[8] Using the IAD framework and comparing cases, models, and experimental outcomes might allow scholars eventually (after several years of research design, implementation, data collection, and analysis) to develop something like the "design principles" Ostrom derived for local common-property regimes used to govern common-pool resources.[9] Such principles might (or might not) facilitate *predictions* of circumstances in which one combination of public, common, and private rights (and duties) in "common pools" of information might work better (or worse) than alternative combinations. Her primary purpose in setting them out was not to enable prediction but merely to identify "underlying regularities" in local common-property regimes (E. Ostrom 2010a: 16).[10]

A. THE PARAMOUNT IMPORTANCE OF CONCEPTUAL CLARITY

Legends abound of three-hour (or longer) meetings at Vincent and Elinor Ostrom's Workshop in Political Theory and Policy Analysis at Indiana University devoted entirely to defining a single term or concept. These were not mere scholastic exercises but practical and important efforts to facilitate cross-disciplinary understanding, so that scholars from diverse academic backgrounds (including, but not limited to, anthropology, economics, game theory, history, law, philosophy, political science, psychology, public administration, and sociology), using different analytical tools and methods, could work together effectively to describe, diagnose, analyze, and possibly resolve commons problems. In the absence of an agreed vocabulary—or, at least, clearly defined terms— cross-disciplinary communication suffers, and progress toward resolving social dilemmas

---

[8] The value of the IAD framework already has been recognized by IP scholars writing from various disciplinary perspectives about the information or knowledge commons. See, e.g., Madison, Frischmann, & Strandburg (2010); Tenenberg (2008); and Schweik & English (2007).

[9] Ostrom's phrase "design principles" can be misleading. She did not mean necessarily to imply either the implementation of a strategic plan or a designer. See Becker & Ostrom 1995: 122 ("one should not presume that there was a conscious overall plan to develop institutions that met the design principles. Rather, the design principles are an effort of careful observers to identify commonalities that help to account for sustainability of fragile resources over very long periods of time."). Ostrom, herself, has regretted confusion arising from the phrase "design principles" and has suggested "best practices" as an alternative (E. Ostrom 2010c: 14, n.5). However, given the normative implication of the word "best," the substitute phrase might prove just as misleading as "design principles." In any case, a recent meta-analysis testing the "design principles" from *Governing the Commons* found them robust overall (see Cox et al. 2010).

[10] Perhaps the phrase "underlying regularities" (or "regularly observed characteristics") might be more fitting than either "design principles" or "best practices" for denoting the attributes of successful commons-management regimes.

of shared concern is obstructed.[11] That concern motivated creation of the Institutional Analysis and Development (IAD) framework, which is addressed in the following subsection. Scholars adopting that framework essentially commit to "a common set of linguistic elements that can be used to analyze a wide diversity of problems," including potentially those relating to the information or knowledge commons (E. Ostrom 2010b).

Ostrom was not an IP scholar; nor am I. So I will not presume to recommend that IP scholars simply adopt or adapt the shared vocabulary that Ostrom "Workshoppers"[12] developed over the course of many years of long and often contentious discussions. Despite Ostrom's goal of generating a shared vocabulary and framework for analysis universally applicable over the wide range of social dilemmas (E. Ostrom 2005: 6), it is entirely possible that the different attributes and issues of the knowledge commons will require deviations from or emendation of existing frameworks and vocabularies. Indeed, the editors of this book have undertaken to adapt Ostrom's IAD framework to the problems of the information or knowledge commons (Madison, Frischmann, & Strandburg 2010), and this book continues that project. Undoubtedly, however, similar interdisciplinary problems can be expected to arise (if they have not arisen already) among scholars in the "IP wars," who make up an even broader group coming not just from the traditional social sciences and the law but also from informatics, computer science, engineering, and biotechnology.

A few examples might suffice to indicate the types of conceptual issues that require, if not consensus, then at least clarification to allow those various scholars (and non-scholar stakeholders) to understand one another.[13] For one, IP scholars surely will want to heed Ostrom's caution about the potential for confusing or conflating resource systems (which, in the case of IP scholars, are the information, data, or knowledge) with either the humanly devised institutional settings for managing those resources (e.g., property and regulatory systems) or with the actors who (a) create, innovate, or discover new information (re)sources and/or (b) structure the institutional structures for managing information.[14] In the natural commons context, we are careful to distinguish

---

[11] What is achieved in the absence of a clearly defined and agreed-upon vocabulary is what the philosopher David Lewis (1969) referred to as a "babbling equilibrium" (see also Ostrom 2005: 176).

[12] A "Workshopper" is an affiliated faculty member, visiting scholar, graduate student, or staffer in Indiana University's Workshop in Political Theory and Policy Analysis, which in 2012 was named for its founders, Vincent and Elinor Ostrom.

[13] Ostrom insisted that everyone should use each term of art, such as "institution," in precisely the same way. For example, Hess & E. Ostrom (2003: 114) stress the need for "shared meanings." In my view, legitimate reasons exist for scholars to use the same term in different ways, depending on what *functions* those terms are serving in their analysis. See Cole (2013). However, if social scientists and legal scholars are to tolerate diverse meanings of similar terms, it becomes imperative for individual scholars to define with utmost care terms amenable to multiple meanings in every paper they write. Moreover, even if Ostrom's insistence on "shared meanings" is unduly strict, her goal of achieving widespread, or even universal, agreement of a common framework for analysis and of variables within that framework remains crucial for enabling meta-analyses of case studies and coding for quantitative empirical analysis.

[14] Indeed, some IP scholars already have heeded this lesson. See Madison, Frischmann, & Strandburg (2010) and this volume.

common-pool resources (CPRs)—naturally existing systems with various biophysical attributes—and common-property regimes (also CPRs), which are human-created sets of institutions for managing common-pool resources (among others). In the case of the information or knowledge commons, it is equally important to distinguish the information itself, with whatever attributes it might have, from whatever system(s), including IP laws, humans set up to control or manage it and its flow.

Another issue requiring careful attention and clarification is specification of different kinds or types of information and information flows, with diverse characteristics and attributes, perhaps warranting differential governance. Already we have a substantially different governance system, patents, for dealing with certain kinds of scientific information, as compared with artistic information, which is governed by copyright law (or sometimes placed in the "creative commons"). Trade names, trade secrets, fiduciary and other privileged communications, evidence submitted under oath, computer code, and many other types of information and flows are all dealt with in various ways in the legal system.

Likewise various fora of information exchange, such as e-mail, telecommunications, police interrogations, court sessions, legislative and administrative committee hearings, face-to-face business meetings (with or without written minutes), and personal communications are subject to very different kinds of procedural and sometimes substantive rules (not to mention informal social norms). Much has been written already about all of these types of information and information-exchange by scholars and advocates (occasionally one and the same) from various disciplines and a variety of perspectives. Much work remains to be done, however, to systematize and meta-analyze this vast quantity of "data" so as to develop the kinds of theories and "design principles" that Ostrom and her colleagues painstakingly developed and applied over the course of decades, with some measure of success, to specifying and diagnosing problems of the natural commons. The existing IAD framework (or some variation on it) could be very useful to such an effort, and the adapted IAD framework developed and applied in this book paves the way.

B. POTENTIAL FOR APPLYING THE IAD FRAMEWORK TO THE INFORMATION OR KNOWLEDGE COMMONS

As noted earlier, the IAD framework originally was created in large part to facilitate scholarly cooperation by providing a common framework based on a shared vocabulary that would be amenable to diverse assumptions, theories, and models of social interaction. The framework itself is deceptively simple in design, but allows for detailed analyses of highly complex interactions of however many variables (and subvariables) are of interest. It is the most widely used framework in studies of the natural commons (Constantinidis 2012), and has been cited as one of the most important analytical tools of the policy process (Sabatier 2007). As a legal scholar, I have long wondered why a framework so obviously congenial to legal analysis has not found wider application in my own field (including, I confess, in my own work). Perhaps it is due to the overwhelming normativity of legal scholarship, discussed earlier. Regardless, IP scholars (lawyers and nonlawyers alike) should find the IAD framework an immensely useful tool for disentangling the various elements that make up social problems relating to information and information flows, understanding those elements, and diagnosing more precisely where the roots of problems lie, enabling (but never guaranteeing) collective action to resolve those problems via new or amended institutions.

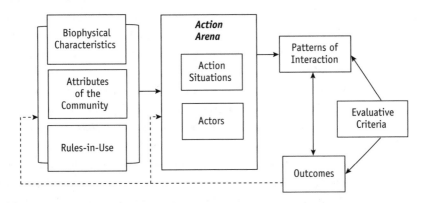

FIGURE 2.1 Institutional Analysis and Development Framework.
Source: Elinor Ostrom & Charlotte Hess, *A Framework for Analyzing the Knowledge Commons, in* UNDERSTANDING KNOWLEDGE AS A COMMONS: FROM THEORY TO PRACTICE 44, Fig. 3-1 (Charlotte Hess & E. Ostrom eds., MIT Press 2007).

Several, marginally different, versions exist of the IAD framework. The version discussed below is fairly standard, and comes from Elinor Ostrom and Charlotte Hess's initial efforts to extend the commons framework to the "knowledge commons."

1. Biophysical Characteristics and Different Types of Goods

Starting with the three boxes vertically aligned along the left side of the framework, the "Biophysical Characteristics" of the resource probably have less significance for information than for a natural commons. After all, ideas have no biophysical attributes (unless we treat them purely as electrical or chemical outputs of cognition via neurotransmission). Nevertheless, Ostrom and co-author Charlotte Hess identified several bases for distinguishing varying physical characteristics of information: *facilities* through which information is accessed, including bookstores, libraries (public, academic, or private), newspapers, the Internet (including both open-access and subscription-based sources of various kinds); *artifacts*, which are the discreet physical forms through which information flows and in which it is accessed, including maps, books, and computer files (to name just a few); *ideas* themselves, which are the "nonphysical flow units" of the resource (E. Ostrom & Hess 2007: 47–48). Obviously, much more work remains to be done elaborating on these tentative categories, and IP scholars (along with others who work in fields diverse as cognitive psychology, informatics, and semiotics) are better positioned to carry out this work than those of us who focus on natural resources.

Related to the discussion of "biophysical characteristics" is a tricky problem of defining just what kind of good (if it *is* a single kind of good) information actually is. Widespread agreement seems to exist that *ideas*, once they are released into the world from any source, are in the nature of *pure public goods*. They meet the strict conditions of nonrivalrousness in consumption and nonexcludability. Very few other public goods (or goods with public attributes) are so pure. Even goods traditionally thought to be virtually pure public goods, such as sunlight, lighthouses, and the atmosphere, are less *pure* public goods than ideas. Solar access disputes have shown that sunlight can, in some circumstances, be rivalrous in consumption.[15] Ronald Coase has argued that, in special cases at least, the external benefits provided by lighthouses can be recaptured by suppliers (Coase 1974; but see Van Zandt 1993[16]). And since the industrial revolution it has become clear that the atmosphere, like waters, forests, and other natural resources, is at best an *impure, subtractable, or congestible* public good. As such, these resources fall somewhere on the spectrum between public goods, as technically defined, and club or toll goods. It is such *impure* public goods to which Ostrom assigned the label "common-pool resources" (Ostrom & Ostrom 1999: 75). She spent no time studying *pure* public goods, which by definition are not candidates for the "tragedy of the commons" because they would survive, undiminished, regardless of whatever institutional structures were introduced to sustain or exploit them. It is doubtful, however, that any natural resources actually meet the strict requirements of nonrivalrousness and nonexcludability.

To the extent information (in the raw form of "ideas") is a pure public good, the implications for governance are quite different from the case of common-pool natural resources, where "open access" (at least where demands on the resource are increasing relative to supply) leads inexorably to "tragedy," as Hardin surmised. All solutions to the "tragedy of the commons" involve the replacement of open access with restricted access and use via private property, common property, or public property/regulatory regimes (Cole 2002). Open access (signifying the absence of restraints on access and use) is *always* the socially optimal governance system for *existing* pure public goods simply because it is inevitable under conditions of nonrivalrousness and nonexcludability. Consequently, if IP scholars were concerned only about information in its purest form—as ideas—then neither Ostrom's analytical framework nor any other approach would be at all useful

---

[15] See, e.g., Prah v. Maretti, 108 Wis. 2d 223, 321 N.W.2d 182 (1982); Fountainebleau Hotel Corp. v. Forty-five Twenty-Five Inc., 114 So. 2d 357 (Fla. App. 1959).

[16] Van Zandt claims that Coase was describing a special case because such a high percentage of global shipping traffic used the Port of London during the period Coase was describing, and notes that the government subsidized private provision of lighthouse services by giving lighthouse owners taxation powers in the Port of London.

because no social dilemmas (or governance problems) would exist. However, that is not the prevailing situation.

In fact, IP institutions matter a great deal not because of the ideas themselves (although IP policy rightfully is concerned with *incentives* for the production of ideas, especially those that contribute to the "stock of useful knowledge" (Kuznets 1965: 85–87)) but with what we might call, to borrow a phrase from mythology and semiotics, "ideas-in-form"— ideas as represented in texts, pictures, symbols and marks, scores or recordings, codes, and so forth. These are what Ostrom and Hess call "artifacts." In contrast to the ideas they contain, the artifacts are not pure public goods; in fact, some of them, such as closely held secrets (think of the formulae for the original Coca-Cola or Kentucky Fried Chicken), are more nearly pure private goods than any kind of public goods.[17] Other artifacts, such as books, are not so easily subjected to institutional control because, even though exclusion is relatively easy, they remain relatively nonrivalrous in consumption. Books are easy to resell, gift, or lend, so that the ideas they contain can be freely accessed by many (with no diminution in the amount available for anyone else to consume, so long as the book itself remains intact). Nonetheless, institutional arrangements can, with greater or lesser success, control the flow of ideas themselves by controlling access to and use of the artifacts that contain them as well as the "facilities" through which information is accessed. In addition, by controlling the flow of ideas, institutions (including IP rights and duties) can impact the rate of production, and/or the direction, of new ideas, as in the case of alleged "patent trolls" (compare Magliocca 2013 and McDonough 2006).

2. Attributes of the Community

The middle box on the left of the IAD framework, labeled "Attributes of the Community," arguably requires fewer adjustments in the move from the natural commons to the knowledge commons. As already noted, the relevant community of the information or knowledge commons is much larger than most of the communities with whom scholars of the natural common-pool resources have dealt. Indeed, moving the IAD framework from the resource commons to the knowledge commons involves a wholly new participant of central concern: the creator (or producer). Typically, a natural common-pool resource has no human producer.[18] Thus, the position of "creator" has not been encountered by scholars employing the IAD framework. The various other "actors" are more familiar,

---

[17] The ideas contained in the formulae are public goods, but the formulae themselves (the "artifacts") are private goods because of ease of excludability, even if they might in theory be nonrival in consumption.

[18] Artificially created "natural" commons do exist; think of stocked fisheries. Moreover, I can easily imagine a philosopher arguing that even what counts as a "natural resource" is, in part, a product of human conceptualization. Thus, all common-pool resources would be at least coproduced or co-created by humans. But I suggest we cabin such issues for purposes of the current discussion, where the distinction between humans as creators of natural and creators of artificial resources seems important regardless of the relation between humans and natural resource systems.

including providers, financers, distributors, millions of potential or actual users, and of course policy makers who establish "rules of the game" for information production, provision, distribution, and consumption.

It is, to repeat, an unusually large community compared to those traditionally studied by Ostrom and other students of the natural commons. Although, problems of the global commons, such as climate change, certainly would challenge the information commons for size and variety of attributes, including number of actors. It is worth observing that Ostrom wrote a good deal about climate change in her later years, but never attempted to apply the IAD framework to that problem of the global commons (see Ostrom 2012; E. Ostrom 2010a). Was she daunted by the scale of the application?[19] If so, might her reluctance signify the scale of the challenge IP scholars face in applying the framework to the information commons? It is worth noting in this context that the few efforts to apply the IAD framework in the realm of the information or knowledge commons so far have focused on discrete subparts of the problem or applied only subparts of the IAD framework, which seems sensible and perhaps inevitable (see Tenenberg 2008 (a full application of the IAD framework to a case study of student software teams in an undergraduate course at the University of Washington, Tacoma); Schewik & Kitsing 2010 (an application of one important aspect of the IAD framework, the various kinds of rules that apply in action arenas or situations, to open-source governance systems)). This book reflects the most significant effort yet to adapt, extend, and apply the IAD framework to the knowledge commons, and in doing so, much more attention is directed toward analysis of the various communities involved.

3. Rules-in-Use

Little needs to be explained to legal scholars (at least) about the box at the bottom-left of the IAD framework, other than that the concept of "rules-in-use" occasionally misleads some social scientists into believing that the "rules-in-form"—the formal legal rules—do not matter at all, as if they could not even influence the rules-in-use (Kinston & Caballero 2009: 158 (mistakenly but approvingly attributing to Ostrom a belief that rules-in-form are "dead letters," while rules-in-use are "rules which are actually followed")). Certainly since Robert Ellickson's famous book on the cattle ranchers of Shasta County, California (Ellickson 1991), if not earlier (Pound 1910; Llewellyn 1949; Friedman 1975), legal scholars have understood the important and highly variable relations between formal legal norms and informal social norms. IP scholars have noted, for example, a disjunction between formal legal rules barring Internet file sharing and social norms of sharing among Internet users (Feldman & Nadler 2006). But no legal scholar doubts that the formal legal rules remain very important (if not always the most important institutional variables).

---

[19] I hasten immediately to cast doubt on the implicit assertion by observing that Elinor Ostrom was not daunted by much of anything during the course of her long career. It is entirely possible that she did not apply the IAD framework to the problem of the "climate commons" merely for lack of sufficient time, given her other innumerable obligations.

The question remains, where do the rules (in form or in use) come from? They are the outcomes (or outputs) of prior action situations taking place at various levels. Constitutional-level interactions result in meta-rules (which may or may not be codified in a single document called a "constitution"), rules that establish processes and procedures for adopting collective choice–level rules (statutes, decisions, administrative rules, etc.). Collective choice–level arenas include (but are not limited to) courts, legislative bodies, administrative agencies, corporate board rooms, club committees, school boards, church conclaves and synods, faculty meetings, and the family kitchen. Rules adopted in those arenas structure everyday interactions at the "operational level." Even at that level, however, rule making goes on. Social norms, which may be as or more powerful than formal legal rules, emerge from regularized patterns of interaction in operational-level situations. The scholar's task, in applying the IAD framework, is to determine, and diagnose perceived problems with, the rules-in-use that govern day-to-day ("operational-level") interactions in the action situations under study. In the IP context, this might be a slightly easier chore than in many natural commons contexts, where determining the rules requires close observation of, and interaction with, local communities for long periods of time. As a highly top-down system of governance, the basic contours of the rule-structure governing various types of information can be discerned from studying national statutes and cases brought under those statutes. In other words, the relative lack of polycentricity in the IP governance system should make it, all else being equal, an easier governance system to comprehend.

In 2005, Ostrom and her Workshop colleague, Sue Crawford, classified (functionally) various types of rules that apply in action situations (E. Ostrom & Crawford 2005: 186–215) including the following (incomplete list):

Position rules	Define positions that actors hold, including as owners of property rights and duties.
Boundary rules	Define: (1) Who is eligible to take a position;
	(2) The process for choosing who is eligible to take a position;
	(3) How actors can leave positions;
	(4) Whether anyone can hold multiple positions simultaneously;
	(5) Succession to vacant positions.
Choice rules	Define what actors in positions must, must not, or may do in their position and in particular circumstances.
Aggregation rules	Determine whether a decision by a single actor or multiple actors is needed prior to acting at a decision point in a process.
Information rules	Specify channels of communication among actors, as well as the kinds of information that can be transmitted between positions.
Payoff rules	Assign external rewards or sanctions for particular actions or outcomes.

Ostrom (2005: 189, Fig. 7.1) provides the following graph to illustrate how the various rules affect activity within the action arena or situation.

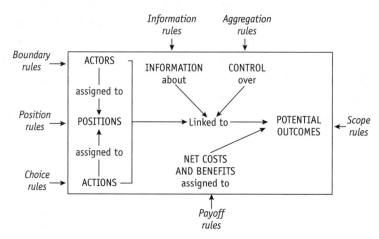

FIGURE 2.2 Rules as Exogenous Variables Directly Affecting the Elements of an Action Situation.
Source: ELINOR OSTROM, UNDERSTANDING INSTITUTIONAL DIVERSITY 189, Fig. 7.1 (Princeton University Press 2005).

Among the more significant positional rules, for both natural commons and the information or knowledge commons, are property rights and duties. In 1992, Ostrom and Edella Schlager identified several components of private property ownership (Schlager & E. Ostrom 1992: 250–51; compare with Honoré 1961: 107, identifying nine distinct rights and two duties in the full, "fee simple" ownership):

Access	Right to enter a defined area and enjoy its benefits without removing any resources.
Withdrawal	Right to obtain specified products from a resource system and remove that product from the area for prescribed uses.
Management	Right to participate in decisions regulating resources or making improvements in infrastructure.
Exclusion	Right to participate in the determination of who has, and who does not have, access to and use of resources.
Alienation	Right to sell, lease, bequeath, or otherwise transfer any or all of the preceding component rights.

4. Not "Exogenous Variables" but "Initial Conditions"

One further point of clarification about the three boxes on the left side of the IAD framework needs to be made before we bring them, as inputs, into the action arena or situation: Ostrom sometimes referred to those three boxes as "exogenous variables" (E. Ostrom 2005: 15, Fig. 1.2). But that is inaccurate. Because of the recursive nature of the framework—feedback from outcomes of action situations effects, either directly or mediated through evaluative criteria, resource attributes, community attributes, and rules-in-use—they are endogenized within the framework. At best, they constitute sets of "initial conditions" immediately preceding any particular social interaction. It might make even more sense to say that they are the prevailing conditions (or "entry conditions") upon a social interaction.[20]

5. The Action Arena (or Situation): Where Collective Action Happens (or Not)

The action arena (or situation) is where social interactions occur. It is the place—often these days a *virtual* place—where: individual actors make decisions that affect social welfare; collective action succeeds or fails; rules are made; entitlements to resources are allocated; exchanges take place (or not); and disputes are adjudicated. If and when institutional change occurs, it occurs in action arenas or situations (Hess & E. Ostrom 2007: 54).

As already noted, action arenas or situations exist at three different levels of governance in the IAD framework: the constitutional-choice level, the collective-choice level, and the operational level. And what happens in various action arenas at those different levels impacts on relevant resources (e.g., how information is provided, to whom, and under what circumstances), attributes of the relevant community, and the rules-in-use (both formal and informal). Ostrom and Hess, for example, have used the creation of digital repositories of scholarship to exemplify how rule systems are created through collective-choice interactions, and affect the *incentives* of individual actors in operational-level interactions (Hess & E. Ostrom 2007: 54–57).

The individual actors participating in action arenas or situations are typically presumed to be either completely or boundedly rational (following Herbert Simon, who greatly influenced Ostrom's work) (Simon 1972: 161), depending on the theory-based preference of the analyst; either way, actors can be expected to behave strategically to further their own interests (as subjectively determined). This feature makes Ostrom's IAD framework almost uniquely compatible with multiple theories and models, including: neoclassical theory, game theory, public choice theory, and behavioral economics, with the exception of (usually deterministic) models of irrational behavior (see, e.g., Berridge 2003: 17).

Pursuant to rules discussed above, actors in action arenas hold a variety of "positions," depending on the choice-level (constitutional, collective-choice, or operational). At the constitutional level, they may be appointed members of the constitutional convention, members of state ratifying conventions, journalists, scholars, members of interest groups

---

[20] Madison, Frischmann, & Strandburg (2010) modify the IAD framework in part to account for the complex feedback mechanisms and interactions across the framework components in the knowledge commons context.

attempting to affect the outcomes of constitutional negotiations, judges determining compliance with constitutional process rules, and so forth. At the collective-choice (or policy) level, positions include legislators (junior and senior) with various congressional or party leadership roles, as well as committee assignments and positions, legislative and committee staff members, lobbyists, hearing witnesses, parliamentarians, official reporters, and journalists, among others. In operational-level action arenas, participants include buyers, sellers, owners, renters, contractors, disputants, fiduciary, beneficiary, player, coach—the whole panoply of roles that humans take on in social interactions of all kinds in everyday life.

Operating within the scope of their respective positions (that is, according to the rules), and strategically according to their own (boundedly) rational interests and preferences (as they subjectively see them), actors choose among available action alternatives in light of information they possess about how potential actions (as well as inaction) link to potential outcomes, including costs and benefits (McGinnis 2011: 173–74). In addition to the costs and benefits internalized to the individual actors, their individual decisions may well have social consequences, entailing significant net costs or benefits for the community. Indeed, if that were not the case, society would not confront any social-cost or public-goods problems (broadly put, social dilemmas) requiring collective action.

Studying social interactions at constitutional, collective-choice, and operational levels allows scholars to observe regularities (and irregularities) in patterns of interaction. In many cases, regularized patterns of interaction will represent an equilibrium (although not necessarily a unique, efficient, or Nash equilibrium) for the actors. In other cases, the equilibrium might be difficult to discern or, in especially conflicted and contested situations, might not actually exist (even over long periods of time). When an equilibrium or regularized pattern of interactions is observed, *patterns* of interaction themselves may constitute or reflect *norms* of social behavior previously known (from the "rules-in-use" box) or unknown. Most importantly, apparent equilibria may be subject to shocks (exogenous or endogenous) that can alter patterns (or norms) of interaction, depending on their robustness and resilience.

6. Outcomes

In a sense, observed patterns of interaction are *outcomes* of social interactions. For example, in the legal action situation of automobile accident disputes, out-of-court settlements are both an observed regularity of interactions among actors (or parties) and outcomes of the proceedings (Ross 1980: 179 (2,123 of 2,216 cases disposed of by settlement before trial)). Similarly, in the legislative action arena of Congress, the so-called "Mickey Mouse rule" of IP policy, whereby Congress extends copyright terms retroactively whenever the Disney character Mickey Mouse is about to fall into the public domain, reflects an observed regularity of interactions (among players including legislators, lobbyists, and expert witnesses), amounting to an equilibrium situation (which is not to say the equilibrium necessarily is efficient) (see, e.g., Posner 2003). That pattern of interaction is itself a predictable *outcome* of the structure of interests and incentives created by existing sets of institutions (pursuant to theories of public choice) (Landes & Posner 2004). Meanwhile, the equilibrium patterns of interaction yield *predictable* outcomes of specific legislative processes to extend the copyright law at regular intervals.

Importantly, outcomes of interactions frequently entail effects that extend beyond the interacting parties to the broader society. So, in a natural commons setting outcomes frequently include consequences for the resource systems and resource units themselves, as well as for those who use the resources (on a broad interpretation of the word "use"). A collective choice–level interaction that displaces "open access" governance with "regulated access and use" naturally would entail outcomes for the relevant resources and users beyond any observed pattern of social interactions in the action arena. In the same vein, a collective-action decision to enclose completely the information commons (e.g., by prohibiting the creation or maintenance of a "creative commons") would produce various predictable and unpredictable outcomes relative to the production and dissemination of information.

Ostrom and Hess provide an unfortunately misleading table of "potential positive or negative outcomes in various knowledge commons" (Hess & E. Ostrom 2007: 61, Table 3.1), which conflates outcomes with *normative* evaluations of those outcomes. For example, they treat enclosure as a "negative" outcome and maintenance of an information commons as a "positive" outcome. This is presumptuous (and as noted above, contrary to their usual practice). It certainly is true that enclosure is an *outcome* of a proprietary (and gated) scientific database, and "open access" likewise is a consequence of an "open access research library." However, whether one institutional arrangement is "positive," "negative," or preferable is a decidedly normative evaluation for which Ostrom and Hess provided no analysis. They should have been more circumspect. Normative assessments of outcomes as "positive" or "negative" will always be in the eye of the beholder, depending on her or his preferences, interests, and subjectively chosen (but hopefully expressly manifest) "evaluative criteria." Even from a social perspective, a normative assessment of outcomes depends on the selection and application of inherently contestable evaluative criteria.

In other words, the IAD framework itself provides no greater basis for normative presumptions about alternative governance systems for information than it provides for normative presumptions about alternative governance systems for natural common-pool resources. Depending on what function we are trying to maximize, it is entirely possible that neither entirely closed-access nor entirely open-access information systems would maximize it. From a social welfare perspective, some combination of open- and closed-access is overwhelmingly likely to be more socially efficient than complete open- or close-access (David 2003: 19). The trick, of course, would be getting the combination just right. And, again, the IAD framework itself will not help that determination, except to the extent applications of the framework result in meta-analyses that yield something like the "design principles" Ostrom derived in *Governing the Commons*. In addition, the IAD framework can be said to facilitate evaluation by making it easy for evaluators to separate out the various elements that combine to affect outcomes.

7. Evaluative Criteria

In applying the IAD framework, we should not simply assume one or another social goal. It might or might not be social efficiency (on some definition). The "evaluative criteria" box in the IAD framework has long been the most neglected and underdeveloped element of the framework. Even in her most elaborate account of the IAD framework, in *Understanding Institutional Diversity*, Ostrom devotes only three pages to a discussion of the "evaluative criteria" box, and offers only some general contenders for populating it, including (1) economic efficiency; (2) fiscal equivalence; (3) redistributional equity; (4) accountability; (5) conformance to values of local actors; and (6) sustainability. In the more specific context of the knowledge commons, Ostrom and Hess suggest (without citation) that six evaluative criteria are "frequently used": (1) increasing scientific knowledge; (2) sustainability and preservation; (3) participation standards; (4) economic efficiency; (5) equity through fiscal equivalence; and (6) redistributional equity (Hess & E. Ostrom 2007: 63). They devote a paragraph to describing each discrete criterion (or set of criteria), amounting to just over three pages, without any detailed analysis of how any of the criteria would actually operate within the context of action situations, either separately or in combination with other evaluative criteria.

Ostrom's lack of detailed and critical attention to the "evaluative criteria" in the IAD framework may reflect, more than anything else, her focus on natural common-pool resources, where little (if any) disagreement existed among diverse scholars about the ultimate goal, which was universally assumed to be long-run resource sustainability. Ostrom, Hardin, Demsetz, and virtually every other scholar writing about common-pool resources concurs in ultimate aim, no matter how strongly they disagree about institutional means of achieving it. Consensus about ends makes for easier agreement on evaluative criteria for assessing alternative means (including privatization, public/state regulation of access and use, or local, common-property management) in various circumstances.

In other realms to which the IAD framework might usefully be applied, including the information or knowledge commons, there is unlikely to be agreement with respect to ultimate social goals. Some may argue that the ultimate goal of IP law is to reward innovators, in accordance with well-established property theories based on labor and just deserts, regardless of social welfare (Hughes 1988). Others might argue that the ultimate goal is to build the stock of useful knowledge to facilitate economic growth (representing a social-welfare function) (Kuznets 1965). Still others might assert that *the* goal is to disseminate knowledge as widely as possible for its own sake (Hettinger 1989; Boyle 2003; but see Wagner 2003 (arguing that strong IP rights are *more* likely to ensure a flourishing public domain of ideas)).

In the absence of consensus about ultimate ends, agreement on evaluative criteria for assessing means is unlikely (to say the least). As a consequence, individual scholars have greater freedom to select from among alternative evaluative criteria (at least within some conventional range) for adjudging the outcomes of social interactions. However, that freedom should be constrained by the general scientific principle that evaluative criteria must be clearly specified along with *reasons* for preferring them, either across the board or in the circumstances, so that the basis for evaluation can be understood and/or contested.

Somewhat more hopefully, scholars of the information commons, like scholars of the natural common-pool resources, might achieve consensus on a certain maximand (e.g., an agreed social-welfare function) for information and information-flows in society, which would enable a more fruitful focus on alternative institutional means of achieving that goal. Alternative presumptions and hypotheses about relations between institutional means and social outcomes could then be subject (at least potentially) to testing and comparison across runs of cases, as Ostrom did in *Governing the Commons* and her earlier studies of police department performance relative to size.

Finally, the evaluative criteria (however chosen) provide a basis for *interpreting* as well as evaluating outcomes. Those interpretations and evaluations become part of the feed-back loop into resource systems, community attributes, and rules-in-use. When members of the relevant community evaluate outcomes of social interactions as "bad" (according to whatever criteria), they may push (successfully or unsuccessfully) for further action in subsequent action situations at the collective-choice level, to alter or curtail "bad" outcomes. Thus, the recursive aspect of the IAD framework accounts for institutional change (or inertia) over time (even though the framework cannot by itself determine, ensure, or even predict institutional change).

IV. Conclusion

IP scholars already have begun applying the IAD framework to good effect. Charlotte Hess, writing with Elinor Ostrom and on her own, has been a pioneer in calling for application of the framework to problems of the information or knowledge commons (see, e.g., Hess & E. Ostrom 2003, 2006, 2007; Hess 2005, 2008). Charles Schweik has applied the IAD framework to "software commons" (Schweik 2005; Schweik & English 2007). Josh Tenenberg has applied it to study software development teams (Tenenberg 2008). And Jorge Contreras, in this volume and elsewhere, applies the IAD framework to the "genome commons" (Contreras, this volume, ch. 4; Contreras 2011). Other scholars might examine these groundbreaking efforts to assess whether the framework might usefully be applied to their own problems and projects.

These are still early days in the social-scientific study of information as a good, whether public, common, or private. But, as noted earlier, students of the information or knowledge commons should not expect quick and decisive results about appropriate governance institutions. That is one of the chief lessons of the large and growing literature on natural common-pool resources. After several decades of data collection and careful construction of analytical frameworks, theories, and methods to analyze and diagnose commons problems, much has been learned but probably not nearly as much as remains to be learned.

Thanks primarily to Elinor Ostrom and her colleagues at the Ostrom Workshop in Political Theory and Policy Analysis, we have learned that common-property regimes are a viable third category of governance regimes for successfully managing natural common-pool resources over long periods of time.[21] And we have gained some idea of the conditions under which common-property regimes seem more or less likely to succeed based on the "design principles" Ostrom derived from her meta-analyses of hundreds of individual cases. Since then, despite increasing data collection and efforts to improve analytical methods, further progress toward understanding and diagnosing (let alone resolving) commons problems has been marginal (though hardly insignificant).

Scant reason exists to expect easier and more rapid progress toward describing, diagnosing, and explaining issues relating to information and information-flows. Indeed, as noted earlier, important questions remain about just how applicable the existing literature of natural common-pool resources is to the information commons. Even when information arises or is placed in common pools, it may not have the same kinds of attributes of natural resources found in common pools. As defined many years ago by Vincent and Elinor Ostrom, common-pool resources share certain attributes with public goods, but are not themselves pure public goods. Specifically, they lack nonrivalrousness in consumption, which is to say they are subtractable or congestible. This is not true of information (though it may be true of the various vehicles by which information is provided or disseminated). Thus, whereas "open access" is potentially tragic, and only very rarely preferable,[22] for a natural resource commons, IP scholars often make arguments promoting "open access" (see, e.g., Willinsky 2006; Swan 2007). And those arguments make sense in that context (even if they are not completely convincing) to the extent that information approximates a *pure* public good.

Even if the natural resource commons and the information commons were more similar than they are, IP scholars hoping to find support for normative arguments about the preferability of common-property management (let alone full-blown open access) will not find much in the work of Elinor Ostrom and others employing her frameworks, theories, and models. As argued in the first part of this chapter, Ostrom's own normative commitments were few and contingent; her work on natural common-pool resources *never* argued as a general rule that common-property regimes were preferable to private, individual property systems or public property/regulatory systems. It was only in specific

---

[21] That is, of course, the primary lesson of Ostrom's *Governing the Commons* (1990).

[22] Arguably, "open access" is optimal (that is, preferable to all alternative property/regulatory systems) for natural resource commons only so long as the rate of demand remains quite low relative to the supply—that is to say, prior to some known or presumed congestion point. See Cole (2002); Frischmann (2012: ch. 11).

circumstances that we might (or might not) find that one type of property/regulatory regime functioned as well as or better than others. She would surely caution IP scholars not to expect to find panacea solutions for problems of the information or knowledge commons.

Acknowledgments

In 2011, Lin Ostrom and I traveled together to the conference that resulted in this book. This chapter, though a poor substitute for what was to have been Lin's contribution to the volume, is dedicated to her memory. I am grateful to Brett Frischmann and Mike McGinnis for several helpful comments and suggestions.

References

James M. Acheson, *Ostrom for Anthropologists*, 5 INT'L J. COMMONS (Sept. 5, 2011), http://www.thecommonsjournal.org/index.php/ijc/article/view/245/209.

MASAHIKO AOKI, TOWARD A COMPARATIVE INSTITUTIONAL ANALYSIS (MIT Press 2001).

DOUGLAS G. BAIRD, ROBERT H. GERTNER, & RANDALL C. PICKER, GAME THEORY AND THE LAW (Harvard University Press 1998).

C. Dustin Becker & Elinor Ostrom, *Human Ecology and Resource Sustainability: The Importance of Institutional Diversity*, 26 ANN. REV. ECOLOGY & SYSTEMATICS 113 (1995)

Kent C. Berridge, *Irrational Pursuits: Hyper-Incentives from a Visceral Brain, in* THE PSYCHOLOGY OF ECONOMIC DECISIONS, VOL. I: RATIONALITY AND WELL-BEING 17 (Isabelle Brocas & Juan D. Carillo eds., Oxford University Press 2003).

James Boyle, *The Second Enclosure Movement and the Construction of the Public Domain*, 66 LAW & CONTEMP. PROBS. 33 (2003).

R. H. Coase, *The Lighthouse in Economics*, 17 J. LAW & ECONOMICS 357 (1974).

DANIEL H. COLE, POLLUTION AND PROPERTY: COMPARING OWNERSHIP SYSTEMS FOR ENVIRONMENTAL PROTECTION (Cambridge University Press 2002).

Daniel H. Cole, *The Varieties of Comparative Institutional Analysis*, 2013 WISCONSIN L. REV. 383.

PANOS CONSTANTINIDIS, PERSPECTIVES AND IMPLICATIONS FOR THE DEVELOPMENT OF INFORMATION INFRASTRUCTURES 43 (IGI Global 2012).

Jorge L. Contreras, *Bermuda's Legacy: Policy, Patents, and the Design of the Genome Commons*, 12 MINNESOTA J.L. SCI. & TECH. 61 (2011).

Michael Cox, Gwen Arnold, & Sergio Villamayor Tomás, *A Review and Reassessment of Design Principles for Community-based Natural Resource Management*, 15 ECOLOGY & SOCIETY 38 (2010).

Paul E. David, *The Economic Logic of "Open Science" and the Balance between Private Property Rights and the Public Domain in Scientific Data and Information: A Primer, in* THE ROLE OF THE PUBLIC DOMAIN IN SCIENTIFIC AND TECHNICAL DATA AND INFORMATION 19 (Julie M. Esanu & Paul F. Uhlir eds., National Academies Press 2003).

Decentralization: A Sampling of Definitions, Working Paper Prepared in Connection with the Joint UNDP—Government of Germany Evaluation of the UNDP Role in Decentralization and Local Governance (Oct. 1999), http://web.undp.org/evaluation/documents/decentralization_working_report.pdf.

ROBERT C. ELLICKSON, ORDER WITHOUT LAW: HOW NEIGHBORS SETTLE DISPUTES (Harvard University Press 1991).

Yuval Feldman & Janice Nadler, *The Law and Norms of File Sharing*, 43 SAN DIEGO L. REV. 577 (2006).

LAWRENCE M. FRIEDMAN, THE LEGAL SYSTEM: A SOCIAL SCIENCE PERSPECTIVE (Russell Sage 1975).

BRETT FRISCHMANN, INFRASTRUCTURE: THE SOCIAL VALUE OF SHARED RESOURCES (Oxford University Press 2012).

Brett Frischmann, *Two Enduring Lessons from Elinor Ostrom*, 9 J. INSTITUTIONAL ECONOMICS 387 (2013).

Garrett Hardin, *The Tragedy of the Commons*, 162 SCIENCE 1243 (1968).

Michael Heise, *The Past, Present, and Future of Empirical Legal Scholarship: Judicial Decision Making and the New Empiricism*, 2002 U. ILLINOIS L. REV. 819 (2002).

Charlotte Hess, *A Resource Guide for Authors: Open Access, Copyright, and the Digital Commons*, CPR DIGEST (March 2005), http://www.iasc-commons.org/sites/all/Digest/cpr72.pdf.

Charlotte Hess, *Mapping the New Commons*, presented at "Governing Shared Resources: Connecting Local Experience to Global Challenges," the 12th Biennial Conference of the International Association for the Study of the Commons, University of Gloucestershire, Cheltenham, England (July 14–18, 2008), http://dlc.dlib.indiana.edu/dlc/handle/10535/304.

Charlotte Hess & Elinor Ostrom, *Ideas, Artifacts, and Facilities: Information as a Common-Pool Resource*, 66 LAW & CONTEMP. PROBS. 111 (2003).

Charlotte Hess & Elinor Ostrom, *A Framework for Analysing the Microbiological Commons*, 58 INT'L SOCIAL SCIENCE J. 335 (2006).

CHARLOTTE HESS & ELINOR OSTROM EDS., UNDERSTANDING KNOWLEDGE AS A COMMONS: FROM THEORY TO PRACTICE (MIT Press 2007).

Edward C. Hettinger, *Justifying Intellectual Property*, 18 PHILOSOPHY & PUBLIC AFFAIRS 31 (1989).

Toni Honoré, *Ownership, in* OXFORD ESSAYS IN JURISPRUDENCE 107 (A. G. Guest ed., Oxford University Press 1961).

Justin Hughes, *The Philosophy of Intellectual Property*, 77 GEORGETOWN L.J. 287 (1988).

Christopher Kinston & Gonzalo Caballero, *Comparing Theories of Institutional Change*, 5 J. INSTITUTIONAL ECONOMICS 151 (2009).

NEIL K. KOMESAR, IMPERFECT ALTERNATIVES: CHOOSING INSTITUTIONS IN LAW (University of Chicago Press 1994).

SIMON KUZNETS, ECONOMIC GROWTH AND STRUCTURE: SELECTED ESSAYS (Norton 1965).

WILLIAM M. LANDES & RICHARD A. POSNER, THE POLITICAL ECONOMY OF INTELLECTUAL PROPERTY LAW (Harvard University Press 2004).

RICHARD LEMPERT & JOSEPH SANDERS, AN INVITATION TO LAW AND SOCIAL SCIENCE (Longman 1986).

DAVID LEWIS, CONVENTION: A PHILOSOPHICAL STUDY (Harvard University Press 1969).

Karl N. Llewellyn, *Law and the Social Sciences—Especially Sociology*, 14 AMER. SOCIOLOGICAL REVIEW 41 (1949).

Michael J. Madison, Brett M. Frischmann, & Katherine J. Strandburg, *Constructing Commons in the Cultural Environment*, 95 CORNELL L.REV. 657 (2010).

Gerard Magliocca, *Blackberries and Barnyards: Patent Trolls and the Perils of Innovation*, 82 NOTRE DAME L. REV. 1809 (2013).

James F. McDonough III, *The Myth of the Patent Troll: An Alternative View of the Function of Patent Dealers in an Idea Economy*, 56 EMORY L.J. 189 (2006).

Michael D. McGinnis, *An Introduction to IAD and the Language of the Ostrom Workshop: A Simple Guild to a Complex Framework*, 39 POLICY STUDIES J. 169 (2011).

JOHN MONAHAN & W. LAURENS WALKER, SOCIAL SCIENCE IN LAW (7th ed., Foundation Press 2009).

DOUGLASS C. NORTH, INSTITUTIONS, INSTITUTIONAL CHANGE, AND ECONOMIC PERFORMANCE (Cambridge University Press 1990).

ELINOR OSTROM, GOVERNING THE COMMONS: THE EVOLUTION OF INSTITUTIONS FOR COLLECTIVE ACTION (Cambridge University Press 1990).

ELINOR OSTROM, UNDERSTANDING INSTITUTIONAL DIVERSITY (Princeton University Press 2005).

Elinor Ostrom, *A Diagnostic Approach for Going beyond Panaceas*, 104 PROCEEDINGS OF THE NATIONAL ACADEMY OF SCIENCES U.S. 15181 (2007).

Elinor Ostrom, *Polycentric Systems as One Approach to Solving Collective-Action Problems, in* CLIMATE CHANGE AND SUSTAINABLE DEVELOPMENT: NEW CHALLENGES FOR POVERTY REDUCTION 17 (M.A. Mohamed Salih ed., Edward Elgar Publishing 2009a).

Elinor Ostrom, *A Polycentric Approach for Coping with Climate Change*, World Bank Policy Research Paper 5095 (Oct. 2009b).

Elinor Ostrom, *A Long Polycentric Journey*, 13 ANN. REVIEW POLITICAL SCIENCE 1 (2010a).

Elinor Ostrom, *Polycentric Systems for Coping with Collective Action and Global Environmental Change*, 20 GLOBAL ENVTL. CHANGE 550 (2010b).

Elinor Ostrom, *Beyond Markets and States: Polycentric Governance of Complex Economic Systems*, 100 AMER. ECONOMIC REVIEW 641 (2010c).

Elinor Ostrom, *Institutional Analysis and Development: Elements of the Framework in Historical Perspective, in* HISTORICAL DEVELOPMENTS AND THEORETICAL APPROACHES IN SOCIOLOGY (C. Crothers ed.), vol. II, UNESCO ENCYCLOPEDIA OF LIFE SUPPORT SYSTEMS (UNESCO-ELOSS 2010d).

Elinor Ostrom, *Background on the Institutional Analysis and Development Framework*, 39 POLICY STUDIES J. 7 (2011).

Elinor Ostrom, *The Challenges of Achieving Conservation and Development*, THE ANNUAL PROCEEDINGS OF THE WEALTH AND WELL-BEING OF NATIONS, VOL. IV (Emily Chamlee-Wright ed., Beloit College 2011–2012).

Elinor Ostrom, *Nested Externalities and Polycentric Institutions: Must We Wait for Global Solutions to Climate Change before Taking Actions at Other Scales?*, 49 ECONOMIC THEORY 353 (2012).

Elinor Ostrom & Sue Crawford, *Classifying Rules, in* ELINOR OSTROM, UNDERSTANDING INSTITUTIONAL DIVERSITY 186 (Princeton University Press 2005).

Elinor Ostrom & Charlotte Hess, *A Framework for Analyzing the Knowledge Commons, in* UNDERSTANDING KNOWLEDGE AS A COMMONS: FROM THEORY TO PRACTICE 41 (Charlotte Hess & Elinor Ostrom eds., MIT Press 2007).

Elinor Ostrom, Marco A. Janssen, & John M. Anderies, *Going Beyond Panaceas*, 104 PROCEEDINGS OF THE NATIONAL ACADEMY OF SCIENCES U.S. 15176 (2007).

ELINOR OSTROM, ROGER PARKS, & GORDON WHITAKER, PATTERNS OF METROPOLITAN POLICING (Ballinger Pub. Co. 1978).

Vincent Ostrom, *Polycentricity*, *in* POLYCENTRICITY AND LOCAL PUBLIC ECONOMIES: READINGS FROM THE WORKSHOP IN POLITICAL THEORY AND POLICY ANALYSIS (M. McGinnis, ed., University of Michigan Press 1999).

Vincent Ostrom & Elinor Ostrom, *Public Goods and Public Choices*, *in* POLYCENTRICITY AND LOCAL PUBLIC ECONOMIES: READINGS FROM THE WORKSHOP IN POLITICAL THEORY AND POLICY ANALYSIS (M. D. McGinnis ed., University of Michigan Press 1999).

Vincent Ostrom, Charles M. Tiebout, & Charles Warren, *The Organization of Government in Metropolitan Areas: A Theoretical Inquiry*, 55 AMER. POLITICAL SCIENCE REV. 831 (1961).

Richard A. Posner, *The Constitutionality of the Copyright Term Extension Act: Economics, Politics, Law and Judicial Technique*, *in* Eldred v. Ashcroft, 2003 THE SUPREME COURT REV. 143 (2003).

Roscoe Pound, *Law in Books and Law in Action*, 44 AMER. L. REV. 12 (1910).

H. LAURENCE ROSS, SETTLED OUT OF COURT: THE SOCIAL PROCESS OF INSURANCE CLAIMS ADJUSTMENT 179 (Rev. 2d ed., De Gruyter 1980).

PAUL SABATIER, THEORIES OF THE POLICY PROCESS (2d ed., Westview Press 2007).

Edella Schlager & Elinor Ostrom, *Property-Rights Regimes and Natural Resources: A Conceptual Analysis*, 68 LAND ECONOMICS 249 (1992).

Charles M. Schweik, *An Institutional Analysis Approach to Studying Libre Software "Commons,"* 6 UPGRADE 17 (2005).

Charles M. Schweik & Robert English, *Tragedy of the FOSS Commons? Investigating the Institutional Designs of Free/Libre and Open Source Software Projects*, 12 FIRST MONDAY no. 2 (Feb. 5, 2007), http://firstmonday.org/htbin/cgiwrap/bin/ojs/index.php/fm/article/view/1619/1534.

Charles M. Schweik & Meelis Kitsing, *Applying Elinor Ostrom's Rule Classification Framework to the Analysis of Open Source Software Commons*, 2 TRANSNAT'L CORPORATIONS REV. 13 (2010).

Herbert A. Simon, *Models of Bounded Rationality*, *in* DECISION AND ORGANIZATION (C. B. McGuire & Roy Radner eds., North-Holland 1972).

Alma Swan, *Open Access and the Progress of Science*, 95 AMER. SCIENTIST 198 (2007).

Josh Tenenberg, *An Institutional Analysis of Software Teams*, 66 J. HUMAN-COMPUTER STUDIES 484 (2008).

David E. Van Zandt, *The Lesson of the Lighthouse: "Government" or "Private" Provision of Goods*, 22 J. LEGAL STUDIES 47 (1993).

R. Polk Wagner, *Information Wants to Be Free: Intellectual Property and the Mythologies of Control*, 103 COLUMBIA L. REV. 995 (2003).

JOHN WILLINSKY, THE ACCESS PRINCIPLE: THE CASE FOR OPEN ACCESS TO RESEARCH AND SCHOLARSHIP (MIT Press 2006).

3   Between Spanish Huertas and the Open Road: A Tale of Two Commons?

Yochai Benkler[*]

I. Introduction

Why are highways, city streets, and sidewalks in almost all cases, in all market economies, managed as open access commons? Should databases be in the public domain as in the United States, or subject to some form of copyright-like regime as in Europe? Is there a role for next-generation Wi-Fi spectrum commons strategies in the construction of the ubiquitous computing environment, or should we auction off all remaining spectrum in property-like models? These and similar institutional design questions, great and small, require us to have a general understanding of the role commons play in contemporary market economies.

Elinor Ostrom's 1990 *Governing the Commons* marked a turning point in the legitimacy of talking about the commons on the background of a dominant neoclassical understanding of property and the tragedy of the commons, leavened only mildly by new institutional economics. If in 1986 Carol Rose's *Comedy of the Commons* was an outlier (Rose 1986), by 2011 the subject has become mainstream. But in the process of creating a legitimate space for studying the commons, Ostrom's emphasis on a very carefully delineated subset of limited common-property regimes (CPRs), that can productively manage a very carefully defined class of physical resources, common-pool resources, largely

* Yochai Benkler is Jack N. and Lillian R. Berkman Professor of Entrepreneurial Legal Studies, Harvard Law School, Cambridge, Massachusetts, USA, and faculty co-director, Berkman Center for Internet and Society.

ershadowed and obscured the exploration that Rose began, of understanding basic, ubiquitous elements of market economies in terms of the interaction of property and commons. Indeed, part of securing a safe intellectual domain for CPR studies included a strict insistence on "the difference between property regimes that are open access, where no one has the legal right to exclude anyone from using a resource, and common property, where members of a clearly defined group have a bundle of legal rights including the right to exclude nonmembers from using that resource" (Hess & Ostrom 2003: 121). Since then we have had two lines of inquiry under the umbrella term of "the commons," each concerned with quite different classes of problems and solutions. Perhaps there is no grand unified theory of commons. Perhaps there is. But the basic theoretical framework of contemporary studies of the commons needs to deal with two distinct paradigm cases that mark our understanding of commons. On the one hand, we have the pastures and irrigation districts (called huertas) that symbolize the work Ostrom pioneered; on the other hand, we have highways, streets, and sidewalks, as well as the traditional, uncontroversial aspects of the public domain: like patent and copyright term limitation, or the necessity of inventive step or nonobviousness for patentability. No theory of the commons can afford to exclude either. Understanding what it is that can include, on the one hand, Alicante's refined water scrip market, with its highly liquid market in divisible and tradable rights, and, on the other hand, highways and the public domain in knowledge, information, and culture, is the challenge of any comprehensive theory of the commons.

The hallmark of the first line of work is a focus on local, non-state-based institutional design for sustainable governance of resources as to which a defined set of claimants—farmers who are part of an irrigation district or a pasture, members of a patent pool—lay claim in common. Common-property regimes are property regimes applied to resources that require larger scale utilization than would be efficient in small, individually owned parcels. If this line of work indeed includes Alicante, then what makes it "commons" must be an absence of a state-created property system. The primary policy implications of this line of work are that in the management of resources, sometimes introducing a government management policy will undermine a well-functioning, collectively created system better tailored to local conditions than a standardized institutional framework could (Hess & Ostrom 2003: 123 and nn. 56–59 (extensive bibliography)). This line of work is capacious enough to have been claimed by authors concerned with much more state-based systems for managing resources whose scale requires common ownership, such as corporations (Hess & Ostrom 2003: 123, citing Eggertsson 1990: 223–28; Eggertsson 1993: 41; Lueck 1994: 93–108) and partnerships (Dagan & Heller 2001).

A second line of work is concerned with substantial resource sets in modern market economies, increasingly so in the global networked information economy, governed so that more-or-less anyone may use the resource set and no one, or no group, has exclusive rights as against anyone else. These include both resources that are provisioned and regulated by government, but whose governance entails open access under symmetrical use constraints, like highways, as well as privately provisioned resources whose outputs were not subject to exclusive property rights, but rather subject to a regime of full or partial open access, like inventions and cultural goods subject to the public domain out of which patent and copyright claims are carved, and into which the creations return after a while or under certain conditions. This was the line of work that Rose launched in her exploration of the idea of "inherently public property" under the title *Comedy of the Commons*, where "inherent" meant that common law doctrine created rights in roads, waterways, or public squares for the unorganized public, rather than a particular subset of users or government as proprietor (Rose 1986). This was the concern that animated much of the work that focused on the public domain in copyright and patents since 1990, from Litman and Samuelson to Boyle, which emphasized the neglected importance of the public domain as a resource set to which anyone has access without permission (Litman 1990: 975). And this was the concern that I emphasized in my work on the commons (Benkler, 1998a, 1998b, 2000, 2001, 2003), that Lessig emphasized in his (Lessig 1999, 2002), and whose most recent well-worked-out version is Frischmann on infrastructure and commons management (Frischmann 2005a, 2005b). The most comprehensive and thoughtful map of this terrain is Charlotte Hess's (2008) *Mapping the New Commons*. The practical design and theoretical questions of why and how you would sustainably manage an irrigation system as common property held by several hundred or even thousands of claimants is quite distinct from the question of why and how you would manage a transportation infrastructure that handles hundreds of millions of people a day as a commons, or a common carrier; why you would insist that patents expire after twenty years, or that data be insusceptible to exclusion, so that anyone, member of a patent pool or not, can build on that innovation or data. There are important and useful overlaps between the two lines of research. Studying Wikipedia's internal governance benefits greatly from the CPR literature. Understanding the transformative implications of Wikipedia, or why it ultimately overshadowed Microsoft's Encarta, requires more of an understanding of commons unmodified; in this case, the benefits of open access to knowledge to the public at large and to the rate of innovation (refinement and accession) of the public goods—information and knowledge—treated as commons.

Commons, including open access commons, almost never means lawlessness or anarchy (e.g., Dagan & Heller 2001). It means freedom to operate under symmetric constraints, available to an open, or undefined, class of users. Rules of the road on the open highway are the most basic instance. They are marked by an absence of asymmetric power to determine disposition of the resource. Experiments to institute minimal pricing systems, such as pay access to HOV lanes (Strahilevitz 2000), or congestion pricing, are (a) the exception, not the rule, and (b) available on nondiscriminatory, fixed terms to anyone, more like common carriage than a spot market in roadway capacity. In Hohfeldian terms, they are marked by privileges and immunities for an undefined public, rather than rights and powers for a defined person or persons.

Markets provide the flexibility needed for specialization and innovation by easing trade in diverse goods and services through a standardized medium of exchange. Their openness and capacity for dynamic reallocation of resources is subject to standard limitations: transactions costs, information shortfalls, and strategic behavior in the presence of market power where competition is lacking. Commons provide similar flexibilities for dynamic allocation and reallocation of the resources they govern, so that no one's permission is necessary. (Note that with markets, at least some*one's* permission is necessary, the prior owner of a resource or flow unit). The primary limitation of managing resources as commons is capacity: either because the resources are underprovisioned in the absence of appropriation-seeking investment, or because of congestion, where the resources are congestible. Whether markets or commons will provide a better institutional framework for a given resource will depend on whether the resource is more or less prone to transactions costs, public goods characteristics, and the exercise of market power, on the one hand, and the extent to which it is susceptible to congestion or underprovisioning, given available solutions to either limitation, on the other hand. That is why classic public goods like information goods are subject to a default commons institutional framework—the public domain—and why even partially congestible resource with high positive externalities and high risk of the presence of market power—like highways or public utilities—are managed as commons provisioned with high levels of public investment to compensate for the risk of underprovisioning, or using regulated monopoly frameworks that allow rent extraction to cover the provisioning costs but insist on nondiscriminatory terms of use to preserve the flexibility of transaction-free, permission-free use of the resource, for at least the parts most prone to market power, like last mile electricity distribution systems.

Once we accept that public highways or the public domain in copyright and patent law are no less paradigm cases of the commons than the Spanish huertas or Swiss pastures, it becomes clear that commons are not only, or even primarily, instances of self-governance applied to discrete resource sets. They are as ubiquitous in, and fundamental to, the global networked information economy as is property; neither institutional system can thrive without the other. Few scholars who study patent pools believe that this study replaces exploring the effects of, say, patent term or nonobviousness.[1] The two lines of inquiry complement each other: the former is a study in the tradition of CPRs, the latter a study of the proper demarcation of property and commons in designing a well-functioning innovation system. The CPR work is fundamentally a challenge to the logic of collective action, to the claim that property is necessary to achieve coordinated use. The hallmark of its subjects of observation is the absence of the state in the structure of entitlements.

---

[1] It is possible to interpret some work that focused purely on transactions costs, like Merges's work on collective rights organizations, to imply that if transactions costs were largely eliminated, the public domain would be unnecessary and counterproductive (Merges 1996). This seems to be too strong of an interpretation that would completely ignore the nonrivalry and positive externalities implications of information, knowledge, and culture, where any exclusion involves trade-offs.

Commons unmodified is primarily a challenge to the property-centric view of market societies. It emphasizes that commons are a fundamental element in any well-functioning market economy. This includes paradigmatic commons like roads, highways, and urban sidewalks, basic data, scientific research, and the majority of human knowledge that has entered the public domain; as well as, public utilities like electricity, water, and sewage; major shipping lanes and standards, from weights and measures to shipping container specifications; telecommunications networks; and legality itself. These are all commons, in the symmetric-freedom-to-operate sense, without which the property system could not function. They include allocation models for classic public goods, major infrastructure, and platforms for trade and innovation. Without ubiquitous, sustained, open commons the global networked information economy would come to a standstill.

Both questions are critical; but the widespread attention to the CPR literature has obscured the fact that there are two distinct (though related and complimentary) lines of literature and fundamental questions at stake. My goal here is not to criticize the CPR literature; the work that Elinor Ostrom herself did and inspired is of enormous significance. But I do want to insist that we locate that work in conversation with the work on commons unmodified, so that we can begin to incorporate productively the critique of the role of property in market society with the critique of the logic of collective action, rather than subsume open commons into the CPR approach. Otherwise we will miss the centrality of the *freedom to operate* that commons provide in market societies, and risk adopting institutional approaches that try to shoehorn problems that are fundamentally about more-or-less universal freedom to operate into CPR solutions that are fundamentally about managing shared scarce resources not amenable to privileging freedom to operate in the resource set.

The contributions to this book seek to bring the contextually sensitive Institutional Analysis and Design (IAD) framework to the study of knowledge commons. In this they offer us an important window into the detailed, complex interactions that groups engage in as they govern the relationships among diversely motivated individuals, with diverse levels of explicit and tacit knowledge, availability, and creativity. These studies offer a rich approach to understanding the actual dynamics of collaborative knowledge development communities. But they must be read on the background of an understanding that they do not represent the full scope of the commons. Particularly in information, knowledge, and culture, commons unmodified, open commons, usable by an undefined set of users, relying on diverse and often unstructured motivational models, and based on symmetrically-applicable rules of engagement that in the public domain mean simply "anything goes" after a while, are the foundation. The tension between commons and property defines the institutional foundations for all organizational forms relying on the existing universe of knowledge resources. The defined communities, clubs, and membership models described here are institutional elements of an organizational layer built on top of either the public domain knowledge commons or its proprietary alternative.

II. Commons, Common-Property Regimes, and Legal Scholarship on Information Policy

In the past two decades, the concept of the commons has gradually been rehabilitated in law, economics, political science, and environmental sciences after a long period in the cold. In legal academia, Carol Rose's *Comedy of the Commons* in the mid-1980s was the first important move, looking at roads, public squares, and navigable waters as core examples. Rose emphasized what would later be named in economics "network effects" and positive spillovers, as well as hold-out problems for socially valuable activities as the core answers to the puzzle of why, even where well-defined property rights preexist commons, some core economic resources absolutely central to the proper functioning of an economy built on trade gravitated from property to commons. The most important boost to this newfound respectability came from the extraordinarily careful work of Elinor Ostrom and her many collaborators and colleagues on common-pool resource systems that were managed as common-property regimes, which she encompassed under the label of "commons" in her book title. The commons became sexy (academically) within the decade, and the term was incorporated into other concepts, including famously "anticommons" (Heller 1998), "semicommons" (Smith 2001), and "creative commons,"[2] as well as "contractually reconstructed commons" (Reichman & Uhlir 2003), "liberal commons" (Dagan & Heller 2001), and "culturally constructed commons" (Madison, Frischmann, & Strandburg 2010a).

In 2001, at the first conference organized by the Center for the Public Domain at Duke Law School, Ostrom first addressed a crowd of legal academics then interested in applying the concept of the commons to problems of information and cultural production. A paper Ostrom co-authored with Charlotte Hess identified three definitions then in use in the legal literature. The earliest, Jessica Litman's definition as part of her 1990 description of *The Public Domain*: "In the intellectual property context, the term describes a true commons comprising elements of intellectual property that are ineligible for private ownership. The contents of the public domain may be mined by any member of the public" (Litman 1990: 975). Next was my definition in *The Commons as Neglected Factor of Information Production*: "The commons refers to institutional devices that entail government abstention from designating anyone as having primary decision-making power over use of a resource. A commons-based information policy relies on the observation that some resources that serve as inputs for information production and exchange have economic or technological characteristics that make them susceptible to be allocated without requiring that any single organization, regulatory agency, or property owner clear conflicting uses of the resource" (Benkler 1998a). And finally, Larry Lessig's formulation in *Code and the Commons*: "The commons: There's a part of our world, here

---

[2] Http://www.creativecommons.org.

and now, that we all get to enjoy without the permission of any" (Lessig 1999). Hess and Ostrom's primary critique of our work was that we in the legal academy were too focused on the public domain as the core instance, and were unable to answer the question of what is the commons: "Is it a given right, a nonassigned right, an unclaimed right, an unmanaged resource, or something that should just be there in a democracy?" (Hess & Ostrom 2003: 114). Hess and Ostrom then proceeded to lay out the analytic framework that made *Governing the Commons* and the work on common-property regimes so successful an institutionalist method of critiquing the neoclassical model of property. In particular, on the characteristics of the resource set, Hess and Ostrom emphasized the centrality of high subtractibility to the definition of common-pool resources, and underscored that what these resources shared with public goods was the difficulty of exclusion, not the nonrivalry (Hess & Ostrom 2003: 120). On the characteristics of the institutional regime, they emphasized, as Ostrom had in *Governing the Commons*, the "confusion between common-property and open access regimes." The combination of these distinct characteristics of common-property regimes led Hess and Ostrom to caution that "analyzing the whole ecosystem of scholarly information is much more tenuous than in *Governing the Commons*. . . . Information . . . often has complex tangible and intangible attributes: fuzzy boundaries, a diverse community of users on local, regional, national, and international levels, and multiple layers of rule-making institutions. . . . Distributed digitized information, such as that on the Internet, adds more layers of complexity to the flow. . . . [D]igital information, though subject to congestion, is generally nonsubtractive; thus, the resource flow is not subject to erosion (deterioration) in that same way that physical information artifacts are (books, journals, newspapers, etc.)" (Hess & Ostrom 2003: 132–34). To overcome these difficulties, Hess and Ostrom chose to apply their familiar framework to the most "well-behaved" problem associated with information and knowledge: libraries. Libraries are "easy" for the literature on common-pool resources because they are hard to characterize as problems of information economics. Unlike their knowledge content, copies of books are rival and excludable. Library stacks, reading rooms, and budgets are constrained. These problems were the familiar problems of congestible facilities and subtractable (or rival) goods, meant to be shared by a moderately large and definable set of users, applied near a domain that raises the real challenges to the traditional model of property when applied to innovation, knowledge, culture, and communications.

The challenge that Ostrom posed in her 2001 presentation, and that Hess and Ostrom emphasized in their paper for that conference: the need for a stable shared definition within law and legal analysis of "the commons" has not been resolved. As recently as 2010, when Madison, Frischmann, and Strandburg were pressed to provide such a definition as part of their project to focus legal academic work on "culturally constructed commons" on the model of Ostrom's studies, they responded with: "The commons framework for collecting case studies is grounded on the premise that existing theories may prove to be inadequate. New theories may need to be developed" (Madison, Frischmann,

& Strandburg 2010b: 840). While the effort of these and other authors to leave a big tent and draw in many diverse scholars is worthy and legitimate, the challenge presented by Ostrom a decade ago and others since is also a legitimate one. As legal scholars, rather than as social scientists observing various cultural production practices, what can we say about the characteristics of "commons" as a distinct legal institutional framework that distinguished "commons" from "property," or from any other institutional arrangement? Any such definition would have to be capacious enough to include both highways and the Spanish irrigation districts, as well as distinguish between them. From the Spanish irrigation districts we take that the absence of the state from the definition of the governance structure is an important component. That is the only plausible marker of systems that include a well-functioning market in private, divisible, tradable exclusive entitlements like Alicante's water scrip as a "commons." From the roads, we take that it cannot in fact *require* an absence of the state; for roads almost everywhere are provisioned and regulated by the state, and yet are the quintessential case of open commons. If the paradigm case is roads, then the definition will most likely be anchored in a shared element of the three articulations that Hess and Ostrom criticized ten years ago. Lessig emphasized "without the permission of any"; Litman emphasized that "the contents of the public domain may be mined by any member of the public." I underscored the absence of asymmetric decision-making power backed by state power. Because so much more work has been done by Ostrom and others following her work to define and explain common-property regimes, I will primarily focus on the form of commons characterized by the absence of asymmetric decision-making power backed by state power, and only then will return to how it can be unified with CPRs.

Law and legal scholarship are concerned with the organization of the application of state power. Whether one anchors one's understanding in American progressive legal thought or in Weberian sociology, the core question is what characterizes commons in terms of the predictions of when the sheriff will show up, at whose behest, and with what range of options for action.

The core institutional attribute of property *as law*, that is, as a framework for applying the power of the state in its domain of application, is the delegation and allocation to individuals, of calls on the state, to enforce their will with regard to the use, allocation, management, and disposition of resources. In Hohfeldian terms, property is characterized by rights and powers. Commons, by contrast, are characterized by Hohfeldian privileges and immunities. In commons, freedom to operate outweighs power to appropriate. The main function of commons is to institutionalize freedom to operate, free of the particular risk that any other can deny us use of that resource set, subject to symmetric known constraints and the risk of congestion applicable to that resource set, under those rules, within the expected population of users. These symmetric constraints and the freedom to operate within them, in turn, are protected by either the modern state or by social norms backed by a sufficiently balanced system of individual or collective self-help.

It is critical that we understand this because the question of commons versus property is not an abstract theoretical problem, but one with immense and continuing significance for material growth and political freedom. As we study various specific commons-based practices, we continue to contribute to a set of ongoing debates over the extent to which nations apply their power to actors and facilities in the global networked environment that will emphasize control and power to appropriate over freedom to operate. As recently as the spring of 2011, then-President Nicolas Sarkozy of France put the networked information economy on the agenda of the G-8 for the first time; his core effort was to increase control of the Internet for purposes of securing appropriation of the fruits of the music and film industries (Howard 2011). In the summer of 2011, as Congress was playing brinkmanship with the U.S. debt ceiling, Republican staffers tried to introduce spectrum auction provisions; had they been law in the 1980s, Wi-Fi would simply have never developed; had it passed when in fact proposed, these provisions would have effectively killed future expansion of the enormously successful spectrum commons of Wi-Fi into its next technological iteration (Benkler 2012). In part, these examples of blindness to the importance of commons may be a function of the lobbying power of incumbents who benefit from asymmetric power to appropriate. But in part they come from a mindset that persists among global elites that growth and innovation depend on perfecting property rights. The role of the commons in dynamic market economies must be integrated into that basic shared understanding, so that the same global elites will have, in their baseline understanding of how the world functions, an interplay between commons and property, the proper mix of the two institutional frameworks, as their core design goal.

III. Commons Distinguished; Ubiquity Thereof

The most important contenders as functioning commons that play a fundamental role in modern market economies are roads and highways, urban sidewalks and squares, and the public domain in information, knowledge, and culture. No capitalist economy functions with the majority of these platforms subject to a property regime or to any common-property regime short of a commons: an institutional framework where private parties do not possess asymmetric power to call on the state to back their decisions to exclude, use, dispose, or transfer with legitimate application of its power. The most recent global-scale platform with similar characteristics is the Internet Protocol, TCP/IP, which has played a similar role for connectivity and communications and information technologies. On a much lesser, but growing scale, unlicensed wireless is a commons that is coming to play a similar role in constructing the capillaries of Internet connectivity. Recognizing this helps to distinguish commons unmodified from other concepts used in contemporary discussions.

As Rose emphasized in her groundbreaking *Comedy of the Commons*, roads and public squares are the greatest puzzle for the Demsetzian narrative of enclosure following increasing value (Demsetz 1967: 347–59). In many cases private turnpikes or fields turn through common law doctrines of prescription and fictional grants to open access commons (Rose 1986). Smith, as he begins to define a subclass of resource management approaches in *Semicommons*, nevertheless explicitly uses highways as the classic example of a commons, rather than a semicommons, emphasizing that though an occupant of a vehicle has a usufruct-like right in the specific location of her vehicle at any given moment, the dominant aspect of highways are their "commons" aspect (Smith 2001: 133–34). Any other interpretation would be implausible, else one treated an open access pasture as "semicommons" because the cows were private. By contrast to roads, as Hess and Ostrom express quite clearly, "[m]ost of the property systems that are called 'common-property' regimes involve participants who are proprietors and have four of the above rights [access,[3] extraction,[4] management,[5] and exclusion[6]], but do not possess the right to sell their management and exclusion rights even though they most frequently have the right to bequeath it to members of their family and to earn income from the resource" (Hess & Ostrom 2003). Highways, sidewalks, and squares clearly provide only the first form of what Ostrom call "rights," and what we in law would properly call "privileges," because they do not entail a call on the power of the state to cause another to permit such access. The public domain includes access, certainly, and perhaps "extraction" to the extent that a given use causes a transformation that results in a proprietary right, like copyright or patent, that partly burdens use of the same information or knowledge by another, although does not formally exclude it.

It is possible to get to a common-property regime from either a commons baseline or a property baseline. Acheson's classic study of the *Lobster Gangs of Maine* is an instance of formal open access commons (no one may call on the state to exclude anyone else from lobstering)—the legal state of lobster fishing in Maine—turned to common-property regime through custom and continuous vigilante violence (Acheson 1988). By contrast, patent pools are the classic case of a private-property regime (owners can call on the state to prohibit infringing products) turned into a common-property regime by a set of mutual licenses. This is the class of practices that Reichman and Uhlir called "contractually reconstructed commons" (Reichman & Uhlir 2003), and the core of what Madison, Frischmann, and Strandburg called "constructed cultural commons" (Madison, Frischmann, & Stranburg 2010a). We can think of contractually reconstructed commons or constructed cultural commons as legal and/or social practices in communities of practice for whom the background legal framework does not provide an adequate or appropriate solution. This may occur because the background law imposes a property regime where a commons would be preferable, given the nature of the resource and needs. Much

---

[3] "The right to enter a defined physical area and enjoy nonsubtractive benefits (for example, hike, canoe, enjoy nature)" (Hess & Ostrom 2003: 125–126).

[4] "The right to obtain resource units or products of a resource system (for example, catch fish, divert water)." Ibid.

[5] "The right to regulate internal use patterns and transform the resource by making improvements." Ibid.

[6] "The right to determine who will have access rights and withdrawal rights, and how those rights may be transferred." Ibid.

of the effort on scientific data and open-access scholarly publication is of this type. Free software and creative commons are important contemporary instances as well.

Classification of free software, another core example claimed by anyone who wants to claim generality for their version of "the commons," has presented some problems in the past. Clearly, BSD takes property and creates an open access commons. This license is extremely popular and, critically, is the model of the Apache Software License that governs most web-server software in the world, and now governs many aspects of Android, one of the two major smartphone operating systems. GPL, on the other hand, as well as Creative Commons ShareAlike licenses, most importantly governing Wikipedia materials, are more challenging. These licenses in no way limit the identity of people licensed to read the materials, or use them as inputs/resources into new production, or to distribute them, including charging for them. In this regard they implement open access commons. They do, however, require modifications that are publicly distributed to come under the same license. They do include, therefore, limits on management and exclusion. Some aspects of free software development projects, notably the process of committing code that can be part of official releases, clearly developed organizational and institutional forms that make them similar to common-property regimes. On the other hand, the capacity to take, modify, and use you own version that will not count as "official" replicates characteristics of an open access commons. The difficulty emerges from the double loop. Step 1: the state creates a private-property regime by recognizing software as copyrightable. Step 2: developers precommit irrevocably to permitting anyone access to their works, and to limit management and exclusion rights from it. Step 3a: Some developers (e.g., Apache Software Foundation) create social institutional practices, not legal devices, which, like the lobster gangs of Maine, create a non-state-based method of management of the most important instance of the work that, while preserving the freedom to operate granted in step 2, denies the management power to the extent it applies to recognition by the community of developers of inclusion in the core code. Step 3b: some developers choose a license that does rely on the power of the state, and is therefore a legal device, to limit extraction rights so that they can only be for personal use. To the extent that extraction is used for software publicly distributed, the extraction right is conditioned on reseeding the commons with whatever improvements one has made. The closest analog from the literature on commons in natural resources are state laws that require various preservation measures, such as reseeding oyster beds with cultch, as a use rule applied to an open commons fishery. This can be done in the alternative to Step 3a, as in application of the GPL in smaller projects that have not developed an organizational structure, or cumulatively with Step 3a, as in the Linux kernel development community. What step 3b does is permit access and extraction, but limits management and exclusion to the extent that a developer (a) distributes their output to others, and (b) wishes to distribute on terms other than those preserving access and extraction to the next round of users. Because it preserves the symmetric freedom to operate open to anyone that characterizes commons, free software, even GPLed software, cannot be classified as a limited common-property regime. No person retains the right to exclude person X, but permit person Y, to make and distribute proprietary modifications, or to determine all management of the resource. Because it depends on the baseline grant of state power of copyright in the software, it is a commons regime carved out of, and with the tools created by, property-like law.

It may occur because a commons does not fit the nature of the resource or the community of practice. The lobster gangs of Maine are an obvious example of these. And, as we saw, at the extreme, some structures included under the umbrella of "common-property regimes," like the water scrip system of Alicante (Ostrom 1990: 78–81), are effectively property regimes, classified under the umbrella of the "commons" only because they institute a call on a community's enforcement mechanisms, often one that preexists the modern state in whose jurisdiction it lies, rather than on the state's enforcement powers.[7]

Two terms that incorporate the word "commons" have become highly used and need to be distinguished here. First, Heller's *anticommons* concept refers to a situation of extreme Coasian inefficiency. Coase's actual theory (as opposed to the misnamed Coase Theorem) states that given transactions costs, markets will fail to move entitlements to their best use; markets move entitlements only to uses whose marginally higher value exceeds present uses by more than the transactions costs associated with shifting. That is why it is important for judges to assign rights to their best use or lower transactions costs: they cannot rely on markets to effect transfers given transactions costs. Heller, observing the bizarre construction of rights in the post-Soviet economies, identified a state in which property rights in critical dependencies lead to stasis. Given sufficient mismatch between the shape of entitlements and the usable packets of resources, and sufficient transactions costs for the recomposition of resources in usable packets, resources will go unused. This then became an excellent model for identifying the problems with patenting of small-scale research tools and gene sequences by Heller and Eisenberg (Heller & Eisenberg 1998: 698–701), and what others, following Shapiro, called patent thickets (Shapiro 2001). It is critical to understand that as a matter of legal theory and institutional design, the implication of identifying anticommons problems is not necessarily the introduction of commons or a common-property regime (although it might be). The first and most direct implication is

---

[7] The term "liberal commons" tried to apply the term "commons" to refer to yet a third class of common ownership regimes, including family co-ownership, partnerships, and condominium associations (Dagan & Heller 2001). That effort defined itself in opposition to liberal utilitarianism, overbearing communitarianism (which the authors saw in some of the common-property regimes), and anarchic, lawless "open access" commons (Dagan & Heller 2001: 552–53). The effort there was to make commons mainstream by, it seems, stripping the concept of a distinct institutional core other than common ownership. Below, I try to explain why commons is not defined by common ownership, or by lawlessness, but by absence of ownership defined as asymmetric calls on the state.

the need to understand the scope and definition of usable units of the resource in question. Then, one may either need to redefine the property rights in question to fit usable units of the covered resource, or to define a commons in the resource, depending on whether it is the type of resource that is best governed by commons or property. But if the answer to a perceived anticommons problem is not obtainable by a redefinition of private-property rights around the resource in question, but rather requires instantiation of a commons, like a highway, then the core problem for the resource is not an anticommons problem at all: it is one of misapplying property where commons are the appropriate institutional form. In other words, "anticommons" rather than "lack of commons" is the best description of the diagnosis only if "better-defined property rights" is the primary treatment.

The second important use of the term "commons" is Smith's *semicommons*. Semicommons, backed out of Smith's study of the open-fields system in England, refers to a situation where the same resource is used best for production at different scales. In the case of the fields, wheat growing, which was done on private allocations within the open fields, was a small-scale event; while animal grazing was a large scale event with costs (trampling) and benefits (manure) for wheat growing. A well-functioning semicommons divided the individual tracts such that small-scale production was inefficient, and free riding or defecting in the common uses was hard. Several papers have tried to analyze policy problems directly applicable to the Internet by comparing to semicommons: telecommunications regulation (Smith 2005), information production and intellectual property (Heverly 2003; Smith 2007; Frischmann & Lemley 2007), or the Internet more generally (Grimmelman 2010: 2799–2842). Of these, the application to intellectual property seems most apt. In particular, it helps to understand that debates over the proper scope of intellectual property are never between property and commons, but rather are debates over delineating the boundaries (a) within a semicommons between the private and common aspects (e.g., debates over term of coverage, or the definition of fair use); and (b) between where there is a semicommons and where there is commons *simpliciter* (e.g., rights in data; status of government publications; future status of academic publishing straddles the two types of debate). Given that information goods are nonrival, the exclusion of pure property-like systems is unsurprising. Even the efforts of Hollywood and the recording industry to create an effectively perpetual copyright are an instance of debate about where the boundary within a semicommons is located; none of the industry lobbyists are suggesting that scenes-a-faire doctrine be changed to force them to pay owners of standard plot lines a royalty; none are suggesting that Shakespeare's or Dickens's heirs be located so as to facilitate a market in clearances of rights to make new versions. Finally, the application of semicommons to the Internet generally, based on the private ownership of computers and physical connections to an open network, seems to suffer from the same mistake as treating highways as semicommons would because they are used in private cars. TCP/IP is at its very core a protocol for symmetric, best-efforts clearance of calls on the resources of the network free of any calls on the state to prioritize one person's preferences for clearance over the network over another's. It epitomizes a commons. HTML and the Web similarly do so. Indeed, recent efforts by such bastions of socialism as the *Financial Times* to develop an HTML5-based version for the iPhone and remove Apps from the App store is precisely and instance of organizations leveraging the commons aspect of HTML to get out from a property system applied in a platform context that gave Apple the leverage to demand 30 percent of every app-based transaction (BBC 2011).

IV. Back to Basics: Property vs. Commons in Hohfeldian Terms

Don't roll your eyes! If you think Wesley Hohfeld's century-old characterization of rights, privileges, duties, no-rights, privileges, powers, liabilities, immunities, and disabilities are old-fashioned, just think of them functionally. The basic question is whether someone does, or does not, have the legal ability to call upon the power of the state to back their preference for how a given resource will, or will not, be accessed, used, and managed, and by whom, or to transfer those calls on the state to others. The terminology is simply a tried-and-true way of not getting confused about which of these very real world questions is being asked, what is the answer, and to whom it pertains.

> A has a *right* against B vis-à-vis Use U of Resource R means: A can call on the state to send the sheriff to make B make or not make U of R.
> B has a *duty* to A not to U in R means the same thing: A can call on the sheriff to stop B from U in R.
> If B has a *privilege* to U in R, that means that if A calls the sheriff to stop B from U in R, the sheriff will refuse to come. In that case A has *no right*.
> If A can change B's duty or privilege, for example, by selling his right to B so that B no longer has a duty toward A, but has a right as against him, then A has *power* over B's state vis-à-vis U in R. Alienation of property is a *power* in this sense, because it changes the rights, privileges, duties, and privileges of the buyer and seller, as well as the addressee of the duties of any third parties. B is then said to have a *liability* to have B's duties or privileges to U in R altered by A.
> If B's legal relations to U in R cannot be changed by A, then B has *immunity* in regard of B's privileges and duties regarding U in R. If B has an immunity, then A is said to have a *disability* with regard to B's U in R.

A property regime instantiates vis-à-vis the resources to which it applies a baseline state where some A or identifiable group A has rights over some class of uses of the resources, which may or may not, but usually do, include powers to change the identity of who occupies the position of A with regard to all or some uses or parts of the resource. Everyone else is usually in the position of B, owing duties and susceptible to liabilities to have their jural relations changed. Markets in property-governed resources are markets in permissions, where buyers buy off sellers to make them selectively remove the threat to call the sheriff if the would-be buyer were to make a given use of the stated resource subject to the transaction.

Commons in a resource means that the baseline state is that there is no A or group of A that has asymmetric power to call on the state as above. Instead, the baseline state is that all A have a privilege against anyone else calling the state to prevent them from making use of the resource, and that all A are immune from any B who would like to change that state. B then has no-right, and is under a disability in the Hohfeldian sense that B cannot alter A's privileges.

Note well that a commons so defined does not mean "anything goes." Having rules regulating usage are equally compatible with commons, as long as the core feature of property—the allocation of asymmetric calls on the state among individuals (or to a group of owners) whose use is the subject of markets—is not there. An overly regulated "commons" will likely fail of its core purpose, because it will undermine the very freedom of action for which commons are useful. A highway on which time, travel path, identity, and load are all regulated by the state fits the definition of "commons" as I classify it here; it is a "commons" that is as misregulated as any property system that defines its property rights poorly enough to make it unusable. A poorly defined property system is no less a property system; so too a poorly designed commons is no less a commons.

The boundaries of "commons" versus "property," when diagnosing real-world problems, need not be marked according to formal law. If by common practice in a given region hunters may cross property boundaries in wooded lands in pursuit of game without asking the owner's permission, and if the local authorities will be very hesitant to respond to a property owner's call to exclude a "trespasser," then even if the state does not formally recognize this privilege of hunters, we can say that for purposes of hunting during hunting season, the woods are a commons. We would then classify those as a semicommons, to use Smith's term, because they are mostly private property, but have an important and distinct role as hunting grounds that are commons during some significant portion of their use. It is on this understanding that I proposed the functional definition of the public domain as: "the range of uses of information that any person is privileged to make absent individualized facts that make a particular use by a particular person unprivileged.... These definitions add to the legal rules traditionally thought of as the public domain, the range of privileged uses that are 'easy cases.'"[8]

The hallmark of commons, then, as a legal institutional matter, is symmetric freedom to operate vis-à-vis a resource set, generally or with respect to a class of uses "in the commons." The hallmark of property is asymmetric allocation of calls on the state to determine use, exclusion, extraction, management, and disposition of the resource or class of

---

[8] Benkler 1999: 362 (the omitted text is: "Conversely, The enclosed domain is the range of uses of information as to which someone has an exclusive right, and that no other person may make absent individualized facts that indicate permission from the holder of the right, or otherwise privilege the specific use under the stated facts."). For a survey of the range of definitions used, see Samuelson 2006.

uses of a resources. That is why a common-property regime is "property" on the outside, vis-à-vis nonmembers, and commons on the inside—the interventions and usage rules among the common appropriators do not derive from a right to call on the state to exclude any other among them, even if under formal law they do have that right.

Since we all need both freedom to operate and stable reliance on access to and use of resources to plan and execute our plans, and since both property-based markets and commons-based resources have limitations on the extent to which they can offer either, modern capitalist economies are pervaded by both property and commons. A Wall Street trader may wake up in her private-property apartment (whatever complications co-ops and condos present are outweighed by the core private-property nature of the apartment), gets out of her private-property bed, and goes into her proprietary bathroom. But then she turns on the light. The electricity is provided by either a private company, in New York, or in many other places a publicly owned utility does so; whether the company is privately or publicly owned, however, public utility law prevents Con-Edison from refusing service to our trader unless she pays a higher amount than her less wealthy neighbors. If she wants to make toast, the company has no right to prevent her from connecting any toaster she wishes, or advantage her over her neighbors, for a fee, in doing so, as long as the equipment complies with symmetrically imposed safety laws. Even after electricity market deregulation, distribution to homes continues to include a provider of first and last resort, the utility, whose terms of service are regulated and symmetrically available to all. The electric utility cannot offer tiered service to some who are willing to pay more while throttling back use and creating brownouts for those not willing to pay more. Whatever debates there are about proper rates, they do not include the option of rolling brownouts based on willingness and ability to pay.

She turns on the tap in her sink, and the water that flows is also a commons. The same applies to the sewage system she uses as the water leaves the sink. She walks out her door; if she lives in Tribeca and walks, she will use the commons that is the sidewalk. If she hops in a taxi, that private business will use the commons called the street. The freedom to operate of the commons assures that she has not only a Yellow Cab, but can also call any one of a wide range of private carriers, all of whom use the commons to take her from A to B without needing to transact to receive permission from an owner of the streets. If she lives in Connecticut and drives in, she uses I-95 or any of many highways and parkways, all of which are commons, despite the theoretically and occasionally attempted alternatives: private turnpikes, bridges, and ferries. She might take the subway or commuter rail. Again, each is a publicly provisioned commons-managed system. As she walks into her office building, she relies on its private property for a place to work. She then turns on her private-property computer, although it was likely imported over an ocean whose shipping lanes are commons, shipped in a container whose standard size reduced its cost and is an international commons managed by an international standards-setting organization, and was brought through the Panama Canal, which is required by international treaty to allow all peaceful shipping without discrimination, and denies to the

Canal Authority the rights to exclude or manage passage, or to alienate its powers.[9] She might read a proprietary news service, but that news service likely relied in part on facts collected elsewhere, or data generated by the government: these facts are in the public domain and governed as commons, and the newsletter harvests from the commons and bundles into a private product. If she uses the Internet, she may be using a private connection, or a public connection subject to common-carriage requirements. Common carriage, in turn, is a set of legal arrangements that assures a private owner that provisions goods subject to this regime will make them available without discrimination. In other words, while it is a property regime, it is limited property precisely along the dimension of asymmetric exclusion. It functions as a commons. This is true everywhere outside the United States (Benkler et al. 2010). In the United States it was certainly true for DSL services prior to 2005, and arguably true to cable broadband as well. Since 2005, the debates over Net neutrality have circled around how much of the nondiscrimination requirement inherent in common carriage to reintroduce after the structural designation was removed. If our trader is using a laptop, chances are it is connected to a Wi-Fi network, and Wi-Fi is a commons. The Internet itself, riding on top of the wires or wireless, is a commons, as is the Web to the extent that that is what she uses. If she accesses any website online, the probability is roughly 3 to 1 that the web-server software is an open access commons governed by a FOSS license.[10] Market prices she needs to know are in the commons, although her employer likely pays for privileged early access to the information, and so for an economically relevant instant they are a proprietary club good and available only to those who buy access. In this regard membership in the stock exchange was historically a club good model of access to instantaneous information on market prices that utilizes physical real property law—the right to exclude from where the board is—to exclude from the real target—market prices—that are, as a matter of law, commons. And so the day goes on. If she makes trades, these depend on the legal system, which defines contract and property rights and promises to enforce them. The legal system is available to all on nondiscriminatory terms, and no person has the right to exclude anyone else from using it. It is a publicly provisioned commons.

In personal and commercial life, property is ubiquitous and highly visible to us. What is less visible is that this property system is suspended in commons that undergird and are interpolated throughout the proprietary system elements. Perhaps there is a libertarian

---

[9] Organic Law Panama Canal Authority Section (1997), Article 3, no rights of alienation ("The Canal constitutes an inalienable patrimony of the Panamanian nation; therefore, it may not be sold, assigned, mortgaged, or otherwise encumbered or transferred."). Article 5 requires nondiscriminatory access ("The fundamental objective of the functions attributable to the Authority is that the Canal always remain open to the peaceful and uninterrupted transit of vessels from all nations of the world, without discrimination, in accordance with the conditions and requirements established in the National Constitution, international treaties, this Law, and the Regulations. Because of the nature of the highly essential international public service provided by the Canal, its operation shall not be interrupted for any reason whatsoever.").

[10] Apache's most recent market share number is roughly 65%; nginx has another 7%. At 3%, the market share for the license used by Google is unclear.

utopia in which all these functions are subject purely to a proprietary regime. But no actual country in the world, whether it professes to be capitalist or socialist, functions purely on property or purely on commons.

V. Why Are Commons So Common?

A. MICROEFFICIENCY UNDER UNCERTAINTY AND CHANGE

Commons and property trade off freedom to operate for security in holdings and power to appropriate. Imagine that John wants to organize a picnic with his friends. He can rely on a commons or on property. Imagine that John has a small back yard in a private home he owns or rents; he can invite people to his back yard. In this case, we can say that he invested in buying (renting) secure (for a period) access to the capacity to invite up to fifteen people to an outdoor event in his home. He could also invite them to meet in the park. Then, he runs the risk of not finding exactly the right spot he wants, or congestion if it is a beautiful sunny day in Sheep's Meadow. But he gets the benefit of being able to invite thirty or fifty friends, if that's what he wants. He does not have the security of holdings, but he does have a greater freedom of action with regard to the size of the lawn he can use, and therefore the size of the social network he can engage in this form. Because the park is large and open for all to use, he can be fairly certain that there will be enough room, although he may be uncertain as to its precise quality relative to his yard. If he wants to issue an open invitation for friends of friends to come as well, the freedom to operate, in this case to expand the amount of space used on spec, the probability that such space will be available in the park compared to the certainty of an available but potentially cramped space in his back yard begins to be more appealing. Again, if he were planning to charge admission, then the loss of power to appropriate by excluding nonpaying participants would outweigh the benefits of flexibility. There, he might choose to expand capacity by renting space from a private party that owns a larger garden. But here again, he runs the risk of either overinvesting or underinvesting relative to the actual number of participants, which requires that he limit invitations, require clearer RSVPs, and so forth to avoid overcrowding or unnecessarily expensive overprovisioning. He also runs into transactions costs, which may well make contracting too expensive to justify the transaction to begin with. Once he invests and invites people to a private, precleared, secure proprietary location, expanding or contracting capacity through market exchanges, and moving people to the new space, is likely to be difficult. It is trivial in the park.

In a highly uncertain, changing environment, with needs and plans that call for continuously updating the required resources, the freedom to operate provided by commons has important valuable attributes relative to the security in holdings and power to appropriate of property. This trade-off is far from hypothetical or limited to parties in the park. When presented with major spikes in its network after introduction of the iPhone, AT&T had major congestion problems with its mobile data network (Benkler 2012). It could have gone to the secondary spectrum markets set up by the FCC a few years earlier to buy more spectrum, where it could have leased the additional capacity in a spot market (Noam 1998).[11] It did not. Instead, the company's rapid response (while still searching for longer-term spectrum purchases) consisted of going to the commons: it invested in Wi-Fi hotspots and encouraged users to offload traffic to their home and public Wi-Fi spots. SFR in France, the second largest mobile provider and third largest home broadband provider, went one further, and harnessed all of its home broadband subscribers, about 22 percent of the French market, to become Wi-Fi load-balancing points for all their mobile data subscribers. Wi-Fi offloading by carriers has become the norm, carrying anywhere from 35percent to 65 percent of mobile data.[12] The dramatic rate of increase in required data-carrying capacity meant that carriers found the commons—Wi-Fi—a more flexible and responsive resource management strategy for spectrum than secondary markets, which are the closest thing to straight property in spectrum that the FCC has ever developed. Even though carriers charge mobile users based on usage, and usage over Wi-Fi connections does not count toward monthly caps and overage charges, the benefits of the flexible deployment and network growth outperformed a more slow-moving, expensive, spectrum property-based approach.

The more diverse and uncertain the needs and plans of users—consumers or producers—are, the more attractive the freedom of action associated with having a resource in the commons is to these users. We can conceptualize it as the commons having a private option value to private users (distinct from its welfare effects), whose price is (a) the reduced certainty of availability of a stated quantity of the resource as available in markets, itself a function of how perfect or imperfect the relevant market is, and how susceptible to failure; (b) the lost appropriation opportunity from not having the resource controlled in a proprietary form; (c) the cost differential between the desired use in the market, given its imperfections (e.g., market power over essential facilities) and the cost of using the commons; and (d) the risk that the commons will be congested. The greater the background uncertainty as to the required quantity or quality of the resource and the market imperfections, the higher the option value—that is, the more of the benefits of property an agent would be willing to forgo in exchange for the greater flexibility offered by commons. The symmetric constraints mean that the need for transactions at the margin is eliminated, and with it transactions cost barriers, strategic behavior for platform or essential facilities, imperfect information with its widespread risk of unmatched offer-ask differences, and so forth.

Because freedom of action (to adapt to changed circumstances) is every bit as important under conditions of uncertainty as security in holdings (whose value and utility are

---

[11] Noam's vision of a spot market in spectrum replacing auctions of stable long-term property rights is most closely implemented by SpectrumBridge. See Spectrum Bridge (2008).

[12] See Benkler (2012). The scale and scope of use, rather than the precise numbers, are what is important for purposes of this theoretical essay.

part of the uncertainty) and power to appropriate outputs (whose coming into being is part of the uncertainty), we need, and find ubiquitously around us, both commons and property. Perhaps with perfectly frictionless markets, under perfect information, we wouldn't need commons. But this is no more relevant than saying that with perfectly self-less individuals under perfect information and frictionless social exchange we wouldn't need property. Given imperfect markets, imperfect information, and diversely motivated individuals, some mix of property and commons is necessary for reasonable planning and pursuit of goals. This is from the *private returns* perspective, setting aside collective goals like efficiency and growth. From an individual agent's perspective, having a mix of resources, some commons, some property, will increase their utility over time, given imperfect markets, persistent uncertainty, and change.

VI. Positive Externalities

Over the years, several arguments have been made for when commons are the appropriate institutional framework for a class of resources. In *Comedy of the Commons*, Rose discussed what she called "inherently public property," rather than commons, as the operative concept, but the analysis outlines the foundation of much that followed. These were classes of resources which were to be managed by no one, either private or government, as a proprietor would manage, but rather were, by common law doctrines of prescription or public trust, made public whether or not there was a government action to make them so, or a government manager to provision or manage the resource. Most importantly, these applied to roads and waterways. Rose's critical intervention here was triplefold. First, she identified commons as central to the economy, rather than peripheral. Roads and navigable waterways were, in the periods she described, the central enabler of trade in a growing continental economy. Second, she did not focus on limited common-property regimes, or defined classes of users, but specifically on those doctrines that created use privileges for the public at large, and in this really does speak of the commons as symmetric privilege or freedom to operate for an undefined open class, "the public." And third, she identified the role of commons, in particular their positive returns to scale or positive spillovers, as a core enabler of commerce and the core reason to identify relevant commons (Rose 1986: 768).

The most complete articulation of an answer to this question to date is Frischmann's work on infrastructure, using the concept of infrastructure capaciously to explore the determinants of when open access, or symmetric access to an undefined public, is the desirable institutional framework (Frischmann 2005a; Frischmann & Lemley 2007; Frischmann 2012).[13] Frischmann begins with nonrivalry and what he calls partial nonrivalry. Nonrival goods, in particular nonrival goods that can be used as

---

[13] Frischmann's (2012) book, *Infrastructure: The Social Value of Shared Resources*, was published after the original version of this paper was presented, but I will try to incorporate one or two insights from that work here.

inputs into further production, are resources that are particularly important to keep in the commons, to the extent feasible. The most obvious case for this is information, knowledge, and culture, and the importance of the public domain. By "partial nonrivalry" he means resources that are renewable or cannot be depleted that are subject to potential peak load congestion. These include highways, lake beaches, the Internet, and wireless communications capacity. I would use partial congestability, rather than partial nonrivalry, for this term, because these are not nonrival goods at all. They are more-or-less renewable goods with substantially variable demand and significant periods of nonscarcity interlaced with periods of congestion. The question for all of these is: how much of the benefits we get from running them as a commons (freedom to operate; positive externalities) are we willing to sacrifice in exchange for more efficient allocation than the model of "first come, first served" over the periods of congestion? The difference between these various resources and Hardin's classic fable is that the commons is not depleted. It is renewable and offers nonscarce resource flows over substantial periods which could be degraded by application of a property regime to solve the less common, but acutely experienced, periods of congestion. Even within this group, there are competing theories about how to attain renewability. Sometimes, as in the case of highways, it will require public investment so as to spread the costs of attaining the positive society-wide effects without requiring the imposition of asymmetric exclusion. Sometimes, it will require a limitation of the degree to which the resources are indeed subject to a commons—as in the case of intellectual property seeking to entice private provisioning of a public good. The precise contours of the trade-off become the main institutional battleground. Sometimes, as in the case of my own claims about the functioning of unlicensed wireless device markets, the freedom of action generated by shifting the resource (wireless "spectrum") from property to commons will create a market in some other goods (like Wi-Fi devices) that will provide the desired outcome (wireless data carriage) (Benkler 1998; Benkler 2002).

We could say that resources in modern market economies are usefully managed as commons when:[14]

(a) Efficient allocation of the resource, once provisioned, throughout much of its range of uses, is not a paramount management concern; this includes
   (1) nonrival resources; or
   (2) partially congestable resources, that have variable loads such that over significant ranges of time and usage patterns their use is uncongested;
   in both cases the costs of expected congestion in the commons are lower than anticipated for more classically proprietary resources.

---

[14] I am primarily synthesizing here from Rose (1986); Frischmann (2012); and Benkler (1998a, 2006).

(b) Significant positive externalities are involved in the social value of the resource set.

(c) The resource is used as input into goods, services, innovations, or other sources of value.

(d) The resource is provisioned in a diverse set of market, public, or social processes.

The first characteristic means that the allocation problem of the resource, once provisioned, is either none at all or variable in its intensity so that the good is nonscarce over significant ranges of its relevant usage. The value of instituting a property regime in the resource is then to be found not in its contribution to efficient allocation, but to initial provisioning, if at all. Moreover, the value to the individual of being able to buy secure access to a given flow of the resource is lower where the risk of congestion under a commons framework is lower. The second characteristic suggests that property, to the extent it works to solve either provisioning of a nonrival or partially congestible resource, or allocation problems in congested ranges of uses, involves significant costs in terms of social welfare, because it will limit the positive spillovers from the activities that use the resource. This is most acute in the case of the public domain, but so too would be the social cost of forgone trips if travel were restricted, or if innovations implemented on the Internet would require permission by the private builders of the last mile of connectivity. The third characteristic is a subset of the second, in that it emphasizes the importance of the resource to production in particular. The fourth and final component is the diversity of outputs and modalities of production. The diversity is critical to explaining the importance and function of the symmetry of restrictions and the absence of a gatekeeper who has the right to exclude. Asymmetric exclusion would, at a minimum, bias the productive uses of the resource set toward those whose social value is closest to their private value, with the lowest quotient of positive externalities, and those that tend to be provisioned by market organizations rather than in nonmarket processes. In innovation, the classic commons of the public domain, we see patents, for example, biasing investment toward applicable innovation rather than basic science, which in turn is reflected in, say, pharmaceutical interventions that may or may not have high positive externalities but whose private benefit to the producer is high (follow-on innovations; acne medicine), whereas nonmarket organizations tend to focus on high positive externalities, such as basic science or broad vaccinations with nonpatented vaccines, for example, measles. The trade-off between a broad property regime and a narrow public domain, and vice versa, is between these two broad classes of innovation. To generalize, treating critical inputs into production processes as property will tend to favor market-based producers with uses susceptible to well-defined appropriation opportunities who can evaluate the monetary value of the input and borrow money to meet the costs of access where they can show a clear appropriation path over producers aiming to produce more remote, or less appropriable (higher positive externalities) outputs, who will be less able to pay the social value of their use.

VII. Between the Huertas and the Public Domain: Self-governing Commons in the Networked Environment

The term commons has, over the past twenty years, been used by different scholars, in different scholarly and policy debates, to mark two very different problems that occur at very different scales. In one class of problems, the resource set is highly rival, or subtractable, but the scale of its utilization and maintenance does not lend itself to efficient allocation into individually owned units, the number of sustainable appropriators is defined and not too large. Under these circumstances the extensive and careful work of those who have studied CPRs shows us that the binary conception of governance of scarce resources, as either state planning or market mechanisms, is a false binary. Groups of appropriators in resource sets that meet the characteristics of common-pool resources have successfully sustained common-property regimes that allowed them to exclude others from overusing and congesting the resource, and sustainably sharing its value among them. CPRs are not the only way of appropriating such resources. As Ellickson explained, if the scale of utilization is such that large ownership must be on a large scale, private property is likely to be burdened by transactions costs and inefficiencies relative to common property (Ellickson 1993), but such uses, governed by common law doctrines such as riparian water law and nuisance, have certainly existed and flourished for centuries. Similarly, state-imposed regimes of, say, water drawing rights, or emissions controls and so forth, also have wide application. In each of the three cases, local conditions may affect which of these three types of imperfect systems—private property mediated by property, contracts, and torts law; public regulatory law; or formal or informal governance systems among neighbors—will be most productive. As research about prosocial motivations increases, and the range of work, in a broad range of disciplines, that shows that people do sustainably maintain cooperation without either strict monitoring and material interests or perfectly designed material incentives, we can turn increasingly to cooperative regimes to solve problems that states and markets can solve only very imperfectly, as we seem to be doomed to relearn to our detriment every decade. Work on these small to mid-scale collaborative resource governance systems is a critical part of learning how to construct the governance of what is increasingly becoming a viable form of production—social production by distributed, networked collaborators.

We might say that CPRs are most appropriate for resources whose scale of efficient utilization is large but defined. What defines their scope of application is the need to insulate the resource they govern from the population at large. What defines their classification as common-property regimes is that the usable resource set is larger than usable by a single household or firm, and that the allocation of the resource is based on a set of rules for use, management, and exclusion whose source is a nongovernment process, by which the defined set of users governs its collectively exclusive use of the resource. While often better tailored to historical use patterns of the resource, CPRs are not a flexible institutional form. Even where uncertainty is a major issue, such as with irrigation districts and annual rainfall, the domain and range of uncertainty are reasonably well known, and the range of responses and affected parties well known. The flexibilities in the system allow transaction-free adjustment, but only within well-known bounds. Contrast this with a major shock, such as regional urbanization or a global shift in the location of agricultural production away from the country where the irrigation systems exist, both markets and commons will be substantially more flexible at allocating away from the class of use around which the CPR has developed.

By contrast, open commons are institutional arrangements that cover much larger ranges of resources in modern society, and these resources are generally open to the entire public or at least to some very large, and largely undefined, set of users, both individual and corporate. Their defining feature is not finely designed allocation of well-behaved and predictable (with known uncertainties) resource sets and needs, but high flexibility and an absence of power of exclusion by early users and uses of the resource against later users or uses (Benkler 2011; Frischmann 2012: 112–13). This fluidity comes from their defining institutional feature—the dominance of privileges and immunities rather than rights and powers; is captured by their core function—creating a freedom to operate available to more or less all actors in the economy they serve; and represents their defining contribution to innovation and trade over time under conditions of persistent uncertainty—that is, to growth. The particular instantiations of the freedom to operate will differ from resource to resource, based on (a) the costs of provisioning the resource, and (b) the degree of congestability, and hence the social cost of freedom to operate with the resource expressed as lost capacity at times of congestion, smoothed out over the value of the range of likely congested and uncongested uses over time. Table 3.1 organizes classic instances of resource utilization along the dimensions of whether they are provisioned publicly or privately, and whether their institutional form is property or commons. Table 3.1 helps to explain why the past decade has seen so much overlap between the two concepts of the commons.

The rise of networked information economy has led to an increase in the salience and economic role of (a) information production generally, and (b) social production, based on social motivations and organizational models, rather than markets, states, or firms (Benkler 2006). This has meant that the greatest commons of all, the public domain, has come to play a vastly larger, and more visible, role in the economy as a whole (such as a self-serving industry report claiming that fair use industries account for one-sixth of U.S. GDP and 23 percent of U.S. growth between 2002 and 2007) (Rogers & Szmosszagi 2010) at a time when increasing emphasis on market-based model of provisioning everything was obscuring the publicly provisioned commons from the prevailing model. It has also meant that an increasing amount of goods and services from which we derive value continuously falls into the rubric of socially provisioned, commons-managed resources.

Free and open source software was the first major, measurable, and economically powerful instance of this trend, and Wikipedia has become the instance that no one can avoid as one of the two central knowledge utilities of first resort (the other being Google, which itself in significant measure is built on harnessing socially provisioned information alongside state and market-provisioned information). The models of contractual reconstruction of commons—be it in specific, more CPR-like models of closed research communities or patent pools (which fall more in the rubric of privately provisioned, CPR-managed resources) or in more open access models like Creative Commons—have since begun to grow in visibility and importance precisely because the capitalization model—radically decentralized—and organizational model—distributed, have enabled more resources that are important in the networked, global information economy to be provisioned socially. As such, they do not necessarily depend on market-oriented property rights. Indeed, given the extensive work on motivation crowding out, market-oriented property rights applied to socially provisioned goods and services can be affirmatively counterproductive. Moreover, because they do not need to be provisioned by the state, in the absence of market provisioning, their governance can be self-given. And here is

TABLE 3.1.

Provisioning	Institutional design	
	Property	Commons
Public	Military bases; European government data	Roads; sewage; urban water systems; public utilities; roads, highways; mass transportation; standards; weather, geo data; most basic research
Market-based	Hot dog stands; homes; land; iPhones; Wi-Fi equipment	Some public utilities; telecommunications common carrier regimes; unlicensed spectrum capacity
Social	Club-based social networks; patented academic research outputs	Freely shared academic research; von Hippel innovation; TCP/IP; the Web; Wi-Fi standards; standards of decency and trust-enabling norms; Wikipedia; some CPRs; contractually reconstructed commons; culturally constructed commons
Nature	Land; private oyster beds; river water under riparian common law	Fisheries; some CPRs like pastures; lobsters; oceans; air

the primary overlap with the literature on CPRs beyond the common intellectual front against the claims of dominance of individual private property, which in terms of intellectual history is the basis of a critical alliance. The commons that we have seen most visibly, and that have become the poster children for the new commons, share this feature of self-organization with the classic subjects of the literature on CPRs. Indeed, as in the case of free software and creative commons, they are self-conscious hacks of the state-created system designed to carve a commons out of a legal regime intended to foster its opposite: the individual property-like rights of copyright law.

VIII. Conclusion

Over the past twenty-five years the study of commons has slowly emerged from under the shadow of the dominant property model. As it has done so, it has developed two distinct arms. The first, more prominent and extensive literature has been the work on common-property regimes. This work played an enormously important role in destabilizing the binary, state/market understanding of how production and the utilization of resources can be governed. But its implications for the design of a modern, networked, global information economy are relatively narrower than those of the other arm. The less-well-worked-out branch began with the observation that commons—in the forms of waterways and roads—were central in the development of national, trade-based economies. It continued with observations that, as information, knowledge, and culture increased in importance, as innovation became more clearly understood as the central driver of material welfare, and as networked cooperation made social production ubiquitous, symmetrically privileged freedom to operate is a central aspect of the institutional design of contemporary economies, complementing and completing asymmetrically allocated rights to control.

The literature on CPRs is primarily concerned with collective action in the absence of state regulation (or, to a lesser extent, corporate management). Its primary insight is that under conditions of relatively stable communities, and relatively known resource sets, appropriators can solve collective action failures and manage their shared resources sustainably and more efficiently than either converting these resources to a state-provisioned, state-regulated system, or a market-provisioned, market-cleared system. CPRs emphasize that both state regulation and market mechanisms require abstraction of input, outputs, and processes, so that they can be codified either for command or for pricing and exchange. In the process of necessary abstraction, both knowledge and motivation are harmed. There are levels of nuance in a given resource set—this particular ditch or hill in the irrigation district, or that particular set of glens in the Alpine pastures—that are too fine-grained, knowledge of which is too tacit—to make it through the abstraction process. In addition to their information shortfalls due to abstraction, state- and market-based solutions tend to crowd out intrinsic and extrinsic-social motivation. The result, when this is true, is that a farmer who sees monitoring local conditions and adjusting his own or his neighbors drawing as part of a religious or cultural practice will both engage in greater self-monitoring and compliance (motivation), and know more precisely what to do (tacit local knowledge) than that same farmer would or could have under a more abstract and rationalized system. In terms of both information and motivation, CPRs in these settings outperform markets and states.

The literature on commons unmodified is concerned specifically with the limits of a particular mechanism for overcoming collective action problems: exclusive property rights. It recognizes that defining exclusive property in a resource entails certain asymmetries, imperfections, and power, while the absence of exclusive property enables certain production, innovation, and social dynamics. It sees the ubiquity and necessity for modern complex economies of having large classes of resources managed under symmetric access rules, available for flexible, dynamic use without being subject to the exclusive control of any given party or parties. It emphasizes the critical role that commons play, together with property, in economic systems typified by imperfect information, change and uncertainty, transactions costs, spillovers, and innovation.

In addition to their shared name, the two approaches to the commons overlap primarily for some classes of governance mechanisms around commons resources—those that entail a moderately closed group of actors who rely on the commons or contribute to it, but organize their affairs through relatively interdependent, self-organized institutions that are neither state- nor market-based.

For many years the alliance between these two lines, in the face of a dominant proprietary paradigm, trumped close investigations of their differences. Certainly, as the other chapters in this volume, or Schweik & English (2012), amply demonstrate, there is extensive work that can be done using the IAD framework to study the institutional details of communities of practice and the governance mechanisms of commons-based peer production that are themselves built on a foundation of open commons. But as recognition of legitimate inquiry into the commons has become mainstream, it is important not to allow the synergies between the two concepts of the commons to overshadow the need for new emphasis on refining our understanding of the very different intellectual and policy agendas implied by these two related, but nonetheless very different lines of thought. The open commons in particular, the commons of the open road and the public domain, the electric utility and the Internet, is the one that offers the greatest room for work. It is less studied than are CPRs, while its implications reach to the very definition of what constitutes the institutional platform of well-functioning contemporary economies.

Acknowledgments

This chapter was prepared as a paper for the Convening Cultural Commons workshop at New York University, September 23–24 2011. I am grateful to comments from participants in the workshop, and in particular to Charlotte Hess for productive comments and engagement on the draft.

References

JAMES H. ACHESON, THE LOBSTER GANGS OF MAINE (University Press of New England 1988).

BBC, *FT Pulls App over Customer Data Dispute with Apple*, BBC (Sept. 1, 2011), http://www.bbc.co.uk/news/business-14734911.

Yochai Benkler, *The Commons as a Neglected Factor of Information Policy*, Remarks at the Telecommunications Policy Research Conference (Sept. 1998a).

Yochai Benkler, *Overcoming Agoraphobia: Building the Commons of the Digitally Networked Environment*, 11 HARVARD J.L. & TECH. 287 (1998b).

Yochai Benkler, *Free as the Air to Common Use: First Amendment Constraints on Enclosure of the Public Domain*, 74 NEW YORK UNIVERSITY L. REV. 354 (1999).

Yochai Benkler, *From Consumers to Users*, 52 FEDERAL COMMUNICATIONS L.J. 561 (2000).

Yochai Benkler, *Property, Commons, and the First Amendment: Towards a Core Common Infrastructure*, White Paper for the First Amendment Program Brennan Center for Justice at NYU School of Law (2001), http://www.benkler.org/WhitePaper.pdf.

Yochai Benkler, *Some Economics of Wireless Communications*, 16 HARVARD J.L. & TECH. 25 (2002).

Yochai Benkler, *The Political Economy of Commons*, 4 UPGRADE 6 (2003).

YOCHAI BENKLER, THE WEALTH OF NETWORKS: HOW SOCIAL PRODUCTION TRANSFORMS MARKETS AND FREEDOM (Yale University Press 2006).

Yochai Benkler, *Growth-Oriented Law for the Networked Information Economy: Emphasizing Freedom to Operate over Power to Appropriate*, in RULES FOR GROWTH: PROMOTING INNOVATION AND GROWTH THROUGH LEGAL REFORM (R. Litan ed., Ewing Marion Kauffman Foundation 2011).

Yochai Benkler, *Open Wireless vs. Licensed Spectrum: Evidence From Market Adoption*, 26 HARVARD J.L. & TECH. 60 (2012).

Yochai Benkler et al., *Next Generation Connectivity: A review of broadband Internet transitions and policy from around the world*, Report of the Berkman Center for Internet and Society for the Federal Communications Commission (February 2010), http://cyber.law.harvard.edu/pubrelease/broadband/.

Hanoch Dagan & Michael Heller, *The Liberal Commons*, 110 YALE L.J. 549 (2001).

Harold Demsetz, *Toward a Theory of Property Rights*, 57 AM. ECONOMIC REV. 347 (1967).

THRÁINN EGGERTSSON, ECONOMIC BEHAVIOR AND INSTITUTIONS (1990).

Thráinn Eggertsson, *The Economic Rationale for Communal Resources*, in A CONFERENCE ON COMMON PROPERTY REGIMES: LAW AND MANAGEMENT OF NON-PRIVATE RESOURCES, VOL. I 41 (Erling Berge ed., Ås, Norway: The Agricultural University of Norway 1993).

Robert C. Ellickson, *Property in Land*, 102 YALE L.J. 1315 (1993).

Brett M. Frischmann, *An Economic Theory of Infrastructure and Commons Management*, 89 MINNESOTA L. REV. 917 (2005a).

Brett M. Frischmann, *Infrastructure Commons*, 89 MICHIGAN STATE L. REV. 121 (2005b).

BRETT M. FRISCHMANN, INFRASTRUCTURE: THE SOCIAL VALUE OF SHARED RESOURCES (Oxford University Press 2012).

Brett M. Frischmann & Mark A. Lemley, *Spillovers*, 107 COLUMBIA L. REV. 257 (2007).

James Grimmelman, *The Internet as Semicommons*, 78 FORDHAM L. REV. 2799 (2010).

Michael A. Heller, *The Tragedy of the Anticommons: Property in the Transition from Marx to Markets*, 111 HARVARD L. REV. 621 (1998).

Michael A. Heller & Rebecca S. Eisenberg, *Can Patents Deter Innovation? The Anticommons in Biomedical Research*, 280 SCIENCE 698 (1998).

Charlotte Hess, *Mapping the New Commons*, presented at "Governing Shared Resources: Connecting Local Experience to Global Challenges," the 12th Biennial Conference of the International Association for the Study of the Commons, University of Gloucestershire, Cheltenham, England (July 14–18, 2008), http://dlc.dlib.indiana.edu/dlc/handle/10535/304.

Charlotte Hess & Elinor Ostrom, *Ideas, Artifacts and Facilities: Information as a Common Pool Resource*, 66 LAW & CONTEMP. PROBS. 111 (2003).

Robert A. Heverly, *The Information Semicommons*, 18 BERKELEY TECH. L.J. 1127 (2003).

Alex Howard, *At the eG8, 20th Century Ideas Clashed with the 21st Century Economy*, O'REILLY RADAR (May 27, 2011), http://radar.oreilly.com/2011/05/eg8-2011-internet-freedom-ip-copyright.html.

Lawrence Lessig, *Code and the Commons*, Keynote Address at the Conference on Media Convergence, held at Fordham University Law School (Feb. 9, 1999), http://cyber.law.harvard.edu/works/lessig/fordham.pdf.

LAWRENCE LESSIG, THE FUTURE OF IDEAS: THE FATE OF THE COMMONS IN A CONNECTED WORLD (Random House 2002).

Jessica Litman, *The Public Domain*, 39 EMORY L.J. 965 (1990).

Dean Lueck, *Common Property as an Egalitarian Share Contract*, 25 J. ECONOMIC BEHAVIOR & ORGANIZATION 93 (1994).

Michael J. Madison, Brett Frischmann, & Katherine Strandburg, *Constructing Commons in the Cultural Environment*, 95 CORNELL L. REV. 657 (2010a).

Michael J. Madison, Brett Frischmann, & Katherine Strandburg, *Reply: The Complexity of Commons*, 95 CORNELL L. REV. 839 (2010b).

Robert P. Merges, *Contracting into Liability Rules: Intellectual Property Rights and Collective Rights Organizations*, 84 CALIFORNIA L. REV. 1293 (1996).

Eli Noam, *Spectrum Auctions: Yesterday's Heresy, Today's Orthodoxy, Tomorrow's Anachronism*, 2 J. LAW & ECONOMICS 765 (1998).

Organic Law Panama Canal Authority Section (1997).

ELINOR OSTROM, GOVERNING THE COMMONS: THE EVOLUTION OF INSTITUTIONS FOR COLLECTIVE ACTION (Cambridge University Press 1990).

J. H. Reichman & Paul Uhlir, *A Contractually Reconstructed Research Commons for Scientific Data in a Highly Protectionist Intellectual Property Environment*, 66 LAW & CONTEMP. PROBS. 315 (2003).

THOMAS ROGERS & ANDREW SZMOSSZEGI, Computer and Communications Industry Association [CCIA], FAIR USE IN THE U.S. ECONOMY: ECONOMIC CONTRIBUTION OF INDUSTRIES RELYING ON FAIR USE (Washington, D.C.: CCIA 2010).

Carol Rose, *The Comedy of the Commons: Custom, Commerce, and Inherently Public Property*, 53 U. CHICAGO L. REV. 711 (1986).

Pamela Samuelson, *Enriching Discourse on Public Domains*, 55 DUKE L.J. (2006).

CHARLES M. SCHWEIK & ROBERT C. ENGLISH, INTERNET SUCCESS: A STUDY OF OPEN SOURCE COMMONS (MIT Press 2012).

Carl Shapiro, *Navigating the Patent Thicket: Cross Licenses, Patent Pools, and Standard-Setting*, *in* INNOVATION POLICY AND THE ECONOMY 119 (Adam B. Jaffe, Josh Lerner, & Scott Stern eds., MIT Press 2001).

Henry E. Smith, *Semicommon Property Rights and Scattering in the Open Fields*, 29 J. LEGAL STUDIES 131 (2001).

Henry E. Smith, *Governing the Tele-Semicommons*, 22 YALE J. ON REG. 289 (2005).

Henry E. Smith, *Intellectual Property as Property: Delineating Entitlements in Information*, 116 YALE L.J. 1742 (2007).

Spectrum Bridge, *The Secondary Spectrum Market: A Licensing & Leasing Primer* (2008), http://spectrumbridge.com/Libraries/White_Papers/The_Secondary_Spectrum_Market_A_Licensing_Leasing_Primer.sflb.ashx.

Lior Jacob Strahilevitz, *How Changes in Property Regimes Influence Social Norms: Commodifying California's Carpool Lanes*, 75 INDIANA L.J. 1231 (2000).

4 Constructing the Genome Commons
Jorge L. Contreras*

I. Introduction

In Chapter 3, Yochai Benkler explores the tension between two competing conceptions of the "commons": one which is frequently espoused in the academic legal literature and focuses on regimes of open access and limited propertization, and another which is addressed in the literature of common-pool resources pioneered by Elinor Ostrom, and focuses on social structures for the management of shared resources.[1] In economic terms, basic scientific research is typically classified as a "public good," a resource provisioned by the state that is susceptible to neither exclusion nor depletion by use (i.e., has the economic characteristics of nonexcludability and nonrivalry). Common examples of economic public goods include lighthouses and public highways. Though the analogy is imperfect, in legal discourse public goods often are associated with the public domain,

---

* Jorge L. Contreras is Associate Professor of Law, American University Washington College of Law, Washington, D.C., USA. He has served as legal counsel to the SNP Consortium, a public-private partnership devoted to the public dissemination of a single nucleotide polymorphism (SNP) map of the human genome. He recently co-edited (with Dr. James Cuticchia) *Bioinformatics Law: Legal Issues for Computational Biology in the Post-Genome Era* (ABA Publishing 2013). Professor Contreras currently serves as Co-Chair of the National Conference of Lawyers and Scientists and is a member of the Advisory Council of the National Center for the Advancement of Translational Sciences (NCATS) at the U.S. National Institutes of Health (NIH).
[1] See Benkler, this volume, ch. 3.

a category that implies free access and a lack of ownership by any particular entity. The public domain is often evoked in the context of intangible ideas and scientific discoveries that are free from intellectual property encumbrances because the relevant rights either have expired or were never procured in the first place. Examples include the works of Shakespeare (in which copyright has expired) and discoveries that have been published but as to which patent applications have not been filed. So conceived, the fruits of scientific research (to the extent not protected by intellectual property) generally fall into Benkler's first broad class of commons: the public domain.

The output of genomics research, however, is more amenable to analysis as a common-pool resource along the lines developed by Ostrom and her colleagues. By genomic research, I refer to the large-scale study of the genetic makeup of humans and other organisms that began with the Human Genome Project (HGP) in the late 1980s and continues today in numerous government and privately funded projects. These projects have made a vast quantity of genetic information available in public databases across the globe. This massive accumulation of data is what has been referred to collectively as the "genome commons" (Angrist 2010: 72–73; Contreras 2010: 393; Contreras 2011: 63).

Today the free availability of genomic data is a fundamental feature of the research landscape. The size of this public aggregation of data is matched only by the breathtaking rate at which it is expanding. Over its decade-long existence, the HGP mapped the 3.2 billion DNA nucleotide base pairs that form the human genome. To do so, it sequenced tens of gigabases (billions of bases), creating what was then an unprecedented accumulation of data. Today, one current research project (aptly named "1000 Genomes") is projected to generate 200,000 gigabases of data—approximately 20,000 times the quantity generated by the HGP (NHGRI 2012). And the rate at which DNA is being sequenced continues to increase. According to one 2011 report, "a single DNA sequencer can now generate in a day what it took 10 years to collect for the Human Genome Project" (Pennisi 2011). What's more, most of this data is available for free to anyone with the ability to download it from one of several governmental and private websites. The public availability of this data over the past decade has yielded significant advances in medical genetics, molecular biology, and bioinformatics; reduced research costs; and enabled greater reproducibility of results, all of which have contributed to the acceleration of scientific discovery and biomedical research (Williams 2013; Collins 2010; 1000 Genomes Project Consortium 2012: 60–61). According to one recent study, the U.S. economic output attributable to advances made by the HGP and follow-on projects totaled $65 billion in 2012 alone (Batelle 2012).

The existence of this invaluable public resource was by no means assured when the HGP was initiated in the early 1990s. Rather, it was widely believed (and feared by some) that the majority of genomic data would be placed in proprietary databases, protected by intellectual property or confidentiality restrictions, and made available only under costly subscription agreements. This alternative model, in fact, was the one initially proposed by Celera Genomics, which raced with the public HGP to complete the human genomic sequence between 1998 and 2001.

The fact that the genome commons is today a global, public resource owes much to a 1996 accord reached in Bermuda by scientific leaders and policy makers. The ground-breaking "Bermuda Principles" required that all DNA sequences generated by the HGP be released to the public a mere twenty-four hours after generation, a stark contrast to the months or years that usually preceded the release of scientific data (Bermuda Principles 1996). The Bermuda Principles arose from early recognition by scientists and policy makers that rapid and efficient sharing of data was necessary to coordinate activity among the geographically dispersed laboratories working on the massive project. But site coordination was not the only factor motivating the unorthodox rapid-release requirements of the Bermuda Principles. More importantly, this approach arose from the conviction among project leaders that rapid release of genomic data was necessary for the advancement of scientific research and the public good (International Human Genome Consortium 2001: 864).

The Bermuda Principles continue to shape data release practices of the genomics research community and have established "rapid prepublication data release" as the norm in this and other fields (Kaye et al. 2009: 332). Advances in science and technology, however, together with increasingly challenging ethical and legal issues, have complicated the data release landscape and given rise to policy considerations not foreseen in Bermuda. Among these are the need to protect human subject data, even at the genomic level, and the desire of scientists who generate large data sets to analyze and publish their research before others take advantage of it. The emergence and recognition of these considerations has led to an evolution of genomics data release policies and norms that are more restrictive and complex than those of the HGP, but which nevertheless preserve the fundamental shared nature of the genome commons. In this respect, the genome commons resembles the managed common-pool resources studied by Elinor Ostrom and her colleagues more than it conforms to the simpler models of the public domain/public goods that are often associated with basic scientific research.

Ostrom pioneered the analysis of common resource structures, whether physical or informational, using a conceptual tool known as the Institutional Analysis and Development (IAD) framework. More recently, as described in Chapter 1, Michael Madison, Brett Frischmann, and Katherine Strandburg have undertaken a thorough reexamination of the IAD framework in relation to commons in the "cultural environment," seeking to combine the functionalist IAD approach with metaphorical and narrative accounts of commons formation (Madison, Frischmann, & Strandburg 2010: 659, 671–74, 681–83). In this chapter, I engage the theoretical framework of Chapter 1 to elucidate both the structural and the narrative elements of the genome commons. The IAD methodology offers a systematic means for examining the characteristics of a commons structure: the common resource, the "action arena" in which stakeholders interact with the commons, and the resulting patterns of interaction (Ostrom & Hess 2007: 44–45). Each of these broad areas is subdivided into further analytical components, so that the common resource, for example, is assessed with respect to its basic characteristics, the attributes of the relevant community, and its applicable "rules in use." In particular, I chart the evolution of the genome commons from what was initially a public domain vehicle established to deter the proprietary designs of emerging biotechnology companies, into a unique polycentric governance institution for the growth, management, and stewardship of a massively shared public resource.

II. Attributes of The Genome Commons

A. RESOURCE CHARACTERISTICS

The genome commons is, at its most basic level, a massive collection of data stored in electronic databases across the world and made available through public networks. In order to understand the unique nature of this resource, it is useful to consider both the data contained within it and the databases that house it, as well as the underlying legal environment that applies to such aggregations of data.

1. Genomic Data

Deoxyribonucleic acid (DNA) is a chemical substance that exists in almost every living organism. Each DNA molecule is composed of four basic building blocks or nucleotides: adenine (A), thymine (T), guanine (G), and cytosine (C). These nucleotides form long strings of linked pairs (A-T and G-C) that are twisted in a ladder-like chain: the famous "double-helix" first described by James Watson and Francis Crick in 1953. Each rung of this ladder is referred to as a "base pair," and the full complement of DNA found within an organism is its "genome." The genome of a simple organism, such as the *E.coli* bacterium, contains approximately five million base pairs, that of the fruit fly contains approximately 160 million base pairs, and that of *Homo sapiens* contains approximately 3.2 billion base pairs. Each human genome is approximately 99.5 percent identical, but the very small differences are responsible for the great variability in human physical and physiological traits.

Some segments of DNA within an organism's cells form functional units called "genes," which range in size from as few as a hundred to more than two million base pairs. It is currently estimated that each human possesses between 20,000 and 25,000 genes. Genes are responsible for the inheritance of traits from one generation to the next, and they encode the many proteins responsible for the biochemical functions within a cell. The observable characteristics of an individual, including physical, physiological, behavioral, and demographic characteristics, are referred to as that individual's "phenotype." One of the principal goals of genomic science has been to associate particular genes or genetic variations (mutations) with phenotypic traits.

Early in the twentieth century, hereditary diseases began to be associated with genes passed from parents to their offspring. But while simple inheritance explained numerous conditions, from benign traits such as hair coloration to debilitating ailments such as cystic fibrosis, Down syndrome, and Huntington's disease, it was not until the 1970s that scientists could identify the individual genes responsible for these conditions. Even then, each of these discoveries took years of painstaking research and a healthy dosage of good luck. In 1986 a revolutionary new process for copying DNA fragments, the polymerase chain reaction (PCR), was developed. PCR enabled the large-scale, rapid sequencing of DNA. PCR technology soon gave rise to ambitious plans to sequence not only genes identified with specific diseases, but the entire human genome.

The HGP, which is discussed in detail below, took a decade to complete, and resulted in the first detailed map of the 3.2 billion base pairs that constitute the human genome. Since the completion of the initial draft of the human genome in 2001, the HGP and follow-on projects have generated vast amounts of genomic data, including the full genomic sequences of hundreds of individual humans and thousands of other organisms. Today, additional international efforts are under way to sequence the genomes of thousands of additional individuals to create still more complete and detailed reference maps of the human genome (Hayden 2008: 378; Travis 2010), and to sequence the genomes of the multitude of microorganisms residing within the human body (Turnbaugh et al. 2007: 804).

The public human genome map has also enabled researchers to conduct studies to determine complex combinations of genetic factors contributing to disease. Whereas earlier studies took years to identify single genes responsible for specific inherited conditions, recent "genome-wide association studies" (GWAS) have been credited with identifying variants in multiple genes that increase susceptibility for complex conditions such as diabetes, cancer, hypertension, and numerous other diseases. Such studies, which involve scanning the entire human genome for variants that are common among affected individuals, have been made possible by dramatic advances in sequencing and data analysis technology.

2. Data and Databases

For hundreds of years, the traditional means of disseminating scientific information has been the peer-reviewed scholarly journal. Scientists are judged, for purposes of career advancement and the awarding of government grants, on the quantity of their publications, giving scientists a significant personal incentive to publish and share their data with others (Merton 1979: 316). Yet, despite the prevalence of scientific publications, there are two principal reasons that journal publication has proven to be inadequate for the dissemination of genomic data.

First, the sheer quantity of genomic data is far too large to allow it to be published in any traditional journal format, and the data is only useful if it is made available for electronic manipulation and analysis. Hess and Ostrom accurately observe that modern biology has been transformed into an *information* science (Hess & Ostrom

2006: 335). A journal article typically includes only a brief presentation of significant experimental findings, often made in summary or tabular fashion, together with the researcher's analysis and conclusions. While journal articles often provide some data essential to support the analysis, the published data typically represent only a small fraction of the "raw" data set. Yet in order to enable the verification and reproduction of an experiment by other scientists, access to the full data set in a usable, electronic format is often required.

Second, there is usually a lengthy delay between the collection of data and journal publication. This delay reflects the time required for the investigators to analyze their results, gather additional data, refine their analysis, prepare a paper based on their findings, and submit the paper to journals; for the journals to conduct their peer review and editorial processes; for the investigators to make revisions required by the journals (including, at times, to conduct additional experiments) or, if the paper is rejected by the journal, to revise it and submit it to different journals; and, finally, for the journal to edit, format, and prepare the accepted paper for publication. Studies report that the average delay between the completion of scientific work and publication can range from twelve to eighteen months and longer, depending on the field (Amat 2008: 379; Garvey & Griffith 1964: 1656; Roland & Kirkpatrick 1975: 1274). Clearly, in a field in which rapid access to experimental data is required to enable additional studies and analysis, these lengthy delays are highly undesirable.

These two considerations have led to the practice of making large scientific data sets available independently of journal articles. Many science funding agencies now require that genomic data be released into public databases shortly after it is generated. A growing number of scientific journals also require that authors make the data underlying their published results available to readers on a website accessible through the journal or the authors' institutions or in a government-maintained database. These databases have enabled the efficient, rapid and cost-effective sharing of new knowledge and the pursuit of studies and analyses that otherwise might have been impossible.

The principal databases for the deposit of genomic sequence data are GenBank, which is administered by the National Center for Biotechnology Information (NCBI) (a division of the U.S. National Institutes of Health (NIH)'s National Library of Medicine), the European Molecular Biology Library (EMBL) in Hinxton, England, and the DNA Data Bank of Japan (DDBJ). NCBI also maintains the RefSeq database, which consolidates and annotates much of the sequence data found in GenBank. In addition to DNA sequence data, genomic studies generate data relating to the association between particular genetic markers and disease risk and other physiological traits. This type of data, which is more complex to record, search, and correlate than the raw sequence data deposited in GenBank, is housed in databases such as the Database of Genotypes and Phenotypes (dbGaP), operated by the NIH's National Library of Medicine. dbGaP can also accommodate phenotypic data, which includes elements such as de-identified subject age, ethnicity, weight, demographics, exposure, disease state, and behavioral factors, as well as study documentation and statistical results. Given the potential sensitivity of phenotypic data, dbGaP allows access to data on two levels: open and controlled. Open data access is available to the general public via the Internet and includes nonsensitive summary data, generally in aggregated form. Data from the controlled portion of the database may be accessed only under conditions specified by the data supplier, often requiring certification of the user's identity and research purpose.

A final important observation regarding the nature of the genome commons arises from its sheer size and the breathtaking rate at which it is expanding. As noted above, current genomics projects can generate as much data as the entire HGP in a matter of weeks. Statistics like these have led to talk of a "data tsunami" in genomic science, in which the capacity to manage and analyze such vast quantities of data could severely lag the rate at which it is being produced (Green 2011: 207–08; Royal Society 2012: 88). Given these challenges, researchers have experimented with new approaches to the storage, handling, and public release of these large data sets. Data from the 1000 Genomes Project, for example, is currently being made available through the "cloud" via Amazon Web Services (Waltz 2012: 376).

The organizational implications of the rapid growth of the genome commons are significant. The institutional rules and structures surrounding genomic data were created when the size of this common resource was several orders of magnitude smaller than it is today. Just as rules established among the early American colonists, numbering in the mere tens of thousands, could not be expected to anticipate the issues involved in governing today's American nation of more than 300 million (particularly if this spectacular growth had occurred over the course of just two decades), it is not surprising that rules established in the days of the HGP did not contemplate many of the complexities associated with today's genome commons. Indeed, it is doubtful that any shared resource described in the common-pool resource literature has grown at a rate anywhere close to that of the genome commons. Considered in this light, the rules and norms established by the HGP, which continue to shape policy today, have fared remarkably well.

3. Legal Background Environment

Madison, Frischmann, and Strandburg emphasize that an understanding of the "natural" environment in which a cultural commons exists is critical to understanding the attributes and operation of that commons (Madison, Frischmann, & Strandburg 2010: 684–88). In the case of collections of intangibles, this natural environment necessarily includes the intellectual property rules that govern rights and permissions with respect to the elements of the common resource. The genome commons presents a complex picture, as it embodies both biomedical discoveries, which are typically addressed via the patent system, and large aggregations of data, which are typically addressed via access restrictions, contractual obligations, and copyright rules.

a. Patents and DNA

Patents may be obtained in most countries to protect novel and inventive articles of manufacture, compositions of matter, and processes. Excluded from patentable subject matter, however, are laws of nature and natural phenomena.[2] The fundamental question, thus, is whether DNA sequence information and medical conclusions drawn from DNA information are more akin to "inventions" that are protectable by patents, or "products of nature" that are not.

The debate regarding the patentability of DNA sequence information began in earnest in the 1980s, shortly after large-scale DNA sequencing became feasible. The U.S. National Institutes of Health (NIH) was among the first to seek patent protection for DNA sequences. In 1991, a group led by NIH researcher J. Craig Venter filed patent applications claiming 337 short genetic sequences known as expressed sequence tags (ESTs), accompanied by an announcement that the NIH would seek to patent thousands more ESTs in the coming months (Anderson 1991: 485; Roberts 1991: 184). There was a public outcry in response to this announcement, triggering what Robert Cook-Deegan has called "an international firestorm" (Cook-Deegan 1994: 330–31). The debate over gene patenting within the NIH was equally vehement and led to a turning point in the NIH's attitude toward patents on genetic material. By 1994, the agency elected not to appeal the Patent and Trademark Office's rejection of its initial EST patent applications (Institute of Medicine 2003: 36–37), and it has since adopted a consistently lukewarm, if not outright averse, attitude toward the patenting of genetic sequences. This attitude is clearly reflected in the agency's support for the patent-deterring Bermuda Principles and subsequent policies.

Nevertheless, the patenting of genetic information by academic research institutions and private enterprises has been the subject of substantial controversy. According to many sources, the number of such patents has continued to rise (Jensen & Murray 2005: 239; Huys et al. 2010: 903; Rosenfeld & Mason 2013). In *Mayo Collaborative Services v. Prometheus Laboratories, Inc.*, the U.S. Supreme Court reaffirmed the long-standing exclusion of so-called "laws of nature" from patentability[3] and in *Ass'n for Molecular Pathology v. Myriad Genetics*, the Court denied the patentability of native DNA sequence data and isolated human genes.[4] Elsewhere, I have analyzed the specific patent deterrent effects of the genomic data release policies adopted by the NIH during and after the HGP (Contreras 2011: 86–87). While a full discussion of this topic is beyond the scope of this chapter, suffice it to say that policies requiring rapid release of genomic data, together with the evolving understanding of the "utility requirement" under U.S. patent law, have had a substantial dampening effect on the issuance of patents

---

[2] Diamond v. Diehr, 450 U.S. 175, 185 (1981).
[3] Mayo Collaborative Servs. v. Prometheus Labs., Inc., 132 S. Ct. 1289 (2012).
[4] Ass'n for Molecular Pathology v. Myriad Genetics, 133 S. Ct. 2107 (2013).

covering "raw" DNA sequence information. Thus, the bulk of so-called "gene patents" issued in recent years have instead claimed specific functions of DNA sequences or the use of particular DNA sequences in diagnostic tests or as the basis for treatment decisions. Thus, while the raw sequence data contained in public repositories such as GenBank is not itself generally subject to patent protection (save for a dwindling number of early "composition of matter" patents, such as the ones litigated in the *Myriad* case), the practical uses of such sequence data might be constrained by patents covering specific diagnostic or therapeutic uses of that data. The debate regarding the proper legal scope of such restrictions will doubtless continue.

b. Protection of Data and Databases

Under U.S. law it has long been held that "facts" such as scientific data are not subject to copyright protection. Databases that merely contain simple compilations of factual information similarly lack formal legal protection.[5] Nevertheless, access to data that is contained in electronic databases can be controlled by the database operator via technical means, such as password-restricted access, as well as by limitations built into contractual access agreements. Thus, while data itself may not be subject to legal protection, circumvention of such technical protection or contractual measures can be challenged under a number of legal theories. In this way, scientific information that might otherwise be in the public domain can become encumbered when compiled in proprietary databases (Reichman & Uhlir 2003: 335). Such restrictions were adopted by Celera Genomics when it announced its intention to sequence the human genome in competition with the publicly funded HGP and offer the resulting data to commercial users pursuant to license agreements. The threat of propertization of the genome in this manner has fueled continuing public support for GenBank, dbGaP, and other publicly accessible repositories for genomic data.

B. ACTORS AND STAKEHOLDERS

Much early work regarding common resource governance was devoted to understanding the attributes of the communities that shared the commons, whether herdsmen grazing cattle on a common pasture or fishermen trolling ocean stocks. This analysis is equally important in the context of the genome commons. While genomic data release policies are typically drafted and adopted by funding agencies, the NIH in particular has given substantial deference to the views and opinions of the scientific community, while also seeking to represent the interests of the general public. Thus, the roles and influence of other stakeholder groups are not to be underestimated: the development of data release policies in the genome sciences has been a polycentric process of negotiation and

---

[5] Feist Publ'ns, Inc. v. Rural Tel. Serv. Co., 499 U.S. 340 (1991).

compromise. The principal stakeholder communities relevant to the genome commons, both initially and as it has evolved over time, include the following:

1. Funders

The HGP, which cost approximately $2.7 billion (in 1991 dollars) (Nat'l Human Genome Research Inst. 2010), has been called "the largest and most visible large-scale science project in biology to date" (Institute of Medicine 2003: 29). The NIH and the U.S. Department of Energy (DOE), which funded the bulk of the massive project, together with their counterparts at the Wellcome Trust in the United Kingdom, exerted significant influence over the project's technical and policy direction. Public funding from sources such as the NIH and the Wellcome Trust still plays a crucial role in genomic research, though smaller-scale and disease-specific studies today frequently are conducted in the private sector.

2. Data Generators

Prior to the HGP, genetic research was conducted in hundreds of academic laboratories across the world and funded primarily by small grants directed toward the investigation of specific genetically-linked diseases. The HGP, in contrast, treated the mapping of the human genome as a campaign of large-scale data production (Roberts 2001: 1182). The NIH funded three major genome centers (Baylor College of Medicine, Washington University, and the Whitehead Institute), which worked closely with the DOE's Joint Genome Institute and the Sanger Centre in Cambridge, England (funded by the Wellcome Trust) (Institute of Medicine 2003: 39). The intensity of this work, the amount of capital equipment required to undertake it, and the degree of specialization demanded by the emerging science of genomics led to the creation of a new breed of scientist: one whose principal research aim was the generation of data rather than the development and testing of hypotheses. This distinction persists today as the number of data-generating projects in the biosciences continues to increase. Like other researchers, data-generating scientists share two principal concerns: (a) obtaining funding for their work and (b) advancing their careers through publication and peer recognition. But while governmental funding of new data-production projects continues, data-generating scientists face challenges when it comes to publishing their work in traditional scientific journals, as the creation of large data sets has not traditionally been viewed as meriting recognition in the most prestigious journals (Toronto Authors 2009: 169–70).

Another trend having a significant impact on the generation of genomic data is the continuing decline in the cost of DNA sequencing equipment. During the HGP and through the early 2000s, genomic sequencing work was typically carried out at large-scale, specialized research centers. But, according to recent estimates, since 2004 the cost of DNA sequencing has dropped by 50 percent every five months (Pennisi 2011: 666; Royal Society 2012: 88). This precipitous price decline has enabled even the smallest labs to acquire sophisticated gene-sequencing equipment, and has shifted much sequencing work from large specialized centers to disaggregated labs across the world. As the community of data-generating researchers expands, the willingness of this new corps of data generators to abide by the policies and norms forged by old-guard sequencing centers may be tested.

3. Data Users

Prior to the completion of the HGP, researchers studying a particular genetic disease devoted substantial time and effort to isolating and sequencing the relevant gene: work that often would take years of painstaking trial-and-error experimentation. The data generated by the HGP and subsequent projects has eliminated the need for researchers to conduct much of this groundwork. Unlike the original close-knit community of data generators at large-scale sequencing centers, the population of data users no longer forms a coherent community. Today, users of genomic data include scientists around the world in nearly every biological discipline. The emergence and growth of this large constituency of data users, and its divergence from the more tightly-knit community of data generators, has had a significant impact on policies for the release and use of genomic data.

4. Scientific Leaders

Many of the scientists involved in the early planning and execution stages of the HGP were globally prominent. The group included numerous Nobel Prize winners. This leadership by preeminent and respected scientists was critical to the HGP and gave the group's decisions a *gravitas* that they otherwise might have lacked. It also engendered among the project's leadership a sense of public stewardship that contributed to the nature of several HGP policies (Watson 1997: 633–34; Juengst 1996: 63). The public-spirited character that permeated the discourse of these scientific leaders appears to have developed independently of the potential role that such individuals may have played either as funders, data generators, or data users. As such, the role of scientific leader is worth considering independently from these other categories.

5. Data Intermediaries

The individual researchers and laboratories that generate genomic data seldom make it available to others directly. In most cases, scientists rely on data intermediaries, whether scientific journals that publish their analyses and results or centralized database managers that host large quantities of raw data. Data intermediaries may operate either as commercial entities (as in the case of commercial publishers and paid database services) or nonprofit/governmental entities (such as the GenBank and dbGaP databases and "open access" journals such as those published by the Public Library of Science (PLoS)). Not surprisingly, the interests of commercial and noncommercial data intermediaries differ in several regards, most notably in the area of pricing access to information. Nevertheless, these stakeholders also share a number of common motivations, including the desire to disseminate information in ways that are effective, secure, and accurate and the need to maintain some level of financial sustainability. In 2000, the journal *Science* was instrumental in securing public access to the genomic data produced by Celera Genomics in competition with the public HGP (Jasny 2013: 5–7).[6] Recently, the critical role of scientific journals in the creation and sustainability of the genome commons has been recognized, particularly with respect to the need to offer meaningful and career-enhancing publication opportunities to data-generating scientists (Sharing Data 2003: 4; Toronto Authors 2009: 170; Jasny 2013: 12).

6. Data Subjects

Human genomic information, by definition, is derived from human subjects. Because the goal of the HGP was to generate a baseline map of the human genome without regard to the particular physiological and pathological traits associated with genetic variation among individuals, the genomic sequence data generated by the HGP was anonymous and retained no association with the individual subjects whose DNA was sequenced (National Human Genome Research Institute 2010). In later projects, however, and particularly with the commencement of large-scale GWA studies, concerns with the potential identification of human subjects has grown (Toronto Authors 2009: 170). Because a GWA study seeks to *associate* genotypic information (e.g., genetic markers) with disease risk, information regarding donor demographics, disease state, and treatment is necessary to interpret genotypic findings. The prospect of releasing clinical and phenotypic data to the public sparked substantial concern and has led to the recognition of human data subjects as important stakeholders in the genomic data equation. Public concern has only been heightened by the publication in 2008 of a paper suggesting that the presence of an identifiable individual's DNA can be statistically inferred from a group of otherwise anonymous samples (Homer et al. 2008). Such findings increasingly suggest that the interests of data subjects may require substantial attention as genomic science advances and have led to numerous proposals for heightened protection of individual identity in publicly released genomic data (P3G Consortium et al. 2009; Ossorio 2011: 908; Jones 2012; Jasny 2013: 9).

7. The Public

The general public cannot be ignored as a key stakeholder with respect to scientific research. Recent studies reveal that the majority of American adults seek health-related information online, including by reviewing the primary medical literature (Davis

---

[6] See Section III.C below.

& Walters 2011: 212–13). The field of genomics, in particular, has captured the public attention and is regularly featured in the popular news media. Beyond general interest, however, there are several significant aspects of public engagement with genomics. First, government-sponsored research is largely taxpayer-funded, meaning that taxpayers and their representatives in Congress have a legitimate and intense interest in the direction and results of research. Second, members of the public who are themselves affected, directly or indirectly, by genetic disorders may form patient advocacy and disease interest groups. These groups frequently possess a high degree of familiarity with the relevant scientific literature and have both the motivation and the financial wherewithal to lobby for changes in research policy (Lee 2009: 986–90; Terry et al. 2007: 157–62). Finally, even members of the general public beyond patient advocacy groups have begun to take an interest in, and to express concern regarding, genomic research and the data sharing practices of genomics researchers (Haga & O'Daniel 2011: 320). Thus, the public is an important stakeholder in both the creation and the use of the genome commons.

Figure 4.1 depicts the relationships between the various actors in the genome commons.

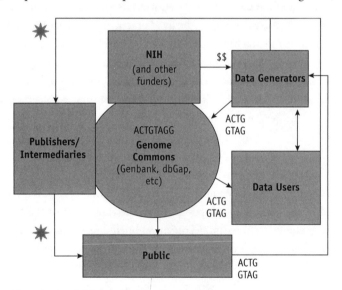

FIGURE 4.1. Organizational Schematic of the Genome Commons.

Figure 4.1 depicts the organizational structure of the genome commons and its associated stakeholder groups. The NIH and other funding organizations support research by data generators that creates the common resource, using biological samples collected from members of the public. The resource is used by data generators and data users, who are often collaborators or even identical, and, to a lesser degree, by the general public. Data generators and data users release results through publishers (typically in the form of scientific articles designated by the "*" symbol), which enrich the understanding of the public. The resource itself is housed within large databases maintained by government funding agencies (e.g., the NIH's National Library of Medicine) and by some journals.

III. Rules-In-use of the HGP

Under the IAD framework, the "rules-in-use" or governance structure of a commons system constitutes its third primary attribute. When considering physical resource commons, the common resource, whether a forest, a pasture, or a body of water, typically exists prior to the imposition of rules regarding its use. Rules-in-use, in this case, typically allocate access and usage rights with respect to this preexisting resource and, while such rules necessarily affect the sustainability of the common resource and the rate at which it is depleted and replenished, they do not create or define it. As observed by Madison, Frischmann, and Strandburg, however, the rules governing a knowledge commons dictate its very nature, including, in the case of the genome commons, features such as its size and content and the speed at which data is deposited in it, as well as when and how it can be accessed and used.

Ostrom defines the "rules in use" of a commons as its formal *de jure* rules coupled with the informal (but often forceful) norms that govern its members' behavior. As explained by Peter Boettke, "it is the 'rules in use' (the lived practice of everyday life) that matter for social cooperation, not so much the 'rules in form' (on the books)" (Boettke 2012). In the case of the genome commons, the formal rules established at the outset of the HGP were strongly influenced by the norms of the scientific community at the time. These formal rules, which have grown in complexity over the years, continue to play a critical role in the governance of the genome commons.

A. EARLY YEARS OF THE HGP

Several factors contributed to the impetus, from the initiation of the HGP, to release the data generated by the project to the public. First, the early work of the HGP involved sequencing the genomes of simple model organisms including the mouse and roundworm (*C. elegans*). The small scientific communities that worked on these organisms traditionally abided by strong "open science" norms and were accustomed to sharing data freely, laying a strong precedent for the HGP (International Human Genome Consortium 2001: 864; Cook-Deegan 2003: 89; National Research Council 2006: 54–56). Moreover, and perhaps more importantly, there was a sense among the leadership of the project that genomic data possessed a special and unique character. In the words of Ari Patrinos, the DOE's Associate Director for Biological and Environmental Research, the genome "belongs to everybody" (Marshall 2001a: 1192). Accordingly, in 1988 the National Research Council recommended that all data generated by the HGP "be provided in an accessible form to the general research community worldwide" (National Research Council 1988: 8).

In 1992, shortly after the project was launched, the NIH and the DOE developed formal guidelines for the sharing of HGP data (U.S. Dept. of Energy & Nat'l Insts. of Health 1993). These guidelines were viewed as essential to achieve the program's goals, avoid unnecessary duplication of effort and expedite research in other areas. But the need for project coordination did not require immediate *public* release of the HGP data. The HGP policy makers in 1992 recognized the need to provide data generators with "some scientific advantage from the effort they have invested" in generating the data. This "advantage" manifested itself in a six-month maximum period from the time that HGP data were generated until the time that they had to be made publicly available. During this six-month hold-back period, HGP researchers could analyze their data and prepare publications.

The 1992 guidelines, in sharp contrast with later policies, also indicated that the agencies would not disfavor investigators who wished to secure patent rights in HGP-funded discoveries. This pro-patent attitude arose contemporaneously with NIH's unsuccessful attempt to seek patents on ESTs, and had waned significantly by the mid-1990s.

B. THE BERMUDA PRINCIPLES

1. The Birth of Rapid Prepublication Data Release

The year 1996 marked a turning point for the HGP. Not only was it the year in which sequencing of the human genome was scheduled to begin, it also signaled a sea change in the data release landscape. That February, approximately fifty scientists and policy makers from the United States, Europe, and Japan met in Bermuda to deliberate over the speed with which HGP data should be released to the public, and whether the six-month "holding period" approved in 1992 should continue (Marshall 2001a: 1192; Cook-Deegan & McCormack 2001: 217). The resulting Bermuda Principles established that all DNA sequence information from large-scale human genomic sequencing projects should be "freely available and in the public domain in order to encourage research and development and to maximize its benefit to society" (Bermuda Principles 1996). Most importantly, the Bermuda Principles required that this data should be released to public databases within a mere *twenty-four hours*.

The Bermuda Principles achieved several of the most important policy objectives held by the HGP funders. First, the Bermuda Principles greatly enhanced project coordination by enabling HGP sequencing centers to avoid duplication of effort and to optimize their respective tasks (Bentley 1996: 533; Bostanci 2004: 174). Waiting six months to obtain data under the 1992 policy was simply not practical if the project was to function effectively. Second, the funders, particularly the project leaders, argued that rapid data release was the best way to maximize scientific advancement (i.e., making sequence data as broadly available as possible as quickly as possible to accelerate discoveries for the benefit of society) (Bentley 1994: 533; Cook-Deegan & McCormack 2001: 217 supp.).

2. Rapid Data Release and Patents

In addition to the effects described above, rapid data release under the Bermuda Principles was also believed to limit the ability of researchers to obtain patent protection on data generated by the HGP. In particular, the Bermuda Principles ensured that HGP data would be made publicly available before data generators could file patent applications covering "inventions" arising from that data in most countries, and in a manner that ensured its availability as prior art against third party patent filings at the earliest possible date (Contreras 2011: 86-87). This result, though lauded by many, was also criticized by those who believed that the NIH's adoption of this antipatenting approach contravened the requirements of the Bayh-Dole Act of 1980, which expressly allows the patenting of federally funded inventions for the benefit of the U.S. economy.[7] In response to this criticism, the NIH's 1996 policy adopting the Bermuda Principles pays lip service to the Bayh-Dole Act, acknowledging that recipients of NIH funding have the right to seek patents on inventions that "reveal convincing evidence for utility." But in the next breath the agency warns that it "will monitor grantee activity in this area to learn whether or not attempts are being made to patent large blocks of primary human genomic DNA sequence" (Nat'l Human Genome Research Inst. 1996). The consequences of violating this prescription are left unstated. The NIH's approach is thus one of norms-setting rather than imposition of legally enforceable penalties, a tactic that will be seen repeated throughout the evolution of the genome commons.

The significance of the NIH's implementation of the Bermuda Principles cannot be overstated. Prior to 1996, the NIH's position with respect to data release and intellectual property was not very different from that of other federal agencies. But in the negotiations at and leading up to the Bermuda meeting, the scientific community's acknowledgment of the collective norms of data sharing seems to have captured the agency's imagination. These norms have since become ingrained as part of the NIH's basic position that genomic data should be widely available and unencumbered.

C. PUBLIC VS. PRIVATE: THE RACE WITH CELERA

By 1998, the HGP had begun the monumental task of sequencing the human genome at research centers in the United States, Europe, and Japan. Then, in May of that year, J. Craig Venter, a former NIH scientist, famously proclaimed that he, funded by substantial commercial backers, would utilize a novel technological approach called "whole-genome shotgun sequencing" and a battalion of 300 state-of-the-art machines to complete the sequencing of the entire human genome a full four years before the expected completion of the publicly funded HGP (Shreeve 2004: 22–23; Roberts 2001: 1187; Wade 1998). Venter's announcement, which shocked the scientific establishment, quickly led to a technological "arms race" between his new company, Celera Genomics, and the HGP, a race in which competing claims and accusations became regular features in the scientific literature and the popular press (Roberts 2001: 1188; Shreeve 2004: 22–23; Venter 2007; Ridley 1999: 6–10). Ultimately, a truce was brokered by the preeminent scientific journal *Science*, which agreed

---

[7] Bayh-Dole Act of 1980, 35 U.S.C. §§ 200–12 (2012).

to publish the genomic sequence generated by Celera, while its rival *Nature* would publish the sequence assembled by the public HGP (Marshall 2001b: 1189–93; Marshall 2000: 2042; Kaiser 2005: 775; Jasny 2013: 4–5). In June 2000, Francis Collins, director of the HGP, and Venter joined President Bill Clinton at the White House to announce that a "first draft" of the human genome sequence had been completed, and both sides declared a major scientific victory (NY Times 2000; Roberts 2001: 1188; Wade 2000).

Despite the eventual détente between Celera and the HGP, the two sequencing efforts approached the release of their genomic data very differently. Unlike the public HGP, Celera initially deposited its data on its commercial website, rather than in GenBank. The company allowed scientists from nonprofit and academic institutions to access the data without charge but required scientists who wished to use the data for commercial purposes to enter into license agreements (Marshall 2000: 2042; Jasny 2013: 6–7). This approach outraged much of the scientific community and led to a highly publicized debate regarding public access to human sequence data. Prominent in this debate were contentions regarding the need to release data broadly and publicly in order to promote scientific advancement and medical breakthroughs, sentiments that Celera found hard to contest. Ultimately, in the settlement brokered by the journal *Science*, Celera agreed to make its data broadly available under a somewhat less restrictive licensing agreement (Marshall 2001b: 1189–93). The HGP draft sequence was published in GenBank in 2001 (International Human Genome Consortium 2001: 911–13), and by 2003 most of the genes contained in Celera's database had been resequenced and released publicly by the HGP. Celera's subscription-based data business was ultimately unsuccessful and in 2005 the company released its genomic data to GenBank (Kaiser 2005: 775).

IV. The Action Arena: Evolution of Rules and Norms

Under the IAD framework, the "action arena" constitutes the set of scenarios in which the participants interact with respect to the common resource (Ostrom & Hess 2007: 53–59). "Patterns of interaction" emerge from these exchanges, resulting in outcomes that in turn affect the characteristics of the community and the common resource and its rules-in-use. Madison, Frischmann, and Strandburg equate these outcomes and patterns of interaction in the context of knowledge commons, arguing that "[h]ow people interact with rules, resources, and each other … is itself an outcome that is inextricably linked with the form and content of the knowledge or informational output of the commons" (Madison, Frischmann, & Strandburg 2010: 682).

In the case of the genome commons, interactions occur at both scientific and policy levels. The vast majority of day-to-day scientific interactions—involving the generation and analysis of scientific data, the securing of funding for research projects, and the publication of results—occur relatively independently of the policy-level debates described above. Yet policy decisions fundamentally affect the manner in which the scientific enterprise is conducted. Data must be released to public databases on a frequent basis, these databases are consulted regularly both to supplement and to validate collected data, and the preparation and submission of publications is constrained by the rules of the commons. During the conduct of this day-to-day scientific work, scientists and researchers accumulate experiences and preferences regarding the rules under which they must operate. They form opinions and draw conclusions regarding the difficulty of regularly depositing data into public databases, the ease with which this data may be used, the usefulness of public data, and the rate at which competing groups seem to be utilizing "their" data to compete with them. These opinions and conclusions manifest themselves in the next set of policy discussions regarding the next project to be proposed. Thus, as anticipated by Ostrom and Madison, Frischmann, and Strandburg, a feedback loop develops, in which policy-level decisions affect interactions within the action arena and cause participants to seek policy-level changes in subsequent iterations of policy making. These patterns emerge in the successive genomics projects that followed the HGP, whether publicly or privately funded.

A. DATA GENERATORS VS. DATA USERS

In their effort to promote the policy goals of the HGP, the project organizers knowingly subrogated the interests of data generators to those of the public. That is, the rapid data release requirements of Bermuda effectively eliminated the ability of data generators to publish their analyses and conclusions before others could access "their" data (Church & Hillier 2009: 105.1). The reasons for this move are not well documented. However, it can perhaps be attributed to the perceived importance of the HGP to worldwide scientific progress, coupled with the fact that the data generators selected for the HGP would be paid significant sums for their work. This funding would enable them to produce the massive quantities of data needed for the HGP, while at the same time establishing their reputations as the world's leading genome sequencing centers. Indeed, this reputation persists for the three principal HGP sequencing centers, the Sanger Centre at Cambridge, the Whitehead Institute at MIT (now part of the Broad Center of MIT/Harvard), and Washington University in St. Louis, which are still regarded as dominant players in the academic sequencing world. Whatever the reasons, the data generators clearly acceded to the rapid data release policies established in Bermuda.

The broader implications of this relinquishment of rights by data generators were not realized immediately, but in the years following the HGP, a number of large-scale, publicly funded genomics projects began to recognize the inherent tension between data generators and data users. This tension was first addressed formally in a new NIH policy adopted in 2000 (Nat'l Human Genome Research Inst. 2000). The policy reaffirmed the Institute's Bermuda-based requirement that DNA sequences be deposited into GenBank within twenty-four hours of assembly. For the first time, however, it also imposed formal requirements on *users* who downloaded this data. The policy references "the widely accepted ethic in the scientific community that those who generate the primary data freely should have both the right and responsibility to publish the work in a peer-reviewed journal." The policy goes on to prohibit users from using publicly released HGP data "for the *initial* publication of the complete genome sequence assembly or other large-scale analyses," thereby reserving this right to the data generators. This concession to the requirements of data generators may not have been large, but it laid the groundwork for many of the post-HGP policy shifts that followed.

B. FT. LAUDERDALE AND COMMUNITY-RESOURCE PROJECTS (CRPS)

The HGP largely completed its work in 2001. Two years later, in 2003, the Wellcome Trust convened a summit of funding agencies, sequencing centers, database managers, biological laboratories, and scientific journals in Ft. Lauderdale, Florida, to revisit rapid data release issues in the "post-genome" world (Wellcome Trust 2003). The Ft. Lauderdale meeting coincided with the spread of genomic research beyond the traditional genomics community to researchers in fields such as oncology, virology, and microbiology. These researchers, who were trained in non-genomics research traditions, did not share the same basic norms of data sharing and openness as the original HGP research groups (Cook-Deegan & McCormack 2001: 217 supp.). Thus, while the Ft. Lauderdale participants "enthusiastically reaffirmed" the 1996 Bermuda Principles, they also expressed reservations about extending these broad principles to every aspect of scientific research and discovery. They drew a distinction between HGP-like "community resource projects" (CRPs) that were "specifically devised and implemented to create a set of data, reagents or other material whose primary utility will be as a resource for the broad scientific community" and "hypothesis-driven" research, in which the goal is to answer a particular scientific question through the interrogation of experimental data. In hypothesis-driven research, success is typically measured by the degree to which the scientific question is answered rather than by the completion of a quantifiable data set or other product. Scientists engaged primarily in hypothesis-driven research generally resisted the early release of data. Giving data away before theories were finalized or published might enable a competing group to "scoop" the data generator, a persistent fear among highly competitive scientists. This risk, and the "legitimate interest" of data-generating scientists to be the first to publish the results of their work, were also recognized by the NIH (Wellcome Trust 2003; Nat'l Human Genome Research Inst. 2003). Accordingly, the Ft. Lauderdale participants agreed that, while the twenty-four-hour rapid release rules of Bermuda would continue to apply to CRPs, there would be no requirement that the Bermuda Principles apply to scientific research projects *other* than CRPs.

C. SECOND-GENERATION DATA RELEASE POLICIES

In the years following the Ft. Lauderdale meeting, numerous large-scale genomic research projects were launched with increasingly sophisticated requirements regarding data release. Moreover, increasingly sophisticated database technologies have enabled the provision of differentiated levels of data access, the screening of user applications for data access, and improved tracking of data access and users.

1. Genetic Association Information Network (GAIN)

The Genetic Association Information Network (GAIN) was established in 2006 by the Foundation for the National Institutes of Health (FNIH), the NIH, and several corporations (GAIN 2007: 1045). GAIN's purpose was to conduct GWA studies of the genetic basis for six common diseases. Data generators selected to participate in the GAIN program were required to sign an agreement calling for immediate release of data generated by the project (GAIN 2007: 1048). Over the course of the three-year project, approximately 18,000 human DNA samples were genotyped, and the resulting data was deposited in dbGaP (Manolio 2009: 236). As described above, dbGaP allows the data producer to segregate the data into open and controlled access portions to protect the privacy of research subjects. Researchers wishing to access GAIN data from the controlled portion of the database were required to obtain approval from the GAIN Data Access Committee (GAIN 2007: 1049). Once approved, they were required to agree to keep the data secure, use it only for approved research purposes, refrain from patenting the data or conclusions drawn directly from it, acknowledge data generators in their publications, and refrain from attempting to identify individual study participants (GAIN 2008: 1–6). Perhaps most importantly, the GAIN policy was the first genomic data release policy to introduce a temporal restriction on the *users* of released data. That is, in order to secure a period of exclusive use for data generators, data users are prohibited from publishing and making presentations based on GAIN data for a specified embargo period (GAIN 2007: 1049). The duration of the embargo period for a given data set is identified in the relevant data repository and may vary by data set, but has generally been set at nine months.

2. The NIH GWAS Policy

In response to the growing number of GWA studies being funded by the NIH and the large amount of genomic data generated by such studies, in August 2007 the NIH released a new policy regarding the generation, protection, and sharing of data generated by federally funded GWA studies (NIH 2007: 49294–97). The NIH GWAS Policy requires that researchers submit descriptive information about each GWA study for inclusion in the "open access" portion of dbGaP. Grantees are also "strongly encouraged" to submit study results, including phenotypic, exposure, and genotypic data, for inclusion in the "controlled access" portion of the database "as soon as quality control procedures have been completed."

Among the principal concerns raised concerning GWA study data were those surrounding the public release of phenotypic or clinical information that could eventually be traced back to individual subjects (Ossorio 2011: 915–19; Lowrance & Collins 2007;

Jasny 2013: 15).[8] To address this concern, the NIH GWAS Policy requires that GWAS data be de-identified in accordance with applicable regulatory guidelines. Moreover, the data in the controlled-access portion of the database may be released only after approval of the proposed research use by a Data Access Committee, and then only under a signed Data Use Certification that contains stringent protective clauses.

The NIH GWAS Policy addresses the publication priority concerns of data genera-tors by announcing an "expectation" that users of GWAS data will refrain from pub-lishing or presenting their analyses and conclusions during an "exclusivity" period of up to twelve months from the date that the data set is first made available. The agency also expresses a "hope" that "genotype-phenotype associations identified through NIH-supported and NIH-maintained GWAS datasets and their obvious implications will remain available to all investigators, unencumbered by intellectual property claims" (NIH 2007: 49296). Regarding patents, the GWAS policy states that "[t]he filing of patent applications and/or the enforcement of resultant patents in a manner that might restrict use of NIH-supported genotype-phenotype data could diminish the potential public benefit they could provide." However, in an effort to show some support for pat-ent seekers, the GWAS Policy also "encourages patenting of technology suitable for sub-sequent private investment that may lead to the development of products that address public needs."

3. 1000 Genomes

The 1000 Genomes Project is an international cooperative effort begun in 2008 to study human genetic variation by sequencing the genomes of approximately 2500 individu-als from 25 diverse populations (1,092 genomes from 14 populations were completed by 2012) (Via, Gignoux, & Burchard 2010: 1; 1000 Genomes Project Consortium: 2012). Much of the project's $120 million budget has been funded by the NIH. As noted above, the project has generated unprecedented quantities of data and has given rise to novel approaches to data handling and management. Genomic data generated by 1000 Genomes is released to the public through Amazon Web Services with very few restric-tions. The project classifies itself as a community resource project (CRP) and cites the Ft. Lauderdale Principles. Though no formal embargo requirements are imposed on the data, the project's data release policy states an expectation that data generators will be allowed to "make the first presentations and to publish the first paper with global analyses of the data" (1000 Genomes 2012). Other guidance regarding the order of publication for different types of analyses is provided, though the extent to which these guidelines are legally binding is uncertain.

---

[8] See Section II.B.6 above.

4. The Human Microbiome Project

The Human Microbiome Project (HMP) is a large-scale community resource project initiated in 2007 and fully launched in 2010 that aims to identify and sequence the genomes of many of the myriad microorganisms inhabiting the human body (Human Microbiome 2010: 994). While much HMP data is subject to rapid Bermuda-like disclosure requirements, investigators are permitted to withhold certain other data from the public for a period of several months (NIH Common Fund 2011). This hold-back period is intended to permit HMP researchers to analyze their data and prepare publications using it before it is released to competing researchers. The reasons that researchers, who are driven by intense competitive pressure to publish and claim credit for discoveries, have pushed for such hold-back periods is clear. However, it also appears that, in the case of HMP, the NIH has not vigorously advanced the patent deterrent arguments that previously motivated policy decisions during the HGP and its immediate aftermath. Patents were not a significant topic of discussion or negotiation in developing the HMP policy, and any patent-deterrent effects of the policy are likely to be incidental. Whether the experience of the HMP indicates a new direction for the NIH or simply a minor deviation from its overall policy approach is not clear.

5. The ENCODE Project

In 2007 the NIH launched the ENCODE project, based on a 2003 pilot program, to identify functional elements in the human genome (i.e., the physiological functions for which particular genetic sequences are responsible) (Celniker et al. 2009: 927). In 2012, ENCODE scientists released a massive series of findings in thirty simultaneously published papers (Maher 2012: 46). The ENCODE data release policy designates the project as a "community resource project," but also requests that users of released data refrain from publishing or presenting re   d on the data for a nine-month embargo period (ENCODE Consortia 2008: 1).   CODE policy distinguishes between published and unpublished data, verified a   fied data, and offers several examples of the data use implications for different ty   idies. The length and complexity of the policy evidences the funders' and the p   ts' desire for clear guidelines and the avoidance of misunderstandings regarding   e of data, in light of the fact that the diversity of participants, organisms, and data   expanded dramatically beyond those originally considered by the framers of the   Principles. But even with such a detailed data sharing policy, the project has at   iticism from its own data analysis coordinator, Ewan Birney. He writes that "clumsy etiquette-based restrictions on…publication…are starting to show their age and a lack of clarity" and that "the new era of data analysis calls for a rethink." (Birney 2012: 51) To this end he cites the 1000 Genomes Project as a model for emulation, suggesting that the data sharing practices of that group, which favor the release of intermediate analyses over raw data, have evolved beyond the relatively straightforward Bermuda-based statements contained in the 1000 Genomes formal policies.

D. PRIVATE SECTOR INITIATIVES

In addition to the HGP and other public sector sequencing efforts described above, a number of private sector projects have made substantial contributions to the genome commons, many with data release policies informed by the principles established in Bermuda and Ft. Lauderdale. These private sector initiatives were important, as they both reacted to, and were closely observed by, the publicly funded projects that continued to operate alongside them. While it is certainly the case that many private-sector research efforts have been undertaken within the highly proprietary environments of pharmaceutical and biotechnology companies, the existence of privately funded activities that contribute to the public genome commons suggests that the common resource structure established by the NIH and its publicly funded projects has taken hold as an accepted mode of organizing genomic research, even in the private sector.

1. Merck Gene Index

Beginning in 1994, pharmaceutical giant Merck initiated a project to identify and publicly release a large number of expressed sequence tags (ESTs) (Merck & Co., Inc. 1995). By 1998, the so-called Merck Gene Index included more than 800,000 ESTs, which were also released through GenBank (Tapscott & Williams 2006: 166). A full analysis of motivations fueling industrial scientific research is beyond the scope of this chapter. However, in the case of the Merck Gene Index, it is generally believed that Merck chose to release these potentially valuable assets because of a combination of philanthropic intent and corporate self-interest (i.e., preempting patenting of ESTs by biotech companies, several of which had already announced business plans that involved the patenting and licensing of ESTs and other genetic information) (Marshall 2001a: 1192; Tapscott & Williams 2006: 166; Rai 1999–2000: 134). To achieve these goals, Merck found it most expedient to release EST information directly to the public, without material restrictions, much as the HGP would do. The development of an organizational structure to oversee the use of the Merck Gene Index does not seem to have been necessary for Merck to achieve its immediate goals.

2. SNP Consortium

A related but distinct approach was adopted by the SNP Consortium. This nonprofit entity was formed in 1999 by a group of pharmaceutical companies and the Wellcome Trust to identify and map genetic markers known as "single nucleotide polymorphisms" (SNPs) (Holden 2002: 22). Responding at least in part to the threat that biotechnology companies might identify and patent these SNP markers first, the SNP Consortium made all SNPs that it identified available to the public (Holden 2002: 26; Tapscott & Williams 2006: 168). It also sought to deter patenting of SNPs by third parties using an innovative "protective patenting" strategy that has been cited as a model of the private industry's potential to contribute to the public genome commons (Marshall 2001a: 1192;

Cook-Deegan & McCormack 2001: 217 supp.). In short, the consortium's approach was to file U.S. patent applications covering SNPs that it discovered, and then contribute these applications to the public domain prior to issuance. This approach ensured that the consortium's discoveries would act as prior art defeating subsequent third-party patent applications, with priority dates extending back to the initial filings.

3. International SAE Consortium

Since the completion of the SNP Consortium project, several other privately funded research collaborations have adopted similar data release models and have made large quantities of genomic data publicly accessible. One of these collaborations is the International SAE Consortium (iSAEC), a group of pharmaceutical and healthcare companies organized in 2007 to fund research seeking to identify DNA markers associated with serious drug side effects (adverse events) (International SAE Consortium 2010). The iSAEC seeks to minimize patent encumbrances on the genetic markers and associations that it identifies via a "protective" patent strategy modeled on that of the SNP Consortium. Like the other policies discussed in this section, the iSAEC imposes various security, research, and non-patenting restrictions on data that is publicly released. It also secures for data-generating scientists a period of exclusivity (up to twelve months) during which they have sole access to the data (International SAE Consortium 2009). Unlike previous private sector efforts such as the Merck Gene Index and SNP Consortium, iSAEC has created a managed common resource subject to rules that echo those of contemporary NIH-funded projects (Contreras, Floratos, & Holden 2013). The fact that this commons-based organizational structure has emerged in the private sector is particularly noteworthy, as the research funded by iSAEC is more akin to hypothesis-driven research than to a community resource project, a fact that might have been expected to push the project toward a more proprietary model, even in the government-funded realm. As such, the iSAEC approach is a testament to the unusually strong shared community norms within the genomics research community, even among scientists employed in the private sector.

4. Personal Genome Project

An interesting recent addition to the genome commons is the Harvard-led Personal Genome Project (PGP) (Personal Genome Project 2012; Angrist 2010). The PGP, launched in 2008 to significant press coverage, solicits volunteers to submit tissue samples and accompanying phenotypic data. Researchers are then authorized to analyze the submitted samples and publish any resulting genomic information on the PGP website. All such data is released without restriction under the "CC0" Creative Commons copyright waiver (Creative Commons 2012). The PGP approach differs markedly from that of the government and privately funded projects described above, in that it dispenses entirely with any attempt to restrict the use of its genomic data (Conley, Doerr, & Vorhaus 2010: 339–41). PGP requires its contributors to waive all privacy-related rights when contributing their tissue samples to the project, and gives no preference to use of the data by researchers of any kind. As such, the PGP policy returns to the broad "public domain" character of the Bermuda Principles and may signal, at least among some researchers, a reconception of genomic data as a public good.

V. Rules and Complexity in the Genome Commons

A. THE GROWTH OF RULES

The genome commons has experienced rapid and unanticipated growth over the past two decades. The rise of this valuable public resource has seen an accompanying growth of complexity in the formal rules governing the commons. Whereas the initial HGP required the rapid release of genomic data to the public, effecting what might be considered a *public good* in economic terms, later projects added increasingly complex rules governing human subject protection and publication priority. Table 4.1 summarizes the principal features of the policies described in Part IV, above.

TABLE 4.1.

GENOMICS DATA RELEASE POLICIES

Program (Year of Initiation)	Data Type(s)	Data Release	User Restrictions	Patents
NIH-DOE 1992 Guidelines	Materials and data produced by the HGP	6 months after generation	None	IP protection "may be needed" for some data and materials
Merck Gene Index (1994)	ESTs	Not specified	None	Unspecified
Bermuda Principles (1996)	Initial genome sequence reads > 1Kb	24 hours after generation	None	Unspecified
NHGRI 1996 Policy	Human genomic DNA sequence data	As rapidly as possible	None	"[R]aw human genomic DNA sequence… is an inappropriate material for patent filing"
NHGRI 1997 Policy	Large-scale genomic DNA sequence data	24 hours after generation	None	Unspecified

Program (Year of Initiation)	Data Type(s)	Data Release	User Restrictions	Patents
SNP Consortium (1998)	SNP map and association data	Monthly/ quarterly releases to website	None	Protective filing strategy to release data to public domain
NHGRI 2000 Policy	Sequence trace data and ancillary information	Deposited weekly into the NCBI Trace Repository	Users may not use data for the initial publication of the complete genome sequence assembly or other large-scale analyses	Unspecified
Ft. Lauderdale Principles (2003)	All data from community-resource projects	Reaffirms Bermuda Principles for sequence assemblies > 2kB	Citation of data generator	Unspecified
NHGRI 2003 Policy	Large-scale sequence data	24 hours after generation	Citation of data generator	Unspecified
Intl. HapMap Project (2003)	SNP and Haplotype data	Rapidly	Citation of data generator	User click-wrap agreement prohibits filing of patent applications on project data or uses thereof, unless unrestricted use is allowed
ENCODE Pilot (2003)	Various data types generated by the project	Deposited as soon as data is verified	Citation of data generator	encourages data generators to consider placing information in the public domain

Program (Year of Initiation)	Data Type(s)	Data Release	User Restrictions	Patents
GAIN (2007)	GWAS data	Immediate	Data use certification; Variable-length embargo (generally 9 months); Security, transfer, and use restrictions	Data users *agree* not to pursue patents that would block access to data or conclusions drawn directly from data
NIH GWAS Policy (2007)	GWAS data	Strong encouragement to submit data as soon as quality control procedures completed	Signed data use certification; 12-month embargo ; Citation of data generator Security, transfer, and use restrictions	Patenting of results discouraged
Intl. SAE Consortium (2007)	Human genotypic and phenotypic data	12 months after data validation	Signed membership agreement Up to 9-month embargo; Citation of data generator Security, transfer, and use restrictions	Data users agree not to pursue patents that would block access to data or conclusions drawn directly from data
ENCODE (2008)	Multiple data types	Deposited as soon as data is verified	9-month embargo; Citation of data generator	NHGRI monitoring of patenting activity and potential consideration of click-wrap agreement ala HapMap Project

Program (Year of Initiation)	Data Type(s)	Data Release	User Restrictions	Patents
1000 Genomes (2008)	Human genomic DNA sequence data	Rapid data release through Amazon cloud services	Allow data generators to make first presentation/ publication of aggregate data analysis Others may publish on more extensive analyses concurrently with the data-generators' paper; Others may publish on methods, specific disease studies, and population comparisons prior to the data-generators' paper	Unspecified
Human Microbiome Project (HMP) (2008)	Microbial genomic and metagenomic sequence data, human clinical and phenotypic data, microbial strains and reagents	Sequence data to be rapidly released, assemblies within 45 days of generation, SNPs within 30 days of validation, other data types by agreement of the steering committee Reagents and microbial strains to be made available before sequencing	12-month embargo; Allow data generators to make first presentation/ publication of aggregate data analysis; Respect Ft. Lauderdale attribution principles	Unspecified

Program (Year of Initiation)	Data Type(s)	Data Release	User Restrictions	Patents
Personal Genome Project (2008)	Human sequence and phenotypic data	Not specified	No restrictions on use	Unspecified (copyright waiver under CC0 License)

B. RULE MAKING IN THE GENOME COMMONS

From the HGP through current genomic research projects, the collection and analysis of genomic data has to a large degree been funded by governmental agencies, and by the NIH in particular. Many of the rules that govern the use and release of genomic data are thus embodied in policies applicable to the recipients of NIH grants. As such, one might expect such rules to be developed and promulgated solely by the funding agency. But, in practice, this has not been the case.

Beginning with the HGP and continuing today, the rules and policies applicable to large-scale NIH-funded genomic research projects are developed by agency personnel in close collaboration with the scientific advisory boards associated with such projects. The composition of these advisory boards is often reflective of many, if not all, of the stakeholder groups discussed in Section II.B (data generators, data users, scientific leaders, data intermediaries, data subjects, and the public). Moreover, most such advisory groups today include at least one individual with training in the "ethical, legal and social implications" (ELSI) of genomic research. And, while the data-generating grant recipients themselves are not form___ ___bers of the project advisory boards, they are typically invited to participate in p____ ____ation discussions both to provide their input and to voice their concerns. In t___ ___er, considerations of publication priority, intellectual property, and patient co____ity have all manifested themselves in genomics research policies over time. And ___ hat the private sector projects described above have adopted policies evidencing ___ ___nsiderations further suggests that these policy changes are motivated more by i___ ___ stakeholder group concerns than by governmental fiat.

Thus, though the ___ ___les applicable to NIH-funded genomics projects are ultimately promulgated ___ y policies, the environment in which they are developed is more akin to the polycentric governance systems studied by Ostrom and others than to authoritarian or top-down rule-making models. As such, these rules have evolved to address the concerns of the different stakeholder groups involved in genomics research, as well as the experiences of the community, positive and negative, with prior projects. As Ostrom observes, "[p]olicy changes are experiments based on more or less informed expectations about potential outcomes" (Ostrom 2005: 243). This progressive experimentation has resulted in the growth of rules surrounding the genome commons.

C. RULES AND COMPLEXITY

Figure 4.2 illustrates the relative complexity of the formal policies governing the major public U.S. genomic research projects from the HGP through current projects, comparing their data release policies on the basis of a straightforward word count algorithm (a measure inspired in part by Milton Friedman's study of the growth of complexity in the U.S. Federal Register year over year via a simple page count). This metric, unfortunately, does not lend itself to a comparison with private sector policies, which are embodied in bylaws, membership agreements, and other documents of significantly greater detail than the governmental policies studied.

There are several possible explanations for the trends shown in Figure 4.2. Despite the significance and lasting influence of the Bermuda Principles, they were drafted to address one specific type of data ("raw" genomic sequences) generated by a specific, unique project (the HGP). It soon became clear that, while the spirit and intent of the Bermuda Principles were attractive to many, the extension of these principles to different projects and data types required additional explication and, in some cases, compromise. By the mid-2000s, the sophistication of genomic studies, the types of data being collected, and the range of researchers participating in genomic science had broadened significantly. Thus, as described above, the rules governing the commons grew, both in terms of length and complexity.

But Figure 4.2 also suggests that the NIH's 2007 GWAS policy may represent a "peak" in the expansion of the rules governing the genome commons. The post-2007 policies represented in the figure are significantly less complex (or at least less verbose) than the 2007 GWAS policy (though still much more complex than the original Bermuda Principles). This effect may simply be a result of growing public and

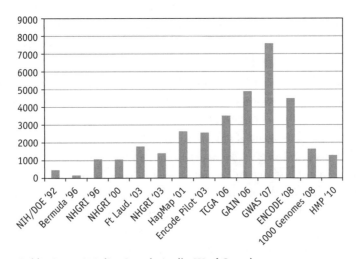

FIGURE 4.2 Public Genomic Policy Complexity (by Word Count).

scientific familiarity with the concepts set out in data release policies and a concomitant reduction in the need for explanation. But it may also represent a lessening community interest in, or need for, specifying the details surrounding data release. Unlike the carefully, and cautiously, drafted policies adopted by the NIH in the early 2000s, the later policies say little if anything about patents. Could this absence indicate a waning concern by the agency with the patenting of genomic information? Or might it indicate, instead, a growing sense within the agency that patent law has stabilized to a degree that further agency pronouncements and guidance are not necessary? The comments made by Birney upon the release of the ENCODE project results suggests that managerial decisions and informal practices may now be more important in large data sharing projects than formal rules that pay lip service to the Bermuda Principles (Birney 2012: 51).

As of this writing, the NIH is in the process of considering further revisions to its institutional data release policies (NIH 2013, Contreras 2013). Though this latest round of revisions has not yet been completed, it is likely that any new NIH data release policy will continue to refine the rules of rapid prepublication data release to take into account the policy considerations and objectives described above. It is thus important that stakeholders with an interest in the future structure of the ever-expanding genome commons participate in such deliberations.

VI. The Genome Commons as a Knowledge Commons

Madison, Frischmann, and Strandburg offer their modified IAD framework in order to encourage the broad analysis of resource commons in the cultural environment and to counter the prevailing functionalist account of knowledge production. In particular, they challenge the notion that the majority of knowledge production can be explained in terms of incentive/exclusion-based intellectual property rules or governmental subsidy. To this end, they claim that "[i]nnovation and creativity are matters of governance of a highly social cultural environment" (Madison, Frischmann, & Strandburg 2010: 669).

Scientific research is often portrayed as an area adhering to the traditional functionalist view of "IP rights and government subsidies" (Madison, Frischmann, & Strandburg 2010: 669). General scientific knowledge resulting from research often is characterized, in economic terms, as a public good. But these paradigmatic views of scientific research do not capture the complex organizational attributes of the scientific enterprise. Scientific knowledge production is characterized by a pervasive and rich set of norms that govern both the incentives and the behaviors of its participants (Merton 1979: 293–305; Rai 1999–2000: 133–35; Merges 1996: 147–52). The foregoing analysis of the genome commons supports this view, both as to researchers in the public sector, and also, to a degree, as to researchers within the private sector.

From the early days of the HGP, NIH policy makers and scientific leaders expressed strong aversion to the encumbrance of genomic information with patents (as evidenced by the EST patenting debate) or database access restrictions (as evidenced by the HGP's competition with Celera Genomics). While the HGP and subsequent public genomics projects were funded, in large part, by governmental grants in the United States and a major philanthropy in the United Kingdom, scientists funded by private efforts such as the SNP Consortium and the International SAE Consortium exhibited similar values. This level of consistency suggests that neither the traditional account of economic property-based incentives nor a simplistic focus on government subsidies fully explains the organizational structure or dynamics observed in the genome commons.

In the years following the completion of the HGP, genomic data release policies became more complex and, to a degree, more restrictive. However, these restrictions arose not from efforts to impose traditional intellectual property rights on the fruits of genomic research, but from competition among scientific groups to achieve publication priority from their data, as well as from the ethical complications arising from the increasing richness of the data generated by genomic research. As the HGP neared conclusion, it became evident that a purely public domain/public goods structure for the vast pool of genomic information being produced by researchers worldwide simply would not suffice. Instead, a set of negotiated compromises emerged from the multistakeholder interactions of government, researchers, and the public. These interactions resulted in sophisticated rules-in-use, both formal and norms-based, to govern the commons. By the late 2000s, the genome commons less resembled the public domain than a managed common resource of the kind studied by Ostrom and her colleagues. Thus, while some may seek to characterize genomic data as an unrestricted public good, the vast majority of genomic data exists within a complex and formalized structure of rules, a structure that both enables and encourages the growth of the resource and its continuing use in further research.

In this sense, the genome commons can, and should, be viewed as a knowledge commons of the type conceptualized by Madison, Frischmann, and Strandburg. As such, it is crucial to study and understand its complex rule structure. Failing to do so, and too quickly embracing either a simple public good/public domain model or a highly proprietary, protectionist model, would lose sight of the carefully negotiated compromises achieved over the past two decades. Complex considerations of human subject protection, data generator priority, patent deterrence, and scientific advancement all contributed to the current policy landscape of the genome commons. Failing to appreciate the structural rules implemented to address these issues, or seeking to dispense with them in favor of a more broadly "open" public goods models such as those advanced in the Public Genome Project and, to a lesser degree, in later NIH-funded projects, could have adverse consequences. In particular the elimination of rules regulating human subject protection could limit the willingness of individuals to participate in genomic research, and the elimination of data-generator priorities could weaken the incentives of data-generating scientists. Each of these effects could negatively impact the growth of the commons itself (Contreras

2013). Thus, policy makers today and in the future should carefully consider the rules structure that has evolved to govern this invaluable global resource and take heed before introducing changes likely to upset its delicate and well-functioning balance of interests.

References

1000 Genomes, A Deep Catalog of Human Genetic Variation (2012), http://www.1000genomes. org/data/.

1000 Genomes Project Consortium, *An Integrated Map of Genetic Variation from 1,092 Human Genomes*, 491 NATURE 56 (2012).

Carlos B. Amat, *Editorial and Publication Delay of Papers Submitted to 14 Selected Food Research Journals, Influence of Online Posting*, 74 SCIENTOMETRICS 379 (2008).

Christopher Anderson, *US Patent Application Stirs Up Gene Hunters*, 353 NATURE 485 (1991).

MISHA ANGRIST, HERE IS A HUMAN BEING—AT THE DAWN OF PERSONAL GENOMICS (HarperCollins 2010).

Ass'n for Molecular Pathology v. Myriad Genetics, 133 S. Ct. 2107 (2013).

Batelle Technology Partnership Practice, *The Impact of Genomics on the U.S. Economy* (2012), http://www.unitedformedicalresearch.com/wp-content/uploads/2013/06/The-Impact-of-Genomics-on-the-US-Economy.pdf.

Bayh-Dole Act of 1980, 35 U.S.C. §§ 200–12 (2012).

David R. Bentley, *Genomic Sequence Information Should Be Released Immediately and Freely in the Public Domain*, 274 SCIENCE 533 (1996).

THE BERMUDA PRINCIPLES, SUMMARY OF PRINCIPLES AGREED AT THE FIRST INTERNATIONAL STRATEGY MEETING ON HUMAN GENOME SEQUENCING (1996), http://www.ornl.gov/sci/techresources/Human_Genome/research/bermuda.shtml.

Ewan Birney, *Lessons for Big-Data Projects*, 489 NATURE 49 (2012).

Peter J. Boettke, LIVING ECONOMICS: YESTERDAY, TODAY, AND TOMORROW (Independent Inst. 2012).

Adam Bostanci, *Sequencing Human Genomes, in* FROM MOLECULAR GENETICS TO GENOMICS 158 (Jean-Paul Gaudilliere & Hans-Jörg Rheiberger eds., Routledge 2004).

S. E. Celniker et al., *Unlocking the Secrets of the Genome*, 459 NATURE 927 (2009).

Deanna M. Church & LaDeana W. Hillier, *Back to Bermuda: How Is Science Best Served?*, 10 GENOME BIOLOGY 105.1 (2009).

Francis Collins, *Has the Revolution Arrived?*, 464 NATURE 674 (2010).

John M. Conley, Adam K. Doerr, & Daniel B. Vorhaus, *Enabling Responsible Public Genomics*, 20 HEALTH MATRIX 325 (2010).

Jorge L. Contreras, *Prepublication Data Release, Latency and Genome Commons*, 329 SCIENCE 393 (2010).

Jorge L. Contreras, *Bermuda's Legacy: Policy, Patents, and the Design of the Genome Commons*, 12 MINNESOTA J.L. SCI. & TECH. 61 (2011).

Jorge L. Contreras, *Comments in Response to Draft NIH Genomic Data Sharing Policy Request for Public Comments* (Nov. 19, 2013), *reproduced in* NIH, Compiled Public Comments on the Draft NIH Genomic Data Sharing Policy, September 20, 2013-November 20, 2013 at 78, http://gds.nih.gov/pdf/GDS_Policy_Public_Comments.PDF.

Jorge L. Contreras, Aris Floratos, & Arthur L. Holden, *The International Serious Adverse Events Consortium's Data Sharing Model*, 31 NATURE BIOTECHNOLOGY 17 (2013).

ROBERT COOK-DEEGAN, THE GENE WARS—SCIENCE, POLITICS, AND THE HUMAN GENOME (Norton 1994).

Robert Cook-Deegan, *The Urge to Commercialize: Interactions Between Public and Private Research Development, in* NATIONAL RESEARCH COUNCIL, THE ROLE OF SCIENTIFIC AND TECHNICAL DATA AND INFORMATION IN THE PUBLIC DOMAIN: PROCEEDINGS OF A SYMPOSIUM 87 (National Research Council 2003).

Robert Cook-Deegan & Stephen J. McCormack, *A Brief Summary of Some Policies to Encourage Open Access to DNA Sequence Data*, 293 SCIENCE 217 supp. (2001).

Creative Commons, *Creative Commons Statement of Purpose*, CREATIVE COMMONS (2012), http://creativecommons.org/publicdomain/zero/1.0/legalcode.

Philip M. Davis & William H. Walters, *The Impact of Free Access to the Scientific Literature: A Review of Recent Research*, 99 J. MEDICAL LIBRARY ASS'N 208–17 (2011).

Diamond v. Diehr, 450 U.S. 175 (1981).

ENCODE Consortia, *Data Release, Data Use, and Publication Policies* (2008), *available at* http://www.genome.gov/Pages/Research/ENCODE/ENCODEDataReleasePolicyFinal2008.pdf.

Feist Publ'ns, Inc. v. Rural Tel. Serv. Co., 499 U.S. 340 (1991).

GAIN, Data Use Certification Agreement, DATABASE OF GENOTYPES AND PHENOTYPES (2008), https://dbgap.ncbi.nlm.nih.gov/aa/wga.cgi?view_pdf&stacc=phs000021.v1.p1.

The GAIN Collaborative Research Group, *New Models of Collaboration in Genome-wide Association Studies: The Genetic Association Information Network*, 39 NATURE GENETICS 1045 (2007).

William D. Garvey & Belver C. Griffith, *Scientific Information Exchange in Psychology*, 146 SCIENCE 1655 (1964).

Eric D. Green, Mark S. Guyer, & Nat'l Human Genome Research Inst., *Charting a Course for Genomic Medicine from Base Pairs to Bedside*, 470 NATURE 204 (2011).

S. B. Haga & J. O'Daniel, *Public Perspectives Regarding Data-Sharing Practices in Genomics Research*, 14 PUBLIC HEALTH GENOMICS 319 (2011).

Erika Check Hayden, *International Genome Project Launched*, 451 NATURE 378 (2008).

Charlotte Hess & Elinor Ostrom, *A Framework for Analyzing the Microbiological Commons*, 58 INT'L SOCIAL SCIENCE J. 335 (2006).

Arthur Holden, *The SNP Consortium: Summary of a Private Consortium Effort to Develop an Applied Map of the Human Genome*, 32 BIOTECHNIQUES 22 (2002).

Nils Homer et al., *Resolving Individuals Contributing Trace Amounts of DNA to Highly Complex Mixtures Using High-Density SNP Genotyping Microarrays, in* 4 PLoS GENETICS, no. 8 (2008), at e1000167.

The Human Microbiome Jumpstart Reference Strains Consortium, *A Catalog of Reference Genomes from the Human Microbiome*, 328 SCIENCE 994 (2010).

Isabelle Huys et al., Legal Uncertainty in the Area of Genetic Diagnostic Testing, 27 NATURE BIOTECHNOLOGY 903 (2010).

INST. OF MED. & NAT'L RESEARCH COUNCIL, LARGE-SCALE BIOMEDICAL SCIENCE (Washington, D.C.: Natl. Research Council, 2003).

Int'l HapMap Consortium, *The International HapMap Project*, 426 NATURE 789 (2003).

Int'l Human Genome Consortium, *Initial Sequencing and Analysis of the Human Genome*, 409 NATURE 860 (2001).

INT'L SAE CONSORTIUM, DATA RELEASE AND INTELLECTUAL PROPERTY POLICY (2009) (on file with author).

Int'l SAE Consortium, *iSAEC's Background and Organizational Structure*, INTERNATIONAL SAE CONSORTIUM (2010), http://www.saeconsortium.org.

Barbara R. Jasny, *Realities of Data Sharing Using the Genome Wars as Case Study—An Historical Perspective and Commentary*, 2 EJP DATA SCIENCE 1 (2013).

Kyle Jensen & Fiona Murray, *Intellectual Property Landscape of the Human Genome*, 310 SCIENCE 239 (2005).

Matt Jones, *White House Bioethics Commission Unveils Draft of Genomic Privacy Policies*, GENOMEWEB DAILY NEWS (Aug. 3, 2012), http://www.genomeweb.com/sequencing/white-house-bioethics-commission-unveils-draft-genomic-privacy-policies.

Eric T. Juengst, *Self-Critical Federal Science? The Ethics Experiment within the U.S. Human Genome Project*, 13 SOCIAL PHILOSOPHY & POL'Y 63 (1996).

Jocelyn Kaiser, *Celera to End Subscriptions and Give Data to Public GenBank*, 308 SCIENCE 775 (2005).

Jane Kaye et al., *Data Sharing in Genomics—Re-shaping Scientific Practice*, 10 NATURE REVIEWS GENETICS 331 (2009).

Peter Lee, *Toward a Distributive Commons in Patent Law*, 2009 WISCONSIN L. REV. 917 (2009).

William W. Lowrance & Francis S. Collins, *Identifiability in Genomic Research*, 317 SCIENCE 600 (2007).

Michael J. Madison, Brett M. Frischmann, & Katherine J. Strandburg, *Constructing Commons in the Cultural Environment*, 95 CORNELL L. REV. 657 (2010).

Brendan Maher, *The Human Encyclopaedia*, 489 NATURE 46 (2012).

Teri A. Manolio, *Collaborative Genome-wide Association Studies of Diverse Diseases: Programs of the NHGRI's Office of Population Genomics*, 10 PHARMACOGENOMICS 235 (2009).

Eliot Marshall, *Storm Erupts over Terms for Publishing Celera's Sequence*, 290 SCIENCE 2042 (2000).

Eliot Marshall, *Bermuda Rules: Community Spirit, with Teeth*, 291 SCIENCE 1192 (2001a).

Eliot Marshall, *Sharing the Glory, Not the Credit*, 291 SCIENCE 1189 (2001b).

Mayo Collaborative Servs. v. Prometheus Labs., Inc., 132 S. Ct. 1289 (2012).

Merck & Co., Inc., Press Release, *First Installment of Merck Gene Index Data Released to Public Databases: Cooperative Effort Promises to Speed Scientific Understanding of the Human Genome* (Feb. 10, 1995), http://www.bio.net/bionet/mm/bionews/1995-February/001794.html.

Robert P. Merges, *Property Rights Theory and the Commons: The Case of Scientific Research*, in SCIENTIFIC INNOVATION, PHILOSOPHY, AND PUBLIC POLICY 145 (E. F. Paul et al. eds., Cambridge University Press 1996).

Robert K. Merton, *Priorities in Scientific Discovery: A Chapter in the Sociology of Science*, 22 AM. SOC. REV. 635 (1957), *reprinted in* THE SOCIOLOGY OF SCIENCE: THEORETICAL AND EMPIRICAL INVESTIGATIONS 286 (R. K. Merton ed., University of Chicago Press 1979).

Nat'l Human Genome Research Inst. (NHGRI), *NHGRI Policy Regarding Intellectual Property of Human Genomic Sequence* (1996), http://www.genome.gov/10000926.

Nat'l Human Genome Research Inst. (NHGRI), *Current NHGRI Policy for Release and Database Deposition of Sequence Data* (1997), http://www.genome.gov/10000910.

Nat'l Human Genome Research Inst. (NHGRI), *NHGRI Policy for Release and Database Deposition of Sequence Data* (2000), http://www.genome.gov/10000910.

Nat'l Human Genome Research Inst. (NHGRI), *Reaffirmation and Extension of NHGRI Rapid Data Release Policies: Large-scale Sequencing and Other Community Resource Projects* (2003), http://www.genome.gov/10506537.

Nat'l Human Genome Research Inst. (NHGRI), *ENCODE Project Data Release Policy (2003–2007)* (2007), http://www.genome.gov/12513440.

Nat'l Human Genome Research Inst. (NHGRI), *The Human Genome Project Completion: Frequently Asked Questions* (2010), http://www.genome.gov/11006943.

Nat'l Human Genome Research Inst. (NHGRI), *1000 Genomes Project Data Available on Amazon Cloud*, NIH NEWS (Mar. 29, 2012), http://www.nih.gov/news/health/mar2012/nhgri-29.htm.

NIH Common Fund, *HMP Data Release and Resource Sharing Guidelines for Human Microbiome Project Data Production Grants*, NIH COMMON FUND (last modified Jan. 1, 2011), http://commonfund.nih.gov/hmp/datareleaseguidelines.aspx.

NIH, *Policy for Sharing of Data Obtained in NIH Supported or Conducted Genome-Wide Association Studies (GWAS)*, 72 FED. REG. 49290 (2007).

NIH, *Notice on Development of Data Sharing Policy for Sequence and Related Genomic Data*, NATIONAL INSTITUTES OF HEALTH: OFFICE OF EXTRAMURAL RESEARCH (Oct. 19 2009), http://grants.nih.gov/grants/guide/notice-files/NOT-HG-10-006.html.

NIH, *Draft NIH Genomic Data Sharing Policy Request for Public Comments*, 78 FED. REG. 57,860 (Sept. 20, 2013).

NAT'L RESEARCH COUNCIL, MAPPING AND SEQUENCING THE HUMAN GENOME (National Research Council 1988).

NAT'L RESEARCH COUNCIL, REAPING THE BENEFITS OF GENOMIC AND PROTEOMIC RESEARCH (National Research Council 2006).

N.Y. Times, *Reading the Book of Life: White House Remarks on Decoding of Genome*, N.Y. TIMES (June 27, 2000), at F8.

Pilar N. Ossorio, *Bodies of Data: Genomic Data and Bioscience Data Sharing*, 78 SOCIAL RESEARCH 907 (2011).

ELINOR OSTROM, UNDERSTANDING INSTITUTIONAL DIVERSITY (Princeton University Press 2005).

Elinor Ostrom & Charlotte Hess, *A Framework for Analyzing the Knowledge Commons*, in UNDERSTANDING KNOWLEDGE AS A COMMONS: FROM THEORY TO PRACTICE 41 (Charlotte Hess & Elinor Ostrom, eds., MIT Press 2007).

P3G Consortium et al., *Public Access to Genome-Wide Data: Five Views on Balancing Research with Privacy and Protection*, 5 PLoS GENETICS, no. 10 (2009), at e1000665.

Elizabeth Pennisi, *Will Computers Crash Genomics?*, 331 SCIENCE 666 (2011).

Personal Genome Project, *Personal Genome Project Mission*, PERSONAL GENOME PROJECT (2012), http://www.personalgenomes.org/mission.html.

Arti Kaur Rai, *Regulating Scientific Research: Intellectual Property Rights and the Norms of Science*, 94 NORTHWESTERN U. L. REV. 77 (1999).

J. H. Reichman & Paul F. Uhlir, *A Contractually Reconstructed Research Commons for Scientific Data in a Highly Protectionist Intellectual Property Environment*, 66 LAW & CONTEMP. PROBS. 315 (2003).

MATT RIDLEY, GENOME (HarperCollins 1999).

Leslie Roberts, *Genome Patent Fight Erupts*, 254 Science 184 (1991).

Leslie Roberts, *Controversial from the Start*, 291 Science 1182 (2001).

Charles G. Roland & Richard A. Kirkpatrick, *Time Lapse Between Hypothesis and Publication in the Medical Sciences*, 292 New England J. Medicine 1273 (1975).

Jeffrey Rosenfeld & Christopher E. Mason, *Pervasive Sequence Patents Cover the Entire Human Genome*, 5 Genome Medicine 27 (2013).

The Royal Society, Science as an Open Enterprise: Final Report (2012), http://royalsociety.org/uploadedFiles/Royal_Society_Content/policy/projects/sape/2012-06-20-SAOE.pdf.

James Shreeve, The Genome War (Knopf 2004).

Don Tapscott & Anthony D. Williams, Wikinomics: How Mass Collaboration Changes Everything (Penguin 2006).

Sharon F. Terry et al., *Advocacy Groups as Research Organizations: The PXE International Example*, 8 Nature Reviews Genetics 157 (2007).

Toronto Int'l Data Release Workshop Authors, *Prepublication Data Sharing*, 461 Nature 168 (2009).

John Travis, *U.K. to Sequence 10,000 Genomes in 3 Years to Shed Light on Diseases*, Science Insider (June 24, 2010), http://news.sciencemag.org/scienceinsider/2010/06/uk-to-sequence-10000-genomes.html.

Peter J. Turnbaugh et al., *The Human Microbiome Project*, 449 Nature 804 (2007).

U.S. Dept. of Energy & Nat'l Insts. of Health, *NIH, DOE Guidelines Encourage Sharing of Data, Resources*, 4 Human Genome News no. 5 (Jan. 1993), at 4, http://www.ornl.gov/sci/techresources/Human_Genome/publicat/hgn/pdfs/Vol4No5.pdf.

J. Craig Venter, A Life Decoded: My Genome, My Life (Penguin 2007).

Marc Via, Christopher Gignoux, & Esteban G. Burchard, *The 1000 Genomes Project: New Opportunities for Research and Social Challenges*, 2 Genome Medicine 3 (2010).

Nicholas Wade, *Scientist's Plan: Map All DNA Within 3 Years*, N.Y. Times (May 10, 1998), at A1.

Nicholas Wade, *Genetic Code of Human Life Is Cracked by Scientists: A Shared Success*, N.Y. Times (June 27, 2000), at A1.

Emily Waltz, *1000 Genomes on Amazon's Cloud*, 30 Nature Biotechnology 376 (2012).

James D. Watson, *Genes and Politics*, 75 J. Molecular Medicine 624 (1997).

The Wellcome Trust, *Sharing Data from Large-Scale Biological Research Projects: A System of Tripartite Responsibility: Report of meeting organized by the Wellcome Trust and held on 14–15 January 2003 at Fort Lauderdale, USA*, National Human Genome Research Institute (Jan. 2003), http://www.genome.gov/Pages/Research/WellcomeReport0303.pdf.

Heidi L. Williams, *Intellectual Property Rights and Innovation: Evidence from the Human Genome*, 121 J. Political Economy 1 (2013).

4B Governing Genomic Data: Plea for an "Open Commons"
Geertrui Van Overwalle*

I. Introduction

In their foundational paper, *Constructing Commons in the Cultural Environment*, further described in Chapter 1 of this volume, Madison, Frischmann, and Strandburg (2010a) develop a theoretical framework for analyzing and systematizing knowledge commons, thereby tilting the Institutional Analysis and Development (IAD) framework approach, originally developed by Ostrom and her colleagues for natural resource commons (Ostrom 1990), in a new direction. Madison, Frischmann, and Strandburg offer the modified IAD framework to provide further systematic analysis of knowledge commons systems and hope that other scholars will consider using the framework as part of their own work. That is exactly what Jorge Contreras has done in Chapter 4 of this volume, where he applies the modified IAD framework in order to get a better grip on the systemic elements of the genome commons. Contreras sketches the evolution of genomics

* Geertrui Van Overwalle, Dr. Iur., is professor of Intellectual Property Law at the University of Leuven (Belgium) and Professor of Patent Law and New Technologies at the Tilburg Institute for Law, Technology and Society (TILT) at the University of Tilburg (the Netherlands). In her recent research, she has focused on patents, genetics and their impact on access to health care. The results of this research have been published in *Nature* and *Science,* among other journals, and in her books *Gene Patents and Public Health* (Brussels: Bruylant 2007) and *Gene Patents and Collaborative Licensing Mechanisms. Patent Pools, Clearinghouses, Open Source Models and Liability Regimes* (Cambridge University Press 2009).

data release policies, applying the framework described in Chapter 1 to examine the characteristics and components of the genome commons structure.

Rather than attempt a full analysis of the Contreras chapter, this chapter elaborates on one important issue. Looking at the genome commons through the lens of the modified IAD framework, this chapter zooms in on the constitutive characteristics of the genome commons, in particular on the elements revolving around *provisioning* and *consumption* of the commons. Studying the modified IAD framework and the genome commons in depth reveals that property plays a vital role in *both* the provisioning *and* the consumption of the commons. The property/nonproperty dichotomy plays a key role in the legal regimes and entitlements provisioning the commons, as well as in the legal institutions governing access to and use of resources to create a knowledge commons.

Interrogating the specific example of the genome commons through the modified IAD framework and through contemporary insights in the commons literature leads to the conclusion that the current genome commons is managed as a "common property" or, more specifically, as a limited research commons. This chapter argues that it would be desirable to manage genomic resources more often under an "open commons" model with symmetric access and use rules.

The present chapter starts, in Section II, with a look at the concepts of resources and actors, which are important to understanding provisioning and consumption: *what* resources constitute the genome commons and *who* is involved? This examination is rather brief, as it is meant to be a prelude to the main theme, explored in Sections III and IV, namely the governance or rules in use: *how* are the resources provisioned and *how* can the resources be used? When discussing governance, this chapter also will look into closely related issues, such as background environment, openness regime, and entitlement regime. The chapter then analyzes delicate qualification and normative issues in Section V: Can the genome commons be characterized as a (knowledge) commons and is that a desirable approach? The chapter finishes off with some suggestions for further research in Section VI and concluding remarks in Section VII.

II. Resources and Actors

As discussed in Chapter 1, a knowledge commons may hold a variety of types of resources. According to Contreras, the resources held in the genome commons are genomic data. No definition of "genomic data" is provided, but one can infer from Contreras's descriptions in Chapter 4 that "genomic data" may refer to raw DNA sequence data (encompassing genomic sequences of individual humans, micro-organisms residing within the human body, and other organisms), to physiological data (e.g., data relating to the association between particular genetic markers and disease risk), and to phenotypic data (including elements such as de-identified subject age, ethnicity, weight, demographics, exposure, disease state, and behavioral factors). This vast amount of genomic data is predominantly stored in publicly managed electronic databases around the world, usually available independently of journal publication. Principal databases for the deposit of genomic sequence data are GenBank,[1] EMBL,[2] and the DDBJ.[3]

A variety of types of knowledge commons participants also may be identified. Contreras points out that the "principal stakeholder communities" relevant to the genome commons include funding agencies (playing a crucial role in drafting and enforcing release policies, such as NIH), data generators (specialized scientists playing a vital role in generating large data sets), data users, data intermediaries (commercial or nonprofit entities playing a vital role in the creation and management of databases), data subjects (human subjects from whom the genomic information is derived), and the public. Contreras's discussion suggests that all of these actors and stakeholders constitute a community sharing the commons. It would seem more appropriate, however, to distinguish between the community *per se* which actually produces and shares the commons (including the data generators, data users, and data intermediaries) and the *larger* community, or social environment, in which the community *per se* is nested and which facilitates and empowers the construction of the commons. This social environment includes funding agencies and members of the public, especially as represented by patient advocacy and disease interest groups.

III. Provision of Resources—Construction of the Commons ("How")

Once it is clear *what* resources can be part of the commons and *who* is involved, the question arises *how* those resources become part of the commons: the construction or provision of the commons. This question may be answered by considering the background propertized environment, various institutions that deviate from that environment, and various entitlement structures.

---

[1] GenBank is the National Institutes of Health (NIH, U.S.) genetic sequence database, encompassing approximately 126,551,501,141 bases in 135,440,924 sequence records in the traditional GenBank divisions and 191,401,393,188 bases in 62,715,288 sequence records in the WGS division as of April 2011 (see http://www.ncbi.nlm.nih.gov/genbank/).

[2] The EMBL Nucleotide Sequence Database (also known as EMBL-Bank) constitutes Europe's primary nucleotide sequence resource. Main sources for DNA and RNA sequences are direct submissions from individual researchers, genome sequencing projects, and patent applications. The database is produced in an international collaboration with GenBank (U.S.) and the DNA Database of Japan (DDBJ). Each of the three groups collects a portion of the total sequence data reported worldwide, and all new and updated database entries are exchanged between the groups on a daily basis. Over the years EMBL-Bank has grown exponentially and currently contains over 96 million entries corresponding to 170 gigabases of sequence from over 280,000 organisms (see http://www.embl.org/).

[3] DDBJ, the DNA Data Bank of Japan, is the sole nucleotide sequence data bank in Asia, which is officially certified to collect nucleotide sequences from researchers. Collected data are exchanged with EMBL-Bank and with GenBank on a daily basis. The principal purpose of DDBJ operations is to improve the quality of the International Nucleotide Sequence Database (INSD) (www.insdc.org).

A. BACKGROUND ENVIRONMENT

In the modified IAD framework described in Chapter 1, provisioning is treated first in the context of the background environment. Two starting points are envisaged: a "natural" cultural environment without intellectual property (IP) and a "default" IP-based cultural environment, corresponding respectively to the public domain and to a propertized environment. Chapter 1 also suggests that the natural cultural environment is the appropriate starting point for discussing knowledge commons in which IP rights are available but play a marginal role. The natural environment may be the most appropriate baseline for viewing a cultural commons even if IP protection is available for the resources contributed to the commons, and even if IP law plays some role in its construction.

According to Contreras's analysis in Chapter 4, the genome commons presents a complex picture, as the commons encompasses "biomedical discoveries," which are in principle subject to patent law, as well as large aggregations of data, which may be subject to copyright rules or technical protection measures.

I fully concur with Contreras on this point. The background environment of the genome commons is indeed a mixed nonproprietary/proprietary environment. Two distinct background environments apply to genomic data, encompassing DNA sequence data, physiological data, and phenotypic data. First and foremost, it is fair to say that the genomic commons emerged as a "natural" cultural environment in which data were not covered by IP. From the initiation of the Human Genome Project (HGP),[4] the scientific communities collecting genomic data traditionally abided by a strong open science norm, under which data were provisioned and subsequently shared. Statements from the NIH in 1991[5] and the Human Genome Organisation (HUGO) in 1995[6] bear witness to this open science

---

[4] Begun formally in 1990, the U.S. Human Genome Project was a thirteen-year effort coordinated by the U.S. Department of Energy and the National Institutes of Health (NIH). The project originally was planned to last fifteen years, but rapid technological advances accelerated the completion date to 2003. Project goals were to identify all the approximately 20,000–25,000 genes in human DNA, to determine the sequences of the three billion chemical base pairs that make up human DNA, to store this information in databases, to improve tools for data analysis, to transfer related technologies to the private sector, and to address the ethical, legal, and social issues (ELSI) that may arise from the project. For more details, see http://www.ornl.gov/sci/techresources/Human_Genome/project/about.shtml.

[5] The NIH DOE Guidelines 1991 state that "[a]fter extensive discussion with the community of genome researchers, the advisors of the National Institutes of Health (NIH) and the Department of Energy (DOE) genome programs have determined that consensus is developing around the concept that a six-month period, from the time data or materials are generated to the time they are made available publicly, is a reasonable maximum in almost all cases. More rapid sharing is encouraged" (NHGRI 1991).

[6] The HUGO Position Statement 1995 states: "Sequence data should immediately and publicly be disseminated without restrictions on its use" (HUGO 1995). Contreras does not discuss the HUGO policy documents. It is unclear why he does not do so.

norm. With the signing of the Bermuda Principles in 1996,[7] the principle of free availability and rapid data release (within twenty-four hours) was firmly embedded.[8] The collective norm of rapid and unencumbered data sharing became an integral part of the NIH's[9] and HUGO's[10] policies soon after. In the years to follow, many genome sequencing initiatives also applied the open science norm with regard to the provisioning of the data.[11] In 2003, the Ft. Lauderdale Principles were introduced. Projects such as the SNP Consortium and the international HapMap project,[12] which were classified as Community Resource Projects (CRPs)—"specifically devised and implemented to create a set of data, reagents or other material whose primary utility will be as a resource for the broad scientific community"[13]— reaffirmed the Bermuda Principles requirement that generated data be released rapidly.[14]

At the same time, however, quite a few pieces of data were shielded with IP rights, such as patents, following a property logic. Somewhat unfortunately, Contreras does not review the data release policy documents systematically from this IP angle, let alone from a global perspective, for he focuses mainly on the United States and does not look at Europe at all. On the global level, and from the outset of the HGP, HUGO accepted

---

[7] The 1996 Bermuda Principles state that "[i]t was agreed that all human genomic sequence information generated by centres funded for large-scale human sequencing, should be freely available and in the public domain in order to encourage research and development and to maximise its benefit to society." The 1997 Bermuda Principles set forth that "[t]he principles enunciated at the first International Strategy meeting, of rapid data release and public access to the primary genomic sequence, are reaffirmed."

[8] According to Marshall (2001), researchers first pledged to share the results of sequencing "as soon as possible," releasing all stretches of DNA longer than 1000 units, and "second, they pledged to submit these data within 24 hours to the public database known as GenBank."

[9] The National Human Genome Research Institute (NHGRI) Policy 1997 sets forth that "[i]n conformity with the existing spirit and philosophy of the Human Genome Project (HGP) and in response to the recommendations of advisors and the expressed wishes of the community, NHGRI seeks to make DNA sequence information available as rapidly and freely as possible"; "[i]t is therefore NHGRI s intent that human genomic DNA sequence data, generated by the projects funded under RFA HG-95-005, should be released as rapidly as possible and placed in the public domain where it will be freely available."

[10] The HUGO Statement 1997 "[u]rges all large-scale sequencing centres and their funding agencies to adopt the policy of immediate release, without privileged access for any party, of all human genome sequence information" and "[s]tresses that only the policy of rapid publication and free availability of human genome sequence information will secure further international co-operation of large-scale sequencing centres" (HUGO 1997).

[11] As Contreras explains in Chapter 4, commercial companies, such as Celera, ultimately also applied the same approach and released their data.

[12] "The [HapMap] project is committed to rapid and complete data release, and to ensuring that project data remain freely available in the public domain at no cost to users. The project follows the data-release principles of a 'community resource project'" (see hapmap.org).

[13] Wellcome Trust (2003). As Contreras explains in Chapter 4, CRPs are distinguished from "hypothesis-driven" research, in which the goal is to answer a particular scientific question.

[14] The Wellcome Trust Ft. Lauderdale Principles of 2003 stipulate that "[t]he meeting attendees enthusiastically reaffirmed the 1996 Bermuda Principles, which expressly called for rapid release to the public international DNA sequence databases (GenBank, EMBL, and DDBJ) of sequence assemblies of 2kb or greater by large-scale sequencing efforts and recommended that that agreement be extended to apply to all sequence data, including both the raw traces submitted to the Trace Repositories at NCBI and Ensembl and whole genome shotgun assemblies," and further set forth that "[r]esource producers...make the data generated by the resource immediately and freely available without restriction" (Wellcome Trust 2003).

the possibility that researchers might acquire patent protection on DNA sequences for which a function had been demonstrated.[15] The Bermuda Principles from 1996 also recognized the right to opt for patent protection as long as utility had been demonstrated. Moreover, the Bermuda Principles applied only to CRPs.[16]

As discussed in Chapter 4, starting with the Ft. Lauderdale Principles, a second generation of data release requirements emerged, which were increasingly complex and sophisticated.[17] Patent protection, though discouraged, was permitted in non-CRPs—such as the ENCODE Pilot Project—if a function had been identified. In the United States, the NIH also allowed—directly or indirectly—the patenting of DNA and the U.S. Patent and Trademark Office (USPTO) accommodated DNA patents as well.[18] In Europe, the patentability of human genes demonstrating a function was formally recognized by the European Parliament in 1998 in the EU Biotechnology Directive,[19] an approach which

---

[15] The HUGO Statement of 1992 explains that "[p]atenting DNA segments of unknown function are considered unjustified." However, the HUGO Statement of 1992 sets forth that DNA sequences having a function should be considered patentable: "Patents should be restricted to genes or other DNA elements of which the function is elucidated." The same line of policy is set forth in the HUGO Statement of 1995 ("Future patent rules, rather than rewarding routine discoveries should provide protection for the much more intellectually challenging work of determining biological function and application of gene sequences") and of 1997 ("Reaffirms its Statements on Patenting DNA Sequences of 1992 and 1995, clarifying that HUGO does not oppose patenting of useful benefits derived from genetic information, but does explicitly oppose the patenting of short sequences from randomly isolated portions of genes encoding proteins of uncertain functions"; HUGO "[e]xpresses the hope that the free availability of raw sequence data, although forming part of the relevant state of the art, will not unduly prevent the protection of genes as new drug targets"). The HUGO Statement of 2000 applies the same approach.

[16] The Wellcome Trust Lauderdale Principles of 2003 set forth that "[b]eyond community resource projects, many valuable data sets could come from other sources. Still different issues arise in the case of resources that emerge from research efforts whose primary goal is not resource generation. In such cases, contribution of the data to the public domain as a resource is more a voluntary matter" (Wellcome Trust 2003). See also the discussion in Contreras, this volume, ch. 4.

[17] See, e.g., the National Human Genome Research Institute (NHGRI) Guidelines of 2003.

[18] The NHGRI-DOE Guidelines 1991 state that "in order to assure that novel ideas and inventions are rapidly developed for the benefit of the public, intellectual property protection may be needed for same of the data and materials." The NHGRI Policy 1997 says that raw DNA should not be considered patentable: "In NHGRIs opinion, raw human genomic DNA sequence, in the absence of additional demonstrated biological information, lacks demonstrated specific utility and therefore is an inappropriate material for patent filing"; even though the NIH recognizes that patents demonstrating function may have undesired side effects, patent protection is not ruled out: "NIH is concerned that patent applications on large blocks of primary human genomic DNA sequence could have a chilling effect on the development of future inventions of useful products. Companies are not likely to pursue projects where they believe it is unlikely that effective patent protection will be available. Patents on large blocks of primary sequence will make it difficult to protect the fruit of subsequent inventions resulting from real creative effort. However, according to the Bayh-Dole Act, the grantees have the right to elect to retain title to subject inventions and are free to choose to apply for patents should additional biological experiments reveal convincing evidence for utility" (NHGRI 1997).

[19] Directive 98/44/EC of 6 July 1998 of the European Parliament and of the Council on the legal protection of biotechnological inventions (Official Journal L 213, 30/07/1998 p. 0013). The EU Biotechnology Directive stipulates that "[a]n element isolated from the human body or otherwise produced by means of a technical process, including the sequence or partial sequence of a gene, may constitute a patentable invention, even if the structure of that element is identical to that of a natural element" (Article 5 (2), provided that industrial application of a sequence or a partial sequence of a gene is disclosed (Article 5 (3)).

was implemented in the European Patent Convention (EPC).[20] Over the past decades, a large fraction of DNA sequences that have been generated have been protected with patents, as quantitative and qualitative studies have documented (see, e.g., Jensen & Murray 2005: 239–40; Huys et al. 2009: 903–09), putting more and more pressure on the "natural" cultural environment and increasingly turning the "natural" environment into an IP-based cultural environment.

B. DEVIATING INSTITUTIONS (CREATIVE ENVIRONMENTS)

At first sight, it would appear that the wide array of DNA sequences shielded with IP, in particular patents, would not be part of the genomic commons (see Figure 4B.1). Chapter 1 point outs, however, that identifying the background environment is only the beginning of the analysis. Institutions may have been established to govern deviations from that background structure. A knowledge commons analysis recognizes that creative environments often are shaped by deviating from both the purely natural and the purely propertized regimes.

This claim begs the question what institutions have been developed in the genome commons to govern deviations from the propertized regimes, and, in particular, what creative measures have been designed in the genome commons to govern deviations from the patent regime. Contreras does not address this question in his chapter, but such institutions do exist, and they play a vital role in the construction of a genome commons. One such measure, established by intervention from public authorities (legislatures or judiciaries), is the research exemption. Research exemptions, where available, allow the use, and by inference also the release, of patented DNA sequences for research purposes. Research exemptions differ in scope between jurisdictions, but genomic sequences burdened with patents tumble into the genome commons in those countries in which research exemptions are established (van Zimmeren & Van Overwalle 2014). (See Figure 4B.1.)

A second measure, applied by private or public/private data generators is so-called defensive patenting. Data generators may apply for patent rights with the sole purpose of avoiding the possibility that others might acquire rights in the sequences they have generated.[21] In a defensive patenting strategy, the patent application is withdrawn before it is examined. Data generators who employ this strategy waive patent protection themselves, while preventing others from obtaining patents, since the knowledge embedded in patent applications becomes part of the prior art. This approach enables the resources to fall within the nonproperty regime (Figure 4B.1). A third measure, which also may be employed by data generators, is licensing. Through nonexclusive licensing, resources shift from a pure property environment toward a "take now, pay later" or so-called liability regime (Calabresi & Melamed 1972: 1089–92; Reichman 2000: 1743–98).

---

[20] See Rule 29 Implementing Regulations of the European Patent Convention (EPC).
[21] Cf. Contreras, this volume, ch. 4.

Closely related is yet a fourth measure. Looking at the genome commons through the lens of collaborative institutions theory teaches us that patent pools and clearinghouses may also be helpful in transforming the property regime into a liability regime (Van Overwalle et al. 2006, 2009, 2010). Patent pools and clearinghouses also change the right to exclude into a "take now, pay later" rule, allowing everyone to use the patented inventions (with or without payment, depending on the context) and ultimately resulting in a commons.[22]

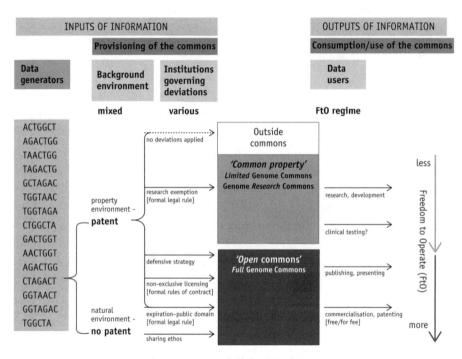

FIGURE 4B.1 Provisioning and Consumption of the (Genome) Commons.

Looking at the mixed nonproperty/property environmental background in genetics, and taking into account the legal instruments that are available to deviate from the property regime (such as research exemptions, defensive patenting, nonexclusive collaborative licensing), it becomes clear that the genetic commons is *provisioned* by both nonpatented and patented sequences, namely those patented sequences which have been "opened up" through creative public and private ordering mechanisms. It is interesting to see that both public actors (the legislator, the judiciary) and private actors (data generators) have legal

---

[22] It has to be admitted that patent pools are less open in terms of membership, and that they manage shared resources in a fashion that is much less focused on sustaining joint production than, say, Wikipedia. Wikipedia is quite open in terms of membership, contributions, and participation in various aspects of the project largely because it focuses on sustaining joint production (see Madison, Frischmann, & Strandburg 2010a: 684).

tools at their disposition (formal legal norms such as the research exemption or term expiration, or legal norms of contract including nonexclusive bilateral licensing or patent pools and clearinghouses) to deviate from the pure property regime or (further) impinge on the mixed nonproperty/property regime and apply the legal regimes at their disposition to assist in constructing a genome commons.

C. ENTITLEMENT STRUCTURES

In the modified IAD framework, the provisioning of the genetic commons is also touched upon when exploring the characteristics of the cultural commons that relate to its governance. The analysis of entitlement structures is "intend[ed] to capture how the resources are made part of the commons, and to understand the mechanisms by which resources are provisioned to the commons, *whether via legal entitlements* or otherwise" (my italics) (Madison, Frischmann, & Strandburg 2010a: 700). It thus seems to me that patented DNA sequences may form part of the commons. The legal institutions described above to deviate from the property regime seem to be the type of entitlement structures Madison, Frischmann, and Strandburg had in mind.

IV. Consumption of the Resources—Access and Use

Once it is clear *what* resources can be part of the commons, *who* is involved, and *how* those resources may become part of the commons, the question of *how* resources can be accessed and used comes to the fore: the question of consumption.

A. ACCESS

Turning to the question of access to the resources, two layers can be distinguished in the complex setting of the genome commons. Indeed, in the context of genetic resources, access is a two-faceted concept. First, there is access to the informational content of genetic sequences. Second, there is access to the tangible component of genetic sequences. In his chapter, Contreras pays considerable attention to the first aspect, namely the access to the informational content. Over the years, as he describes, increasingly sophisticated database technologies have enabled the provision of differentiated levels of access to the information content, with both open and controlled access portions.[23] In principle, patents do not hinder access to information; on the contrary, patent law guarantees access to the information embedded in the patent description, through the disclosure requirement. So, the property/nonproperty discussion—at least with regard to patenting—is

---

[23] This is the approach applied in the Genetic Association Information Network (GAIN) and in the NIH Genome-Wide Association Studies (GWAS) Policy of 2007 (GAIN 2010; NIH 2007).

not relevant here. Access to informational content is not much of an issue when patent is the dominant IP regime. The property/nonproperty debate, and the subsequent access issue, are, however, important where copyright comes into play.

Contreras pays little attention to the second aspect—the tangible content of a resource—and hardly addresses material transfer agreements and the limiting effect such agreements may have on access to genetic resources. Studies have revealed that material transfer agreements may have a blocking effect on research.[24] Especially when research becomes more high level (involving not just raw material but more complex information) it might be necessary for researchers to have access to the tangible resource itself, rather than to the data. It has been demonstrated that this is the case for stem cell research, but it might be worthwhile to revisit this issue for genomic material. It remains to be seen, however, how important access to tangible resources is in the framework of the commons discourse.

B. USE

More important than the issue of access is the question of to what extent data users really can work with the informational content to which they have access. Rather than hindering access to the information embedded in patented subject matter,[25] patents potentially block the unencumbered use of such data.

In the modified IAD framework described in Chapter 1, access and use are discussed in the context of the third constitutive characteristic, namely openness. Commons regimes are defined by the degree of openness and control that they exhibit with respect to contributors, users, and resources.[26] With respect to resources, openness is described as the capacity to relate to a resource by (*accessing and*) *using* it, including the extent to which there are barriers to possession or use. The framework does not disentangle the various dimensions of use or the purposes for which use might be envisaged: for mere philosophical inquiry? for further (commercial/non-commercial) use? for improvement? for exploitation? With respect to actors, openness refers to the capacity to relate to the community as a contributor or user of resources. The modified IAD framework includes an analysis of the extent to which there are criteria for or barriers to membership or participation in the creative/innovative processes that the knowledge commons intends to support. For example, *use* of the shared resources may be open to anyone, even if the ability to contribute to the shared resources is limited.

The modified IAD framework described in Chapter 1 also touches upon (access and) use in its inquiry into the governance of a knowledge commons. An important cluster of

---

[24] Walsh, Cohen, & Cho (2007) point out that practical excludability is rarely associated with the existence of a patent in academic settings, but is more readily achieved through secrecy or not sharing research materials.

[25] On the contrary, patent law facilitates access to information embedded in technology by way of the disclosure requirement.

[26] See Frischmann, Madison, & Strandburg, this volume, ch. 1.

questions in this regard relates to entitlement structures. The inquiry into entitlement structures is intended not only to capture how resources are made part of the commons and to understand the mechanisms by which resources are provisioned to the commons (whether via legal entitlements or otherwise) but also to inquire as to entitlements to *use* and consume those resources once they are part of that commons.

Contreras's chapter provides an interesting historic account of access and use rules in the genome commons and meticulously analyzes the freedom to use (often called "freedom to operate") in each and every project. But what has been the degree of freedom to operate over time?[27] In light of the various projects and policy documents discussed here and in Chapter 4, three levels of freedom to operate can be discerned in my view. A first level is freedom to use data for *research* (see Figure 4B.1). Most, if not all, policies allow use of the released data for research purposes. A second level is freedom to *publish* (see Figure 4B.1). A wide series of clauses relates to the use of data for publishing or presentation purposes. Some restrict use at this level. The Genetic Association Information Network (GAIN), established in 2006, was the first genomic data release policy to introduce temporal restrictions on the use of released data for publishing or presenting. Data users are prohibited to publish and make presentations based on GAIN data for a specific embargo period.[28] In 2007, the NIH adopted similar restrictions for the GWA studies[29] and ENCODE project. Such restrictions also were imposed by the international SAE Consortium (iSAEC).[30] A third level relates to freedom to use data for *commercial/mixed research–commercial* purposes. Many policies forbid or seriously restrict use for such purposes (see Figure 4B.1).

V. A Commons?

Now that I have carefully dissected the elements and characteristics of the genome commons in terms of their provisioning and consumption, two further questions come to

---

[27] "Freedom to operate" is defined as a situation in which "the commercial production, marketing and use of a product, process or service does not infringe the patent rights of others ('third party patent rights')" (van Zimmeren, Vanneste, & Van Overwalle 2011).

[28] "In accord with the NIH GWAS Policy for Data Sharing, and as expressed through the submission of the DAR, Approved Users acknowledge the NIH's expectation that they will not *submit* GAIN March 1, 2010 version Page 5 of 11 findings using the GAIN dataset(s), or updated versions thereof, for publication or presentation for a period of exclusivity for Contributing Investigators concluding with the Embargo Date identified on the dbGaP or other NIH genomic data repository homepage" (GAIN 2010).

[29] NIH (2007).

[30] "To qualify for data access researchers must agree to the following restrictions: Not to submit for publication or presentation, or make any other use or disclosure of, any Public Data or any abstract, article or other information that is based on, includes or uses Public Data for a specified time period not to exceed nine (9) months following the Consortium's initial disclosure of such Public Data (the specific restriction period for such Public Data shall be indicated in the database entry for such Public Data)" (International Serious Adverse Event Consortium (iSAEC), *s.d.*).

the fore. First, can one conclude that the genome commons is indeed a commons, in particular a knowledge commons (definitional question)? Next, is a commons structure the most appropriate institutional format for the provision and consumption of genomic data (normative question)?

A. DEFINITIONAL QUESTION

Examining the terminological ambiguity with regard to the commons and comparing the various terms and qualifications is a daunting task, which goes beyond the scope of the present chapter. It will suffice to say that in the commons literature two distinct strands have developed and two major regimes of commons have been discerned, as discussed in Yochai Benkler's chapter in this volume.[31] On the one hand, there is the "common property" regime[32] in which "members of a clearly defined group have a bundle of legal rights including the right to exclude nonmembers from using that resource" (Hess & Ostrom 2003: 121). Most "common property" regimes involve participants who are proprietors and have four rights: access (the right to enter a defined physical area and enjoy nonsubtractive benefits), extraction (the right to obtain resource units or products of a resource system), management (the right to regulate internal use patterns and transform the resource by making improvements), and exclusion (the right to determine who will have access rights and withdrawal rights, and how those rights may be transferred) (Hess & Ostrom 2003: 125–26). On the other hand, there is the so-called "open commons" regime, where "no one has the right to exclude anyone from using a resource" (Hess & Ostrom 2003: 125–26) and where anyone can access/use the resource and cannot exclude others. As Benkler discusses in Chapter 3, the hallmark of "open commons" is "symmetric freedom to operate vis-à-vis a resource set, generally or with respect to a class of uses in the commons." The defining institutional feature of an "open commons" is captured by its core function: "creating freedom to operate, available to more or less all actors in the economy they serve."

At this point, two observations can be made. First and foremost, both approaches to commons study give great weight to the *governance* dimension of commons (how is the commons managed once it has been established?), rather than looking at the *provisioning* dimension of commons (how was the commons established?) to distinguish the two types of commons regime. In modified IAD framework terms, this means that more attention is given to the consumption component than to the provisioning component in defining the type of commons.

---

[31] Benkler, this volume, ch. 3. See also Hess & Ostrom (2003: 121).

[32] Some authors speak of a "positive commons" in this regard, referring to "a common in which resources are jointly owned and so use of those resources by any one commoner depends on all the commoners having consented" (Drahos 2006).

Furthermore, two major criteria can be discerned that can be used to discriminate between the two types of commons regimes. The first criterion is the scope of *use* of the resource. In a "common property" regime only the members can access/use the resource and can exclude nonmembers. In an "open commons" regime more or less anyone may use the resource set, and no one, or no group, has exclusive rights against anyone else. Moreover, the outputs in an open commons regimes are not subject to exclusive property rights, but rather to a regime of full or partial open access. The second criterion is the range of *users* of the resources. In a "common property" regime a clearly defined group (Hess & Ostrom 2003), a defined set of claimants (Benkler, this volume, ch. 3), or a particular subset of users (Rose 1986) is entitled to access and use. In contrast, in an "open commons," resources are available "for the unorganized public" (Rose 1986) or, as Benkler puts it, "to an open or undefined class of users."

Where do knowledge commons fit in this analysis? Chapter 1 defines knowledge commons as "environments for developing and distributing cultural and scientific knowledge through institutions that support pooling and sharing that knowledge in a managed way." Such environments are designed and managed with limitations tailored to the character of those resources and to the communities involved rather than left to evolve via market transactions grounded solely in the traditional property narrative. This specification does not provide a fine-meshed definition, but rather leaves "a big tent," inviting scholars to contribute to assess existing theories (Madison, Frischmann, & Strandburg 2010b).

And how can the genome commons be characterized? Contreras refers to the genome commons as the global resource of genetic data which originated with the HGP and the sweeping Bermuda Principles and which was made freely available in public databases (Contreras 2011). As he explains in Chapter 4, the genome commons is a "massive accumulation of data," a "vast quantity of genetic information" made available in public databases across the globe, or "a massive accumulation of data." According to Contreras, the genome commons is a "global public resource" which, thanks to its "fundamental shared nature," resembles a "common-pool resource" as studied by Elinor Ostrom and her colleagues, rather than the simpler models of the public domain or public good that are typically set forth in the context of basic scientific research. He takes the view that the genome commons evolved from a public domain vehicle into a "polycentric governance institution for the growth, management and stewardship of a massively-shared public resource."

Contreras's observations are not sufficient to classify the genome commons as a "common property" or an "open commons," however, since he focuses mainly on data *release*, rather than systematically assessing access and *use* of the released data. Put differently, Contreras pays attention mostly to construction/production/provisioning rules and policies. And for the most part, he analyses only those governance/consumption/utilization restrictions resulting from copyright law, ignoring those resulting from patent law and policy. The latter are equally important in the study of the commons, however.

Looking at the utilization dimension of the genome commons in more detail, it seems fair to say that the genome commons may have been rather successful in offering equal rights to all users for *accessing* genetic information and data, thanks to the Bermuda Principles and further efforts. However, the genome commons as it stands today does not offer equal rights to all to *use* the genetic data, burdened as the related discoveries may be with patents and subsequent restrictions on freedom to use. Following Ostrom, and characterizing a "common property" regime as a regime where access, use (or extraction), management, and exclusion are available to a well-defined set of users, the genome commons appears to be a "common property" regime or, more specifically, a limited commons or "genome *research* commons," in which access and use of resources is restricted to researchers for research purposes. Following Benkler, and characterizing an "open commons" as an institution in which all have symmetric freedom to operate with respect to the resource, it is highly unlikely that the genome commons as depicted by Contreras can be properly characterized as an "open commons." Some genome commons regimes, however, in which access and use of the resources is offered to all (data holders/date generators and data users) for a variety of purposes (ranging from research through clinical practice[33] to commercialization), are managed as "open commons" or, equivalently, "*full* genome commons."

B. NORMATIVE PERSPECTIVE

Madison, Frischmann, and Strandburg (2010a) set forth that "[e]xamples of constructed cultural commons for which the 'natural' environment is the most appropriate baseline likely include the commons of scientific research results and tools." As the genome commons may be regarded as a commons of scientific research results and tools in the basic sciences, their view may be interpreted as suggesting that the appropriate background environment for the genome commons is the "natural" cultural environment without IP and unmediated by rights of exclusion. Benkler suggests that "common property" regimes are most appropriate for resources whose scale is large but defined, whereas "open commons" arrangements are more adequate for the management of larger ranges of resources open to the entire public or at least to some very large, and largely undefined, set of users (Benkler, this volume, ch. 3). As genomic data resources are large and both access and use of these resources to develop follow-on innovations greatly benefit society, the ideal type of management structure would be the "open commons" model, in which resources are managed under symmetric access and use rules and where access and use cannot be refused—in other words, permission from a (data) owner is not needed.

However, it has been argued that complete open access to genomic data without any publication embargoes might compromise the incentives of *upstream* researchers. Further research is needed to test this argument. Reichman & Uhlir (2003) have argued that, in order to preserve the incentives of *downstream* innovators, follow-on applications of genomic databases for commercial purposes should be permitted, subject to requiring the

---

[33] It is still being debated whether clinical testing can fall under the research exemption. See Van Overwalle et al. (2006).

follow-on innovators to pay a reasonable compensation for such uses. I fully endorse such an approach, which would turn the "common property" character of the commons into a "for all" approach, by way of a "take now, pay later" or liability regime (Reichman 2000).

VI. Suggestions for Further Research

With respect to the study of the genome commons, I would like to invite Contreras to look further into two issues. The first issue relates to geographical scope. Contreras focuses on the situation in the United States, but devotes almost no attention to initiatives going beyond the confines of the United States, which include, for example, the international policy guidelines from HUGO, European guidelines,[34] and the European legal framework, with its *sui generis* database protection, lack of grace period in patent law, and so forth. Can one speak of the genetic commons as a "global resource of genetic data which was produced in the context of the human genome project" while considering only the U.S. context?

The second topic is enforcement. Contreras's chapter devotes wide attention to the history and development of policy guidelines, but pays little attention to how these formal and informal policies are enforced. In particular, one would like to know how compliance with the policies is monitored and how noncompliance is sanctioned. Funding often is conditioned on data release: no data release, no funding.[35] Use for publication often is embargoed. But how is all of this enforced? Are there (empirical) data highlighting current practices in that regard?

On a more detailed (and far less important) level, it would be helpful if Contreras clarified the nature of the resources that are part of his genome commons a little more. Does the genome commons include only DNA sequences of which the function is *elucidated,* *or* does it also include DNA sequences with *unknown* functions (expressed sequence tags (ESTs), short randomly cloned c-DNA segments)? And does the genome commons include protein structure data? What about clinical data?

VII. Conclusion

Interrogating the specific example of the genome commons through the modified IAD framework and through contemporary insights in the commons literature has led to the conclusion that the current genome commons is managed mainly as a "common property" or, more specifically, a limited research commons. (See Figure 4B.1). As genomic

---

[34] Aymé et al. (2008).

[35] The GWAS policy states that "[t]he NIH *expects* that investigators who contribute data to the NIH GWAS data repository will retain the exclusive right to publish analyses of the dataset for a defined period of time following the release of a given genotype-phenotype dataset through the NIH GWAS data repository (including the precomputed analyses of the data)" (my italics) (NIH 2007).

data encompasses large classes of resources, which benefit society greatly when they are accessed and used to develop follow-on innovations, it would be desirable to have more genomic resources run under an "open commons" model, in which resources are managed under symmetric access and use rules, with no permission needed for access and use.

Given the great importance of genomic data for the progress of science and innovation and of open availability and unhindered use of genomic resources, further exploration of the genome commons and of the various commons narratives is certainly warranted. An in-depth (re)examination of U.S. and European approaches and of the impact of European *sui generis* data protection systems merits further attention if one is to speak of a "global" and open genome commons. An analysis and discussion of legal, economic, and policy tools to combat pressures to privatize *clinical* data related to the human genome,[36] which could disrupt the genome commons, would be most welcome as well.

References

S. Aymé, G. Matthijs, & S. Soini, on behalf of the ESHG Working Party on Patenting and Licensing, *Patenting and licensing in genetic testing. Recommendations of the European Society of Human Genetics*, 16 EUR. J. HUMAN GENETICS S3 (2008).

Guido Calabresi & A. Douglas Melamed, *Property Rules, Liability Rules, and Inalienability: One View of the Cathedral*, 85 HARVARD L. REV. 1089 (1972).

Robert Cook-Deegan, John M. Conley, James P. Evans, & Daniel Vorhaus, *The Next Controversy in Genetic Testing: Clinical Data as Trade Secrets?*, 21 EUR. J. OF HUMAN GENETICS 585 (2012).

Jorge L. Contreras, *Bermuda's Legacy: Policy, Patents and the Design of the Genome Commons*, 12 MINNESOTA J.L. SCI. & TECH. 61 (2011).

Peter Drahos, *A Defence of the Intellectual Commons*, 16 CONSUMER POLICY REV. 2 (2006).

GAIN, Data Use Certification Agreement (March 1, 2010, version), https://dbgap.ncbi.nlm.nih. gov/aa/wga.cgi?view_pdf&stacc=phs000021.v1.p1.

The GAIN Collaborative Research Group, *New Models of Collaboration in Genome-wide Association Studies: The Genetic Association Information Network*, 39 NATURE GENETICS 1045 (2007).

Charlotte Hess & Elinor Ostrom, *Ideas, Artifacts and Facilities: Information as a Common Pool Resource*, 66 LAW & CONTEMP. PROBS. 111 (2003).

Human Genome Organization (HUGO), *HUGO Statement on the Patenting of DNA Sequences* (January 1995).

Human Genome Organization (HUGO), *Intellectual Property Committee Statement on Patenting Issues Related to Early Release of Raw Sequence Data* (May 1997), http://www.genome.gov/ Pages/About/InstitutePolicies/ip_sequencedata_1997.pdf.

Isabelle Huys, Nele Berthels, Gert Matthijs, & Geertrui Van Overwalle, *Legal Uncertainty in the Area of Genetic Diagnostic Testing*, 27 NATURE BIOTECHNOLOGY 903 (2009).

---

[36] See Cook-Deegan, Conley, Evans, & Vorhaus (2012). See also *The Governance of Large Research and Medical Databases in Clinical and Research Multi-Centre Trials*, 4th Meeting of the EC International Dialogue on Bioethics, Copenhagen, June 19, 2012.

Kyle Jensen & Fiona Murray, *Intellectual Property Landscape of the Human Genome*, 310 SCIENCE 239 (2005).

Michael J. Madison, Brett M. Frischmann, & Kathering J. Strandburg, *Constructing Commons in the Cultural Environment*, 95 CORNELL L.REV. 657 (2010a).

Michael J. Madison, Brett M. Frischmann, & Katherine J. Strandburg, *Reply: The Complexity of Commons*, 95 CORNELL L. REV. 839 (2010b).

Eliot Marshal, *Bermuda Rules: Community Spirit, with Teeth*, 291 SCIENCE 1192 (2001).

Nat'l Human Genome Research Inst. (NHGRI), *NIH-DOE Guidelines for Access to Mapping and Sequencing Data and Material Resources* (1991), http://www.genome.gov/10000925.

Nat'l Human Genome Research Inst. (NHGRI), *Current NHGRI Policy for Release and Database Deposition of Sequence Data* (1997), http://www.genome.gov/10000910.

NIH, *Policy for Sharing of Data Obtained in NIH Supported or Conducted Genome-Wide Association Studies (GWAS)*, 72 FED. REG. 49290 (Aug. 28, 2007).

ELINOR OSTROM, GOVERNING THE COMMONS: THE EVOLUTION OF INSTITUTIONS FOR COLLECTIVE ACTION (Cambridge University Press 1990).

J.H. Reichman, *Of Green Tulips and Legal Kudzu: Repackaging Rights in Subpatentable Innovation*, 53 VANDERBILT L. REV. 1743 (2000).

J.H. Reichman & Paul F. Uhlir, *A Contractually Reconstructed Research Commons for Scientific Data in a Highly Protectionist Intellectual Property Environment*, 66 LAW & CONTEMP. PROBS. 315 (2003).

Carol Rose, *The Comedy of the Commons: Custom, Commerce, and Inherently Public Property*, 53 U. CHICAGO L. REV. 711 (1986).

Geertrui Van Overwalle, *Of Thickets, Blocks and Gaps: Designing Tools to Resolve Obstacles in the Gene Patents Landscape*, in GENE PATENTS AND COLLABORATIVE LICENSING MODELS: PATENT POOLS, CLEARING HOUSES, OPEN SOURCE MODELS AND LIABILITY REGIMES (Geertrui Van Overwalle ed., Cambridge University Press 2009).

Geertrui Van Overwalle, *Designing Models to Clear Patent Thickets in Genetics*, in WORKING WITHIN THE BOUNDARIES OF INTELLECTUAL PROPERTY: INNOVATION POLICIY FOR THE KNOWLEDGE SOCIETY (Rochelle C. Dreyfuss, Harry First, & Diane L. Zimmerman eds., Oxford University Press 2010).

Geertrui Van Overwalle, Esther van Zimmeren, Birgit Verbeure, & Gert Matthijs, *Models for Facilitating Access to Patents on Genetic Inventions*, 7 NATURE REVIEW GENETICS 143 (2006).

Esther van Zimmeren & Geertrui Van Overwalle, *A False Sense of Security Offered by Zero-Price Liability Rules? Research Exceptions in the United States, Europe and Japan in an Open Innovation Context*, in PATENT LAW IN GLOBAL PERSPECTIVE (Ruth Okediji & Margo Bagley eds., Oxford University Press 2014)

ESTHER VAN ZIMMEREN, SVEN VANNESTE, & GEERTRUI VAN OVERWALLE, PATENT LICENSING IN MEDICAL BIOTECHNOLOGY IN EUROPE: A ROLE FOR COLLABORATIVE LICENSING STRATEGIES? (Leuven: Academic Cooperative Publishers 2011).

John P. Walsh, Wesley M. Cohen, & Charlene Cho, *Where Excludability Matters: Material versus Intellectual Property in Academic Biomedical Research*, 36 RESEARCH POLICY 1184 (2007).

WELLCOME TRUST, SHARING DATA FROM LARGE-SCALE BIOLOGICAL RESEARCH PROJECTS: A SYSTEM OF TRIPARTITE RESPONSIBILITY (report of a meeting held at Fort Lauderdale, Florida, USA, Jan. 14–15, 2003.

5 The Rare Diseases Clinical Research Network and the Urea Cycle Disorders Consortium as Nested Knowledge Commons

Katherine J. Strandburg, Brett M. Frischmann, and Can Cui*

I. Introduction

Concerns about the productivity of the pharmaceutical industry, the accessibility of treatment, and the expense of healthcare have led to numerous experiments with "openness" at various stages of research. "Open" approaches are particularly attractive in the rare disease context, given the small numbers and geographical dispersion of potential research subjects and the inapplicability of the "blockbuster drug" business model.

Estimates suggest that there are between 5000 and 8000 rare diseases (Field & Boat 2011), where, in the United States, rare diseases have been defined legislatively as diseases affecting fewer than 200,000 individuals.[1] In the aggregate, rare diseases affect millions of Americans. Moreover, as scientific understanding of disease advances, it appears that more and more diseases may be "rare" for treatment purposes. For example, while one

---

* Katherine J. Strandburg is the Alfred B. Engelberg Professor of Law and a faculty director of the Engelberg Center for Innovation Law and Policy at the New York University School of Law, New York, New York, USA. Brett M. Frischmann is Professor of Law and Director of the Intellectual Property and Information Law Program at the Benjamin N. Cardozo School of Law, Yeshiva University, New York, New York, USA. Each is also a member of the Affiliated Faculty of the Vincent and Elinor Ostrom Workshop in Political Theory and Policy Analysis. Can Cui, a member of The Order of the Coif, holds a Ph.D. from Harvard University and a J.D. from New York University School of Law. He is an associate resident in the Hong Kong office of Morrison & Foerster and teaches intellectual property law at The Chinese University of Hong Kong Faculty of Law, Hong Kong SAR, China.

[1] Federal Food, Drug, and Cosmetic Act, 21 U.S.C. § 360bb (A)(2)(A) (2012).

used to speak of a "cure for cancer," it now seems evident that there will, if we are lucky, be many and various cures for the various forms of the disease, perhaps tailored to the characteristics of individual patients. Moreover, some adverse reactions to trauma and to interventions such as chemotherapy and surgery also appear to be driven by genetic variations similar to those underlying many rare diseases.

These developments make it all the more pressing to find effective approaches to rare disease clinical research. Information sharing, collaboration, and community building among researchers, doctors, and patients are critical to rare disease research. It is very difficult to do clinical research on rare diseases; rareness means small numbers of patients, who usually are dispersed among geographically scattered medical centers. As summarized in a National Academies Report, *Rare Diseases and Orphan Products: Accelerating Research and Development*:

> Because the number of people affected with any particular rare disease is relatively small and the number of rare diseases is so large, a host of challenges complicates the development of safe and effective drugs, biologics, and medical devices to prevent, diagnose, treat, or cure these conditions. These challenges include difficulties in attracting public and private funding for research and development, recruiting sufficient numbers of research participants for clinical studies, appropriately using clinical research designs for small populations, and securing adequate expertise at the government agencies that review rare diseases research applications or authorize the marketing of products for rare conditions.

The Rare Disease Clinical Research Network (RDCRN) is a program of the National Institutes of Health (NIH) which aims to develop infrastructure and methodologies for rare disease clinical research by creating a network of rare disease research consortia. Each RDCRN consortium (RDCRC) creates a collaboration involving researchers, other healthcare professionals, and patients at a group of geographically dispersed clinical sites that focuses on a cluster of at least three related diseases. Essentially, the RDCRN constructs a commons (or, more precisely, a nested set of commons arrangements). The RDCRN also includes a Data Management Coordination Center (DMCC), tasked with developing databases and other information technology for coordinating the research of the consortia.

Knowledge about medical treatment is an inherently nonrivalrous resource, which can be used to treat any number of patients without diminishing its value to the next patient. RDCRCs nonetheless face resource governance challenges, including (1) managing some rivalrous resources, such as research funding, that are necessary inputs to producing knowledge about medical treatments; (2) managing some rivalrous resources, such as authorship credit, that incentivize and reward members' work; (3) overcoming potential "anticommons"-type problems arising from researchers' incentives to respond to the scarcity of research subjects by hoarding access to patients and their data; (4) reducing the transaction costs of cooperation between widely dispersed researchers; and (5) managing interactions with outsiders, such as pharmaceutical companies and the NIH.

There is a tension inherent in all scientific research between the need to apportion scarce resources (such as funding and the time and attention of good researchers) and the value of sharing research results and certain infrastructural data and research tools as broadly as possible. The general mechanisms developed by society and by scientific research communities for managing this tension include public funding, reputation-based systems of peer review and publication for disseminating knowledge and apportioning funding, and scientific norms encouraging what Merton famously described as communism (better described today as openness or sharing), universalism, disinterestedness, and organized skepticism. In the clinical research context, there is further tension between the potential value of the research and potential risks to research subjects, which is addressed by measures such as informed consent regulation, medical profession ethical requirements prioritizing duty to patients, and various institutional review boards (IRBs). These general governance mechanisms form part of the backdrop of the specific resource management strategies of the RDCRN and its associated consortia.

This chapter reports on a case study of the RDCRN's Urea Cycle Disorders Consortium (UCDC) that employed the knowledge commons framework described in Chapter 1 of this volume. This case study is a step toward understanding whether and in what ways the RDCRN contributes to progress in combating rare diseases. Government funding for research is limited, and it is important to try to understand how various ways of structuring that funding influence the outcomes. Moreover, a government program such as the RDCRN inevitably interacts with preexisting collaborative arrangements, strengthening or undermining them. Observations from close study of the UCDC generate hypotheses about the RDCRN approach that can be tested in comparative studies of other consortia.

The UCDC is considered one of the most successful RDCRN consortia. One important indicator of its success is that it has created and continues to build a relatively large pool of research subjects and patient data through a longitudinal study of urea cycle disorder patients at all fifteen of its clinical sites. The common pool of patient data facilitates both collaborative and individual research projects by consortium researchers. It also reduces the expense and difficulty of clinical treatment trials. The UCDC's strong relationship with the National Urea Cycle Disorder Foundation (NUCDF), the patient advocacy group for those with urea cycle disorders, has been critical to this effort. The UCDC also appears to have been reasonably successful in pursuing several other important objectives: sustaining and growing a community of researchers with expertise and interest in urea cycle disorders; promoting knowledge and idea sharing within the community; cooperating with patients in framing research and disseminating research results to patients; and translating research into treatments by interacting with pharmaceutical companies.

Our case study suggests that several factors have contributed to the UCDC's success thus far. Trust in and respect for the consortium leadership appears to facilitate informal decision making and avoid conflict. Shared goals and norms, arising in part from the fact that the consortium grew out of a long-standing and close-knit group of researchers, serve similar purposes. The study also identifies several aspects of the RDCRN structure that appear to have been particularly important to the UCDC's successful operation, including the longitudinal study requirement, the mandate for involvement of the patients advocacy group, the requirement of regular monthly teleconferences, and the DMCC's provision of data aggregation services. Finally, the study identifies several areas on the horizon that may pose challenges to the UCDC's current approach to governance in light of its heavy dependence on informal interpersonal relationships, including pending leadership transitions, the need to incorporate a growing number of new researchers and clinical sites, and data sharing and intellectual property issues that may arise out of increasing interactions with pharmaceutical companies.

Part II explains the methodology of this case study. Part III briefly sets out the background contexts for the UCDC, focusing primarily on the RDCRN. Part IV describes the UCDC's goals and objectives and its history. Part V describes the various participants in the UCDC and their roles. Part VI identifies some of the important resources used, generated, and disseminated by the UCDC and touches upon some of the governance challenges they pose. Part VII describes the UCDC's overall approach to governance and decision making. It also explores how the UCDC handles the governance issues that arise in some specific action arenas. Part VIII concludes by setting forth several hypotheses about factors that may contribute to consortium success, which can be tested in future comparative studies.

II. Methodology

Our overall approach follows the modified version of the Institutional Analysis and Development (IAD) framework described in Chapter 1. Specifically, we:

- *Conducted a literature review.* We reviewed available public documentation about the RDCRN and UCDC, using the knowledge commons framework to structure our observations. Based on what we observed, we identified questions to investigate as we continued our research by interviewing various participants. We later obtained permission to review some documents available on the UCDC's members-only website, including Publication and Data Use Policies, executed Industry Agreements, and minutes of consortium meetings.
- *Conducted a series of semi-structured interviews.* We interviewed sixteen professionals involved with the UCDC: four NIH officials, including the head of the Office of Rare Diseases Research, the director of extramural research for the Office of Rare Diseases Research, and the science and program officers for the UCDC; the three UCDC consortium principal investigators (CPIs); the UCDC program manager; a principal investigator at one of the UCDC

clinical sites (SPI) in the United States; an SPI in Europe; a former SPI in the United States; a site study coordinator; a neuropsychologist at one of the clinical sites; an attorney at Children's National Medical Center; the Director of U.S. Commercial Operations for one of the pharmaceutical companies involved with the UCDC; and the executive director of the associated patient advocacy group, the NUCDF. NUCDF is a volunteer organization with activities ranging from education, research, and fundraising to support groups.

The interviews ranged in length from 45 minutes to 120 minutes, with average duration of about 85 minutes. Though interview questions were tailored to each interviewee, we used the modified IAD framework to structure the interviews, keeping them focused on relevant issues. Our analysis procedure focused on organizing information provided by interviewees according to that framework.

- *Attended a UCDC conference as observers.* During the course of our interviews, the UCDC researchers invited us to attend their annual conference in July 2012. We attended a pre-conference dinner, where the UCDC CPI Mark Batshaw introduced us to the attendees. The first day was a scientific research workshop during which, for the most part, we sat in the back of the room as silent observers and took notes. We also spoke informally with various participants about their interactions and experiences with the UCDC. Our aim was to observe the interactions among researchers, their methods of communication and interaction, the social dynamics, and anything else relevant to the UCDC's stated objectives of facilitating research collaboration.

The second day of the conference was sponsored by the NUCDF for the benefit of urea cycle disorder (UCD) patients. During much of the day, UCDC researchers, as well as one of the NIH officials we interviewed, gave presentations to clinicians, patients, and their families about the state of research and treatment, responded to questions, and engaged with patients and their families informally. Again, we acted mostly as silent observers.

- *Conducted an online survey of UCDC researchers and administrative staff.* The survey was designed to supplement our interviews, both by obtaining additional perspectives and by testing some of our observations. We used the e-mail list from the UCDC website to solicit responses. After eliminating those who were no longer associated with the UCDC or whose roles (such as research assistant or volunteer) limited their familiarity with the issues addressed by the survey, we were left with 95 potential respondents, 56 of whom began the survey. The average number of responses to a question was 51. Somewhat more respondents answered earlier questions, so that the number of responses tapered off to about

45 near the end. Though our sample sizes are quite small, the fact that they represent a large fraction of the entire population gives us some confidence in the accuracy of our results. In analyzing the survey results, we included data from partially completed surveys, since the questions were generally independent of one another. Unless otherwise noted, all percentages reported here were calculated in terms of the number of respondents to the given question.

For the most part, we broke down the responses by role for comparison. We received an excellent response rate from principal investigators and study coordinators. Fifteen out of twenty principal investigators responded, representing ten out of the fifteen research sites to which the survey was sent. Seventeen of twenty-five study coordinators responded, representing fourteen of the fifteen sites to which the survey was sent. The remaining respondents included thirteen other researchers, eight providers of clinical or testing services, and three with other responsibilities. While it is possible that there were selection effects based on the fact that the survey was voluntary, we would expect such effects to be fairly minimal for principal investigator (PIs) and study coordinators, given the very high response rate. The response rate for other categories appears to have been considerably lower, though we were unable to determine with certainty whether non-respondents who were not PIs or study coordinators remained active in the UCDC. Nonetheless, for purposes of this qualitative study, we believe it is useful to consider respondents in all categories in generating hypotheses.

III. The UCDC's Complex Environment

The UCDC is shaped by a larger context, which includes the biological realities of urea cycle disorders, the cultural contexts of medicine and academic research, and the more specific contexts of rare disease research and NIH research funding. The UCDC also is nested within the RDCRN and constrained by the requirements of the consortium grants. The complexities of the background environment in which these consortia "live" inevitably affect the degree to which and means by which these commons-type approaches can produce the desired result—improved medical treatment.

A. THE BIOLOGICAL CONTEXT: UREA CYCLE DISORDERS

A consortium's progress in understanding and treating its focal diseases depends unavoidably on the underlying biology of the diseases and on the extent of current scientific understanding. UCDs result from inborn errors of ureagenesis, a metabolic process. Thus far, eight different enzyme deficiencies have been linked to inborn errors of ureagenesis. UCDs range in severity and may be fatal when not detected and treated quickly enough. Symptoms may begin at birth, during childhood, or in adulthood. Ammonia, which is produced during protein digestion, accumulates to toxic levels in the bodies of individuals with UCDs. While elevated ammonia in the blood is a strong indication of a UCD, definitive diagnosis requires a combination of family history, clinical presentation, and a battery of laboratory tests, which may include amino acid and orotic acid measurements, molecular genetic testing (lab tests), and measuring enzyme (arginase) activity from a liver biopsy specimen or red blood cells. Treatments employ various methods for reducing the amount of ammonia in the blood or attenuating the effect of hyperammonemia, such as special diet, medication to assist in the excretion of ammonia, interventions aimed at reducing the risk of brain damage by hyperammonemia, and, in some cases, infant liver transplant. Research regarding treatment options, diagnostic methods, and diagnosis for newborns and children is ongoing. Gene therapy may be possible, an option which provokes some controversy within the consortium.

B. THE MEDICAL RESEARCH CONTEXT

The medical research context in which the RDCRCs are situated lies at the intersection of at least three background systems of laws, norms, and regulations. First, RDCRCs are situated in the medical environment. They involve patients, physicians, and other caregivers, invoking medical norms and practices guided in part by physicians' ethical duties toward their individual patients and toward their fellow physicians. Some of our physician interviewees suggested that the norms of the pediatrician community are particularly important to UCDC researchers' ability to collaborate successfully for the benefit of their patients. The medical environment also involves health insurance and healthcare regulation, including concerns with patient privacy and the costs of treatment.

Second, RDCRCs sit in the academic research environment. The consortia are funded by the NIH and the research mostly is performed at academic medical centers, which are governed by additional regulations and practices, including the requirements of their IRBs, which must approve all human subjects research. Academic research is both cooperative and competitive by nature. Practices regarding when and with whom to share data and results vary among academic disciplines.

Third, because RDCRCs seek to develop drugs and other medical treatments, they interact with the pharmaceutical environment, which includes the commercial sector, with its norms and practices of proprietary control of data and patenting of discoveries, and the regulatory regime of the Food and Drug Administration.

C. THE RARE DISEASE CONTEXT

The rare disease context involves a number of publicly and privately funded projects and organizations. It is importantly shaped by patient advocacy groups, which engage in political advocacy, education of physicians and patients, and research promotion and funding. Many patient advocacy groups, including the NUCDF, long preexist the NIH's establishment of the RDCRN.

Within the NIH, rare disease research is coordinated by the Office for Rare Diseases Research (ORDR), but funding comes from many of the NIH's twenty-five institutes and centers, each of which focuses on a particular field of disease research. Many other NIH initiatives also contribute to rare disease research. According to one of the ORDR officials we interviewed, ORDR recently has calculated that approximately 10 percent of NIH research spending, or about $5 billion, goes toward research on rare diseases, though only about $12 million of that funding is dedicated to clinical research.

D. THE RDCRN CONTEXT

The Rare Disease Act of 2002 mandated the establishment of "Rare Disease Regional Centers of Excellence."[2] The NIH responded to this mandate by creating the RDCRN in 2003. The RDCRN is funded by contributions from relevant NIH institutes and centers, along with direct funding from ORDR. Though there are thousands of rare diseases, funding is limited and RDCRN consortia cover only a small fraction of them. In 2003, ten RDCRCs were funded, along with a Data and Technology Coordinating Center (DTCC).[3] In a second round of funding in 2009, the NIH selected nineteen consortia,[4] including five of the original ten.[5] The DTCC was reconfigured and retitled DMCC at that time. Another round of proposals, peer review, and funding is scheduled for 2014.

1. RDCRN Goals and Objectives

The overarching goal of the RDCRN is to address obstacles that hamper clinical research in the rare disease context as a result of the small numbers and geographic dispersion of rare disease sufferers. The RDCRN thus is designed to promote research collaborations across multiple sites. Interviewee Stephen Groft, head of the NIH ORDR, explained the considerations that went into the design of the RDCRN:

> [W]e were facing a lot of perceptions about research on rare diseases. One, it couldn't be done; two, you couldn't get enough patients; three, you can't get researcher interest; and four, if you did, you could not get grants to do research on rare diseases.

---

[2] Rare Diseases Act of 2002, §§2(a)(6), 2(b)(1), 3 and 4. According to one interviewee, "The ideas of funding of creating consortia have been circulated amongst our [UCDC] community for a long time but nothing serious has happened until the RDCRN had been established."

[3] NIH Establishes Rare Diseases Clinical Research Network, NIH NEWS (Nov. 3, 2003), http://www.nih.gov/news/pr/nov2003/ncrr-03.htm.

[4] NIH Announces Expansion of Rare Diseases Clinical Research Network, NIH NEWS (Oct. 5, 2009), http://www.nih.gov/news/health/oct2009/od-05.htm.

[5] For a list of former RDCRCs, see https://rarediseasesnetwork.epi.usf.edu/about/rdcrn1.htm#bmfc.

So, we thought with a little bit of money...we get a critical mass of investigators together under one consortium from different sites around the country....We also want an active role for the patient advocacy group in a patient community because again we felt they were essential to whatever we do. We felt there's the tremendous need for a training component that we had to train the next group of investigators who got to get ready for it so that was a requirement. And then we had the requirement of natural history studies and we've realized that for most rare diseases...[w]e don't have good information and so [for the consortia we had the] requirement to do natural history studies. [A consortium also gives us] the potential to do clinical studies, clinical trials that if we discover a compound that...industry could contribute money for research studies. We would have the investigators on board. We'd have the patients on board ready to go....[T]o prepare the way to start these clinical trials, we needed to have this infrastructure in place, which we didn't have back in 2000.

Groft emphasized the importance of involving the entire rare disease community in the research:

[W]e call them rare diseases community because it involves everyone. [You] need all the partners working together to effect the best treatment and best care...[T]he group of urea cycle disorder [researchers]...had been able to affect the care even...before there were [pharmaceutical] interventions coming[.]...Even if you don't have an intervention, just getting that clinical picture, getting the clinicians, getting the nursing staff, the respiratory therapists, the physical therapists, all the partners together, all the specialists, they'll say, "What is the best thing for the patients with this disease? What's the best thing for this disease? How can we manage this better?...Why do some patients seem to be doing better? Is there a genetic mutation or genetic difference? [] What is this center or consortium site doing that this site may not be doing and how do we extend the knowledge from here to here to here then out to the entire community?" [Then] that knowledge of how best to treat the patients comes in to place. A lot of these thoughts were running through our minds as we [put] [the RDCRN] together....

These general ideas led to a set of specific objectives:
The purpose of each RDCRC is to facilitate clinical research in rare diseases through support for

- collaborative clinical research in rare diseases, including longitudinal studies of individuals with rare diseases, clinical studies and/or phase I, II and II/III trials;
- training of investigators in clinical research of rare diseases;
- pilot/demonstration projects; and

- access to information related to rare diseases for basic and clinical researchers, academic and practicing physicians, patients, and the lay public. (Website resource for education and research in rare diseases)[6]

The RDCRN seeks not only to develop treatments for the focal diseases of the funded consortia[7] but also to develop a shared body of knowledge and experience about the problems involved in rare disease clinical research and approaches to solving them. While the NIH thus views the RDCRCs partly as pilot programs exploring the effectiveness of the consortium approach, we did not uncover much evidence of inter-consortium sharing of methodologies and resources, with the exception of the DMCC. One interviewee suggested that perhaps there could and should be more "cross- fertilization" among consortia, but that it might be difficult to pull off without additional NIH support:

To be specific, they could, if they wished to, encourage neural imaging. Because many of these diseases affect brains especially the pediatric diseases. So the NIH could create and could invest in a series of neural imaging facilities that will furnish services at a subsidized cost to registrants or participants in each of these consortia. It could do the same in the world of genetics. It could consider, I don't know if it will work, creating tissue banks. It could offer expertise in experimental design. But so far it's not done that. It hasn't been invested in. Perhaps they think it's enough to just get Penn and Hopkins and Harvard on the same page.

2. RDCRN Structure

The basic structural components of the RDCRN, illustrated in Figure 5.1, are the individual consortia, the DMCC, a Coalition of Patient Advocacy Groups (CPAG), and various institutions with network-wide governance responsibilities. Grants for RDCRCs provide a maximum of $1.25 million per year over a five-year period and are intended to facilitate collaborative efforts beyond the small-scale collaborations typical of individual research projects. The NIH uses two basic mechanisms to try to ensure that RDCRCs meet NIH goals: mandating certain activities as a condition of funding and structuring the funding so as to ensure cooperation between researchers at different institutions.

The "request for applications" (RFAs) for RDCRC funding required that each consortium's proposed activities include the following components:

1. Clinical Research Projects for Observational/Longitudinal Studies and/or Clinical trials (At least two projects are required, *one of which must be a longitudinal study*)

---

[6] RDCRC Slides from March 17, 2008, preapplication meeting, http://rarediseases.info.nih.gov/asp/resources/extr_res_archived.asp.

[7] See, e.g., Conference, *Advancing Rare Diseases Research through Networks and Collaboration*, July 16, 2009), video available at http://videocast.nih.gov/summary.asp?live=7739.

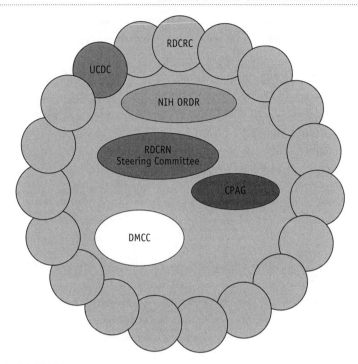

FIGURE 5.1 RDCRN Structure.

2. Pilot/Demonstration Projects (At least one project is required)
3. Training (career development) Component
4. Website resource for education and research in rare diseases
5. RDCRC Administrative Unit
6. Collaboration with Patient Advocacy Group[8]

The DMCC is an important central infrastructure for the RDCRN. All consortia have access to and are in some respects required to use the DMCC for data collection and management, website management, maintaining a patient registry, and various other functions, including audits of each site's compliance with data collection protocols. The DMCC has been housed at the University of South Florida since the initial funding round in 2003. The site was chosen via a peer review process similar to that used to select the consortia. We discuss the DMCC's role in more detail in the section on resources used by the UCDC.

RDCRC grants are implemented by the NIH's "U54" funding mechanism for Specialized Center–Cooperative Agreements, for which "[t]he spectrum of activities comprises a multidisciplinary attack on a specific disease entity or biomedical

---

[8] 2003 Request For Applications (RFA), http://grants.nih.gov/grants/guide/rfa-files/RFA-OD-08-001.html# SectionI (emphasis added).

problem area."[9] A key feature of the U mechanism is substantial programmatic interaction between the NIH and the grantee.[10] As one interviewee explained:

> Normally you have a single investigator doing an RO1 in a single institution, and there is no relationship to patient advocacy group or to pharmaceutical industry. But this U54 mechanism [collaborative research projects]...allows you to do team science in a broader sense. [The NIH Science Officer] is part of the group. She contributes scientifically, and she is our advocate in the NIH, which you don't normally have.... [The] combination of philanthropy, NIH, advocacy groups, and the pharmaceutical industry and then the team scientists and investigators is quite extraordinary for a single NIH grant.

Unlike the standard "R" funding mechanism for individual grants, U funding ensures cooperation between different institutions. As one principal investigator explained:

> [T]he advantage of a U is that they will force the different centers to cross-fertilize and cross-collaborate more, which is akin to the example of UCDC. Because what happens now is in [a differently funded consortium] the money goes to core laboratories in each center. What that means is everybody winds up with a genetic center and everybody winds up with a statistics center and it's inefficient. So the NIH insists upon centralization and more cross-fertilization in terms of access to clinical populations....

When asked why a special funding mechanism is needed to facilitate this kind of collaboration, the interviewee continued;

> Quite honestly the R [individual NIH grant] mechanism is inherently competitive. It disfavors collaboration because it goes to each center. It says here is a million dollars. Do with it what you want. There is no incentive to share populations or anything. It's the opposite because we know we are competing with one another for renewal so you want to be the best. There is no incentive to cooperate.... [Under the U mechanism], the measure of our success in NIH's eyes is our ability to realize a collaboration of major medical centers. Without that collaboration we fail.

---

[9] National Institutes of Health (NIH), Office of Extramural Research, Grants & Funding, Activity Codes Search Results, http://grants.nih.gov/grants/funding/ac_search_results.htm.

[10] National Institiutes of Health (NIH) Funding Mechanisms in the P and U series 2012, http://www.ospa.umn.edu/announcements/documents/NIHmechanismsSess12.pdf.

Each RDCRC must include at least one patient advocacy group. Currently, there are more than eighty-five patient advocacy groups associated with the RDCRN, which together form the CPAG. The NIH has not specified the extent or type of "collaboration" that individual consortia are to have with patient advocacy groups. ORDR director Groft told us that patient advocacy groups are "the hub of all activities related to rare disease" because "[t]hey touch everybody:" "the patients are so few and scattered many times and you have some group that coordinat[es] that patient aspect. You also need them to bring in the scientific and medical experts and the other medical advisory boards and technical advisory boards." Groft also noted that patient advocacy groups are crucial "research partners" who contribute, among other things, to understanding and communicating rare disease patients' "willingness to accept risk" in medical research "because for many diseases, there are no treatments and there's a very, very low hope of survival over X number of years."

Groft further expounded on the importance of patient advocacy groups to consortium success:

> For the most part, I would say the successful consortia are the ones who have a good working relationship with the patient advocacy group. Their staffs are responsive to the patients and the families. They have a way to answer questions when [they] come[] in. They share information and extend information out to everyone and so I think that's one of the keys. I mean, there are a lot [of] keys we can click on depending on what we're talking about but it's a sharing of information and knowledge so that people—families and patients—know how to respond if a situation develops. As the disease moves forward, they know how to respond if something starts happening. I think it's part of what we're trying to do, too: build up that knowledge about the disease and how to treat it so that as the disease progressed, the whole community would know and here's what we have to do to address this complication that's occurring.

Another NIH official noted that the relationships between patient advocacy groups and the research communities vary considerably across consortia. We discuss the relationship between the UCDC and the NUCDF below.

The RDCRN is governed by a Steering Committee composed of the CPIs, the principal investigator (PI) of the DMCC, representatives from the NIH's in-house scientific staff and the ORDR, and the chair of the CPAG. Research protocols for all consortia are overseen by an NIH-established Protocol Review Committee (PRC), which "provides in depth scientific review of protocols developed by the consortia," and a Data and Safety Monitoring Board (DSMB), which "monitors study protocols, ensures the safety of study participants and the integrity of studies" (Seminara et al. 2010).

IV. UCDC History, Goals, and Objectives

The UCDC is one among many RDCRCs and necessarily shares characteristics with other RDCRN consortia. The UCDC is also a very particular organization, with its own history and community. In this part, we discuss the UCDC's goals and objectives, which are reflected in its significant action arenas. We then briefly describe the UCDC's history.

A. UCDC GOALS AND OBJECTIVES

To understand a knowledge commons such as the UCDC, we must understand its goals and objectives. The makeup of a knowledge commons, the resources it creates and employs, and its governance structure all tend to be centered on its goals and objectives. The UCDC's goals and objectives generate specific action arenas, which in turn generate a need for governance. Meeting UCDC objectives requires cooperative efforts among UCDC members, who may differ as to how best to accomplish those objectives, how to apportion responsibility and credit, and so forth. Moreover, constraints on funding, time, and attention mean that the UCDC must prioritize and make trade-offs between efforts addressed to the various objectives. The determination and updating of goals and objectives is itself an action arena, for which formal or informal decision-making procedures are needed. The group's goals and objectives also provide metrics for assessing success. The UCDC's Mission Statement explains that:

> The Urea Cycle Disorders Consortium is a group of health care professionals and researchers dedicated to improving the lives of patients with urea cycle disorders.... The UCDC strives to provide current and useful information on urea cycle disorders to health care professionals and families. The Consortium is also dedicated to research in clinical and scientific issues in urea cycle disorders. To better understand the nature of these diseases, the Consortium has established a National Registry for patients, and is conducting long-term studies on the outcome of patients with urea cycle disorders. The Consortium also has laboratory researchers working to develop new treatments and new understandings for urea cycle disorders. With better understanding of these diseases, we hope to improve the future for our patients and their families.

Our interviews, survey, and document review all suggest that UCDC members are focused on the substantive goal of treating patients with urea cycle disorders, while meta-questions of how to conduct rare disease research play a decidedly secondary role. Nonetheless, NIH requirements and the specific challenges of rare disease research necessarily influence the UCDC's approach. As a result, the overarching goal of patient treatment is resolved into five main objectives: (1) creating a pool of research subjects and patient data; (2) sustaining and growing a community of researchers with expertise and interest in urea cycle disorders; (3) promoting knowledge and idea sharing within the community; (4) cooperating with patients in framing research and disseminating research results to patients; and (5) translating research into treatments by interacting with pharmaceutical companies. We consider each of these objectives in turn.

1. Creating a Pool of Research Subjects and Patient Data

The primary action arena through which the UCDC pursues its goal of creating a pool of research subjects and data is the *longitudinal study of patients with urea cycle disorders*, which tracks various biological, mental, and behavioral indicators of how the disorders affect patients over time. Longitudinal study data collected at various UCDC sites is pooled using the data management facilities of the DMCC. Data from the longitudinal study may be used in several distinct ways. It may be mined to obtain better understanding of the disorders,[11] used to identify and characterize participants for research studies involving further patient testing or intervention, or used to reduce the costs and increase the efficiency of clinical trials of pharmaceuticals or other treatments.

All UCDC sites take part in the longitudinal study, which is the activity that most closely binds UCDC members. Nearly 90 percent of our survey respondents were actively involved in the longitudinal study in some fashion. Though the longitudinal study is required by the NIH, its importance is enthusiastically endorsed by UCDC members. For example, nearly 80 percent of survey respondents agreed or strongly agreed (and none disagreed) that every rare disease research consortium should conduct a longitudinal study, while more than half agreed or strongly agreed that the longitudinal study is the UCDC's most important project. Indeed, the UCDC's growth over its ten-year existence seems to have been organized for the most part around adding clinical sites so as to obtain larger numbers of patient participants in the longitudinal study.

2. Sustaining and Growing a Community of Researchers with Expertise and Interest in Urea Cycle Disorders

The rarity of the UCDs means limited funding for research and some degree of isolation for researchers. Even the most involved UCD researchers spend only part of their time studying UCDs and treating UCD patients. UCDC leaders are quite cognizant of the need to sustain the research community as some of the pioneers approach retirement age. Researchers may be drawn to particular research topics by various factors, including the availability of funding, the sense of excitement afforded by participation in cutting-edge

---

[11] See, e.g., Ah Mew, N., Krivitzky, L., McCarter, R., Batshaw, M., & Tuchman, M; Urea Cycle Disorders Consortium of the Rare Diseases Clinical Research Network, *Clinical Outcomes of Neonatal Onset Proximal versus Distal Urea Cycle Disorders Do Not Differ*, 162 J. PEDIATRICS 324 (2013); Morgan, T. M., Schlegel, C., Edwards, K. M., et al., *Vaccines Are Not Associated with Metabolic Events in Children with Urea Cycle Disorders*, 127 PEDIATRICS 1147 (2011).

research, the support and mentorship available from a particular research community, and the perception that a particular research area has the potential to lead to a successful and fulfilling career. Long-time UCD researcher interviewees discussed the importance of providing mentoring, training, and pilot funding to new UCD researchers. While pilot funding and research fellowships are most clearly directed toward new UCD researchers, other UCD activities, such as monthly telephone conferences and annual face-to-face meetings, are intended in part to promote a sense of community and inclusiveness among UCDC members.

Sustaining a growing community of UCD researchers presents a variety of challenges, ranging from obtaining and managing additional funding to dealing with the logistics of organizing face-to-face meeting and teleconferences for a growing number of participants to maintaining a collaborative culture within an increasingly large and dispersed community.

3. Promoting Knowledge and Idea Sharing within the Community

Sharing knowledge and ideas internally is one of the most basic reasons to form a research consortium. In the ordinary course, informal knowledge sharing is most likely between researchers at the same institution, between collaborators, and at conferences and workshops that bring researchers together. The challenge for the UCDC is to provide structures and an atmosphere that promotes informal sharing of knowledge and ideas among a group of widely dispersed researchers, study coordinators, and others, only some of whom know each other well.

4. Cooperating with Patients in Setting Research Objectives, and Communicating Research Results to Patients

Several of our interviewees discussed the importance of involving patients as research partners in the consortium's activities. Several UCDC structures and activities are focused on this objective. Probably most importantly, the executive director of the NUCDF participates in many of the UCDC's decision-making processes. UCDC researchers also serve on the NUCDF's advisory board and participate in an annual NUCDF meeting, at which they update patients on research and treatments, answer questions, and socialize informally with patient attendees. Many interviewees also emphasized how their clinical relationships with patients and their families, especially as pediatricians, motivated and shaped their research.

5. Translating Research into Treatments through Interactions with Pharmaceutical Companies

In general, UCDC members are focused on bringing treatments to patients, a goal for which pharmaceutical company interactions are essential. Indeed, interactions with pharmaceutical companies are growing in importance to the UCDC as its research progresses. Involvement with pharmaceutical companies also is mandated implicitly by the NIH's inclusion of phase II and phase III clinical trials among the RDCRN's goals. Cooperation with pharmaceutical companies raises a variety of issues for a consortium such as the UCDC, including issues of intellectual property policy, conflicts of interest, and treatment costs.

B. UCDC HISTORY

The UCDC has its roots in a community of collaborators that preexisted the RDCRN's establishment in 2003. As Mendel Tuchman, one of the three CPIs, described it, "Our cohesive group was formed way before the Rare Diseases Clinical Research Center." Similarly, when asked whether he has "previously collaborated with other members of the UCDC," another CPI, Marshall Summar, replied: "Absolutely, since the 1980s. Mendel and others, we [had] been working together for over 10 years. It's a very collegial community."[12]

Several current UCDC CPIs and SPIs spearheaded an effort to develop standardized treatment guidelines for UCDs several years before the establishment of the RDCRN. A "consensus conference" held in 2000 resulted in a series of treatment protocols and documents describing what then was the state of the art. Those consensus guidelines, which have been updated in subsequent years, have been very important for treatment of

---

[12] One important incident, though not described by our interviewees as having a direct impact on the UCDC's governance, occurred during the time the UCDC was being established. In 1999, Dr. Batshaw was associated with a highly publicized tragedy in urea cycle disorder research. Jesse Gelsinger, a UCD patient with ornithine transcarbamylase deficiency, died during a gene transfer trial conducted at the University of Pennsylvania by Batshaw in collaboration with Drs. Steve Raper and James Wilson. The FDA immediately began an investigation. Jesse's family later filed a lawsuit against those involved. The family's suit settled almost immediately in 2000. Charges stemming from the government investigations were finally settled in 2005. The most serious sanctions stemmed from conflict of interest allegations against Wilson, who had financial interests in a gene therapy company with connections to the trial. Batshaw and Raper agreed to a three-year period of restrictions on their human subjects research and to various forms of supervision and oversight. The *Gelsinger* case is discussed regularly in health law and bioethics classes and was one impetus for a series of institutional changes in the regulation of gene transfer trials and of human subjects research more generally during the early 2000s. See, e.g., Johnson et al. 2009: ch. 11; Steinbrook 2008.

None of our interviewees mentioned the *Gelsinger* case as a significant factor in UCDC structure and governance, except in relation to the UCDC's reluctance, thus far, to engage in gene therapy research. (Batshaw continues to conduct NIH-funded gene-therapy related research outside of the UCDC framework.) To probe more deeply, after some readers of a draft of this chapter asked about the apparent absence of impact, we conducted follow-up interviews of Mark Batshaw, Marshall Summar, Stephen Groft, and Jennifer Seminara. Seminara's observations are particularly relevant because her initial interactions with Batshaw were in an oversight capacity during the monitoring period required by the settlement. We did not uncover any significant impact of the *Gelsinger* case on the structure and governance of the UCDC in particular, which is the focus of this study. In part, this is because the changes in the oversight and conduct of human subjects research that the tragedy inspired have become part of the background environment at the NIH and in the researchers' universities in which the UCDC operates. It is, of course, possible that there are effects that our interviewees did not share with us or of which they themselves are unaware. Having done only this single case study so far, we cannot comment on how likely it is that our study missed any such effects.

UCDs. The 2000 conference also was an important precursor to the RDCRN. UCDC CPI Marshall Summar explained the connection:

> The nucleus of the idea came in 2000. A company acquired a main drug in our field and asked around different centers what they should do. We decided to have those consensus conferences because there was no industry protocol at that time and no one had come up with a consensus protocol. Mendel had this idea and it...was a great success. When the RDCRN came into being three years later, Mark [Batshaw] said that this was obviously the way to put all these groups together. [E]veryone had their own recipe until we got together and pulled all the information together. Some of it was guess work. We wanted to set a baseline. This doesn't mean that it can't be modified. The idea "once you get it down in writing you can't deviate from it" is actually not the way to do it. We got the idea that longitudinal study would be useful. I spoke with someone at NIH and several years later, it worked. We were so far ahead at that point being used to working together that Mark wrote grants. That's one of the reasons ours was the top scoring grant among the initial grants.

As the informal collaboration of UCDC researchers has become formalized into the UCDC, the original group of researchers has remained deeply involved, as explained by CPI Mark Batshaw:

> All the people who were there at the beginning are still there. There is very little turnover over the years. But we have been able to add people. The nice part about that is we now have three generations of investigators. I am the grey-haired in his 60s; Marshall Summar is a less grey-haired in his 50s. And we have junior investigators who are 35–40 to carry this on. So it's really important.

Since its establishment in 2003, the UCDC has grown substantially. At its inception, the UCDC involved ten investigators at five clinical research institutions. By 2009, it had grown to "43 faculty investigators and 26 research staff members" (Seminara et al. 2010). Today, there are fifteen sites, twelve dispersed throughout the United States, one in Canada, and two in Europe.

One interviewee described this growth:

> So as we have started with these five sites that we got a terrific score and we got funded, we started adding soon thereafter other sites because we quickly realized that we have to have a geographic coverage of most of the United States in order to be effective because these diseases are distributed all over the country and patients have a hard time traveling, right? So you don't expect somebody to come frequently flying from California to for example Tennessee or something like that.

So we wanted to make sure that we have coverage, and the only way to have coverage with respect to having patient access these sites would be to have them in as many places.

The UCDC's expansion beyond the original five sites has meant the inclusion of researchers who are less focused on UCDs. As Tuchman explained:

[Some of the more recently added sites] have a general interest, not a specific interest. They had patients with these disorders at their location, but they didn't do primary research in these disorders. But nevertheless, they have agreed [to participate] because of the need of the patients who joined this consortium. And so they have basically collaborated with us on executing the studies that we have.

V. UCDC Community Members and Their Roles

The UCDC includes fifteen dispersed clinical sites. Consortium-wide leadership is provided by three CPIs and a Program Manager. The programmatic NIH involvement central to the U funding mechanism is provided by a science officer and a program officer. The NUCDF and its director are critical participants in the UCDC. The UCDC also interacts with the DMCC and with several pharmaceutical companies.

A. UCDC CONSORTIUM-WIDE LEADERSHIP

The UCDC's central leadership team, located at Children's National Medical Center (CNMC) in Washington, D.C., is composed of CPIs Mark Batshaw, Mendel Tuchman, and Marshall Summar, all of whom are physician researchers, and Program Manager Jennifer Seminara, MPH. The CPIs take primary responsibility for the overall scientific direction of the consortium and for grant-writing and fundraising. They also lead and manage the consortium in other ways, discussed in the section on governance below. Program Manager Seminara participates in consortium decision making at a high level and has overall administrative responsibility. She also plays a particularly important role in training and managing the study coordinators at UCDC clinical research sites.

All three CPIs are well-established and well-funded researchers, with significant additional responsibilities at CNMC and long-standing relationships with the NIH. Dr. Batshaw has been the UCDC's project director since its inception and is its acknowledged leader. He is a pioneer (indeed, "the" pioneer) in urea cycle disorder research. Drs. Tuchman and Summar are part of the core group of researchers who started the UCDC and both were heavily involved in the 2000 UCDC consensus conference. Summar was SPI at the UCDC's Vanderbilt University site before moving to CNMC.

B. PARTICIPANTS AT UCDC CLINICAL RESEARCH SITES

The UCDC today is composed of fifteen clinical research sites. As explained in Seminara et al. 2010, "each consortium site is led by a principal investigator, who is a board-certified metabolic specialist, with a team consisting of a study coordinator, a neuropsychologist, and at some sites a co-investigator, research fellow, and/or nutritionist."

1. SPIs

The PI for each UCDC research site has overall responsibility for UCDC research performed at the site and provides scientific direction for the site's UCDC-related research. All UCDC SPIs are medical doctors and some also have PhDs. According to our survey, about half had performed UCD research before joining the UCDC, while 75 percent had performed research on closely related subjects. In addition, 80 percent of SPIs had treated UCD patients clinically before joining the UCDC. Of about a dozen potential motivations for joining the UCDC, top choices of PI survey respondents were interest in researching UCDs, metabolic disorders, or rare diseases generally and desire to participate in a research community. SPIs are for the most part highly published. Nearly three-quarters of PI survey respondents reported more than fifty publications. Most have published about UCDs, though only 40 percent had more than twenty publications focusing on UCDs, while 20 percent had three or fewer UCD publications. Though all SPI respondents had co-authored with other UCDC members, most reported that only about a quarter of their publications were co-authored with other UCDC members.

Our survey responses reflect the extent to which the UCDC has grown out of preexisting relationships between PIs. All fifteen PI respondents reported some type of prior relationship with another UCDC member, with about half of PIs reporting prior personal friendship and/or collaboration. Nearly all were professionally acquainted with other UCDC members before joining.

2. Site Study Coordinators

Study coordinators at the clinical research sites are critically important to UCDC activities. One UCDC leader went so far as to say that "[t]he key to the success is the site coordinators, not the doctors" and that "[s]tudy coordinators are the guts of this thing, without whom nothing happens." Study coordinators are centrally involved in recruiting patients and have major responsibilities for patient contact, arranging appointments, following up with patients about participation in the longitudinal study, and so forth. Nearly half of survey respondents agreed that "patient recruitment is primarily the responsibility of site coordinators," while more than half agreed that "making sure that patients continue participating in the longitudinal study is primarily the responsibility of site coordinators." Study coordinators also are responsible for ensuring that data are entered into the DMCC databases correctly, completely, and in accordance with DMCC protocols, obtaining informed consent and otherwise ensuring IRB compliance at their study sites, and handling general administrative duties.

Study coordinators tend to be relatively young, most are female, and their professional backgrounds include genetic counseling, public health, and nursing. About half of site coordinator survey respondents had previous experience in medical research. Less than a third reported any kind of relationship with another UCDC member before joining the UCDC, with few of those reporting anything other than professional acquaintance. While interest in metabolic disorders and in participating in a research community were important to study coordinator decisions to join the UCDC, the top factors selected were "UCDC activities are part of my job responsibilities" and "I was recruited to work on the longitudinal study." Most, but not all, study coordinators reported few or no publications.

3. Other Researchers and Clinicians

As noted in the quote above, at many sites non-PI researchers and clinicians are involved in UCDC research. Some are PhD scientists, some are MDs, and some have other relevant degrees. Most of the UCDC's MD researchers specialize in pediatrics and are experts in metabolic disorders generally or in genetics. Some non-PI researchers are graduate students or postdoctoral researchers, while others are more established. Clinicians are involved in various aspects of UCDC activities. For example, testing by neuropsychologists is an important part of the longitudinal study. Because diet is a central aspect of UCD treatment, nutritionists and dieticians are involved. Because UCDs are genetically triggered, genetic counselors also are important members of the healthcare teams at UCDC sites.

C. NIH REPRESENTATIVES

The UCDC interacts closely with two NIH officials, a program officer, and a scientific officer, as required by the U54 grant mechanism. Both work with multiple consortia. The scientific officer is effectively "embedded" in the research community, participating in monthly telephone calls, helping to develop research protocols, and even assisting with grant proposals. One PI interviewee explained:

> When I tell you we have a monthly phone conference, there is an NIH person who is on the phone and she is a participant. So there is an ongoing relationship with them. They are part of the project.... [The scientific officer participates] in every sense. In other words, they have the right to voice an opinion. And actually we often solicit their advice. Again, these are people whom we've known for a long time. It's an enabling relationship, not paternalistic or adversarial. They are part of the group.

The program officer's role focuses mostly on administrative oversight, though it also involves assisting the consortium with its interactions with the NIH. The program officer gives the "official [] approval for protocols." As the UCDC's program officer explained:

> They say they are going to go ahead and do this. This is the plan, but then they have to submit a detailed protocol…that has a description of what they're going to do, how much blood they're going to take, or what they're going to give the patient or whatever, and then they also have to submit the consent forms because to me, that's really important. It is what they do to the patient or get from the patient or ask the patient or test with the patient, and then how they explain what is the risk, can it be done, and what have they told the patient as an educated lay person, would I be able to understand, and do the patients understand whatever risk there may be to them and are they willing to do that.… [U]sually, I'll have questions and so it goes back and they respond and until I'm completely comfortable with the fact that they're not asking too much from the patient. Then I approve it. It gets the NIH watermark and then it goes to the IRBs and their institutions.

The program officer emphasized that in reviewing protocols she considers ethical issues and feels responsible "for making sure the patient's perspective is taken into account."

The program officer also assists junior researchers in attempting to obtain individual NIH grants of their own:

> I've interacted with some of the more junior investigators to look and to discuss with them their grant applications. I see my role as sort of oversight for the consortium, but also a mentor for the more junior investigators.… [S]ome of them will turn to me and I'll talk to them and help them both with the administrative ways of getting things coming in to the NIH and submitting a grant and those kinds of administrative issues. I will take a look at their grant. If they send it to me, I'll review it and see if it's structured correctly. I do this for all. It's not just for UCDC.

D. THE NUCDF PATIENT ADVOCACY GROUP

The UCDC collaborates with a single patient advocacy group, the NUCDF, which undertakes a wide range of activities, including education, research, fundraising, and organizing support groups. Both the NUCDF and its relationship with many of the UCDC's PIs predate the RDCRN. Currently seven out of nine members of the NUCDF's Medical Advisory Board are UCDC PIs. The NUCDF reaches out to patients to inform them about clinical research studies and hosts an annual conference for patients, families, healthcare professionals, and researchers. The NUCDF's website (which is independent of the UCDC's public website) summarizes research results for patients and contains information about ongoing UCDC studies and patient registries.

Pharmaceutical company clinical trials also are listed on the NUCDF's website. Though not performed under UCDC auspices, these trials often are offshoots of research by UCDC members. NUCDF also helps match patients to UCDC sites that will fit their needs. As NUCDF's executive director, Cynthia Le Mons explained: "It's almost like a personality match sometimes to make sure [patients] are going to communicat[e] with someone who is [] going to be able to help them."

NUCDF executive director Le Mons is a voting member of the Steering Committee of the UCDC. Primarily through her involvement, NUCDF has a role in a wide range of UCDC activities and decisions, including setting the research agenda, designing the longitudinal study, developing study protocols, and deciding whether to add new clinical sites to the UCDC. As one of the NIH officials explained, "Don't forget that the patient advocacy groups are on every call, on a monthly call, and their comments are solicited.... Cindy is extremely involved and her point of view is solicited and listened to."

Interviewees stressed the importance of Cindy Le Mons's leadership in facilitating effective interactions between the UCDC and the NUCDF. As one researcher explained:

Fortunately for us, by the way, the patient parent group is very well organized. The NUCDF, the credit to that belongs really to Cynthia Le Mons []. She made it her lifetime work to advocate for these children and provide support to these families. She's been very successful.

The UCDC's NIH program officer also noted that "leadership personality" is important to the success of a patient advocacy group:

You've met Cindy and so you know that she will speak her mind and she will speak for the needs of the patients and the different concerns and issues that they have, and actually she is right on target because if patients complain, they know their illness, what they're feeling, etc., really, really well. And so if there is enough noise, there must be a reason for it and you listen to it and you begin to examine so that's why this was just a fantastic idea when it was established. And so the urea cycle has been particularly successful in harnessing the families, the researchers both the M.D. types and also the Ph.D. types, all of your other clinical personnel, and the companies.

Annual joint meetings between the UCDC and NUCDF facilitate relationships between researchers and patients. As one PI explained: "When we do meet, we make an effort to meet in concert with the patient group. So I've actually become friendly with families not only in Philly but also in LA.... When we have the Philadelphia meeting, the social part was in my home, not just here at the institution. The association is very gratifying for both sides."

A site coordinator interviewee noted other ways in which the NUCDF helps to bridge the gap between patients and physicians, while at the same time hinting at some tensions that can arise between researchers and patient advocacy groups:

I talk to [NUCDF executive director] Cindy fairly frequently. If I have a patient whom I am unable to help I reach out to her. I usually give out information to new families, information about our conference. [The patient advocacy group] is good and bad. It's generally good to have other patients who are going through the same thing. It's really good for the kids, I think, to meet other kids who are like them. The bad is the discussions that happen regarding medical things amongst themselves instead of talking to doctors, as with any other internet thing, which is going to happen. They have groups and forums and whatever and they talk about "oh you should try this and this." It would be better for you to call your doctors and nutritionists than asking these other moms who may have a completely different situation or what have you. If you hear those things, I still think going back to the doctors or nutritionists is the right thing to do....I think Cindy generally makes sure that people talk to the doctors. I think it's hard to put her in such a position that she can help fix everything. But generally she encourages them to go see the doctors and succeeds in doing that.

Finally, at least one interviewee believed that the NUCDF's involvement had been important to the UCDC's selection as an RDCRN consortium:

I think the presence of that advocacy group made it a certainty that we would be included as a consortium. Because let's face it. NIH is sensitive to public pressure. Here you have a very articulate and forceful advocacy group who insisted that their children get a hearing.

E. PHARMACEUTICAL COMPANY REPRESENTATIVES

While pharmaceutical company representatives are not members of the UCDC, they are important enough to UCDC activities to warrant discussion here. It was our expectation going into the study that there would be little interest from pharmaceutical companies in developing treatments for these rare diseases. The UCDC, however, is cooperating with six different pharmaceutical companies working on UCD treatments. When asked about the reason for pharmaceutical company interest in developing treatments for diseases with such a small number of patients, many of our interviewees emphasized the importance of the fact that the UCDC, through its longitudinal study, has data on a large number of potential research subjects, cutting the costs of clinical trials.

These are not "Big Pharma" companies, but smaller companies focusing on rare and orphan diseases. These specialized companies are much more integrated into the rare disease community than would be likely for a large pharmaceutical company focusing on more prevalent diseases. For example, representatives from these companies attended both days of the annual conference and gave presentations at the research workshop. At least some of these specialized pharmaceutical companies have been involved with the UCDC from close to its inception. As one pharmaceutical company representative explained:

> I don't know when we [Orphan Europe] started collaborating with [the UCDC] but it's probably not from inception but very close. [For the study of UCD drug] Carbaglu…we've always collaborated with [the PI] for the development and marketing approvals specifically in the U.S. He has accompanied us for the approval in the U.S. which we actually got approved based on the European data. We want to develop Carbaglu into other indications that are also urea cycle disorders so we're doing this study together where [the PI] does the study and we provide the study drug and we provide some financing. So we've always been present at the consortium meetings. Scientifically, we leave them alone pretty much. I mean of course with this trial because it's [an] improved [drug], we want to use [the data] for the approval afterwards. There has been some back and forth on the timing of the whole thing on what data you could use when for approval.

VI. Resources Used, Generated, Shared, and Disseminated by the UCDC

The UCDC uses, generates, shares, and disseminates a variety of resources, most of which it must manage in some way. This section describes many of these resources and identifies challenges and social dilemmas involved in their creation, use, sharing, and/or dissemination.[13] To organize our discussion we have divided the resources into four categories: (1) resources obtained from outside sources; 2) resources generated by the UCDC primarily for internal use; (3) resources generated by the UCDC for both internal and external use; and (4) resources generated primarily for external use. These categories are somewhat blurry. In part, this is because of the nonrivalrous nature of many of the resources, which means that it is possible to provide external access to them even if

---

[13] In analyzing the resources generated and used by the UCDC, we began by making as comprehensive a list as possible. We then analyzed the ways in which various resources were used to pursue particular UCDC objectives. We found it helpful to distinguish resources along various axes: (1) level at which the resource is shared (i.e., across medical research generally, across rare disease researchers generally, across the RDCRN generally, within the UCDC, etc.); (2) locus of generation (e.g., outside of the UCDC or within the UCDC); (3) locus of use (e.g., outside of the UCDC, within the UCDC, or both). We then narrowed the list to those discussed here, which our study suggests are most important to UCDC objectives. This preliminary step was critical, as scrutinizing a wider list of resources helped us to move beyond preconceived notions based on more traditional research contexts.

they were generated for internal use. In part, it is because some of the UCDC's activities require collaboration with outsiders. It is also possible for resources to migrate from one category to another, particularly if external uses grow in importance over time.

A. RESOURCES OBTAINED FROM OUTSIDE THE UCDC

1. Research Funding

The UCDC obtains research funding from the NIH and from private donors. Many of its researchers also have individual grants that support UCD or related research. Importantly, the amount of funding distributed through the RDCRN U54 grants is relatively small—only about $1.25 million per year per consortium. As an interviewee explained, "The RDCRN funding is essential but not sufficient." Philanthropic funding, much of which comes from a few donors with family members suffering from UCDs, accounts for a proportion of UCDC funding on a par with NIH funding. The NUCDF also raises money for the UCDC. As one of the site PIs explained:

> There are families who will raise money for us. By the way that's not only for UCDs but for many [rare disease research activities]. We must be getting 50–100K a year, very moving, from families who organize bake sales, from marathon racers to help us do our research. I can't tell you it [] compare[s] with the millions of dollars from NIH but it plays a role and does help to support [young researchers especially]. On an emotional level that's very gratifying.... We meet these people once a year in July...and it's a very important morale boosting event.

Pharmaceutical companies also "supplement the funding of the government and the philanthropy" in various ways. The relationship with these companies is complicated, as it is in medical research generally, by concerns about conflicts of interest. Therefore, companies do not provide research funding directly to the UCDC. Some of the senior PIs consult with the pharmaceutical companies and, in accordance with conflict of interest policies, fees are returned to the UCDC general coffers. Pharmaceutical companies also support clinical trials stemming from UCDC research by donating the drugs being tested and other support services.

The UCDC deploys its funding in three primary ways, all of which are closely connected to the goals and objectives identified above. First, each research site is allocated funding for its participation in the longitudinal study, which pays for the time of study coordinators, neuropsychologists, and other clinicians involved in the study, among other things. Second, UCDC funding supports certain central consortium functions, such as the project manager, annual meetings, biostatistics support, and so forth. Third, the UCDC funds a few pilot projects intended, as one interviewee explained, to support "new program project development...to specifically enable research by younger people because younger people with no track record have a lot of trouble getting grants at NIH." UCDC pilot funding advances the goal of recruiting more researchers into UCD research not only directly but also because researchers hope that UCDC participation will serve as a "springboard for future research funding." Indeed, that possibility motivated many researchers to join the UCDC. Nearly 60 percent of PIs and about 30 percent of other researchers responding to our survey rated this factor "very important" or "essential" to their decision to join.

Because funding is limited, the UCDC faces challenges in allocating it among sites, researchers, and uses. Funding limitations also drive decisions about whether to add new clinical sites and continue to fund existing ones.

2. DMCC Services

The RDCRN's DMCC provides a number of resources to the UCDC, including a central repository of study data for the consortium's geographically dispersed sites; support for data analysis and biostatistics, enforcement; and auditing services for data collection protocols, assistance with the creation and structuring of data collection protocols, training and assistance for study coordinators, assistance with the human subjects research requirements of IRBs, and a patient contact registry.

The DMCC also maintains an online registry of patients who might be interested in participating in research studies. Based on our literature review, we expected that the DMCC Patient Registry would be a very important resource for patient recruitment. However, multiple interviewees told us that the DMCC patient registry has played a rather minor role in patient recruitment. As one interviewee explained to us, "only 14% of our patients actually came through the [DMCC] registry." On average, survey respondents gave the DMCC patient registry about the same ranking, somewhat below "important," that they gave to IRB compliance assistance.

Interviewees varied in their conjectures about why the DMCC patient registry had not worked very well for the UCDC thus far. The initial design of the registry relied on notifying patients by e-mail about relevant studies, but did not permit researchers to contact patients directly. According to one interviewee, that approach was premised on an overly restrictive interpretation of the Health Insurance Portability and Accountability Act (HIPAA) privacy regulations. In an attempt to improve its effectiveness, the DMCC's patient registry procedure was modified to permit patients to give researchers permission to contact them directly about studies.[14] However, that option was not endorsed by the NUCDF. At one point, its website stated:

> At the end of registration, you may consent to allow a researcher or institutional representative to contact you directly, which may result in outside access by third

---

[14] Https://rarediseasesnetwork.epi.usf.edu/rdnwebapp/registry/RDCRNRegistryConsent.aspx?OwnerId=11&DiseaseType=1, accessed Aug. 15, 2013.

parties to your contact information. NUCDF recommends you do not give consent to release your contact information.[15]

Currently, the NUCDF website does not mention the DMCC patient registry, referring patients to the UCD International Patient Registry,[16] which promises that "[t]he Registry will not release your name to the researcher."[17]

The DMCC also performs various other information technology functions. For example, it maintains a members-only web-based e-mail communication platform and document repository and public-facing websites for the RDCRN and for each individual consortium.

B. RESOURCES GENERATED PRIMARILY FOR INTERNAL USE

1. Pool of Research Participants and Data about Them

As already discussed, creating a pool of research participants and data about them is one of the UCDC's most important overarching objectives. Creating this resource is a cooperative effort involving patients, UCDC researchers, study coordinators and clinicians, and the DMCC. The longitudinal study is the most important part of this effort. It is the primary source of the data in the common pool and is also the main way in which patients become involved in UCDC research. The longitudinal study tracks many indicators—biological, mental, and behavioral—of how the disorders affect patients. As explained by one of the SPIs:

> The data includes biochemical markers (ammonia and amino acids and so forth) and it includes demographic information (age, height, weight and so forth), and it includes neuropsychological profile of the child. The funding provides that each kid enrolled undergoes a very detailed series of tests that can take as long as six hours depending on the child's age. We identify IQ and specific areas of weakness, difficulties in spatial relationships or mathematics. They have emotional problems, anger, hostility and all sorts of things. All of that is resident and deposited in the databank in South Florida.

To generate a pool of research participants and patient data, the UCDC must overcome challenges in three main areas: patient participation, researcher cooperation, and data aggregation and management. The UCDC also must manage internal use of the

---

[15] See Internet Archive, http://www.nucdf.org/research.htm, version of March 24, 2013, http://web.archive.org/web/20130324103130/ and http://www.nucdf.org/research.htm.

[16] Http://www.nucdf.org/research.htm, accessed Aug. 15, 2013.

[17] Https://ucdparegistry.patientcrossroads.org/index.php?option=com_comprofiler&task=registers&pid=1&lang=en, accessed Aug. 15, 2013.

pooled data and determine whether and under what circumstances to make the data available to external users (including those in the private sector). Sharing data with outsiders, especially for-profit companies, raises issues of informed consent and patient privacy.

2. Human Capital and Tacit Knowledge

The purpose of attracting additional researchers to the UCDC is to create a growing pool of human capital focused on UCD research. UCDC members contribute and continually generate important human capital, in the form of knowledge about and skills related to many aspects of rare disease research, which includes specialized medical and scientific knowledge, knowledge about and skills in methodologies for dealing with the particular challenges of rare disease research, clinical knowledge and skills, knowledge about and skills in interacting with patients and their families, and so forth. As the UCDC grows and new researchers, site coordinators, and clinicians are brought on board, the UCDC must pass on this knowledge, some of which is, and is likely to remain, tacit. As already discussed, the NIH requires each consortium to have a plan for training young investigators. Researchers are only one part of the picture, however. Site coordinators are critical in obtaining patient participation over time and in ensuring the accuracy and standardization of the UCDC's pool of patient data. Training study coordinators is a challenge that the NIH framework does not address. The UCDC appears to have recognized the importance of this challenge, however, and recently has appointed one of its experienced site study coordinators to head up study coordinator training.

C. RESOURCES GENERATED BY THE UCDC FOR BOTH INTERNAL AND EXTERNAL USE

1. Knowledge and Ideas about Research, Treatment, Clinical Trials, and Other Related Subjects

Knowledge and ideas are the lifeblood of all scientific and medical research; indeed, generating them essentially defines research. A wide variety of knowledge and ideas generated by UCDC activities are important resources for internal use in ongoing consortium activities. Some of the knowledge and ideas generated by the UCDC also are intended to be disseminated to outsiders, including outside researchers, treating physicians, and patients, in the guise of "research results." Individual researchers will, of course, share some knowledge informally with colleagues and associates outside of the UCDC. Before being disseminated more widely, research results are reviewed and validated internally and generally are codified and translated into publications, treatment guidelines, research reports, newsletters, and the like intended for particular types of audiences.

Examples of such codified forms of knowledge are scientific publications and treatment guidelines for physicians. The UCDC website lists seven scientific articles stemming from the longitudinal study, thirteen articles coming out of other UCDC protocols, and an article about the design of the consortium itself. The earliest of these were published in 2008, five years after the consortium's inception in 2003, evidencing the considerable start-up time required to obtain publishable results. Managing publication of UCDC research results raises issues of authorship and credit, as well as the need to decide when research findings are ready for external release.

As already discussed, the development of consensus treatment guidelines played a very important role in the UCDC's history. The community continues to develop and refine treatment guidelines that can be used not only by its members in treating their own patients but by physicians who are less familiar with the disorders. A section of the UCDC website specifically aimed at physicians includes information about the diagnosis of UCDs and detailed treatment guidelines. As Mark Batshaw explained:

> In terms of education we have a website where we go all out to the peripheries. We talk to neonatologists about all these kinds of things. We standardized care. We held a series of consensus conferences in five-year intervals. We published that and it's on our website so that everyone can have a standard therapy. They are generally followed. So I can now get the person on our website and walk them through the treatment process, which wasn't something that was done because people didn't know who to call. There is the website and the Internet.

Knowledge generated by the UCDC also may be brought to bear on interactions with pharmaceutical companies aimed at developing, validating and gaining regulatory approval for new or improved drugs. Each of these three dissemination contexts brings its own set of challenges for UCDC governance.

D. RESOURCES GENERATED BY THE UCDC (MOSTLY) FOR EXTERNAL USE

1. Educational Materials about Urea Cycle Disorders for Patients and the General Public

The NIH requires each consortium to maintain a website information resource aimed at basic and clinical researchers, academic and practicing physicians, patients, and the lay public.[18] The public-facing websites maintained by the DMCC for each consortium fulfill this requirement. The UCDC website provides (besides the study recruitment information and research results already discussed) general information about urea cycle disorder symptoms, diagnosis, and treatment. Much of this information also is available through the NUCDF website. The UCDC and NUCDF websites reinforce and refer to one another. However, the UCDC website does not provide information for patients about support groups, coping, and the experiences of others, which are an important

---

[18] RDCRC Slides from March 17, 2008, preapplication meeting, http://rarediseases.info.nih.gov/asp/resources/extr_res_archived.asp.

focus of the NUCDF's website and activities. The NUCDF website provides more extensive educational materials than the UCDC website, and it seems likely that the NUCDF's website plays the more important role in patient education.

2. Diagnostic Tools and Tests

Diagnostic methods for UCDs range from clinical assessments of symptoms to genetic tests. To be useful, a diagnostic test must be developed and validated, based upon basic and clinical research. Developing diagnostic tests is not the whole story, however, since these tests must be made available to physicians outside of the UCDC.

Dissemination of diagnostic methods poses several particular challenges in the rare disease context. Some diagnostic methods can be (and are) disseminated effectively simply by educating physicians, by means such as the UCDC website. According to one interviewee, however, it can be difficult to communicate diagnostic methods to general practice physicians effectively because they do not have experience with rare diseases. Moreover, to use diagnostic information, physicians first have to know both that the disease exists and may be relevant for their patients and where to find information about it, both of which are difficult for rare diseases.

In addition, to disseminate some diagnostic tests, it may not be enough to inform physicians about them. Testing for genetic disorders such as the UCDs often requires specialized laboratory expertise. To make these tests available for patients, then, the UCDC must transfer technology and expertise to commercial laboratories. For example, an interviewee explained that the UCDC developed expertise in gene sequence testing for mutations associated with UCDs and then passed the relevant information on to an industry partner so that it could provide the test commercially. The potential for commercial involvement in providing diagnostic tests raises the question of whether a particular test can, or should, be patented. The UCDC PIs we interviewed had differing views about whether diagnostic methods should be patented and there did not seem to be a consensus policy on the subject.

The dissemination of newborn screening tests involves a further wrinkle. Undiagnosed UCDs can be fatal during the neonatal period. At the urging of the patient advocacy group, the UCDC has worked to develop and validate newborn screening tests for the UCDs. However, outside authorities, including the Department of Health and Human Services (HHS), define the standard suite of newborn screening tests. If screening is to be broadly available, UCD screening must be included in this standard suite. As a result, UCDC also is engaged in advocating that testing for UCDC to be included within the HHS standard newborn screening suite.

VII. UCDC Governance

In this part, we explore the ways in which the UCDC governs its various activities. We begin by discussing the UCDC's general governance structure, which affects the way that decisions are made in virtually all of the UCDC's action arenas. We then discuss some specific action arenas related to the UCDC's primary objectives. We focus in most detail on the governance of the creation and use of the pool of research participants and patient data created by the longitudinal study. This action arena appears to be particularly central to the UCDC's goals and objectives and structure. It raises a number of important and interesting challenges and dilemmas, and illustrates several different aspects of UCDC governance. We also include brief discussions of UCDC approaches to knowledge sharing within the consortium, interactions with pharmaceutical companies, and interactions with patients in setting research priorities and sharing research results. Notably, overcoming the standard "free rider" problem that dominates discussions of intellectual property policy is only a small piece of the governance picture for this knowledge commons.

A. GENERAL GOVERNANCE STRUCTURE

The UCDC is formally governed by a Steering Committee "composed of the UCDC directors [CPIs], the principal investigator from each site [SPI], the executive director of the National Urea Cycle Disorders Foundation, the NIH scientific and program officers, the DMCC director, the project manager, and the grant manager" (Seminara et al. 2010). Yet our interviewees and survey respondents did not emphasize this formal structure. Instead, they overwhelmingly emphasized more informal aspects of governance and, in particular, the importance of *leadership* and the *collegiality* of the community. This is not entirely surprising; while the UCDC is not a purely "grassroots" commons, it grew out of and takes advantage of grassroots relationships between research collaborators, and between researchers and the NUCDF. The UCDC's governance practice reflects the interplay between these relationships and the structure imposed by the RDCRN.

1. Leadership

The importance of the UCDC's current leadership to its success was one of the most definitive findings of our study. Virtually every interviewee emphasized the importance of Mark Batshaw's leadership to the success of the UCDC. Batshaw is highly respected, not only for his pioneering scientific work on UCDs but also for his organizational and people skills. One interviewee, for example, described Batshaw as the "glue that holds everyone together." Another described him as a "master" of leadership. Still another stated that Batshaw "may be the best administrator I've ever known. He is very aggressive, very smart, and very fair, always in possession of himself and never loses his cool." More abstractly, our survey asked respondents to rank collegiality, funding, leadership, patient advocacy group, relationship with the NIH, and the DMCC in order of importance to UCDC success. Each subgroup of respondents ranked leadership, collegiality, and funding highest, with leadership receiving the largest number of first place votes overall.

In light of this affirmation of the importance of leadership, we attempted to ascertain what aspects of leadership characterized the current UCDC leaders and which of those aspects were deemed important by UCDC members. When asked to choose three words that "best describe the current UCDC leadership," approximately 75 percent of respondents included the word "dedicated" among their choices, making it by far the most popular choice.[19] There was somewhat less agreement about other characteristics, though "trustworthy" and "determined" were chosen next most often overall. We asked respondents to consider which characteristics they thought would be most important in choosing leaders for a *new* rare disease consortium. "Dedicated," selected by more than 80 percent of respondents, topped the list of desired characteristics, while "trustworthy" and "determined" solidified as second and third choices. Respondents put more emphasis on trustworthiness when considering a hypothetical new consortium.

Our interviews also suggested that certain leadership *skills*, including grant writing, fundraising, scientific insight, communication, organization, and community building, also were important to UCDC success. Our survey asked respondents to rank these skills in order of importance to the success of the UCDC. There was little overall consensus as to the ranking, with different subgroups appearing to emphasize different skills. One possibility is that all of these skills are necessary for a successful UCDC leader.

The UCDC expects to undergo a leadership transition before long, since Mark Batshaw plans to retire (or at least step down from his role as project director for the UCDC) sometime in the next few years. Leadership transitions may be especially difficult for institutions, such as the UCDC, that rely heavily on informal governance and on the skills and personality of a strong leader. Our survey did not inquire specifically about concerns about the impending leadership transition, though two answers to an open-ended question about the UCDC's growth raised the issue. One respondent expressed the view that "it will depend on the future leadership if [growth of the UCDC] will work," while the other more bluntly referred to the "leadership transition," commenting that "there are few Mark Batshaws in the world."

The UCDC leadership has taken specific steps to prepare for the upcoming transition. At the July 2012 conference, Batshaw announced to the group that Marshall Summar eventually would be succeeding him as project director. Bringing him into the official UCDC leadership as a CPI was part of a plan for leadership succession. As Batshaw explained:

> The other thing is you need to have a succession planning. Marshall is my successor planning. When I talked to the NIH I said I wanted Marshall to be a co-PI so that when I run off to the sunset he will be here.

---

[19] Respondents were given a list of ten positive descriptors and "other" to choose from. Those choosing "other" were given the opportunity to write in some other characteristic. The ten terms were: articulate, confident, decisive, dedicated, determined, friendly, outgoing, trustworthy, perceptive, and persistent. We selected positive descriptors because our interviewees overwhelmingly expressed positive views of the UCDC leadership, and the goal of this question was to determine which leadership characteristics were considered most important.

Though Summar is the most recently appointed, and youngest, CPI, he has considerable experience as a leader of the UCD research community and in research involving genetic and metabolic disorders more generally. He is the Chief of the Division of Genetics and Metabolism at CNMC and plays a major role in the clinical research center at CNMC, working with Clinical and Translational Science Award grants. Before becoming a CPI in 2012, Summar was the SPI at the UCDC's Vanderbilt University site. As mentioned earlier, he was part of the core group of researchers who participated in the 2000 consensus conference. Though he thus has much in common with the other two CPIs, Summar has what he described as an "unconventional" approach to research funding, with an emphasis on the private sector. He told us that he receives approximately 60 percent of his individual research funding from tech transfer. He is an inventor on a number of patents and patent applications filed since 2000. While all of the PIs we interviewed emphasized the importance of working with the private sector to deliver treatments to patients, Batshaw, Tuchman, and the substantial majority of SPIs obtained and filed for no patents during that period.

2. Collegiality and Inclusiveness

Our interviewees and survey respondents also agreed on the importance of collegiality to the UCDC's success. The UCDC's roots in a close-knit community of colleagues are important in understanding its present structure and governance. The PIs we interviewed all had been in this original group and most emphasized the collegiality of the UCDC research community as the first or second (depending on the interviewee) most important factor in the consortium's success (with leadership generally taken the other slot). Interviewees also emphasized the importance of personal relationships to the UCDC's success, explaining that they had visited one another's homes, attended celebrations such as weddings and bar mitzvahs, and so forth. Interviewees also emphasized that shared commitment to the patients brought the group together. Several interviewees suggested that the researchers' common backgrounds as pediatricians made collaboration more successful (the implication apparently being that pediatricians are more caring and less self-centered than those in other specialties because their patients are children). Interviewees also mentioned the mutual respect between researchers that had developed over a long period of interactions.

It is well known that close-knit communities sometimes can govern themselves effectively through systems of informal norms. The UCDC would not be a success, however, if it had not expanded beyond its original group of five institutions. In light of the priority given to expanding the number of sites and researchers involved and the perceived importance of collegiality to the success of the UCDC, it is important to understand whether, and if so how, the group has maintained the sense of collegiality and community as the number of research sites has expanded. Unfortunately, because our selection of interviewees was made before we realized the importance of understanding how new members are incorporated into the consortium, our interviews were for the most part conducted with core UCDC members. We thus have two primary sources of information about the way in which the growth in research sites and consortium members has affected the collegiality of the group: interviews with core members about efforts made to incorporate newer members into the group and responses to some of our survey questions.

The original members of the UCDC we interviewed all reported conscious efforts to be inclusive, in part because the research itself demands widespread geographic coverage. For example, when asked whether there are researchers who work on UCDs but are not included in the UCDC, Batshaw indicated that there "are a few, but we have about 90%. If I had more money I would get the other 10%. We wanted to make sure that we cover the entire U.S. The northeast tends to have more academic institutions than do other areas. So there are a few areas that are not covered." Another PI responded to the same question:

> Very few and I think that's an important point because our psychology has always been to be inclusive. I would actually be curious if that's typical of all of the consortia. I think for some people there is the tendency when they get the money, make it an old boys' club. We have avoided that.... From the beginning our goal was to enroll every person in the world in our studies, every patient in the world. So today I think we have 550 people out of probably a few thousands.

Several of the UCDC's activities (some required by the NIH) provide opportunities for interaction among UCDC members and presumably provide opportunities for newer members to be integrated into the collegial group. The UCDC now holds face-to-face meetings annually, though they were held more often in earlier years. Our observations at the 2012 meeting suggest that the face-to-face meetings facilitate collegiality between consortium members in various ways. We observed a general sense of engagement and community within the group attending the meeting. The NIH program officer also noted her experience of the openness of the UCDC:

> I've only been part of UCDC for a year. In fact, my first real contact with the UCDC was that meeting in Colorado last year when I was brand new, and this last meeting was amazing because it's like I'd known them all my life.

We also noted several times when Batshaw took actions that seemed designed to facilitate collegiality and inclusiveness. For example, at a dinner prior to the substantive meeting, Batshaw made a point of going around the room so that each attendee could introduce himself or herself to the group. This same ritual was repeated at the beginning of the research meeting the following day. We also observed him leading several discussions about potential research directions. During those discussions, he sometimes solicited input from particular researchers in what appeared to be an effort to ensure that all views were heard.

Our survey asked how the value of face-to-face meetings had changed with the consortium's expansion. More than 85 percent of the PIs reported that the value of face-to-face meetings had increased with consortium growth, though other respondents were most likely to report no change in the value of face-to-face meetings. Unfortunately, our survey did not ask about the absolute value of face-to-face meetings (but only about whether the value had changed), so we cannot assess whether members of these other groups believed that face-to-face meetings were valuable and remained so or were not particularly valuable and remained so. Two of the responses to our open-ended question about what respondents would change about the UCDC did address face-to-face meetings, with one PI simply suggesting "more face to face meetings" and one site coordinator advocating "more opportunity for face-to-face meeting, especially for site coordinators and individuals involved in the research who are not the PIs (young physicians, dieticians, genetic counselors, etc.)." This second response suggests at least some concern about the integration of non-PIs into the UCDC community.

The UCDC holds regular monthly conference calls, which are attended by PIs and study coordinators, along with the NIH science officer and the executive director of the NUCDF. It appears from our interviews and review of the minutes of these calls that the monthly conference call is a very important venue both for scientific discussion and for deliberation about decisions and issues facing the UCDC. It seems likely that these calls also help to integrate newcomers into the group, but we did not address that question directly in our interviews or survey. Certainly, the survey confirmed that UCDC members value the monthly calls. Only about 7 percent of the PIs and 20 percent of study coordinators agreed that "participating in monthly conference calls takes too much time from my other responsibilities." Given that these individuals are all extremely busy, with many responsibilities, this is a fairly resounding endorsement of the value of the conference calls. While they apparently value the monthly calls, only 43 percent of the PIs agreed that the calls contribute to their research, suggesting that the conference calls are valued for other reasons, perhaps including reinforcing the collegiality of the group.

We also asked survey respondents to assess the effects of consortium growth on the monthly conference calls. Most respondents believed that the value of monthly conference calls had been unaffected by the growth in the number of consortium sites and most were not at all or only slightly concerned that as the UCDC continues to grow, the monthly phone conferences would become less effective.

In the next section, we consider how the emphasis on leadership and collegiality is reflected in UCDC decision making.

3. UCDC Decision Making

While the UCDC formally is governed by a steering committee, our interviews suggested that many (perhaps most) decisions are made by a much more informal process involving discussion among UCDC members, often during the monthly teleconferences, with final decisions made by the CPIs (and especially Mark Batshaw) in consultation with the Program Manager. Interviewees repeatedly described a process of active (sometimes even "loud") discussion of issues followed by general agreement. Several interviewees also noted, however, that if push came to shove Batshaw's decisions would carry the day because of his "status" as a pioneer in the study of UCDs. Our observations at the UCDC conference also suggested a kind of hybrid approach. Though votes were occasionally taken, it was not evident to us, at least, that voting was limited to steering committee members or to formal members of the UCDC. Voting seemed more like an informal show of hands than a formal process. We did not observe any votes on contentious issues. According to our interviewees, however, this informal approach was taken even on issues that might have been expected to be contentious, such as allocation of funding among sites or even dealing with sites that were not succeeding in recruiting patients to participate.

We also asked a number of survey questions aimed at characterizing UCDC decision making. The responses gave a mixed, and apparently contradictory, picture. On average, respondents were slightly inclined to agree that "most UCDC decisions are made by the leadership" and that "the UCDC is hierarchical." Yet they also were inclined to agree that "UCDC decisions are based on consensus" and that "UCDC decisions are made by majority vote." Looking at responses by subgroup or excluding responses from those who selected the option "neither agree nor disagree" did not resolve the apparent contradiction. In light of our interviews and observations, we believe that the most reasonable interpretation is that the survey responses reflect the complexity, variability, and informality of UCDC decision-making processes. One interviewee's description nicely captured this sense of what one might call hierarchical democratic governance:

> It's all majority type of decisions. Mark then makes the final decision but he makes it based on the discussion....I can think of several things that we voted the majority was completely wrong but they still adopted it because it is very hard to go against the majority....And you want them to be dedicated to the mission of the consortium.

One apparent exception to the UCDC's generally informal approach to decision making is its process for selecting among proposals for pilot funding. That process is somewhat more formalized. As one interviewee explained:

> Mark Batshaw is in charge of a committee consisting of other members of the consortium. It will be anonymous. They will render a verdict. They read the proposal. There was a deadline. There will probably be I guess 3–6 proposals. I think two of them will be funded so we are spending 70K a year on two proposals.

We can speculate that this procedure is more formal because it would be undesirable for various reasons for the entire UCDC membership to debate the merits of these proposals, and yet it is important that members perceive the decisions to be fair. A process of this sort is a means to give legitimacy to the pilot funding awards.

During our interviews, we also asked specifically about conflict resolution, a vital area of group decision making. We were told that although there is no formal conflict resolution procedure or policy for the UCDC, there are occasional conflicts, which are usually resolved amicably after discussion or "negotiation" with the parties involved, in which UCDC leaders play the role of "mediator." As NUCDF's Le Mons put it: "[T]hese are people that have worked together for a long, long time and have the mutual respect and are able to work out conflicts reasonably. So there's nobody going to war." When we asked one interviewee how conflicts were resolved, we were told about the following example:

A couple of years ago several PIs wanted to add organic acidemia to the diseases covered by the UCDC. The idea was presented at the annual meeting by the PI who felt most strongly about it. There was vigorous discussion and disagreement about whether doing so would dilute resources. The NUCDF representative said that patients would feel betrayed because they had been so supportive of the UCDC, including financially. There was concern about funding and where it would come from. In the end, there was a vote and the consortium decided, by majority, not to add it.

Our survey also gave respondents a chance to indicate their satisfaction with the present UCDC decision-making process. Despite the strong support for describing the UCDC as collegial, there was some dissatisfaction with the inclusiveness of the decision-making process. Thus, 33 percent of respondents agreed that SPIs should have more say in decisions, while only 8 percent disagreed (leaving 59 percent who neither agreed nor disagreed). Similarly, 33 percent agreed that non-PI researchers should have more say in decisions, while only 14 percent disagreed, and 40 percent agreed that site coordinators should have more say in decisions, with only 18 percent disagreeing. Responses to open-ended questions also indicated some concern about the inclusiveness of the decision-making process for those outside of the core group of PIs. One PI, for example, would want "more participation in decision making process at least for site PIs, ideally coordinators would also have a role, neuropsychologists have somewhat of a role." Several site coordinators indicated a desire for greater involvement in decision making, particularly as related to data collection. One wrote, for example, that "study coordinators are rarely acknowledged, listed to or even allowed to contribute to a variety of decisions that involve data collection or contribution to the UCDC.... There is much disconnect between the site PIs involved in UCDC and the site coordinators." Another suggested "greater reception and discussion concerning practical suggestions from site coordinators with UCDC investigators and leadership." One respondent complained that "neuropsychologists were constantly undervalued (e.g. not invited to meetings, not funded adequately)."

In light of these findings, both the upcoming leadership transition and the UCDC's growth may pose challenges to its informal approach to governance. As one survey respondent wrote: "[C]onflict resolution is getting sticky because…when we were a small group of 20 people, [we would] literally just stand up and say anything reasonable and talk as a group. Now when there are 55 or 60 people, it's not conducive to people standing up and saying, 'Well, I don't think that or I disagree with that.' Some will, but I think people are intimidated by that."

B. GOVERNANCE OF THE POOL OF RESEARCH PARTICIPANTS AND PATIENT DATA

Perhaps the most important resource created by the UCDC is the pool of research participants and patient data associated primarily with the longitudinal study. In creating this pool, the UCDC has to manage challenges associated with the need to recruit rare and dispersed patients to participate in the research and the need to overcome barriers to cooperation by researchers at geographically dispersed clinical sites. The UCDC also must have mechanisms for managing use of the pooled data internally and by external researchers, including those from pharmaceutical companies.

1. Patient Participation

In the rare disease context, recruiting study participants is both difficult and crucial to the objective of creating a pool of research subjects and patient data. The UCDC's public website reflects this reality:

> The purpose of this consortium is to provide a way for patients to join with doctors and researchers by participating in research studies. The greater the collaboration between doctors and patients, the more we can learn about Urea Cycle Disorders. This important first step is necessary if we are ever to find newer treatments.

To recruit study participants, UCDC researchers must identify and make contact with a small and scattered patient population. According to our interviewees, patients, rather than their physicians, institute most contacts with the UCDC. Patients most often learn about the UCDC and its studies through the NUCDF. Some patients also find about the UCDC through its own website (and, as discussed above, some come to the UCDC through the DMCC's patient registry). The UCDC's clinical sites, which have specialists who treat UCDs and other metabolic disorders, also bring some of their own patients into the studies.

Once identified, patients (or more often, their families) must be convinced that study participation is worthwhile, either because they expect to benefit directly or because they feel a commitment to other UCD patients. They also need to trust that the researchers will conduct the research in as safe and fair a manner as possible. The NUCDF has been critical to the UCDC's success in recruiting patients to participate in UCDC studies. NUCDF staff makes direct contact with patients to determine their interest in participating in UCDC research studies. NUCDF's Le Mons emphasized in our interview with her that the NUCDF's role is to inform patients, not to persuade them to participate in studies, "to make sure the patients understand the clinical trial, the risks, the benefits if any, and exactly what they're getting before they jump." Through its annual meeting of patients and researchers, the NUCDF also helps to forge the necessary trusting and reciprocal relationships between patients and researchers.

Unlike many clinical research studies, UCDC research depends on engaging patients' participation over long periods of time. UCDs are chronic genetic diseases that run in families. Fortunately, current treatments often make it possible to avoid early fatalities. It is thus both possible and important for particular patients and families to participate in UCDC studies over significant periods of time. Long-term participation provides some direct benefits to patients, in that they are monitored by experts on the disorders, receive neuropsychological testing that may be used to obtain special education benefits, and so forth. Participating in the longitudinal study is time-consuming, however, often requiring travel. Though the tests are not very invasive or risky, which makes patients more likely to want to participate, long bouts of testing can be frustrating and unpleasant for patients and their parents, especially because inattentiveness is a common symptom of UCDs.

The RDCRN's structure attempts to address the challenges of identifying UCD patients, recruiting them to participate in the longitudinal study, and sustaining their ongoing participation by involving geographically dispersed clinical sites, requiring patient advocacy group participation in the consortium, and providing IT infrastructure for a patient contact registry. In the UCDC's case, by far the most important of these elements with respect to patient identification and recruitment seems to have been the involvement of the patient advocacy group, with the infrastructure provided by the DMCC playing a relatively minor role. Patients seem to prefer to engage with the UCDC through the NUCDF intermediary, rather than directly, suggesting that patient advocacy groups not only serve as easily findable hubs for information but also are important in establishing research legitimacy and trust.

The availability of dispersed clinical research sites reduces the costs of patient participation in research and thus facilitates sustained patient participation. Beyond that, however, the RDCRN structure does not appear to address the challenge of sustaining patient participation in research. Our interviews and observations suggest that maintaining long-term participation depends importantly on two factors: (1) the follow-up efforts of study coordinators and (2) relationships that patients form with UCDC researchers and study coordinators. Study coordinators are the front line for patient recruitment and follow-up. They are the most frequent point of contact with study participants who see participants every time they come for data collection and testing, phone them to remind them of their appointments, answer their questions, and work with the NUCDF to help them in various ways. UCDC researchers also are clinicians and most, as several interviewees emphasized, are pediatricians. They provide clinical care to some UCD patients on a regular, though perhaps infrequent, basis over long periods of time. The UCDC also fosters trusted relationships with researchers by partnering with the NUCDF at annual meetings in which researchers make themselves available to explain the results of their research and interact informally with patients.

It would be interesting to investigate the impact of these factors in more detail to determine whether the RDCRN should consider requiring consortia to participate in joint meetings with patient advocacy groups and whether study coordinators, in particular, should be given some kind of training aimed at making their interactions with patients more useful in sustaining participation.

2. Researcher Cooperation

A second challenge is to motivate researchers to contribute to a common data pool. Barriers to data pooling can arise out of the natural tension between researchers' recognition that sharing data increase the pace of research and their interests in obtaining credit for their individual efforts. The small number of rare disease patients, along with the scarcity of funding to study any particular rare disease, creates particular incentives for researchers to "hoard" access to patients so that they can publish whatever they can learn from case studies of their own patients.[20] As some of our interviewees noted, the NIH competitive individual grant process plays inadvertently into this dynamic because success depends on having one's own group of patients to study. Because both funding and access to patients are limited in the rare disease context, competition for individual grants may well result in research concentrated at a few independent sites, with study participants drawn from a few local areas (or brought in from other areas at great expense and inconvenience). This situation is particularly disastrous for rare diseases because clinical research is critically dependent on involving enough patients to support sound statistical analysis. In essence, meaningful studies of rare diseases depend on collaboration between widely dispersed researchers, but, within the standard model of individual competitive grants, the scarcity of research subjects and of funding in the rare disease context erects barriers to cooperation.

The RDCRN's structure addresses this problem head on by (1) mandating a longitudinal study, (2) monitoring and displaying each site's progress in recruiting patients to participate in the longitudinal study, (3) providing funding targeted at facilitating the longitudinal study, especially for hiring study coordinators, and (4) providing infrastructure, especially through the DMCC, to make it easier for researchers to contribute to the common data pool.

Based on our study, we believe that there also are several inherent features of the longitudinal study that make it a particularly good foundation for overcoming barriers to

---

[20] Hoarding may be too strong a word, although we did hear it used once or twice during the interviews. The point is that without a consortium to bring people together, doctors tended to focus on their own patients and not work with others across the country.

researcher participation in creating a common data pool. First, once the protocols for data collection are in place and with the DMCC providing data management services, participating in the longitudinal study is a relatively low-cost way for researchers to become part of the consortium, enabling it to grow beyond a core group of researchers who are highly dedicated to the study of UCDs. Second, the pool of data produced by the longitudinal study can be used not only for consortium-wide research projects but also as a resource for independent research projects, through which researchers can establish individual competence and reputation.

Despite these features, the creation of the pool remains vulnerable to free-rider issues if researchers are permitted to use the pooled data and to be given authorship on consortium-wide publications without regard to their contribution of data. Aspects of the RDCRN structure seem designed to mitigate this problem, however. Most importantly, patient recruitment numbers are available to RDCRN participants on the members-only website. Cumulative and current year totals for each consortium are displayed to all participants, while totals for each clinical site are displayed to UCDC members. The availability of this information means that social norms can be effective in discouraging free riding. Monthly teleconferences involving UCDC members and NIH officials perform many functions, but one result of these frequent group calls may be to strengthen the effectiveness of norms against free riding. The availability of patient recruitment information also makes it possible for a consortium to de-fund a clinical site that is not pulling its weight, if necessary.

As the UCDC collects more and more data about more and more UCDC patients, it also becomes a self-reinforcing focal point for everyone interested in UCD research, including patients, researchers, and pharmaceutical companies, thus potentially creating an "if you can't beat 'em, join 'em" dynamic for researchers.

3. Coordinating Data Collection and Entry

A third major challenge is to coordinate the collection and entry of data from a large number of clinical sites.

Standardizing data collection protocols requires coming to an agreement about what data should be collected and what test should be run. This is a challenging activity, because it requires the UCDC to balance factors including the desire to collect as much data as possible, different researchers' views about what data is most important, the practical need for protocols that can be implemented by all UCDC sites, and limits on patients' willingness to submit to a large battery of tests. Input from nearly every participant in the UCDC, including PIs, study coordinators, neuropsychologists, genetic counselors, and other clinicians, as well as from patients is important to getting the balance right. As a study coordinator interviewee explained:

> The general idea across the board, the initial goal, not just for neuropsych, is to get as much data as possible, right? If there is a longitudinal natural history study, you

want to get everything. Over time, we adjusted things that we collected, because it didn't turn out as feasible or as logical as they thought it would be. So initially the way they captured family history was totally crazy and clearly they didn't involve a genetic counselor in doing it. Right, you have to look at a pedigree where they are assigning numbers, make a mathematical weight and analyze it. This doesn't really work. So it sort of shifted on how things were collected and there are a lot of examples to that. When you are gathering so much data from so many patients that over time we realize what works better just from direct experience.

The UCDC's collegiality and informal democratic/hierarchical governance apply to the making of protocol changes, such as this one. While participants seem generally satisfied with the informal decision-making system, designing the longitudinal study protocol may be the kind of decision for which complaints about lack of voice for study coordinators and neuropsychologists have some force.

Besides establishing a standard study protocol to be used at all sites, challenges associated with coordinating data collection and entry have to do with creating a shared database with an interface that facilitates data entry and later data use and ensuring that data is entered in a timely and accurate fashion. The RDCRN deals with these issues by centralizing data management in the DMCC, thereby providing a central source of database expertise and relieving individual consortia of many of the costs of data management. There was widespread agreement among our survey respondents about the importance of the DMCC's role in "managing the central data repository," with thirty-four out of forty-five rating it as "very important" or "essential." The DMCC activity next most highly valued by survey respondents was "data analysis and statistics support." DMCC auditing and enforcement of research protocols, assistance in protocol design, and site coordinator training and assistance also were considered "important" on average. DMCC assistance with IRB compliance was ranked somewhat below "important" on average, with some interviewees suggesting that IRB compliance would be more effectively addressed by the establishment of a cross-institutional IRB for RDCRN projects, so as to cut down on the time and expense of obtaining approvals from multiple clinical sites.

We speculate that "outsourcing" certain enforcement tasks, such as auditing the clinical sites' compliance with study protocols and posting patient recruitment numbers online, to the DMCC may have possibly unappreciated benefits in reducing conflict and maintaining collegiality among consortium members.

4. Managing Internal Use of the Data

If researchers are permitted to use the data pool for individual research projects (which is one of its major purposes), there is the potential for conflicts of two sorts. First, there may be disagreements over data use, especially if more than one researcher wants to pursue a similar project. Second, there may be disagreements over publication and authorship of publications reporting research based on the data pool. The UCDC has formal written policies dealing with each of these issues.

The UCDC's Data Use Policy stipulates that all UCDC researchers have access to the data (stripped of identifying information, such as name, address, phone number) generated by the longitudinal study. However, data-mining studies must be approved by the CPIs "to ensure that there is not redundancy or overlap in concurrent analysis." According to one CPI, "a request for data mining is expected to be accompanied by a reasonable research idea or proposal approved by the PIs, the request has to be approved by the steering committee, and relevant data needs to be extracted out of the DMCC database before it can be shared with others for mining." Other uses of longitudinal study data do not require CPI approval. Consortium members wishing to use data generated by other UCDC research projects, such as the pilot projects, are to "work closely" with the PIs of those projects to "define roles for analysis and drafting a publication (or other use)." Informal norms appear to be important in implementing these policies. As the Program Manager explained, there is a concept of joint ownership of consortium data, but, nonetheless, researchers would not use data generated by projects at other sites if the researchers who collected the data objected.

Our survey asked about respondents' familiarity with the UCDC data sharing policy. All PIs, about half of study coordinators, and smaller fractions of other respondents reported familiarity with the policy. About 70 percent of PIs reported that it was important to them to have input into the data sharing policy.

Publications are the primary means by which researchers gain reputation, which is the "coin of the realm" in scientific research. Thus, authorship credit is very important to researchers. A consortium in which a large number of members contribute to the collection and analysis of a pool of data also effectively creates a "pool" of authorship credit, which must be allocated among consortium members. The UCDC's Publication Policy "addresses the coordination, development, and communications related to the orderly and timely release of information generated by the UCDC." It "defines authorship roles and responsibilities—including communications and notifications among co-authors, other investigators, the consortium Principal Investigator, and relevant NIH science and project officers." It provides that "[m]ajor publications resulting from the Longitudinal Study will include all UCDC Site PIs, UCDC leadership, project director (Jennifer Seminara), co-PIs [at certain sites] and [certain] former PIs []." Major publications are defined to include "publications describing the Longitudinal Study or reporting on the overall results of the specific aims of the study." Study coordinators are to be acknowledged by name. Authorship of individual analyses of longitudinal study data is to include those (including study coordinators where appropriate) who have "significantly contributed to the analysis and publication," as defined in the policy. The author list for such individual analyses also must include "Members of the UCDC," who are to be listed in a footnote. The publication policy defines the "first author" as the researcher who takes primary responsibility for the project and gives the first author responsibility for determining the timeline of publication. The policy also provides for internal quality review of all UCDC manuscripts by UCDC leadership before publication and sets out various other requirements for acknowledgments and compliance with NIH policies.

All PI survey respondents expressed familiarity with the publication policy, while only about half of site coordinators and even fewer non-PI researchers and clinicians were familiar with the policy. Nearly all PIs reported that it was important to them to have input into the publication policy. Moreover, all PI respondents agreed that authorship of UCDC research was assigned fairly. Most respondents from other subgroups neither agreed nor disagreed with that statement, though a small number of site coordinators and clinicians disagreed.

The written data sharing and publication policies appear to be important for managing the use and publication of the UCDC's data pool. But they do not appear to be deployed for conflict resolution in any formal way. Our interviewees emphasized that conflicts, including conflicts about data sharing, generally are resolved informally as described in the section on UCDC general governance. Interviewees also emphasized that researchers' commitment to advancing knowledge about the disorders and helping patients tended to ward off conflict. As one of our interviewees explained:

> [P]eople in the consortium are collaborative and they have that in mind: yes everybody wants to be the first author on a publication, and things like that; but they are also thinking about the impact of the publication. It's not just about being a lead on something. It's about the impact of the work. It's important not just for your own career advancement but for the impact. There are so many more pluses to collaborate.

The same interviewee also explained how belonging to the UCDC mitigated concerns about being "scooped" by competing researchers:

> There is an advantage to being in a large consortium. If you combine everybody, instead of having 100 subjects, you will have thousands of subjects and that's going to make a much higher impact than a bunch of individual smaller papers.

5. Managing External Use of the Data

The NIH requires that, after a specified period of time (generally five years), data obtained by its funded projects be contributed to a data repository that is available to the scientific community. Over and above complying with this policy, the UCDC sometimes makes data available to particular outsiders, including pharmaceutical companies, in response to specific data requests. Data collected by the longitudinal study has been critically important in interesting pharmaceutical companies in pursuing treatments for UCDs. As CPI Batshaw explained:

> The last partner is really the pharmaceutical companies. We are involved with six pharmaceutical companies. Three of them were actually involved in, for a long period of time, very intensive ways. The fact that we have six pharmaceutical companies in a disease that occurs 1 on 30,000 is quite remarkable. And the reason this happened is because we provide to them 600 patients that represent the entire population. They are in Europe as well as in the U.S. They are all being treated in exactly the same way so that their clinical pathway is the same. And for natural history you have to pull a number of years, the cognitive function, biomarkers.... So the cost for them to do clinical studies is about 1/10 of what it would have been if they had to do this on their own. And it worked wonderfully.

Thus, sharing data with pharmaceutical companies is central to the UCDC's objective of developing improved treatments for patients. While patients also welcome pharmaceutical company interest in developing treatments, however, they also are concerned about data sharing with pharmaceutical companies for privacy reasons and because of the extremely high cost of many treatments that are developed using patient data.

According to the UCDC Data Use Policy, all external uses of UCDC data must be approved by UCDC leadership. Moreover, "[t]o ensure that the confidentiality and privacy of study participants are protected, all external investigators seeking access to data from UCDC studies must execute and submit an appropriate standard data use agreement prior to obtaining UCDC data." Unless research subjects have consented explicitly to the use of data that does not meet HIPAA's definition of de-identified data, only de-identified data is made available to external investigators. Academic researchers may obtain access to UCDC data by collaborating with a UCDC member or by obtaining approval from UCDC leadership. Commercial users are given access only through specific service agreements, which set out a "scope of work" to be performed by the UCDC and deal with fees to be paid by the user, ownership of intellectual property, confidentiality, and so forth.

Though the Data Use Policy addresses the form of data sharing agreements with external parties, it has little to say about the standards for deciding whether to allow data to be shared. Nor does it address how issues of data ownership and intellectual property are to be handled in agreements with external data users, stating only (and rather opaquely) that "[e]ach site owns the data collected at their own site. The Urea Cycle Disorders Consortium owns the complete set of data collected at all sites (collective ownership)." The policy thus apparently leaves such questions to be resolved by UCDC leaders when they negotiate data use agreements. Despite its formal data use policy, UCDC's approach to decision making about external use of data thus appears consistent with its general approach to decision making, which is strongly dependent on members' respect for UCDC leadership (and in particular, for Mark Batshaw) and on informal discussion and debate.

Up to this point, there appear to have been few conflicts within the consortium about the interactions with pharmaceutical companies. Our interviews suggest that this lack of conflict is due to a combination of factors: (1) relationships with pharmaceutical companies are handled according to general conflict of interest policies for medical research, which have become stricter in recent years, (2) the pharmaceutical companies involved so far are specialized companies, with which consortium researchers have interacted for many years, and (3) UCDC researchers are very pleased to have succeeded in attracting pharmaceutical company interest in developing drugs for these rare conditions. As UCDC research progresses toward the development of more treatments, however, issues of data sharing with pharmaceutical companies may become more pressing.

C. SHARING KNOWLEDGE AND IDEAS WITHIN THE UCDC

As far as we were able to ascertain, most UCDC members are intrinsically motivated to share their knowledge and ideas with other consortium members because they enjoy collaborating and see the benefits of the exchange for their research and for UCD patients. One interviewee described the core group of researchers, who had sought to work collaboratively even before the RDCRN was established as "just the type of people that were collaborative and wanted to work together and were committed and they were interested in science and they were also compassionate about patients." As another interviewee put it: "[t]he whole reason people are in the consortium is because they are willing to collaborate." Both interviewees and survey respondents agreed that the UCDC has succeeded in improving the exchange of knowledge between researchers. For example, in answering a question about how the UCDC affected his "day to day research or interaction with the other collaborators or researchers in the urea cycle disorders," one interviewee explained:

> The first thing I see is a great exchange of ideas. You see, I have a laboratory research portfolio, quite a good one, I think. I have like 12 people in the lab and have several NIH grants. But you know, the ideas that we exchange are mainly between us. Here, we have a consortium and any time we have some kind of an idea, we vet it out, among everybody, suddenly you get all kind[s] of perspectives. So exchange of ideas and new ideas is something that is clearly facilitated.

Along similar lines, another interviewee explained:

> We meet often. We discuss treatments. Some issues puzzling patients, we talk about those. We have a couple of groups embedded in NIH. Peter McGuire, a fellow we trained, is now in NIH....A good case in point is the curiosity a few years back about vaccine safety in UCDs. I talked to other people in the group and wanted

to get vaccine records. We pulled 1,200 vaccine records and examined whether the patients fell sick after vaccination and it turned out they didn't. The vaccines were actually quite safe. That's a case where we were sitting down and just talking about some idea, asking for opinions and others thought it was a good idea.

More than 85 percent of survey respondents "agreed" or "strongly agreed" that without the UCDC UCD researchers "would have shared ideas less often" and "would have done less data sharing." A similar fraction "agreed" or "strongly agreed" that "the UCDC has increased collaboration among urea cycle disorder researchers." An equally large number of survey respondents "agreed" or "strongly agreed" that "without the UCDC, geographical dispersion would have been a much greater barrier to collaboration," confirming that the UCDC has been effective in addressing this particular obstacle to rare disease research.

Interestingly, our interviewees suggested that the structure provided by the consortium, such as the regular monthly teleconferences and annual meetings was important in facilitating knowledge sharing, despite the fact that many, if not all, UCDC researchers are inherently motivated to share. Thus, for example, one interviewee told us that "[s]imply having the grant with leadership provides cohesion to the effort and people feel invested and responsible." We speculate that a regular structure for communication, such as the required monthly conference calls, may be particularly important to promoting knowledge sharing in circumstances in which participants are separated geographically and have many responsibilities clamoring for their time and attention. In this respect, the consortium structure seems to serve as a mechanism for coordination and commitment, rather than as a mechanism for overcoming a collective action problem of the prisoner's dilemma variety.

D. MANAGING INTERACTIONS WITH PHARMACEUTICAL COMPANIES

There are many facets to the UCDC's interactions with pharmaceutical companies. We discussed some of the issues related to data access in Section A, above. Here, we briefly consider the issues raised by more direct involvement between UCDC researchers and pharmaceutical companies. Currently, for example, UCDC researchers are involved (though not always directly under UCDC auspices) with a UCDC-sponsored surveillance study of patients who are being treated with Orphan Europe drug, Carbaglu; with clinical trials of HPN-100, a drug produced by Hyperion Therapeutics, which drastically improves the palatability of treatment for certain UCDs; and with studies of a human liver cell infusion treatment sponsored by Cytonet GmbH & Co. KG; and with studies of additional UCD indications for Carbaglu.

As already discussed, the development of new drug treatments is an important goal of the UCDC's research. When research results suggest new or improved treatments, UCDC researchers often interact with pharmaceutical companies as they develop and test the drugs. UCDC researchers are also likely, because of their expertise in UCDs, to be involved with the development and testing of pharmaceutical treatments that do not initially stem from UCDC research. As already mentioned, perhaps the primary way in which the UCDC influences the interaction with pharmaceutical companies in the rare disease context is by creating a pool of data about potential research subjects that dramatically reduces the cost of recruiting and characterizing patients for clinical trials.

As interactions with pharmaceutical companies increase, there are likely to be more issues for the UCDC to address. While institutional conflict of interest policies address general concerns raised by interactions between researchers and pharmaceutical companies, they cannot address conflicts that arise out of differences of opinion between UCDC members about issues such as choice of appropriate pharmaceutical company partners, terms of data sharing and intellectual property agreements and so forth.

Patients may also want input on these issues. For example, in our interview, NUCDF's Le Mons emphasized the importance of transparency in collaborations between pharmaceutical companies, the UCDC, and the patient advocacy group, describing a successful collaboration in which information learned in clinical trials was shared with researchers and led to advances in scientific understanding of the disorders.

Some of our interviewees suggested that the UCDC may need to develop policies for dealing with intellectual property issues that are likely to arise in interactions with pharmaceutical companies. At present, the UCDC does not have an intellectual property policy and there appears to be some significant disagreement about the issues among PIs. For example, researchers (both PI and non-PI) and study coordinators all were evenly split as to whether the decision to apply for a patent "should be up to the individual researcher" and close to evenly split as to whether "patents based on UCDC research should be jointly owned by all UCDC participating institutions." While a majority of PIs agreed that licensing policy for such patents "is the business of that patent's inventors and their institutions," nearly 30 percent of PIs disagreed. Nearly all PIs agreed, however, that licensing policy should be established by the UCDC Steering Committee and that it was important to them to have input into the UCDC's intellectual property policy.

E. INTERACTING WITH PATIENTS TO SET RESEARCH PRIORITIES AND SHARE RESEARCH RESULTS

Interactions with patients serve many important purposes for the UCDC. We already discussed the issue of recruiting participants for UCDC studies in Section A, above. Here, we consider interactions between patients and researchers that involve the setting of research priorities and the communication of research results.

As already mentioned, one of the goals of the RDCRN is to treat patients as "research partners." Our study suggests that the UCDC has been relatively successful in that regard. NUCDF executive director Le Mons appears to take an active part in discussions of proposed research directions and protocol design. A CPI confirmed the importance of NUCDF input: "Cindy is part of our steering committee so her input is critical. If we want to do something and she doesn't think it's a good idea, we listen very carefully because she knows.... She has her finger on the pulse of the patient. So she knows what the patients are interested in." Le Mons herself emphasized the collegial relationship she has with UCDC researchers and especially with CPI Batshaw. As she explained: "I can pick up the phone any time and talk to Mark [Batshaw] and I have."

At the annual meeting we attended, NUCDF's Le Mons participated both in the NUCDF-sponsored gathering for patients and researchers and in the more technical research workshop that preceded it. NUCDF was acknowledged along with various researchers in many of the researchers' PowerPoint presentations. One interviewee described a specific situation in which the NUCDF helped the UCDC identify patient needs and adjust research priorities:

> [T]his U54 mechanism [collaborative research projects]... really allows you to do team science in a broader sense.... Cindy Le Mons has been extremely helpful, and not only helpful; she's told us what's important to parents. And she lets us know if we are not doing certain things. So for example, the grant did not tell us to do newborn screening, to develop screening for UCDs. We hadn't focused on that; we really focused on natural history and developing therapies. The advocacy group's point was: many of these kids were not diagnosed in the newborn period, and so they are dying without being diagnosed, without any treatment. And these parents keep having additional patients, additional children who were dying without diagnosis. And so newborn screening has to be part of this, even though you are not funded to do it; you gotta do it. And she was absolutely right. So that really impacted, changed the directions, and added to what we were going to do.

In communicating research findings to patients, the UCDC faces two main challenges: the difficulty of translating research results into terms that patients will understand and incentivizing the investment of time, energy, and other resources necessary to translate and disseminate research findings to patients. UCDC researchers' concern for patient welfare, particularly as pediatricians, undoubtedly motivates them to invest time and effort in these activities, as do the longstanding relationships between UCDC researchers and the NUCDF's director. Translating research results for rare disease patients may also be made easier by the fact that many patients and their families have invested heavily in self-education about the diseases and are extremely well informed.

The NUCDF plays an important role in ensuring that patients gain timely access to research results by reporting research results on its website, newsletter, and e-mail updates to patients. The NUCDF annual conference, which we attended in 2012, provides an important bridge between the research community and UCD patients and families. Researchers devote a day to presenting research findings to patients and their families who attend. As one interviewee explained: "[t]o her credit, Cindy Le Mons has been extremely proactive in making sure when families get together every year in their meeting that scientists are there to sit down and answer questions and tell the families about what their studies have done." Le Mons explained that the annual meetings can also play an important role in getting patients' local physicians "into the fold." Just as the consortium structures, and thereby encourages, communication between UCDC researchers, the NUCDF's activities appear to structure, and thereby encourage, communication of research findings to patients.

VIII. Conclusion

The UCDC is considered one of the most successful consortia in the RDCRN, and we have largely taken that as a given here. From what we can tell at this stage, having performed only this single case study, the UCDC is effective, at least in so far as it has been successful in meeting many of its own self-professed goals, as well as those set by the NIH. Though we do not have independent metrics for assessing UCDC outcomes, the NIH peer review process in 2009 gave the UCDC its highest score. Because this is our first RDCRC case study, we cannot reliably identify the characteristics responsible for the UCDC's success, nor can we entirely disentangle characteristics resulting from the structure imposed by the RDCRN from characteristics stemming from the UCDC's particular community. Nonetheless, we believe that our study of the UCDC allows us to identify characteristics that seem to have contributed to the UCDC's success and to posit hypotheses that such characteristics that may be important for consortium success more generally. We hope to expand our study to several more rare disease research consortia to allow us to perform systematic comparison and analysis. Our interviews thus far suggest that existing rare disease research consortia vary considerably along many dimensions, including their success.

To begin at a rather general level, our study suggests that the following have been important for UCDC success and may be important to the success of other consortia: strong CPI leadership, strong program manager leadership, a close-knit core researcher group coupled with inclusiveness/openness to new members, and a strong patient advocacy group with a good working relationship with the consortium leadership. Strong PI leadership in the UCDC seems to involve the following important characteristics: dedication, collegiality, trustworthiness, fundraising capability, respected decision-making capability, scientific credentials, and sincere interest in serving patients. While formal governance was not important in most respects, the UCDC's publication policy and internal data sharing policies served to clarify and set consortium norms. Involving the patient advocacy group with the research community seemed to have several benefits, including better understanding of patient needs, more successful patient recruitment for research studies, and strengthening of researcher motivations to collaborate because of shared concern for patient welfare. We hypothesize that cooperation is more likely to succeed when (1) the patient advocacy group is an empowered member of the consortium; (2) patient advocacy group participation is visible to other community members; and (3) the patient advocacy group is itself successful and has strong leadership. Along the same lines, we note that most UCDC researchers are pediatricians and most of the patients are children and hypothesize that collaborative research may be more likely to succeed when this is the case.

Certain aspects of the RDCRN's structure also seemed to have been particularly important to the UCDC's success. The longitudinal study formed a backbone for developing a shared data pool, developing collaborative practices, and facilitating consortium growth. Monthly teleconferences appeared to be extremely important both for scientific communication and for implementing the consortium's informal governance approach. The DMCC's data management activities provided important infrastructure for the creation of a shared pool of data, and its auditing and enforcement activities may have alleviated a potential source of conflict between consortium members.

Finally, the study identified several areas on the horizon that may pose challenges to the UCDC's current approach to governance and decision making, with its heavy dependence on leadership style and informal, though hierarchical, decision making. As various interviewees noted, the UCDC will undergo a leadership transition in the next few years and such transitions can be difficult. Continued growth in the number of sites and community members may increase transaction and management costs and put additional pressure on the consortium's informal governance mechanisms. Other loci for potential stress include pursuing research on gene therapy and various interactions with pharmaceutical companies.

Our list of potentially important contributors to the UCDC's success is rather long and many of them may seem evident in hindsight. Nonetheless, the list is not quite what we anticipated after a reasonably extensive review of the UCDC website, RDCRN documentation, and other publicly accessible documents. We had anticipated, for example, that factors such as a formal conflict resolution policy or procedure, a history of involvement by all SPIs in UCD research, the DMCC patient contact registry, and the UCDC's public-facing website would be much more important for the UCDC's success than our detailed case study showed them to be. The difference confirms our view that structured and detailed case studies are needed to understand knowledge commons.

In our view, the modified IAD framework was an extremely useful tool for identifying and studying the governance issues faced by the UCDC and its approaches to managing them. Though RDCRN consortia aim to produce nonrivalrous knowledge, the study demonstrated that they have a variety of related goals and objectives. These goals and objectives produce action arenas involving the generating, sharing, and managing of many different types of resources—rivalrous and nonrivalrous, tangible and intangible. These action arenas involve a variety of social dilemmas, which governance systems must resolve. A superficial focus on knowledge sharing runs the risk of missing important facts on the ground that shape success or failure. The study also provided us with many ideas about how the modified IAD framework might be further adapted to better fit these research commons. For example, we found that the inquiry into goals and objectives is more foundational here than it might often be in the natural resources context because, to a significant extent, goals and objectives precede, generate, and organize both resources and community and define important action arenas.

Acknowledgments

Professor Strandburg acknowledges the generous support of the Filomen D'Agostino and Max E. Greenberg Research Fund.

References

Marilyn J. Field & Thomas F. Boat (Eds.), Committee on Accelerating Rare Diseases Research and Orphan Product Development; Institute of Medicine of the National Academies, Rare Diseases and Orphan Products: Accelerating Research and Development (Washington, D.C.: National Academies Press 2011).

Sandra H. Johnson, Joan H. Krause, Richard S. Saver, & Robin Fretwell Wilson, Health Law and Bioethics: Cases in Context (Aspen Publishers 2009).

Jennifer Seminara, M. Tuchman, L. Krivitzky, J. Krischer, H. S. Lee, & C. Lemons et al., *Establishing a Consortium for the Study of Rare Diseases: The Urea Cycle Disorders Consortium*, 100 (Suppl. 1) Molecular Genetics and Metabolism S97 (2010).

Robert Steinbrook, *The Gelsinger Case, in* The Oxford Textbook of Clinical Research Ethics (Ezekiel J. Emanuel et al. eds., Oxford University Press 2008).

6 Commons at the Intersection of Peer Production, Citizen Science, and Big Data: Galaxy Zoo

Michael J. Madison*

I. Introduction

Policy analysis of scientific research, particularly in recent decades, has focused on tensions between norms of open science and knowledge sharing, on the one hand, and political and economic pressures to embed scientific research in market-based institutions based on proprietary claims to knowledge, such as modern patent law, on the other hand (Eisenberg 1989; Rai 1999; Reichman & Uhlir 2003). Twenty-first century technologies offer additional challenges and opportunities for science, grounded in the emergence of the Internet as a communications medium and in the explosion in the quantity of data available for study. If contests between norms of open science and the expectation that new knowledge should be propertized frame one (older, but still meaningful) debate about scientific research, then the emergence of so-called Big Data, often referred to more descriptively as data-intensive science (Hey et al. 2009), frames a second, related, and broader new debate. The new question is this: How should new scientific knowledge be governed? Do the historical poles—open science based on the norms of a scientific discipline, versus propertized knowledge grounded in the patent system—still offer the key alternatives? This chapter suggests that they do not. It offers a study of the organization

* Michael J. Madison is Professor of Law and Faculty Director, Innovation Practice Institute, University of Pittsburgh School of Law, Pittsburgh, Pennsylvania, USA.

and practices of scientific research in a contemporary astronomy project, Galaxy Zoo. The intuition explored below is that *commons*, rather than either the market or the social norms of science taken alone, offers a superior analytic framework for understanding the changing futures of science.

Galaxy Zoo supplies a wildly successful model of what popular media refer to at times as "citizen science" and at other times and in other respects as peer production or "crowd-sourcing." Academic researchers in astronomy in 2007 created a website that invited any and all comers to undertake the task of classifying approximately 900,000 galaxies, by looking at images downloaded from a recent sky survey. The classification exercise involved only a handful of relatively simple criteria and could be undertaken by non-experts after a brief online tutorial. The sponsoring researchers expected to rely on the results as part of preparing traditional scientific papers. (In the main, that has been the case, with some exceptions, as discussed in more detail below.) The researchers had modest expectations at the start regarding the number of visitors to the site and regarding the length of time that completing the classification exercise would take. Not only were those expectations rapidly and vastly exceeded, but the number of volunteer classifiers and their enthusiasm led in short order to continuing the project both in depth and in breadth. The initial Galaxy Zoo enterprise has been extended multiple times, to include classification of additional astronomical data and also to facilitate additional and different types of social and scientific engagement by public volunteers. The sociotechnical "zoo" architecture that evolved in conjunction with the original Galaxy Zoo project has been refined and applied to additional and similarly structured scientific research projects, all of them collected since December 2009 under the umbrella name, the "Zooniverse."[1]

Galaxy Zoo and its success teach many things. Foremost among them, for present purposes, is the proposition that large-scale scientific research projects, particularly those involving extremely large sets of data, can be managed productively by threading a careful path between the idea that scientific research is (or should be) fully and completely open and the idea that large-scale knowledge-based enterprises are best governed via patent law. Galaxy Zoo relies on both openness and on property norms, and in that sense it serves as a useful case of commons.

"Commons," as the term and concept are used in this chapter, is an umbrella idea that refers to a broad array of possible institutional arrangements for sharing information and knowledge (that is, products and sources of human culture) and for sharing legal rights that might pertain to that information and knowledge. Accessible examples of such

---

[1] Zooniverse, https://www.zooniverse.org/. The citizen science/e-science projects housed at the Zooniverse as of this writing all are classified as relating to space, to the Earth's climate, to biology, to nature, and to the humanities. They include the Galaxy Zoo, the Moon Zoo, Solar Stormwatch, Planet Hunters, the Milky Way Project, Planet Four, Spacewarps, Old Weather, Cyclone Center, Ancient Lives, WhaleFM, Seafloor Explorer, Bat Detective, Notes from Nature, and Cell Slider. The original Galaxy Zoo was chosen for this case study based on the fact that its design and success were foundational to the rest.

commons include patent pools; contemporary online, networked digital resources such as Wikipedia; modern analog knowledge production and distribution collectives such as news-reporting wire services; and older, conventional knowledge sharing institutions such as public lending libraries and universities.

Commons and commons governance refer to resource sharing and therefore to openness, but in present usage it refers to *structured* openness, with formal and informal institutional mechanisms in place to manage or govern that openness. Commons is governance, and commons is constructed, or built. In this sense commons should be distinguished from the unrestricted formal openness which defines the concept of the public domain in intellectual property law and which is sometimes attached to the term "commons" in casual, rhetorical, or political usage. I refer to commons as "constructed" because of the important sense in which commons are human institutions, often produced purposefully but sometimes emerging from or evolving out of historical happenstance. Below, I refer to the "knowledge commons research framework" as the analytic framework presented in Chapter 1 and in Madison, Frischmann, & Strandburg (2010).

The case study yields certain tentative conclusions and some hypotheses to be tested in future research. First, at a high conceptual level, there exists a dynamic relationship among scientific practice, forms of knowledge and knowledge structures, and social organization. This is hardly novel; it merely documents, again, what has been described by a diverse array of scholars, including Brown & Duguid (2000), Hilgartner & Brandt-Rauf (1994), Kuhn (1962), Mandeville (1996), Polanyi (1946), and most famously, Merton (1973). Second, at a more concrete level, relevant forms of social organization—including both the shape of astronomy and astrophysics disciplines and the character of their commons governance—are dependent on changing conceptual and material (technologically grounded) understandings of the data that scientists generate and use. Modern astronomy and astrophysics are, to significant degrees, large and complex exercises in information and knowledge governance, in addition to celestial observation. The growing computational character of these disciplines is in many respects akin to the computational character of contemporary geophysics. In light of that dynamism, none of these disciplines is itself static. What "is" science (or what "is" astronomy), what "is" relevant scientific research, and how individuals and groups bind themselves to those understandings are parts of the processes by which commons are constituted and by which commons constitutes those disciplines. I suggest, in other words, that institutional order and knowledge governance such as commons are mutually constitutive.[2] One exists largely because of the other. Finally, and despite the popular view that citizen science projects such as Galaxy Zoo primarily involve participation by undifferentiated "crowds" of volunteers, in practice the knowledge community that makes up the project succeeds in large part because it incorporates a defined social structure and a layered matrix of visions and purposes, from "this is astronomy" to "this is how the astronomical data should be

---

[2] For a related view based on a review of crowdsourced citizen science projects, see Mansell (2013).

classified," that both produce that social structure and are reinforced by it. More specific and detailed implications follow, below.

The chapter is organized as follows. Part II describes Galaxy Zoo in broad outline and explains the motivations for this examination. Part III provides an overview of the knowledge commons concept detailed in Chapter I. Part IV applies the knowledge commons research framework to the Galaxy Zoo, both by supplying a brief narrative of its history and functioning and by breaking down its components in light of the detailed clusters of research inquiries suggested by the framework. Part IV also contrasts the Galaxy Zoo case with some hypothetical and actual institutional alternatives, in order to bolster the argument for evaluating Galaxy Zoo as knowledge commons. Part V offers implications and lessons, and Part VI concludes.

II. Galaxy Zoo and Its Contexts

Humans have long looked to the stars to understand how they should look at each other and at their world. Humans likewise have long looked to each other to understand how they should look at the stars. That reciprocal relationship gave us the disciplines of astrology, astronomy, and astrophysics and ever greater understandings of literal and metaphorical influence and force. Along the way, and beginning with early astronomers, cultures of scientific inquiry and research emerged, with their own influence and force both on scientists themselves and on the institutions of science and related public policy. Comte (1830: 135–37) characterized astronomy as the first science and the foundation of all other sciences. Kuhn (1957) used the history of astronomy to frame a communitarian theory of the advancement of scientific knowledge. Traweek (1988) focused on an adjacent discipline, high-energy physics, to inaugurate the contemporary anthropological study of scientific disciplines as communities. The present chapter examines an astronomical research project partly because of the antiquity of the questions that the project addresses, partly because of the strong historical lineage of cultural questions of openness and access in communal terms, and partly because of the powerful and dramatic changes that these disciplines are now undergoing as a result of technological innovations described below.

Despite the cultural valence of earlier inquiries into the research communities of astronomers, physicists, and astrophysicists, the goal of this chapter is not to explore the anthropological or sociological character of the communities that constitute Galaxy Zoo. Rather, the goal here is to use this case to explore the dynamics of knowledge production, sharing, and dissemination in one particular scientific research community.

Galaxy Zoo began as a single solution to a pair of research problems. One of these was the domain of Kevin Schawinski, who in the early-2000s was a graduate student in astronomy at the University of Oxford. Schawinski was researching the evolution of elliptical galaxies (Clery 2011), that is, he was pursuing morphological analysis of galaxies, distinguishing elliptical from spiral-shaped galaxies. Galaxy morphology is closely linked to color. Most spiral galaxies have a distinct blue tinge, which is associated with the younger, hotter stars in their spiral arms; elliptical galaxies usually appear red, indicating the older ages of their stars and low levels of star formation. Blue ellipticals suggest the existence of gas reservoirs sufficient to support significant levels of star formation and are therefore of special interest to researchers (Schawinski et al. 2009). Schawinski aimed to examine a massive amount of digital astronomical data recently made available by the Sloan Digital Sky Survey (SDSS), a project of an international consortium of seven universities, other participating research institutions, several governments, and the Alfred P. Sloan Foundation (as principal funder). The SDSS had undertaken the largest comprehensive electronic map of the northern sky produced to date. Using a special purpose telescope on Apache Point, New Mexico, beginning in 2000 it imaged 10,000 square degrees of the sky, 70 million stars, and 50 million galaxies, resulting in approximately 15 trillion bytes of data, all of which were made publicly available as images to the research community (Margony 1999; Szalay et al. 2002). Schawinski planned to review and classify approximately 900,000 galaxies disclosed in the SDSS data. He tried, briefly, to do this himself, but he abandoned the effort because it was simply too time-consuming.

The second problem was the domain of another Oxford researcher, a postdoctoral fellow named Chris Lintott. Lintott was trying to understand spiral galaxies, also within the SDSS dataset. Whereas Schawinski was after blue ellipticals, Lintott was after red (that is, mostly dead) spirals (Lintott et al. 2008). (In each instance, the existence of these galaxies would suggest new research problems having to do with galaxy evolution and the birth and death of stars.) Schawinski's conversations with Lintott yielded the idea that the classification exercise that interested each of them could be outsourced, in a manner of speaking, to the public. Borrowing insights and some elementary technology from other, recent online scientific "crowdsourcing" efforts, notably Stardust@Home,[3] the first, public, Galaxy Zoo website (http://www.galaxyzoo.org) made the SDSS image data available online beginning in July 2007. The images were accompanied by a brief tutorial describing the classification dimensions that visitors were invited to learn and apply. (The phrase "Galaxy Zoo" evokes the idea of a zoo of galaxies—a somewhat unruly collection of "animals" with distinct appearances.) A handful of simple questions were asked, directed to morphological issues. Based on a brief online tutorial, users were asked: Is this an elliptical galaxy or a spiral galaxy, or something else? If it is a spiral galaxy, which way does it appear to be rotating? Related publicity (principally through the BBC) described the launch of the project and pointed visitors to the website (McGourty 2007).

The project was a tremendous success almost overnight, in several senses. In the first place, the classification problem that Galaxy Zoo was intended to solve was solved far more quickly and thoroughly than the organizers anticipated. "Within 24 hours of

---

[3] The Stardust@Home project began in 2006 and is located at http://stardustathome.ssl.berkeley.edu/. It engages ordinary citizens, who refer to themselves as "dusters," to examine movies of the universe to detect interstellar dust particles collected by the Stardust mission, launched by NASA in 1999 to explore the comet Wild 2.

launch, the site was receiving 70,000 classifications per hour. More than 50 million classifications were received by the project during its first year, from almost 150,000 people."[4] Galaxy Zoo is now the world's largest database of galaxy shapes (Masters 2013).

In the second place, the model of citizen science data analysis that Galaxy Zoo introduced appears to have been accepted by the community of professional astronomers. The original Galaxy Zoo project is now complete, but it has been succeeded by follow-on astronomical research projects using closely related protocols: Galaxy Zoo 2, which asked participants to classify more finely a subset of 250,000 galaxies from the original SDSS Main Galaxy Sample, using a different and more detailed set of questions; Galaxy Zoo: Hubble, which asked participants to classify a different group of older and more distant galaxies using data derived from images obtained through the Hubble Space Telescope; and now Galaxy Zoo Quench, which offered volunteers the opportunity to both classify and analyze galaxy data. In the case of the original Galaxy Zoo, Galaxy Zoo 2, and Galaxy Zoo: Hubble, the zoo-produced data either has been incorporated into a continuing series of scientific research papers published in scholarly journals or is being prepared for publication. (Galaxy Zoo Quench is still in progress, as of this writing.) More than thirty peer-reviewed papers have followed from analysis of the original Galaxy Zoo data.[5]

In the third place, Galaxy Zoo has had unanticipated spillover benefits. Galaxy Zoo volunteers organized themselves into an online forum, creating and sustaining a community that is adjacent to and that in some respects overlaps with the community of professional astronomers. Through their forum, member "Zooites," that is, amateur Galaxy Zoo participants,[6] have made a number of important discoveries based on the original SDSS data shared via Galaxy Zoo, such as the object known as Hanny's Voorwerp and the so-called "Green Pea" galaxies (Fortson et al. 2009). Those discoveries have themselves been the bases for a number of scholarly papers. All of these Galaxy Zoo projects are now part of the larger cluster of citizen science projects described in the introduction to this chapter, known as the Zooniverse. Nearly 200,000 people are registered users of one or more Zooniverse projects, and more than 800,000 have participated in one way or another.[7]

The introduction to this chapter noted that exploring Galaxy Zoo as a commons case means observing an institution at the intersection of several distinct but sometimes overlapping phenomena: peer production or crowdsourcing; citizen science; and Big Data, or data-intensive science. Before turning to the knowledge commons framework and institutional analysis of Galaxy Zoo as commons governance, it is appropriate briefly to note the meaning and significance of these concepts in the Galaxy Zoo context.

---

[4] Galaxy Zoo, http://www.galaxyzoo.org/#/story, accessed June 12, 2013.

[5] A list of published papers appears at http://www.galaxyzoo.org/#/papers, accessed June 12, 2013.

[6] The term "Zooite" is, of course, highly informal. Its principal meaning captures volunteers who participate in the Galaxy Zoo forum, but its broader meaning includes all those who contribute to the classification project.

[7] The home page of the Zooniverse, https://www.zooniverse.org/, posts a tally of total participants.

Crowdsourcing is a popular and relatively recent term that denotes a product- or service-producing enterprise or exercise in which most of the relevant labor, if not all of the labor, is supplied from a so-called "crowd"—a large number of distributed individuals who are loosely coordinated, who offer their labor and/or expertise mostly as volunteers, and who are organized, if at all, mostly in nonhierarchical relationships. Benkler (2006) uses the phrase "peer production" to describe the phenomenon as follows. Some very large group of "peers," that is, individuals coordinated through a network rather than hierarchically through a firm, cooperatively and effectively produce some "thing," typically directed to knowledge, information, or culture, such as an online encyclopedia. The contents of Wikipedia are said to have been produced by crowdsourcing, for example, because of the very large number of volunteer Wikipedia contributors and editors and because the vast majority of them operate anonymously or pseudonymously and without formal supervision or discipline in a firm-based hierarchy.

It is important not to overstate the novelty of crowdsourcing or peer production, even if the Internet seems to make them much easier. The *Oxford English Dictionary* was produced in large part based on the contributions of thousands of volunteer lexicographers, who found and submitted slips of paper containing old literary references for unusual words (Ogilvie 2012; Winchester 2004). Nonetheless, the original Galaxy Zoo is in a sense an exemplary case of peer production or crowdsourcing. Thousands of anonymous and pseudonymous classifiers cooperated in producing an extraordinary database of morphologically classified galaxies.

The phrase "citizen science" captures a slightly different if sometimes related phenomenon and a different source of the significance of Galaxy Zoo. Citizen science describes the contributions of nonprofessionals to the work of professional scientists, in data collection and curation, analysis, or even production of scholarship based on that data (Cooper 2012a; Cooper 2012b; Reed et al. 2012). Citizen scientists may operate in large groups (in that sense, a large group of citizen scientists may crowdsource scientific data), in small groups, or even as solo contributors. Both halves of the phrase "citizen science" are significant. Individual nonprofessionals are engaged in *science* in some meaningful sense. And they are *citizens*, both in the sense that they are citizens of the world (that is, lay practitioners) rather than citizens of the scientific community and also in the sense that indirectly, at least, they subscribe to some flavor of the norms of citizenship that define that scientific community.

Although the phrase citizen science dates only from the early 1990s, the practice is, like crowdsourcing, relatively old. Examples come from both England and the United States. During the 1840s American sailors were charged by the head of the Depot of Charts and Instruments of the Navy Department with the systematic collection of weather data that were used to create wind and current charts (Cooper 2012a).[8] In England, during the 1830s, with the blessing of the British Admiralty, a scholar named William Whewell coordinated the collection of tidal information at more than 650 locations by volunteers

---

[8] One of the Zooniverse projects is titled "Old Weather" and involves the transcription of old ship logs.

who partook in the "great tidal experiment" (Cooper 2012b).[9] Charles Darwin relied on observations collected by a host of others, transmitted via post, for evidence consistent with his theory of evolution by natural selection (Browne 1996).

Some might quibble with characterizing data collection or even data analysis as "science" and characterizing these historical examples or Galaxy Zoo (which clearly follows in their tradition) as science. Stardust@Home, one of the modern models for Galaxy Zoo, is "science" in the same sense. Individual Stardust@Home citizen "dusters" and Galaxy Zoo citizen "Zooites" are credible citizen scientists because they actively apply their own critical faculties in selecting and/or analyzing data.[10] As discussed below, that identity appears to be an important factor in the success of Galaxy Zoo. From the perspective of citizen volunteers, SETI@Home, a longer-standing project through which individuals allow spare computing cycles in their Internet-connected computers to be harnessed as part of a larger-scale "distributed" computing project that analyzes radio signal data to detect signals that might indicate the existence of extraterrestrial intelligence, likely is not science. The distinction is the nature of the individual agency involved. SETI@Home is a scientific research project, and its data is peer produced (or crowdsourced), but volunteer participants are not necessarily citizen scientists. They have merely loaned their technology to the actual researchers and become passive participants in a computing exercise.

Big Data is the third significant domain in which Galaxy Zoo is situated. Contemporary commentators now often use the more prosaic and less media-friendly phrase "data-intensive science" to refer to what is simultaneously field, problem, and opportunity: how to make productive use of the massive quantities of digital data now made available by widely distributed sensor networks and highly sensitive observing instruments coupled with massive data storage facilities (Manyika et al. 2011). Exploring, classifying, searching, visualizing, and otherwise using this information—which is quantified in terms of petabytes—now constitutes a healthy research agenda in itself, because doing all of these things requires and will continue to require a host of new technological tools. Both *Nature* and *Science* have devoted special issues in recent years to the nuances of the challenges of Big Data, testifying to the scale and significance of this development (Nature 2011; Science 2011). The National Research Council of the National Academies of Science recently released a report synthesizing contemporary thinking across the scientific and policy domains implicated by data-intensive science (National Research Council 2012). Much of the report is taken up by surveys of the scientific disciplines

---

[9] William Whewell is also credited with being the first to publicly associate the term "scientist" with a person who practiced science, although the term did not achieve widespread acceptance for several decades (Whewell 1840: cxiii). The terms "philosopher" and "natural philosopher" were no longer sufficient to distinguish among practitioners of different scientific disciplines.

[10] This summary intentionally excludes the vast emerging infrastructure of online networked technical resources that bring observational opportunities to astronomical amateurs and professionals like by bringing high-resolution imaging to the desktop, including Google Sky (http://www.google.com/sky/) and the Microsoft WorldWide Telescope (http://www.worldwidetelescope.org/).

that have begun to tackle Big Data challenges, notably geophysics and astronomy. It also directs attention to underlying governance problems in light of the fact that much of this data is being generated and distributed in open networked environments funded by many different institutions and researchers. How will this data be managed?

Galaxy Zoo is an obvious candidate for discussion as an exemplar of a Big Data project. The SDSS dataset that formed the foundation of Galaxy Zoo constituted more than 10 terabytes of data. It is only one of several data releases provided by SDSS. Future SDSS surveys will produce even more data; technology improvements mean that astronomical data is likely to be created at the rate of multiple terabytes *per night* (Goodman & Wong 2009; Lawrence 2009; Škoda 2007). It is not only the case that new technologies and organizational models must be created and/or adapted to analyze that data but also that those technologies and models must be conceptualized. Peer production and citizen science are two possible conceptual sources that inspire and are inspired by Galaxy Zoo itself, but the challenges of data-intensive science are greater than Galaxy Zoo alone.

Making Galaxy Zoo the primary subject of the present chapter is prompted by interest in the sources and implications of each of these three perspectives. The type of data considered by Galaxy Zoo might lead observers to conclude that classification and aggregation of that data—the governance challenge—should be either a case of pure open science (as a traditional research scientist might suppose), or a case of market-based transfers of intellectual property (IP) rights (as a conventional intellectual property lawyer might suppose). In other words, Galaxy Zoo might have been conceived as a large version of a conventional research protocol, or as a marketplace for thousands of small-scale IP transactions. Each of the three perspectives highlighted above suggests that Galaxy Zoo is, to a significant degree, both more than and different from either of these things. Each of those perspectives is, in itself, incomplete. Treating Galaxy Zoo solely as a case of peer production or as a case of citizen science captures a great deal of the labor dynamics of the project but fails to capture fully its normative dimensions as scientific research. Treating it as a case of Big Data goes further in explaining those normative dimensions but potentially undervalues the significance of the contributions of the citizen scientists. Looking for transactions undervalues the seamlessness of the work in practice and the collaborative character of the relationships among the astronomical experts and the volunteers. What follows in the remainder of this chapter is largely an effort to synthesize the insights of each of those perspectives, using the broader rubric of the knowledge commons research framework. The hypothesis here is not that Galaxy Zoo "is" a commons, but instead that the commons framework offers a particularly useful way to understand how and why Galaxy Zoo functions as it does.

III. The Knowledge Commons Framework

This part reviews the knowledge commons research framework, outlined in detail in Chapter 1 of this volume, for the sake of the internal completeness of this chapter.

Readers who are acquainted with the purposes and details of the framework may skip ahead to Part IV.

The knowledge commons framework builds on a series of related intuitions (Madison, Frischmann, & Strandburg 2010). Commons governance means knowledge and information management characterized by domains of managed openness and sharing of relevant resources, and the first intuition is that commons governance is in broad use in day to day practice in a variety of domains and across a variety of scales. Documenting evidence to justify that intuition is the first goal of the framework. The second intuition is that such structured openness in the management of both natural and cultural resources is likely to lead to socially beneficial and/or socially productive outcomes. Salient among the class of cases where commons governance is successful and sustainable are contexts where social interest in positive spillovers from bilateral, market transactions is high. Commons may sustain the production of spillovers when the market otherwise may not. Testing that intuition by applying the framework in a series of case studies is the second goal of the framework. The final intuition is that a standard framework for identifying and assessing commons across a variety of domains can support the development of more sophisticated tools for realizing the potential for commons solutions in new institutional settings and for distinguishing commons solutions from other solutions in settings where some other approach, such as an approach grounded in proprietary rights, might be preferred. Applying the knowledge commons research framework is an exercise in analyzing colloquial commons institutions, such as "scientific research" taken in the aggregate (Merges 1996), in a nuanced way via comparative institutional analysis.

Examining constructed commons in the cultural context builds on the Institutional Analysis and Development (IAD) framework pioneered by Elinor Ostrom and her colleagues (Ostrom 1990; Ostrom 2011), but it adds some important modifications. The IAD framework has been used principally to structure analysis of solutions to collective action problems in natural resource contexts (so-called action arenas, or action situations) such as forests, fisheries, and irrigation systems. IAD analysis is premised largely on choice-processing, goal-oriented behavior by self-interested individuals. (Individual agents may fully informed and rational or operating under conditions of bounded rationality.) It looks to explain sustainable collective action that produces measurable, productive results. The insight from applying the IAD framework to a large number of governance institutions and resources is that commons solutions can be as robust as market-oriented solutions to classic "tragedy of the commons" overconsumption dilemmas involving depletable natural resources. Shared governance can lead to sustainable fisheries and forests and to regular supplies of usable water.

The knowledge commons framework differs in certain key respects. It does not assume the agency of rational, choice-selecting, self-interested individuals. It accepts the role of historical contingency and of inward-directed agents in the evolution of collective or commons institutions. At the front end of the analysis, it also requires understanding the contingency of the underlying resources themselves. Natural resource commons largely take the existence of their resources for granted: fish, trees, water, and the like. Knowledge commons identify resource design and creation as variables to be analyzed. As cultural resources (that is, as forms of knowledge and information), patents, copyrights, and underlying inventions, creations, and data are shaped by a variety of institutional forces rather than by nature.[11] Critically, the knowledge commons framework does not assume that the relevant resources are rival and depletable. The knowledge commons framework generally assumes precisely the contrary: that intangible information and knowledge resources are nonrival, nonexcludable public goods. The dilemma to be solved is not primarily a classic "tragic commons" overconsumption problem. Instead, it is more likely (in part) an underproduction problem and (in part) a coordination problem. In the absence of a governance mechanism to moderate consumption, producers of resources will fail to invest in creating new goods or in preserving them, either on their own or in combination with others, because of uncertainty regarding their ability (either individually or collectively) to earn returns that justify the investment.

Against that background, the knowledge commons framework proposes to undertake comparative institutional analysis by evaluating cases of commons resources via a series of questions, or clusters, to be applied in each instance. Several of these are borrowed or adapted from Ostrom's IAD framework. Some are developed specifically for the knowledge commons context. The full list is described here, and an abbreviated version is applied to Galaxy Zoo in Part IV.

The initial question is whether the relevant resource or case is characterized from the outset by patent rights or other proprietary rights, as in the case of a patent pool, or by a legal regime of formal or informal openness, as in the case of public domain data or information collected in a government archive. A particular regime might involve sharing data and information, or sharing rights in information, or sharing both. The character of the commons solution might involve coordinating holders of different IP interests or holders of different public domain knowledge resources, for example.

Answering that question sets a default baseline against which a commons governance regime is constructed. Within that regime, one next asks definitional questions. What are the relevant resources, what are the relationships among these resources, the baseline, and any relevant legal regime (for example, what a scientist considers to be an invention, what patent law considers to be an invention, and the boundaries of the patent itself are three related but distinct things), and what are the boundaries and constitution (membership) of the community or communities that manage access and use of those resources? How is membership acquired (this may be informal, formal, or a blend of the two), and how is membership governed? What is good behavior within the group, what is bad behavior, who polices that boundary, and how?

---

[11] Institutional forces and technologies bear on the constitution of natural resources as well, to be sure. But the biophysical dimensions of resources in natural resource commons analysis are both materially and conceptually different from the metaphysical dimensions of knowledge and information "things" in knowledge and information commons (Madison 2005).

Next are questions concerning explicit and implicit goals and objectives of commons governance, if there are any. Is there a particular resource development or management dilemma that commons governance is intended to address, and what commons strategies are used to address that dilemma?

How "open" are the knowledge and information resources and the community of participants that create, use, and manage them? Madison, Frischmann, & Strandburg (2010) argue that commons governance regimes involve significance measures of resource and community sharing and openness. Their details, however, should be specified, along with their contributions to the effectiveness of commons. Some commons and commons resources have precise and fixed definitions of both resources and community membership. Or, either resources or membership or both may be more fluid, with boundaries defined by flexible standards rather than by rules.

A large and critical cluster of questions concerns the dynamics of commons governance, or what Ostrom refers to as the "rules-in-use" of commons: the interactions of commons participants and resources. Included in this cluster of questions are (1) stories of the origin and history of commons; (2) formal and informal (norm-based) rules and practices regarding distribution of commons resources among participants, including rules for appropriation and replenishment of commons resources; (3) the institutional setting(s), including the character of the regime's possibly being "nested" in larger scale institutions and being dependent on other, adjacent institutions; (4) relevant legal regimes, including but not limited to intellectual property law; (5) the structure of interactions between commons resources and participants and institutions adjacent to and outside the regime; and (6) dispute resolution and other disciplinary mechanisms by which commons rules, norms, and participants are policed.

At this point it becomes possible to identify and assess outcomes. In Ostrom's IAD framework, outcomes are typically assessed in terms of the resources themselves. Has a fishery been managed in a way that sustains fish stocks over time? Do commons participants, such as the members of a fishing community, earn returns in the commons context that match or exceed returns from participation in an alternative governance context? In knowledge commons, resource-based outcome measures may be difficult to identify and assess. Sustaining the resources and their uses, individually or in combination, may be the point. In a patent pool, pooled resources may constitute components of larger, complex products that could not be produced but for the pooling arrangement that reduces transactions costs among participants. Outcomes take different forms. It may be the case that patterns of participant interaction constitute relevant outcomes as well as relevant inputs. Agency, in a manner of speaking, may be less important than identity; the group and its participants, in a particular institutional setting, may be ends as well as means. Levels of interaction and combination matter. Participant interaction in the context of a shared resource pool or group may give rise to (or preserve, or modify) an industrial field or a technical discipline. In that specific case, such spillovers may be treated as relevant outcomes. One might characterize these phenomena *ex ante* as different "types" of commons (Benkler, this volume, ch. 3). The knowledge commons framework deems them all fair game for comparative inquiry.

Having identified relevant outcomes, it becomes possible to look back at the problems that defined commons governance in the first place. Has the regime in fact solved those problems, and if not, then what gaps remain? How do the outcomes produced by commons governance differ from outcomes that might have been available if alternative governance had been employed? On the other side of the assessment ledger, has commons governance created costs or risks that should give policy makers and/or institution designers pause? Costs of administration might be needlessly high; costs of participation might be high; and commons governance might offer a risk of negative spillovers that offsets the initial instinct that commons produce positive spillovers. A collection of industrial firms that pool related patents in order to produce complex products may produce those products but may also engage in anticompetitive, collusive behavior. Commons governance may facilitate innovation; it may also facilitate stagnation, or worse.

IV. Galaxy Zoo as Knowledge Commons

In this part, the knowledge commons framework is applied to Galaxy Zoo. The results are derived primarily from examining publicly accessible online materials that describe and implement the project (http://www.galaxyzoo.org), which are extraordinarily rich and detailed. The information is supplemented by personal interviews that I conducted with the initiator of the project, Kevin Schawinski; with Brooke Simmons, a researcher at the University of Oxford and previously (with Kevin Schawinski) at Yale University; and with Kevin Schawinski's initial collaborator at the University of Oxford and the coordinator of the emerging Zooniverse, Chris Lintott. I have also relied on a number of research papers and conference posters reporting on studies of and by Galaxy Zoo participants. The results are reported below initially according to the clusters of questions framed by the knowledge commons research framework, although as will become clear, not all of those questions are useful or applicable here. Following that discussion, I consider the strengths and weaknesses of Galaxy Zoo as commons in light of possible alternative institutional frameworks. In that setting I briefly discuss a different Big Data astrophysics scientific research project, the Nearby Supernova Factory, that appears to be governed not as commons but instead as something approximating a traditional firm.

A. GALAXY ZOO: APPLICATION OF THE FRAMEWORK

Applying the knowledge commons framework begins with some supplemental detail about the origins and outcomes of Galaxy Zoo.

Galaxy Zoo emerged from efforts to answer a research problem. The broad challenge, and the focus of the discussion below, was morphologically classifying roughly 900,000 known galaxies revealed in images collected in the Sloan Digital Sky Survey. The narrower challenges consisted of identifying blue elliptical galaxies, which are relatively rare, and red spiral galaxies. The results would (and now do) form the backbone of a database about galaxy types to help astronomers understand the evolutionary dynamics of galaxies. Schawinski, then a University of Oxford graduate student, had attempted initially to do the blue elliptical classification work himself. In a week's time, working full-time at the task, he classified 50,000 galaxies, separating spirals from ellipticals. He realized quickly that this approach was not likely to be time-effective, but his classification rate (50,000 galaxies in a week) became known within the Galaxy Zoo community as a "Kevin week," a unit of analysis (Adams 2012).

Schawinski and an Oxford postdoc also interested in galaxy morphology, Chris Lintott, determined that the classification task could not be undertaken accurately by computer technology acting alone. The images were too indistinct for image- and pattern-recognition software of the time to be trusted (Lintott et al. 2008). Astronomers had been looking for solutions in various computation-based methods: artificial neural networks, computational algorithms, and model-based morphologies coded into software. Instead, Lintott and Schawinski and a third Oxford researcher, Kate Land (working with a Slovenian astronomer, Anže Slosar), who was interested in the "handedness" of spiral galaxies (do they seem to spin to the left or to the right?), took their inspiration from the Stardust@Home citizen science project. Via a website tutorial and an invitation distributed initially in July 2007 with a press release picked up by British television (Lintott was a copresenter on the BBC's Sky at Night program) and the online BBC News and repeated via other online media, they invited public volunteers to answer a brief set of questions about galaxy images displayed on a public website (Fortson et al. 2009).[12] The central questions were: Is the galaxy elliptical or spiral? Does it appear to be something other than a galaxy, such as a star? Does the image appear to contain galaxies that are merging? And if the galaxy is spiral, is it spinning counterclockwise or clockwise, or does the rotation appear to be "edge on" (facing the viewer)? Volunteers were asked to register an account (a username or pseudonym was accepted) and to run through a trial set of fifteen sample galaxies. If they correctly classified eight or more, then they were permitted to move ahead into classifying further images.[13]

The scale of the response was unexpected and overwhelming. The researchers anticipated five to ten classifications per galaxy over a period of three years, so that the entire classification exercise would be completed in five years' time. Instead, within forty-eight hours of the site's going live, Galaxy Zoo was receiving more than 50,000 classifications per hour. The three-year target of 30,000 registered users was reached before the end of the first week. By the end of the first year, roughly 150,000 registered volunteers had

---

[12] A contemporaneous blog post by Chris Lintott captures the history in more minute detail (Lintott 2007). A professional design team was retained to assemble the original Galaxy Zoo website.

[13] The full original Galaxy Zoo site is still online in archive form at http://zoo1.galaxyzoo.org.

submitted more than 50 million classifications. Because the servers storing the galaxy images did not withdraw an image after it had been classified previously, each galaxy had been classified more than 30 times. The original Galaxy Zoo project closed in February 2009. The accumulated data was publicly released and remains available at http://data. galaxyzoo.org/ (Lintott et al. 2010).[14] Papers analyzing the data are collected at https:// www.zooniverse.org/publications.

Unexpectedly but noteworthy for present purposes, the explosion of volunteer interest in the project was accompanied by a demand by volunteers for answers to thousands of both scientific and technical questions. At least one celebrity with a noted interest in astronomy, Brian May, former lead guitarist of the band Queen and now a PhD astrophysicist, publicly promoted the Galaxy Zoo project, a fact that undoubtedly help stir public interest. But the sheer volume and intensity of the response suggests that Galaxy Zoo tapped into a huge, latent demand for amateur scientific—particularly astronomical— exploration. The Galaxy Zoo team launched a blog in which they discussed their work with the galaxy classification data. An online forum (still at http://www.galaxyzooforum. org) was added quickly—within a month of the launch of Galaxy Zoo—where volunteers could post interesting images and questions and talk among themselves as well as with the team leaders. Importantly, the images on the Galaxy Zoo site were served directly by the SDSS archive (more on the SDSS, below), and each image was accompanied by a link, via a disclosed galaxy reference number, to the SDSS Object Explorer for that image (currently located at http://skyserver.sdss.org/public/en/tools/explore/obj.asp). The Object Explorer allows users to explore objects in that image in greater details. The Galaxy Zoo exercise asked volunteers one relatively limited set of questions, but the website served volunteers an opportunity to explore the sky with very sophisticated tools.[15]

The Galaxy Zoo forum has remained an integral part of Galaxy Zoo and its successors (Galaxy Zoo 2, Galaxy Zoo: Hubble, and Galaxy Zoo Quench). Users of the forum, which has evolved into a longer list of moderated message boards, refer to themselves as "Zooites." From the beginning, moderation has been handled largely by volunteer Zooites who were appointed, informally, by Lintott. In turn, Zooites refer to the professional astronomers who lead the Galaxy Zoo team (at least partially in jest) as "zookeepers."[16] Among the successes of the Zooite community are the discovery of and

---

[14] Each volunteer's classifications are treated as "votes," and the Galaxy Zoo team developed software that converted these votes into final classifications. The Galaxy Zoo data release includes full detail regarding the number and distribution of classification "votes" for each image.

[15] A related SDSS tool, the SDSS Viewer, at http://ncastro.org/Contrib/SDSS/SdssViewer.htm, created additional opportunities for what Cohen (2012) might refer to as "play." Much like a contemporary online digital music service, using the Viewer SDSS users or groups of SDSS users could explore attributes of SDSS objects and create playlists of their favorite images. Those playlists are public, along with the image data itself. Using the link above, explore "GZ Take My Breath Away," "GZ Best Spirals Short List," and "GZ Best Spirals Full" playlists.

[16] A list of current and former zookeepers is posted at http://hubble.galaxyzoo.org/team.

published scholarship regarding additional "irregular" astronomical objects not targeted for initial analysis by the team (the object known as "Hanny's Voorwerp," discovered by a Dutch Zooite volunteer named Hanny Van Arkel, and a group of so-called "Green Pea" galaxies) (Clery 2011), and the fact that some of the more active volunteers have been inspired to move from amateur astronomy to acquisition of professional, academic training in the discipline (Adams 2012).

I now turn to the clusters of commons-related questions suggested by the knowledge commons framework.

1. The Character of Commons Resources and of the Community

What are the relevant governable resources relevant to Galaxy Zoo? The resources here are of several kinds. The original resources are the underlying SDSS image data; Galaxy Zoo volunteers were presented with images of galaxies from this data archive. The next set of resources is the individual time and expertise of each Galaxy Zoo team member and volunteer, which is translated into some number of galaxy classifications. The third and final set of resources is the aggregated Galaxy Zoo data and the scholarly papers that resulted from it. Each set of resources should be characterized and analyzed in turn.

The SDSS image data deserve the greatest exploration and explanation. However one might characterize the innovation and impact of Galaxy Zoo, there is no doubt that the Sloan Digital Sky Survey is, itself, a transformative resource for astronomers (Finkbeiner 2010). The Sloan Digital Sky Survey is a seven-university cooperative enterprise that will result in the most precise, high-resolution electronic map of the northern sky ever realized. It has been analogized to a cosmological Human Genome Project (Hey 2013). The technical specifications alone suggest its massive scope. The SDSS was launched in 1998 and relies on data gathered from the Apache Point Observatory, a dedicated, 2.5-meter telescope on Apache Point, New Mexico operated by the Astrophysical Research Consortium that is equipped with a 120-megapixel camera. The camera can image 1.5 square degrees of sky at a time (about eight times the area of the full moon), and a pair of related spectrographs fed by optical fibers can measure spectra of (and therefore distances to) more than 600 galaxies and quasars in a single observation (York et al. 2000). A custom-designed set of software pipelines manages the enormous data flow from the telescope. The SDSS completed its first phase of operations, SDSS-I, in June 2005, and its second phase, SDSS-II, in 2008.

Over the course of five years, SDSS-I imaged more than 8,000 square degrees of the sky, detecting nearly 200 million celestial objects, and it measured spectra of more than 675,000 galaxies, 90,000 quasars, and 185,000 stars. Annual data releases beginning in 2005 and extensions of the SDSS phase of operations mean that the volume of data disclosed to the public, initially measured in terabytes, is now measured in petabytes. (The first and second SDSS programs can be accessed at http://www.sdss.org; the continuing program, SDSS-III, is accessible at http://www.sdss3.org. The SDSS-I and SDSS-II data releases form what is referred to as the "Main Galaxy Sample" and were the foundations for the original Galaxy Zoo.) As one scholar put it as the survey got underway:

The imaging survey of 10,000 square degrees of the sky, 70 million stars, and 50 million galaxies will result in approximately 15 trillion bytes of data, an amount that will rival in quantity the total information content of the Library of Congress. Even amateur astronomers will be able to use the data to search for rare celestial objects, to study particular regions of the sky, or to search for unexpected similarities or differences in collected data (Fuchs 2001: 51).

Funding for the creation and distribution of the SDSS archive has been provided by the Alfred P. Sloan Foundation, the "Participating Institutions," the National Aeronautics and Space Administration, the National Science Foundation, the U.S. Department of Energy, the Japanese Monbukagakusho, and the Max Planck Society. The SDSS is managed by the Astrophysical Research Consortium (ARC) for the Participating Institutions. The Participating Institutions are the University of Chicago, Fermilab, the Institute for Advanced Study, the Japan Participation Group, the Johns Hopkins University, Los Alamos National Laboratory, the Max Planck Institute for Astronomy (MPIA), the Max Planck Institute for Astrophysics (MPA), New Mexico State University, University of Pittsburgh, Princeton University, the United States Naval Observatory, and the University of Washington.[17]

Making SDSS data accessible and usable to astronomers has required more than simply dumping the data onto servers linked to the Internet. Critical to use of SDSS image data generally and to the operation of Galaxy Zoo in particular was the development of the Sky Server, a collection of databases and associated websites and interfaces that offer SDSS data to the public. Production and management of the Sky Server (currently located at http://cas.sdss.org/dr7/en/ and hosting SDSS Data Release 7) is coordinated principally among Johns Hopkins University (with respect to the underlying data archive) and Microsoft Research (with respect to the Sky Server technology itself). When the Galaxy Zoo website went live, it was hosted on Johns Hopkins University servers (later, because of the volume of traffic, it was moved to a commercial vendor). As noted above, the images themselves were served to Galaxy Zoo volunteers, via the Galaxy Zoo website, directly from the Sky Server.

The abundant technical and organizational detail that accompanies discussion of the SDSS data are important in part to demonstrate the complex and layered character of the source knowledge resources that lie at the center of Galaxy Zoo. A massive and sensitive astronomical instrument obtained a daunting amount of data, which was processed,

---

[17] A thorough yet accessible summary of the SDSS is available at http://cas.sdss.org/dr7/en/sdss/. The Sky Survey is part of an international consortium of publicly accessible astronomical data archives that collectively make up what is now known as the Virtual Observatory (VO).

sorted, and organized into particular images stored in a networked data archive and then made available for public viewing and analysis via yet another sophisticated collection of information technologies. In one sense, these images and the collection of galaxies they represent are wholly manufactured by experts using sophisticated technology, and the scope of the resource pool is limited by the scope and pace of the experts' time and manufacturing capabilities. At some formal or technical level, moreover, each image and the observable characteristics regarding the objects in that image are unique, and they are necessarily unique because they relate to an underlying physical reality.

For all practical purposes, however, none of the limitations implied by the manufactured character of the images seems to constrain how that pool of knowledge resources is created or governed. Despite the uniqueness of each image, it remains part of a pool of knowledge that is neither exhaustible, rival, nor depletable. The nondepletable character of the relevant resource (the pool of image data) is central to the success of the Galaxy Zoo project. First, the night sky itself, of course, is an effectively inexhaustible resource. Second, the continuing SDSS venture and its associated data releases demonstrate that ever-improving observational, image processing, and data storage technologies are increasing the size of the knowledge pool more rapidly than astronomers can develop tools to classify and analyze it. Third, as the Galaxy Zoo project leaders learned, any particular image of a galaxy can be used or "consumed" many times over, and in fact the unexpectedly large number of classifications of the same galaxy by Galaxy Zoo volunteers turned out to be beneficial to the project as a whole. The increased number of classifications increased the level of confidence in the accuracy of the data as a whole (Lintott et al. 2008).

The sociotechnical detail surrounding SDSS is also relevant to the next cluster of questions, which goes to the default baseline or expectations regarding the shareability of that information, as well as to questions regarding how those resources might have been governed otherwise. Before turning to those questions in the next section, I note (with less detail) two other resource sets: Galaxy Zoo volunteers themselves, and the collected Galaxy Zoo data and associated scholarly papers.

The time and expertise of those who contributed to Galaxy Zoo is conventionally viewed as labor resources rather than as knowledge or information resources and is, therefore, correspondingly challenging to describe in terms of the commons framework. Yet it is precisely this pool that inspires interest in Galaxy Zoo as commons governance. Chris Lintott and Kevin Schawinski and other professional astronomers associated with creating and managing Galaxy Zoo and producing scholarship based on Galaxy Zoo data (that is, their scholarly colleagues, postdocs, and graduate students) were contributing and sharing their time and professional expertise with one another and with the broader astronomical research community much as any research scientists ordinarily would do. It is straightforward to draw a clear distinction between them and the corps of Galaxy Zoo volunteers, then to find a formal link between the expert contributions and those of the amateurs, given the fact that the latter were invited initially to conduct relatively elementary classification tasks and nothing more.

There is a meaningful sense, however, in which the time and expertise of Galaxy Zoo volunteers and experts alike may be viewed as information or knowledge resources as well as labor, so that governance questions become interesting at this second level. Consider, first, the time and expertise of Galaxy Zoo leaders. Most observers would reasonably conclude that the leaders' participation in the project involved sharing knowledge resources with each other and (potentially) with Galaxy Zoo volunteers. The leaders conceived of the project drawing on their astronomical expertise, designed it, and shared its concept, its execution, and aspects of the underlying expertise (some of which was explicit in the design of Galaxy Zoo, and some of which presumably was implicit) with the world of potential volunteers. Consider, next, the volunteers themselves. Galaxy Zoo conveyed knowledge sufficient for volunteers to effectively participate and invited participants to exercise human judgment. Having been invited to share their judgment as to relatively simple tasks, they were motivated to share their judgment—a kind of knowledge-based expertise. Through the Galaxy Zoo forum, they were given opportunities to share that judgment as to other, less-structured opportunities, such identifying and questioning the significance of celestial objects that volunteers could see alongside the galaxies. That expertise might not be characterized in terms of professional training and education, but the documented contributions of volunteers to the discovery of celestial objects beyond the galaxy classifications suggests that they were doing more than merely sharing clicks of a computer mouse. Some of those contributions led to published papers, suggesting that the professional astronomers recognized these volunteer contributions as more than mere thoughtless labor (Cardamone et al. 2009; Lintott et al. 2010).

Should thought*ful* labor be classified as a kind of knowledge resource? In terms of modern intellectual property orthodoxy, which is highly skeptical of any labor-based claims to proprietary rights or interests,[18] the answer might well be "no." But there is a significant difference between resources and legal rights governing those resources, and the former are the topic here. Omitting these resources from an account of the enterprise and treating Galaxy Zoo time and expertise simply in terms of a division of labor between professional and amateur astronomers likely misses some important aspects of what happened. There is abundant evidence of meaningful scholarly collaboration between and among the experts and the volunteers. The record also suggests that the professional astronomers went to some lengths to prevent disciplinary hierarchies from limiting forms of interpersonal interaction. With respect to human contributions, this was a knowledge-sharing enterprise as well as an exercise in distributing and sharing labor. The fit between the resource-character question and the nature of the shared contributions suggests, perhaps, that "knowledge resources" is an insufficiently broad question to be asking. In some respects, what was shared was not only a kind of astronomical judgment

---

[18] See Feist Pub'ns, Inc. v. Rural Tel. Serv. Co., 499 U.S. 340 (1991) (rejecting labor-based "sweat of the brow" justifications for copyright interests).

but also parts of what it means to be an astronomer or a scientist.[19] Akerlof & Kranton (2010) suggest that group and organizational identity may form an important part of an individual's contribution to organizational productivity but is missing from most economic accounts of organizations. In the case of Galaxy Zoo, identity, or identities, may have been shared, and they may have been among the most important "things" shared in terms of advancing the scientific goals of the project.

Partially confirming that hypothesis is the project's pattern of scholarly publication and shared authorship. A number of Galaxy Zoo volunteers are listed as authors on scholarly publications to which they contributed. In the early papers produced by Galaxy Zoo leaders, the professional scientists tried to get journal editors to include as authors the names of all of the Galaxy Zoo volunteers (Schawinski interview 2011). When that approach was rejected, the leaders turned to acknowledging the volunteers in the paper and linking to an online image that includes all of their names (Burton 2012). The image can be viewed at http://zoo1.galaxyzoo.org/Volunteers.aspx. This sort of indirect credit might be viewed only as an effort to compensate volunteers in a way that motivates them to continue to contribute, but it is equally the case that the Galaxy Zoo leadership viewed (and views) the volunteers as genuine collaborators. Biagioli (2006) points out that scientific authorship should always be viewed as codifying contingent scientific norms. Authorship in one sense represents credit for having done some or all of the underlying work, but in a distinct sense it may represent accountability for that work, including errors, flaws, and possible harms that it causes. Galaxy Zoo's pattern of shared authorship neither represents full sharing of credit nor of responsibility, because of the physical and intellectual distance between the vast majority of the volunteers and the expert researchers who prepared the papers themselves. The expert author of the so-called "Green Peas" paper, disclosing and describing a class of objects identified initially by Galaxy Zoo volunteers, recounted the process by which the amateur observations were refined into a scholarly work product (Cardamone 2009; [Sheppard] 2009). At most shared authorship here represents a statement of descriptive and aspirational affinity between and among those who participated in Galaxy Zoo. When I interviewed Kevin Schawinski in his office (then at Yale University) and asked him to identify the members of the Galaxy Zoo team, he pointed to a poster of the Galaxy Zoo volunteer corps mounted on his office door, in effect saying "this is my team." The phrase that he did use, referring to the volunteers, was "direct collaborators" (Schawinski interview 2011).

Last, the Galaxy Zoo dataset itself should be considered as a kind of shared information resource and as a collection of shared resources. The time and expertise of Galaxy Zoo volunteers is not a well-defined shareable "thing" like an image of a galaxy or a galaxy itself or a pool of galaxy images, but via application of software and the volunteer's

---

[19] During 2009 and 2010, the Galaxy Zoo blog featured a series of posts framed as interviews with seven Galaxy Zoo experts and eight Galaxy Zoo volunteers, all women, titled "She's an Astronomer." (Masters 2011).

responses to classification questions (sometimes referred to as "votes") that volunteer's time and expertise is translated into a small smidgeon of metadata about that image. Each small piece of metadata is a tiny information "work" that is shared via the Galaxy Zoo database itself with all other, similar information works. Each such work in itself is of minimal value, but in the aggregate, millions of those works taken as a whole offer fertile ground for further research. The Galaxy Zoo database has been posted online, with all of the detail regarding individually contributed "works" intact, for full and open reuse by other scholars (Lintott et al. 2010).

2. The Default Baseline: What Formal and Informal Expectations Attach to the Relevant Governable Resources?

This cluster of questions looks to distinguish between resources governed in the first place by default intellectual property regimes (patent law, copyright law, trade secret law, and the like) or by an absence of formal legal regimes (material that is in the public domain). The premise of both perspectives is that knowledge resources are nondepletable, and their nondepletable character is an important driver of commons creation and success. In the case of Galaxy Zoo, and continuing the theme introduced in the last section, the following suggests that both the nondepletable character of the relevant resources and the formal legal baseline for their governance may be less significant in practice than relevant community expectations regarding their creation and use.

The SDSS image data that constitutes the initial resources for Galaxy Zoo are potentially copyrightable. Although the images are meant to be absolutely faithful high resolution photographs of natural physical phenomena, it is plausible to suspect that they are characterized by the very modest amount of creative "authorship" that would place them within the scope of copyright. A host of individual researchers contributed to the process that produced the data; any or perhaps even all of them could claim standing, as a formal matter, as copyright "authors." Although the images were obtained by a collaborative that included funding and expertise from U.S. government agencies,[20] there is no suggestion that the images are U.S. government "works" that cannot be protected by copyright.

Functionally, the image data appears to have been treated by the SDSS and users of SDSS data as belonging to the kind of normative public domain of public information that we typically associate with scientific data. The Astrophysical Research Consortium published SDSS data to the world with the intent that it be used for follow-on research. The SDSS project website includes a restrictive notice to accompany any use of SDSS data: "Data from the SDSS public archive may not be used for any commercial publication or other commercial purpose except with explicit approval by the Astrophysical Research Consortium (ARC). Requests for such use should be directed to the ARC

---

[20] The Apache Point Observatory is operated by a consortium of research universities, listed at the observatory's home page at http://arc.apo.nmsu.edu/.

Corporate Office via ARC's Business Manager.... "[21] Note a rhetorical ambiguity embedded in this statement that reinforces its public, shared character. The SDSS data archive is *public*, but it is presumptively *noncommercial*. One commentator has gone so far as to characterize the SDSS direct data release as a novel form of scholarly communication, because disclosing all of the data to the public contravened a scholarly convention that research data remain private or proprietary even so long as scholarly papers are published (Hey 2013). That treatment is consistent with the restrictive legend on the website. In effect, the SDSS data were simultaneously distributed and claimed as a shared scholarly resource.

With respect to Galaxy Zoo itself, the modest ambiguity did not cause any difficulty. The founders were aware of the restriction on use of the data from the beginning (Schawinski interview 2011). There is no evidence that the restriction was communicated formally to the broader Galaxy Zoo community; it seems to have been understood that the Galaxy Zoo project was by its nature a research program and therefore not commercial. There was never any question that SDSS image data could be freely shared within the Galaxy Zoo project and among Galaxy Zoo professionals and volunteers, even as that latter group expanded informally and significantly.

The other two pools of resources related to Galaxy Zoo, the knowledge pool that consists of the experts and volunteers themselves, and the Galaxy Zoo classification data, are somewhat easier to characterize. The leadership group, the professional astronomers, acted at virtually all times in ways that were consistent with "Mertonian" norms of scientific research: communalism (common or shared "ownership" of scientific discoveries); universalism (truth claims being evaluated according to objective or universal criteria); disinterestedness (selflessness); and organized skepticism (truth claims are subjected to community scrutiny) (Merton 1973). The two initiators, Lintott and Schwanski, engaged in what can only be characterized as a significant amount of entrepreneurship and promotion as part of getting the venture off the ground and sustaining interest in it (Lintott interview 2013). Press releases, interviews, and/or media appearances by one or both men were frequent (and remain so, in Lintott's case, with respect to the Zooniverse). Those efforts appear to have been motivated both by the desire to generate sufficient public interest in the project that it could succeed and possibly generate sufficient institutional credibility that it could retain funding from relevant supporters, particularly Johns Hopkins (host of the SDSS image archive) and Oxford (home of the servers with the Galaxy Zoo interface), and their respective public-funding sources. Interestingly, those promotional efforts, while important to the project's success, neither suggested any sort of proprietary claim to any Galaxy Zoo data nor compromised the outward association of the project with Mertonian norms. Hagstrom (1965) translated the Mertonian

---

[21] The notice appears at http://www.sdss.org/collaboration/credits.html, which has been unchanged since 2008. This page does not refer to copyright. There is no requirement that those who use or download SDSS data acknowledge the policy explicitly before they do so.

framework into an economic model framed as gift exchange. Scientific research was given to the broader community in exchange for nonmonetary recognition. It is fair to characterize the Galaxy Zoo team as operating in gift exchange mode, at least to a sizable extent.

Likewise, the volunteer population appears to have expressed little interest in any non-Mertonian perspective on their efforts. They clearly welcomed the fact that their contributions were recognized in Galaxy Zoo's shared authorship practice. Individuals whose names were omitted from the list of the whole group pointed out the omissions, and they were corrected. Not recognized or pursued was the possibility that the volunteers could be regarded, in a class-based sense, as unpaid laborers doing the tedious work needed to enable the higher-profile, better-recognized scholarship of professional experts.[22] The modern phrase "citizen science" in this context replaces the nineteenth-century phrase "subordinate labourers," used by William Whewell (Cooper 2012b). With respect to the data itself, however, the leadership group understood that they had invited the public at large to participate in a science project, and the public understood that they accepted that invitation and thus subscribed to the implicit norms of science (Raddick et al. 2010).

Those two premises, as to the SDSS data and as to the efforts of the Galaxy Zoo team, merge in the character of the Galaxy Zoo classification database, which has been made available for public access. The default baseline with respect to that database is copyright law, and the database as a whole is almost certainly a copyrightable work of authorship. The Galaxy Zoo leadership developed software that aggregated the "votes" represented by individual classifications with respect to each galaxy, identified and segregated outliers, and translated the results into classifications in fact associated with each galaxy (Lintott et al. 2010). The result is undoubtedly and at least minimally creative. Galaxy Zoo pays forward the "no commercial use" restriction that accompanied the SDSS image data by associating the Galaxy Zoo data with a Creative Commons Attribution-Noncommercial-No Derivative Works 2.0 UK: England & Wales License. The Galaxy Zoo summary of its terms is worth quoting in full:

> The design and graphical elements of this site, including the Galaxy Zoo logo, are separately copyrighted and are not part of the Creative Commons license. Design and graphical elements © Galaxy Zoo 2007, All Rights Reserved.
>
> You may print, or download to a local hard disk, any content from this site for personal use. You may use any content from this site for personal or noncommercial use, with the exception of the Galaxy Zoo site design and logo, provided you acknowledge this site as the source of the content with the usage notice above. You may copy content to individual third parties for their personal or noncommercial use, but only if you distribute the content without modification, and acknowledge this site as the source with the usage notice above.

---

[22] The gendered dimension to Galaxy Zoo, as part of professional astronomy as a whole, did not go unnoticed (Masters 2011).

You may not, except with our express written permission, distribute or commercially exploit the content.

All the galaxy images that appear on the Galaxy Zoo site come from the Sloan Digital Sky Survey and are governed by its copyright policy. [Galaxy Zoo links here to the SDSS policy noted above, although what Galaxy Zoo characterizes as a copyright policy does not refer to copyright.]. Essentially, non-commercial personal, educational, or scientific use is granted as long as credit is given to the Sloan Digital Sky Survey, with a link to www.sdss.org. Specific acknowledgement must be given for non-commercial publication. To use the images for any commercial purposes, request permission according to the instructions in the SDSS copyright policy.[23]

Pause here to consider some technical copyright details. If, as this policy suggests, the Galaxy Zoo data comprise a single copyrighted work, then who is the author? One might look to the shared authorship practices of the group, which take a step in the direction of recognizing all Galaxy Zoo volunteers as contributors, if not formal, named authors. Acknowledgment does not an author make, but it should be recognized that between the shared authorship practice, the plausible treatment of each individual classification as a small work of authorship, and the reference by the Galaxy Zoo copyright policy to the SDSS restrictive notice, there is a gap. Individual volunteers are not asked or expected to license, waive, or assign any possible intellectual property interests that they might have in their contributions. SDSS image data are part of a formal IP rights scheme, and the Galaxy Zoo data are part of a formal IP rights scheme. But the volunteer contributions that are merged with the SDSS image data are not part of a formal IP rights scheme. In practice, this seems to matter not at all, and I do not mean to imply that there is anything defective about Galaxy Zoo's strategy. For reasons discussed below, Galaxy Zoo's approach here may be precisely the right one. One possible implication is that the formal IP baseline with respect to commons resources is less important than community or group expectations and how those expectations intersect with proprietary norms.

The other final output of Galaxy Zoo, scholarly papers, are subject to all of the usual expectations associated with scholarship in the astronomy and astrophysics domains. Virtually all of the papers that have used Galaxy Zoo data are, formally speaking, authored by leadership team members. As noted earlier, some papers have had nonteam members as named co-authors, and many have identified the population of Galaxy Zoo volunteers as contributors. But in Hagstrom's terms they, like the data itself, are a kind of gift. The papers are distributed publicly. In this context, e-prints are submitted to and posted on the arXiv website (http://www.archiv.org) that hosts open-access copies of papers in physics, including astrophysics, and some related disciplines.

---

[23] Copyright Notice, http://zoo1.galaxyzoo.org/Copyright.aspx, accessed June 12, 2013.

3. Goals and Objectives: What Commons Problems Are Being Solved?

The point of declaring that the governable resources are subject initially to an intellectual property regime, or are not, is to explore the reasons for the emergence of commons governance. What type or kind of social dilemma prompted a commons solution? The prototypical dilemma in a knowledge production and management context is framed by the formal "tragic commons" hypothesis, that in the absence of individuated, marketable proprietary rights, a resource would be overconsumed. An alternative dilemma posits that the presence of proprietary rights themselves with respect to a given resource might give rise to a kind of coordination or transactions costs problem, if multiple rights and/or owners need to be combined in order for the resource to be exploited effectively. The prototypical response to such a dilemma is to preserve the resource as a formally and fully open or public thing. Commons governance is suggested as a method by which either of these dilemmas might be solved by enterprise participants exiting the default market-based system of proprietary rights, or the default open and public system, and working instead through a blend of formal and informal or norm-based rights and interests.

In the case of Galaxy Zoo, it might be said that neither sort of dilemma directed the commons solution, although the foundation of the galaxy classification problem was, in a sense, an underproduction problem framed in terms of coordination of participants at scale. How could all of those galaxies be studied and a suitable database of metadata created? Classic law-and-economics theory might suggest creating a market defined by transactions in individual interests in particular "votes" or classifications. One need not imagine some kind of public auction or trading floor; the "votes" could be seamlessly and automatically packaged and transferred, with an accompanying transfer of rights, in an online space little different from Galaxy Zoo itself. In practice, as noted above, that theoretical framework did not guide the development of Galaxy Zoo. Lintott and Schawinski did not start from scratch; they started from a position of commons to begin with (SDSS scientific data as a shared communal resource), and they adapted from that point forward. That is, if the discipline of professional astronomy constitutes commons governance with respect to scientific research in the first place, as it likely does, then the challenge that Lintott and Schawinski faced when they needed to classify their SDSS image data was a matter of choosing (1) to maintain the existing professional commons model and coding the data themselves; (2) to abandon the commons model in whole or in part, either by obtaining resources from a public authority, such as coding services or money to hire coders, or by organizing a market of coders with proprietary claims to exchange and housing the market entirely within their enterprise (one could characterize this approach either as a professional commons model accompanied by a clear division of labor, or as abandonment of the commons model and adoption of a firm-based model); or (3) to expand commons governance to include more "commoners."

In effect, this last option, to expand commons governance, is the strategy chosen by Galaxy Zoo. Commons was built adjacent to commons. The line between "building a firm of coders" based on division of labor, on the one hand, and "including more commoners," on the other hand, appears to be a thin one in theory. One person's commoners are another's (human) computers (Fortson et al. 2009). In the first half of the twentieth century, the term "computer" referred to individuals, usually women, who were hired to classify large batches of observational astronomical data (Nelson 2008). The affinity between those computers and contemporary Galaxy Zoo volunteers cannot be overlooked. But in practice, that affinity seems to have mattered less than the distinction. The volunteers believed that they were part of the scientific community, rather than subservient to it.

4. Resource and Community Openness: How Open Are the Relevant Resources and Groups?

"Openness" is not a simple binary, but openness of some sort is part of commons governance. Franzoni and Sauermann, in their recent discussion of "crowdsourced" scientific research, including Galaxy Zoo, focus particular attention on dimensions of openness (2014: 7-10). The idea that knowledge or information resources are shared depends to some extent on their not being fully controlled or controllable by a single agent or individual. The related groups of resources and communities described above operate with different degrees of openness, both as to membership and as to the creation and use of resources.

The pool of SDSS image data can only be added to by the scientific professionals charged with administering the instrument in New Mexico and its associated hardware, software, and database, but in theory it can be used by anyone, once the data is released publicly. In practice, of course, the data set is so large and so complex that few people will be able to make meaningful use of it. That very problem gave rise to Galaxy Zoo itself. The Galaxy Zoo community includes at least three obvious levels of inclusiveness. With some nuance added, several more are revealed. The leadership team of expert astronomers is relatively closed; over time, some leaders have joined and some have departed, but typical scientific and institutional credentials are required to become an active member of that group. The population of Zooite volunteers is open to anyone with access to an Internet connection; in practice anyone *can* (or could) classify galaxies. In between is the population of volunteers who are more active participants in forum discussions both about galaxies and about other astronomical phenomena revealed in the SDSS image data. Registration is all that is required (pseudonymous registration is acceptable); no one is required to meet any quantity or quality threshold in order to remain a Galaxy Zoo or forum member in good standing.

In addition to those three levels of community openness, more subtle distinctions appear among Galaxy Zoo volunteers. Some actively collaborate with professional astronomers in authoring scholarly papers; access to that status is relatively open and depends on substantive contributions to relevant forum threads. Others have taken leading roles in structuring and monitoring message boards on the forum. That status appears to derive from informal arrangements and relationships with the Galaxy Zoo team, particularly with Chris Lintott (Lintott interview 2013) rather than from any formal selection or election process. It corresponds roughly to length and depth of engagement with the forum. As with many Internet forums, more active and more thoughtful participation leads to more substantial responsibilities. While the pool of SDSS data themselves is relatively fixed, with new data added only by professionals and existing data only analyzed by volunteers, the pool of volunteers is quite fluid, especially in the middle and bottom (largest) populations. Leadership and coordination is limited largely but not exclusively to the professional astronomers.

Last, there is the pool of Galaxy Zoo classification data, which has been published (via http://data.galaxyzoo.org/) and which remains available to follow-on researchers. A relevant nuance here confirms the claim above that "openness" is not a simple binary. The Galaxy Zoo leadership team held off releasing the underlying data until after publication of the initial Galaxy Zoo scholarly papers (Lintott interview 2013). The delay neither added to nor detracted from the mechanics of Galaxy Zoo as a scientific project. Instead, it followed from the need to coordinate the novel governance dimensions of Galaxy Zoo with existing imperatives of scholarship and professional advancement by the leadership group.

It is not clear from the description above that "openness" as a separate inquiry adds much to the analysis of Galaxy Zoo, once the sociotechnical dynamics of the enterprise are accounted for. "Open" commons governance does not add resources at the beginning of the process and accounts only for a part of the collaborative work that goes into producing scientific papers. There is no extraction and replenishment process with respect to the knowledge resources involved aside from expansion and management of the pool of Galaxy Zoo volunteers themselves. Membership in the Galaxy Zoo project exists at various levels; the complete openness of the classification project to volunteer contributions means that there is little meaningful boundary between "inside" and "outside" the project. The key variable, already discussed, is the manner in which contributions are coordinated.

5. "Rules-in-Use" (Narratives; Appropriation, Management, and Replenishment; Institutional Nesting; Relevant Legal Regimes; Discipline)

In terms analogous to those set by Ostrom with respect to the IAD framework, Galaxy Zoo is both a resource institution and a kind of "action arena" in which group members interact with resources according to informal and formal rules. Once the system is set up, in other words, then it operates. In practice, of course, distinguishing the elements of the mechanism from its operation is more art than science. This section, however, attempts some of that task.

- *Narrative(s)*
  The stories that Galaxy Zoo tells about itself, and that are told about Galaxy Zoo, do at least two things. In part they frame the analysis here, and in part they frame

how the enterprise understands itself. The discussion in the introduction to this chapter disclosed much of the relevant narrative of Galaxy Zoo. Commentary both internal to the Galaxy Zoo project (such as articles written and interviews given by Galaxy Zoo members) and external to it (articles written by outsiders, either for scientific publications or for the popular media) appear to emphasize "citizen science," "crowdsourcing," and "Big Data" or "eScience" if not in equal measure then at least to a significant extent in each case. The common thread is "science," and within science, "astronomy." Galaxy Zoo is simultaneously characterized as an extraordinary solution to an extraordinary problem and as part and parcel of scientific traditions. That duality seems to be critical in keeping all aspects of Galaxy Zoo functioning well.

As with many extraordinary things, in other words, evidence of continuity is as compelling as evidence of innovation and change. The underlying scientific problem, the classification of galaxies in order to understand their dynamics, is a long-standing challenge for astronomers and was among the questions addressed by Edwin Hubble, for whom the space telescope is named. Amateur support for astronomy, if not necessarily "citizen science," is among the oldest traditions in research science. Galileo, Newton, and Kepler were amateurs in their own times. Patterns of broad amateur participation in observational astronomy have been well documented for decades (Berensden 2005; Ferris 2002; Lankford 1981). In many respects Galaxy Zoo is a broadening and deepening of explicit, long-standing amateur interests, including those of the leaders themselves (Lintott interview 2013). When Lintott and Schawinski invited the public to help them classify galaxies, it is likely that those who responded included many people with existing, if often latent, interests in the field (Raddick et al. 2010). Galaxy Zoo likewise offers a robust platform for teaching lay and youth audiences about astronomy.[24]

- *Appropriation and replenishment processes and rules*
  As to the SDSS image data and related sky survey data, the sky and the associated imaging data are functionally nondepletable. We do not yet know the limits of the universe, and advancements in sensing and detection technologies mean that the quality and quantity of image data continues to improve. Replenishment of the classification data, either by permitting multiple classifications of the same galaxy or by putting forward additional sets of data images for classification (as in Galaxy Zoo: 2 and Galaxy Zoo: Hubble) has proved to be robust in practice, despite the absence of any formal or informal rules that govern how the classification data is created, such as how many times a given galaxy may be classified, or how many galaxies may be classified by a given volunteer.

---

[24] The Zooniverse includes its own set of resources for teachers. See https://www.zooniverse.org/education and http://www.zooteach.org/zoo/galaxy_zoo, both accessed Sept. 10, 2013.

"Depletion" and "replenishment" and accompanying limits and duties are not quite accurate descriptions of the operation of the data analysis project that defined Galaxy Zoo in the first place. The SDSS image data simply "is," although its parameters expanded and continue to expand. The classification data accumulated through repeated "votes" by Galaxy Zoo volunteers, although no additional contributions were expected from existing members. On the one hand, older data did not decay or disappear, so there was no "depletion." On the other hand, new data did not simply add to the existing archive on a one-vote-per-entry basis; the relevant resource was supplemented, or enhanced, but not "replenished." As Lintott explained when the Galaxy Zoo data were released, a complex computer algorithm was developed to convert raw votes into classification data (Lintott et al. 2010).

Moreover, the Galaxy Zoo community identified and pursued additional celestial objects for study, which means that a certain type of resource creation and/or replenishment was possible even while the original Galaxy Zoo task entailed classifying a fixed data set. A technical platform built for one purpose turned out to support a community that was capable of and interested in pursuing many more tasks. Galaxy Zoo facilitated research into additional objects via a series of technical and social decisions. First, the Galaxy Zoo website classification interface included a link next to each image to the Sky Server Object Explorer for that image. Volunteers were not limited narrowly to the classification exercise with respect to each galaxy but had the power, if they had the imagination, to explore further. Second, the creation and support of the Galaxy Zoo forum offered those more imaginative and curious volunteers a venue for sharing their questions and insights, so that questions and possible research about these additional objects could ferment. Third, the Galaxy Zoo team quickly accepted the productive contributions of volunteers and collaborated with the volunteers, rather than directing volunteer time and energy solely to the classification task. Galaxy Zoo was productive commons governance in several senses, not the least of which was the creation of new knowledge beyond what the organizers planned for.

- *Nesting*

Is Galaxy Zoo or any of its constituent parts nested in higher order commons governance regimes? The relationships among the different shared sets of data in Galaxy Zoo initially appear to be mostly linear. SDSS image data were produced. Then, in response to particular research problems, a broad pool of human knowledge resources were brought to bear on data analysis, leading to the creation of a database of metadata about the original data set, to scholarly publications interpreting that metadata, and to new observations and scholarly publications made possible in large part by the construction of the pool of human resources.

That linear characterization is fair in one sense, but the self-reported descriptions of Galaxy Zoo as a collaborative, iterative enterprise should also be taken seriously. Galaxy Zoo both produced new astronomical knowledge and also produced itself. In a broad sense, the creation and disciplinary acceptance of Galaxy Zoo as a research enterprise (via the addition of new team members and via publication of its papers in peer-reviewed journals) seems to be linked to its origins both within the research university setting (Oxford, to begin with, with immediate and direct links to several other universities, including Johns Hopkins and Yale) and within the communities of scientific research generally and of astronomical research in particular. It is noteworthy that following his Oxford experience and after he co-initiated Galaxy Zoo, Schawinski was awarded a postdoc at Yale, which houses a highly regarded astronomy and astrophysics program, and that Yale warmly welcomed Galaxy Zoo as part of his research agenda (Schawinski interview 2011).[25] Each of those things may be fairly characterized as commons governance in their own rights and therefore as material contributors to the success of the Galaxy Zoo as commons itself.

- *Relevant legal regimes and discipline*
  I have not found any legal regimes that bear directly on any features of Galaxy Zoo. The forum is nominally subject to the "safe harbors" for hosted content described in Section 512 of the American Digital Millennium Copyright Act.[26] The image data is now hosted on a commercial third-party cloud storage service, which is subject to both Section 512 of the DMCA and to Section 230 of the Communications Decency Act, which immunizes hosts of that sort from liability for non-IP claims associated with merely hosting the data. But there have been no reported episodes or incidents of bad behavior taking place on the forum that rise to the level of implicating possible legal claims, and there are no reports of moderators having had to intervene on disciplinary grounds other than very infrequently (Schawinski interview 2011). The forum moderators are relatively strict with respect to the use of inappropriate or vulgar language on the forum, in order to ensure that the forum is welcoming and friendly to all comers, including children (Lintott interview 2013).

The disciplinary question is independently noteworthy. There appears to be no formal or informal disciplinary mechanisms with respect to any of the commons communities included within Galaxy Zoo. Nor is there any formal organizational hierarchy within the leadership team (Lintott interview 2013; Schawinski interview 2011). Given the size and presumed diversity of the volunteer population, that seems remarkable, though perhaps it is less so when one considers the relatively narrow scope of "community" participation, at least with respect to classification. The scope of bad behavior available to classifiers is pretty

---

[25] Perhaps coincidentally, the chair of the Yale Astronomy Department at the time was Meg Urry, who is one of a relatively small number of senior women in professional astronomy (Masters 2010).

[26] 17 U.S.C. § 512 (2012).

small; individuals could intentionally mis-describe an object. But the algorithm that translates such "votes" into classifications is set up to anticipate and discard outliers, and there is little reason *ex ante* to prescribe a regime for excluding those individuals from continued participation. In other words, Lintott set himself the initial challenge in 2007 of figuring out how to find *enough* volunteers (Lintott interview 2013), rather than to find the *right* volunteers.

Discipline, to the extent that it exists, is either technical, as just described, or social. Volunteers who did no more than classify galaxies would never trip disciplinary wires set up to catch outlying votes; those who did register for the Galaxy Zoo forum and posted there would be subject to moderation. The fact that little moderation has been required suggests that despite the diversity of background that characterized the volunteers, in fact they mostly shared a commitment to the broad ambitions of the project. I hesitate to characterize that commitment in terms of social norms or norms of any kind, because that term sometimes suggests the existence of a kind of informal rule-set. In the Galaxy Zoo context, the project was characterized by a strong alignment of interests, expectations, and goals both at a high level ("science" and "astronomy") and at ground level (investigating galaxies and black holes).

6. Outcomes and Assessment

In terms of the number of volunteer participants, their passion and focus, the amount of morphological classification data and other scientific data generated, and, importantly, the number of scholarly papers published using that data, there seems to be little reason to question the success of the Galaxy Zoo project, both on its initial terms and on the terms that evolved over time, with the emergence of the forum and with volunteer-initiated discoveries. While its absolute success seems clear, its relative success is less obvious. The next section contrasts Galaxy Zoo's governance, which I characterize as commons governance, with possible alternatives.

B. INSTITUTIONAL ALTERNATIVES

Fully appreciating the institutional character of Galaxy Zoo as commons requires a brief comparison between Galaxy Zoo's governance mechanisms and the most plausible alternatives. How is Galaxy Zoo different, and in what ways have those differences benefited or imposed costs on Galaxy Zoo?

From the standpoint of knowledge and information management, three possible alternatives seem plausible.

The first looks at the galaxy classification exercise as an exemplary scientific research project undertaken by a graduate student or by a faculty researcher. It would represent professional science, rather than citizen science. Under this model, a PI (principal investigator) would undertake responsibility for all of the relevant data acquisition and analysis, alone or by supervising a team of research assistants. Classification would take place by hand, given the judgment early on in the case of Galaxy Zoo that computer algorithms could not perform the task adequately. Given the Kevin-week unit of analysis developed using the manual classification of galaxies by Kevin Schawinski himself, it seems likely that this hypothetical manually created Galaxy Zoo dataset would be inferior to the actual Galaxy Zoo dataset in one or more ways. Fewer galaxies would be classified (and therefore fewer of the target galaxies might be identified), or the classification would be less accurate (because fewer galaxies would be classified multiple times), or the project would take much, much longer to complete and fewer research findings would be produced over the same time span. This alternative construction would lack the spillover benefits that accumulated as a result of exploring objects through the SDSS Object Viewer and the formation of the Galaxy Zoo forum.

A second alternative construction borrows from well-known examples of peer production often characterized as commons: open source software development and Wikipedia. Both Wikipedia and an open source software development project operate approximately as Galaxy Zoo does. A very large number of contributors who may be largely anonymous or pseudonymous contribute small bits of labor and knowledge to a product produced collectively and that is much larger than any single person, or even any smallish group of people, could produce on their own. In the case of Wikipedia, this is the Wikipedia online encyclopedia itself; in the case of an open source software development project, it is the resulting computer program. In both cases the community of participants is itself a kind of ongoing product. In the context of open source projects, Kelty refers to this phenomenon as a "recursive public" (Kelty 2008). What he means is that the social collective both constitutes and is constituted by the product that it produces via knowledge and information sharing. Wikipedia, though not the subject of Kelty's study, bears many of the same hallmarks. The community of Galaxy Zoo Zooites and zookeepers and the database and scholarship that they jointly produce appears to have much in common with the "recursive public" model. Galaxy Zoo is both process and product.

There is at least one key distinction, and that has to do with some details of the governance strategy used by both Wikipedia and open source projects. Open source projects and products are defined in part by their formal software licenses. Each license is an essential part of the open source knowledge governance strategy, ensuring that the knowledge pooled within each project is shared both with active developers and with users and casual modifiers of the program (Madison 2003). Licenses vary in their details, but open source licenses all require that the source code for the program be made available to users and future developers so that they might modify it. In many cases the license requires that users and future developers agree that they will likewise share the source code to their modifications of the program. This duty to share is often a strong informal, normative commitment of open source communities, but it is also formally documented. Each member of an open source community, which is to say, each user of a particular open source computer program, agrees to certain formal terms and conditions that accompany access to that program, and among those terms, typically, is the duty to license back to other users (to share) modifications made by that user. From time to time, when disputes arise about the obligations of users of an open source program, the formal document is the basis for resolving the dispute,[27] and as matter of best practices, it is possible to trace individual contributions and their compliance with licensing obligations. Open source software projects are thus paradigmatic examples of commons governance, but the openness and shared character of the open source project is both norm-based and legally and technologically formal.

Likewise, contributors to Wikipedia often operate under a strong normative commitment to openness, but they, too, must formally subscribe to a form of license (a Creative Commons license) that attaches to each of their contributions, no matter how small, and ensures that those contributions will be available to future Wikipedia users on open terms. When individual contributions are aggregated within particular Wikipedia entries, the underlying Creative Commons licensing that attaches to those contributions is, for practical purposes, pooled as well, so that entire Wikipedia entries are made available to users under Creative Commons licenses. The underlying individual licenses and entries, while fully available in detail to those who would look under Wikipedia's hood to determine how the end product was created, are hidden from immediate view. Wikipedia is thus likewise a paradigmatic example of commons governance (Benkler 2006: 70–74), but like open source software projects, its openness and commitment to knowledge sharing is defined formally, in both technical and legal terms, as well as normatively.

By contrast, Galaxy Zoo (and for that matter, all of the Zooniverse projects) required no equivalent formal license or assignment of legal rights in connection with individual contributions and classifications, and those contributions are far less individuated and traceable in the context of the overall Galaxy Zoo classification database. A number of questions arise. Why does Galaxy Zoo lack the formality of an open source project or Wikipedia? Could Galaxy Zoo have been organized as either of these were? Has Galaxy Zoo's lack of that formality interfered with its development in any way? Could it be said that Galaxy Zoo has succeeded in part because of the lack of formality? If so, then why, and how?

Definitive answers are not possible, but a number of considerations seem to be at work. In the first place, contributions to an open source software project and to Wikipedia, even if trivially small, are arguably protected by applicable copyright law. At the least, it is not implausible under current law that should a dispute arise among Wikipedians or among open source software developers, a court would recognize a copyright interest in an individual contributor/claimant. If that is the case, then developing and using a license to govern knowledge contribution and use seems wise, out of an abundance of caution. The standardized license minimizes a specific type of transactions cost that

---

[27] See Jacobsen v. Katzer, 535 F.3d 1373 (Fed. Cir. 2008).

would otherwise be associated with clearing all rights from individual participants and that would be associated, in particular, with a disruptive outlier who refuses to play by informal norms. By contrast, it is less clear (though as I noted above, in my view not implausible) that galaxy classifications in the Galaxy Zoo project could be treated as copyrightable works of authorship for copyright purposes rather than as contributions of time and effort. Legally speaking, even a cautious copyright lawyer might see no reason for concern. In the second place, both open source software projects and Wikipedia likely have greater needs to for what we might call "lateral" coordination of the contributions of individual programmers and authors/editors. In technical terms, a modification of a computer program must work effectively with the existing program; an edit to a Wikipedia entry must relate in some coherent way to its existing content. The license does not ensure that either of these things will happen, but against a background norm of copyright status for each contribution and each entry, the license permits others—higher level technical coordinators and editors—to have the access to the work that they need in order to make it happen.

Galaxy Zoo is different in key respects. Each contributor's classifications simply go into the database of classifications. Coordination among the classifications is in effect "vertical," in the sense that further algorithmic work is done to analyze the classifications as a group (including, among other things, identifying and distinguishing outliers), but there is no equivalent coordinating "use" of each classification relative to existing classifications. Moreover, and perhaps more important, for reasons and in ways reviewed above, Galaxy Zoo seems to have successfully cultivated an ethos of "science" among its participants, so that the normative constraint on both data creation (everyone will do their best) and on dispute resolution (no one will claim individuated rights in a particular classification that could hold up the productive use of the pooled data) seems to be more than adequate. One cannot say for certain, but the disciplinary idea of "astronomy" seems to hold people together in Galaxy Zoo well enough, as a governance strategy.

Two further details should be noted, both of which suggest that the conclusion of the last paragraph may be on the right track. First, in the domain of commercializable "User Generated Content," or manufacturing platforms that invite end users to share ideas with for-profit companies that may be built into new versions of commercial products, it is typical for those platforms to offer mandatory terms of use by which each end user assigns all relevant rights to the manufacturer in the event that an individual contribution, which may or may not rise to the level of copyrightable authorship protected by applicable law, makes its way into a real product.[28]

Earlier in this chapter, I noted the absence of such a fail-safe provision and noted that it might be part of a wise strategy on the part of Galaxy Zoo. Here is why. Its absence may be traced in part to the fact that for all practical purposes, there are no commercial

---

[28] See, e.g., the LEGO CUUSSOO User Innovation Platform Terms of Service, http://lego.cuusoo.com/terms, accessed June 13, 2013.

implications of individual contributions or of the Galaxy Zoo classification database as a whole. Yet Galaxy Zoo has attached a no-commercial-use Creative Commons license to its own database. So the absence or presence of a formal governance document in the Galaxy Zoo context is not entirely due to the presence or absence of plausible commercial potential.[29] More important, Galaxy Zoo contributors are permitted to submit more than simply the classifications that become part of the Galaxy Zoo database; over time they have contributed additional scientific observations and analysis. There is little doubt that the form of this material is potentially copyrightable, and that its substance may end up in copyrightable material (the research papers) and has ended up there, relatively directly. Yet registered users of the forum are not required to acknowledge any formal restriction, release, or license of material shared there. I conclude that the practice of inclusiveness in terms of shared authorship for Galaxy Zoo papers, coupled with the practice of inclusiveness with respect to participation in Galaxy Zoo generally, has been sufficient to support the project's relative informal governance. Formalizing rules regarding contributions and authorship with respect to forum participants might have had unanticipated harmful consequences, by undermining the normative benefits of associating the entire enterprise and its participants with astronomy. A formal license or release may have signaled that Zooites were not fully welcome as citizen scientists, or that their potentially valuable contributions were being appropriated for less than fair value in return (even in Hagstrom's sense of scientific research as gift exchange)—in other words, that this was not only research science. Either signal could have reduced participation levels or reduced the positive spillover observed in practice. To be sure, either result is speculative.

In sum, it seems clear that Galaxy Zoo could have added a layer of formality (a license or release or both) either to the classification exercise or to the forum, or to both, very much as Wikipedia and open source software projects have done. For the reasons surveyed above, doing so likely was not necessary. The lesson is that peer production comes in many forms. Here, peer-produced "astronomy" itself is a kind of commons.

The third plausible institutional alternative borrows not from a hypothetical research project but from an actual one: the Nearby Supernova Factory. If the first alternative is grounded in traditional scientific organization and the second is grounded in newer forms of peer production, then this third alternative seems to be grounded most plausibly in conventional understandings of the firm. I use this particular example because like Galaxy Zoo, it is an organizational form situated in data-intensive science, particularly astronomy and astrophysics.

The Nearby Supernova Factory (SNfactory), housed at http://snfactory.lbl.gov/, is a formal interinstitutional astrophysics data collection, curation, and distribution enterprise. It is an international astrophysics experiment "designed to collect data on more Type Ia supernovae than have ever been studied in a single project before, and in so doing,

---

[29] Trademark concerns seem to be much more real, however, and Galaxy Zoo's copyright notice takes care to (try to) forbid commercial use of Galaxy Zoo's logo and site design.

to answer some fundamental questions about the nature of the universe."[30] Specifically, it is "an experiment to develop Type Ia supernovae as tools to measure the expansion history of the Universe and explore the nature of Dark Energy. It is the largest data volume supernova search currently in operation."[31] Planned in 2001 and launched in 2002, SNfactory has six participating institutions (three in France, two in the United States, and one in Germany), and several dozen participating individual members, about half of whom are in the United States and the other half in France (a very small number of members are located in other countries). Membership is interdisciplinary; it includes physicists, scientists, and software engineers, among others.

The project uses a CCD camera attached to its primary telescope, originally at the Palomar Observatory near San Diego, California, and now located in Chile, to collect up to 80 GB of data each night, using specifications provided by a geographically distributed group of two to six people.[32] That data becomes part of SUNFALL (SUperNova Assembly Line), "a collaborative visual analytics software system to provide distributed access, management, visualization, and analysis of supernova data."[33] The data is transferred via a high-speed network from Hawaii and Palomar to the Lawrence Berkeley National Laboratory (LBNL), where the data is stored in a giant database.[34] Follow-up spectroscopic screening and analysis takes place at LBNL, at facilities in France, and at Yale (Hules 2011). The search for supernovae, the task of analyzing them to determine whether they are Type Ia supernovae, and addressing the problem of understanding their brightness (a key measure in using Type Ia supernovae as cosmological tools, that is, to understand the rate of expansion of the universe), are undertaken by researchers elsewhere, particularly at Yale.

In sum, the "factory" production process involves three steps. First, broad scans of the sky are obtained. That is the function of the discovery camera, originally at Palomar. Second, specific coordinates of candidate objects are fed through the software to the camera; repeated observations of these objects are important in order to obtain data regarding changes in brightness. The images themselves are processed using spectrographic analysis, and eventually the resulting data is interpreted by human researchers. The project name—the "Factory"—owes its origin to the fact that the task is to produce new "things": so-called "standard candles," or cosmological objects whose brightness can be standardized and therefore used in cosmological analysis.

The distributed, interdisciplinary data curation and management strategies of SNfactory are integral to the project and key contributors to its success. SNfactory and

---

[30] About the SNfactory, http://snfactory.lbl.gov/snf/snf-about.html.

[31] The Nearby Supernova Factory, http://snfactory.lbl.gov/.

[32] The instrument was originally located at the W. M. Keck Observatory in Hawaii but was relocated to Palomar and has since been relocated to Cerro Tololo, in Chile. The coordinates used by the camera are now generated via computer software.

[33] SUNFALL: SUperNova Factory Assembly Line, http://snfactory.lbl.gov/snf/snf-sunfall.html.

[34] The storage facilities are provided by the National Energy Research Scientific Computing Center, or NERSC.

SUNFALL have reduced false supernovae identification by 40 percent, improved scanning and vetting times by 70 percent, and reduced labor for search and scanning from six to eight people working four hours per day to one person working one hour per day. The project has led to ten publications in 2009 in both computer science and physics journals (Hey 2011). It has been able to determine the intrinsic standard brightness of Type Ia supernovae with much improved accuracy. The project has evolved somewhat since its origins (the relocation of the camera suggests as much), and its success has spawned some rivals, such as the Palomar Transient Factory, at Caltech, housed at http://ptf.caltech.edu/iptf/.

As a large-scale, distributed, information technology-based enterprise intended to manage a large volume of astrophysical data, the SNfactory has much in common with Galaxy Zoo.

Yet in important respects, the SNfactory governs itself and its data differently, and the differences are instructive. In effect, the SNfactory is a hierarchical firm, producing scientific products (its standard candles) and otherwise operating, with respect to its data, within the bounds of astrophysics as a professional discipline. Membership in the SNfactory is clearly and publicly defined and limited to the institutional homes of participating researchers. These are defined in the first instance by the several institutions that are listed sponsors of the project. Individual researchers who are members of the SNfactory project are employed by these institutions or are students of faculty and researchers employed there (or both) and are academic scientists from a variety of disciplines: astrophysicists, computer scientists, and engineers from several engineering subfields (including electrical, mechanical, and optical). The physicists work with the data, and the computer scientists and engineers are responsible primarily for design and maintenance of the hardware and software facilities used to analyze the image data. The latter are referred to by the project as "builders" rather than as "members."

In contrast to Galaxy Zoo's informal and undocumented collaborative of zookeepers/leaders and Zooites, the organizational structure of SNfactory is part of a formal, documented governance structure.[35] The SNfactory is managed by the SNfactory Collaboration Board (SCB), which consists of one representative of each sponsoring group, plus the Principal Investigator of the Supernova Cosmology Project at Lawrence Berkeley National Laboratory, a spokesperson for the participating French research consortium, and a project manager. Operation of the project is delegated by the Collaboration Board to an Operations Committee (OC) (a small group of member researchers, and the project manager). Individual graduate students and postdocs can be added to the project at the discretion of the leadership of each participating group. The Collaboration Board must approve admission of new faculty researchers or permanent staff.

---

[35] The formal governance document is posted publicly at http://snfactory.in2p3.fr/people/SNFactory_Organization_v4.1.pdf, accessed June 13, 2013.

Equivalent formality attaches to the SNfactory's approach to governing the shared data itself. As is common in scientific research, and as is common in for-profit firms that rely on confidential technical information or know-how (that is, trade secrets), the enterprise draws a clear and explicit line between sharing data among members of the collaborative, which is expressly permitted, and sharing it with outsiders, which is forbidden except with the permission of the Collaboration Board. More of the collaboration document is dedicated to identifying express standards related to publication of works based on SNfactory data. Where the Galaxy Zoo team informally adopted a shared authorship norm that attributed Galaxy Zoo scholarship to all Galaxy Zoo participants, the SNfactory reached an equivalent conclusion by formal rule: "Any paper written by a collaboration member that uses data, software, or internal group knowledge that comes out of the collaboration's work is assumed to be a collaboration paper unless otherwise agreed to in advance by the SNfactory Collaboration Board."

Whether or not all of this formality is followed strictly in practice, the only thing that surprises about this governance approach is the fact that it has been reduced to writing in such a formal way. The content of the rules is entirely consistent with underlying practice in scientific research and with a linear "production line" concept. There are well-defined roles and responsibilities among collaborating researchers and their institutions, and a firm injunction against disclosing unpublished data without the consent of the team. (That injunction likes serves the entirely ordinary scientific interest in avoiding premature publication of incompletely analyzed data, an outcome that could jeopardize institutions, careers, and funding; the Galaxy Zoo team informally adopted a similar approach.) The sociotechnical architecture that secures this model extends to the data itself. Whereas Galaxy Zoo used publicly accessible data and shared its data publicly rather than via a scholarly platform, SNfactory created its own data and managed access to its by network security protocols, that is, by passwords and an addressing protocol that renders the relevant website hidden from Google and other search engines.

To an observer outside the disciplines relevant to the SNfactory, perhaps the most significant thing about the operation of the project is its very normalcy. In effect, the narrative might explain, this is how science is produced. Within the astrophysics literature, the SNfactory is presented as a technical solution to a very important new scientific problem: understanding the properties of "dark energy," which is now believed to be the key to measuring the rate of expansion of the universe. The collaborative elements of the project and its governance structure are largely hidden from public view. They are not hidden outright, but they appear to be treated merely as scientific or research infrastructure (which, of course, they are). The narratives that accompany Galaxy Zoo stress its extraordinary character. Galaxy Zoo is treated as a novel form of scientific collaboration.

The comparative institutional question is whether it is conceivable that Galaxy Zoo might have been organized roughly as SNfactory has been organized, as a large, complex but ultimately ordinary form of formal hierarchical collaboration among scientific researchers. The scientific problems addressed by SNfactory and Galaxy Zoo are not identical, but they are closely related. In both cases, scientists asked how to coordinate analysis of a massive amount of data about the universe. It is conceivable that institutions to classify galaxies might have been organized in more conventional hierarchical terms, and Galaxy Zoo itself is hardly without its important hierarchies. But it seems doubtful that Galaxy Zoo could have achieved its levels of success by building in the kinds of organizational formality that characterize SNfactory and the sense of proprietary interest in the raw data that specifically concerns that project. Like many if not most scientific research collaboratives, SNfactory is characterized by an acute sensibility with respect to who is "in" the collaborative and who is "out." Galaxy Zoo, by contrast, never imposed such a bright-line boundary, and in many respects went out of its way to express a participatory norm that was both extremely inclusive and that projected the idea that all Galaxy Zoo volunteers were, in effect, part of the scientific team. Even if that idea took hold over time rather than immediately upon the launch of the project, the evidence suggests that it played an important role in encouraging volunteers to participate both in the classification exercise and in the Galaxy Zoo forum.

In sum, if a scientific discipline and scientific research are both forms of commons governance, then the demands of scale imposed by data-intensive science may be satisfied in multiple ways. As in SNfactory, with highly specialized data-processing needs, related commons may be joined in a kind of hierarchical data-processing firm, or, as in Galaxy Zoo, with much simpler data-processing needs. An existing commons may be expanded in scale so that, functionally, almost anyone who wishes to join may do so—so long as the individual plays by disciplinary rules. Of course, a full assessment of the costs and benefits of each approach should account not only for the community governance challenges in each setting and the relative complexity of their data analysis challenges but also for the respective spillovers associated with each. In the case of the SNfactory, spillover effects, if any exist, are likely focused on improving the expertise and impact of the associated researchers and their institutions in connection with this particular project. Progress in the field is achieved as it often is in science, via rival teams of researchers trying to outperform each other. In the case of Galaxy Zoo, spillover effects included unanticipated research findings achieved by or together with volunteer researchers, expansion of the field as volunteers entered academic astronomy, redirection of research trajectories as Galaxy Zoo team leaders expanded and redirected their technical platform to address new research challenges, and, possibly (in the future) new research findings based on the shared Galaxy Zoo data.

V. Analysis and Implications

In the introduction I highlighted several results from the application of the knowledge commons research framework to Galaxy Zoo. Here I elaborate on and extend those results. I divide them into analysis and implications with respect to commons governance, first, and then with respect to the research framework itself.

First, at a high conceptual level, Galaxy Zoo confirms the existence of a dynamic relationship among scientific practice, forms of knowledge and knowledge structures, and social organization. Galaxy Zoo also suggests a similar dynamic relationship with respect to commons governance. Scientific practice has no fixed or necessary institutional or organizational form. Its forms are adapted dynamically to the interests of relevant scientific communities and to the characteristics of the research problems to be addressed and the data to be acquired and tested. The four attributes of Mertonian science are present in this case, but they are put to the test in some respects by the organizers of Galaxy Zoo aggressively building Galaxy Zoo with entrepreneurial zeal and tactics. One attribute of successful entrepreneurs is the ability to "pivot" from one project to the next, whether turning from failure to new opportunity or capitalizing on and institutionalizing early success. The Zooniverse, as an extension of Galaxy Zoo beyond astronomy, seems to be a case of the latter. In the process of Galaxy Zoo's evolution, its commons character evolved as well. What began as community construction to solve questions about galaxies evolved over time into the development of an infrastructural resource—a citizen-science peer-production tool.

Second, at a more concrete level, specific forms of social organization—including both the shape of astronomy and astrophysics disciplines and the character of their commons governance—are dependent on elastic conceptual and material (technologically grounded) understandings of the data that scientists generate and use. Modern astronomy and astrophysics are large and complex exercises in information and knowledge governance in addition to celestial observation. The computational character of the disciplines is in many respects akin to the computational character of contemporary geophysics. In light of that elasticity, none of these disciplines is itself static. What "is" science (or what "is" astronomy), what "is" relevant scientific research, and how individuals and groups bind themselves to those understandings, tightly or loosely, are parts of the processes by which commons is constituted, and by which commons constitutes those disciplines. I suggest, in other words, generalizing Kelty's observation about "recursive publics" in the context of open source software projects. Galaxy Zoo not only produces knowledge; it is in effect a form of knowledge itself. Governance (in this instance, commons) and knowledge and are mutually and recursively constitutive. One exists largely because of the other, and they evolve together.

Finally, and despite the popular view that citizen science projects such as Galaxy Zoo primarily involve participation by undifferentiated "crowds" of volunteers, the knowledge community that makes up Galaxy Zoo in this case succeeds in large part because it incorporates a well-defined (though far from rigid) social structure, with leaders, managers, and followers, and a layered matrix of visions and purposes, from "this is science" to "this is astronomy" to "this is how the astronomical data should be classified," that both produce that social structure and are reinforced by it. In part this is a rhetorical strategy that has the effect of distinguishing the work of volunteer scientists from that of unpaid laborers. In part it seems to be part of a larger, implicit strategy to align the volunteers with the professionals as part of the scientific enterprise. Throughout this chapter I have noted the relevance of appeals to the vision of Galaxy Zoo and to the scientific narrative as constituting a meaningful part of the project's success. The implication is this: If everyone is on the same page from the beginning, then it may be far less necessary to develop and use formal discipline to keep everyone in line with collective expectations and goals.

How do people get on the same page to begin with, and how do we know whether the vision continues to bind them together? Galaxy Zoo benefited from the existence of a large preexisting pool of amateur astronomers and the availability of an enormous, publicly accessible pool of observational data. Galaxy Zoo also benefited from the fact it was able to minimize the gap between what volunteers were doing (actually examining observational data) and what the professionals would do (in fact, the very same thing), despite its reliance on very large-scale and very complex information technology infrastructures. By expanding the opportunities for participation in "real" science, via the Galaxy Zoo forum, and by nominally including volunteers in Galaxy Zoo papers, the Galaxy Zoo team cultivated a meaningful scientific identity among the volunteers. The fact that the volunteers produced high-quality work, and at times even scientifically innovative work, created a virtuous circle, ratifying the initial decision to undertake Galaxy Zoo, reinforcing the collaborative character of Galaxy Zoo and providing a template for extending Galaxy Zoo to other research questions. One should always been alert for signs of exploitation in a case such as this, but there appear to be very few of them here. Galaxy Zoo volunteers were not trained expert researchers, but the work that they were doing was real and important enough that it is not implausible to treat it under the big tent of science. This finding is consistent with the research of the sociologist Harrison White (2008), which models persistent social organizations in terms of patterns of relations, including identity, rather than in terms of the attributes and attitudes of individuals.

The suggestions that the social structure of commons matters a great deal in understanding the effectiveness of commons, and that vision and personal and group identity matter a great deal as well—more so, perhaps that individual knowledge, attributes, and preferences—suggest some modest refinements to the knowledge commons research framework and some hypotheses for future inquiry That framework, as we have seen, focuses much of its attention on the resources that are created and shared within a commons regime and on how individuals make decisions regarding those resources. "Tragedy of the commons" overconsumption dilemmas are typical starting points for investigating cases of commons governance. But whatever the problems or dilemmas may be that give rise to governance challenges, it is typical to frame analysis in terms of decisions by individual actors or agents with respect to the character of specified resources.

More prominent than individual decisions regarding resources and more influential in the success of Galaxy Zoo, I believe, are the presence of a defined research problem to be solved, the need to choose and/or to design an organizational form well suited to solving it, and efforts to define both of those things publicly in terms of a specific vision that linked peer-production to citizen science to data-driven scientific discovery. A kind of collective identity bound members of the group via rhetorical interventions and related sociotechnical designs. Future work on knowledge commons should address from the beginning the underlying problem being solved, which may or may not depend directly on legally determined attributes of the resources in question; the choice of institutional or organizational form with respect to how that problem is being solved; and the ways in which that choice of form leads to or is connected to modes of engagement by individuals.

VI. Conclusion

This chapter has examined Galaxy Zoo, a scientific research enterprise that exists at the intersection of three phenomena: citizen science, peer production, and data-intensive science. Galaxy Zoo was founded in 2007 by astronomers at the University of Oxford as a way to enlist public volunteers to assist with data classification in connection with understanding the evolution of galaxies. Based on the number of volunteers who participated, the amount of data processed, the speed and accuracy with which the project was completed, and the number of scholarly research papers produced, Galaxy Zoo has been a notable success. Its organizers have applied the same crowdsourcing techniques to large-scale data analysis in follow-on astronomy projects and in other areas of scientific research.

Here, Galaxy Zoo is examined not for its own sake but as a case of commons governance, using the knowledge commons research framework proposed by Madison, Frischmann, & Strandburg (2010) and described in Chapter 1 of this volume. The framework was proposed as a way of systematically investigating knowledge governance regimes that rely on resource sharing in settings involving nondepletable resources such as knowledge and information. This case study determined that the most significant aspects of Galaxy Zoo, and the most important reasons for its effectiveness as commons, have less to do with the character of its information resources (scientific data) and rules regarding their usage, and more to do with the expanded community constructed from hundreds of thousands of Galaxy Zoo volunteers. That community was guided from the outset by a vision of a specific organizational solution to a specific research problem in astronomy, initiated and governed, over time, by professional astronomers in collaboration with their expanding universe of volunteers. Future knowledge commons research should be especially attentive to the social organization of commons as a key factor in their success and effectiveness, along with the dynamics of resource production and consumption.

References

Tim Adams, *Galaxy Zoo and the New Dawn of Citizen Science*, The Guardian, Mar. 17, 2012, http://www.guardian.co.uk/science/2012/mar/18/galaxy-zoo-crowdsourcing-citizen-scientists.
George A. Akerlof & Rachel E. Kranton, Identity Economics: How Our Identities Shape Our Work, Wages, and Well-Being (Princeton University Press 2010).

YOCHAI BENKLER, THE WEALTH OF NETWORKS: HOW SOCIAL PRODUCTION TRANSFORMS MARKETS AND FREEDOM (Yale University Press 2006).

Margaret L. Berendsen, *Conceptual Astronomy Knowledge among Amateur Astronomers*, 4 ASTRONOMY EDUCATION REV. 1 (2005).

Mario Biagioli, *Documents of Documents: Scientists' Names and Scientific Claims*, in DOCUMENTS: ARTIFACTS OF MODERN KNOWLEDGE 129 (Annelise Riles ed., University of Michigan Press 2006).

JOHN SEELY BROWN & PAUL DUGUID, THE SOCIAL LIFE OF INFORMATION (Harvard Business Review Press 2000).

JANET BROWNE, CHARLES DARWIN: A BIOGRAPHY, VOL. 1 – VOYAGING (Princeton University Press 1996).

Adrian Burton, *The Ichthyosaur in the Room*, 10 FRONTIERS IN ECOLOGY AND THE ENVIR. 340 (2012).

Carie Cardamone, *The Story of the Peas: Writing a Scientific Paper*, Galaxy Zoo, A Zooniverse Project Blog (July 2, 2009), http://blog.galaxyzoo.org/2009/07/02/the-story-of-the-peas-writing-a-scientific-paper/.

Carolin N. Cardamone et al., *Galaxy Zoo Green Peas: Discovery of a Class of Compact Extremely Star-Forming Galaxies*, 399 MONTHLY NOTICES OF THE ROYAL ASTRONOMICAL SOC'Y 1191 (2009).

Daniel Clery, *Galaxy Zoo Volunteers Share Pain and Glory of Research*, 333 SCIENCE 173 (2011).

JULIE E. COHEN, CONFIGURING THE NETWORKED SELF: LAW, CODE, AND THE PLAY OF EVERYDAY PRACTICE (Yale University Press 2012).

AUGUST COMTE, COURSE OF POSITIVE PHILOSOPHY (Hermann 1975) (originally published 1830) (translated and condensed as H. MARTINEAU, THE POSITIVE PHILOSOPHY OF AUGUST COMTE (2 vols. London 1875) (1st ed. London 1853)).

Caren Cooper, *Victorian-Era Citizen Science: Reports of Its Death Have Been Greatly Exaggerated*, Scientific American Blogs (Aug. 30, 2012a), http://blogs.scientificamerican.com/guest-blog/2012/08/30/victorian-era-citizen-science-reports-of-its-death-have-been-greatly-exaggerated/.

Caren Cooper, *Retro Science, Part 1*, Scientific American Blogs (Aug. 23, 2012b), http://blogs.scientificamerican.com/guest-blog/2012/08/23/retro-science-part-1/.

Rebecca S. Eisenberg, *Patents and the Progress of Science: Exclusive Rights and Experimental Use*, 56 U. CHICAGO L. REV. 1017 (1989).

TIMOTHY FERRIS, SEEING IN THE DARK: HOW AMATEUR ASTRONOMERS ARE DISCOVERING THE WONDERS OF THE UNIVERSE (Simon & Schuster 2002).

ANN K. FINKBEINER, A GRAND AND BOLD THING: AN EXTRAORDINARY NEW MAP OF THE UNIVERSE USHERING IN A NEW ERA OF DISCOVERY (Free Press 2010).

Lucy Fortson et al., *Galaxy Zoo: Morphological Classification and Citizen Science*, in ADVANCES IN MACHINE LEARNING AND DATA MINING FOR ASTRONOMY 213 (Michael J. Way et al. eds., 2009).

Chiara Franzoni & Henry Sauermann, *Crowd Science: The Organization of Scientific Research in Open Collaborative Projects*, 43 RESEARCH POLICY 1 (2014).

Ira H. Fuchs, *Prospects and Possibilities of the Digital Age*, 145 PROCEEDINGS OF THE AM. PHILOSOPHICAL SOCIETY NO. 1 (Mar. 2001).

Alyssa A. Goodman & Curtis G. Wong, *Bringing the Night Sky Closer: Discoveries in the Data Deluge*, in THE FOURTH PARADIGM: DATA-INTENSIVE SCIENTIFIC DISCOVERY 39 (Tony Hey et al. eds., Microsoft Research 2009).

WARREN O. HAGSTROM, THE SCIENTIFIC COMMUNITY (Basic Books 1965).

Tony Hey, *Data Esperanto*, Tony Hey on eScience (Apr. 28, 2011), http://tonyhey.net/2011/04/28/data-esperanto/.

Tony Hey, *A Journey to Open Access—Part 3*, Tony Hey on eScience (Jan. 18, 2013), http://tonyhey.net/2013/01/18/a-journey-to-open-access-part-3/.

TONY HEY ET AL. (EDS.), THE FOURTH PARADIGM: DATA-INTENSIVE SCIENTIFIC DISCOVERY (Microsoft Research 2009).

Stephen Hilgartner & Sherry Brandt-Rauf, *Data Access, Ownership, and Control: Toward Empirical Studies of Access Practices*, 15 KNOWLEDGE 355 (1994).

John Hules, *Discovery of Dark Energy Ushered in a New Era in Computational Cosmology*, NERSC (Oct. 4, 2011), https://www.nersc.gov/news-publications/news/nersc-center-news/2011/nobel-laureate-blazed-new-trails-in-computational-cosmology/discovery-of-dark-energy-ushered-in-a-new-era-in-computational-cosmology/.

CHRISTOPHER M. KELTY, TWO BITS: THE CULTURAL SIGNIFICANCE OF FREE SOFTWARE AND THE INTERNET (Duke University Press 2008).

THOMAS S. KUHN, THE COPERNICAN REVOLUTION: PLANETARY ASTRONOMY IN THE DEVELOPMENT OF WESTERN THOUGHT (Harvard University Press 1957).

THOMAS S. KUHN, THE STRUCTURE OF SCIENTIFIC REVOLUTIONS (University of Chicago Press 1962).

John Lankford, *Amateurs and Astrophysics: A Neglected Aspect in the Development of a Scientific Specialty*, 11 SOCIAL STUDIES OF SCIENCE 275 (1981).

A. Lawrence, *Drowning in Data: VO to the Rescue*, in ASTRONOMY: NETWORKED ASTRONOMY AND THE NEW MEDIA (R. J. Simpson & D. Ward-Thompson eds., Canopus Publishing 2009).

Chris Lintott, *A Week Inside the Galaxy Zoo*, Chris Lintott's Universe (July 18, 2007), http://chrislintott.net/2007/07/18/a-week-inside-the-galaxy-zoo/.

Chris Lintott, Interviewed by Michael Madison, June 25, 2013.

Chris J. Lintott et al., *Galaxy Zoo: Morphologies Derived from Visual Inspection of Galaxies from the Sloan Digital Sky Survey*, 389 MONTHLY NOTICES OF THE ROYAL ASTRONOMICAL SOC'Y 1179 (2008).

Chris Lintott et al., *Galaxy Zoo 1: Data Release of Morphological Classifications for Nearly 900,000 Galaxies*, 410 MONTHLY NOTICES OF THE ROYAL ASTRONOMICAL SOC'Y 166 (2010).

Michael J. Madison, *Reconstructing the Software License*, 35 LOYOLA U. CHI. L.J. 275 (2003).

Michael J. Madison, *Law as Design: Objects, Concepts, and Digital Things*, 56 CASE WESTERN RESERVE. L. REV. 381 (2005).

Michael J. Madison, Brett M. Frischmann, & Katherine J. Strandburg, *Constructing Commons in the Cultural Environment*, 95 CORNELL L. REV. 657 (2010).

THOMAS MANDEVILLE, UNDERSTANDING NOVELTY: INFORMATION, TECHNOLOGICAL CHANGE, AND THE PATENT SYSTEM (Ablex 1996).

Robin Mansell, *Employing Digital Crowdsourced Information Resources: Managing the Emerging Information Commons*, 7 INT'L J. OF THE COMMONS 255 (2013).

JAMES MANYIKA ET AL., BIG DATA: THE NEXT FRONTIER FOR INNOVATION, COMPETITION, AND PRODUCTIVITY (McKinsey Global Institute 2011).

Bruce Margony, *The Sloan Digital Sky Survey*, 357 Philosophical Transactions of the Royal Society London A, No. 1750 93 (Jan. 15, 1999).

Karen L. Masters, *She's an Astronomer: Meg Urry*, Galaxy Zoo, A Zooniverse Project Blog (May 2, 2010), http://blog.galaxyzoo.org/2010/05/02/shes-an-astronomer-meg-urry/.

Karen L. Masters, *She's an Astronomer: Did We Really Need that Series?*, Galaxy Zoo, A Zooniverse Project Blog (Jan. 7, 2011), http://blog.galaxyzoo.org/2011/01/07/shes-an-astronomer-did-we-really-need-that-series/.

Karen L. Masters, *Invited Discourse: "A Zoo of Galaxies,"* 16 Highlights of Astronomy (XXVIIth IAU General Assembly, August 2009, Thierry Montmerle ed.) (2013), http://arxiv.org/pdf/1303.7118v1.pdf.

Christine McGourty, *Scientists Seek Galaxy Hunt Help*, BBC News (July 11, 2007), http://news.bbc.co.uk/2/hi/science/nature/6289474.stm.

Robert P. Merges, *Property Rights Theory and the Commons: The Case of Scientific Research*, 13 Social Philosophy & Policy, No. 2, at 145 (1996).

Robert K. Merton, *The Normative Structure of Science*, reprinted in The Sociology of Science: Theoretical Empirical Investigations 267 (Norman W. Storer ed., University of Chicago Press 1973) (originally published 1942).

National Research Council, The Future of Scientific Knowledge Discovery in Open Networked Environments (National Academy Press 2012).

Nature, *Special issue on "Big Data,"* Vol. 455, Issue no. 7209 (Sept. 4, 2008).

Sue Nelson, *Big Data: The Harvard Computers*, 455 Nature 36 (Sept. 4, 2008).

Sarah Ogilvie, Words of the World: A Global History of the Oxford English Dictionary (Cambridge University Press 2012).

Elinor Ostrom, Governing the Commons: The Evolution of Institutions for Collective Action (Cambridge University Press 1990).

Elinor Ostrom, *Background on the Institutional Analysis and Development Framework*, 39 The Policy Studies J. 7 (2011).

Michael Polanyi, Science, Faith and Society (Oxford University Press 1946).

M. Jordan Raddick et al., *Galaxy Zoo: Exploring the Motivations of Citizen Science Volunteers*, 9 Astronomy Education Rev. 010103-1 (2010).

Arti Kaur Rai, *Regulating Scientific Research: Intellectual Property Rights and the Norms of Science*, 94 Northwestern U. L. Rev. 77 (1999).

Jason Reed et al., *A Framework for Defining and Describing Key Design Features of Virtual Citizen Science Projects*, in Proceedings of the 2012 iConference 623 (Toronto 2012).

J. H. Reichman & Paul F. Uhlir, *A Contractually Reconstructed Research Commons for Scientific Data in a Highly Protectionist Intellectual Property Environment*, 66 Law & Contemp. Probs. 315 (2003).

Kevin Schawinski, Interviewed by Michael Madison, Dec. 1, 2011.

Kevin Schawinski, et al., *Galaxy Zoo: A Sample of Blue Early-type Galaxies at Low Redshift*, 396 Monthly Notices of the Royal Astronomical Soc'y 818 (2009).

Science, *Special issue on "Dealing with Data,"* Vol. 331, Issue no. 6018 (Feb. 11, 2011).

Alice [Sheppard], *Peas in the Universe, Goodwill and a History of Zooite Collaboration on the Peas Project*, Galaxy Zoo, A Zooniverse Project Blog (July 7, 2009), http://blog.galaxyzoo.org/2009/07/07/peas-in-the-universe-goodwill-and-a-history-of-zooite-collaboration-on-the-peas-project/.

Petr Škoda, *The Virtual Observatory and Its Benefits for Amateur Astronomers*, 75 OPEN EUROPEAN J. ON VARIABLE STARS 32 (2007).

Alexander S. Szalay et al., *The SDSS SkyServer—Public Access to the Sloan Digital Sky Server Data*, SIGMOD '02: Proceedings of the 2002 ACM SIGMOD International Conference on Management of Data (2002).

SHARON TRAWEEK, BEAMTIMES AND LIFETIMES: THE WORLD OF HIGH ENERGY PHYSICISTS (Harvard University Press 1988)

WILLIAM WHEWELL, THE PHILOSOPHY OF THE INDUCTIVE SCIENCES: FOUNDED UPON THEIR HISTORY, VOL. 1 (London 1840).

HARRISON C. WHITE, IDENTITY AND CONTROL: HOW SOCIAL FORMATIONS EMERGE (2d ed. Princeton University Press 2008)

SIMON WINCHESTER, THE MEANING OF EVERYTHING: THE STORY OF THE OXFORD ENGLISH DICTIONARY (Oxford University Press 2004).

Donald G. York et al., *The Sloan Digital Sky Survey: Technical Summary*, 120 THE ASTRONOMICAL J. 1579 (2000).

7 Toward the Comparison of Open Source Commons Institutions

Charles M. Schweik*

I. Introduction

In this volume's opening chapter, open source software is offered as a prominent example of knowledge commons that fall under the "default, intellectual-property-rights" baseline environment. But it wasn't always that way. In the earliest days of computing, right up to about 1980, computer software development fell closer to the "natural" cultural environment without intellectual property issues involved. It was standard practice in the academic and computer industry to share and collaborate on software code (Campbell-Kelly 2003). This practice of software sharing and collaboration continued as Internet infrastructure was being built. But around 1980, the legal protection available for software changed. Schwarz & Takhteyev (2009: 22) describe the history:

> Prior to 1964 software was understood to be outside the bounds of copyright law and was offered no protection beyond trade secrecy. In 1964, the Copyright Office extended copyright protection to software, giving software producers a new mechanism for

---

* Charles M. Schweik is an Associate Professor in the Department of Environmental Conservation and the Center for Public Policy and Administration at the University of Massachusetts, Amherst, Massachusetts, USA and is Associate Director of the National Center for Digital Government at UMass Amherst. He is co-author (with Robert English) of *Internet Success: A Study of Open Source Software Commons* (MIT Press 2012), which examines collaborative principles in open source software projects.

making software excludable. This mechanism suffered from an important drawback, however. As other works, software had to be *published* and *registered* to be protected by copyright. Specifically, the *source code* of the software had to be published and deposited with the Copyright Office…Software producers could thus protect their work using either copyright or trade secrets, but not both…To make software truly excludable, the producer needs dual protection: trade secrecy for the source code…and copyright protection for the binary that is offered on the market. A 1980 amendment to the Copyright Act of 1976 offered software producers exactly this protection [by making copyright protection available without registration]. (Emphasis in original.)

These new protections led to more commodification of software—a form of the "second enclosure movement" that Boyle (2003) describes—and these changes led to the free/libre software "movement," initiated by Richard Stallman and colleagues in the 1980s. Stallman's major innovation was his idea of "copyleft" and his brilliant use of copyright law to create software licenses, such as his General Public License (GPL) for software and his GNU Free Document License (GFDL) for accompanying software documentation, that promote sharing and collaboration (FSF 2009).[1] Later, similar open source licenses appeared, containing somewhat different requirements than those of Stallman's GPL. Benkler (2006: 63) describes the collaborative principles that emerged through this history and have since evolved in free/libre and open source software as the "quintessential instance" of commons-based peer production.

As other chapters in this volume recognize, experiments following open source–like commons-based peer production have now emerged in other settings. The obvious example is the open digital content effort, Wikipedia. But this idea has been extended to other arenas of collaborative writing, such as course curriculum (e.g., Rice Connexions, MIT Open Courseware) and to many other areas where digital products can be shared and remixed.[2]

Moreover, peer-production commons experiments have appeared in some surprising new areas. Consider, for example, the use of this production model in national intelligence gathering (Howard 2010) or the borrowing of open source production and crowdsourcing to spur design innovation and efforts to produce "openly designed" physical (not digital) products, sometimes in an effort to solve market failure problems.[3] My particular interest in understanding open source peer-production motivation is to see how these collaborative principles might be applied to encourage sharing and dialog between public sector academics and practitioners[4] or in efforts to solve problems faced across the world in environmental management.[5]

---

[1] See Schwarz & Takhteyev (2009) for more description of Stallman's evolution toward the copyleft idea.
[2] See CreativeCommons.org for many examples.
[3] For a few interesting examples, see LocalMotors (2014) for an effort to crowdsource innovative design ideas in the automotive industry, or Jha & Nerurkar (2010) and Kuniholm (2010) for examples in healthcare, where market failures exist.
[4] See Schweik, et al. (2011).
[5] See Schweik, et al. (2005).

Given that the open source collaborative paradigm was born in the context of computer programming, and that it is in this field that it has been around the longest, it makes sense to study open source software commons empirically. Historically, there has been a great deal of research on open source software from a wide range of disciplines. Prominent book-length related studies include Weber (2004), von Hippel (2005a), Benkler (2006), and Fogel (2006). Many more studies of particular elements of open source software commons can be found in a variety of journals and other outlets.[6]

In this chapter I report some results from a study of the sociotechnical aspects of open source software collaboration. This study took more than five years to complete, and involved a team of researchers at the University of Massachusetts, Amherst. The major product of the study is a book-length manuscript (Schweik & English 2012) that summarizes our efforts to capture what was happening in a close approximation to the overall population of open source projects. Much of the research prior to this study focused on high-profile open source software cases, such as the Linux operating system. The study has three primary goals:

(1) to get a better understanding of what was happening in the broader population of open source software commons, the vast majority of which are small projects, much less visible than the high-profile cases that have been the focus of much of the prior research;

(2) to identify factors that appear to affect whether an open source software commons is successful in terms of maintaining ongoing collaboration—or becomes abandoned; and,

(3) to focus more attention on the governance and rules-in-use of open source commons, and to explore methods for the systematic study of the institutions that govern open source commons.[7]

Underlying the study reported in this chapter is the modified Institutional Analysis and Development (IAD) framework as proposed by Frischmann, Madison & Strandburg (this volume, ch. 1). At the conclusion of this chapter, I provide some reflections on the use of this framework for the study of this important form of knowledge commons.

II. A Summary of the Open Source Commons Success and Abandonment Study

A major incentive driving the initiation of our study was that, at the time we started in 2005, there was very little empirical work trying to capture and document the *population*

---

[6] See, e.g., Feller et al. (2005), for an edited volume containing a variety of empirical studies.
[7] In this chapter "open source commons" and "open source projects" are used interchangeably.

of open source software commons and to study these projects as sociotechnical systems of production. Of course, open source projects are only a subset of the broader population of "default" intellectual-property-based knowledge commons (recall Chapter 1), but open source projects are a very important subgroup of cases to study: (1) they have a relatively long track record, in that programmers were some of the first to use the Internet for collective action in software development; and (2) there are literally hundreds of thousands of projects to study. Consequently, in this chapter we focus on open source projects and ask: "What factors lead some open source software commons to achieve ongoing collaborative success while others become abandoned?"

We should note that this project started in 2005, before the initial publication of the framework described in Chapter 1, and continued until 2011. But it is uncanny how well our study aligns with the framework presented in Chapter 1. We utilized a modified IAD theoretical framework (recall Chapter 1) to guide the research, and with that supporting guidance, we then conducted literature reviews in a number of relevant disciplines—Information Systems, Virtual Teams and Distributed Work, Environmental Commons—and of the emerging literature specifically on open source in an effort to identify testable hypotheses or, where no testable hypothesis could be identified from the existing literature, "subresearch questions." Multiple people on our team worked for a year and a half and identified a variety of variables aligned along the components of the IAD framework. Ultimately, more than forty hypotheses and research questions were identified, each of which we later investigated empirically (Schweik & English 2012). Figure 7.1 provides a summary of some of the variables we researched, organized by components of the modified IAD framework presented earlier in this volume.

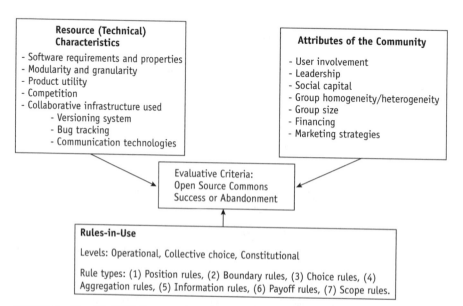

FIGURE 7.1 Simplified IAD Framework* with Independent Variables Identified.
*See this volume, ch. 1.

Like other areas characterized by knowledge commons, open source software is a space that is changing rapidly. At the time we initiated this study, a vast majority of the literature was focused on the central question of why people (volunteers) would contribute their ideas and effort to a public commons, rather than protect their work as private, proprietary property. This "gift culture" (Raymond 2000b) was a particular puzzle to economists and, over time, the motivations driving these contributions became better understood (e.g., self-learning, user-centered need, self-promotion, contributing to a movement, and being part of a community) (David & Shapiro 2008; Schweik & English 2012).

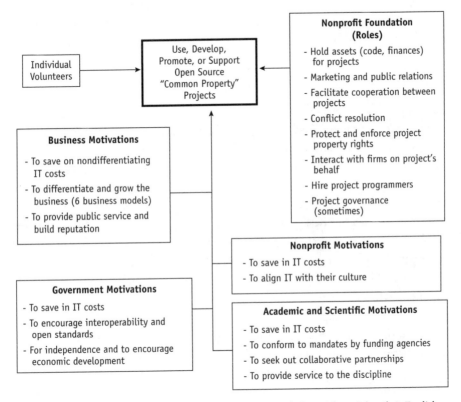

FIGURE 7.2 The Open Source Software Commons Ecosystem (adapted from Schweik & English 2012).

However, in 2005 when we started this study, a shift was occurring, moving open source software from what had largely been described as all-volunteer efforts to a more complex ecosystem (Figure 7.2). Some companies in private industry, such as IBM, embraced the open source collaborative paradigm in an effort to advance their businesses. A variety of business models and motivations connected to the open source commons production now exist.[8] Governments embraced open source in efforts to break the vendor lock-in problem and, in some cases, to jump-start their own countries' software industries (Simon

---

[8] See Krishamurthy (2005); Riehle (2007); and Deek & McHugh (2007: 272-79) for more detail.

2005; Lewis 2010). Not-for-profit organizations became active in this space both in their own efforts to cut information technology costs and also, in some instances, to promote and help open source projects operate through overarching foundations (McQuillan 2003; NOSI 2008). Scientific and academic organizations continued, in some cases as they always had, to share and collaborate on software code, but these efforts expanded into new fields as a result of changing information technology needs.[9]

In short, when we started in 2005 it was apparent that open source was moving from a less complicated setting of volunteers collaborating to a knowledge commons setting in which a variety of organizations could be involved, suggesting that the governance and the rules-in-use guiding collaboration might be more complex and fluid as the open source ecosystem evolved. We set out in our study to investigate this possibility.

A. EVALUATIVE CRITERIA: SUCCESS AND ABANDONMENT IN OPEN SOURCE SOFTWARE COMMONS

After the task of researching relevant theory and empirical work related to factors that contribute to the success or abandonment of open source software commons, we then turned our attention to how to conceptualize and, ultimately, operationalize a means to measure the success of a project for our study. Space limits me from going into a deep discussion of this component of the project. Here, I summarize a few key aspects of this work.[10]

First, we focused on the longitudinal aspects of these commons and identified two key stages in their evolution. As we see it, open source software commons go through an "initiation stage," during which they start up and have yet to produce a first public release, and a "growth stage" during the period after a first public release of code. We hypothesized that the factors affecting collaborative success and abandonment would be different in these two stages.

Second, with these stages identified, we set out to develop solid metrics for collaborative success and abandonment in each of these stages. The measures treat as success stories both projects that grow and gain large development teams and projects that begin and remain as very small collaborations (even if they have only one developer and a small community of users). Our measures build on project "life and death metrics" (Robles-Martinez et al. 2003), as well as "project popularity metrics" (Weiss 2005).

B. DATASETS/METHODS

As I stated above, a key interest at the outset of this project was to analyze a more representative dataset of open source software commons, rather than to focus on more high profile, larger ones. In 2005—and arguably continuing to this day—many of these commons

---

[9] See Courant & Griffiths (2006).

[10] A full discussion on this dependent variable can be found in English & Schweik (2007) (also in Schweik & English (2012: ch. 7)), and the work was generally replicated by Wiggins & Crowston (2010) helping to confirm that a solid measure of these concepts was established.

reside on the project hosting site Sourceforge.net (SF). SF provides a free web-based platform that allows open source software developers to store and manage their code and projects. The SF website is widely known in the software programming world and is a hub on the Internet where users can find open source software projects for potential use. SF is also a somewhat "noisy" dataset, in that it is used by programmers to store, for example, projects they developed for college courses. That said, in Schweik & English (2012) we explain why we think SF still provided the best data available at the time for researchers attempting to characterize the unknown population of open source software commons.

To get SF project data, we turned to an open-access dataset of SF projects called "FLOSSmole" built and provided by researchers affiliated with Syracuse University (Howison, Conklin, & Crowston 2006). The initial FLOSSmole database had 107,747 projects and represented SF in the fall of 2006. After analyzing the 2006 data, we developed an online survey to capture theoretical concepts related to community and institutional variables that are not available in the SF project metadata. We conducted the survey in the fall of 2009. In an effort to ensure that our study included enough data on abandoned projects, we invited a large random sample of SF developers to complete the survey, resulting in over 1400 usable surveys returned (Schweik & English 2012). We then combined our survey data with another "snapshot" of SF project data provided by Madey (2011) for a more conceptually complete dataset representing, roughly, the data available at year end 2009. This dataset covered 174,333 projects.

Summarizing several years of work in one sentence, we carefully categorized each project in these datasets based on our definitions of success and abandonment (Table 7.1). With that dependent variable in place, we then analyzed and investigated the importance for project success of theoretically identified independent variables, using contingency tables, classification, and regression tree and logit regression. Rather than present statistical results here,[11] I will simply extract a few important findings for discussion.

TABLE 7.1.

SUCCESS AND ABANDONMENT CLASSIFICATION RESULTS FOR THE SF 2006 AND 2009 DATASETS (ADAPTED FROM SCHWEIK & ENGLISH 2012).

	SF 2006 Data	SF 2009 Data
Class	# of projects	# of projects
Abandoned Initiation	37,320	67,126
Indeterminate Initiation	13,342	16,806
Indeterminate in Growth	10,711	12,052
Abandoned Growth	30,592	53,450
Successful Growth	15,782	24,899
Total	107,747	174,333

---

[11] Details are described in Schweik & English (2012).

FINDING 1. THE VAST MAJORITY OF OPEN SOURCE PROJECTS HAVE VERY
SMALL DEVELOPMENT TEAMS.

As I have emphasized earlier, much of the research on open source commons to date focuses on high-profile, large development team success stories. Figure 7.3 provides a histogram of the team size distribution of the 174,000 projects in SF in the fall of 2009. Table 7.2 shows team size numerically. Together, they show that the vast majority of SF projects involve only one or two developers. This finding isn't new—Krishnamurthy (2002) was one of the first to make this observation—but it leads to two important points. First, much of the case study research on open source software over the last decade has focused on high-profile projects with larger team compositions. But, looking at open source software as a category of knowledge commons, these statistics demonstrate that open source commons are often (usually) made up of very small teams. Second, even though these projects often have very small development teams, these projects, including the 140,000 single-developer projects, should be characterized as collaborations. It is well understood in open source projects that the end users of the software sometimes contribute to these projects through bug reporting, testing, or even the creation of supporting documentation.

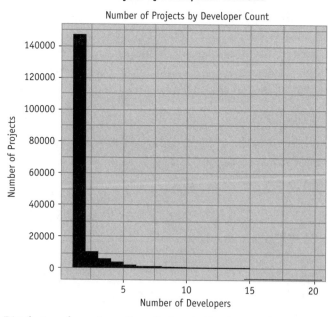

FIGURE 7.3 Distribution of 2009 SourceForge Projects by Development Team Size.

TABLE 7.2.

DEVELOPER COUNTS FOR THE MAY 2009 SOURCEFORGE POPULATION FOR ABANDONED (AG) AND SUCCESSFUL (SG) GROWTH STAGE PROJECTS (PERCENTAGE OF TOTAL* IN PARENTHESES)

Developer Count	SF Population: Class AG	SF Population: Class SG
1	37259 (48)	11765 (15)
2	8329 (11)	4420 (6)
3	3236 (4)	2380 (3)
4	1573 (2)	1515 (2)
5	921 (1)	1076 (1)
6	525 (1)	731 (1)
7	316 (0)	514 (1)
8	198 (0)	424 (0)
9	141 (0)	309 (0)
10	90 (0)	234 (0)
11–20	305 (0)	990 (1)
>20	53 (0)	457 (0)
Totals	52,946 (68)	24,815 (32)

FINDING 2. WE HAVE STATISTICAL SUPPORT FOR "CONVENTIONAL WISDOM" ABOUT HOW OPEN SOURCE PROJECTS OPERATE.

Our broad statistical analysis, described in detail in Schweik & English (2012), tells a story of how open source projects, in general, operate. In the initiation (pre-first release) stage, the most important factors for success depend on the designated leader of the project, who is often the single developer. Projects that are successful at this stage—meaning they continue to be worked on—are those with project leaders who devote larger numbers of hours to the project. In addition, a leader's efforts in putting in place plans for architecture and functionality, project goals, and project documentation, as well as a good project web presence, appear to be important, for these efforts help to attract contributions from volunteers or potential end users before the first release. We found that "putting in the hours" and various other elements of leadership are not simply correlated with success but appear to be causes of success in the initiation stage.

In the growth, or post-first release, stage, the leadership abilities of members of the development team, coupled with the utility of the software itself, begin to attract new users and, eventually, at least one new development team member or other "community" contributors. Developers continue to make contributions to the software, leading to a virtuous circle of continuing improvements and continued collaborative success. In this stage, we found that some aspects of project leadership, slight growth in the development team, and project financing are causal influences for success.

These findings are aligned with what we might call "conventional wisdom" about open source software commons, and may seem obvious to some who have thought about these commons. However, our findings are based on a large empirical dataset (170,000 projects) along with our own survey data of over 1400 developers, not merely on reflections on the participation history of one or two open source projects. In other words, our study confirms what is commonly thought about open source with strong statistical evidence.

FINDING 3. STATISTICAL FINDINGS SUPPORT THE CONTENTION THAT
THE ECOSYSTEM IS NOW MORE COMPLEX THAN IT WAS IN THE EARLIER
"ALL-VOLUNTEER" DAYS OF OPEN SOURCE.

In our analysis of the quantitative data, we had several hypotheses that were related to the emergence of the more complex ecosystem pictured in Figure 7.2. Our SF dataset classified each project using nearly fifty categorical variables. For example, project administrators could identify the operating system for which a particular project was built. They could classify the project with a large set of "software types" (e.g., databases, end-user desktop applications, etc.). Our expectation was that if open source was still being motivated by the more philosophical open source or "free/libre movement," we would find projects aligned with this movement to be more successful in the initiation and growth stages compared to projects not aligned with this movement. In other words, contingency tables would show statistically significant distributional differences between successful and abandoned projects for variables distinguishing projects according to their association with the "free/libre" movement.

In our analysis of the data for our 1400 surveyed projects (Schweik & English 2012), we found no evidence suggesting that projects affiliated with "pure open source" were more successful than projects that did not have such an affiliation. We also found no distributional differences between projects licensed with the General Public License (GPL; the license more often connected to the philosophical free/libre movement) and projects licensed with "non-GPL" licenses. Successful and abandoned projects were evenly distributed across GPL and non-GPL cases, and successful projects were found throughout all different types of software categories. No particular categories or kinds of software projects stood out by having higher numbers of successful collaborations.

Our survey also investigated motivations for participating in open source projects. While a vast majority of respondents felt that software should be open, it was clear that there was a wide mix of motivations driving participation and that many of the participants were paid by firms. Finally, von Hippel's (2005a) concept of user-driven need was widely observed in all projects (successful and abandoned). Our survey provides evidence that user need is a major motivation both for individuals to participate and for their employers to encourage them to participate (because the employing organization needs the software). Taken together, while these findings provide statistical evidence that open source is still driven by an ideological belief that software should be open, the lack of distributional differences in our data suggest that the open source approach is now mainstream and is used in developing software in many contexts. Moreover, open source development is not just about volunteers any longer, but rather reflects the footprint of the more complex ecosystem represented in Figure 7.2.

FINDING 4. SF AND SEARCH ENGINES SUCH AS GOOGLE ACT AS GLOBAL INTELLECTUAL MATCHMAKERS.

Finding 4 is one of our most interesting empirical findings. In our analysis of the 2006 SF dataset, we found that the developer teams in successful growth-stage projects grew slightly while the developer teams for abandoned projects did not. Armed with that knowledge, we investigated this issue further in our 2009 survey of developers. We asked them two questions related to this issue. First, we asked whether, if their development team had more than one individual, the surveyed developer found the other team members using the Internet. Second, we asked whether the geographic location of all project team members was best described as very close; same city; same state/province; same country; same continent or multicontinental. Through these questions, we found that successful projects find new team members on the Internet more often than abandoned projects do and that 52 percent of the successful growth-stage projects had development team members from multiple continents (Schweik & English 2012). Third, we asked respondents about the frequency of face-to-face interaction on their teams. We found that while face-to-face interaction indeed helps to build social capital, there are many successful projects where some team members have never met in person.

Taken together, these findings suggest that SF, perhaps coupled with search engines such as Google, acts as a "power law hub" (Karpf 2010) allowing people with similar interests, passions, and skills to connect with each other and begin to feel each other out as potential collaborators, before eventually joining in coproduction. In the SF case these collaborations are mostly multicontinental collaborations between North America and Europe. I have not seen statistical evidence anywhere else that suggests this multicontinental collaboration is happening, but it appears to be important in open source commons. I think this is a very important finding. Multicontinental collaboration occurs in other knowledge commons situations (e.g., Wikipedia) as well. Here is the key point: In open source commons, success is often not about building a large development team. It *is* about finding "just the right person" with similar interests, skills, and passions somewhere in the world and developing a collaborative relationship with that person. The significance of bringing together the right people for collaboration may be a very important insight for our understanding of knowledge commons more broadly.

FINDING 5. INSTITUTIONS PROVIDE "FRICTION," BUT THEY ALSO EVOLVE.

The governance and institutional design of open source commons is one of the least studied areas, although there are a few scholars who have contributed important work on the topic.[12] A driving motivation for our study was to begin to shed more light on the institutional structure of open source as well as on the evolution of open source institutions.

In his famous essay on open source, *The Cathedral and the Bazaar*, Eric Raymond (2000a) argued that potential contributors to open source software commons will be less apt to participate if the "number of hoops" they have to jump through with is higher. In other words, more formalized rules guiding the process of contributing code will reduce the likelihood of participation. Programmers want to program, and not deal with rules guiding collaboration. In our research, we found strong statistical and qualitative evidence suggesting that this is indeed the case, and this is one way in which open source commons differ quite sharply from the more traditional environmental commons Elinor studied in the past. In most of the SF projects we surveyed, the operational rules are either "very informal" social norms or are coded into the online collaborative systems used to coordinate work (e.g., CVS or Subversion) and, in that sense, quite formalized. We did not find many formal operational rules that were socially enforced. Moreover, we learned from the SF survey data that the dominant governance model was a "benevolent dictator," rather than a model with more democratic processes.[13]

That said, we did also see some indications—as we expected—that institutions evolve and become more formalized as projects grow in numbers of developers. However, our survey data indicates that this evolution tends to be along the lines of "we moved from a *very* informal institutional structure to simply an informal structure," that is, the "very" descriptor was removed. Nonetheless, the survey results did suggest that institutions evolve toward some level of formalization as the number of participants grows.

C. WHAT THIS TELLS US

Two important conclusions come out of the discussion above. First, looking back at Figure 7.3, our interest in understanding and articulating the properties of the population of open source software commons leaves us with conclusions that are, in a sense, weighted toward smaller development projects. This is the case because the population we studied, SF, is vastly dominated by projects driven by very small development teams, with a majority having only one developer. But even in cases of single developer teams, the software is still governed by a form of common-property regime, and the project can still involve collaborative action between the developer and a user community. What we did not do in our data analysis—and what should be done in the future—was a detailed examination of the larger developer team projects that reside in the longer tail on the right in Figure 7.3. In our 2006 data, the largest project involved on the order of 320 developers, but it was only one of 107,747 projects in our dataset. There are roughly a thousand projects in these SF datasets that have

---

[12] See, e.g., O'Mahony (2005, 2007); O'Mahony & Ferraro (2007); Markus (2007).

[13] We think this finding was so strong because we were trying to understand the population of open source, and so many of the projects in our dataset were small development team projects.

developer teams of ten or more people. The institutional design of these projects is likely different from that of the vast majority of others in SF, but any differences are muffled in our statistical analysis because such projects represent such a small proportion of the population.

Second, we have found evidence that the governance (rules-in-use in the modified IAD framework) of projects does indeed evolve. This is an issue that requires further research, in particular for larger projects that involve participants from a variety of organizations. For example, I recently gave an invited talk on this project at an open source software conference focused on software in the U.S. Military (http://mil-oss.org/wg3-agenda). The list of participants at the conference supports the contention that open source software is now "more mainstream" and involves a much more complex configuration of actors. Projects presented involved university partners, private contracting firms, and government agencies. Some presenters, such as Alex Voultepsis of the Office of the Director of National Intelligence, talked about forming a software sharing and development effort that would cross homeland security agencies and involve private contractors. Understanding how the working of such multi-organizational collaborations evolves, and how they are structured institutionally, will be important for the successful design of future larger-scale software projects (and other open-type collaborations outside of software). In other words, mid- to large-size projects are an interesting and important subset of open source software commons "success stories," which represent more "mature" collaborations. They need to be studied more carefully and understood.

In moving toward a systematic study of these larger projects, key questions that we must ask are:

How do we systematically document the institutional designs of larger collaborations or collaborations between organizations?

and,

How do we study the evolution of open source-like commons systematically?

Rich case description is helpful and important. However, it is important to ask how we can compile and analyze, side by side, rich case studies of open source commons institutional designs as well as their evolution. How do we compare, to use two famous projects as an example, how the Debian Linux project has evolved with how the Eclipse project has evolved? This same question is being asked by this book's editors and it was the reason they introduce their modified IAD framework, described in Chapter 1.

In the next part of this chapter, I focus specifically on how to approach the systematic comparison of open source software commons. My effort here thus is narrower than the efforts of this book's editorial team, but the approach I am about to present could easily be extended or applied to the systematic study and comparison of other types of knowledge commons cases.

III. Toward a Systematic Analysis of Knowledge Commons Rules-in-Use: The OSGeo Case Study

In parallel to the quantitative research briefly reported above, my collaborators and I also were interested in understanding open source commons in more depth, for two reasons. First, we wanted to complement our quantitative analysis with a more rich study to see whether what we were learning from the quantitative work aligned with what we could learn from case research. Second, given that we had read a number of descriptive papers on specific, usually high-profile, open source projects, we wanted to take a step toward developing a systematic comparative approach to analyzing open source governance and institutional design.

We selected the Open Source Geospatial Foundation (OSGeo.org) and seven of its associated projects for study. We chose this group of projects because it provided an example of a more complex open source ecosystem, given that nonprofits and private firms are involved, and because of its international scope. A practical reason for choosing this case was that, in full disclosure, I am involved with this foundation, currently acting as the chair of its education and curriculum committee. This participation, I think, gave me more credibility as we moved ahead to interview developers in OSGeo-related projects.

Full descriptions of the analysis of the OSGeo case can be found at Schweik & Kitsing (2010) and Schweik & English (2012: chs. 5 and 6). For our purposes here, my goal is to briefly describe my experience in using IAD as a guiding framework for institutional analysis, coupled with Ostrom's seven categories of rules (Ostrom 2005).

A. A PRIMER ON THE THREE INSTITUTIONAL LEVELS OF IAD AND OSTROM'S SEVEN RULE CLASSES

Summarizing what is more fully described in Ostrom (2005), within the "institutional attributes" component of the IAD framework are three nested institutional levels: operational, collective-choice, and constitutional. These levels are not specifically depicted in Figure 1.1 of Chapter 1, but they are embedded implicitly in the bottom left box in that figure, labeled "Rules-in-Use."

As Ostrom (2005) describes, the operational level is a general label to describe the sets of rules (formal or informal) that influence the daily behavior and actions of commons participants. For example, in an open source software setting, these can be rules about how computer code gets accepted into the next version of the software being developed or rules establishing the process for releasing a new version.

The collective-choice level involves a different set of rules that (1) define who is eligible to undertake operational-level activities, and (2) define who has authority to change operational-level rules and the procedures for making such changes. An example of a collective-choice rule in the context of open source software commons would be a change in the process for committing code to the repository or a change in how code is reviewed prior to adding it to a new release library.

Finally, constitutional level rules specify how the commons is structured or organized constitutionally, but, in addition, include specifications of who can change collective-choice arrangements and of procedures for making those changes. In open source software commons, an obvious constitutional issue is the choice of license to attach to the software (e.g., a GPL or non-GPL type license). But constitutional level rules might also be related to whether the project is associated with a nonprofit foundation, whether there are particular requirements related to an oversight board, and so forth.

As the authors of Chapter 1 note, these three levels of rules in IAD have been guiding commons researchers for at least two decades, particularly in the context of natural resource commons. But what was lacking in case analysis prior to 2005 was more specificity about how to analyze the rules that exist at any of these levels. In her book *Understanding Institutional Diversity*, Elinor Ostrom (2005) once again moved us forward by proposing seven classes of rules that can exist in any of these three levels, as summarized in Table 7.3. The following discussion of the OSGeo projects illustrates how the use of these rule classes helps us to compare the governance of knowledge commons in a systematic way.

TABLE 7.3.

OSTROM'S SEVEN RULE CLASSES

Position rules	Articulate what roles people play in the project.
Boundary rules	Define who is eligible for a position, the process of how he or she is assigned to that position, and rules related to how the person leaves that position.
Choice rules	Define actions that can, cannot, or must be done.
Aggregation rules	Articulate the process for how conflict should be resolved. Within this category, there are three subclasses: symmetric (e.g., unanimity), nonsymmetric (where a leader can make decisions for a group), and lack-of-agreement rules.
Information rules	Specify how and what kind of information flows between project members and other interested parties, as well as how information is archived through the project life cycle.
Pay-off rules	Assign some kind of reward or sanction to specific actions or outcomes.
Scope rules	Specify which outcomes may, must, or must not be affected or produced in a given situation.

(These can apply to any or all of the three nested levels of rules-in-use: Operational, Collective-Choice, or Constitutional).
(Adapted from Ostrom 2005: 193–210).

B. THE OSGEO CASE

OSGeo is a nonprofit foundation that provides overarching support to a number of open source software projects working in the area of geographic information systems (GIS). Broadly speaking, GIS is the label used for computer-based technologies that, in some fashion, deal with data that has positional ties to the earth. If you've ever used Google Earth, MapQuest, or your car's GPS navigation screen, then you've used a form of GIS.

OSGeo's mission is to "support the development of open source geospatial software, and promote its widespread use" (OSGeo 2009). At the time of our research there were ten software projects treated as "full members" of the foundation and several others in "incubation." We chose to study only fully affiliated projects because their institutional designs would be fully formed. We contacted representatives of all ten projects for interviews, but only seven were willing to participate in the study. Here, I report only some of our findings related to institutional design and structure.

Institutional analysis of this case requires not only attention to the three levels and classes of rules that Ostrom describes but also a realization that there is not only an institutional design for each project but also an institutional design at the foundation level. Moreover, the foundation has established mandates with which each project must comply.

Some examples of Ostrom's rule classes that function at the foundation level are summarized in Table 7.4.

TABLE 7.4.

EXAMPLES OF RULES AT THE OSGEO FOUNDATION LEVEL

Aggregation rules	Symmetric: Consensus in committees. Nonsymmetric: Board of directors create committees
Information rules	Minutes meetings required. Meeting notifications required. Annual meetings required. Financial statements required.
Pay-off rules	Executive director and others can be paid. BOD members cannot be paid.
Scope rules	Specified to some extent in organizational and committee mission statements.

Our interviews and interpretation of online documentation permitted us to characterize the rules at this level according to Ostrom's classes as well (Table 7.5).

I present Tables 7.4 and 7.5 not with the expectation that readers will have enough information from this brief discussion to understand the institutional design of the OSGeo Foundation or associated projects, but simply to demonstrate that it is *possible*

TABLE 7.5.

OSGEO AFFILIATED PROJECTS AND SOME OF THEIR ASSOCIATED RULES

Ostrom's Rule Category	Project A	Project B	Project C	Project D	Project E	Project F	Project G
Position rules	Project leader; Project steering committee member; Core developer (informal; often overlaps with the committee member); Developer	Project leader; Project steering committee member; Core developer (informal; often overlaps with the committee member); Developer	No formal project leader; Informal lead team of three people; Project steering committee member; Committers	Project leader; Project steering committee member; Core developer (informal; often overlaps with the committee member); Developer	Project leader; Project steering committee member; Core developer (informal; often overlaps with the committee member); Developer	Project leader; Project steering committee member; Core developer (informal; often overlaps with the committee member); Developer	No formal project leader; Informal lead team of four people; Project management committee member; Core developer (informal; often overlaps with the committee member); Developer
Boundary rules	Formal rules; Community members elect to PSC; No term limits	Formal rules	Formal rules copied from another project	Formal rules copied from another project; Almost never consulted	Formal rules	Formal rules exist but primarily depend on social norms	Formal rules, but not necessarily followed

Ostrom's Rule Category	Project A	Project B	Project C	Project D	Project E	Project F	Project G
Choice rules	Some formalized Program steering committee makes some major rules Primarily social norms Open exchange in the list Mutual expectations	Some formalized available in the wiki Primarily social norms	Some formalized available in the wiki Primarily social norms	Social norms	Social norms	Social norms	Formalized rules written down Program management acts if necessary Social norms important
Aggregation rules	Informal-symmetric: consensus in program steering committee and discussion including developers who are not in the committee Formal voting: rarely occurs, even though formal rules stipulate it	Steering committee: almost all developers are on the committee Voting: if veto vote is used, discussion follows	Informal-symmetric: consensus in program steering committee Formal voting: rarely occurs even though formal rules stipulate it	Steering committee makes decision by consensus or voting All developers can vote as well, but their votes do not count.	Informal-symmetric: consensus in program steering committee Formal voting: rarely occurs even though formal rules stipulate it	Informal-symmetric: consensus in program steering committee and discussion but often back channels used before the decision is reached	Program management committee votes

	Only PSC members can vote		Only PSC members can vote		Only PSC members can vote	Voting is a last resort	
Information rules	Social norm: open exchange of information Unwritten rule that e-mail list is the main communication tool	Limited formal rules Most decisions are made in Internet Relay Chat and mailing list is used as well	Social norms Talking by e-mail and weekly Internet Relay Chat meetings	Social norms Project leaders available on Internet Relay Chat almost all the time	Social norms	Social norms All communication is based on writing	Social norms Weekly Internet Relay Chat meetings Otherwise no clear rules
Pay-off rules	No rules	No rules	No rules	No rules	No rules	No rules	No rules
Scope rules	Design rules	Design rules	Design rules	Design rules	Design rules	Design rules	Design rules

to decompose, articulate, and systematically analyze open source commons institutional designs using Ostrom's seven rule framework.

As described in our book (Schweik & English 2012: ch. 5, Table 5.4), I was also able, based on the description of the evolution of institutions in the Debian Linux case articulated by O'Mahony & Ferrarro (2007), to associate key rules of that project with Ostrom's seven rule classes. In their paper, O'Mahony and Ferrarro describe the evolution of governance structures in this high-profile open source software project. Their description permitted us to categorize in a two-column table the project's rules at two different longitudinal stages according to rule class and institutional level (constitutional, collective-choice, or operational). (For space reasons I decided not to include that table in this chapter). The important point here is that it is *possible* to do this categorization.

The take-home message from the OSGeo case study experience is that it is possible to articulate more systematically the institutional designs of open source software commons (and, by extension, other types of open, digital commons where collaboration occurs). Related to the study of knowledge commons more generally, this feasibility demonstration is vitally important for, as many chapters in this volume demonstrate, there is much happening in this space.

IV. Conclusions and Future Research

In many cases, knowledge commons may, as we have seen with open source software commons, be made up of very small teams with extremely lean institutional designs. Our quantitative work suggests that, for a very large percentage of these, success is not about building a large team of developers. Much can get done, driven in part by user- or organizational-centered need if even two people with similar passion, interest, and skills can find each other and begin to build a working relationship.

At the same time, I would argue that we are just at the cusp of a new period of open collaboration that will involve much more complicated institutional arrangements guiding collective action and evolving over time. The Debian Linux case described by O'Mahony & Ferrarro (2007) is a case in point. Increasingly, there is a need to understand the structure of institutional designs in these larger, more complex commons, and a need to understand how they evolve. Our empirical work on SF projects revealed some evidence that more formalized institutions do emerge as projects get larger, but our findings along these lines are limited because of the large number of small projects in our SF dataset.

All of this leads to a key question: *How do we best analyze the institutional structure of knowledge commons and their evolution in a comparative fashion?* We need methods for systematically articulating these structures and, in my view, the framework introduced in Chapter 1, coupled with Ostrom's (2005) more detailed analysis of rules-in-use levels (operational, collective-choice, constitutional) and her more refined seven rule categories, provides an initial structure for such systematic comparative analysis.

Given that an appropriate theoretical framework is critical to structuring comparative analysis of knowledge commons cases, let me close with some reflections on the utility of the modified IAD framework presented in the beginning of this volume, as it is applied to open source projects as knowledge commons.

First, the modified IAD framework in Chapter 1 introduces the idea of "resource characteristics" on the left side of the diagram (Chapter 1, Figure 1.2). In the context of open source projects as knowledge commons, the resource characteristics would be "technological characteristics" of the project. They include characteristics such as the programming language(s) used, the database systems utilized (if any), the operating system(s) the program is being developed to run upon, and so forth. Frischmann, Madison, and Strandburg are correct in their recognition that knowledge commons differ and that we need to expect that different cultural commons will have different resource characteristics. This fact will lead to challenges concerning how best to compare different knowledge commons. But comparison is important if we want to understand how much similarity exists between different knowledge commons. We might look to comparative studies that have analyzed different natural resource commons cases (e.g., forests or irrigation systems)—to the extent such comparative analyzes exist—as inspiration here.

An additional important point related to resource characteristics that Frischmann, Madison, and Strandburg recognize is that in knowledge commons there may be multiple and distinct shared resources. Indeed, this is the case in open source software, for both the source code and the binary code that is actually run by users, are shared. There may be connections to natural resource commons studies here as well. Consider the idea that a forest commons may provide wood or plant resources for subsistence use, but also provide a habitat for wild animals. In both settings, resource characteristics are complex.

Second, I agree with Frischmann, Madison, and Strandburg's assertion that there are complexities associated with thinking about the attributes of knowledge commons communities. In open source software cases, for example, there are two rather distinct groups: the development team with authority to modify the source code and to control the source code repository, and the end-user community, members of which, in some circumstances, contribute back to the source code commons in the form of bug reporting, testing, or documentation. Analytically, there can be multiple constituencies that fall under the IAD "community attributes" component and that need to be analyzed in terms of their specific roles and contributions to these knowledge commons.

Third, in their discussion, Frischmann, Madison, and Strandburg recognize that knowledge or "intellectual" commons are not rivalrously consumed. Building on this idea and reflecting on open source software as an intellectual commons that exists in digital format, one realizes that the "tragedy of the commons" in digital open source is not about overconsumption and depletion, but, rather, is about the code not being further developed and/or used.

Frischmann, Madison, and Strandburg's modified IAD framework identifies "clusters" or "buckets" of variables relevant to project governance or "rules-in-use" that they suggest are important to explore. One of these buckets is "institutional setting," which includes "…markets and related firm and collective structures" and "social structures that describe the roles and interests of individual actors in the commons." In our statistical work (Schweik & English 2012), we discovered substantial quantitative evidence suggesting that open source software is much more mainstream than popular discussion might suggest, with many projects being collaborations between participants paid by firms or government organizations and volunteers, rather than collaborations composed entirely, or even primarily, of volunteer programmers. Open source knowledge or information commons often serve markets, industries, and firms, rather than simply a voluntary community, as was thought to be the case in the "early days" of open source software research and scholarship. The specific configurations and motivations of participants vary among open source projects based on what kinds of people are the primary project contributors.

Moreover, with regard to governance, in many of Elinor Ostrom's writings she pointed out that the degree of self-governance is important and that commons do better when participants in the "action arena" (see Chapter 1) have a say in governance. Indeed, in open source software projects this is undoubtedly true—but to a degree. What we have learned from our research is that programmers care about the largely informal social norms that help guide their collaborations, but that a greater degree of formality of rules-in-use can *negatively* influence the collaboration and performance of an open source team. Last, we have learned from our analysis that, while it is important for team members to have a say in the rules that govern open source collaboration, in the vast majority of these projects, benevolent dictatorships are the norm. This result is largely due, in our opinion, to the fact that the vast majority of the teams in our sample are so small that hierarchy in decision making is driven by the authority of the individual who started the project or by technical meritocracy. We did, however, also identify signs that, as teams get larger, more formalized governance structures emerge, suggesting that the establishment of formalized rules may be important for larger projects. As mentioned above, more research is needed on the larger development team cases that fall in the tail end of the distribution shown in Figure 7.3.

In conclusion, the modified IAD framework presented in the beginning of this volume clearly has utility in analyzing open source projects as a form of knowledge commons. What is needed now is to continue the effort toward developing a systematic articulation of the variety of knowledge commons "out there" and to work toward constructing a larger database of knowledge commons cases that we can use to analyze similarities and differences, both in one slice in time and longitudinally. It is my hope that in some small way, this chapter, along with the framework presented in Chapter 1, helps move us forward toward establishing methods and approaches to help us articulate the structure and evolution of knowledge commons.

Acknowledgments

Support for this work was provided by a grant from the U.S. National Science Foundation (NSFIIS 0447623). The findings, recommendations, and opinions expressed are those of the authors and do not necessarily reflect the views of the funding agency. The work this chapter builds upon is the result of not just the author but a team of highly capable individuals: Bob English, Sandra Haire, Meng-Shiou Shieh, and Meelis Kitsing. Of course, any mistakes are my responsibility alone.

References

Yochai Benkler, The Wealth of Networks: How Social Production Transforms Markets and Freedom (Yale University Press 2006).

James Boyle, *The Second Enclosure Movement and the Construction of the Public Domain*, 66 Law & Contemp. Probs. 33 (2003).

Martin Campbell-Kelly, From Airline Reservations to Sonic the Hedgehog: A History of the Software Industry (MIT Press 2003).

Paul N. Courant & Rebecca J. Griffiths, *Software and Collaboration in Higher Education: A Study of Open Source Software* (2006), http://www.campussource.de/opensource/docs/OOSS_Report.pdf.

Paul A. David & Joseph S. Shapiro, *Community-Based Production of Open-Source Software: What Do We Know about the Developers Who Participate?*, 20 Information Economics & Policy 364 (2008).

Fadi P. Deek & James A. M. McHugh, Open Source Technology and Policy (Cambridge University Press 2007).

Robert English & Charles M. Schweik, *Identifying Success and Tragedy of FLOSS Commons: A Preliminary Classification of Sourceforge.net Projects*, 8 Upgrade 54 (2007).

Joseph Feller, Brian Fitzgerald, Scott A. Hissam, & Karim R. Lakhani (eds.), Perspectives on Free and Open Source Software (MIT Press 2005).

Karl Fogel, Producing Open Source Software: How to Run a Successful Free Software Project (2006), http://producingoss.com/en/producingoss.pdf.

FSF (Free Software Foundation), *What Is CopyLeft?*, GNU Operating System (2009), http://www.gnu.org/copyleft/.

Alex Howard, *Connecting the Dots with Intellipedia*, O'Reilly Radar (June 3, 2010), http://radar.oreilly.com/2010/06/connecting-the-dots-with-intel.html.

James Howison, Megan Conklin, & Kevin Crowston, *FLOSSmole: A Collaborative Repository for FLOSS Research Data and Analyses*, 1 Int'l J. Information Technology and Web Engineering 17 (2006).

Shishir Kumar Jha & Amrutaunshu Nerurkar, *Expanding Open Source into Other Domains: Analysis of Open Source Biomedical Research*, in Conference Proceedings of JTIP 2010: The Politics of Open Source 160 (Stuart W. Schulman & Charles M. Schweik eds., 2010), http://scholarworks.umass.edu/cgi/viewcontent.cgi?article=1000&context=jitpc2010.

David Karpf, *What Can Wikipedia Tell Us about Open Source Politics?*, in CONFERENCE PROCEEDINGS OF JITP 2010: THE POLITICS OF OPEN SOURCE 2 (Stuart W. Shulman & Charles M. Schweik eds., 2010), http://scholarworks.umass.edu/jitpc2010/1/.

Sandeep Krishnamurthy, *Cave or Community? An Empirical Examination of 100 Mature Open Source Projects*, 7 FIRST MONDAY no. 6 (June 3, 2002), http://firstmonday.org/htbin/cgi-wrap/bin/ojs/index.php/fm/article/view/960/881.

Sandeep Krishamurthy, *An Analysis of Open Source Business Models*, in PERSPECTIVES ON FREE AND OPEN SOURCE SOFTWARE 279 (Joseph Feller, Brian Fitzgerald, Scott A. Hissam, & Karim R. Lakhani eds., MIT Press 2005).

John Kuniholm, *The Open Prosthetics Project*, Presentation at the Military Open Source Software Conference (Aug. 31, 2011), http://mil-oss.org/wg3-speakers-and-presentations.

James A. Lewis, *Government Open Source Policies* (Center for Strategic & International Studies 2010), http://csis.org/files/publication/100416_Open_Source_Policies.pdf.

LocalMotors, http://www.localmotors.com/ (accessed Mar. 28, 2014).

Greg Madey, *SourceForge.net Research Data*, RESEARCH PROJECT ON THE FREE/OPEN SOURCE SOFTWARE (F/OSS) DEVELOPMENT PHENOMENON: UNDERSTANDING OPEN SOURCE SOFTWARE DEVELOPMENT, http://www.nd.edu/~oss/Data/data.html (accessed Sept. 1, 2011).

M. Lynne Markus, *The Governance of Free/Open Source Software Projects: Monolithic, Multidimensional, or Configurational?*, 11 J. MANAGEMENT & GOVERNANCE 151 (2007).

Dan McQuillan, *Open Source Is on the Map*, LASA KNOWLEDGEBASE (2003), http://www.ictknowledgebase.org.uk/opensourceonthemap. NOSI (Nonprofit Open Source Initiative), *NOSI's Survey of FOSS Use in the Nonprofit Sector* (2008), http://nosi.net/node/300.

Siobhán O'Mahony, *Nonprofit Foundations and Their Role in Community-Firm Software Collaboration*, in PERSPECTIVES ON FREE AND OPEN SOURCE SOFTWARE 393 (Joseph Feller, Brian Fitzgerald, Scott A. Hissam, & Karim R. Lakhani eds., MIT Press 2005).

Siobhán O'Mahony, *The Governance of Open Source Initiatives: What Does It Mean to Be Community Managed?*, 11 J. MANAGEMENT & GOVERNANCE 139 (2007).

Siobhán O'Mahony & Fabrizio Ferraro, *The Emergence of Governance in an Open Source Community*, 50 ACADEMY OF MANAGEMENT J. 1079 (2007).

OSGeo, *About the Open Source Geospatial Foundation*, OSGEO: YOUR OPEN SOURCE COMPASS, http://www.osgeo.org/content/foundation/about.html (accessed Mar. 10, 2009).

ELINOR OSTROM, UNDERSTANDING INSTITUTIONAL DIVERSITY (Princeton University Press 2005).

Eric Steven Raymond, *The Cathedral and the Bazaar*, ERIC S. RAYMOND'S HOME PAGE (2000a), http://www.catb.org/~esr/writings/cathedral-bazaar/cathedral-bazaar/index.html.

Eric S. Raymond, *Homesteading the Noosphere*, ERIC S. RAYMOND'S HOME PAGE (2000b), http://catb.org/esr/writings/homesteading/homesteading/.

Dirk Riehle, *The Economic Motivation of Open Source Software: Stakeholder Perspectives*, 40 IEEE COMPUTER 25 (2007).

Gregorio Robles-Martínez, Jesús M. González-Barahona, José Centeno-González, Vicente Matellán-Olivera, & Luis Rodero-Merino, *Studying the Evolution of Libre Software Projects Using Publicly Available Data*, ICSE International Conference on Software Engineering (2003), http://flosshub.org/system/files/111-115.pdf.

Michael Schwarz & Yuri Takhteyev, *Half a Century of Public Software Institutions: Open Source as a Solution to Hold-Up Problem* (National Bureau of Economic Research, Working Paper No. 14946, 2009).

Charles M. Schweik & Robert C. English, Internet Success: A Study of Open Source Software Commons (MIT Press 2012).

Charles M. Schweik, Tom P. Evans, & J. Morgan Grove, *Open Source and Open Content: A Framework for Global Collaboration in Social-Ecological Research*, 10 Ecology & Society 33 (2005).

Charles M. Schweik & Meelis Kitsing, *Applying Elinor Ostrom's Rule Classification Framework to the Analysis of Open Source Software Commons*, 2 J. Transnat'l Corporations. Rev. 13 (2010).

Charles M. Schweik, Ines Mergel, Jodi Sandfort, & Zhirong Zhao, *Toward Public Administration Scholarship*, 21 J. Public Administration Research & Theory 1175 (2011).

Kimberly D. Simon, *The Value of Open Standards and Open-Source Software in Government Environments*, 44 IBM Systems J. 227 (2005).

Eric von Hippel, Democratizing Innovation (MIT Press 2005a).

Eric von Hippel, *Open Source Software Projects as User Innovation Networks*, *in* Perspectives on Free and Open Source Software 267 (Joseph Feller, Brian Fitzgerald, Scott A. Hissam, & Karim R. Lakhani eds., MIT Press 2005b).

Steven Weber, The Success of Open Source (Harvard University Press 2004).

Dawid Weiss, *Measuring Success of Open Source Projects Using Web Search Engines*, presented at First International Conference on Open Source Systems (2005), http://oss2005.case.unibz.it/Papers/26.pdf.

Andrea Wiggins & Kevin Crowston. *Reclassifying Success and Tragedy in FLOSS Projects*, *in* Proceedings of the Sixth International Conference on Open Source Software (Pär Ågerfalk, Cornelia Boldyreff, Jesus González-Barahona, Greg Madey, & John Noll, eds., Springer 2010).

8 Governance of Online Creation Communities for the Building of Digital Commons: Viewed through the Framework of Institutional Analysis and Development

Mayo Fuster Morell*

I. Introduction

Natural commons have been studied substantially using the Institutional Analysis and Development (IAD) framework of Ostrom (1990) and many others. More recently, a new type of commons has also attracted the attention of researchers (Hess & Ostrom 2007). Constructing commons in the cultural environment as characterized by Madison, Frischmann, & Strandburg (2010) refers to a broader set of commons in the field of culture and knowledge. This chapter addresses a specific type of constructed cultural common-pool resource: online creation communities.

With the adoption of information and communication technologies (ICTs), diverse types of communities of individuals following common goals through technologically mediated communication have emerged (Benkler 2006). Online creation communities (OCCs) are a particular type of online community whose goal is knowledge making and knowledge sharing. OCCs are communities of individuals that mainly interact via a platform for online participation, with the goal of building and sharing a common-pool

* Mayo Fuster Morell, PhD, is a Fellow at the Berkman Center for Internet and Society, Harvard University, Cambridge, Massachusetts, USA.

resource (or common pool of resources) resulting from collaboratively systematizing and integrating dispersed information and knowledge resources and cognitive capacities.

A. PREVIOUS WORK ON THE GOVERNANCE OF OCCS

One of the more lively debates in contemporary organizational research concerns how the coordination and governance of distributed knowledge in globally dispersed settings—such as the case of OCCs—takes place, and how it can be accounted for (Becker 2001; Hansen 1999; Orlikowski 2002). Unlike other types of online communities, OCCs must integrate individual contributions into a common pool, which can heighten interdependencies and the need for coordination and governance. Yet little is known about how OCCs which organize around production govern themselves.

The scant empirical research on OCCs governance is mainly concentrated on the case of free/libre and open source software (FLOSS) projects (Crowston & Howison 2005; Lanzara & Morner 2004; O'Mahony 2007; O'Mahony & Ferraro 2007; Weber 2004) and more recently on Wikipedia (Burke & Kraut 2008; Ciffolilli 2003; Kittur, Suh, Pendleton, & Chi 2007; Kriplean, Beschastnikh, McDonald, & Golder 2007; Loubser & Pentzold 2009; O'Neil 2009; Reagle 2004; Stadler & Hirsh 2002; Tkacz 2007; Viégas, Wattenberg, & McKeon 2007). These analyses focus on the community (Konieczny 2009; Greenstein & Devereau 2009; Tkacz 2007), particularly in terms of policy making in the community (Kriplean, Beschastnikh, McDonald, & Golder 2007; Loubser & Pentzold 2009; Viégas, Wattenberg, & McKeon 2007), its decentralized character (Forte & Bruckman 2008; Malone 2004), and forms of conflict resolution (Kittur, Suh, Pendleton, & Chi 2007; Matei & Caius 2011). The nature of authority has also been analyzed (Ciffolilli 2003; O'Neil 2009; Stadler & Hirsh 2002), together with studies on modes of selection of administrators, their roles (Burke & Kraut 2008), and leadership (Reagle 2004). Fuster Morell (2010) considered the institutional frame or, more specifically, the role of the Wikimedia Foundation as platform provider.

Although the number of articles on community governance has increased, their range of topics remains limited. Previous research has mostly focused on analyzing the policy-making processes developed by the participants to govern their interaction. However, there was a gap in the literature, lacking a comprehensive and holistic view of what governance means in collective action online.

This chapter aims to move beyond the analysis of specific aspects of the governance of OCCs, to provide a comprehensive understanding of the diverse aspects that drive governance of OCCs. This chapter provides a set of dimensions that define the governance of OCCs. In particular, most previous work did not consider infrastructure provision in their analysis. In this regard, the chapter challenges previous literature by questioning the neutrality of infrastructure for collective action.

B. EMPIRICAL ANALYSIS: INSTITUTIONAL ANALYSIS AND DEVELOPMENT (IAD) FRAMEWORK

The governance of OCCs will be analyzed though the Institutional Analysis and Development (IAD) framework, building on the work of Madison, Frischmann, & Strandburg (2010), who adapt the IAD framework from natural commons to knowledge commons and commons in the cultural environment. References to Schweik & English's (2012) adaptation of the IAD framework to FLOSS will also be made. In this regard, the chapter will also provide an assessment of the IAD framework in the analysis of OCCs.

The empirical data were drawn from a statistical analysis of fifty cases and four case study comparisons on OCCs conducted in 2010 (Fuster Morell 2010).

For the statistical analysis of fifty units, a code book was used to collect the data from digital threads available on the OCCs websites. In the case of OCCs, random selection is difficult given that the universe is unknown. Nevertheless, the sample tried to reflect the heterogeneity of OCCs. For the sampling, a snowball method was used. The strategy employed in selecting the units for the sample was based on selecting the cases which fulfilled the OCCs definition and had a global scope. From the cases that conformed to these two criteria, the cases covered were a variety of OCCs following two central sampling guidelines. First, there had to be a balance between more recent and older organizations. Second, there had to be a balance between the several types of technological base and knowledge goal central interests of the OCCs (e.g., multimedia archives, libraries, encyclopedias, dictionaries, information nodes, software programs, collective social memory, among others).

The statistical analysis pointed to four models of governance that will be presented though the chapter. These informed the selection of the four case studies, each associated with one of the four models. The four case studies were Wikipedia, wikiHow, Flickr, and the Social Forums Memory project. Wikipedia is an encyclopedia made up of free content that emerged from 2001. Editors collaborate to create encyclopedic articles. Its infrastructure is provided by the Wikimedia Foundation. WikiHow is a collaborative "how-to" manual. The wikiHow provider is a start-up with the same name founded in 2005. Flickr is a platform provided by Yahoo! for sharing and archiving visual materials. Participants interact to improve and comment on each other's pictures, collaborate to create "albums" of photos around a particular topic, or create learning groups around photography techniques. The Social Forums Memory project operates at openesf.net, a platform provided by the European Social Forum, a collectivity of social movements in Europe.[1] Openesf.net was set up to support collectible document forums. The case studies were based on virtual ethnography, interviews, and participative observations at events. Data was collected in 2008 and 2010.[2]

---

[1] See http://www.fse-esf.org/.
[2] A further specification of the methods (code book, criteria for interview selection, etc.) is provided at http://www.onlinecreation.info/outline_design.

II. Online Creation Communities Viewed through an Analytical Framework Directed at Institutional Analysis and Development

This section views OCCs through the Institutional Analysis and Development (IAD) analytical framework. Reference is made to the adaptation of Madison, Frischmann, & Strandburg (2010) of the framework to constructed commons (see Figure 8.1). First, resource characteristics, community attributes, and the governance of OCCs are presented. In the following section, OCCs outcomes are presented along with an analysis of how resource characteristics, community attributes, and rules-in-use/governance might impact upon them.

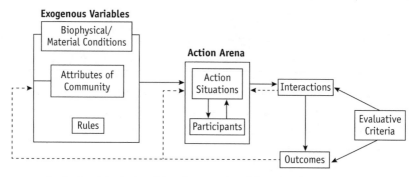

FIGURE 8.1 Institutional Analysis and Development (IAD) framework.

Madison, Frischmann, & Strandburg (2010) provide a characterization of the cultural environment as being that within which commons construction emerges. They also recognize that the background environment for a particular commons may need further specification and analysis in order to situate the description, classification, and analysis of resource characteristics, community attributes, and governance institutions. In the analysis of OCCs, a specific environmental setting is involved and needs to be considered. The Internet is the specific environment within which OCCs emerge and their common-pool resource is hosted. The Internet as an environment is shaped by the digital culture and the technological constraints of virtual spheres, as well as the legal frameworks that regulate it.

A. RESOURCE CHARACTERISTICS OF OCCS

The pooled resources in OCCs are not given resources that need to be "preserved" as in natural commons-pool resources. Rather, they are resources that need to be built. OCCs, indeed, arise from the collective goal of building a specific resource. The building process is characterized by the pooling of dispersed information and cognitive capacities in evolving bodies of shared knowledge. The resource tends to be conceived of as a permanent *work in progress*, and in most of the cases, without a specific moment of definitive conclusion.

The OCCs are immaterial in nature, consisting of information and knowledge. As public goods, they are nonrivalrous and nonexcludable. Madison, Frischmann, & Strandburg (2010) classify constructed commons goals as existing in a milieu of intellectual property (IP) rights, as existing only because of the IP rights, or as mediating among communities with different default norms. Most OCCs, including the four case studies considered here, fall into the first category, as they exist as part of IP rights.

According to Madison, Frischmann, & Strandburg (2010) cultural commons are diverse in terms of the level at which their pooled resources are most easily identifiable or recognized. OCCs form a case where pooled resources are easily identifiable—an archive that gathers and coherently systematizes the contributions. Indeed, the construction of an integrated and identifiable piece of knowledge is what distinguishes OCCs from other online communities such as networking sites or communities of support or shared interest. An encyclopedia is the main common resource in the case of Wikipedia, a picture repository in the case of Flickr, how-to manuals in the case of wikiHow, and organizational information linked to a forum in the case of openesf.net. However, beyond their principal resources, all the cases aggregate other secondary "pooled resources" which deepen one another. For example, Wikipedia is not only an encyclopedia but also hosts a repository of audio-visual sources as a commons. Additionally, even if the knowledge resource is the central goal around which OCCs interact, OCCs also depend on an infrastructure to support interaction, and so an infrastructure architecture also results from the process. However, the term "infrastructure" means something that sustains the main goal but is not itself the central goal of the process.

Schweik & English (2012) have previously attempted to apply the IAD framework to OCCs in the specific case of FLOSS. Regarding resource characteristics, my approach differs in two ways from Schweik and English. On the one hand, Schweik and English do not specify the type of resource. However, when analyzing diverse OCCs as is the case in this chapter, specifying the type of resource is appropriate. On the other hand, Schweik and English present as resource characteristics aspects, such as the participation platform design, that are integrated as part of governance, not as resource characteristics, in the present work.

B. COMMUNITY ATTRIBUTES OF OCCS

It was pointed out above that pooled resources in OCCs are easily identifiable but that the same cannot be said of their communities. In terms of communities of constituents, OCCs are complex. OCCs are open to participation, and it is difficult to identify their boundaries. For none of the four case studies, or in the sample of fifty cases of OCCs looked at herein, were clear boundaries or membership established. The communities of OCCs may include any person potentially willing to contribute to the common-pool resource or to use it.

1. Community Size

OCCs are generally open to participation, but such openness does not necessarily result in actual participation. The size of the community of participants depends substantially on the goal of each OCC, ranging from more broad to more restricted sets of interests. One rightly expects that an encyclopedia attracts more participants than a site organized around visualization techniques.

In terms of the participation in the four cases, Wikipedia achieves a high level of participation. Almost 18 million registered users were part of Wikipedia in November 2012. Flickr also draws a large amount of participation. In 2007, one estimate put the Flickr community at 7.7 million users (Negoescu & Gatica-Perez 2008). WikiHow has substantially fewer participants. As of April 2010, the number of registered wikiHow participants was around 213,204. The levels of participation at openesf.net are low, with less than 1200 people registered at their highest point.[3]

2. Voluntary Engagement

Participants in OCCs are volunteers. They do not have a contractual labor relationship with the community, even if some participants may make their contributions as part of their work outside the community. All four cases share this characteristic of voluntary participation. Notably, however, professional photographers who use Flickr as part of their work form a significant part of the Flickr population (Burgess 2007).

As a consequence of the voluntary character of OCCs, each participant assumes the costs of participation. The participants are able to contribute according to their own resources of time, skills, or money. According to the civic voluntarism model (Verba, Schlozman, & Brady 1995), resources are a key factor in understanding why some people participate whereas others do not. Resource-rich participants with free time, connectivity, skills, and money can contribute more easily than those without such resources. And so the resource-rich tend to be disproportionately represented among participants. However, a lack of resources may not be the only explanatory variable behind nonparticipation. Even people with the necessary resources may decide not to participate for a variety of reasons such as questions of identity or personality. People who identify themselves as creative, for example, and/or are more used to public exposure may be more likely to participate. This is the case for younger generations. According to Preece, Nonnecke, & Andrews (2004), other reasons why people do not participate in OCCs are as follows: thinking that they were being helpful by not posting; wanting to learn more about the community before diving in; not being able to use the software because

---

[3] Wikipedia, http://meta.wikimedia.org/wiki/List_of_Wikipedias#Grand_Total; wikiHow, http://www.wikihow.com/wikiHow:Statistics. See Fuster Morell (2010) for a detailed account of participation in each of the four OCCs.

of poor usability; not liking the dynamics that they observed within the group; or feeling represented in what was said by other participants.

3. Community Heterogeneity

Several authors have pointed out that OCCs are very diverse in terms of the motivations and interest that drive their participation (e.g., Benkler 2006; Weber 2004). However, Schweik & English (2012) point out that their surveys of participants in FLOSS show a high level of homogeneity in terms of social composition, specifically gender (predominantly male), age (predominantly young), and geographical origin (predominantly Europe and United States). Analysis of gender distribution at openesf.net also shows that the predominance of male participation was also repeated in the case of openesf. net, where 36 percent of active participants are women according to their name or/and presentation in their user page. In the case of Wikipedia, previous research has concluded that women accounted for around 12 percent of the editor community (Glott, Schmidt, & Ghosh 2009). According to wikiHow Inc., the wikiHow community has a higher women's participation rate of around 40 percent (Interview with J. Herrick, Dec. 4, 2008, reported in Fuster Morell 2010).

4. External Relationships

Madison, Frischmann, & Strandburg (2010) suggest, with respect to community attributes, analyzing external relationships of community and common-pool resources regarding markets, industries or firms. For the specific case of FLOSS, several studies have pointed out how corporations and foundations engage with the common-pool resource, which Schweik & English (2012: 15) refer to with the label "open-source ecosystem." The external relationships of OCCs may explain their capacity to mobilize participation. However, research in this area is very limited, and there is not a unique pattern of interaction with markets, industries or firms. In the cases presented here, I observe the development of "net districts" similar to an industrial district. OCCs that are part of a "net district" and cooperate with each other. This is the case of Wikipedia and wikiHow, which adopt the same license or protocols to facilitate the flow of content and participation between their platforms.

C. RULES-IN-USE OR GOVERNANCE OF OCCS

Ostrom (2005: 3) defines institutions (referred to herein as bodies with governance or rules-in-use) as "the prescriptions that humans use to organize all forms of repetitive and structured interactions." Institutions raise and channel interaction among participants. They provide direction, control, and coordination of the collective action. Institutions are set by social norms and formalized rules, together with the forms in which those rules are created and enforced (Ostrom 2005).

The governance, or the direction, control, and coordination of a process, is embedded or operates though aspects or points/sources of power. According to the analysis reported here, there are eight main aspects that are in a complex juxtaposition or interaction which determine and drive governance in OCCs. The eight dimensions (that operate at the different operational, collective-choice, and constitutional levels) that give OCCs direction, control, and coordination are:

(1) Collective mission or goal of the process.
(2) Cultural principles and social norms.
(3) Design of the platform of participation (where regulation is embedded in the code).
(4) Self-management of contributions: autonomous condition of participants in allocating their contribution to the building process.
(5) Formal rules or policies applied to community interaction.
(6) License.
(7) Decision-making and conflict resolution systems with regard to community interaction.
(8) Infrastructure provision.[4]

The eight dimensions are interrelated rather than narrowly discrete. Additionally, governance is not "static" but dynamic and might evolve over time. It might not be linear in its evolution, with "incoherent" moves in the diverse aspects on occasion.

Governance is very much shaped on the basis of how and who decides and manages these dimensions. Each of the dimensions might be managed in a more open to participation or inclusive way or not. They may encourage involvement or consideration of the views and interests of the participants as individuals and/or community as a whole. Or they may be contrasted by the infrastructure provider. Another important dimension is whether it is more decentralized/fragmented/ad hoc or more centralized and established.

Some of these aspects are similarly present in other forms of collective action, while others are specific to the OCCs. This might be connected to the background environment within which OCCs operate, particularly the functioning of the digital environment. OCCs take place in an environment that shapes them in terms of technical and legal constraints. The emerging governance of OCCs in this environment cannot be qualified as simple. Indeed it is a highly complex system.

In the following section each of these eight aspects will be presented in detail.

---

[4] Weber (2004: 189) also highlights the role of leadership in FLOSS governance. Here, leadership is integrated as part of social norms where informal, and as part of decision-making mechanisms if formal.

1. Collective Mission or Goal of the Process

In general, the goal or mission of OCCs is building and sharing a common-pool resource. The specific mission is defined by the early participants or by the infrastructure provider. Then, the overall system is shaped by experiences with fulfillment of this initial mission. However, participants do not *need* to identify with the mission or the project as a whole in order to contribute.

It is common in OCCs to define their goals in terms of a sentence that describes their mission. Wikipedia's mission reads, "Imagine a world in which every single human being can freely share in the sum of all knowledge." WikiHow's mission is "to build the world's largest, highest quality, free how-to manual in many languages." Openesf.net does not have its own mission, but is a "tool" for supporting the working groups in their roles within a much larger process, the European Social Forum, whose goal or motto is that "another world is possible." Flickr's mission is "Share your photos. Watch the world."

Generally, the mission is defined by the founder of the OCC. In OCCs culture, the founders tend to be considered relevant and visible figures, especially with Wikipedia, where there is just one. The role of the founder might change over time, from more central and with formal power, to less central or only symbolic, such as the case of Jimmy Wales for Wikipedia, or the founders of Flickr. In the case of wikiHow, the figure of the founder maintained its position over time, as owner of wikiHow Inc. In contrast, openesf.net did not generate such a figure, but the founders of the process are connected, keeping their position. Giving importance to the figure of the founder is connected to a social norm (meritocracy) and is presented in the following section, which considers the importance given to values.

2. Cultural Principles and Social Norms

There is a set of cultural principles and values that tend to be present transversally in the culture of OCCs. These also feed the way these eight dimensions are performed and function. Among these key principles are: openness and "freedom to operate," meritocracy, and flexibility. Openness and "freedom to operate" without seeking permission or pre-clearance by a manager or property owner (in Benkler's terms, see Benkler 2006; Benkler (forthcoming)), might be present though the license that favors freedom to access and use the resource, or freedom though the openness of the process and the autonomy of the participants to allocate his or her own participation. Meritocracy or "do-acracy" refers to valuing individuals on the basis of the quantity and quality of their contributions, not on the basis of "who" they are in terms of external credentials or their opinions. Do-acracy also refers to the tendency in some OCCs for whoever does something to also have authority over it. Flexibility refers to the methods or preestablished formats. OCCs tend to be more mission oriented—to be intended to accomplish something—than method oriented—to do something in a particular manner. Benkler (forthcoming) refers to this question by pointing to the "nondeterminative" governance of peer production.

In the following section, further social norms will be presented, as they are also present in the way the platform is designed.

3. Design of the Platform of Participation (Where Regulation Is Embedded in the Code)

In OCCs, it is relatively rare for individuals to be involved in direct dialogues and negotiations among themselves. Instead, individuals interact with the platform design. Platform design thus influences participation and interaction. In this section, the design of the platform of participation and social norms is presented. As the analysis will show, the way in which the environment is designed by the code of the platforms is very much in line with the OCC's social norms.

The design of the participation platform is embedded and regulated in the code. Many diverse code programs can support a platform of participation. Here I present a set of principles embedded in the platforms that embody and guide participation in OCCs. The provision of the platform is controlled by the infrastructure provider. More or less involvement from the community in the platform design depends on the level of openness of the infrastructure providing community involvement.

a. Openness

I. OPENNESS AS IT APPLIES TO THE ACCESS TO THE RESOURCE. Openness as applied to the access to the resource is defined by Madison, Frischmann, & Strandburg (2010: 695) as "our capacity to relate to a resource by accessing and using it."

In terms of the conditions of access and use of the resources in OCCs, as will be shown later, free licenses favor free use. Yet how the knowledge resources are actually made available also determines the possibility of accessing and using them. In this regard, it is common for the common-pool resource in OCCs to be hosted by a participation platform made accessible in an open-access condition. The open-access condition of the resources should not, however, lead us to think they are not regulated, as they are.

These knowledge resources are open access through their license and through being made openly available online. The open-access condition of the resources does not imply openness when understood as the degree of control and intervention in decision making of those conditions. Deciding the license terms and how the resource is made available online are in the hands of the infrastructure provider. The level of openness to decision making about the conditions of use of the resources (as stated in the license and embedded in the platform of participation), here again, depends on the level of openness of the infrastructure provider.

II. OPENNESS AS IT APPLIES TO THE COMMUNITY BUILDING THE RESOURCE. Openness to interrelation and participation within the community for collaborative common-pool resource building is a significant principle at work in OCCs.

Openness to participation is made operative through the provision of channels that allow intervention in content creation, as well as through the protocols that guide those channels. Protocols refer, for example, to low requirements for credentials to participate.

According to the statistical analysis conducted for fifty cases (Fuster Morell 2010), OCCs usually have an average of four different channels of participation (i.e., the possibility to add comments to a specific section of the content, upload materials, and edit web pages, among others). The protocols that guide participation in OCCs appear to incentivize participation in a high percentage of the cases (i.e., 80 percent of the registration systems allow automatic registration without requiring any filter to become part of the platform). This contributes to lowering the transaction costs involved in becoming an active contributor. In all four case studies discussed here, indicators for the importance of openness are present: they all employ easy to use technology and channels for open participation, and they do not ask for credentials or other requirements in order to intervene.

However, even if openness to participation is embedded in the technology of OCCs, not all OCCs are equally accessible. The level of inclusion of OCCs and the willingness or capacity to ensure there are no barriers to participation vary. For example, an analysis of OCC inclusion shows OCCs to be exclusive in terms of accessibility for people with relevant physical disabilities (Fuster Morell 2010).

The principle of openness to participation is not only embedded in the design of the platform of participation, it is also present in social norms. For instance, in OCC discourses, it is emphasized that the community is provided accessibility for participation. In this line, Wikipedia is presented as the encyclopedia that "anyone can edit."[5]

b. Modularity and Decentralized Participation

Another aspect embedded in the code of the platform of participation is the modular organization of the platform. Essentially, this involves splitting content into separate units (such as articles, software packages, thematic albums of pictures, etc.). The design of OCCs does not imply that all participants are involved in all projects or modules. Instead, and particularly as the OCC grows, there is a tendency for participation to split or fragment into projects or modules. Modularity favors the decentralization of activity. In addition, distributing tasks between modules favors increased participation. The participation of many people in a single (central) place could be more difficult to handle than that of many small groups. Modular design and the resulting decentralization of participation are features present in the Wikipedia, wikiHow, and openesf.net cases.

Concerning the Wikipedia case, activities which involve the entire Wikipedia community are extremely rare. Most of the activities of Wikipedia are based on interactions of small groups. The same finding was uncovered in the wikiHow case. In openesf.net, 41.5 percent of the projects are composed by only one member, and projects with three

---

[5] Http://en.wikipedia.org/wiki/Wikipedia:Introduction.

members are the most frequent following this (20.8 percent) (Fuster Morell 2010). The Flickr case is different because its primary unit of content is not based on collective "projects" such as an article in Wikipedia but on individual acts (uploading photos). In this regard, rather than decentralization as such, structural individualization exists at the base of the design of the participation platform. However, Flickr, too, possesses the feature of the formation of separate groups around common interests. According to Sieberg, there were 300,000 groups on Flickr by 2007 (Sieberg 2007).

c. Participation Is Mostly Asynchronous and Online

As presented in the previous section, participation is decentralized to projects in OCCs. Furthermore, it is not implied in terms of either the platform design or social norms that participants congregate at the same time within the platform. Asynchronous participation in the platform is common to all the case studies.

One moment at which some participants might congregate at the same time and place is during physical encounters. Even if OCCs are mainly developed online, participants do sometimes meet physically. In the Wikipedia and openesf.net cases, regular local meetings of participants are organized. Plus, both of these case study OCCs hold regular meetings. WikiHow and Flickr participants meet much more infrequently.

d. Transparency of Participation

OCCs are developed in public, indeed it would be accurate to say that OCCs *live* in public. The analysis of fifty cases of OCCs showed that in 88 percent of the cases the content of communications among participants is publicly accessible. That is, it is possible to read the content of communications among participants without registering on the site.

The public, or transparent, character of the organizational process favors openness to participation. Public organizing also favors the training of new participants and the building of trust. New participants can see how others perform some tasks. Finally, it also favors the autonomy and decentralization of participation and the coordination of participation without a predefined plan or a gatekeeper distributing roles. Participants themselves can identify where contributions are needed and to what level they wish to get involved. According to O'Mahony's research on FLOSS communities, "a public or transparent development process is necessary to support decentralized decision-making so that a large body of people can learn enough to participate in decisions" (O'Mahony 2007: 148).

In the Wikipedia case the whole drafting process, not only the resulting content, is visible to all. The channels that host the interaction (such as Wikis, mailing lists, meet-ups, etc.) are public by default. The same is true of wikiHow. In the case of openesf.net, each project creator may choose how public each project will be. They decide whether the project will be accessible to the general public, only to people registered at openesf.net, or only to members of that particular project. However, the majority of the projects have a public character. The same may be said concerning Flickr, albeit at an individual level.

On Flickr, each individual chooses if his or her content is publicly accessible or not and, thereby, if the communication surrounding the content is public or not.

4. Self-Management of Contributions: The Autonomous Condition of
Participants in Contributing to the Building Process

As pointed out in the previous section, the design of the platform of participation determines, to a large degree, the type of interaction and actions that can be performed by participants. Still, the participants have great flexibility in terms of the types of activities they develop and degrees of involvement they undertake. Participants decide their level of commitment and how they want to contribute freely and automatically on the basis of personal interests, motivations, resources, and abilities. The distribution of participation is not based on centralized planning of user activities but on decentralized, volunteers deciding for themselves. There is no gatekeeper or similar role in charge of prodding participants along in a particular direction. In the designed platform participants choose what to do. Participation is not driven by command but by self-direction. Additionally, participants "build" or "do." Participation is mainly based on implementing tasks by directly creating or editing content. This is not a major risk. Online interaction facilitates the undoing of actions, and so mistakes are not irreparable. This implies that there is no separation between decision making and implementation, or between a delegation and an implementation body. Those who take care of a task also have the authority to decide how to perform it. This form of participation opens up the idea of *do-ography* or "implementation democracy." Finally, the coordination of participation is not the result of a strict, absolute, and fixed plan. Rather it is open to uncertainty and variation, based on principles of randomness and the serendipitous.

This is so for the four case studies. That said, the Flickr platform is the most restrictive in terms of the types of activities that can be performed. Additionally, for some of the activities on Flickr, in contrast to the other cases, participants must pay for access, which may restrict access to some of the population.

Not all participants necessarily carry out the same tasks. They choose among several, such as adding new content, editing content, and classifying content, among others. One person may contribute unedited information while another participant takes care of editing it and increasing its quality. Some tasks may require more effort and commitment than others, however, and in most cases, tasks are highly divided so that each participant can contribute either just a small part of a module or a large part, facilitating the scaling of participation. Again, this must not be confused with a lack of structure. On the contrary the platforms are highly structured. There are also different levels of commitment to the platform in terms of time and active task performance. Participants' freedom to decide their level of contribution results in a very common distribution feature in OCCs. Research on the distribution of participation suggests a very unequal distribution known as the 90/9/1 principle or power law (Hill, Hollan, Wroblewski, & McCandless 1992;

Nielsen 1997). Ninety percent of visitors to OCCs tend to be lurkers who read or observe but never contribute, 9 percent contribute a little from time to time, and 1 percent contribute often and account for almost all the content and system activity (Nielsen 2006). In other words, there are three main profiles of participation: strong or very active, weak, and nonparticipant, each playing a role. Very active participants have a high degree of commitment to the process and dedicate a great deal of time and a large volume of work or complex effort to it. Low-level participants are people who contribute only sporadically. Weak participation may favor greater connectivity of the OCC with other processes. Weak ties favor reaching larger areas of information (Granovetter 1983). Beyond strong and weak participation, nonparticipation or unintended participation is also present and plays a role.

Nonparticipation could be characterized as free-riding behavior. However, free riding, and in general the fact that a large percentage of people do not contribute, does not necessarily constitute a problem or put at risk the achievement of the common goals of OCCs.[6] With exhaustible goods, such as natural resources which can be "used up" and are costly to extract, free riding constitutes a problem. But in a context where ICTs have substantially decreased the cost of reproduction of information and information-based goods, like those provided by OCCs, OCCs do not necessarily face scarcity problems linked to resource use. When goods are nonexhaustible, noncompetitive, and exclusion from their use is costly, then free riding is not necessarily a problem. It has even been said that OCCs are antirival (Weber 2004). They are not *only* nonrival in the sense that they can tolerate free riding without reducing their stock of value, but are actually antirival in the sense that OCCs positively benefit from free riders. That is, ironically, the *comedy of the commons*, the value of the outcome of OCCs increases when more people use them (Frischmann 2012; Rose 1986). This implies that for any participant, contributor, or "free rider," mere "use" implies a contribution. Nevertheless, this is only so where there is a sufficient number of contributors that assure the building of the resource.

The value of the information resources resulting from OCCs increases through several mechanisms as more people "use" them. First, nonparticipants contribute due to positive network effects. A network effect is the effect that one participant in an OCC has on the value of that OCC for other people, even if this was not intentional. When network effects appear, more people become involved in an OCC, and the more valuable

---

[6] See Frischmann (2012: ch. 8). In addition, Bimber, Flanagin, & Stohl (2005) suggest that the free-riding analysis of costs and benefits as applied to information goods is challenged by some of the emerging characteristics of online communities. In the authors' approach the perceived cost of contributing to collective actions via contemporary electronic tools is a relatively weak or even an unimportant factor in explaining individuals' decisions to contribute to information repositories. In their words: "When (contribution) is costly, boundary crossing typically takes on the characteristics of a discrete decision. When participation is easy and not costly, it is less of an issue of a decision" (Bimber, Flanagin, & Stohl 2005: 378). Also, some contributions do not necessarily involve a decision. For example, in their *side effects* contributions become "unintended," there is no decision to contribute; the contribution is the result of some other intention, such as using the content.

it becomes. For example, as more people use Flickr as a tool to connect with others, the more valuable it becomes since users can potentially connect with a larger number of people through it.

Second, in online environments, most actions are translated into digital information, known as *digital threads*, and the elaboration of these digital threads form a source of very valuable information for the improvement of content and the functioning of the environment. They can provide, for example, relational and attention data. The environment can learn about the connections between content according to how users navigate, or the number of times an article was visited or downloaded could be used as an indicator of the quality of that article.

Third, nonparticipants also play a role as an *audience*. *Free rider audiences* increase the relevance and value of a platform's content and increase the motives for participation.

Finally, it is also worth considering that even though exclusion is present in OCCs, restricting access to nonparticipants can be costly. Technically this might be challenging. Additionally, digital culture values "simple," "easy-to-use" solutions. To incorporate filters might constitute an additional step that reduces the simplicity of the system and restricts its openness.

The distinction between strong/weak/noninvolved participants is also present in the four case studies.

Previous analyses of Wikipedia have addressed the question of participation distribution and showed that contributions to Wikipedia also present strong inequalities. Ortega & Gonzalez-Barahona (2007) and Ortega (2009) conclude that less than 10 percent of the total number of authors are responsible for more than 90 percent of the total number of contributions or, conversely, 90 percent of active editors are responsible for less than 10 percent of the total number of contributions. The evolution of this inequality has remained very stable over time (with a typical value of between 80 percent and 85 percent of content produced by a "core team"). However, the authors also point out that the "core team" of very active participants is not necessarily formed by the same individuals over time.

Concerning the wikiHow case, from the analysis of a random day, it emerged that the top ten participants were responsible for almost half of the content produced that day (46.5 percent).[7] WikiHow interviewees reported a similarly unequal distribution of participation as that found in Wikipedia (Interviews of B. Megas and N. Willson, Aug. 28, 2009, reported in Fuster Morell 2010). In the words of wikiHow's founder: "Wikihow follows power law.... You have to support the very minimal contribution or the very small contributions of people who wouldn't actually interact with it—while it's not obvious that they create value for the whole, they really do. So you need to allow the whole

---

[7] WikiHow daily statistics page for April 16, 2010; see WikiHow statistics page, http://www.wikihow.com/ Special:Statistics.

thing, so the ecosystem flourishes and can be successful" (Interview of J. Herrick, Dec. 4, 2008, reported in Fuster Morell 2010).

Shirky (2008: 123) reports that the top ten participants among the total 118 contributors contributed half of the content on an event uploaded on Flickr. The analysis of openesf.net showed that 18 percent of the participants generated content and 82 percent of the participants did not. Within the 18 percent of content generators, 3.7 percent were very active participants and 14.3 percent were less-active participants.

This unequal distribution of participation does not seem to be interpreted as a problem in OCCs. On the contrary, equal participation and contributions are not expected. GerardM, an active Wikipedian, spoke out in a mailing list against the idea of regular equal contributors and for valuing all community forms: "When you divide people up in groups, when you single out the 'most valuable' ones (because they contribute more), you in effect divide the community....When you label groups of people, you divide them and it is exactly the egalitarian aspect (independently of their contribution) that makes the community thrive" (GerardM e-mail to the mailing list Wiki-research-l, Oct. 21, 2008, reported in Fuster Morell 2010: 116). Additionally, from an outcomes perspective, the Wikipedia community accomplishes its goal. Wikipedia is the largest encyclopedia in history. Sue Gardner, executive director of the Wikipedia Foundation, puts it in these terms: "We need sufficient people to do the work that needs to be done. (...) But the purpose of the project is not participation" (Angwin & Fowler 2009). There does not seem to be a problem with a lack of participation in Wikipedia. On the contrary, in some instances problems linked to "too much participation" occur. This happens when levels of participation are so high that technically the system is not able to sustain the amount of activity and collapses. This occurred after the September 11, 2001, attacks and President Barack Obama's election, when many people wanted to keep Wikipedia updated (Interview of T. Finc, Nov. 20, 2009, reported in Fuster Morell 2010).

5. Formal Rules or Policies Applied to Community Interaction

OCCs, particularly as they evolve from more initial stages, tend to establish formal rules. Formal rules may be restricted and limited to rules defined by the legal framework in which the OCCs operates (terms of use and license), or they may be more or less expansive including a set of principles or complex bureaucratic policies. However, O'Mahony (2003) points out that developers in FLOSS resist formal methods. The existence of too many established rules and procedures is generally perceived as problematic in OCCs. Benkler (2013) points to a relative feature in the nondefinitive character of governance mechanism in peer production: even with formal rules, there is also the social norm that a rule can be broken if that makes sense for fulfilling a task.

Lanzara & Morner (2003) pointed out that it is not that traditional mechanisms of governance and coordination are nonexistent or irrelevant in OCCs. In this sense, the governance of FLOSS projects results in a combination of formal organizational mechanisms and decentralized and spontaneous mechanisms for the community platform (Lanzara & Morner 2003). According to these authors, the presence of formal organizational features, however, does not really play a dominant or pervasive role in FLOSS projects, and taken alone would not be strong enough to account for the impressive performance of large-size projects.

In terms of the possibility to control and intervene in the definition of rules, on some occasions rules (and, when applied, roles) are defined by the communities. According to the analysis of fifty cases, in 51 percent of the cases it is the community that is considered to be in charge of deciding policies and the distribution of tasks and roles. In the rest of the cases, rules are defined by the infrastructure provider.

In the cases of Wikipedia, openesf.net, and wikiHow, the approach is that the community is in charge of defining policies and also of choosing the people to fulfill roles where these are created, such as site administrators.

In the case of Wikipedia, the community collaborates in wiki pages to define common policies, and administrators are chosen through elections. However, there is a general feeling among the participants that there are too many policies and that their overwhelming number results in the exclusion of new participants (Lih 2009).

WikiHow follows the same approach as Wikipedia, although the wikiHow case sees more intervention from the provider. For example, administrators are not selected by the community but by the provider.

In the case of openesf.net, there is no distinction between providers and community and so all infrastructure governance is based on community self-governance. However, these were defined during physical meetings of the web team charged with maintaining openesf.net, not by the openesf.net platform participants as the platform did not generate enough participation to develop a community dynamic of interaction.

In the case of Flickr, although each individual can choose conditions of access and other aspects that will apply to the content they generate, participants cannot decide the policies and rules of overall interaction. Furthermore, no roles or responsibilities for the maintenance of the platform are assigned to participants. Importantly, there is no collective decision making over the roles and rules of the platform; these are defined by Yahoo! In this regard, Flickr participation does not imply participation in governance in terms of defining the rules that govern community interaction.

6. License (of the Common-Pool Resource and Code)

The license is a foundational rule in OCCs in the sense that it defines the resource management regime for the common-pool resource, the resources contributed and shared. The license also mediates the relationships between the constructed commons regime and the intellectual property regimes, where relevant. There are various types of licenses (from copyright, to several options of creative commons licenses that are more flexible on users' rights, and others). The license applies to both the common-pool resource (and the contributions of the participants) and the software code of the platform of participation.

Most OCCs in this study adopted free licenses for their content (68.1 percent of cases) (Fuster Morell 2010). This favors the free use of the common-pool resource by all and the freedom to use the resources under less restrictive conditions. Additionally, where the software is also free (78 percent of the cases), this means that the platform of participation may be replicated somewhere else independently of the infrastructure provider. In this case, content can be moved, and it is possible to relaunch interaction in a different context. This is known as *forking*. Forkability empowers the community with respect to the infrastructure provider as the community can leave and start interacting somewhere else (Weber 2004). However, not all OCCs have the conditions that allow this.

Wikipedia, wikiHow, and openesf.net are all based on FLOSS and collective free licenses and are therefore forkable. Flickr is based on individually defined licenses and proprietary software—its content is free only insofar as individual participants choose free licenses for their content.

7. Decision-Making and Conflict Resolution Systems in Community Interaction

Governance of OCCs depends on decision-making institutions, including conflict resolution. Consensus decision making is common in OCCs, yet they are also characterized by the pluralism of methods or polymorphism that involves the coexistence of several working or decision-making styles. This implies that there is no single way to solve all the situations of the platform but a flexible approach that adopts several methods. The methodological pluralism of OCCs may appear to signal a lack of coherence in the overall system. However, for some researchers, this apparently chaotic diversity becomes a powerful resource for knowledge making and innovation (Brown & Duguid 1991). The plurality of methods is also linked to the fact that OCCs tend to select methods according to their effectiveness in fulfilling their mission. The famous FLOSS catchphrase, "rough consensus and running code" captures the sense that actions which contribute to the accomplishment of the mission are more valuable than the precise use of a method.

In terms of polymorphy or plural methods, in Wikipedia most activity is primarily based on open groups on specific articles using consensus decision making. However, the community combines this with a heterogeneous, sometimes secondary, mechanism to force decision making, block the violation of policies, and contain the process within certain margins. On some occasions alternative forms of decision making such as polls and voting are adopted. There are also administrators with particular powers, tasks assigned historically to respected individuals, and a charismatic leader (the founder).

In terms of plural methods, wikiHow follows a similar approach to Wikipedia. Openesf.net uses mainly consensus decision making. Flickr is different to the other cases because the norms and in general the overall governance system are not defined by the community of participants, but by Yahoo! as Flickr's provider.

8. Infrastructure Provision (Technically, Legally, and Economically Sustaining the Platform of Participation)

Infrastructure provision solves some of the other questions OCCs raise and very much defines the process and shapes OCCs governance. Frischmann (2012) has also approached infrastructure in terms of its management as a commons. Infrastructure providers technically, legally, and economically sustain the platform of participation where the community interacts. It involves the management of the servers and domain name, and covering the costs these involve, among others. O'Mahony (2007) and Lanzara & Morner (2003) have researched provision in the case of FLOSS. However, previous analyses of OCCs have dedicated little attention to this issue, and infrastructure governance is considered a "backstage" question in OCCs.

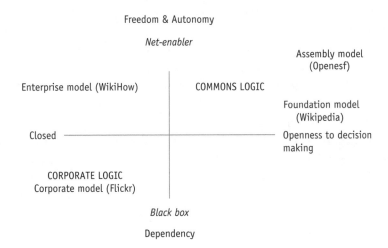

FIGURE 8.2 Models across the Two Axes of Infrastructure Governance.
Legend: Y = Freedom and autonomy of community from the provider; X = Involvement of the community in the provider body.

Infrastructure provision can function and be governed in diverse ways. Two main axes concerning infrastructure provision strategies can be distinguished: open *versus* closed to community involvement in infrastructure provision, and freedom and autonomy *versus* dependency on infrastructure (see Figure 8.2).

Participation in the provider space dimension (axis X in Figure 8.2) is closed when there is no possibility of involvement. Participation in the provider space is considered partly open where this depends on fulfilling certain criteria related to participation in the platform (such as a number of contributions). It is considered open when participation in the provider space is possible for anyone, that is, participation is regulated through self-selection.

Freedom and autonomy *versus* dependency on the infrastructure (net-enabler *versus* black box) dimension (axis Y in Figure 8.2) is linked to the license held for the common-pool resources and to the type of software used for the platform of participation. Net-enabler conditions are defined by a copyleft license and the use of FLOSS code, while black box conditions are defined by copyright and proprietary software. There is a qualitative difference between relational settings in which the OCCs is "locked" into the platform, and those where the community interaction is free and autonomous with respect to the platform. If the platform cannot be reproduced, the community relationship is "closed" within the specific platform, which is dependent on the provider. If the platform can be replicated (can be forkable), the relationships are free from the specific platform provider. FLOSS and copyleft licensing allow platforms to be replicated, while proprietary software and restrictive or less open copyright license regimes do not. In other words, the use of FLOSS and a copyleft license creates conditions in which the community can have greater autonomy and freedom from the platform provider.

An analysis of how fifty cases perform on the two specified axes of infrastructure governance was developed (Fuster Morell 2010). From the analysis resulted four clusters of cases. These four provision models can be defined: corporation service (which is the case of Flickr), mission enterprise (wikiHow), autonomous representational foundation (Wikipedia), and assembly or assemblarian self-provision models (openesf.net) (see Figure 8.2).

The corporation model applies to cases of infrastructure platforms owned by companies with large pools of technological skills such as Yahoo!, the provider of Flickr. The corporate model of infrastructure governance is characterized by a provider body closed to participant involvement and based on black box conditions. It follows a for-profit strategy. Participants are "trapped" in the platform (unless they exit), as the copyright and proprietary software framework restrict the freedom and autonomy of the participants in the platform.

The mission enterprise model is characterized by being for-profit and hence closed to participant involvement. Importantly, the enterprise model is based on net-enabler conditions, which favor the autonomy of collaboration. Furthermore, according to the statistical analysis, the enterprise model is characterized by more net-enabler conditions than the foundation model. The enterprise model applies to start-ups which maintain independence from big communications companies. It is a strategy for developing new business models which are compatible with net-enabler conditions. This is the case of wikiHow.

The autonomous representational foundation model is characterized by a provider body which is (relatively) open to participant involvement as it uses some formal filters. This model is also characterized by promoting the freedom and autonomy of collaboration (a type of access labeled *net-enabler*). Additionally, they are nonprofit. Being relatively open to participant involvement implies that they are formal and involve some requirement to take part, not based only on the self-selection of participants. In this regard it can be considered a hybrid form (partly open, partly closed). OCCs following this model are less open than those following the assembly model, which is based on total openness of the provision body. They are also less net-enabler in its access conditions than the assembly and enterprise models. The foundation model comprises the case of Wikipedia. O'Mahony (2007) researched the governance of FLOSS communities via case studies based on the autonomous representation foundation model. She characterized the foundation model as community management. However, she left open the questions of the characteristics of governance models other than community management and the degree to which community management can be applied to types of providers other than open foundations.

The self-provision assembly model is characterized by being the most open in terms of provision. A self-selected community of participants can be part of the provision body in this model. It follows an informal organizing logic (without a board or legal entity) and is nonprofit oriented. Additionally, the assembly model assures that it applies the most net-enabler access condition. The assembly model applies to openesf.net.

III. Models of OCCs Governance

In the previous sections, the eight dimensions that give direction and govern OCCs were presented. In this section, I present how these eight dimensions link with one another.

The analysis of the juxtaposition or interaction between the eight dimensions reveals that infrastructure provision is central. Infrastructure provision also determines some of the other eight aspects linked to the governance of OCCs. Infrastructure provision involves the provision of the platform of participation and the control over its design (code), the license, formal policies (such as terms of use), and, on some occasions, initiates the process and establishes the mission, and controls decision making on conflicts around community interaction (see Table 8.1). Still some other dimensions, like self-management of contributors in self-directing their action, are not controlled by the infrastructure provider. There is no command mechanism that forces contributors to direct their actions.

In this regard, the modality of governance of the infrastructure also contributes to shaping other dimensions of governance (see Table 8.2). Where there is openness to community involvement in infrastructure provision (representative foundation case of Wikipedia and self-assemblarian models of openesf.net), the community has, structurally, more control over the design of the platform of participation and the license.

Furthermore, according to the statistical analysis of fifty cases, openness to community involvement in infrastructure provision is correlated with a community having a decision-making mechanism (Fuster Morell 2010: 155), a role in conflict resolution at the community level, deciding its formal rules, a free license that also grants

TABLE 8.1.

DIMENSIONS OF OCCS GOVERNANCE THAT MIGHT BE CONTROLLED BY THE
INFRASTRUCTURE PROVIDER (IN ITALICS)

(1) *Collective mission or goal of the process.*
(2) Cultural principles/Social norms.
(3) *Design of the platform of participation (where regulation is embedded in the code).*
(4) Self-management of contributions: autonomous condition of participants in allocating her or his contribution to the building process.
(5) *Formal rules or policies applied to community interaction.*
(6) *License.*
(7) *Decision-making and conflict resolution system with regard to community interaction.*
(8) *Infrastructure provision.*

Legend: In *italics* the dimensions that might be controlled by infrastructure provider.

that the community owns the common-pool resource, and net-enabler conditions (including the right to fork). However, some of these aspects (a community having a decision-making mechanism and a role in conflict resolution at the community level, deciding its formal rules, having a free license) are also present in the mission enterprise model of wikiHow even if this model is closed to community involvement in infrastructure provision.

The corporate model of Flickr is where most sources of control are in the hands of the infrastructure provider, and the community of users (both individually and collectively) is most disempowered in comparison to the other cases. In the corporate model of Flickr, the community does not have control over the design of the platform of participation, does not have decision mechanisms, and does not define the rules, and the license does not favor community autonomy but dependency on the infrastructure provider (see Table 8.2).

In sum, the level of control and power over governance of the community of participants, in contrast to the infrastructure provision, is higher in the self-provision assembly model of openesf.net, followed by the representative foundation of Wikipedia, the mission enterprise of wikiHow, and finally the corporation model of Flickr. However, in all of the cases, participants self-manage their own contribution, and the infrastructure provider depends importantly on the participants in developing the content.

IV. OCCs Outcomes

Following the IAD framework the three *exogenous* aspects presented in the previous section—resource characteristics, community attributes, and governance—contribute to shape the action arena. The action arena is defined by action situations, that is, the design of the situation in which a particular person takes the decision to contribute or

TABLE 8.2.

THE EIGHT DIMENSIONS OF OCC INFRASTRUCTURE IN EACH OF THE MODELS

	Corporation	Mission enterprise	Representational foundation	Self-provision assembly
Mission	Defined by the provider	Defined either by community or provider	Defined either by community or provider	Community
Social norms	Community	Community	Community	Community
Design platform of participation	Provider	Provider	Provider	Provider
Participants self-allocation and management	Yes	Yes	Yes	Yes
Formal policies	Provider	Provider	Community	Community
License	Provider Proprietary license & software	Provider Free license & software	Provider Free license & software	Community Free license & software
Decision-making & conflict resolution at community level	No	Yes	Yes	Yes
Infrastructure provision	Closed	Closed	Open, filtered by representation	Open

not. They can encourage individuals' decisions to participate and collaborate—by solving collective action dilemmas—or on the opposite side discourage them. For Ostrom (2008: 52), action situations are "composed of participants in positions choosing among actions at a particular stage of a decision process in light of their control over a choice node, the information they have, the outcomes that are likely, and the benefits and costs they perceive for these outcomes." Action arenas result in patterns of interaction and, ultimately, those patterns result in particular outcomes. For the sake of space, I will not analyze action situations in the context of this chapter.

Additionally, the IAD framework points out that action arenas impact OCCs' outcomes. OCCs and cultural commons more generally are building processes. They are not provided by nature as in natural commons but are constructed, and this process is organic to common-pool resources. The ability or inability of OCCs to end in outcomes is a relevant aspect for the IAD framework. However, it is not clear if Madison, Frischmann, & Strandburg take outcomes into consideration in their reframing of the IAD framework. However, they do stress that "a cultural commons should be assessed not only in light of its ostensible purposes but also in light of its consequences. This aspect of the case study approach should both identify the consequences and describe relevant criteria for evaluating them" (2010: 705).

In terms of outcomes of OCCs, I differentiate between two sets of outcomes: outcomes in terms of common-pool resources (amount of content, quality of content, usage of content, etc.) and the building process. As common-pool resources in OCCs are built rather than simply "there," I consider it relevant to integrate the capacity of the IAD framework to engage with participation and collaboration in the evaluation of OCCs outcomes, in order to see whether it contributes more benefits than costs and is worth sustaining.

According to the analysis of fifty cases, the four different infrastructure governance models highlighted have different capacities to engage with participation and collaboration in OCCs. First, the analysis suggests that not all the models are able to generate the same size of community. Second, not all the models are able to engage or increase collaboration levels. Third, some models are more suited to complex collaboration than others.

Concerning the two axes ordering infrastructure governance, dependency on infrastructure (black box) favors an increase in the size of communities but impacts negatively on collaboration. Autonomy and freedom from infrastructure (net-enabler conditions) favors more complex collaboration but negatively affects the size of the community. In other words, larger communities do not require freedom and autonomy conditions if it does not involve complexity in the interaction, but the engagement of complex interaction does.

Concerning the axis of open versus closed to community involvement, the effect is more complex. Openness to involvement in provision favors collaboration where there is some formal organization of participation in the infrastructure provision. Being closed to participation in provision favors an increase in size, but only where provision is based on a for-profit strategy.

In terms of how each of the four models shapes the community, none of the models combine a large community size with *collaborativeness*. The corporation model generates the biggest communities, based on lower levels of collaboration, while the foundation and enterprise models are able to raise mid-size communities and are more collaborative. Finally, the assembly model is the weakest in terms of generating (active) OCCs. According to the case studies analysis, these diverse performances could be linked to the diverse ability to generate resources, the ability to manage resources according to organizational strategy, the ability to inspire trust and motivate contributions, and the ability to create conditions favoring collaboration (or not) through the type of license and software and the design of the platform of participation.

In sum, more empowering conditions of the community favor outcomes in terms of *collaborativeness*, but not size. Of the eight "design principles" that Ostrom (1990) identifies in stable local common-pool resource management, two refer to self-governance (collective-choice arrangements that allow most resource appropriators to participate in the decision-making process and self-determination of the community recognized by higher-level authorities). According to the analysis of OCCs, higher self-governance favors collaboration but not a high level of participation in OCCs.

V. Conclusions

OCCs are a particular type of cultural or knowledge commons. In this chapter, I provided a characterization of OCCs governance as a complex system in which eight critical aspects define their direction: collective mission or goal of the process; cultural principles/social norms; design of the platform of participation (where regulation is embedded in the code); self-management of contributions; formal policies applied to community interaction; license; decision-making and conflict resolution systems with regard to community interaction; and infrastructure provision.

Sustainability of this model is also a critical question for OCCs. However, I did not expand on this aspect in the chapter, and it might be considered for further research.

The empirical analysis of fifty statistical cases and four case studies reveals the centrality of one of the dimensions in configuring some of the other governance dimensions and in determining the outcomes. However, the self-direction or autonomy of the contributors in allocating their own resources (without command mechanisms) is also a relevant aspect in determining the power interplays in OCCs.

A. APPLICABILITY OF THE IAD FRAMEWORK TO OCCS

In this chapter, I have adapted and applied the IAD framework to OCCs by analyzing the resource characteristics of OCCs, their community attributes, and their governance, and to then approach how governance of OCCs might explain their ability to raise participation and collaboration.

Clearly this was a very limited application of the IAD framework, as action situations were not analyzed, nor the interplay between the different aspects presented. Still, we hope it provides an overview of OCCs as an important case of constructed commons and how the framework could be applied.

In applying the IAD framework, I build upon previous adaptations (Madison, Frischmann, & Strandburg 2010; Schweik & English 2012). IAD is a very useful framework to analyze OCCs, as it allows us to approach the interplay between the characteristics of a common-pool resource, the characteristics of a community and the political and institutional arrangements for its governance and explain how these link to action arenas and, ultimately, to outcomes.

In line with Ostrom's original IAD framework and Schweik & English's (2012) adaptation of it to the FLOSS case, I consider it useful to retain the differentiation between resource characteristics, community attributes, and rules of law. In contrast, it is stressed less in Madison, Frischmann, & Strandburg (2010). Beyond finding it useful to stress the distinction between resource characteristics, community attributes, and rules of law as Schweik & English (2012) do in their analysis of FLOSS, I do not fully share Schweik and English's organization of aspects within those three areas. In concrete terms, Schweik and English present some technological attributes as resource characteristics that are in my opinion part of the regulatory frame of governance, and not a given characteristic of the resource.

In line with Lessig (1999), *code is law*, and rules embedded in the code refer to features that govern interaction among participants and that are inscribed in the technological design of the platform of participation within which the community interacts. Schweik and English seem to consider design principles that are embedded in the platform pro-gram and code not to be part of the governance but as technological attributes in their own right, similar to biophysical characteristics for Ostrom. In my view, rules embedded in the code govern the interaction as much as other rules and need to be integrated and considered as such in the governance dimension. In a similar vein, Schweik and English consider aspects such as leadership or financing as part of community attributes, while I consider these as part of the governance, too.

Coming back to Madison, Frischmann, & Strandburg (2010), the authors seem to sug-gest de-emphasizing how the clusters of issues to consider are related to the dimensions of outcomes, or the question of the outcome more generally. At least, they note that given the complex dynamics involved, it may be difficult to separate outcomes from the resources and communities that produce them over time. Still, I emphasize that even if difficult, analysis of outcomes is useful. Adopting an IAD-based approach may result in expand-ing the number of variables to consider, which along with the richness of the framework makes it worthwhile. However, without the outcome dimension (or explanatory analysis more generally) I see difficulties for other researchers to adopt the framework, as present-ing the clusters suggested by Madison, Frischmann, and Strandburg becomes a research project of its own without a similar or specific explanatory line to engage with.

The Madison, Frischmann, and Strandburg framework applies to constructing cultural commons as a category. It is the case that constructed cultural or knowledge common-pool resources share some commonalities (more than they do with natural commons); how-ever, it is still a very diverse set. The constructing cultural commons category might be useful for some purposes, but in my view, it is too broad a category to apply the IAD framework equally or uniformly. In this line, the background environment described by Madison, Frischmann, and Strandburg does not totally apply or capture the context of OCCs. As Ostrom (1990) points out, the devil is in the context and the details. Even if the overall IAD framework is useful, the clusters of issues related to resource characteris-tics, community attributes, rules in use, action arenas, and outcomes needed to apply the IAD framework to a particular commons need to be much more specified and contextu-alized for each type of cultural commons.

B. WHAT DEFINES OCCS AS "COMMONS"?

IAD was developed initially to investigate natural "commons." In this last section, I would like to address the question of the conditions that define the diverse types of "commons" as "commons."

Natural "commons" have received substantial attention (Ostrom 1990). OCCs are, together with many others, another typology of "commons." In this regard, Hess (2008) provided a rich classification of "new" types of "commons." However, it remains unclear what "commons" have in common. In this line, Benkler (this volume, ch. 3) addresses this issue by raising a very important question: How can two diverse trajectories of commons—"Spanish huertas" (referring to natural commons) and "open roads"— be integrated in a general theory of "commons"?

Benkler points out that the resources provided under open access—such as open roads, but that is also the case of OCCs—are also "commons." This is independent of whether they are provided by markets, states, nature, or social sources (self-organization). In general, this is a very valuable contribution. Furthermore, it expands the "commons" to other central resources of the system. An open road should be considered a "commons" because of its open-access character, even if it is provided and governed by the state. However, this question becomes more complex when applied to other types of open-access "commons," such as those based on collaborative production and voluntary engagement of the common-pool resource, such as OCCs. What is defined as a "commons" in open roads is diverse for Spanish huertas (referring to natural resources), as Benkler pointed out, but also for OCCs in my view. That "commons" should not only consider instances of self-governance applied to discrete resource sets (Benkler, this volume, ch. 3) does not imply that governance should not be considered for any type of open-access resource.

In my view, for the specific case of OCCs, open access alone is not a sufficient condition. To the open access of the common-pool resource (which Benkler points to) I must add a governance design that maintains community control over the collaborative process of building the common-pool resource. In this regard, both open-access resources provision and community governance should be considered for characterizing OCCs as "commons," to avoid possible confusion. This does not mean that the community governance as a condition for a "commons" in OCCs must adopt the community governance model of natural "commons," but the community governance must be part of OCCs functioning, as characterized in this chapter.

In the following, I argue why I consider both open-access and community governance as conditions for a "commons" in OCCs. In OCCs, the resource is not already available, but needs to be produced and preserved. The production process is based on collaborative and voluntary engagement, and this implies that certain aspects be taken into consideration. On the one hand, the process of production is not based on labor; that is, it is not a contractual relationship of exchanging work per a salary, which tends to be the case when building a road. Rather it is a voluntary and collaborative relationship. This raises the question of whether community could be disempowered from the resource management it produces and lack control equally in voluntary and collaborative production as in labor conditions. Additionally, this disempowerment in voluntary communities might affect prosocial motivation characteristic of OCCs. A key component to drive community governance in OCCs according to my analysis is infrastructure governance, because it is important in itself, and because it is a point of control over other dimensions of the governance. Some level of community control over infrastructure is central for community governance, as I have argued across this chapter.

Furthermore, the idea of detaching the community from the resource might be questioned. In OCCs the outcome is not only the resources in terms of the archive of knowledge, but the community itself. The resource could not be produced or preserved without the community. In other words, the "production" of the community is a precondition for possibly producing the resource. Particularly, in regard to the infrastructure, infrastructure governance is not neutral. As I have noted previously in this chapter, infrastructure provision shapes the community and the resource. Again, this raises the question of whether community could be detached from the resource it produces.

If only open access is considered as a condition for OCCs to be a "commons," Flickr and Wikipedia, both with open-access resources in different degrees, would be considered "commons." But could OCCs produced by and/or dependent on for-profit enterprises such as Yahoo! (Flickr) and based on a noncommunity self-governance model be considered a "commons" just as Wikipedia is based on community self-governance? In order to avoid misinterpretations, I am not pointing to this distinction on the basis of the Flickr corporate for-profit character and the Wikipedia nonprofit character, but on the basis of their governance. WikiHow is also for profit, but this is not in conflict with its being based upon favoring community governance conditions.

I could argue it from another perspective. As Benkler points out, OCCs would be "commons" when based in open access. I would agree, if the open access would not only apply to the resource the community produces but also to the "open access" character of the infrastructure the resource is based upon. This would assure freedom to operate from the infrastructure provider, too.

In sum, common-pool-produced resources should not only be regarded according to how they are provided (open access) and owned (property) but to how they are produced. In other words, the conditions of production and control over the means of production is a highly relevant question.

References

Julia Angwin & Geoffrey A. Fowler, *Volunteers Log Off as Wikipedia Ages*, WALL ST. J. (Nov. 27, 2009), http://online.wsj.com/article/SB125893981183759969.html.

Markus C. Becker, *Managing Dispersed Knowledge: Organizational Problems, Managerial Strategies, and Their Effectiveness*, 38 J. MANAGEMENT STUDIES 1037 (2001).

YOCHAI BENKLER, THE WEALTH OF NETWORKS: HOW SOCIAL PRODUCTION TRANSFORMS MARKETS AND FREEDOM (Yale University Press 2006).

Yochai Benkler, *Peer Production and Cooperation, in* HANDBOOK ON THE ECONOMICS OF THE INTERNET (Johannes M. Bauer & Michael Latzer eds., Edward Elgar Publishing) (forthcoming).

Bruce Bimber, Andrew J. Flanagin, & Cynthia Stohl, *Reconceptualizing Collective Action in the Contemporary Media Environment*, 15 COMMUNICATION THEORY 365 (2005).

John Seely Brown & Paul Duguid, *Organizational Learning and Communities of Practice: Toward a Unified View of Working, Learning, and Innovation*, 2 ORGANIZATION SCIENCE 40 (1991).

J. Burgess, *Vernacular Creativity and New Media*, unpublished PhD dissertation (University of Queensland, Brisbane Australia 2007).

Moira Burke & Robert Kraut, *Mopping Up: Modeling Wikipedia Promotion Decisions, in* PROCEEDINGS OF THE 2008 ACM CONFERENCE ON COMPUTER SUPPORTED COOPERATIVE WORK 27 (New York: Association for Computing Machinery 2008).

Andrea Ciffolilli, *Phantom Authority, Self-Selective Recruitment and Retention of Members in Virtual Communities: The Case of Wikipedia*, 8 FIRST MONDAY, no. 12 (Dec. 1, 2003), http://www.firstmonday.org/issues/issue8_12/ciffolilli/.

Kevin Crowston & James Howison, *The Social Structure of Free and Open Source Software Development*, 10 FIRST MONDAY, no. 2 (Feb. 7, 2005), http://firstmonday.org/ojs/index.php/fm/article/view/1207/1127.

Andrea Forte & Amy Bruckman, *Scaling Consensus: Increasing Decentralization in Wikipedia Governance, in* PROCEEDINGS OF THE 41ST ANNUAL HAWAII INTERNATIONAL CONFERENCE ON SYSTEM SCIENCES 157 (Washington, D.C.: IEEE Computer Society 2008).

BRETT M. FRISCHMANN, INFRASTRUCTURE: THE SOCIAL VALUE OF SHARED RESOURCES (2012).

Mayo Fuster Morell, *Governance of online creation communities. Provision of platforms for participation for the building of digital commons*, unpublished PhD dissertation (European University Institute, Florence, Italy 2010), http://www.onlinecreation.info/outline_design.

Ruediger Glott, Philipp Schmidt, & Rishab Ghosh, *Wikipedia Survey—Overview of Results* (United Nations University UNU-Merit 2010), http://archive.is/d6Pf1.

Mark Granovetter, *The Strength of Weak Ties: A Network Theory Revisited, in* 1 SOCIOLOGICAL THEORY 201 (1983).

Shane Greenstein & Michelle Devereux, *Wikipedia in the Spotlight*, Kellogg Case Number 5-306-507; (Chicago: Kellogg Case Publishing 2009).

Morton T. Hansen, *The Search-Transfer Problem: The Role of Weak Ties in Sharing Knowledge Across Organization Subunits*, 44 ADMINISTRATIVE SCIENCE Q. 82 (1999).

Charlotte Hess, *Mapping the New Commons*, presented at "Governing Shared Resources: Connecting Local Experience to Global Challenges," the 12th Biennial Conference of the International Association for the Study of the Commons, University of Gloucestershire, Cheltenham, England (July 14–18, 2008), http://dlc.dlib.indiana.edu/dlc/handle/10535/304.

CHARLOTTE HESS & ELINOR OSTROM (EDS.), UNDERSTANDING KNOWLEDGE AS A COMMONS: FROM THEORY TO PRACTICE (MIT Press 2007).

William C. Hill, James D. Hollan, Dave Wroblewski, & Tim McCandless, *Edit Wear and Read Wear, in* CHI '92: PROCEEDINGS OF THE SIGCHI CONFERENCE ON HUMAN FACTORS IN COMPUTING SYSTEMS 3 (New York: Association for Computing Machinery 1992).

A. Kittur, E. Chi, B. Pendleton, B. Suh, & T. Mytkowicz, *Power of the Few vs. Wisdom of the Crowd: Wikipedia and the Rise of the Bourgeoisie, in* CHI'07: PROCEEDINGS OF THE SIGCHI CONFERENCE ON HUMAN FACTORS IN COMPUTING SYSTEMS (New York: Association for Computing Machinery 2007).

Piotr Konieczny, *Governance, Organization, and Democracy on the Internet: The Iron Law and the Evolution of Wikipedia*, 24 SOCIOLOGICAL FORUM 162 (2009).

Travis Kriplean, Ivan Beschastnikh, David W. McDonald, & Scott A. Golder, *Community, Consensus, Coercion, Control: CS*W or How Policy Mediates Mass Participation, in* GROUP '07: PROCEEDINGS OF THE 2007 INTERNATIONAL ACM CONFERENCE SUPPORTING GROUP WORK 167 (New York: Association for Computing Machinery 2007).

Giovan Francesco Lanzara & Michele Morner, *The Knowledge Ecology of Open-Source Software Projects*, Paper presented at the 19th European Group of Organizational Studies (EGOS) Colloquium, Copenhagen, Denmark (July 3–5, 2003).

Giovan Francesco Lanzara & Michele Morner, *Making and Sharing Knowledge at Electronic Crossroads: The Evolutionary Ecology of Open Source*, Paper presented at the Fifth European Conference on Organizational Knowledge, Learning and Capabilities, Innsbruck, Austria (2004), http://www2.warwick.ac.uk/fac/soc/wbs/conf/olkc/archive/oklc5/papers/j-3_lanzara.pdf.

LAWRENCE LESSIG, CODE AND OTHER LAWS OF CYBERSPACE (New York: Basic Books 1999).

ANDREW LIH, THE WIKIPEDIA REVOLUTION: HOW A BUNCH OF NOBODIES CREATED THE WORLD'S GREATEST ENCYCLOPEDIA (New York: Hyperion 2009).

Max Loubser & Christian Pentzold, *Rule Dynamics and Rule Effects in Commons-Based Peer Production*, 5th ECPR General Conference, Potsdam/Germany (Sept.10–12, 2009).

Michael J. Madison, Brett M. Frischmann, & Katherine J. Strandburg, *Constructing Commons in the Cultural Environment*, 95 CORNELL L. REV. 657 (2010).

THOMAS W. MALONE, THE FUTURE OF WORK: HOW THE NEW ORDER OF BUSINESS WILL SHAPE YOUR ORGANIZATION, YOUR MANAGEMENT STYLE AND YOUR LIFE (Harvard Business Review 2004).

Sorin Adam Matei & Caius Dobrescu, *Wikipedia's "Neutral Point of View": Settling Conflict through Ambiguity*, 27 THE INFORMATION SOCIETY 40 (2011).

Radu Andrei Negoescu & Daniel Gatica-Perez, *Analyzing Flickr Groups, in* CIVR '08: PROCEEDINGS OF THE 2008 INTERNATIONAL CONFERENCE ON CONTENT-BASED IMAGE AND VIDEO RETRIEVAL 417 (New York: Association for Computing Machinery 2008).

Jakob Nielsen, *Community Is Dead; Long Live Mega-Collaboration*, JAKOB NIELSEN'S ALERTBOX (Aug. 15, 1997), http://www.useit.com/alertbox/9708b.html.

Jakob Nielsen, *Participation Inequality: Encouraging More Users to Contribute*, JAKOB NIELSEN'S ALERTBOX (Oct. 9, 2006), http://www.useit.com/alertbox/participation_inequality.html.

Siobhan O'Mahony, *Guarding the Commons: How Community Managed Software Projects Protect Their Work*, 32 RESEARCH POLICY 1179 (2003).

Siobhan O'Mahony, *The Governance of Open Source Initiatives: What Does It Mean to Be Community Managed?*, 11 J. MANAGEMENT & GOVERNANCE 139 (2007).

Siobhan O'Mahony & Fabrizio Ferraro, *The Emergence of Governance in an Open Source Community*, 50 ACADEMY OF MANAGEMENT J. 1079 (2007).

MATHIEU O'NEIL, CYBERCHIEFS: AUTONOMY AND AUTHORITY IN ONLINE TRIBES (New York: Pluto Press 2009).

Wanda J. Orlikowski, *Knowing in Practice: Enacting a Collective Capability in Distributed Organizing*, 13 ORGANIZATION SCIENCE 249 (2002).

Felipe Ortega, *Wikipedia: A Quantitative Analysis*, unpublished PhD dissertation (Universidad Rey Juan Carlos, Madrid 2009), http://felipeortega.net/sites/default/files/thesis-jfelipe.pdf.

Felipe Ortega & Jesus M. Gonzalez-Barahona, *Quantitative Analysis of the Wikipedia Community of Users, in* WIKISYM '07: PROCEEDINGS OF THE 2007 INTERNATIONAL SYMPOSIUM ON WIKIS 75 (2007).

ELINOR OSTROM, GOVERNING THE COMMONS: THE EVOLUTION OF INSTITUTIONS FOR COLLECTIVE ACTION (Cambridge University Press 1990).

ELINOR OSTROM, UNDERSTANDING INSTITUTIONAL DIVERSITY (Princeton University Press 2005).

Elinor Ostrom, *Developing a Method for Analyzing Institutional Change, in* ALTERNATIVE INSTITUTIONAL STRUCTURES: EVOLUTION AND IMPACT 48 (Sandra S. Batie & Nicholas Mercuro eds., Routledge 2008).

Jenny Preece, Blair Nonnecke, & Dorine Andrews, *The Top 5 Reasons for Lurking: Improving Community Experiences for Everyone*, 20 COMPUTERS IN HUMAN BEHAVIOR 201 (2004).

Joseph Reagle Jr., *Open Content Communities*, 7 M/C J., no. 3 (July 2004), http://journal.media-culture.org.au/0406/06_Reagle.rft.php.

Carol Rose, *The Comedy of the Commons: Custom, Commerce, and Inherently Public Property*, 53 U. CHICAGO L. REV. 711 (1986).

CHARLES M. SCHWEIK & ROBERT C. ENGLISH, INTERNET SUCCESS: A STUDY OF OPEN SOURCE SOFTWARE COMMONS (MIT Press 2012).

CLAY SHIRKY, HERE COMES EVERYBODY: THE POWER OF ORGANIZING WITHOUT ORGANIZATIONS (New York: Penguin 2008).

Daniel Sieberg, *Flickr on the Fly*, 28 TORCH: U. VICTORIA ALUMNI MAG., no. 1 (Spring 2007), http://web.uvic.ca/torch/torch2007s/feature_5.htm.

Felix Stalder & Jesse Hirsh, *Open Source Intelligence*, 7 FIRST MONDAY, no. 6 (June 3, 2002), http://www.firstmonday.org/ojs/index.php/fm/article/view/961.

Nathaniel Tkacz, *Power, Visibility, Wikipedia*, 40 SOUTHERN REV. 5 (2007).

SIDNEY VERBA, KAY LEHMAN SCHLOZMAN, & HENRY E. BRADY, VOICE AND EQUALITY: CIVIC VOLUNTARISM IN AMERICAN POLITICS (Harvard University Press 1995).

Fernanda B. Viégas, Martin Wattenberg, & Matthew M. McKeon, *The Hidden Order of Wikipedia, in* ONLINE COMMUNITIES AND SOCIAL COMPUTING 445 (Douglas Schuler ed., Springer 2007).

STEVEN WEBER, THE SUCCESS OF OPEN SOURCE (Harvard University Press 2004).

9 Creating a Context for Entrepreneurship: Examining How Users' Technological and Organizational Innovations Set the Stage for Entrepreneurial Activity

Sonali K. Shah and Cyrus C. M. Mody*

I. Introduction

It is widely acknowledged that innovation and entrepreneurship drive economic growth and prosperity. But, what drives entrepreneurs? This question is of critical interest to political and business leaders and of scholarly interest to a wide variety of academic disciplines. Start-ups contribute to the health of our economy and society by creating jobs and by providing access to technologies—both novel and established—to those who need and want them. The provision of innovative products and services improves the day-to-day lives of many consumers and citizens.

At the same time, innovation and entrepreneurship are also complex, challenging, and knowledge-intensive activities. The process by which innovative new products and services are developed involves novel insights and considerable learning about technologies and markets (Taylor 2010; Clark & Fujimoto 1991; Brown & Eisenhardt 1995). Hence, from the perspective of the external observer and possibly from the perspective of the entrepreneur, undertaking these activities appears to involve considerable risk, effort, and time.

* Sonali K. Shah is Assistant Professor at the University of Illinois at Urbana-Champaign College of Business, Champaign, Illinois, USA. Cyrus C. M. Mody is Associate Professor of History in the Department of History at Rice University, Houston, Texas, USA.

So, how then do potential entrepreneurs make the decision to commercialize an innovative product or service? Most prior examinations of entrepreneurship have focused on fairly *static* factors. These static factors can be either internal to the entrepreneur (e.g., intrinsic attraction to risk) or present in the entrepreneur's environment (e.g., "culture"). While we acknowledge that such factors play a role in entrepreneurial activity—for example, some individuals are predisposed to entrepreneurial activity, have cognitive traits that help them become successful entrepreneurs, or are situated in environments rife with resources—static approaches ignore the circumstances in which entrepreneurs are *made*, and in which entrepreneurial individuals are coproduced with the environment that supports them. The lesson we illustrate, through our data, is that entrepreneurs are made through a series of interactions with an external and changing environment. Building upon the seminal argument in both classic and contemporary sociology that individuals shape and are shaped by their social context, we show how these interactions affect both the environment and the potential entrepreneur, culminating in entrepreneurship (Giddens 1984; Weber 1904; Coleman 1994).

We illustrate this point by examining the experiences of user entrepreneurs. User entrepreneurs are individuals whose experiences creating or modifying a technology that they themselves used—often combined with their experiences creating and/or participating in a community of other users coalesced to further develop and diffuse the technology—steered them toward founding firms dedicated to commercializing their innovation(s). User entrepreneurs have played pivotal roles in many economically important industries: serving as a source of technological insights to established firms (Winston Smith & Shah 2013), introducing new innovations into established industries (Shah & Tripsas 2007; Baldwin, Hiernerth, & von Hippel 2006), creating technological discontinuities in established industries (Tripsas 2008; Haefliger, Jäger, & von Krogh 2010), and founding the first—or among the first—and often the most successful firms in a new industry (Shah & Mody 2013). Almost 50 percent of firms founded in the Unites States to produce an innovative product or service that survive to age 5 are founded by user innovators (Shah, Winston Smith, & Reedy 2012).[1]

Throughout this chapter, we will supply examples of user entrepreneurship from both high-tech (e.g., biotechnology and microelectronics) and low-tech (e.g., juvenile products) industries. This extensive data, culled from studies in the innovation and history of technology literatures, supplements an intensive examination of two industries: scientific instrumentation, specifically probe microscopes; and sporting equipment, specifically windsurfing boards. We gathered data on probe microscopy and windsurfing through more than two hundred interviews with users and examination of archival materials and published sources generated by or about these user communities.[2]

---

[1] A full 10% of all entrepreneurial start-ups founded in the United States that survive to age 5 are founded by user innovators.

[2] Readers interested in further details of our methodology are referred to our previous work on the role of users in the development of technology and organization in probe microscopy and sporting equipment (Mody 2011; Shah & Mody 2013).

This chapter contributes to entrepreneurship theory by showing how individuals' entrepreneurial proclivities co-evolve with the technology and organizations created to sustain that technology. We build on the insight that users engage in technological innovation and innovation in organizational forms concurrently: technological innovation allows users to create the equipment and techniques that allow them to shape and tame their external environment, whereas organizational innovations allow users to build new and extend existing institutions such that their technological innovations can flourish (Shah & Mody 2013).

This chapter also contributes to our understanding of the role of a particular type of knowledge commons—a user innovation community—in stimulating entrepreneurship and technological development. We show how the interactions that occur in the commons generate information, resources, skills, and affective rewards that contribute to entrepreneurial activities, while maintaining the integrity and stability of the commons.

Finally, in keeping with the theme of this edited volume, we use empirical data to highlight unique characteristics of a particular type of knowledge commons, namely innovation communities constructed by users, as part of an effort to bring nuanced data to bear upon the task of understanding the role, governance, and functioning of knowledge commons. As Madison, Frischmann, and Strandburg point out, the "devil is in the details": adapting Ostrom's Institutional Analysis and Development framework to investigate sharing and resource-pooling arrangements for information- and knowledge-based works will require "significant modifications" (Madison, Frischmann, & Strandburg 2010: 670–71).

One such modification may involve envisioning knowledge commons as means to an end, rather than an end goal or sustaining organizational structure in and of itself. The seminal work of Elinor Ostrom and colleagues views the commons as a means of sustaining natural resources (Ostrom 1990).[3] In the two cases highlighted in this chapter, the user innovation community (a specific type of knowledge commons) is constructed as a means through which technologies can be developed and diffused. However, as users' needs evolve, additional proprietary organizing structures—network exchanges and industries—that draw from and sometimes contribute to the knowledge produced and held within the commons are also built by users. This illustrates the notion that commons-based organizing structures can play a critical role in a technology's development and diffusion, but other organizing structures may be equally necessary and provide the means for developing and diffusing a technology to meet the needs of distinct types of users. A second modification may involve further grappling with the nonrivalrous character of knowledge and the purposive transfer of that knowledge outside the

---

[3] We see no contradiction in actors' interpreting cultural commons as both means and ends simultaneously. For instance, we have interviewed many people who were members of user innovation communities partly out of enjoyment of the relationships and activities fostered by the community (commons as an end) and partly as a way to access resources needed to improve a technology that they intended to use (commons as a means).

commons. Whereas the natural resource commons exist to sustain a resource for the use of a circumscribed set of individuals, many cultural artifacts may be developed within a commons, and later diffused broadly to many through a variety of means. In this chapter, we focus on the role of entrepreneurs and new firms in diffusing a rapidly evolving technology; however, we also acknowledge that diffusion is aided by established firms, private and public universities, privately owned media outlets, and so on. We hope that the cases highlighted here, combined with the other examples highlighted in the volume, serve to provide nuanced and contextualized empirical data that will allow scholars to further develop our understanding of knowledge commons.

We begin by providing a brief review of the literature on entrepreneurial motivation. We then describe the innovative activities of users, highlighting the fact that users create new innovations and new organizations. In fact, it appears that technologies and organizations co-evolve, and—in cases where users create altogether new technologies—are coproduced.

Finally, we show how these activities set the stage for entrepreneurship. We focus on how sharing and collaborative work practices increase the availability of information, expand the set of individuals using the technology, and introduce affective rewards and skill growth that can pave the way to entrepreneurship.

II. Why Do Individuals Engage in Entrepreneurship? Insights from the Existing Literature

We bring an interdisciplinary perspective to our work, as we have training in management studies, engineering, and science and technology studies. We believe that the question of entrepreneurs' motivations lends itself to interdisciplinary investigation, since the problem combines (at the very least) dynamics at the level of individual psychology, organizational capacity, and economic decision making. In this section we briefly review some of the approaches that have informed ours.

A. PSYCHOLOGY

Much popular and political discourse depicts entrepreneurs in psychologistic terms, whether as go-getting "risk-takers" or, more darkly, as norm-defying "psychopaths."[4] Many academic studies have also taken individual cognition as the primary factor in explaining entrepreneurship. Researchers in psychology and, increasingly, neuroscience and genetics have claimed that entrepreneurs possess intrinsic—even, biologically inherited and therefore congenital—traits that predispose them to found firms: intelligence,

---

[4] For the former, see Brockhaus & Horowitz (1986). For the latter, see Ronson (2011); Babiak, Neumann, & Hare (2010).

a capacity to recognize opportunities, openness to new experiences, and both a greater propensity to take risks and less anxiety when confronting risks.[5]

B. BUSINESS HISTORY

Unfortunately for psychologistic explanations, levels of firm formation appear, at least at first glance, to have varied quite widely over time and across regions. If entrepreneurs are born, not made, it is not clear why so many of them would have been born in late eighteenth and early nineteenth century Manchester and Sheffield rather than in Bath or Bristol during the same era (Misa 2011; Becattini 2004; Marshall 1919). Spatially- and temporally-delimited phenomena are ready-made for historical analysis, and business historians have repeatedly examined and debated the reasons why some regions have become entrepreneurial hot spots.

In general, business historians have depicted the motivations for entrepreneurship as emergent from a national or community-level environment external to the entrepreneur. However, how such larger social formations influence entrepreneurship is unclear. One prominent, if now rather dated, view was that "culture" could largely account for why inhabitants of one region were more likely to found firms than inhabitants of another region (Landes 1999).[6] That is, some cultures were said to be more encouraging of risk-taking, more tolerant of failure, and more approving of material gain, while others were said to be more inhospitable to individual undertaking.

Cultural explanations have been roundly criticized for their superficial and reifying characterizations of whole societies or communities and for their inability to specify exactly what culture is. Such studies have, therefore, steadily lost favor in business history and have been replaced by accounts that pay closer attention to concrete phenomena. In particular, many recent studies have examined the role of institutions (such as banking systems or legal regimes) and social networks (e.g., among coreligionists or members of diasporic ethnic communities[7] or colocated artisans) that stimulate firm formation by providing entrepreneurs access to markets, expertise, and resources.

C. GEOGRAPHY AND REGIONAL DEVELOPMENT ECONOMICS

Many of the same themes have also been taken up by geographers and regional development economists. While some prominent works in this literature have fallen back on

---

[5] For an overview of the psychologistic approach to entrepreneurship in which cognitive traits are ascribed to genetic predisposition, see Nicolaou & Shane (2011).

[6] Note that Landes has been making similar arguments since the 1940s and that his views are still influential enough to have been cited in recent speeches by Mitt Romney. The culture thesis has also been pursued in work such as Weiner (1981) and Morris (1967). For an updated version of this argument, somewhat more compatible with our own perspective, see Godley (2001) and Tsang (2006).

[7] E.g., Louri & Minoglou (1997); Dobbin (1996); Kirby (1993); McCabe, Harlaftis, & Minoglou (2005).

rather obscure cultural factors fostering entrepreneurship (e.g., the stimulating role of the "creative class"[8]), much work in this field has been admirably detailed in examining how institutions, ancillary firms, and social networks lower the barriers to entrepreneurship in industrial districts such as Silicon Valley.[9] Individuals who live in a region where there are already many other entrepreneurs have many models to follow if they wish to found a firm themselves, and they have access to local banks, lawyers, public relations firms, universities, and so forth that are used to dealing with entrepreneurs and provide valuable resources.

D. MANAGEMENT

Management scholars have built upon and further explored many of the themes previously mentioned. In addition, the institutional approach to entrepreneurship is gaining traction. This is a relatively new approach, built atop institutional theory. Institutional theory has long been criticized for not providing a role for agency (DiMaggio 1988). In response, recent research has studied individuals who transform existing institutions, referring to these individuals as "institutional entrepreneurs" (Garud & Karnøe 2001; Greenwood, Suddaby, & Hinings 2002). However, until quite recently, institutional theorists have paid far less attention to entrepreneurship in the sense of founding and managing new organizations (Sine & David 2010). This approach to entrepreneurship focuses on how existing institutions shape entrepreneurial opportunities and actions, how entrepreneurs navigate the environments that surround them, and how entrepreneurs modify and build institutions to support new types of organizations. This approach has been credited for its theoretical flexibility in that it does not constrain or put boundary conditions on the rationality of actors, specific historical context, or level of analysis (Thornton 1999). In particular, early work by Van de Ven and Garud has examined how the actions of entrepreneurs have both built firms and shaped the institutions around them; in turn, these institutions provide the infrastructure upon which firms build (Van de Ven & Garud 1993).

Each of these perspectives contributes to our understanding of entrepreneurship. Studies in business history, geography and regional development economics, and management all point to the importance of resources in stimulating and supporting entrepreneurship. Hence, studies of entrepreneurs' interactions with social networks (defined by ethnicity, trade, or region), ancillary organizations (e.g., universities or business groups), and institutions (such as the patent system, financial regulations, and social movements) all inform our understanding of how to help new ventures be successful. However, it

---

[8] E.g., Florida (2005). In a broadly similar, though less reductive, vein are Saxenian (1996) and Castells & Hall (1994).

[9] See especially the essays in Kenney (2000). Organizational sociologists have also offered similar explanations for the development of entrepreneurial clusters (e.g., Owen-Smith & Powell 2004).

appears unlikely that such resources alone are enough to spark the types of high-growth entrepreneurship that many regions desire.[10]

It should be obvious that one of the most important components of the external environment with which potential entrepreneurs must interact before deciding to found a firm is the good or service that they intend their firm to sell. While there are important exceptions, familiarity with the artifact being sold would seem to be as necessary a precondition for entrepreneurship as any cognitive trait or external resource, and it would seem to offer an advantage in leveraging other factors in the entrepreneur's environment. For example, banks, venture capitalists, and social networks may be reluctant to offer money, trust, and access to a variety of resources unless the entrepreneur can demonstrate that she is familiar with the artifact she intends to sell. A vibrant set of studies in economics and management shows that firms founded by entrepreneurs possessing prior experience in a particular industry tend to survive longer than other firms (Klepper & Simons 2000; Helfat & Lieberman 2002; Agarwal et al. 2004).

But what about situations in which the entrepreneur intends to sell a technology or innovation that is so new that it is not currently on the market? In such cases, how can a nascent entrepreneur gain enough familiarity with the innovation to see its market potential and understand how to make and sell it? The answer, surprisingly often, is that prior to founding a firm, the entrepreneur was a user of the premarket version of the innovation and usually also a user innovator.

III. What Do Users Create? Technologies, Social Structures, and Firms

User innovators are distinguished from other innovators by the motives that drive their innovative activities: users innovate because they expect to benefit by *using* the innovations that they develop (von Hippel 1988). In contrast, manufacturers expect to benefit from an innovation by selling it to others. Users have been responsible for key innovations across an astonishing array of "high" and "low" tech, physical and virtual, and industrial and consumer product categories, including medical devices, scientific instruments, semiconductors, software, and sports equipment (von Hippel 1988). Innovative communities of users of one technology have, historically, also been important seedbeds of entrepreneurship in related technologies: ham radio enthusiasts, for instance, were important contributors to the early vacuum tube and personal computer industries (Haring 2007). The Wright brothers invented the airplane partly on the basis of know-how developed from their participation in the bicycle enthusiast community. With the proliferation of new information technologies and the decline of in-house corporate research units since the early 1990s, many firms have come to rely on large, networked communities of

---

[10] Many regions have experimented with providing such resources, with decidedly mixed results. For a national survey of such efforts in biotechnology, see Cortright & Mayer (2002). For case studies of attempts to recreate Silicon Valley, see O'Mara (2005); Leslie & Kargon (1996); and Leslie (2001).

users to make suggestions about, test, or innovate on their products,[11] while others have been surprised when such communities arise (Walker 2012; Raymond 1998). Indeed, in some ways scholarship on user innovation and entrepreneurship is just catching up with attempts to leverage user innovations by the business community, government agencies, and university technology transfer offices.[12]

Early academic studies of users were conducted by scholars in management and in the history/sociology of technology (von Hippel 1988; Kline & Pinch 1996). Both sets of scholars pictured users as innovating only on technologies that were marketed by preexisting firms. That is, firms would sell a product that users identified as relevant to, but not adequately meeting, their needs, and then users would tinker with that product to adapt it to new uses or conditions. We and other scholars, however, have begun to expand the outlook of user studies to include users who invent whole new technologies, form new institutions and social formations to promote diffusion and innovation of those technologies, and found new firms and even *industries* based on those technologies.

What makes users innovative is, unsurprisingly, use. That is, in the course of interacting with their environment—in particular, with the technologies contained in that environment—users often come to see new or better ways of doing things which would be directly beneficial to them. Many users do not act on those insights, but a substantial number do. Studies conducted across various types of technologies find that 19–38 percent of users have, at some point, innovated on a technology for their own use. A recent study conducted in the United Kingdom finds that 6.2 percent of U.K. consumers report having engaged in innovation for their own use (von Hippel, de Jong, & Flowers 2012). The discrepancy between the 6.2 percent statistic and the range of 19–38 percent found in other studies may be due to a form of recall bias; it may be easier for individuals to recall having innovated when asked to think about their activities with a particular class of products than if asked generally.

However, technologies are not the only components of the environment with which innovative users interact. In many cases, *relationships with other users* also have been critical to user innovation and to users' decisions to found firms. For reasons we explicate more fully below, new users often seek out existing users for advice, while existing innovative users (and firms founded by those users) seek out other leading users to gain access to the latest innovations. Especially—but by no means only—when firms do not yet exist to market a technology, communities of users of that technology can become catalysts of innovation and entrepreneurship.

Our approach, therefore, privileges factors external to the individual in attempting to explain entrepreneurship, at least within the rather large and economically important class of user entrepreneurs. In particular, we focus on users' interactions with and

---

[11] Valuable and early insights on this topic often came from practitioners, see Kim (2000); Gabriel & Goldman (2005).

[12] For an example of the military leveraging user innovation among its personnel, see Lindsay (2010).

innovations on a technology, and their relationships with other users of that technology, as external factors that shape individuals' decisions whether or not to found a firm to market that technology. Unlike some approaches that examine the entrepreneur's external environment, however, we pay close attention to the ways the external environment changes over time, and especially to the ways in which potential entrepreneurs influence the environment that, in turn, shapes them. That is, we understand individual motivations (including motivations to found firms) to be *coproduced* with external factors such as the state of the technology and the complexity of the social structure in which the user is participating.[13]

IV. A Framework for Understanding How Users Develop and Diffuse Their Innovations

Coproduction, unfortunately, is a messy way of depicting innovative and entrepreneurial activities, even if it is faithful to the messiness of the phenomena. Even if we narrow our approach down to three components—a technology, a community of users centered on that technology, and individual users who are potential entrepreneurs—the co-evolution of those three components is still complicated enough to require at least a book-length description for just a single technology and user community.[14] To make our analysis simple enough for cross-case comparisons, therefore, we build upon a framework of four "modes" of user innovation and user community complexity developed in previous work (Shah & Mody 2013).

Our four modes are distinguished from each other by the characteristics of the social structure associated with the technology. Each mode fulfills a distinct purpose with respect to a technology's development and diffusion and serves the needs of a unique category of users. As a result, each of these modes will be constructed by users as necessary to develop and diffuse the technology in the direction that users prefer at the time—and therefore these nodes need not appear in any particular order. Like all frameworks, however, ours is an abstraction, albeit an empirically grounded one; reality is riddled with complexities.

We draw on established definitions used by technology scholars to differentiate between a technology and its constituent innovations: a "radical" innovation establishes the basis for a technology and is followed by a number of subsequent "conservative" (or "incremental") innovations that serve to improve and refine the technology (Nelson & Winter 1982; Hughes 1987; McKelvey 1996). It is useful to note that both "radical" and "conservative" innovations—that is to say, the first groundbreaking innovation that

---

[13] We take "coproduction" in the sense developed in the science and technology studies field, as exemplified by the chapters (particularly the introductory essay) in Jasanoff (2004).

[14] Of which there are many in the history of technology literature. Some interesting examples include Lucsko (2008); Akera (2007); and Smith Hughes (2011).

defines a new technology and subsequent follow-on innovations—tend to be developed in the inventor mode.

A. THE INVENTOR MODE

In the inventor mode, there is almost no social structure to speak of: the technology's inventor and perhaps one or two very close associates compose the complete set of users of the technology. In probe microscopy, both the first successful probe microscope (the scanning tunneling microscope, or STM) and a failed precursor (the Topografiner) were invented by small groups located within large research organizations: for the STM, two PhD-level staff scientists (one senior and one junior) and two technicians at IBM's laboratory near Zurich in the early 1980s; for the Topografiner, one mid-career PhD-level staff scientist and one to two technicians at the US National Bureau of Standards in the late 1960s. In both cases, the inventors were able to secure resources from their employers by claiming that the microscope would contribute to those employers' objectives; however, the STM (and possibly the Topografiner) were intended primarily for their inventors' own use, and in both cases the inventions grew out of the inventors' prior use of related technologies. The dozens of later variants of the STM, such as the (more commercially important) atomic force microscope, were invented by similarly sized groups of academic, corporate, or government researchers; the majority of these variants were invented primarily for their inventors' own use. The size and organizational location of the groups that formed around user inventors in probe microscopy is very typical for the broader class of scientific instruments (with exceptions for so-called "Big Science" experiments such as observatories, particle accelerators, nuclear fission and fusion reactors, etc.).[15]

Similarly, the windsurfer was invented by Newman Darby, a Pennsylvania sailboat enthusiast and amateur boat builder, with help from his wife and brother-in-law (i.e., Darby would qualify as an "occasional inventor" unaffiliated with an organization related to the windsurfer). The majority of subsequent innovations made in windsurfing were also made by users under similar circumstances, that is, these user innovators were unaffiliated, occasional inventors, often working alongside close personal affiliates (usually friends rather than relatives). They were led to their inventions both by prior use of related technologies (e.g., surfboards, waterskis) and by a desire to personally use windsurfing equipment in a way that currently available products did not accommodate.

---

[15] Some examples of scientific user innovation (in circumstances where small, localized groups of users were networked into a wider, distributed community of users working on similar technologies) can be found in Kohler (1994); Reinhardt (2006); and Landecker (2007). Even in Big Science fields, many innovations originate in small groups embedded in a larger organization. For some examples, see McCray (2004); Hoddeson, Kolb, & Westfall (2008); Galison (1997).

In both probe microscopy and windsurfing we observed the interplay of equipment, technique, and need. For example, users' need or desire to use particular products for particular applications sometimes led them to alter their equipment. Those alterations in turn sometimes opened new possibilities in technique; for example, the conducting of aerial acrobatic tricks on a windsurf board. As users sought to hone and refine such new techniques, they sometimes altered their equipment further. Modifications in equipment, technique, or needs often drove subsequent modifications.

B. THE COMMUNITY MODE

In the community mode, a small number (up to a few dozen) of users—whom we call "modifiers"—have heard about and then replicated an invention for themselves, often after establishing contact with the inventor. The transition to a true "community" mode comes when these modifiers have begun to innovate on the original technology (thereby becoming user innovators) and have formed connections among themselves (rather than just being connected to the inventor). At that point, improvements to the technology can move rapidly among modifiers, often through one-to-many modes of communication, and innovations can be taken up, tested, and discarded or retained at an accelerating pace.

In transitioning into the community mode, inventors and modifiers often make use of preexisting organizations and communication channels associated with related technologies or potential applications of the technology. The inventors of the STM recruited modifiers, for instance, by publishing in journals and attending conferences aimed at physicists and electron microscopists, in the belief that those fields would be most receptive to their invention. Their success also persuaded IBM Research managers to incentivize other IBM groups to build STMs, which in turn led IBM's rivals (especially Bell Labs) to encourage their groups to build STMs. In windsurfing, Newman Darby published a description of his invention in *Popular Science*, which gradually led a few modifiers to copy his design and/or contact him for more details. However, it took almost a decade and the efforts of subsequent user innovators for a large and interconnected user community to form. We can see here several motivations for inventors to cultivate a community: a desire to improve the technology, the fame, or the prestige associated with publication in a forum such as *Physical Review Letters* or *Popular Science*, the emotional satisfaction of being taken seriously by a powerful organization such as IBM or an established association of one's peers such as the American Physical Society, and the excitement and enthusiasm associated with being part of the development of something new.

Once enough modifiers have been recruited, however, they and the inventors may find that preexisting organizations and institutions do not suffice for communicating information quickly enough regarding innovations to the technology. In both probe microscopy and windsurfing, users created new mechanisms for one-to-many communication and for copresence very soon after entering the community mode: probe microscopists started an annual international conference (with published proceedings), while windsurfing enthusiasts began holding informal competitions and distributing information through newsletters and, eventually, dedicated windsurfing magazines. Such new, technology-specific organizations and institutions support technology development and diffusion by enabling collective and cooperative work, and highlight a second motivation for inventors and modifiers to form a community: the pleasure of working closely, collaborating, and competing with other individuals who share one's dedication to a new technology. Over and over again, our interviewees mentioned the emotional satisfaction associated with spending time with other community members. That satisfaction derived from many sources: the opportunity to meet new and interesting people and to travel to interesting locales (early probe microscopy conferences took place in Cancun, the Austrian Alps, and Oxford; windsurfing competitions in Hawaii); the pleasures of demonstrating one's own innovations or particularly skillful use of the technology, as well as learning about others' innovations and uses; and the intellectual ferment of discussing new innovations and uses with other members of the community in an atmosphere in which new ideas flow easily.[16]

Many inventions do not enter the community mode. Creating a community is difficult, thankless work; for inventors, the community mode also has the drawback of diluting their control over the invention. Some inventors may wish to transition to the industry mode by starting firms and commercializing their ideas.[17] In some scientific communities, the desire to standardize measurements leads inventors to move quickly to the network exchange mode, in which a limited number of user-producers ("kitmakers" in our terminology) supply noncommercial versions of the technology to user-consumers ("kitters").[18] In probe microscopy and windsurfing, the inventors did foster the creation of user communities soon after they got their inventions to work. However, in probe microscopy at least, the inventors pointedly drew a contrast between their actions and those of inventors of other instruments (such as the field ion microscope) who had blocked development of strong user communities. That is, the inventors of the STM knew there was nothing inevitable about the community mode and made a conscious decision to cultivate a network of modifiers who would build their own versions of the instrument.

C. THE NETWORK EXCHANGE MODE

In the community mode, almost all community members are both users and producers of the technology, and new members generally build their own versions of the technology

---

[16] The relationship between innovation and emotional cohesion in small groups has been well documented by Parker & Hackett (2012).

[17] E.g., Sara Blakely, founder of Spanx, see *Sara Blakely*, FORBES (Mar. 2012), http://www.forbes.com/profile/sara-blakely/; or Mark Stadnyk, founder of MadStad Engineering and a vocal critic of the disadvantages conferred on user entrepreneurs by the U.S. patent system. See Lohr (2012).

[18] See Kohler (1994); Murray (2009).

before being recognized by existing members. Not everyone who wishes to use a new technology, however, also wishes to build it. In the absence of firms that sell the technology, such users must find someone who will build all or part of the technology for them. If that happens, then the user community will now include users who are not producers, and it will include a few producers who produce for someone other than themselves. We call this the "network exchange" mode.

Network exchange contains some features of both the industry and community modes, but it is qualitatively different from both. The network exchange mode, unlike the community mode, will not form unless the technology has reached a stage where it is sufficiently easy to replicate and, typically, sufficiently easy to use. However, no one participating in network exchange is able to live off of providing copies of the technology to new users, as those in the industry mode do, and no formal organizations are dedicated to providing copies to new users. Moreover, the version of the technology that is provided to new users is often an incomplete "kit" rather than a fully operational product: for that reason we refer to providers as "kitmakers" and their "customers" as "kitters." In probe microscopy, for instance, some kitmakers provided the physical apparatus but not the electronics, others provided the electronics but not the apparatus, and others provided control software, but not the electronics or the apparatus.

Network exchange further differs from full commercialization in that kitters do not necessarily pay cash for their kits. In probe microscopy, some kitters offered kitmakers access to interesting experimental materials, or to expertise in difficult sample-preparation techniques, or helped them break into journals and conferences that otherwise would have been difficult for them to access. In both probe microscopy and windsurfing, kitmakers sometimes provided kits out of a sense of obligation. As one windsurfer kitmaker put it, "People asked for copies of our stuff... friends, friends of friends, friends of friends of someone." In probe microscopy, kits were given to kitmakers' current and former postdoctoral fellows, to fellow employees of the same university or company, and to friends from college or graduate school. In both windsurfing and probe microscopy, cash gradually became a token of exchange, but in amounts below market value. Windsurfer kitmakers initially gave kits away for free, then (as the volume of requests increased) for an amount equivalent to the cost of materials, and finally (as their time became consumed with kitbuilding) for cost-plus amounts. In probe microscopy, a few kitmakers were graduate students who (either on their own initiative or at their advisers' request) sold cheap kits to their advisers' former students, collaborators, or other professional contacts—with goodwill from their advisers or potential employers making up the difference between the exchange price and market value.

D. THE COMMERCIAL MODE

The most studied and most familiar of our modes is, of course, the one in which firms exist to sell products to consumers who do not have the time, skill, and/or interest to build a technology for themselves. In this mode, new members of the user community are overwhelmingly consumers rather than producers, and consumers' relationship to producers is primarily transactional (unlike in the community or network exchange modes where producers and consumers often form, or have preexisting, long-standing relationships). One precondition of the commercial mode, therefore, is that the technology has developed in a direction that is attractive to consumers—it is reliable and user-friendly enough that the costs incurred in casual use do not outweigh the benefits.

As noted earlier, plenty of consumers still modify commercial products to meet their specific requirements. Indeed, firms can decide to market specifically to tinkering users. In probe microscopy, for instance, the dominant manufacturer (with approximately 50 percent market share) built very reliable "black-boxed" products which were difficult to modify extensively; other manufacturers therefore carved out niches by selling products that were more easily modified and appealed to customers with unusual or rapidly changing requirements. Almost all of the firms manufacturing windsurfing boards that were not founded by users sought to create one-design mentality in the sport; one-design is a racing method in which all boats share identical or very similar designs. Many user-founded firms, however, sold equipment and components that allowed owners to customize their boards and practice the sport in more creative ways.

In general, though, the commercial mode is associated with standardization of the design and use of the technology in order for firms to achieve economies of scale. In this mode, as well, firms often attempt to capture the innovation process, either by forming their own in-house R&D units or by forming alliances with leading innovative users. In both windsurfing and probe microscopy, bringing innovative users in-house or into alliances with firms significantly enhanced those firms' reputations in the larger user community.

E. MOVING BACKWARD, FORWARD, OR NOT AT ALL

In the case of very novel innovations, we observe that these modes often appear in the order in which we presented them above: inventor, community, network exchange, and industry. This ordering is intuitively appealing in that it is the order of increasing social complexity on several dimensions: the number of types of actors involved increases, the absolute number of users increases, and the primary set of users served by each mode is increasingly unwilling to build copies of the innovation for themselves.[19] In addition, an innovation's functionality and usability tend to be refined as it progresses through modes in this direction. As a result, most entrepreneurs will find it easiest to commercialize an innovation that has progressed from the inventor to the community to the network exchange mode, as the innovation will be further developed, will have diffused further, and the value of the innovation to potential customers (and therefore to potential

---

[19] Identifying a singular, precise metric of complexity might be an interesting topic for future research.

entrepreneurs) will be more clear. However, an entrepreneur might also choose to commercialize an innovation that has not passed through these modes; that entrepreneur would then have to expend greater personal resources to develop both the innovation and the potential market for the innovation.

However, it is important to stress that our modes do not necessarily form a chronological sequence. Recall that each mode fulfills a distinct purpose with respect to an innovation's development and diffusion and serves the needs of a unique category of users. Most individual user innovations in probe microscopy, as well as the field itself, moved through all four modes in the order that we have presented them. Most—but not all—user-generated innovations in windsurfing moved through the four modes in the order presented; some user innovations made late in the product life cycle skipped either the community or network exchange modes, as innovators believed that there was an established market for the technology and—in a shocking turn of events—Darby's original design for the windsurfer was ostensibly copied and then streamlined by two entrepreneurs (not users) who quickly patented and commercialized the innovation.

Many other user-created innovations have taken other routes. As we have noted, some inventors have commercialized their inventions almost immediately upon using them to their satisfaction (thereby skipping the community and network exchange modes), while others have skipped straight to network exchange. Many technologies remain in the inventor, community, or network exchange modes for long periods (perhaps indefinitely) without proceeding to the commercial mode. This situation is very common in scientific instrumentation, where the total number of users may be small and where almost all users may wish to build the technology for themselves to meet their own specific requirements.

Technologies can also proceed "backward" from a more complex mode to a less complex mode. For instance, when all firms that market a particular technology cease doing so (e.g., because doing so is no longer profitable or because a more profitable alternative has appeared), the commercial mode collapses. If there is still interest in the technology, however, then its users may regroup into the network exchange or community modes. This has occurred with a few beloved technologies of the early PC era, including the TRS-80 personal computer and the Apple Newton PDA (Muñiz & Schau 2005; Lindsay 1997). This pattern is also arguably observable in many hobbyist technologies, such as knitting or woodworking, where the pleasures of interaction with other users and of making something for oneself motivate users to form communities that exclude manufacturers of the technology (though firms that sell tools such as saws or materials such as yarn may still be incorporated into the community) (Maines 2009).

In other cases, a technology may be taken up in more than one mode simultaneously. This pattern was seen repeatedly in both probe microscopy and windsurfing. For instance, in probe microscopy a large number of distinct variants were invented. Some users (e.g., life scientists) perceived disincentives to use anything other than commercial, off-the-shelf instruments, while other users (e.g., physicists) perceived disincentives to use anything other than largely home-built instruments. Most users—"consumers"—were best served by the commercial mode, in which firms sold them instruments that they could use and modify modestly. A substantial minority of users, however, continued to invent variants and to cultivate small subcommunities of modifiers who would innovate on those variants. In a few cases, firms encouraged their employees to participate in these parallel user communities in order to maintain awareness of (and expertise in) these variants and to commercialize them when the technology and market potential had matured sufficiently. In some cases, when existing firms declined to commercialize a variant, that variant's inventors or modifiers were driven to found new firms.[20]

V. Entrepreneurship in Context: How Users' Technological and Organizational Activities Give Rise to Entrepreneurship

We are now able to examine more closely how user innovation—in technology and organization—can lead to entrepreneurship. While firm formation is most typical of the commercial mode, we find that all four modes possess unique characteristics that can foster (or hinder) entrepreneurship. We find that the experience of participation in earlier modes provides some individuals with the skills and motivations necessary for successful entrepreneurship.

A. ENTREPRENEURSHIP ARISING FROM THE INVENTOR MODE

In the cases we have examined, there does not seem to be a direct link between invention of an altogether new technology (as opposed to innovation on an existing technology) and entrepreneurship in that technological category. In probe microscopy, the initial inventors of the scanning tunneling microscope, its precursor (the Topografiner), and the STM's most important variant (the atomic force microscope) all remained with their original employers (Stanford, IBM, and the Bureau of Standards), and none showed any interest in persuading those employers to market their inventions. The inventor of the windsurfer, Newman Darby, halfheartedly attempted to found a firm, but found little success.

Based on our findings and knowledge of the actions of user entrepreneurs in other fields, we hypothesize a few conditions that would encourage the inventors of an *altogether new technology* to become entrepreneurs:

- The inventor's use of the technology must be so satisfying and so evidently not specific to the inventor's own needs or personality that the inventor could imagine others benefiting from the invention. This happens frequently when a technology or the context in which it is to be used is well established, and therefore

---

[20] For an extended description of user innovation and entrepreneurship in probe microscopy, see Mody (2011).

supporting institutions and a market for the technology exist (or can be created by the entrepreneur) and the entrepreneur can draw support and/or resources from these sources. Many examples of novel medical devices fit in this category.[21]

- The invention should be complex enough or have sufficient value added to its constituent components that other users will find it more attractive to buy it rather than make their own. Note that this condition may require significant adaptation from the original form of the invention—in which case the inventor may spend a significant amount of time between inventing and marketing the product and/or may seek a transition to the community mode (in order to access others' innovations on the technology) prior to founding a firm.

- Inventors who do not form the *first* firms to commercialize their inventions may view those firms as inducements to found their own firms if they feel the initial firms have not commercialized the technology properly or have not given the inventor sufficient credit or monetary reward, or if they see their status as the inventor as enabling them to capture market share from the initial firms.

- Inventors' experience with inventing and/or commercializing prior technologies (or watching their technologies be commercialized by someone else) may confer expertise or insight that will make entrepreneurship seem more feasible and/or rewarding with respect to a new technology they encounter.

This last circumstance was particularly notable in probe microscopy. One of the inventors of the STM, Gerd Binnig, went on to co-invent the atomic force microscope but refrained from commercializing either invention. However, he later went on to co-invent a probe-based data storage technology (the "millipede"), which IBM has tentatively sought to commercialize. Binnig later invented a number of software algorithms and founded a company, Definiens, to commercialize them.

The examples of other user innovators in probe microscopy serve to further underscore the aforementioned point that, while participation in the inventor mode is not necessarily linked to entrepreneurship, *repeated* participation in the inventor mode (which often allows for observation of the commercial process, its requirements, and its benefits— even if across different technologies) appears to be associated with entrepreneurship. In academic probe microscopy, those professors who either founded or allied with the first generation of firms were serial inventors, most of whom had some prior experience commercializing their ideas. Professors who invented probe microscope variants but had little prior inventing or entrepreneurial experience almost uniformly allowed their inventions to be commercialized by other parties. In several prominent cases, however, professors who did not found or ally closely with firms to commercialize their first inventions did do so after their second or third inventions.

---

[21] See, for instance, the case studies of several new medical imaging technologies in Blume (1992).

The cases of innovative probe microscopists embedded within firms further substantiate this pattern, although, in these cases, little commercialization occurred. The sole probe microscope variant that IBM commercialized—the SXM—was invented by an IBM scientist, Kumar Wickramasinghe, who had previously invented several other probe microscopes which neither he nor IBM had commercialized. Other corporate researchers (at IBM, Bell Labs, and Intel) who invented only one probe microscope variant did not pursue commercialization either by themselves or through their employers; instead, they waited for their inventions to be commercialized by third parties.

B. ENTREPRENEURSHIP ARISING FROM THE COMMUNITY MODE

In the community mode, many more individuals are innovating on the technology and rapidly communicating those innovations to one another than in the inventor mode. Even the most astute creators of altogether new technologies cannot consider every possible improvement to their inventions; indeed, they may neglect or actively resist even obvious improvements. In probe microscopy, for instance, the initial inventors of the STM were reluctant to computerize control of the microscope, whereas most of the first modifiers in the community mode saw computerization as a much-needed addition. In windsurfing, Darby did not envision a need for footstraps to help the rider remain on the board; once a windsurfing community took root, almost ten years after Darby's original invention, members of that community very rapidly added footstraps to the windsurfing board.

In both probe microscopy and windsurfing, subsequent user innovators who participated in the community mode were significantly more likely to found firms or to encourage others to commercialize their innovations than were the technology's original inventors. These user innovators have no chance to gain prestige by reinventing the technology; instead their claim to status in the community is secured by adapting it to a new use or by making it more powerful or easier to use. Improvements to the usability of a technology are closely linked to the commercial potential of the technology. In probe microscopy, most initial variants were extremely unreliable and were not regarded as commercializable; when innovations on those variants made them more reliable, however, commercialization generally followed quickly.

Similarly, adapting a technology to new uses can increase its market potential dramatically. In windsurfing, the original invention was only suitable for use on relatively placid lakes and rivers; subsequent user innovators adapted the technology for use on ocean waters with high wind and waves, thereby making its use more enjoyable and more marketable to existing users of surfboards. In probe microscopy, several subsequent user innovators were recruited by the initial inventors of the STM in the belief that they would adapt the STM for use in fields in which the inventors had little expertise (e.g., surface science or electrochemistry). These individuals therefore became expert in tailoring the technology for a new class of users—users who could become a potential market for a commercial version of the technology.

As mentioned before, the community mode is also associated with emotional satisfaction derived from rapid innovation and camaraderie with other innovating users. While the role of these emotive aspects of the community mode in fostering entrepreneurship is hard to measure, we observe that many of the most successful entrepreneurs in the fields we studied referred to the satisfactions of entrepreneurship in the same language they used to describe their earlier participation in the community mode. Entrepreneurs told us of the emotional rewards of learning the new skills associated with running a business, or their satisfaction in successfully competing against other entrepreneurs, or the pride they felt in making a quality product, or the camaraderie that bound the members of their start-up company. All of these are emotional rewards that are also typical of the community mode, where new skills must be learned, and where close relationships, involving both competition and collaboration, often develop among community members.

We hypothesize that, as long as these emotional rewards are forthcoming in the community mode, community members may be less likely to found firms. However, if the community mode enters a less exciting phase, community members may see entrepreneurship as a way to recover some of their earlier emotional satisfaction. It is perhaps telling that, in probe microscopy, the earliest entrepreneurs were people who had not generated rich affective bonds with other community members. The second generation of entrepreneurs, however, were people who had participated vigorously in the early community mode, but who viewed the later rapid growth of the community as diluting the affective rewards of membership (e.g., by making conferences too large and impersonal).

In addition, the affective ties among participants generated in the community mode can aid user innovators who later become entrepreneurs in that they may have readier access to their peers' innovations and a larger reserve of their peers' good will than entrepreneurs who do not engage in the community mode. Entrepreneurs can also make significant use of the new institutions and one-to-many communication mechanisms created during the community mode. These mechanisms allow entrepreneurs to gauge the market potential of the technology and then to advertise the debuts of their products. The competitions that brought together early participants in the windsurfing community, for instance, soon acquired corporate sponsorship, while the transition from windsurfing newsletters to windsurfing magazines was enabled by the emergence of firms that could advertise in those magazines. In probe microscopy, the first serious entrepreneur decided to found his firm only after attending an international STM conference to gauge the market; he then brought his first product to market somewhat before it was fully ready so that he could display it at the next year's STM conference. His company then became one of the major sponsors of that conference in following years, as did competing firms.

C. ENTREPRENEURSHIP ARISING FROM THE NETWORK EXCHANGE MODE

In this mode, we see a few actors come right up to the edge of entrepreneurship in its usual sense. The questions to be answered then are why, and what factors encourage them to cross or back away from that line? We observe that inducements toward or away from entrepreneurship in the network exchange mode depend heavily on actors' positions within a user community and the nature of their relationships forged with other users—reinforcing our view that social determinants are as important as intrinsic personality characteristics in determining entrepreneurship.

In windsurfing, the network exchange period lasted a very short time, yet it was critical in shaping the emergence of an industry in several ways. First, it accentuated distinctions among windsurfer builders that had begun to emerge in the community mode: only some modifiers received large volumes of requests for boards, and only those who were willing to become kitmakers received further requests. Modifiers who were willing to become kitmakers were then primed to become entrepreneurs: they had acquired experience building boards for others, they were visible to (and appreciated by) large numbers of current users who were willing to recommend them to potential users, and they were able to gauge the size of the market and even to roughly determine price points. Forming a firm became attractive as a way to devolve some of the burden of board-making onto others.

In probe microscopy, the network exchange mode lasted for a longer period, although it ran in parallel with the emergence of a robust commercial mode. That is, once firms began appearing in 1987, they commercialized variants that had already passed through the network exchange mode for two or three years. New variants, however, continued to be invented and to transition into network exchange; some variants were then commercialized, others were not. A few groups that gained reputations as particularly innovative modifiers in the community mode became kitmakers upon receiving large numbers of requests for copies of or access to their microscopes.

Two main types of network exchange were common in probe microscopy. In one, low-status individuals who had some close tie to a high-status person used that connection to make a little cash on the side by selling cheap copies of the technology. Several graduate students used their advisers' network of contacts in this way, as did a few technicians who worked for well-known corporate, government, or academic probe microscopists. This type of network exchange was almost always short-lived since kitmakers had other duties that were more pressing. This type of exchange generally did not, therefore, lead to firm formation.

In the second type, well-known (mostly academic) probe microscopists received large numbers of requests from other academic specialists who wanted to collaborate. These specialists were sometimes given all or part of a microscope, in return for which they contributed knowledge of how to prepare samples, the samples themselves, journal articles co-authored with the kitmaker, and access to or increased credibility with the specialists' home disciplines (e.g., biochemistry, geology, surface science, etc.). Members of the kitmakers' lab groups (their students, postdocs, and technicians) received feedback from kitters regarding how to make the microscope more user-friendly and more narrowly tuned to the needs of the kitters' disciplinary colleagues. In this way, feedback from kitters in the network exchange mode translated easily into adapting microscopes for new markets in the commercial mode. Network exchange preceded—and likely primed—kitmakers' interest in commercializing their microscopes. A few high-profile kitters founded firms themselves; several others encouraged their students and postdocs to found firms (and then joined those firms' boards); still others sought out new firms and persuaded them to sell commercial versions of the kitmakers' microscopes.

Thus, network exchange can lead both to a more marketable technology and to a more market-savvy kitmaker. However, network exchange can also hinder, or at least complicate, entrepreneurship. Property rights—to materials and intellectual output—can be blurry in the network exchange mode. Kitters and kitmakers sometimes make explicit trades, but more often the exchange is ill-defined. Certainly, scientific kitters are often not given explicit instructions as to how they may or may not use their kits. In the biotechnology industry, there are many famous examples of kitters who modified and then commercialized gifted biological materials or intellectual property without due regard for the kitmaker.[22] In some instances this mismatch between the property rights regimes of the network exchange and commercial modes has led to messy lawsuits.[23]

D. ENTREPRENEURSHIP ARISING FROM THE COMMERCIAL MODE

Obviously, this is the mode for which there are many explanations already advanced for why entrepreneurs emerge. However, much less has been written about the benefits entrepreneurs and new firms can derive from their relationships with members of a user community and vice versa. Particularly early in the commercial mode, new firms may lag behind members of the user community in producing new innovations, while individuals in the user community may look to new firms as a source of revenue or resources. In windsurfing, diversifying firms who entered the industry often lagged behind user innovators in terms of innovation, as well as brand and image. A number of these firms sought to associate themselves with the user community to gain visibility. For example, some arranged photo shoots with prominent user innovators, asking the user innovators to place decals emblazoned with the company logo on the innovator's homemade equipment. In probe microscopy, start-ups formed alliances with users to gain access to innovations but also to accrue status, visibility, and credibility from those users. For instance, the dominant probe microscope manufacturer in the 1990s ran a famous advertising campaign called "We Have Science Covered" in which their microscope stood next to seven covers of the journal *Science* featuring cover images generated with the company's products. The articles in *Science* associated with those covers were authored by prominent members of the user community, and four of the articles were actually co-authored with employees of the company.

---

[22] See Smith Hughes (2011); Jones (2005); Fortun (2008); Strasser (2011).
[23] See Murray (2009); Swanson (2007).

From the other end, some prominent innovative users closely allied with start-up companies in part to generate royalties from licenses on their patents. However, users also benefited from alliances with firms in a variety of nonmonetary ways. Alliances boosted their productivity and profile in the probe microscopy community—they had access to free microscopes and ancillary equipment, including beta-tested equipment that was not yet on the market (and therefore not available to competing groups). Alliances also helped users shape the design of start-ups' products that they knew would eventually become their own lab equipment—thereby ensuring that their own requirements would find their way into the firm's products. Also, allying with a start-up was one way to increase the size of the research subfield in which a user was working, so that the user's work would gain wider acceptance—if more people could replicate and extend a user's experiments, the user's work would gain more citations. Finally, allying with or founding a start-up also led to employment for users' current and former lab group members—indeed, personnel trained by prominent users rose very high in several firms and a few have gone on to found second- and third-generation spin-off firms.

VI. Concluding Thoughts

Many of our current theories, practices, and policies privilege profit and status as explanations for what drives innovators and entrepreneurs. By showing that entrepreneurship can be rooted in creative, collective activities, we suggest that existing theories may not provide a complete picture of our innovation and industrial ecosystems. These findings, alongside the findings of other scholars, point to the importance of the commons as a seedbed for economic, cultural, and social development. In particular, the effects of policies influencing innovation and entrepreneurship—be they focused on intellectual property law (Heller & Eisenberg 1998; Lessig 2001; Benkler 2004), support for start-up firms, or education and training—on user innovators and commons of various sorts ought to be considered.[24]

In this chapter we have tried to show some ways that user innovation paves the way for successful firm formation and even industry creation. In particular, we have shown that the social structures created by users support the formation of skills, attitudes, and relationships that can later be translated into entrepreneurship. The specific structure and content of a particular mode—how complex it is and how mature its technology is—affects how and why its members approach entrepreneurship. Each of our four modes—inventor, community, network exchange, and industry—offers users a different path toward (or obstacles to) entrepreneurship.

---

[24] The other chapters in this book, as well as the work of Madison, Frischmann, and Strandburg, provide a glimpse at the various sorts of commons that so pervasively and quietly develop the technologies and cultural artifacts available to us (Madison, Frischmann, & Strandburg 2010).

Acknowledgments

The National Science Foundation (under Cooperative Agreement No. 0531184) and Alfred P. Sloan Foundation provided support for this work. Our work has benefited from interactions with Emily Cox, Pierre Mourad, Mary Tripsas, and participants at the Convening Cultural Commons workshop at New York University School of Law. We are grateful to the many innovators, community participants, and entrepreneurs who graciously shared their time and experiences.

References

Rajshree Agarwal et al., *Knowledge Transfer through Inheritance: Spin-out Generation, Development and Performance*, 47 ACADEMY OF MANAGEMENT J. 501 (2004).

ATSUSHI AKERA, CALCULATING A NATURAL WORLD: SCIENTISTS, ENGINEERS, AND COMPUTERS DURING THE RISE OF US COLD WAR RESEARCH (MIT Press 2007).

Paul Babiak, Craig S. Neumann, & Robert D. Hare, *Corporate Psychopathy: Talking the Walk*, 28 BEHAVIORAL SCIENCES & LAW 174 (2010).

Carliss Baldwin, Christoph Hienerth, & Eric von Hippel, *How User Innovations Become Commercial Products: A Theoretical Investigation and Case Study*, 35 RESEARCH POLICY 1291 (2006).

GIACOMO BECATTINI, INDUSTRIAL DISTRICTS: A NEW APPROACH TO INDUSTRIAL CHANGE (Edward Elgar Publishing 2004).

Yochai Benkler, *Commons-Based Strategies and the Problems of Patents*, 305 SCIENCE 1110 (2004).

STUART BLUME, INSIGHT AND INDUSTRY: ON THE DYNAMICS OF TECHNOLOGICAL CHANGE IN MEDICINE (MIT Press 1992).

Robert H. Brockhaus & Pamela S. Horwitz, *The Psychology of the Entrepreneur, in* THE ART AND SCIENCE OF ENTREPRENEURSHIP 25 (Donald L. Sexton & Raymond W. Smilor eds., Cambridge, MA: Ballinger Publishing 1986).

Shona L. Brown & Kathleen M. Eisenhardt, *Product Development: Past Research, Present Findings and Future Directions*, 20 ACADEMY OF MANAGEMENT REV. 343 (1995).

MANUEL CASTELLS & PETER HALL, TECHNOPOLES OF THE WORLD: THE MAKING OF TWENTY-FIRST-CENTURY INDUSTRIAL COMPLEXES (Routledge 1994).

KIM CLARK & TAKAHIRO FUJIMOTO, PRODUCT DEVELOPMENT PERFORMANCE (Harvard Business School Press 1991).

James S. Coleman, *A Vision for Sociology*, 32 SOCIETY 29 (1994).

JOSEPH CORTRIGHT & HEIKE MAYER, SIGNS OF LIFE: THE GROWTH OF BIOTECHNOLOGY CENTERS IN THE US (Washington, D.C.: Brookings Institution 2002).

Paul J. DiMaggio, *Interest and Agency in Institutional Theory, in* INSTITUTIONAL PATTERNS AND ORGANIZATIONS: CULTURE AND ENVIRONMENT 3 (L. Zucker ed., Ballinger Publishing 1988).

CHRISTINE DOBBIN, ASIAN ENTREPRENEURIAL MINORITIES: CONJOINT COMMUNITIES IN THE MAKING OF THE WORLD-ECONOMY 1570–1940 (Curzon 1996).

RICHARD FLORIDA, CITIES AND THE CREATIVE CLASS (Routledge 2005).

MICHAEL A. FORTUN, PROMISING GENOMICS: ICELAND AND DECODE GENETICS IN A WORLD OF SPECULATION (University of California Press 2008).

RICHARD P. GABRIEL & RON GOLDMAN, INNOVATION HAPPENS ELSEWHERE: OPEN SOURCE AS BUSINESS STRATEGY (San Francisco: Morgan Kaufmann 2005).

PETER GALISON, IMAGE AND LOGIC: A MATERIAL CULTURE OF MICROPHYSICS (University of Chicago Press 1997).

Raghu Garud & Peter Karnøe, *Path Creation as a Process of Mindful Deviation*, in PATH DEPENDENCE AND CREATION 1 (Raghu Garud & Peter Karnoe eds., Mahwah, NJ: Lawrence Erlbaum Associates 2001).

ANTHONY GIDDENS, THE CONSTITUTION OF SOCIETY: OUTLINE OF THE THEORY OF STRUCTURATION (Cambridge: Polity Press 1984).

ANDREW GODLEY, JEWISH IMMIGRANT ENTREPRENEURSHIP IN NEW YORK AND LONDON (Palgrave MacMillan 2001).

Royston Greenwood, Roy Suddaby, & C. R. Hinings, *Theorizing Change: The Role of Professional Associations in the Transformation of Institutionalized Fields*, 45 ACADEMY OF MANAGEMENT J. 58 (2002).

Stefan Haefliger, Peter Jäger, & Georg von Krogh, *Under the Radar: Industry Entry by User Entrepreneurs*, 39 RESEARCH POLICY 1198 (2010).

KRISTEN HARING, HAM RADIO'S TECHNICAL CULTURE (MIT Press 2007).

Constance E. Helfat & Marvin B. Lieberman, *The Birth of Capabilities: Market Entry and the Importance of Pre-History*, 11 INDUSTRIAL & CORPORATE CHANGE 725 (2002).

Michael A. Heller & Rebecca S. Eisenberg, *Can Patents Deter Innovation? The Anticommons in Biomedical Research*, 280 SCIENCE 698 (1998).

LILLIAN HODDESON, ADRIENNE W. KOLB, & CATHERINE WESTFALL, FERMILAB: PHYSICS, THE FRONTIER, AND MEGASCIENCE (University of Chicago Press 2008).

SALLY SMITH HUGHES, GENENTECH: THE BEGINNINGS OF BIOTECH (University of Chicago Press 2011).

Thomas P. Hughes, *The Evolution of Large Technological Systems*, in THE SOCIAL CONSTRUCTION OF TECHNOLOGICAL SYSTEMS 51 (Wiebe E. Bijker, Thomas P. Hughes, & Trevor Pinch eds., MIT Press 1987).

SHEILA JASANOFF (ED.), STATES OF KNOWLEDGE: THE CO-PRODUCTION OF SCIENCE AND SOCIAL ORDER (Routledge 2004).

Mark Peter Jones, *Biotech's Perfect Climate: The Hybritech Story*, unpublished PhD dissertation (University of California San Diego 2005).

MARTIN KENNEY (ED.), UNDERSTANDING SILICON VALLEY: THE ANATOMY OF AN ENTREPRENEURIAL REGION (Stanford University Press 2000).

AMY JO KIM, COMMUNITY BUILDING ON THE WEB: SECRET STRATEGIES FOR SUCCESSFUL ONLINE COMMUNITIES (Berkeley, CA: Peachpit Press 2000).

Maurice Kirby, *Quakerism, Entrepreneurship, and the Family Firm in North-East England, 1780–1860*, in ENTREPRENEURSHIP, NETWORKS, AND MODERN BUSINESS 105 (Jonathan Brown & Mary B. Rose eds., Manchester University Press 1993).

Steven Klepper & Kenneth L. Simons, *Dominance by Birthright: Entry of Prior Radio Producers and Competitive Ramifications in the U.S. Television Receiver Industry*, 21 STRATEGIC MANAGEMENT J. 997 (2000).

Ronald Kline & Trevor Pinch, *Users as Agents of Technological Change: The Social Construction of the Automobile in the Rural United States*, 37 TECHNOLOGY & CULTURE 763 (1996).

ROBERT KOHLER, LORDS OF THE FLY: DROSOPHILA GENETICS AND THE EXPERIMENTAL LIFE (University of Chicago Press 1994).

HANNAH LANDECKER, CULTURING LIFE: HOW CELLS BECAME TECHNOLOGIES (Harvard University Press 2007).

DAVID LANDES, WEALTH AND POVERTY OF NATIONS: WHY SOME ARE SO RICH AND SOME SO POOR (W.W. Norton 1999).

Stuart W. Leslie, *Regional Disadvantage: Replicating Silicon Valley in New York's Capital Region*, 42 TECHNOLOGY & CULTURE 236 (2001).

Stuart W. Leslie & Robert H. Kargon, *Selling Silicon Valley: Frederick Terman's Model for Regional Advantage*, 70 BUSINESS HISTORY REV. 435 (1996).

LAWRENCE LESSIG, THE FUTURE OF IDEAS (Random House 2001).

Christina Lindsay, *From the Shadows: Users as Designers, Producers, Marketers, Distributors, and Technical Support*, in HOW USERS MATTER: THE CO-CONSTRUCTION OF USERS AND TECHNOLOGY 29 (Nelly Oudshoorn & Trevor Pinch eds., MIT Press 1997).

Jon R. Lindsay, *War Upon the Map: User Innovation in American Military Software*, 51 TECHNOLOGY & CULTURE 619 (2010).

Steve Lohr, *Inventor Challenges a Sweeping Revision in Patent Law*, N.Y. TIMES (Aug. 26, 2012), http://www.nytimes.com/2012/08/27/technology/mark-stadnyk-challenges-sweeping-revision-in-patent-law.html.

Helen Louri & Ioanna Pepelasis Minoglou, *Diaspora Entrepreneurial Networks in the Black Sea and Greece, 1870–1917*, 26 J. ECONOMIC HISTORY 69 (1997).

D. N. LUCSKO, THE BUSINESS OF SPEED: THE HOT ROD INDUSTRY IN AMERICA, 1915–1990 (Johns Hopkins University Press 2008).

Michael J. Madison, Brett M. Frischmann, & Katherine J. Strandburg, *Constructing Commons in the Cultural Environment*, 95 CORNELL L. REV. 657 (2010).

RACHEL P. MAINES, HEDONIZING TECHNOLOGIES: PATHS TO PLEASURE IN HOBBIES AND LEISURE (Johns Hopkins University Press 2009).

ALFRED MARSHALL, INDUSTRY AND TRADE (London: Macmillan and Co. 1919).

INA BAGHDIANTZ MCCABE, GELINA HARLAFTIS, & IOANNA PEPELASIS MINOGLOU EDS., DIASPORA ENTREPRENEURIAL NETWORKS: FOUR CENTURIES OF HISTORY (Oxford: Berg 2005).

W. PATRICK MCCRAY, GIANT TELESCOPES: ASTRONOMICAL AMBITION AND THE PROMISE OF TECHNOLOGY (Harvard University Press 2004).

MAUREEN D. MCKELVEY, EVOLUTIONARY INNOVATION: THE BUSINESS OF BIOTECHNOLOGY (Oxford University Press 1996).

THOMAS J. MISA, FROM LEONARDO TO THE INTERNET: TECHNOLOGY AND CULTURE FROM THE RENAISSANCE TO THE PRESENT (Johns Hopkins University Press 2011).

CYRUS C. M. MODY, INSTRUMENTAL COMMUNITY: PROBE MICROSCOPY AND THE PATH TO NANOTECHNOLOGY (MIT Press 2011).

David Morris, *Values as an Obstacle to Economic Growth in South Asia: An Historical Survey*, 27 J. ECONOMIC HISTORY 588 (1967).

Albert M. Muñiz, Jr. & Hope Jensen Schau, *Religiosity in the Abandoned Apple Newton Brand Community*, 31 J. CONSUMER RESEARCH 737 (2005).

Fiona Murray, *The Oncomouse That Roared: Hybrid Exchange Strategies as a Source of Productive Tension at the Boundary of Overlapping Institutions*, 105 AM. J. SOCIOLOGY 1105 (2009).

RICHARD R. NELSON & SIDNEY G. WINTER, AN EVOLUTIONARY THEORY OF ECONOMIC CHANGE (Belknap Press of Harvard University Press 1982).

Nicos Nicolaou & Scott Shane, *The Genetics of Entrepreneurship*, *in* HANDBOOK OF RESEARCH ON INNOVATION AND ENTREPRENEURSHIP 471 (David B. Audretsch, Oliver Falck, Stephan Heblich, & Adam Lederer eds., Edward Elgar Publishing 2011).

MARGARET PUGH O'MARA, CITIES OF KNOWLEDGE: COLD WAR SCIENCE AND THE SEARCH FOR THE NEXT SILICON VALLEY (Princeton University Press 2005).

ELINOR OSTROM, GOVERNING THE COMMONS: THE EVOLUTION OF INSTITUTIONS FOR COLLECTIVE ACTION (Cambridge University Press 1990).

Jason Owen-Smith & Walter W. Powell, *Knowledge Networks as Channels and Conduits: The Effects of Spillovers in the Boston Biotechnology Community*, 15 ORGANIZATON SCIENCE 5 (2004).

John N. Parker & Edward J. Hackett, *Hot Spots and Hot Moments in Scientific Collaborations and Social Movements*, 77 AM. SOCIOLOGICAL REV. 21 (2012).

Eric Raymond, *The Halloween Documents* (1998), http://www.opensource.ac.uk/mirrors/www.opensource.org/halloween/index.html/ (accessed Mar. 28, 2014).

CARSTEN REINHARDT, SHIFTING AND REARRANGING: PHYSICAL METHODS AND THE TRANSFORMATION OF MODERN CHEMISTRY (Sagamore Beach, MA: Science History Publications 2006).

JON RONSON, THE PSYCHOPATH TEST: A JOURNEY THROUGH THE MADNESS INDUSTRY (New York: Riverhead Books 2011).

ANNALEE SAXENIAN, REGIONAL ADVANTAGE: CULTURE AND COMPETITION IN SILICON VALLEY AND ROUTE 128 (Harvard University Press 1996).

Sonali K. Shah & Mary Tripsas, *The Accidental Entrepreneur: The Emergent & Collective Process of User Entrepreneurship*, 1 STRATEGIC ENTREPRENEURSHIP J. 123 (2007).

SONALI K. SHAH, SHERYL WINSTON SMITH, & E. J. REEDY, WHO ARE USER ENTREPRENEURS? FINDINGS ON INNOVATION, FOUNDER CHARACTERISTICS & FIRM CHARACTERISTICS (Ewing Marion Kauffman Foundation 2012).

Sonali Shah & Cyrus C. M. Mody, *How Do Users Develop & Diffuse Their Innovations? Resources, New Social Structures & Scaffolding* (Working paper 2013) (on file with authors).

WESLEY D. SINE & ROBERT J. DAVID EDS., INSTITUTIONS AND ENTREPRENEURSHIP (RESEARCH IN THE SOCIOLOGY OF WORK, vol. 21) (Bingley, UK: Emerald Group Publishing 2010).

Sheryl Winston Smith & Sonali K. Shah, *Do Innovative Users Generate More Useful Insights? An Analysis of CVC Investment in the Medical Device Industry*, 7 STRATEGIC ENTREPRENEURSHIP J. 151 (2013).

Bruno J. Strasser, *The Experimenter's Museum: Genbank, Natural History, and the Moral Economies of Biomedicine*, 102 ISIS 60 (2011).

Kara Swanson, *Biotech in Court: A Legal Lesson in the Unity of Science*, 37 SOCIAL STUDIES OF SCIENCE 357 (2007).

Alva Taylor, *The Next Generation: Technology Adoption and Integration through Internal Competition in New Product Development*, 21 ORGANIZATION SCIENCE 3 (2010).

Patricia H. Thornton, *The Sociology of Entrepreneurship*, 25 ANNUAL REV. SOCIOLOGY 19 (1999).

Mary Tripsas, *Customer Preference Discontinuities: A Trigger for Radical Technological Change*, 29 Managerial & Decision Economics 79 (2008).

Denise Tsang, The Entrepreneurial Culture: Network Advantage within Chinese and Irish Software Firms (Edward Elgar Publishing 2006).

Andrew H. Van de Ven & Raghu Garud, *Innovation and Industry Development: The Case of Cochlear Implants, in* 5 Research on Technological Innovation, Management & Policy 1 (Robert Burgelman & Richard Rosenbloom eds., Bingley, UK: Emerald Group Publishing 1993).

Eric von Hippel, The Sources of Innovation (Oxford University Press 1988).

Eric A. von Hippel, Jereon de Jong, & Stephen Flowers, *Comparing Business and Household Sector Innovation in Consumer Products: Findings from a Representative Study in the UK*, 58 Management Science 1669 (2012).

Rob Walker, *Freaks, Geeks and Microsoft*, N.Y. Times (May 31, 2012), http://www.nytimes.com/2012/06/03/magazine/how-kinect-spawned-a-commercial-ecosystem.html.

Max Weber, The Protestant Ethic and the Spirit of Capitalism (1904).

Martin Wiener, English Culture and the Decline of the Industrial Spirit: 1950–1980 (Cambridge University Press 1981).

10 An Inventive Commons: Shared Sources of the Airplane and Its Industry

Peter B. Meyer*

I. Introduction

In 1809 a scientific journal published a paper describing a fixed-wing aircraft design that could carry a person. Author George Cayley bravely wrote in its first paragraph that by publishing his observations on the subject he might be "expediting the attainment of an object that will in time be found of great importance to mankind; so much so, that a new era in society will commence from the moment that aerial navigation is familiarly recognized."

That paper launched the phrase "aerial navigation," which was then used for over a century in an international discussion among experimenters and scientists about how to make an aircraft that could be piloted and controlled better than a balloon or projectile. Participants in this discussion published articles, created new journals, filed patents, formed clubs, and attended exhibitions and conferences. After a century, this line of thought and work led to the invention of the modern airplane.

---

* Peter B. Meyer was a software engineer and is now a research economist in the Office of Productivity and Technology at the U.S. Bureau of Labor Statistics, Washington, D.C., USA. He has a longstanding interest in technical invention and open-source processes. Views expressed here are the author's and do not represent the Bureau.

This chapter explores the ways in which documents, information, and networks associated with the century of aeronautical texts represented a *knowledge commons* space in the sense of Madison, Frischmann, & Strandburg (2010). Their work inherits from the discussions of natural resource commons by Ostrom (1990) and of the informational commons by Ostrom & Hess (2007).

This case study of commons management describes structures encouraging the creation and maintenance (also called "provision" or supply) of the common resources and of structures controlling or encouraging appropriate use of the common assets. In general the participants in the development of the airplane were self-motivated experimenters, interested in flight partly as a dream and partly as an intellectual challenge, so the fundamental source of provision of shared knowledge was intrinsic to each of them. Provision was subsidized by their own enthusiasm.

Key institutions enabled and supported their internally motivated pursuit of "aerial navigation." They created and used a pool of ideas, often codified in publicly available documents. For a natural resource such as a river, usage must be controlled; for a stream of information, which is inherently nonrivalous, that is not generally the case. As has been demonstrated by studies of "user innovation," usage may replenish or improve a shared resource of knowledge about a particular technology (von Hippel 2006). Such was the case with the common pool of knowledge about aerial navigation through 1905.

The *inventive commons* described here differs from most commons examples in certain critical ways. First, this commons was diffuse—neither the group of participants nor the common documents and ideas were clearly bounded or delineated. Second, there was not much enforcement of rules or norms, even within local groups. There were norms of behavior with respect to shared resources and various leaders and organizers encouraged "good" behavior, but we do not see formal rules across national boundaries or enforcement by agreed-on punishments. There were occasional instances of some kind of cheating; of a person who did not share; of a person who disliked or was angry with another; and perhaps many instances of shunning. Primarily, these arose in the later period of invention of aerial navigation when the stakes were higher because airplanes were real, there were real revenues and real military buyers, and the scope for a great reputation had expanded. Just as there was no strong paradigm for the scientific field of aeronautics or for the technical and industrial field of aviation, there was no strong social paradigm for the aeronautical commons.

The next sections lay out some of the history of the interactions by which these driven dreamers experimented, communicated, and slowly advanced the field of aeronautics toward modern airplane aviation. It is useful to think in four stages: an early stage in which individuals worked alone, a stage in which aeronautics became more unified as a field across the world, a stage of start-up industrialization and, finally, a stage when World War I military use drove the story. Knowledge was governed and managed differently in each of these stages as the issues faced by aeronautical science and practice changed.

II. Efforts toward "Aerial Navigation," 1809–1905: Overview

Modern airplanes can be traced conceptually back to George Cayley's early designs.[1] Cayley was an inventor, scientist, and public official. He conducted years of experiments, then published papers in 1809–1810 presenting original fixed-wing aircraft designs and discussing his experiments on them.[2] He stated that he expected an era of aerial navigation to come, which must have surprised readers. The rest of his text was empirical. The papers described his experiments on gliders, giving a dozen diagrams and reporting scores of measurements including comparisons to birds. Cayley referred implicitly to the work of predecessors who had published studies of ballistics and air pressure in scientific and engineering publications, including Isaac Newton, Giovanni Borelli, and Benjamin Robins; though Leonardo da Vinci's aeronautical designs were not known to him. Cayley's papers adopted an open science approach and were works of scientific engineering, not fantasy. By adopting this approach, Cayley set a pattern or precedent of treating the issue scientifically.

Cayley's scientific approach to aerial navigation garnered the attention of others partly because he had earned their respect in other scientific and technological endeavors. In the 1830s he was a founding member of the British Association for the Advancement of Science and became the first chairman of the Royal Polytechnic Institution, which taught practical science and technology. In the 1840s others finally started to use glider designs similar to his in their studies of flight. Cayley returned to experimentation periodically and launched gliders with a person on board in the 1850s.

Cayley seems to have reached out repeatedly for a network of colleagues with whom to develop aerial navigation. He published quickly and enthusiastically in response to publications on aviation and ballooning topics by others, analyzed technical topics with enthusiasm, and predicted a bright future for aerial navigation. He proposed government funding and a broad subscription to create an organization to focus on the topic. But for most of his life he was too far ahead of others to have valuable peer or network relations related to aircraft; indeed, his last works, which included many features of the modern airplane, were not even cited by others in the field, perhaps because they did not understand the issues (Gibbs-Smith 1962).

Cayley operated in an environment in which ballooning was recognized as a respectable leisure activity for the wealthy, as was the case throughout this period. Although there was not much technological overlap between balloons and the kites and gliders that eventually would lead to the airplane, balloon clubs were natural places for people interested in winged craft to find one another. In 1852 the first society that included

---

[1] This historical account is drawn from Meyer (2013) and many earlier works.

[2] Cayley (1809, 1810) in the *Journal of Natural Philosophy, Chemistry and the Arts*. They are analyzed in context by Gibbs-Smith (1962).

aerial navigation along with ballooning and meteorology in its mission, the Société Aérostatique et Météorologique de France, was established. Cayley lived long enough to republish some of his papers in translation in its brief-lived journal and to write a substantial original paper for that journal.[3] Thus, the networks and practices of aeronautics built on the social and institutional infrastructure of the balloonists.

During the century of these developments, a number of creative experimenters, including Alphonse Penaud, Louis Mouillard, Lawrence Hargrave, Samuel Langley, Otto Lilienthal, and Octave Chanute, tried to figure out how to control gliders in flight. These individuals came from a variety of backgrounds and locations and did not know one another prior to their experiments in this field. They published their studies in a scientific literature that was generally less formal than today's, and also in journals associated with ballooning.

To summarize some of their aeronautical contributions briefly: Penaud designed rubber-band-powered models and showed that an aircraft would be more stable if it had a tail that, like the main wings, brought lift. The tail helped the craft to maintain stability in the air. Mouillard studied birds and their flapping and soaring wings in detail. He tried to imagine and build wings that would match a human in the way that a bird's wings match its body. Hargrave ran many experiments, notably showing that box kites are more stable in gusty winds than flat kites are. Lilienthal experimented with wings and published detailed data about his experiments in a book in 1889. He then built gliders and flew them himself, leaping from a hill. These exploits drew crowds, and Lilienthal became a kind of celebrity. Langley published a book about a series of his scientific experiments investigating the lift experienced by flat wings with an airflow going past them. He went on to build a model aircraft that flew a substantial distance in the open air in the late 1890s. These were among the most important of hundreds of authors, experimenters, and theorists associated with aeronautics during this time.

III. Institutions Supporting an Aeronautical Commons

The technically focused and self-motivated individuals who worked on flight during the nineteenth century had to be willing to work alone, and often did. When possible they also joined into networks through clubs, societies, conversations, correspondence, exhibitions, conferences, and journals. Many of these activities were well documented, and my ongoing research involves building databases of them. Over time, these activities

---

[3] Gibbs-Smith (1962: 158–76). Cayley did not apparently feel a constraint against publishing original work on this subject in a French journal. Earlier in life he had suggested that aerial navigation was a suitable project for the British nation—its government or subscribers/investors in a particular project. It seems he cared about getting the project underway, not about who exactly would undertake it. He said aerial navigation would be good for spreading civilization generally and did not think there were any near-term military consequences.

changed what had been primarily an activity of individuals into a community activity supported by shared knowledge resources.

A. CLUBS, CONFERENCES, AND EXHIBITIONS

In the 1860s, societies oriented toward aeronautics appeared in London, Paris, and Berlin. Ballooning was popular in France. A dozen organizers of French ballooning societies, including photographer Gaspard-Félix Tournachon (known by the single pseudonym Nadar) and science fiction author Jules Verne, also took an active interest in heavier-than-air craft. Over time, clubs and societies associated with ballooning began to include more and more people interested in aerial navigation issues and in fixed-wing flying machines. Two especially relevant societies were the Aeronautical Society of Great Britain (founded in 1866) and the Aéro-Club de France (founded in 1898). Through their meetings, journals, and general legitimacy, these societies enabled experimenters to find one another and to build on one another's discoveries and designs. Available documents about the membership and activities of these societies suggest that interest in aerial navigation trended up over time, though there were periods of booming and flagging interest.

Conferences and exhibitions attracted curiosity and interest to the quest for flight. The number of meetings in which aeronautics played a significant part grew over time. There were at least four related conferences in the 1880s, six in the 1890s, then more than one a year after 1900.

B. PUBLICATIONS

There was no single central publication with all the latest in aeronautics globally. Then, as now, scientific publishing was partly a public good and partly a business. For example, Cayley's first key aerial navigation papers appeared in a relatively informal journal published by one man as a somewhat uncertain business enterprise. Papers in these journals were sometimes formally commented upon, but were not peer-reviewed in the modern sense.

There was a long-lasting public goods problem of collecting aeronautical findings and making them available. Without venues for collecting such findings, progress would have been considerably slower. By the 1880s, aeronautical societies in Paris, Berlin, and London published journals. These were central places to find hundreds of aeronautics articles, including accounts of voyages, celebrity balloonists, contests, and meetings and plans for future events. Many such articles were no more than two pages long. Aeronautics articles also appeared in general magazines, such as *Scientific American*, and occasionally in general scientific journals. A number were published as books or pamphlets. Many included diagrams or equations. Importantly, as discussed in the next subsection, several bibliographies appeared starting in the late 1880s to help those who wanted to survey the subject overall.

Figure 10.1 illustrates how the number of aeronautics-related articles, pamphlets, and books published annually grew over time.[4] (Please refer to "Figure 10.1 Count of Aeronautics-Related Publications Each Year. Source: Brockett's *Bibliography of Aeronautics* (1910)," located between pages 346 and 347.) This data comes from the books of aeronautical bibliography published by Smithsonian librarian Paul Brockett. The first volume of the *Bibliography of Aeronautics* in 1910 listed more than 13,000 publications related to aeronautics, including many that the Smithsonian did not itself hold.[5] Some of these publications were oriented toward the subject of ballooning; others to aerial navigation; others to meteorology and the ways birds and animals move. Throughout this period, journals started and disappeared. Paris-based *L'Aerophile*, founded in 1893, became the most central journal by 1900, according to historian Gibbs-Smith (1968: 75), and it is the publication with the most articles in the bibliography data.[6]

C. INFORMATION INTERMEDIARIES IN THE LATE NINETEENTH CENTURY

The publications of Langley, Lilienthal, and others were insightful, detailed, one-way transmissions about particular sets of experiments, rarely citing the work of others. The establishment of a commons dynamic was given a large boost by the activities of Octave Chanute. Chanute had become wealthy as a civil engineer and railroad manager. He retired to write about and experiment with flying machines. In 1893, during the World's Fair in Chicago, he helped to organize a major conference and exhibition on flying machines. He published many articles reporting his work and summarized the state of the art in an 1894 book with the optimistic title *Progress in Flying Machines*. By surveying flying machine activity broadly, Chanute served as a kind of technology information broker or moderator, identifying key persons and technologies and incorporating their work into his summary and his own designs and experiments.

---

[4] Such growth over time in a data set can be an artifact of backward-looking ("retrospective") data, since respondents remember recent events more easily than previous ones, so counts of remembered events are naturally increasing over time. I do not think that is the main reason for the growth in the data here. The Smithsonian was collecting and indexing its library for a long time, and it drew information from long-lasting serials and bibliographies that explicitly referred to previous work, which they would also find and include. The growth pattern of publications is similar to that of patents, which do not have the retrospective problem since each accepted patent is recorded officially in the category at the time—we draw samples from the complete set of accepted patents. Based on all this, I believe earlier aeronautical publications are well represented and the growth pattern is not biased.

[5] Brockett's 1910 bibliography has been scanned and made available online at archive.org by Cornell University and the University of Michigan. I have cleaned up the electronically scanned text and made its entries into a database. For most of these articles, the bibliography includes the title, authors, years of publication, journal of publication, language of the text, and country of publication. This database can be used to track the evolution of this technical literature, but it is necessary to exclude many entries for which these data elements are not complete.

[6] *L'Aerophile*'s name means literally lover-of-the-air. Discussing a version of this paper, law professor Joseph Scott Miller characterized the name as telling because the overall history was a love story—an epic, multigenerational love story. These men indeed loved flight, and dreamed to make flight work. For most, their love was unrequited.

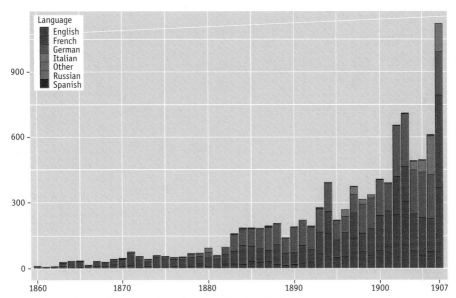

FIGURE 10.1 Count of Aeronautics-Related Publications Each Year.

Source: Brockett's *Bibliography of Aeronautics* (1910).

Progress in Flying Machines cited 190 experimenters from around the world. The frequency with which the book referred to various persons, a kind of citation count, provides a proxy measure of their significance and contribution according to Chanute's vision of the network of airplane creators. Penaud and the others listed above, whose work was later recognized as highly significant, are among those most often mentioned in the book. Chanute's description of the field in 1894 was broad and treated as definitive. Other bibliographies were published at around the same time. As a result, there was a general upturn in the size of the common pool of information and the number of publications about aerial navigation. The environment had changed. While Lilienthal's 1889 book and Langley's 1891 book cited almost no one else, successful experimenters in the mid-1890s could refer to a broad range of past experiments. Chanute's 1894 book is a convenient marker of the beginning of a unified global search for a better technology informed by a connected technical literature; a global pool of knowledge.

Chanute was a leader and moderator of the commons. He wrote repeatedly of his attempts to help others to behave as if they belonged to a community with a norm of reciprocal sharing. For example, an 1895 letter to Langley exhorted: "I propose to let you avail of whatever novelty and value there may be in my own models or ideas. I should expect in return a like frank access to your results."[7]

The Smithsonian Institution in Washington, D.C., was another important information intermediary during this period. It began collecting aeronautical studies in the 1880s, particularly after experimenter Samuel Langley became the Smithsonian's director in 1887 and brought his personal collection of publications there. The Smithsonian developed a large library of works on aeronautics and an associated bibliography. The Smithsonian library played a direct part in the history of the invention of the airplane when Wilbur Wright wrote them in 1899 to ask for any papers they had published on the subject and a list of other works. In reply, he received four pamphlets and a list of key books, which he obtained and used to begin his technical training in aeronautics.[8] The same library is the source for the publications data shown in Figure 10.1.

D. AERIAL NAVIGATION PATENTS

Thousands of ballooning and aerial navigation patents were taken out in the nineteenth century, particularly in France, Germany, Britain, and the United States. Colleagues and I have identified over 3000 relevant patents before 1910 so far, and thousands more were filed worldwide.[9] Perhaps surprisingly from a twenty-first-century perspective, patents

---

[7] Chanute to Langley, 1895, quoted by Short (2011: 208).

[8] Anderson (2002: 85–87).

[9] A dozen eclectic sources may be used to identify particular patents as relevant to aeronautics. The patents themselves are visible online from the U.S. Patent and Trademark Office, espacenet.com, and Google-patents. The data set is expanding and improving over time. To get the data, please contact the author. The national patent

appear to have played a role similar to that of scientific publications in the early aviation commons, rather than a role as intellectual property.

Ballooning was a small business at this time, and presumably many of the patents associated with ballooning functioned as traditional intellectual property. Aeronautical patents seem to have played a different role. While the specific experimental tools, devices, and machines that experimenters built to embody these patents were not shared in a commons, the patent texts and diagrams became part of a commons zone. They were shared and discussed in ways that suggest that experimenters were expected to copy and make use of them in their own projects. While there were occasional discussions of selling rights to a flying-machine (aeronautical) patent—by Henson and colleagues in 1842–1843, and by Lilienthal for his hang gliders, I have not found any cases of actual licensing or claims of infringement before 1906, when the basic Wright airplane patent was granted.

Why, then, did these inventors patent? I have not found clear statements of their reasons, though perhaps many patenters hoped they might eventually have a chance to license their inventions. I speculate that most patenters also hoped both to receive credit for and to enable others to use their inventions. Patenting also was normal engineering practice, which perhaps needed no special motivation.

There is a great overlap between the population of experimenters who published articles and those who patented. However, a number of the most prolific patentees did not publish any articles that were noted in Brockett's *Bibliography* and were not mentioned by Chanute or by subsequent airplane makers.[10] Few of their patents contributed technology directly to the development of the first airplanes. It is not clear why these inventors chose to patent, but not to publish. Perhaps some of them did not have a better, more central or more convenient way to make their work known, though patenting required paying fees and I am not aware that publication would have been unavailable to them. In any event, although these patentees did not generally engage in the published discussion as far as we can tell, I believe it is sensible to say that their contributions were de facto part of the commons, since they shared their designs at least through the patents and are not known to have made property claims. This is a speculative interpretation, however, since it is not clear that the work of these nonpublishing patentees ever was adopted by others.

IV. Analysis of This Informational Commons

A. GOALS, OBJECTIVES, AND DILEMMAS

Having now seen some key elements of the environment for studies of "aerial navigation" in the late nineteenth century, let us evaluate the period before the rise of the

---

systems were different from one another, but it is not difficult to combine the patent data into a single data set once it has been gathered.

[10] Meyer (2013: 124).

airplane industry—before 1908, that is—as a story of a commons. The basic goods and institutions—including experiments, publications, patents, clubs, and network interactions—were produced by the enthusiasm, resources, and ideas of the early experimenters themselves. These were self-motivated experimenters, interested in flight partly as a dream and partly as an intellectual challenge, so the fundamental source of provision was very much internal to them. During this period, participants who published designs or experimental results did not realistically expect to appropriate any financial rewards. Realistically, the best an experimenter could expect by way of payoffs from others was to be cited and respected and to contribute to the eventual achievement of the goal of controlled flight. Wilbur Wright's first letter on this subject, to the Smithsonian Institution in 1899, said that this was what he hoped for—to contribute a little to the future person who would achieve aerial navigation in a flying machine.

Users of a technological platform generally are better off if there are more users because of the positive network effects. A platform with more users has more developers, making it easier to use, providing add-ons, and enabling more people to train others to use it. This phenomenon has been studied in the contexts of user innovation (e.g., von Hippel 2006) and jambands, for example. Simcoe (2014) makes a similar point in the context of standards-setting organizations and other technological platforms, contrasting them explicitly with natural resource commons where there is a risk of overuse.[11] Indeed, while usage of a natural resource, such as a river, must be controlled, usage of a stream of information can replenish or improve the stream, as in this case of scientific experimentation.

Consistent with this observation, the institutions associated with the invention of aerial navigation were generally organized in such a way as to expand the use of the common expertise and designs. Expanding participation was interwoven with substantive progress. With successful experiments, there would be positive network effects from having many people engaged in the activity—more fun, more resources, more positive public perception, and positive feedback generating more progress toward the participants' technical goals. If instead the overall network did not produce valuable results, the enterprise would decline and perhaps collapse.[12] The following behaviors or situations represented threats to the aerial navigation enthusiasts' progress and their network:

- **Secrecy or inaccessibility**. If too many members kept their best findings secret, that would produce a failure-to-make-progress problem, because the others would

---

[11] This fundamental difference between natural-resource commons and informational commons is recognized in Ostrom & Hess (2007), Madison, Frischmann, & Strandburg (2010), Simcoe (2014), and Coriat (2013). Natural resources are subtractible, meanings use by A reduces what B can use, so institutions are designed to measure and constrain usage. Informational resources are generally nonrivalrous and have positive network effects so their commons seek more users.

[12] The same dynamics are faced by open source projects, many of which do not attract new participants beyond their founders. Similarly, technological standards need to accumulate a critical mass of users and developers. Simcoe (2014) discusses formal standards organizations in this context.

have too little to read, copy, and build upon. The problem would be extreme if the secret-holders were more successful than the commons participants; then the point of the commons would largely have evaporated. Accessibility was also a serious problem. Results were scattered throughout a wide variety of publications and written in different languages, making them difficult for interested parties to find and thus making it hard for the field to progress in a cumulative fashion.

- **Costly participation.** Difficulties and costs associated with accessing and learning from existing knowledge about aerial navigation would act as friction to slow down future contributions and associated progress.

- **Competition for one-of-a-kind opportunities.** One kind of "subtractibility" that did exist was that there were one-of-a-kind opportunities in this field, most notably the opportunity to make a working airplane for the first time. On a smaller scale, there were one-of-a-kind opportunities to make contributions that would help move the field toward that goal. In principle, competition for such opportunities could be a source of contention among the participants and a reason not to contribute to the commons. Many contributed anyway. Why? I think the central reasons was that most participants believed that they had little chance to reach that threshold and that only by working with other experts would they have any chance at all. Moreover, especially after bibliographies were compiled, publication provided a mechanism for documenting priority and establishing credit for contributions toward the shared goal.

- **Conflict or discouragement.** If members had unpleasant battles or broke into factions, participants would withdraw and the overall effort would again fail to make progress. Perhaps to avoid this problem, the phrasings in the texts of the era are often positive and encouraging—notably in Chanute's book *Progress in Flying Machines.*

- Dramatic technological **failure or humiliation.** All network efforts would be put at a disadvantage if flying machine efforts were put in a bad light, as dangerous or ridiculous. There was one event which seemed to have such an effect. The fatal crashes of glider-pilot Otto Lilienthal in 1896 and of his principal student, Percy Pilcher, in 1899 eliminated the men most likely to put a motor on a glider and fly a powered craft. They also put a damper on optimism about glider activity more broadly. Gibbs-Smith (1966: 54) writes that European aviation was "moribund" for six years after Lilienthal's death. The reaction is understandable. Lilienthal was an expert, hero, and celebrity. The crashes gave naysayers evidence of the difficulties and dangers of flight. As a result, progress slowed.[13]

- Dramatic technical **success**, too, would eventually represent a kind of threat to the network, since it would bring about competition and new economic forces

---

[13] As the databases on publications, patents, letters, and so forth improve, it may become possible to characterize that decline quantitatively.

and take away the motive of reaching for and contributing to that dramatic success. The participants do not seem to have written much about this possibility. They cared much more, I think, about making scientific and technical progress than about protecting the commons and its sharing norms.

B. SHARED RESOURCES

Published texts and patents were de facto shared resources. Published ideas were available for use in the search for functional flying machines, essentially without restriction, as long as they were able to locate and gain access to the texts. Relevant ideas were scattered among a variety of journals, books, and pamphlets, however. The lack of citations to one another's work in the publications of early experimenters suggests that the field evolved in a fairly disconnected manner in the early period. The bibliographies of aeronautical works that started appearing in the 1880s played an important role in turning a set of nominally public knowledge into a truly common pool of information. Chanute's 1894 survey book was particularly important in this regard. These published bibliographies constituted a layer of indexing and knowledge of the field on top of the underlying ideas, which provided interested experimenters with the *awareness* of, and the capacity to find, the spectrum of useful texts and people.

C. COMMUNITY MEMBERSHIP, OPENNESS, AND MOTIVATING VISIONS

A participant in the commons, here, was simply anyone who showed up at meetings or read, or especially published, articles containing new findings, discoveries, designs, or inventions. There were certainly hundreds, and perhaps thousands, of these self-selected participants. The community was global—participants were believers in natural laws, and that those laws would apply in Paris, London, or high in the air. They had an interest in those natural laws and debated exactly what they were.

There also seems to have been an inner core of participants who had been educated (or educated themselves) to be expert on natural science and acculturated to follow something like the norms of science (Merton 1973). Communications in the major French and British aviation societies had such a tone—that the participants were expert and high-minded and thought of society at large. In Chanute's letters and publications he also took this tone, as did those who wrote to him. I infer from reading these documents that certain leaders thought of themselves as an inner circle of wise experts and that others also thought of them that way. The desire to be part of, or gain access to, this inner circle of expert correspondents also would have motivated others to adhere to norms of sharing scientific and technical information and to make efforts to be seen as advancing the frontiers of scientific knowledge.[14]

---

[14] I am indebted to Katherine Strandburg for pointing this out.

Who did not participate? Though some of the aviation clubs had membership rules and certain club assets—such as equipment or access to landing fields—may have been available only to some members, I am not aware that those rules were used to exclude people with any regularity. We can, however, identify some aircraft designers who were doing relevant technical work but basically did not participate in the commons. Their stories illustrate some of the constraints on participation.

Clément Ader, a French engineer, oriented his attention to military purposes in the early 1890s, received funding from the military, and generally did not publish or widely share his aeronautical designs or findings. He appears not to have known of the best practices of others, either (Gibbs-Smith 1968). His story exemplifies the issue of secrecy mentioned above.

Chuhachi Ninomiya of Japan made elegant bird-like kites and model gliders and anticipated putting engines on them in the early 1890s, but does not appear to have known of the Western literature on the subject and never contributed to it. Richard Pearse of New Zealand, a poor farmer, knew something of the literature and made a powered but uncontrolled craft that flew in 1901–1903. He did not continue his experiments and did not become known to other aviation pioneers until much later. These stories illustrate the exclusive power of logistical issues such as geographical location, language, and education. Financial resources were another important constraint, given that aeronautical experimentation could be an expensive hobby. The communities and materials of aeronautical experimenters were thus open, but not universally accessible.

D. GOVERNANCE OF THE AVIATION KNOWLEDGE COMMONS

I have not found explicit rules about use and consumption of the flow of information in publications about aerial navigation in the nineteenth century. Rules or norms were implicit in behavior.

1. Leaders as Exemplars and Norm Entrepreneurs

Technological leaders of the network—such as Cayley, Chanute, Lilienthal, and many of the journal editors—encouraged norms of positivity, encouragement, and openness. Formation of the commons was powerfully influenced by particular characters such as these. Cayley was a published scientist, an inventor, and also a baronet and a politician. Chanute was a moderator, evangelist, and source of encouragement. By flying his hang gliders in front of crowds, Lilienthal brought a kind of charismatic celebrity and public legitimacy to the effort, and thus recruited new interested people to the subject. Langley was a recognized academic scientist who had bought in to the vision of aerial navigation. Generally these figures actively protected and nurtured the norms that would sustain and grow the commons.

Chanute was a central figure in encouraging norms of sharing and openness. Over and above the importance of his book in collecting the literature and putting aircraft builders in touch with one another, his many speeches and writings were "noteworthy for fostering a spirit of cooperation and encouraging a free exchange of ideas among the world's leading aeronautical experimenters." (Stoff 1997: iv). Chanute believed that cooperation and free exchange would make success possible. Chanute also engaged in the cooperative free exchange he advocated. He visited and corresponded with many of the key experimenters. His letters exemplified gracious writing and an encouraging tone. He sent over two hundred letters to the Wright brothers alone.[15] Simine Short, author of a biography of Chanute (Short 2011) located hundreds more addressed to other experimenters. Chanute routinely credited others for their wisdom and accomplishments, which must have been rewarding for them. Chanute's open approach facilitated his substantive role as a kind of information broker. Because of his open interactions with other experimenters, Chanute was well connected and knew approximately what there was to know in this incipient field.[16]

These leaders exemplified appealing norms and laid down a kind of "soft law" of expectations. They did not rely on systems of control or power in which experimenters were actually ensured of recognition for their accomplishments or punished for failing to recognize the accomplishments of others.[17]

2. Norms about Patenting

There was certainly no general norm against patenting in the aviation community. Indeed, most of the productive aviation experimenters obtained patents. I have found no explicit statement as to why they did so, since these patents seem never to have been enforced. It seems likely these experimenters used patents as a means to document their achievements and ensure credit for priority in making an invention. It also seems likely that there was a good faith norm that one should not sue one's colleague in the search for aerial navigation. Experimenters saw themselves as members of an isolated minority and perhaps felt some fraternal bond. Even after 1906, when the Wrights began enforcing their patent with lawsuits, their opponents responded by attempting to undermine their suits, but did not sue the Wrights for infringing earlier patents. (I do not know whether

---

[15] Most were published in McFarland (1953).

[16] Technology moderators and organizers with this frame of mind have helped other new technologies along, including steam engines, iron blast furnaces, steel rolling mills, personal computers, the World Wide Web, and open source software. For details, see Meyer (2003).

[17] Modern scientific and technological communication more explicitly keeps score. For example, participants and others can track the number of postings someone made to an open source project, or to Wikipedia. In software development these are sometimes explicitly visible to and shared with potential employers or funders. This evidence has led to a line of economic argument that open source software developers might be justified in giving their code away because of the career benefits; but in early aeronautics career benefits were unlikely and formal incentives were weak. In this environment, the drive for intrinsically satisfying progress is a more relevant incentive.

such suits would have been viable given the patents in force at the time.) Another reason that there were no infringement suits before 1906 may have been that there was so little market value in the patents during that period.

At least two of the major experimenters, Lawrence Hargrave and Alberto Santos-Dumont, decided not to file for patents. In the early 1890s, Hargrave took the view that the technology was entirely uncertain and that it would be counterproductive to dispute ownership of designs until after airplanes worked, at which time there would be credit and money to spare. He wrote: "Workers must root out the idea that by keeping the results of their labors to themselves a fortune will be assured to them. Patent fees are so much wasted money. The flying machine of the future will not be born fully fledged…Like everything else it must be evolved gradually. The first difficulty is to get a thing that will fly at all. When this is made, a full description should be published as an aid to others. Excellence of design and workmanship will always defy competition."[18] Hargrave expressed faith that experts in aerial navigation would have a durable advantage in any commercial market because of complementary assets—their skills, knowledge, experience, and past designs. Hargrave seemed to think that these complementary assets were so valuable that there would be no need for intellectual property claims. In the event, his prediction did not seem to come true; the very few holders of key patents came out well and the founders of some new companies made money, but the past experience of the aeronautical developers did not bring them any long-lasting competitive advantage in the later market. Hargrave expressed a kind of idealism that many early technologists share. Such idealism helps progress along and certainly sustains sharing in a commons.[19]

Santos-Dumont also eschewed patenting. In the earlier period when he made dirigibles, "Santos-Dumont did not believe in patents. He made the blueprints of his airships freely available to anyone who wanted them. He saw the flying machine as a chariot of peace, bringing estranged cultures in contact with one another so that they could get to know one another as people, thereby reducing the potential for hostilities" (Hoffman 2003). In 1906, Santos-Dumont flew the first controlled powered airplane in Europe. A couple of years later he became involved in the commercial manufacture of airplanes, but continued to avoid patenting: "They urged him to patent *Demoiselle*. He refused. It was his gift to humanity, he said, and he would rather end up in the poorhouse than charge others for the privilege of copying his invention and taking to the skies." (Hoffman 2003: 4, 274.)

The antipatent norm advocated by these researchers did not take hold, however. Instead, patents were obtained, but generally not enforced, during this period.

---

[18] As quoted in Chanute (1894: 218). Chanute expressed respect for this point of view, but he himself continued to apply for patents.

[19] Analogous norms come up in the open-science context and in free or open source software context—that a scientist who creates a database or a software developer has an obligation to make the data or source code available because it is a norm of good practice, with likely good outcomes for people overall, and if everyone would do it, the world would be a better place.

3. The Direct Imitation Norm

Fairly direct copying, even of patented designs, played an important role in the development of the first successful airplanes. Well-known and respected figures in the community seem to have engaged in it and it appears to have been a community norm.

For example, having surveyed the state of the field in his well-known book, Chanute synthesized a glider from earlier examples in an 1896 design, built jointly with Augustus Herring and experimented with in 1896–1897. The glider incorporated Penaud's design of the fuselage and a tail which had lift to help the craft stay longitudinally stable. From Lilienthal, Chanute drew the critical idea that a person had to ride on, or pilot, the glider to learn control in the air. The new glider's wings were arched ("cambered") like bird's wings and like the wings of Lilienthal's glider. Drawing from Hargrave's box kite designs, Chanute made a biplane arrangement, with two wings connected by a rigid frame. Two wings would bring more lift than one. In order to keep the stacked wings light, he copied from his own bridge-building experience what he called a Pratt truss—an angled arrangement of wires to hold the wings parallel all along their length. Chanute then patented the resulting design.[20]

Eventually, Chanute was contacted by Wilbur Wright. Wilbur and his brother Orville had tackled a number of entrepreneurial and technical projects together and were running a bicycle making and repair shop in the late 1890s when Wilbur took an interest in flying machines. Among other things, Wilbur thought about why Lilienthal had crashed and what might be done to avoid future crashes. In 1899, Wilbur Wright wrote the Smithsonian Institution for advice about what to read on the subject and then wrote to Chanute directly. In his very first letter to Chanute, on May 13, 1900, Wilbur stated explicitly that he intended to build on the work of Lilienthal and would use a design like Chanute's own:

> Assuming then that Lilienthal was correct... [Wilbur explained what he will do differently].... my object is to learn to what extent similar plans have been tested and found to be failures, and also to obtain such suggestions as your great knowledge and experience might enable you to give me. I make no secret of my plans for the reason that I believe no financial profit will accrue to the inventor of the first flying machine, and that only those who are willing to give as well as to receive suggestions can hope to link their names with the honor of its discovery. The problem is too great for one man alone and unaided to solve in secret..... The apparatus I intend to employ...is very similar to the "double-deck" machine with which the experiments of yourself and Mr. Herring were conducted in 1896–7.

---

[20] U.S. Patent no. 582,718 and British Patents nos. 13372, 13373, and 15221, all from 1897.

Chanute agreed quickly, replying back on May 17, 1900:

> I believe like yourself that no financial profit is to be expected from such investigations for a long while to come.

These phrasings give us some insight into the copying norms of the aviation commons at this time.

The Wrights made a series of aircraft similar to Chanute's, and Chanute and the Wrights exchanged hundreds of letters and telegrams. They exchanged both information and encouragement. The Wrights continued to follow open practices in the following years. Wilbur Wright accepted an invitation by Chanute to describe the brothers' experiments in an address to an engineering society. The brothers published articles about aeronautics and about their experiments. They invited visitors, including Chanute himself, to their beach camp at Kitty Hawk, North Carolina, where they performed their flight experiments. Kitty Hawk was hard to get to, but like Hargrave and Chanute, who had chosen beaches for their experiments, the Wrights wanted a strong wind from the ocean so a glider could get a lot of lift without having to travel fast, and they wanted any landings or crashes to be on a soft beach so the craft would survive and could be used again. We also know that the relationship between Chanute and the Wrights was specifically important to the Wrights' later invention of controllable powered aircraft.

Others copied the Wrights. Ferdinand Ferber, an aerial navigation experimenter in France, had worked with a glider designed along the lines of Lilienthal's. In 1902, Chanute sent Ferber copies of a lecture by Wilbur Wright and included illustrations of the Wright gliders. Ferber then abandoned the Lilienthal design and built a glider of the Wright type. After a talk by Chanute in Paris in 1903, further photographs and drawings of Wright craft were published in France and Wright-type craft were built by other important French experimenters, including Ernest Archdeacon and Robert Esnault-Pelterie. (Gibbs-Smith 1966: 54–56; Gibbs-Smith 1974). The Wright craft were directly imitated in Europe more than a year before the Wrights had flown their first airplane successfully and continued to be copied until they began enforcing their later patent.

Thus in key instances, imitation led to advances. The designs of Penaud, Lilienthal, and Hargrave were copied by Chanute; the Wrights copied Chanute's glider; then the Wright gliders were ancestors of most airplanes in Europe as well as the United States. It seems that the experimenters had a norm—even if a design had been patented, copying it was allowed.

4. Inculcation, Monitoring, and Enforcement

The exchange between Wright and Chanute quoted above shows one way sharing norms were nurtured. In writing that "only those who are willing to give as well as to receive suggestions can hope to link their names with the honor of its discovery," Wright may have stated his actual beliefs; we cannot know for certain, but it is certainly the case that he chose to make statements of belief in cooperative sharing in his uninvited first letter to an important man in the field. In essence, this letter was Wright's bid to become part of the inner circle of Chanute's correspondents. Chanute was a unique and authoritative figure, an important author on the subject of aeronautics and aviation, a person who knew the major experimenters, a man who had done major experimentation himself, and a person whose preferred norms of scientific interaction were known. Wright likely knew that Chanute propounded sharing norms and chose phrases that would harmonize with Chanute's preferred norms. In this way, Wright asserted his qualification for membership in an implicit community that Chanute was known to imagine and believe in. Wright acknowledged in advance his intellectual debt to Lilienthal and to Chanute himself in the design that he would put into practice.

In our language as analysts of commons: Chanute, a central figure in the community, had asserted that there was or should be an aviation commons. He had declared his preferred norms for this commons and invited interaction on the basis of those norms. Wright was interested in aircraft, but probably not as interested in the scientific commons as Chanute was.[21] Nonetheless, Wright stated his acceptance and belief in those norms in his request for Chanute's acceptance, support, and advice. Both parties understood that if he were going to make aircraft, Wilbur Wright would benefit from Chanute's experience, contacts, and mastery of the field, possibly including tacit knowledge that Wright would not get from public documents. Wilbur also wanted to be in good standing with the influential Chanute, apart from any specific information he might get.

The parties understood, I think, that intellectual property laws were not likely to limit Wright's future actions. There was no history of using the mechanisms of intellectual property law on designs and devices for aerial navigation. We do not know what either of these men actually believed about whether or not the imagined future inventor of the airplane would make a profit. The exchange suggests, however, that support for the copying norm may have been an important step in obtaining entry to the inner circle of correspondents in the field.

One important scientific norm is the norm against making exaggerated or dishonest claims, particularly as to priority of discovery. In science generally, punishments for violating this norm are rare, spotty, and slow, however. That also was the case among aviation experimenters. For example, while there were criticisms of the honesty of experimenters Gustave Whitehead and Augustus Herring, they were not actually punished very much so far as I can tell. Whitehead claimed to have flown a real airplane in 1901, but the evidence for this is weak, and it is not clear why, if he had done this, he would have stopped

---

[21] Chanute imagined a scientific society and acted as if it were there. In sociological language, it was an *imagined community* in his mind. He made it more real—reified it, and institutionalized it—by using his influence to declare it existed and by acting according to its norms. There were no sharp membership definitions identifying a single community of investigators of aerial navigation. The analysis of Macey (2010) helps frame socially constructed commons such as this one.

his experiments. Herring convinced engine expert Glenn Curtiss to cofound a company with him based partly on the false claim that Herring held aviation patents. Presumably, the reputations of Whitehead and Herring suffered in the 1900s, but any such punishment in the commons context was weak.

Clément Ader, the military engineer mentioned earlier, who did not participate in the commons, made claims after 1906, that he had flown in the air in the 1890s. His claims produced a great deal of conflict. A widespread nationalistic view developed among French aeronauts and aviators that Ader had flown first and been cheated of credit. Aviation historian Charles Gibbs-Smith carefully investigated Ader's experiments and claims and found convincing contemporaneous evidence that Ader did not make a controlled flight in the 1890s. The documented evidence of the time by Ader's funders in the French military did not report a controlled flight; the wings on his craft were too small and weak for controlled flight; his main experiments occurred along a circle not on a straight runway that would have enabled his craft to build up speed; the military eventually withdrew his funding; and Ader, who was independently wealthy and probably could have continued his experiments, ceased his aviation experiments at that time. Moreover, Ader's claims to have flown in the 1890s first appeared only after 1906, by which time others were known to have achieved flight (Gibbs-Smith 1968).

Examples such as these were rare, however, and the norm of giving proper credit appears to have functioned reasonably well. The viability of these norms probably was important to the success of the commons. In principle, potential contributors to a commons will refrain from contributing if they believe others are likely to profit from their contributions, while they themselves do not benefit. People are averse to being made "saps" or "suckers" (Gordon 2010). In the aeronautical context, potential participants had several reasons to expect not to be put in such a position, however. Potential participants could see that there were systems of documenting contributions through publications, patents, and other mechanisms of visibility. These mechanisms of recording priority of discovery made misappropriation of credit more difficult. They could observe that smart and wise people were contributing to the published literature and that there was no history of anyone misappropriating credit for such contributions. Because aeronautical knowledge wasn't very useful during this period, there may not have been particularly large incentives for misappropriation. As a result, though there were exceptions such as Ader, misappropriation of credit does not seem to have been a serious problem for which a serious punishment system was needed.

There was also a norm against secrecy. It was understood within the community that if an experimenter was keeping key findings secret he was implicitly choosing not to support progress by others. There were gentle criticisms of secrecy in some cases, for example by Chanute against Clément Ader. Since Ader was not an active participant in the commons, however, he was not particularly sensitive to any reputational sanctions.

These norms were sustained informally, as "soft law." I find little evidence that there were any formal processes to inculcate, monitor, or enforce them. It seems to me that it was possible to violate the norms nearly with impunity; a violator would not even lose access to open-minded figures such as Chanute. The significance of the norms, to my mind, is that they were strong enough to sustain the developments that in fact led to the invention of the airplane. The story of the Wrights is utterly interwoven with these developments. Without Chanute and the open scientific community of which he was a part, the invention of the airplane would have taken longer and it does not seem likely that the Wrights would have stuck with their research experimentation long enough to do it.

V. After Reaching the Goal of Controlled Flight

The aviation knowledge commons did not survive its own success in reaching the goal of controlled flight. As airplane manufacture became a new industry, assertions of exclusive rights increased. Eventually, the competing assertion of such rights posed serious problems for the supply of aircraft to the military during World War I. The U.S. government then stepped in to create a new kind of patent-based sharing regime—a patent pool.

A. JOCKEYING FOR POSITION IN THE NEW INDUSTRY

By late 1902, the Wrights had made important technological advances in control systems and in the shapes of wings and propellers. They behaved strategically, according to principles different from those of the commons. Crouch (1989: 296) puts it this way:

> The brothers had been among the most open members of the community prior to this time. The essentials of their system had been freely shared with Chanute and others. Their camp at Kitty Hawk had been thrown open to those men who they had every reason to believe were their closest rivals in the search for a flying machine. This pattern changed after fall 1902.
>
> The major factor leading to this change was the realization that they had invented the airplane. Before 1902 the Wrights had viewed themselves as contributors to a body of knowledge upon which eventual success would be based. The breakthroughs [of 1901 and 1902] had changed their attitude.

The environment changed after the Wrights obtained their patent, which was filed in 1903 and granted after much back and forth in 1906. According to one historian, the Wrights tried to avoid photographers, reporters, and other visitors from 1903 all the way up to 1908, when they felt ready to manufacture and sell airplanes and to enforce their patent (Tise 2009: 37–41). They started a U.S. company, attempted to get military contracts, and started to license to new companies in Europe. Their patent was interpreted broadly by the U.S. courts, and they enforced it vigorously, not only against manufacturers but also against aerial performers and exhibition companies.

Effectively, the Wrights switched away from the commons narrative entirely. They adopted another nineteenth-century narrative: the narrative of the great inventor (such as Thomas Edison or Alexander Graham Bell) who makes a breakthrough, then owns it through a patent, and manufactures it in quantity. That narrative incorporates a public purpose too: mass production makes new breakthroughs broadly available to ordinary people, and prices fall.

The Wrights' secrecy and tight hold on patent rights led to conflicts with Chanute, airplane maker Glenn Curtiss, and others. For narrative clarity it would be easy to personalize this story as a conflict between Chanute and the Wright brothers. But the conflict was intrinsic to the new situation; even if Chanute and the Wrights disappeared, the conflict would remain as the environment underlying the earlier commons changed. By 1908, multiple inventors had flown airplanes, both in Europe and in North America. The basic technological uncertainty had been resolved; specialists knew that airplanes would work and believed there would be a market for them and for related inventions and patent rights. The aviation commons would be under strain once a truly useful airplane was on the verge of appearing. Indeed, counts of aeronautical patents jumped in 1907, as shown in Figure 10.2, and went much higher after that. (Please refer to "Figure 10.2 Count of Aeronautics-Related Patents by Year, 1860–1907. Source: Author's sample, under development," located between pages 362 and 363). In this sample of patents, the annual flow had been increasing at a rate of 4–5 percent up to 1907, then in this start-up industrial period it spiked sharply at a much faster rate.

A wave of airplane companies appeared starting in 1908. Many were relatively open to outside visitors and to clubs, but they also were driven toward the industrial logic of competition, of conducting product-focused research and development, and of keeping certain findings and inventions secret. Though patents per se were old news, a new population of aeronautical experimenters entered the scene with different norms about sharing information. Intellectual property principles came to the field of flying machines.

After the modern airplane was invented and an industry of airplane makers was established, social activity centered around aviation shifted. There were huge and growing numbers of local aviation clubs and a growing number of aviation publications. The new clubs could focus on aviation as a real activity, using manufactured airplanes and parts, as well as on the long-standing goals of discovery and invention. The makers of airplanes were mostly manufacturers; the manufacturers had patents; and now the patents functioned as intellectual property.

The numbers of aviation-related conference and exhibitions grew, according to my data, from somewhat more than one a year from 1900 to 1907 to four in 1908, eleven in 1909, and thirty-five in 1910. An enormous ten-day exhibition near Los Angeles in January 1910 drew 250,000 attendees. In 1911 or 1912, after many people already had seen the flying machines for the first time, the numbers declined.

B. THE ENFORCED PATENT POOL

The Wrights sued exhibition companies that showed aircraft that infringed on their key 1906 patents, as well as Curtiss's manufacturing company. In the process, they lost public support, but they were generally successful in U.S. courts, which defined theirs as a "pioneering" patent, deserving of broad scope. European courts judged it to cover, more literally, a particular kind of control system in which the tips of the wings were controlled and were wired directly to the tail.

The legal battles over the Wright patents became more vicious, and the positions of the opposing parties more entrenched. Allies of Glenn Curtiss made extended efforts to undermine the Wright patent by claiming that it purported to cover designs that were prior art. Allies of the Wrights, allies of Curtiss, and others accumulated patents and used them to block one another's progress (Johnson 2004). The companies were investing more and more, but it was in a zero-sum battle, not resulting in significantly better aircraft from the U.S. industry.

The conflict occurred partly because the earlier commons was too weak and had not prepared the community to manage a situation in which participants held such an important patent. The information was never legally in a commons and the norm-based equilibrium was destabilized when the technological situation and paradigm changed. The Wrights were able to use their technological edge to get a legal monopoly on almost all aircraft, normal competitive industrial dynamics were stymied, and there were unproductive battles in the courts.

Experts disagree on whether this "patent thicket" and its associated hostility delayed the progress of either aviation technology or commercial aviation in the United States. (With future data, I hope to determine quantitatively whether there were significant differences between U.S. and European firms, publications, patents, and so forth after 1910.)

Eventually, the U.S. government intervened to end the patent battles. During World War I, the U.S. military intended to buy airplanes, but the largest airplane makers, associated with the Wrights and with Glenn Curtiss, were locked in patent battles. In 1917, top officials of the U.S. government pressured the major airplane makers to enter a cross-licensing agreement—a patent pool—and to create a joint organization called the Manufacturers Aircraft Association. According to the analysis of Bittlingmayer (1988), this government intervention enabled the airplane makers to overcome anticommons in which at least two companies—the Wright-Martin Company and the Curtiss Aeroplane Company—had mutually blocking patents. While this arrangement was a commons, it was not a return to the old style that was open to all; in this cross-licensing commons, only airplane companies were members, and the property in common was well defined (Johnson 2004).

VI. Conclusions

The inventive commons of the 1810–1910 period built up shared knowledge of discoveries and designs in the aeronautical field. Devoted, self-directed experimenters, in many countries were driven by their own enthusiasm to create aircraft, models, and other key inventions, which after a very long time brought forth actual airplanes that could carry passengers, thus addressing a long-time dream. By contrast hierarchical, directed research and development on this problem was rarely attempted and did not solve it. Technological uncertainty was very great, and so it was left to a public commons, with experimenters following open-source practices, to solve it.

There is ambiguity about what materials were in this implicitly shared scientific library, because for one thing the boundaries of useful aeronautics research were not clear. The point I emphasize is that the patterns of behavior which worked to advance the field were specifically advocated by a number of the most effective experimenters. They had a vision of what the open scientific enterprise could achieve, and very slowly, it achieved that vision. Many of the materials that made up the commons were not legally in the public domain and initially were not easy to access. It was important that some, notably Chanute, specialized in communications, sending hundreds of letters, advocating sharing, and writing a clear book that brought dispersed knowledge together in an accessible place. Chanute was an active evangelist. Others showed leadership in other ways: Hargrave published his experimental results without filing any patents; Langley demonstrated that a serious academic could study the subject of aerial navigation and flying machines; Lilienthal was a respectable engineer but also a charismatic demonstrator of gliders who got public attention. Thus there was a kind of space for potential entrants to see that the field of flying machines was a real one.

The commons space supported the copying by one innovator of another's design, which helped them to specialize and, in a way, standardize on a design. The actors in the commons space also did not attempt to enforce their patents in the early stage before the goal of aerial navigation was achieved. When an airplane finally was built, it was based mostly on designs which were in common view. Once an airplane was built, however, the commons was vulnerable to commercial pressures and patent enforcement. When patenting lead to stalemate, the government stepped in to impose a different kind of knowledge commons—a patent pool. Thus, a knowledge commons supported the creation of a new industry which has grown for a century afterward.

Acknowledgments

The author thanks Ceceile Kay Richter, Adam Hyland, Leo Zimmermann, John Russell Herbert, and Richard Meyer for valuable research assistance and Katherine Strandburg

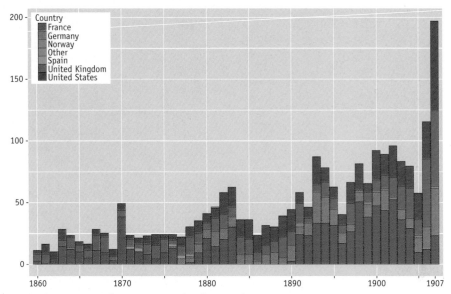

FIGURE 10.2 Count of Aeronautics-Related Patents by Year, 1860–1907.

Source: Author's sample, under development.

for valuable comments. A version of this chapter was presented at the Convening Cultural Commons workshop at NYU School of Law, September 23–24 2011. This chapter builds on Meyer (2013, forthcoming).

References

John D. Anderson, Jr. The Airplane: A History of Its Technology (Reston, VA: American Institute of Aeronautics and Astronautics 2002).

George Bittlingmayer, *Property Rights, Progress, and the Aircraft Patent Agreement*, 31 J. Law and Economics 227 (1988).

George Cayley, *On Aerial Navigation*, parts 1–3, J. Natural Philosophy, Chemistry, and the Arts (1809, 1810).

Octave Chanute, Progress in Flying Machines (New York: American Engineer and Railroad Journal Press 1894).

Benjamin Coriat, *From National-Resource Commons to Knowledge Commons: Common Traits and Differences*, paper presented at PROPICE conference (April 2013), http://www.mshparis-nord.fr/ANR-PROPICE/seminaire.html.

Tom D. Crouch, A Dream of Wings: Americans and the Airplane, 1875–1905 (2d ed. New York: Norton 1989).

Charles Gibbs-Smith, Sir George Cayley's Aeronautics, 1796–1855 (London: Her Majesty's Stationery Office 1962).

Charles Gibbs-Smith, The Invention of the Aeroplane, 1799–1909 (London: Faber & Faber 1966).

Charles Gibbs-Smith, Clément Ader—His Flight Claims and His Place in History (London: Science Museum 1968).

Charles Gibbs-Smith, The Rebirth of European Aviation: 1902–1908 (London: Her Majesty's Stationery Office 1974).

Wendy J. Gordon, *Response: Discipline and Nourish: On Constructing Commons*, 95 Cornell L. Rev. 733 (2010).

Paul Hoffman, Wings of Madness: Alberto Santos-Dumont and the Invention of Flight (New York: Theia/Hyperion 2003).

Herbert A. Johnson, *The Wright Patent Wars and Early American Aviation*, 69 J. Air Law and Commerce 21 (2004).

Gregg P. Macey, *Response: Cooperative Institutions in Cultural Commons*, 95 Cornell L. Rev. 757 (2010).

Michael J. Madison, Brett M. Frischmann, & Katherine J. Strandburg, *Constructing Commons in the Cultural Environment*, 95 Cornell L. Rev. 657 (2010).

Marvin W. McFarland ed., The Papers of Wilbur and Orville Wright, vol. 1 (New York: McGraw-Hill 2001) (originally published 1953).

Robert K. Merton, The Sociology of Science: Theoretical and Empirical Investigations (University of Chicago Press 1973).

Peter B. Meyer, *Episodes of Collective Invention* (U.S. Bureau of Labor Statistics Working Paper WP-368 2003), http://www.bls.gov/ore/abstract/ec/ec030050.htm.

Peter B. Meyer, *The Airplane as an Open-Source Invention*, 64 Revue économique 115 (2013).

Peter B. Meyer, *The Catapult of Riches: The Airplane as a Creative Macroinvention, in* Institutions, Innovation, and Industrialization: Essays in Economic History and Development (Avner Greif, Lynne Kiesling, & John Nye eds., Princeton University Press forthcoming).

Elinor Ostrom, Governing the Commons: The Evolution of Institutions for Collective Action (Cambridge University Press 1990).

Elinor Ostrom & Charlotte Hess, *A Framework for Analyzing the Knowledge Commons, in* Understanding Knowledge as a Commons: From Theory to Practice 41 (Charlotte Hess & Elinor Ostrom eds., MIT Press 2007).

Simine Short, Locomotive to Aeromotive: Octave Chanute and the Transportation Revolution (University of Illinois Press 2011).

Timothy Simcoe, *Governing the Anti-commons: The Institutional Logic of Standard Setting Organizations, in* Innovation Policy and the Economy, vol. 14 (Josh Lerner, & Scott Stern eds., University of Chicago Press 2014).

Joshua Stoff, *Introduction* to Octave Chanute, Progress in Flying Machines (Mineola, NY: Dover Publications 1997).

Larry E. Tise, Conquering the Sky (Palgrave Macmillan 2009).

Eric von Hippel, Democratizing Innovation (MIT Press 2006).

Wilbur Wright, *Angle of Incidence, in* The Published Papers of Orville and Wilbur Wright (Peter L. Jakab & Rick Young eds., Smithsonian Institution 2000) (originally published 1901).

11 Exchange Practices among Nineteenth-Century U.S. Newspaper Editors: Cooperation in Competition
Laura J. Murray*

I. Introduction

> Messrs. J. Munroe & Co. have published a second edition, revised, of *Slavery, by William E. Channing*. The same publishers have also issued, in a pamphlet form, *A Letter to the Hon Harrison G. Otis, Peleg Sprague, and Richard Fletcher.*
>
> This letter appeared originally in the Boston Courier. We believe it to be our property; although, from "the mere" form of publication, we are excluded from the privilege of copy-right. We believe our claim to it, *in morals*, though not *in law*, to be as good as that of Messrs Munroe & Co. to Dr. Channing's essays on *Slavery*. We should certainly not think of re-printing that work entire in another form, without at least, informing them of our intention beforehand, as well as sending them a copy with our "respects" after publication. (*Boston Daily Courier*, February 11, 1836)[1]

* Laura J. Murray is Professor of English and Cultural Studies at Queen's University, Canada. Her work in Indigenous Studies, American literary history, and advocacy informs her work on copyright law. With Samuel E. Trosow, she is author of *Canadian Copyright: A Citizen's Guide* (Between the Lines 2007, 2013). With S. Tina Piper and Kirsty Robertson, she is the author of *Putting Intellectual Property in Its Place: Rights Discourses, Creative Labor, and the Everyday* (Oxford University Press 2014).

[1] Article dated February 9. The following day, the paper issued a retraction: "the author of a 'Letter to the Hon. Harrison G. Otis, Peleg Sprague, and Richard Fletcher,' alluded to in our paper yesterday, informs me, by a note, that whatever impropriety there may have been for the publication of that Letter in the pamphlet form, is to be attributed solely to himself, and not to the publishers" (article dated February 10).

In this item, a newspaper editor identifies a difference between U.S. law's treatment of books, which could be copyrighted, and periodicals, which at this time could not be. The *Courier's* editor, J. T. Buckingham, is not happy. But note that while he is well aware of the distinction in the legal status of copying books and copying from newspapers, he is not exactly begging for the "privilege of copy-right." Rather, he asserts that a moral code operates at a more profound level, which entitles him to advance notice and thanks, and that is what he wants properly observed. In fact, he assumes toward his brother publishers in the book trade a tone of slightly patronizing correction. Book publishers, it seems, just do not know how to behave. Outside the newspaper community, the *Courier* editor implies, Messrs. J. Munroe & Co. blithely think that copyright is the only regulating mechanism for copying, and that anything outside its parameters is simply free for the taking.[2] But the newspaper editors know differently.

Indeed, in this period, an editorial paragraph or two of a newspaper might be generated "in-house," but apart from two pages or so of advertising, the rest of the four-page paper would be material clipped from other papers. In the absence of copyright, editors copied without clearance or payment. But to describe the situation in terms of lack in this way is contaminated by hindsight, and a misrepresentation of how editors thought of it at the time. Nonmonetized circulation was an affirmative practice, not compensatory.[3] It was the essence of an editor's job. While at first glance the daily newspaper of the 1830s and 1840s may appear to be awash with piracy, or at least laziness, in its large-scale reprinting of material from other papers, it was this very compendium that editors sought to craft and readers sought to read (McGill 2003). Copying was not anarchic. Immersed in each others' papers, editors developed and policed profession-specific expectations about appropriate and inappropriate copying of each others' material. They did not reprint material from books with impunity; one can find many references to the constraints of copyright[4]—except of course if the books were British or European, in which case they were fair game as not copyrighted in the United States. Neither did newspaper editors accept an outsider reprinting their material without due proprieties; in fact, the editor of the *Courier* asks for more of Messrs. Monroe & Co.—advance notice—than he would of his fellow newspaper editors. Newspaper exchange practices applied only

---

[2] In fact, "courtesy of the trade" practices did to some extent regulate the republication of U.K. books in the United States; see Everton (2011: 44–47), Groves (2007: 139–48).

[3] The present study stands alongside recent scholarship on creative activities "outside IP's domain" (see Fagundes (2012); Fauchart & von Hippel (2008); Loshin (2010); Oliar & Sprigman (2008); Raustiala & Sprigman (2006, 2009), and yet this framework sits somewhat awkwardly in my context. The "IP's negative space" line of research on the whole takes copyright regulation to be the bottom-line incentive for creative activity and seeks to identify, in its absence, its functional equivalents. This seems a bit backward; it represents an attempt to reinstall copyright at the center of discussions in which it played no part.

[4] For example, the editor of the *Angelica (NY) Reporter* writes: "We had laid aside the whole number of N.P. Willis' letters for publication, at our leisure, but we are informed that the proprietors of the *Mirror*, Willis' paper, have taken out a copy-right—and we do not consider them of so much value and importance as to give a dollar a piece for the *privilege* of publishing them" (August 27, 1845).

within the newspaper network. Participation in that network defined the profession, and determined the newspaper's aesthetic of aggregation; the form of both the industry and the newspaper as artifact emerged from exchange practices. Newspapers are one instance of intersecting but specific literary economies in the period. As Leon Jackson puts it, "authorship in the antebellum period…was transacted through a multitude of distinct economies, each of which had its own rules and reciprocities, its own exchange rituals and ethical strictures, and even, sometimes, its own currencies" (2008: 2).

Other dimensions of the material conditions of production—the mechanics of news-gathering, production, and transmission—dovetailed with exchange practices.[5] This was a time before the telegraph, before reporters; papers were printed on flatbed press by hand, filled with material delivered by hand or word of mouth; they were transported by newsboys in the cities and by train, steamship, and horses beyond. The main and often only reporter of a newspaper in this period was its editor. Other than what he learned by going down to the docks or the courthouse, by loitering in an oyster saloon with some well-informed cronies, or from occasional letters from correspondents, he only knew from reading other newspapers. Information from abroad came only when the ships did, which was at intervals, bearing news at least a month old (Mott 1941: 244). The eastern seaboard urban editor's job was to be the first to read the newspapers on those ships, and to digest their contents. He also read or at least sifted papers from New Orleans, Washington, Montreal, and all other North American points large and small, aiming to make a selection of their content most pleasing to his readership, and hence to his advertisers. The editors of all those papers did the same. A paper was thus only as good as its editor's exchange relations with other papers. Original material was generated not only with paying readers in mind, but to offer to other editors as currency of exchange.[6]

Essential to the functioning of the exchange system were postal regulations specifically designed to encourage the spread of print information (John 1995: ch. 2; Casper 2007). Newspapers traveled cheaply to subscribers, and they traveled free between editors. In 1830, 16 million newspapers passed through the U.S. mail, not including newspapers exchanged by editors; 1832 figures show newspapers to constitute 90 percent of the mails,

---

[5] Brauneis (2009) describes a related range of "technological and social conditions" that produced the "result" that "newspapers had little or no need for copyright" (343). While his account is detailed and compelling, my aim here is to emphasize that the practice or culture of editing was also determinative, not merely epiphenomenal. In terms of the everyday experience of editors, "doing one's job" was what made the newspaper what it was, and the consensus about what that job was came most immediately from doing it. It was not merely or directly a result of economic or political forces.

[6] See Nerone (2007: 233). Sometimes a sense of collaboration is explicit, as when the *Philadelphia North American* notes, "The following record of the state of the Thermometer at London and Philadelphia, for a week in March, we place in our journal, with the hope that the table may be enlarged by additions by our editorial friends in different parts of the United States. We shall feel particularly obliged if some of our exchange papers at New Orleans, St. Louis, Detroit, Troy, Boston and New York, will furnish the information as to their respective points" (May 21, 1839).

though only 1/9 of the revenue; in 1843, 7 million newspapers passed through the mail for free as exchanges.[7] As Henkin explains the principles,

> Letters were priced beyond the reach of most Americans, not because technological developments had yet to lower the costs of transmitting the mail, but because letters were expected to finance the main business of the post. From its creation, the U.S. Post Office was committed principally to facilitating the wide circulation of political news, allowing an informed citizenry to live far from the metropolitan centers of government while remaining active in its affairs. Individual letter-writers, typically merchants, were depended upon to absorb the costs of this political commitment by subsidizing an extremely low rate on newspapers. (2006: 21)[8]

To provide what we now call "access" to information reasonably easily in all regions, a postal subsidy was offered on both the front and back end of newspaper production: exchange and circulation. It worked. Nord attests that

> [a]t the time of Tocqueville's visit in the early 1830s, the United States had some nine hundred newspapers, about twice as many as Great Britain, its nearest rival. By 1840 the census counted 1631 papers; by 1850 the figure reached 2,526, with a total annual circulation of nearly half a billion copies. The decades from 1820 to 1850 might be called the take-off stage for daily newspapers. From a handful of 24 dailies in 1820 the daily newspaper industry grew to 138 papers in 1840 and to 254 in 1850. (2001: 94)

This was not merely some kind of "natural" development. Regulation in the postal domain prioritizing mass communication over individual communication fostered the emergence of both a profession and a profitable industry.[9]

---

[7] Henkin (2006: 43); Mott (1941: 194); post office figures quoted in "Post Office Statistics," VERMONT PHOENIX (Brattleboro), February 2, 1844.

[8] See also Casper (2007).

[9] John makes a specific claim about the growth of the rural press: "By the 1820s, these [exchange] newspapers sometimes made up between one-third and one-half of the total weight of the mail. By the 1840s, every newspaper published in the United States received free of charge an average of 4,300 different exchange newspapers every year. No less important, the policy provided a major boost for what would quickly come to be known as the 'country press.' By guaranteeing printers located throughout the United States regular access to the information that they needed to fill their pages, it ended the monopoly that had formerly been enjoyed by printers located in close physical proximity to the seat of power, and in this way created the 'country editor' as an occupational class" (1995: 37). In his authoritative account of the early history of U.S. postal policy, John also observes that free transmission of exchange papers actually antedated the Revolution: "Long before the establishment of the American postal system, postal officers had encouraged postriders to permit printers to exchange one copy of their newspaper with fellow printers and in this way to provide their journalistic peers with the nonlocal information on which they relied to fill their pages" (1995: 32). So later policy followed existing practice.

But what about copyright? McGill has shown how "for much of this period, copyright laws were unenforced and technically unenforceable; they played more of a shadow role than a central part in the growth and regulation of the market for printed materials" (2007: 159). For periodicals, copyright was an even more marginal factor than for books, and among periodicals, the daily newspapers seemed furthest from its reach. The legal rationale for copyright's absence from the periodical realm was only rarely articulated in the period. In *Clayton v. Stone* (1829),[10] Justice Smith Thompson lumped newspapers in with the "price current" at issue in the case (a conversion table for values of bills issued by various banks) as he considered Congress's constitutional responsibility "to promote the progress of science":

> The term science cannot, with any propriety, be applied to a work of so fluctuating and fugitive form as that of a newspaper or pricecurrent, the subject-matter of which is daily changing, and is of more temporary use. Although great praise may be due to the plaintiffs for their industry and enterprise in publishing this paper, yet the law does not contemplate their being rewarded in this way; it must seek patronage and protection from its utility to the public and not as a work of science. The title of the act of congress is for the encouragement of learning, and was not intended for the encouragement of mere industry, unconnected with learning and the sciences.

This reasoning would seem to apply to a price current more than it would a newspaper where originality, selection, and arrangement are factors—although both types of publication are ephemeral as Thompson observes. Brauneis (2009) has contextualized *Clayton* in a group of early cases concerning facts and charts, and later discussions of labor and originality as grounds of copyright, but acknowledges that "there was never any chance to find out more about the impact of *Clayton* on daily newspapers, because, in spite of the dominance of nonfiction works in American copyright litigation over the next fifty years, no reported case concerned a newspaper" (339).[11] Editors may or may not have known about *Clayton*; I have seen no mention of it in the newspapers I have surveyed. They knew that it was impossible as a practical matter to register copyright given the formalities required. Copyright registration required a fee, and a copy of the work had to be deposited in the district court; obviously, this was incompatible with the continuous cycle of daily or weekly periodicals.[12] But in the hundreds of big city and small town dailies I have perused, I have come across no instance of an editor chafing against this. In

---

[10] 5 F. Cas. 999 (C.C.S.D.N.Y. 1829).

[11] It is perhaps worth noting that constitutional craftsman Thomas Jefferson did not think of newspapers as "mere industry"; Jefferson sought the abolition of postage on newspapers "to facilitate the progress of information," a phrase if not identical to "the progress of science," certainly analogous to it. See Kielbowicz (1989: 36).

[12] McGill (2007: 160). Homestead (2005) notes that the 1834 *Wheaton v. Peters* case (33 U.S. 591) asserted the necessity of following all formalities to the letter (156). It was not until the 1880s that some newspapers found it practicable to copyright some of their articles; see Slauter (2014).

terms of government policy affecting their trade, editors complained plenty about late delivery of the mail, but never about absence of copyright protection. Copyright was simply not perceived as pertinent to newspapers at this time.[13]

As a case study of social practices of cultural production, this chapter shows how essential recirculated material was to newspapers of this period, and it articulates, from the face of the papers, editors' expectations about appropriate ways to circulate materials. Business papers and correspondence amongst editors do not survive, and besides, because of the differential postal rates for papers and letters, editors tended to communicate through their papers rather than through private correspondence; other than balls and brawls shared by editors in the same city,[14] relationships and controversies played out where we can still see them. A description of typical practices can allow us to view disputes over attribution not as signs of crisis, but as rituals of maintenance and adjustment. The whole culture of exchanges worked on its own logic, asserting proprietary or quasi-proprietary rights over both more and less than copyright and therefore aligning well with the constructed information and knowledge commons frameworks with which this book is concerned. The study of this early period provides a baseline for understanding later efforts to invoke intellectual property (IP) law as circumstances in the industry changed.

Mid-nineteenth-century journalism may be characterized as a case of constructed cultural commons of the sort framed by the initial chapter of this volume: structured or managed sharing of knowledge and intellectual content within a community of practice (Madison, Frischmann, & Strandburg 2010). This particular approach to commons is more appropriate for the present study than other treatments of commons[15] in that it does not position commons as essentially antithetical to or subversive of the market. Newspapers were businesses and, within the same region at least, in competition with each other. While they did not refrain from boasting about their crucial role in democracy, it is difficult to locate any idealism about custodianship of shared resources. Newspapers were commercial in their content (the prevalence of advertisements), their primary address (to men of commerce), their business model, and their political vision. Thus if we are to understand shared newspaper articles or subsidized postage as a kind of commons, we are speaking of commons in Yochai Benkler's sense of a "fundamental element of well-functioning market economy" rather than as an alternative to that market

---

[13] Magazine editors showed a little more interest in copyright. Slauter (2014) discusses Noah Webster's assertion of copyright in his *American Magazine* (4–5). Melissa Homestead (2005) shows how slightly later, in the 1850s, the *Musical World* used the threat of copyright proceedings to ensure proper credit for reproduction of Fanny Fern's work, rather than permission or remuneration (162).

[14] Even the brawls often served as material; James Bennett, the editor of the *Herald*, described his caning at the hands of fellow editor James Watson Webb with great gusto (NEW YORK HERALD, Jan. 20, 1836; see also Mindich 1998: ch. 1).

[15] See Bollier (2003); Hyde (1979).

economy.[16] Behaviors and priorities associated with commercial markets were actually imbricated with commons.

Exchange practices did not come to an end until the private telegraph replaced the public mail as the fastest conveyance for news, and even then they lingered, because the telegraph was expensive and used at first only for materials whose value depended on rapid transmission. Later the telegraph became the tool of the wire services, which were followed by the syndicates in the business of packaging and selling news, an altogether different business model than the exchanges. However, news collecting remains a collective enterprise, and some aspects of journalism's early practices survive in the statutory provision of fair use and the more fraught legal concept of "hot news." Commons, in other words, remains a relevant framework for considering modern journalism. In the last section of the chapter I show that the off-kilter relationship between copyright law on one hand and the news industry's ideas about appropriation and misappropriation on the other continues. Considering that journalism is a major part of the "copyright industry," this is surely rather remarkable, and evidence that copyright's categories and provisions are not self-evident or universal in any way.

The following sections lay out, first, the nature of recirculation of newspaper materials; and second, the attribution practices that accompanied this. In the last section, I discuss the later development and present-day mobilization of the concepts of fair use and hot news.

II. Scissors and Paste

> This world we live in is a world of wonders: but of the wonders it contains, the most wonderful of all is, the unaccountable impudence of some of its inhabitants! An editor of a newspaper talking about plagiarisms! Just conceive it! and say can there possibly be anything more supremely ridiculous? A man, whose scissors are in his hand; a man who lives by cutting and cabbaging, here a column, and there a paragraph; here an anecdote and there an advertisement; here a hairbreadth escape, and there a laughable adventure; here strange news, and there mysterious accidents ... a man who lives so entirely on others, extracting compiling, compiling, condensing and gathering fragments here and there, to fill up his daily or weekly sheet; for such a man to sit down and coolly talk about plagiarism—Good Heavens! I can think of nothing like it, unless it be sir John Falstaff reading a lecture on temperance.

---

[16] Benkler, this volume, ch. 3, distinguishes between a commons and a "common property regime," where the latter may be limited to a specific group of participants; this is probably the more appropriate term for the newspaper exchanges, although my contexts are not bureaucratized or contractually formalized like most of those he discusses—even though he does concede that "[a] overly-regulated 'commons' will likely fail of its core purpose, because it will undermine the very freedom of action for which commons are useful." Benkler contends that "without ubiquitous, sustained, open commons the global networked information economy would come to a standstill"—and while his emphasis is on the digital information economy, that would have been the case equally in the nineteenth century.

In this piece from the *Port Huron Representative*, reprinted with attribution by the *Washington County Post* (Salem, NY) on August 15, 1839, the lineaments of newspaper editorial practice in the Jacksonian period are clearly sketched. The task of the editor was to compile materials from other papers to create a tableau of current events and a pleasing miscellany. Offering a recipe to keep paste from getting moldy, one editor observes that "next to scissors paste is an invaluable editorial assistant" (*Ohio Statesman* [Columbus], August 25, 1847). The editor of the *New Orleans Times Picayune*, complaining that his coworkers were all away and he was left with the flu to run the operation, laments, "we are so deaf that we cannot hear the compositors call for copy but through an ear-trumpet, so hoarse that we cannot call for paste, and so bad with the rheumatism that we cannot use the scissors" (July 19, 1843). Copied material included everything from congressional proceedings and election returns, political prospects and military affairs, to murders, poems, and news of strawberry socials and large pumpkins. Some papers had section headings such as "Variety," "News Gleanings," "By Last Night's Mails," "Selected Miscellany," and "Spirit of the Press,"[17] but such designations were largely superfluous in an environment where borrowed material may even have included advertisements.[18] This was not just "filler." People read papers to find out about events beyond their locality, so they actively sought exchange materials. Thus in 1838, the *New Hampshire Patriot and State Gazette* (Concord) actually apologized for allowing legislative news to take over the paper: "The Legislature will adjourn on Tuesday. In order to present a full report of the proceedings we have necessarily excluded almost every thing else, as well original articles as interesting selections with which our exchange papers are filled. After this week we shall be able to furnish the usual variety" (July 2). And the author of the epigraph to this section even offers, later in the same piece, a broad sociophilosophical justification for the paste-and-scissors approach to editing: "This doctrine of never borrowing, of saying nothing but what you yourself originated, is cruel in the extreme. It would condemn most men to perpetual silence. In the halls of legislation, in the courts of law, in drawing rooms, and at dinner parties, what a long, sad, solemn stillness there would be!"

Despite the ubiquity of borrowed materials, it seems to have been generally expected that editorials, brief as they were, would be generated in-house—that the editor's voice would speak his own words. The *Nashville Banner* outlined the pertinent distinctions in 1838:

The editor of the *Columbia Democrat* stoutly maintains that as far as *writing* is concerned, he edits all the editorials in his sheet. We now [*sic*] not what he means by

---

[17] See the YORKVILLE COMPILER ("Variety," March 26, 1841); the CHERRY VALLEY GAZETTE ("News Gleanings," January 1, 1857); the EVENING TATTLER ("Selected Miscellany," January 25, 1840); and the DAILY NATIONAL INTELLIGENCER (Washington, D.C.), with lengthy extracts from the *Albany Evening Journal, Western Citizen*, and other papers ("Spirit of the Press," Sept. 5, 1835).

[18] Sometimes advertisements included requests for reprinting. For example, the *Milwaukee Sentinel* prints a "Stop thief" with a note at the bottom: "exchange papers please copy" (June 12, 1845).

this, unless he calls *copying* editing. We presume such to be his meaning, and we doubt not the thing is as he says, namely, that as far as *writing* the editorials is concerned, he edits his own paper. *Inditing* seems to be another business altogether, with this *editor of writing*.[19]

When it came to editorials, borrowing was understood not as the end but as the beginning; it generated writing or "inditing" in its turn. Editors proceeded by "examining the contents of our exchange papers, inditing such paragraphs as they suggested to us" (*Milwaukee Sentinel*, March 11, 1845). Thus, when in spring 1835 the editor of the *Mobile Register* found the postal service remiss in its service, he took its agents to task with a full sense of entitlement:

> If they will not give us mails, out of which to make a paper, they must look to figure in a paragraph, for the want of a better subjects. We have for two months, rung all the changes upon mail failures, till we are tired of looking for new phrases of complaint, and shall now be obliged to give it up from mere barrenness of invention. When that end is fairly reached, and there is no change for the better, we shall be obliged to leave a column or two blank. (March 13; reprinted in the *New Orleans Courier*, March 18)

An editor could not be expected to "perpetrate a paragraph" (*St. Augustine News*, November 3, 1838) without raw material.[20]

But this was not just about access to facts. It was very important for an editor to perform connection in order to perform his own role as a facilitator and interpreter of civil and political dialogue. Consider the verbs in the *Freeman's Journal* (Cooperstown, NY): "We learn from the Columbian (Ct.) Register that on the 8th inst., as the Albany and Springfield stage was passing from Chatham to Stockbridge, in Massachusetts, a small bridge broke in, which threw the driver from his seat and nearly killed him.... We learn that a laborer on the Genessee Valley Canal, was killed at the Portage Tunnel....A correspondent of the Yarmouth Register informs that paper that.... The Buffalo Commercial Advertiser mentions the arrest of Hollis A. Sampson, for bigamy.... The Hamilton, U.C. Gazette states that.... The Geneva Courier says...." (July 29, 1839). The editor sits in one place "learning," and passes his collected knowledge on to readers. He has also used a letter received by someone in the village to

---

[19] Actually this paragraph is taken from the *St. Augustine News* (November 17, 1838). The *News* uses this paragraph from the *Nashville Banner* to cast doubt on the originality of the editorial material of its sister St. Augustine paper, the *Herald*, by suggesting they in turn copy the paragraph "for the amusement of your readers."

[20] The *Auburn (NY) Daily News* states, "There seems to be but little news, of consequence, in any of the papers by today's mail. It's hard catering for news when there is none" (May 18, 1838).

confirm and amplify reports coming via the *Sunday Morning News* of labor unrest in Jamaica. He has his finger on the pulse.[21]

Furthermore, editors staged their personae and their politics, what we would now call the "brand" of their paper or even their city or state, by the way in which they commented on the opinions and writings of other editors. The editor who announces "The following article…meets our views and we agree to the conclusions…and therefore we give the article to our readers" (*Washington County Post* [Salem, NY], August 15, 1839) is only putting into words what is implied in many other acts of reprinting. Whig editors reprinted and praised other Whig editors; Democratic editors reprinted and praised Democratic editors.[22] The *Richmond Compiler* (a significant title in itself) uses a comment from the *Augusta Chronicle* to indulge in a little Virginia boosterism: "The Correspondent of the Augusta Chronicle refers to a bill for preventing frauds at elections, which was lost, in the Georgia Legislature.…The writer says that such a provision, it is said, exists in the laws of Alabama, and some other of the States; 'but,' he concludes very justly, 'no system is so correct, and so promotive of the manly virtues of independence, as the *viva voce* plan of Virginia'" (December 29, 1840). Despite many such instances of mutually congratulatory comments, particularly between papers of the same partisan stripe or same region, a snider tone predominated. Party-baiting was common. In 1845, the *Mohawk Courier* in Upstate New York teased the *Herkimer Democrat*, which has "suddenly fallen in love with the principles and opinions promulgated by the Goshen Independent Republican," suggesting that the Herkimer paper "find a place in its columns" for an extract from that Goshen paper that clashes with Democratic views (March 20). The New York City editors were constantly at each other's throats with insinuations and threats. Comments, critiques, and vile insults between editors in fact generated a considerable part of the papers' energy. They dramatized a masculine game of connection, interaction, and verification, and gave the reader the opportunity to watch the show from the sidelines.[23] Thus, practices that derived from practical necessity fostered key generic and aesthetic qualities of the newspaper.

---

[21] To perform the role of window to the world even more materially, some urban newspapers offered reading rooms where subscribers could consult exchange papers directly (BOSTON EMANCIPATOR AND WEEKLY CHRONICLE, July 16, 1845). The *New-Hampshire Gazette* (Portsmouth) also states, "Subscribers to the Gazette, who are not in arrears, and who regularly pay their subscription to this paper, may have the privilege of reading our exchange papers, at our counting room, free of expense. Our exchange probably comprises the most extensive and valuable in the place. The room will be opened during the hours of business" (July 3, 1838).

[22] Pasley (2001) dates the first party-inflected exchange practices to the 1790s: "Each editor began to focus on selecting materials that expressed his own views and helped promote his own political goals, arranging the newspapers he received along a political spectrum into which he could also insert himself. Having identified some journals as political opponents, editors looked through them for outrageous remarks to score points against, arguments to answer, and misinformation to correct" (173).

[23] The fact that readers consumed the papers simultaneously adds to the collective experience. See Anderson (1983: 29) on the "mass ceremony" of simultaneous newspaper reading; Henkin takes this up in his superb study of urban reading (1999: 122).

Counterintuitively perhaps, even attacks between editors could have the effect of bolstering the credibility of the whole system or profession. Editors often made a point of questioning reports from other editors, or making fun of what would later be called "broken telephone" qualities of exchanges, but in so doing they performed, publicly, a kind of consolidation and validation of the profession as a whole (perhaps much as newspaper corrections function even today). The *National Intelligencer* (Washington, D.C.) complained in 1835 that

> [t]he editor of the Argus and his subalterns concoct lies for the columns of that dirty sheet, and the Globe gives them farther currency by extracting them, and adding its characteristic comments. These comments rebound back again in to the Argus, and so the game is kept up; the victim of it, in the mean time, being similarly situated with a man who is placed midway between two enraged skunks. (September 25)

The *New York Spectator* observes that while "Rumor says that Mr. Berrien has resigned the office of Attorney General," "it wants official confirmation" (June 7, 1831). Reports from the uprising in Poland in 1831 reprinted and cross-referenced as many European sources as possible, admitting quite openly how difficult it was to discern the truth.[24] And the *Auburn (NY) Daily News* in 1838 publicly rejected its sources: "We see a paragraph going the rounds of the papers, that Lord Durham Governor of Canada, has demanded the delivery of those concerned in the burning of the Sir Robert Peel Steamboat, and if not delivered up to the British authorities, in Canada, he will declare war against the United States. That's a very likely story to circulate! we don't believe a word of it" (June 25).[25] Even if they attack or criticize specific other newspaper sources, these kinds of remarks make claims both about the vitality of the network and its verification mechanisms.

Before an editor could play such a monitoring role, of course, he had to have papers from which to quote. Despite the fact that postage for exchanged papers was free, it cost money to print each one, and thus editors did not scatter them randomly. They only sent them to editors who offered valuable content in return.[26] And one's exchange list was clearly an indicator of status and affiliation. Thus, when the *New York Weekly Whig* celebrated its first year of publication in 1839, it prepared an advertisement trumpeting, along with its commitment to "expose corruption, speculation, Jacobinism, disorganization, and demagoguism in high places, with no mealy-mouthed phraseology or craven

---

[24] See, for example, the PHILADELPHIA INQUIRER, June 9, 1831.

[25] See also the article entitled "Unicorns," about how unicorns don't exist even though "the above paragraph has been going the rounds" (RHODE-ISLAND AMERICAN (Providence), June 14, 1831).

[26] The *Georgia Telegraph* (Macon) reports that "[o]ut of the 30,000 sheets struck off" per week by Georgia newspapers, "*one-tenth* are exchange papers"—this in addition to those given way "to clerks, sheriffs, correspondents...beggars and borrowers," those left dead in the post office, and those for which subscribers fail to pay (February 12, 1839).

spirit," the fact that "[t]he News of the Day will be carefully made up from an ample list of Exchanges in this country and in Europe, aided by a valuable Foreign Correspondence." Its exchange list was what established its credibility and range of material. And how did it circulate this advertisement? It appended a note to it: "All Publishers of Country newspapers who will insert the above Prospectus three times, shall be entitled to an exchange with us for one year. Our exchanges with country papers will necessarily be limited to those who may find it convenient to do so." Accordingly, the *Geneva (NY) Courier* reprinted the notice (April 16, 1839).

The *Weekly Whig* sought rural subscribers; the rural papers sought urban material; the exchange worked. Sometimes too, urban editors appreciated local color from the small-town papers. A paper in Ravenna, Ohio, reported that a city editor had "urged upon the country press to adopt a home column, and to notice even minute affairs, asserting that things, often regarded as too trifling for notice, would be read with much interest, and would furnish topics or extracts for the daily papers," noting that "a re-hash of news and miscellaneous reading were comparatively valueless as exchanges" (*Portage County Democrat*, April 19, 1854). Nonetheless, there was friction. In late summer 1839, the *Herkimer (NY) Journal* inveighed against competition from urban papers: "'Brother Jonathan' is one of that numerous and pestilent class of papers, of the hotchpotch, Johnny-cake-ginger-bread order, put forth with almost no expense by the daily publishers in the cities, to the constant detriment and frequent ruin of country publishers" (August 15).[27] Printing weeklies from standing type accumulated over the week's run of dailies, featuring a great deal of noncopyright European fiction, and benefiting from very low postal rates, the urban papers went head to head with rural and small-town papers with higher production costs. Small-town editors argued that the local press was also an economic and social good. Thus the exchange system, based on a certain homogenization of national and local needs, was not without its tensions, and over the 1840s these produced considerable controversy over postal rates.[28]

III. Credit and Cabbaging

Having established the fact of cutting and pasting, and some of its causes and effects, I now wish to turn to the question of attribution. Even if recirculation of material between newspapers did not require permission or payment, it was not exactly a free-for-all; editors often expected attribution. Modes and degrees of attribution were quite complex, however. No manual or "best practices" document existed. Editors learned appropriate behavior just as I did—by reading papers. Perusing them, one can see that jokes

---

[27] See also the WASHINGTON COUNTY POST (Salem, NY), August 15, 1839.

[28] One proposal to level the playing field was to eliminate postage for newspapers within the county in which they were printed. See "New Postage Regulations," DAILY MADISONIAN (Washington, D.C.), February 5, 1844.

or little squibs on "amazing facts" from history or natural science were often copied without indication of source. Indeed, the proximate source would be rather insignificant information as these kinds of items circled around and around. Poems were marked "For the Sun" or "For the Patriot" if they were original; if not so marked, they could be taken to come from another periodical, which was sometimes named and sometimes not. Literary materials from European periodicals usually displayed the source above the text. Small news items, on the other hand, were often tracked by a citation at the end of the text: "—*Quincy Patriot*," "—*Rochester Daily Whig*," or "[Eve. Star," "[Pensacola Gaz.," "[N.E. Farmer." Other times, they were simply sourced to "Exchange paper" or "Western paper."[29] Sometimes the two practices were mixed:

> "*California is Coming*."—Under this head, the United States Journal says, "we see by our exchange papers that the citizens of California have organized an independent government similar to that of Texas and the United States." (*Republican Farmer* [Bridgeport, CT], August 5, 1845)

Citing exchange papers in general might seem rather pointless, but its purpose emerges in its performativity. An editor who read so many papers he could hardly remember where he heard what was playing the role, already well-established, of the harried but well-informed figure at the center of the action. And if several exchange papers reported the same fact, the fact gained authority. Thus, the apparently empty "exchange papers" citation is further evidence of a self-conscious and affirmative practice of circulation among the papers.

While an editor might hope that others would attribute his writing if they copied it, having paragraphs picked up without citation was still good for business, as a comic sketch in the *Philadelphia Inquirer* in 1831 indicates. It tells of an editor who agreed to publish poems written by another editor in order that his own paper be "puffed" in all the Democratic papers; when he did so, "my editorial articles were copied all over the United States, and although many papers re-printed them without credit, and sometimes as original communications, yet on the whole I found my fame rising rapidly. My subscribers increased…every thing promised that I should establish myself on a higher eminence than ever editor reached before" (March 9). Note that this editor is not fussed by the fact that not all the reprintings were credited, and some were downright plagiarized; it seems to have been acceptable that the credit system be somewhat "leaky." In fact, I only once found the term plagiarism in newspapers of the period (in the passage that forms the epigraph to the previous section); instead, editors protest "cabbaging," a term that

---

[29] See "Public Lands," OHIO STATESMAN (Columbus), November 19, 1845, for an example of citing only "Exchange paper"; commentary on that squib is sourced to "Western paper." Also see "They Have Found Me Out," PHILADELPHIA PUBLIC LEDGER, July 14, 1840.

originates in tailors' habits of amassing extra scraps of fabric left over from custom-made clothing.[30] In the tailoring context, which was still understood in this period, cabbaging was reprehensible not so much for its thievery—whether scraps belonged to the tailor or the customer was somewhat open to question—but its pettiness. Thus plagiarism was hardly a crime of high degree; it was more embarrassing than unethical to be charged with cabbaging.

Cribbing and copying were alternate terms in vogue, as was the language of credit.[31] Consider for example the *New York City Evening Tattler*'s tone as it generates copy out of complaints about uncited material. "The Mirror, in copying from our paper that exquisite bit of poetry, 'Love at Sea,' (one of the sweetest lyrics of the age)," they chastise, "has given us a credit mark for it, but so small and at such a formidable distance from the article, as to amount to hardly any credit at all." They go on:

> There are a precious set of these fellows afloat on the sea of periodical literature, now-a-days—perfect wreckers.
>
> The Saturday Courier, of Philadelphia, cribs one article of ours about "S.P.Q.R."—and gives no credit.
>
> The Ledger, of the same city, cribs the "Epitaphs on the Living," which we procured form the manuscript of the authors—and gives no credit.
>
> We might name many other instances. But those are fair (or rather foul) samples of the whole. It is too, *too*, TOO bad. (January 27, 1840)

Editors constantly belittled and berated each other on the grounds of party politics, religion, or sartorial style, and this editor reaches for plagiarism charges as a weapon at this particular moment. I would argue that the claim about the evils of cribbing provided an occasion, or a means, for performative flagellation of the editor of a competitive publication; I have a hard time believing that the editor of the *Tattler* is really shocked at a practice he no doubt indulges in himself.

When politics are in the picture, it is even clearer that plagiarism, or response to it, is the weapon, not the primary cause of, dispute. For example when the *Hudson River Chronicle* (Sing-Sing, NY) took on the *New York Sun* for unacknowledged reuse in 1841, it observed archly that "the Sun is deeply imbued with the spirit of Locofocoism, and consequently entertains great horror for the credit system, and a proportionate love for the 'largest liberty,' or, in other words, for 'equal rights,'—which meaneth, according to the true Locofoco definition, a right to take your neighbor's property wherever you can find it, and convert it to your own use" (June 29). From 1837 to 1839, a protracted battle emerged between two newspapers in upstate Oxford, New York: the *Republican*, a

---

[30] For a definition of cabbaging in the tailoring context, see the *Daily National Intelligencer*, September 23, 1840.
     For a U.S. controversy, see "Trouble among the Tailors," ESSEX GAZETTE (Haverhill, MA), June 1, 1833.
[31] See Slauter (2014: 9–11).

locofoco paper, and the more recently established *Times*, a Whig paper. The *Republican* teased the *Times* about being a "new-fledged" "Bantling" (November 5 and December 5, 1838), and after that both highly partisan papers flung charges of "cabbaging" back and forth with verve. By September 1839 the *Times* was moved "to unhorse the valiant Knight of the Scissors at the first onset" by comparing a paragraph from the *Albany Evening Journal* with its own version of the same story, asserting their differences, and taking the occasion as well to dredge up prior charges against the *Republican* (September 4, 1839). The essential charge seems to be laziness, related, one supposes, to insinuations of stupidity in political judgment.

It seems important to consider that there are many reasons why an editor might attribute borrowed material. Good manners is only one of them. One might also attribute in order to increase credibility. One would want to associate a crime story with a source close to the crime, for example, or a political analysis with a well-known commentator. Or, on the other hand, one might attribute in order to ridicule. This is harder to identify for a reader further from the political ecosystem of papers in the period, but it is clear that sometimes attribution is provided in order to ridicule the information provided. If a Democratic editor praises an initiative or candidate, the verbatim passage is all that is needed to provoke guffaws from readers of a Whig paper. There were also reasons not to cite. The *Evening Tattler* in New York City reproduced a slightly salacious report of a divorce from the *Baltimore Clipper* asking: "Whom did you steal that paragraph from, Clip? If you don't remember, *we* can tell you" (January 25, 1840). From other innuendo in this paper we can presume that the *Clipper* got the squib from a "racy paper," but chooses (as does the *Tattler*) not to say so, skating on the edge of propriety by allowing certain readers to make the attribution themselves. So the practice was exceedingly complex, one might even say virtuosic. To reduce it to a set of rules would be both impossible and inappropriate.

There was one type of material where failure to attribute seems to have provoked controversy more vehement than the usual teasing and soft shaming. As urban newspapers started to get into the business of active newsgathering beyond visiting the docks and saloons, they became protective of the labor they expended on that material. This is not to say that there was any sense that reproduction ought to require permission or payment. Rather, it was competition with the market (immediate republication within the same city) that was the issue. For example, in September 1840 the *New York Herald* sent a reporter to Patchogue on Long Island to cover a speech by celebrated orator Senator Daniel Webster and an express to race the transcription back to town. Editor Bennett was incensed by the behavior of a competitor paper:

> [T]hey waited till our Special Express from Patchogue had reached this city, and by hook or by crook, they got hold of a Herald, and actually published the speech as reported by us, accompanied by the atrocious falsehood that they had got it by their own Special Express.... The Special Express cost us some money, and we are

certainly entitled to the benefit of our enterprize and expenditure, without being at the mercy of plunderers and pilferers, without acknowledgement.

Bennett does not even deign to name his misbehaving competitor at first. But its misdeeds produced even further insult to the *Herald*, and here he does name names:

> …worst of all is the mean conduct of the "Commercial Advertiser," conducted by Francis Hall and William L. Stone. Not content with pilfering our report they have the malignity to ascribe it to a penny paper that stole it from us without acknowledgment. This is done knowingly and wilfully. We do not expect any just treatment from such a contemptible creature as Stone, but Mr. Hall makes pretensions to honor and religion. How can he reconcile such conduct with the sound moral principles taught him by the Methodist Church? (September 24)

The next day, the tirade continued:

> …common honesty, as men of business, ought to have restrained these papers from appropriating to themselves our labors without acknowledgment. Yesterday we were compelled to detain the publication of the Herald till 5 o'clock in the morning, in order to prevent the pilferers from perpetrating more theft. We have the consolation, however, to know that the public understand the question. The Wall street press having failed to affect, in the remotest degree, the prosperity and character of the Herald by open denunciation and violent abuse, have now assumed the principles of pickpockets, and stole our news—our reports, and our intelligence, without the least acknowledgment on their part. This is a game, however, that cannot last long. (September 25)

There are a few things to note here. First, the use of Lockean language when Bennett denominates his charge, "appropriating to themselves our labors." Comparisons with pickpockets, theft, and, in another squib, "piracy," confirm the property discourse. However, note that it is not the material that is stolen, but the "news." News is an interesting object; it is not simply information, but *new* information, and is thus ephemeral as such. No theft would have been perpetrated had the material been reprinted with a longer delay.[32] So this complaint is more fine-grained than anything copyright usually addresses; it concerns a certain timing of appropriation rather than appropriation in itself. The complaint also focuses on the lack of acknowledgment, a component of European *droit d'auteur* traditions absent from U.S. copyright. So we see here emerging a language of rights, but the rights in question are not *copy*-rights.

---

[32] For a good discussion of the issue of lead time and priority in this period, see Brauneis (2009: 342).

Note too that the charges were part of a larger business "game" between Bennett and the other penny papers and the older "Wall Street" six-cent papers. Bennett used the occasion to advertise the speed and quality of his enterprise, and the following weeks display much trumpeting and crowing on the subject. Sometimes editors took the game idea a step further. In 1831 the *New York Courier & Enquirer*, "so frequently annoyed at the practice of the Daily Journals borrowing our news, and giving no credit for it," "resolved to set a trap to catch some of the rats who nibble at our cheese" (reprinted as "The Bitter Hit" in the *Republican Star and General Advertiser* [Easton, MD], November 15, 1831). They concocted a fake story from Poland and gloated when the *Gazette* and *Journal of Commerce* reprinted it verbatim without credit.[33] Some years later, this strategy was also pursued energetically by Melville Stone, who founded the *Chicago Daily News* in 1876. To shame the "pirating" McMullen brothers, editors of the *Post and Mail*, he fabricated a story headlined, "Sad Story of Distress in Servia." It went like this:

> A few days ago the mayor of the provincial town of Sovik issued a proclamation ending with the ominous words: "*Er us siht la Etsll iws nel lum cmeht*" (the municipality cannot aid).
> Upon reading this, the people, led by the women of the town,
> organized a riot, in the course of which a dozen houses were pillaged and over twenty persons were brutally murdered. (Stone 1921: 63)

When the *Post and Mail* accordingly reprinted the story, including its reversed direct insult to the McMullen brothers, the paper was, as Stone tells it in his memoirs, "literally laughed to death. In less than two years we bought all that was left of it, including its franchise in the Associated Press and its material, for $15,000" (64). Stone played another trick on the *Chicago Tribune* a few years later, engineering a fake telegraph from Matthew Arnold; on this occasion, "The Chicago Tribune was not merely convicted of having stolen the 'dispatch,' which was not worth stealing, but of adding humbug and deluding the readers" (124). Note that the court here was the court of public opinion, and the crimes were, well, not crimes. Stone was relying on the public's inclination to share his sense of journalistic professionalism.

All in all, while it is not inaccurate to say that attribution was expected in many aspects of newspaper reuse of material, it must also be noted that it was not demanded, but rather silently practiced—or not. Lack of attribution was rarely contested, and even then in erratic, opportunistic, and performative ways. What governed these situations was an abstract sense of "*morals*, not…*law*," as the editor of the *Boston Courier* put it. In this period, the exchange system both represented and supported an emerging profession that preferred to govern itself through a performance of editorial virtuosity or community rather than through appeals to legal authority. There was, however, as shown above, an

---

[33] For more on this incident, see Rosewater (1930: 18–19).

emerging sense that maybe news stories could belong to their collector, and this is the development I will pursue in the next and final section.

IV. Fair Use and Hot News

Stone's patience with shaming techniques as a cure for "piracy" did not last. In 1883, he became a director of the Associated Press, and he spent a huge amount of effort over the following thirty-five years pursuing legal avenues for protecting news, culminating in his victory in *International News Service v. Associated Press (INS v. AP)*.[34] Indeed, the climate and circumstances of the news industry began to change a good deal in the 1840s. For one thing, as cities grew, markets expanded and diversified for newspapers. Advertising became more lucrative, wider swaths of the population read newspapers, and printing presses became faster. On the heels of already intensifying and competitive mechanisms for express newsgathering (pigeons, fast ships, horse relays), the telegraph was introduced, followed quickly by the Associated Press (AP), which offered news to its members, not to all. Access to news from afar thus became differentiated; whereas all editors were formerly dependent on the mail, which traveled at the same speed for (more or less) all, now they could choose to invest in faster methods. Newspapers started to put more resources into hiring reporters and correspondents. Free postage for exchange of papers between editors was revoked by Congress in 1873 (Kielbowicz 1989: 155). In *Harper v. Shoppell* (1886),[35] a judge ruled that periodicals could be registered for copyright, and by 1909 Congress had confirmed the change (Easton 2004: 539, 542).

So the question is, did these changes completely overturn industry circulation practices from the earlier period described above? Are those practices of merely historical interest from our present point of view? Most have claimed yes,[36] and of course it is true that an emphasis on originality and competition rose to the fore in journalism compared to the earlier model of copying and exchange. But the change was not total, and the news industry still manifests fundamentally cooperative practices. The reasons for cooperative practices outlasted the economic, cultural, or technological conditions of a nascent industry. Newsgathering remains a cooperative activity in important ways; it is simply not within the capacity of even the most moneyed conglomerates to be everywhere at once. News organizations compete; they also are inherently dependent on each other. Hence, now that the law is more often called upon in journalism disputes, it has to address itself, however awkwardly, to practices both less and more proprietary than copyright law would tend to prescribe or permit. I will turn in this closing section to fair use and hot news as important, if fraught, indicators of industry-specific practice surviving from long ago.

---

[34] 248 U.S. 215 (1918).

[35] 28 Fed. 519 (C.C.A. 2d, 1886).

[36] See Ekstrand (2005: 16–17); Barnhurst & Nerone (2001: 102–03).

The reproduction of the exact words of people close to an event gives news reports authority and presence. A legal requirement to ask permission for every sequence of reproduced words would burden publishers and journalists logistically and financially, and impede the circulation of information. In some circumstances, that is, a speaker or writer would not give permission to reproduce embarrassing material for any price. Interestingly, it seems that in the context of news reporting, the threshold for permission for reproduction remained high long after the end of newspaper exchanges, if done in reasonable quantities and with attribution as appropriate. In all the cases defining "fair use" through the common law before 1976 surveyed by Patry (1985), not a single one concerns journalism. Newspapers did not argue about fair use because they had a well-developed self-monitoring practice of quoting and commenting on each other that does not seem to have provoked legal controversy over more than a century.[37] When in 1976 the United States made fair use a statutory provision in the Copyright Act, it followed the United Kingdom's lead from 1911 in including "news reporting" in its list of permitted fair uses, suggesting a recognition and accommodation of still-existing practice. In other words, this provision appears to recognize that industry practice requires shared resources in a manner not otherwise guaranteed under an intellectual property regime.

Hot news, on the other hand, represents an area where journalism organizations have sought *more* protection than copyright offers. In 1883, Melville Stone recalled, "I dreamed a dream. There was a defect in the law which should, and perhaps might, be remedied" (1921: 357). He hired lobbyists to convince Congress to extend copyright protection to news, on the rationale that "everything having an exchangeable value" (360) ought to be considered intellectual property—or, indeed, property. That is, the request was not for copyright protection in news reporting (which, while politically relatively easy, would not have prevented the recirculation of facts that incensed the AP), but for something more controversial: some kind of property, however temporary, in information. This idea went against the grain of the emerging Berne, Berlin, and Pan-American copyright negotiations, and it failed in Washington as well, largely because of the effective resistance from rural papers and fears that it would not "promote the Progress of Science and useful Arts" as the Constitution entrusted Congress to do (Cloud 1996).

Interestingly, one bill tabled during this effort acknowledged not only the concerns of rural editors but also expectations from within the newspaper community by limiting copyright to eight or twenty-four hours. This seems to match, for example, the *Herald*'s expectations with regard to Daniel Webster's speech; the *Herald* wanted to be first, and it wanted to be credited, but later reprintings would have been considered less inappropriate. A right as expansive as copyright or property rights was simply not needed. More generally, despite the hugely visible self-interest in the AP's pursuit of this legislation, it

[37] Brauneis (2009) notes that the Berne Convention as drafted in the 1880s allowed for free copying of news stories (373). The United States was not a party to Berne, but this indicates a broader practice and set of expectations that would be interesting to explore.

would be too simple to dismiss the effort as a pet project only of one particularly power-ful news agency. Borrowed facts had been objects of controversy in earlier years along with borrowed words.[38] The *New York Spectator* was charged by the *Journal of Commerce* in 1837 with "cabbaging facts," for example. Its response articulates one difficulty of trying to act on such complaints, whether through shaming or law; it is very hard to trace where a fact comes from.

> Touching the cabbaging, we deny the charge, and pray you to point out the mat-ter of our misdoing. The election news in our paper yesterday was made up from twenty different sources—from letters, from slips, from all the morning papers, and from the reports of friends, who were coming in to us with tidings, all the morning. You might as well say that the very air we breathed was "cabbaged" from your testy worships. (November 13)

Essentially, the *Spectator* claims that any borrowing it did from the *Journal of Commerce* was amplified and corroborated from other sources. This industry practice of working from tips continues as essential to reporting. No offense obtains if a prior story has been checked and refabricated. Exchange practices lack a strong distinction between repro-ducing facts and reproducing expression, but demonstrate a tradition of tolerating repro-duction of both if delayed or done in a spirit of newsgathering or commentary. This is very far from a property or copyright right way of thinking.

In 1918, after a long crusade, Stone did find success at the Supreme Court when it ruled in *INS v. AP* that

> one who gathers news at pains and expense, for the purpose of lucrative publica-tion, may be said to have a *quasi*-property in the results of his enterprise as against a rival in the same business, and the appropriation of those results at the expense and to the damage of the one and for the profit of the other is unfair competition against which equity will afford relief.[39]

The nature of this idea of "quasi-property" has been endlessly discussed, but it is at least uncontroversial to note that he refrained from speaking of "property."[40] Epstein has argued that this case follows industry custom, even if it does not acknowledge this fact (1992: 106), and I too would emphasize all the ways that the right described is constrained

---

[38] For an account of copyright's protection of facts in this period, see Brauneis (2009).

[39] 248 U.S. 215, 216 (1918).

[40] Baird (2006) asserts that the issues arising in *INS v. AP* properly had "more to do with the regulation of a natural monopoly than with property rights" (10). I do not disagree; here once more is confirmation that some of the most crucial disputes in the news business are not as related to IP law as is sometimes thought or argued. IP or even property discourse becomes a way of adding strength to other claims, or obscuring distaste-ful circumstances.

or defined differently than property, or, for that matter, intellectual property. The idea that one might have a right of property against some parties (other newspapers) but not others (the general public or other sorts of publishers outside the exchange circuit) certainly matches community-based exchange practice as I have documented it. As the Court put it,

> [t]he right of the purchaser of a single newspaper to spread knowledge of its contents gratuitously, for any legitimate purpose not unreasonably interfering with complainant's right to make merchandise of it, may be admitted, but to transmit that news for commercial use, in competition with complainant—which is what defendant has done and seeks to justify—is a very different matter.[41]

The ruling also acknowledges, if somewhat grudgingly, a space for working from tips:

> The circuit court of appeals found that the tip habit, though discouraged by complainant, was "incurably journalistic".... We are inclined to think a distinction may be drawn between the utilization of tips and the bodily appropriation of news matter, either in its original form or after rewriting and without independent investigation and verification; ... both parties avowedly recognize the practice of taking tips, and neither party alleges it to be unlawful or to amount to unfair competition in business.[42]

In his independent concurrence, Justice Holmes suggested a refinement that also matched what I take to be a version of industry custom: "I think that ... the defendant should be enjoined from publishing news obtained from the Associated Press for hours after publication by the plaintiff unless it gives express credit to the Associated Press, the number of hours and the form of acknowledgment to be settled by the district court."[43]

Balganesh (2011) has recently offered a reframing of *INS v. AP* that nuances its logic and complements my approach. Balganesh sees the news industry turning to the courts at the point when the exchange system, to which all belonged, gave way to another cooperative system, the news agency, to which only some belonged, a situation that rendered the problem of free riding more visible. But he insists that Judge Pitney's ruling shows an awareness that "an individual property right granted to each news collector might deter free riding, but could potentially affect the nature of cooperation in the market" (426):

> one detects in the Court's opinion a deep concern with the effects of superimposing a regime of individual ownership on an industry that had until then governed news

---

[41] 248 U.S. at 239.
[42] 248 U.S. at 246–48.
[43] 248 U.S. at 248.

collection as a common pool resource. Referring to the news as a form of common property among newspapers, as an item of publici juris, and as stock in trade little susceptible to absolute ownership, the misappropriation strategy seemed consciously directed at retaining the public domain nature of factual news. (450)

Melville Stone may have sought property rights in information, but, Balganesh argues, *INS v. AP* did not capitulate, despite the ways the case has been subsequently interpreted.[44]

To present-day copyright watchers, the most familiar part of *INS v. AP* is Justice Brandeis's dissent, with the ringing lines:

> The general rule of law is that the noblest of human productions—knowledge, truths ascertained, conceptions, and ideas—became, after voluntary communication to others, free as the air to common use. Upon these incorporeal productions the attribute of property is continued after such communication only in certain classes of cases where public policy has seemed to demand it.[45]

Indeed, the idea of property, even quasi-property, in news, would seem to go against all good public policy and common sense. It would certainly advantage those already equipped with newsgathering capacity, as opposed to those who needed access to news. In the light of more recent lawsuits by the AP and other large news outfits against bloggers and aggregators, *INS v. AP* may represent a last cash grab from a dying industry, and an attack on new modes of circulating information and commentary.[46] But the journalistic community has defined itself with respect to circulation practices for a very long time, and claims to some sort of property in news are not novel any more than claims to some sort of fair use are. As new enterprises have emerged, such as news aggregators, it is not surprising that the professional news community should have considered them outsiders, and thus not participants in whatever sharing it may have done within its boundaries. It is at this point that a community may turn to the law to resolve disputes—even if the law may not suit its practices and expectations very well. The idea that ideas upon publication are "free as the air to common use" would never have quite made sense within the news industry—and it was not an argument presented by the INS in its defense (Baird 2006). The grand public agora Brandeis invokes was in fact subtended and produced by

---

[44] Balganesh (2011) is right to criticize the "doctrinal feedback" loop by which courts "readily infer the existence of an ex ante legal entitlement [property in hot news] over a type of use/copying when licenses describe the entitlement in those terms" (434). Just because risk-averse entities agree to pay for certain uses does not necessarily mean that those uses actually require permission.

[45] 248 U.S. at 250 (Brandeis, J., dissenting).

[46] *The Associated Press v. All Headline News Corp.* et al., 08-cv-00323-PKC (S.D.N.Y. 2008). For other disputes and commentary, see, for example, Roy Greenslade, "Papers to website: stop quoting our stories. Website to papers: you'll be the loser," THE GUARDIAN, July 9, 2010; Saul Hansell, "The A.P., Hot News and Hotheaded Blogs," NEW YORK TIMES, June 16, 2008; and Nate Anderson, "Who owns the facts? The AP and the 'hot news' controversy," ARSTECHNICA, http://www.arstechnica.com, May 6, 2009.

practices more local and complex than he recognizes. The commons operative in journalism may have had (and still have) quite a fraught relationship to the information commons more generally construed.

I might turn in closing to the relationship between collective resources conceived in terms of rights, and those conceived in terms of practices. Balganesh again:

> Elinor Ostrom…argues that in numerous situations participants do not readily abandon holding a resource in common pool while attempting to extract value from it, but instead choose to develop governance structures to regulate and deter free riders and ensure an efficient allocation of the resource among participants. In the intangible (i.e., intellectual property) context, such common pool arrangements can involve participants pooling their property rights together to minimize transaction costs and achieve organizational efficiency. Alternatively, participants can pool their efforts—prior to any legal recognition of property rights in their individual contributions—to achieve an efficient outcome. The latter type of pooling arrangement emerged as the common practice in the newspaper industry. The cooperation among participants that had emerged was directed at collectively producing the very resource in question—timely, comprehensive news—rather than pooling together preexisting rights in an intangible resource and administering them collectively. (450–51)

Precisely that sense of collective or community action to produce and manage intellectual or cultural resources underlies the concept of commons as it is described in the introductory chapter of this book (Madison, Frischmann, & Strandburg 2010). The example of nineteenth-century newspaper exchanges suggests that commons practices need not be understood as independent of state actions; free postage between editors definitely enabled exchange practices. If we are to see the exchange network as a constructed commons, we must acknowledge that in a sense it was constructed by postal policy, not by editors. But its daily workings emerged out of prior and ongoing news-gathering practices—what Madison et al. would call a baseline "natural environment" (25). In the mid-nineteenth century, there was no editors' or newspapers' association, no formal understanding of rules for sharing or attribution, and no rules governing who was "in" and "out" of exchanges. To say that this commons was "policed," "managed," or even "constructed" by its participants would be too strong—especially in comparison with the workings of the later cooperative wire services. Sanctions were relatively mild; the shaming that came with inappropriate behavior was not that different from the insults that flew from paper to paper all the time. Nonetheless, I do perceive shared practices of circulation and attribution in papers of this period, and in fact would observe a kind of symbiosis between participation in those practices and a sense of membership in an emerging profession.

Popular conceptions of the history of journalism have tended to foreground competition instead of cooperation. Indeed, given the imperative of brand loyalty, any editor worth his salt represented his paper as independent and autonomous. And yet, the competition was (and is) enabled by cooperation. And cooperation was (and is) regulated by both government and industry custom. A case study such as this reminds us that commons may not be innocent or isolated from capital, that capital is not produced solely by individual enterprise, and that copyright is not always a useful tool for incentivizing innovation. Retrieving the collectivist past of the news industry may seem an exercise in nostalgia, except of course that in the Internet we find a similar set of practices subtending new modes of civic education and debate. Bloggers expect credit for republication or quotation, but demand no permission or payment. Perhaps in understanding the relation between rights and innovation we would be wise to reverse common wisdom and presume high awareness and enforcement of IP rights to be signs of an industry's demise, unless proven otherwise, rather than underpinnings of its inception.

Acknowledgments

I am grateful to the American Antiquarian Society for financial support of this research and for generous assistance with their ample collections, and to Nicholas Kennedy for research assistance on the topic of "hot news." Research in primary sources was also conducted at New York University, New York Public Library, and via the Readex resource, "America's Historical Newspapers." This chapter is adapted from a chapter in Murray, Piper, & Robertson (2014).

References

BENEDICT ANDERSON, IMAGINED COMMUNITIES: REFLECTIONS ON THE ORIGIN AND SPREAD OF NATIONALISM (London: Verso 1983).

Douglas G. Baird, *The Story of INS v. AP: Property, Natural Monopoly, and the Uneasy Legacy of a Concocted Controversy, in* INTELLECTUAL PROPERTY STORIES 9 (Jane C. Ginsburg & Rochelle Cooper Dreyfuss eds., Foundation Press 2006).

Shyamkrishna Balganesh, *"Hot News": The Enduring Myth of Property in News,* 111 COLUMBIA L. REV. 419 (2011).

KEVIN G. BARNHURST & JOHN NERONE, THE FORM OF NEWS: A HISTORY (New York: Guilford Press 2001).

DAVID BOLLIER, SILENT THEFT: THE PRIVATE PLUNDER OF OUR COMMON WEALTH (New York: Routledge 2003).

Robert Brauneis, *The Transformation of Originality in the Progressive-Era Debate over Copyright in News,* 27 CARDOZO ARTS & ENT. L.J. 321 (2009).

Scott E. Casper, *The Census, the Post Office, and Governmental Publishing, in* A HISTORY OF THE BOOK IN AMERICA. VOL. 3 THE INDUSTRIAL BOOK, 1840–1880 178 (Scott E. Casper, Jeffrey D. Groves, Stephen W. Nissenbaum, & Michael Winship eds., University of North Carolina Press 2007).

Barbara Cloud, *News: Public Service of Profitable Property?*, 13 AM. JOURNALISM 141 (1996).

Eric B. Easton, *Who Owns the "First Rough Draft of History"? Reconsidering Copyright in News*, 27 COLUMBIA J.L. & THE ARTS 521 (2004).

VICTORIA SMITH EKSTRAND, NEWS PIRACY AND THE HOT NEWS DOCTRINE: ORIGINS IN LAW AND IMPLICATIONS FOR THE DIGITAL AGE (New York: LFB Scholarly Publishing 2005).

Richard A. Epstein, International News Service v. Associated Press: *Custom and Law as Sources of Property Rights in News*, 78 VIRGINIA L. REV. 85 (1992).

MICHAEL J. EVERTON, THE GRAND CHORUS OF COMPLAINT: AUTHORS AND THE BUSINESS ETHICS OF AMERICAN PUBLISHING (Oxford University Press 2011).

David Fagundes, *Talk Derby to Me: Emergent Intellectual Property Norms Governing Roller Derby Pseudonyms*, 90 TEXAS L. REV. 1093 (2012).

Emmanuelle Fauchart & Eric von Hippel, *Norms-Based Intellectual Property Systems: The Case of French Chefs,* 19 ORGANIZATION SCIENCE 187 (2008).

Jeffrey G. Groves, *Courtesy of the Trade, in* A HISTORY OF THE BOOK IN AMERICA. VOL. 3 THE INDUSTRIAL BOOK, 1840–1880 139 (Scott E. Casper, Jeffrey D. Groves, Stephen W. Nissenbaum, & Michael Winship eds., University of North Carolina Press 2007).

DAVID HENKIN, CITY READING: WRITTEN WORDS AND PUBLIC SPACES IN ANTEBELLUM NEW YORK (Columbia University Press 1999).

DAVID HENKIN, THE POSTAL AGE: THE EMERGENCE OF MODERN COMMUNICATIONS IN NINETEENTH-CENTURY AMERICA (University of Chicago Press 2006).

MELISSA HOMESTEAD, AMERICAN WOMEN AUTHORS AND LITERARY PROPERTY, 1822–1869 (Cambridge University Press 2005).

LEWIS HYDE, THE GIFT: IMAGINATION AND THE EROTIC LIFE OF PROPERTY (Vintage Books 1979).

LEON JACKSON, THE BUSINESS OF LETTERS: AUTHORIAL ECONOMIES IN ANTEBELLUM AMERICA (Stanford University Press 2008).

RICHARD R. JOHN, SPREADING THE NEWS: THE AMERICAN POSTAL SYSTEM FROM FRANKLIN TO MORSE (Harvard University Press 1995).

RICHARD B. KIELBOWICZ, NEWS IN THE MAIL: THE PRESS, POST OFFICE, AND PUBLIC INFORMATION, 1700–1860S (New York: Greenwood 1989).

Jacob Loshin, *Secrets Revealed: Protecting Magicians' Intellectual Property without Law, in* LAW AND MAGIC: A COLLECTION OF ESSAYS 123 (Christine A. Corcos ed., Durham: Carolina Academic Press 2010).

Michael J. Madison, Brett M. Frischmann, & Katherine J. Strandburg, *Constructing Commons in the Cultural Environment*, 95 CORNELL L. REV. 657 (2010).

MEREDITH MCGILL, AMERICAN LITERATURE AND THE CULTURE OF REPRINTING, 1834–1853 (University of Pennsylvania Press 2003).

Meredith McGill, *Copyright, in* A HISTORY OF THE BOOK IN AMERICA, VOL. 3: THE INDUSTRIAL BOOK 1840–1880 158–78 (Scott E. Casper, Jeffrey D. Groves, Stephen W. Nissenbaum, & Michael Winship eds., University of North Carolina Press 2007).

DAVID T. Z. MINDICH, JUST THE FACTS: HOW "OBJECTIVITY" CAME TO DEFINE AMERICAN JOURNALISM (New York University Press 1998).

FRANK LUTHER MOTT, AMERICAN JOURNALISM: A HISTORY OF NEWSPAPERS IN THE UNITED STATES THROUGH 250 YEARS 1690 TO 1940 (New York: Macmillan 1941).

Laura J. Murray, S. Tina Piper, & Kirsty M. Robertson, Putting Intellectual Property in Its Place: Rights Discourses, Creative Labor, and the Everyday (Oxford University Press 2014).

John Nerone, *Newspapers and the Public Sphere, in* A History of the Book in America Vol. 3 The Industrial Book, 1840–1880 230–47 (Scott E. Casper, Jeffrey D. Groves, Stephen W. Nissenbaum, & Michael Winship eds., University of North Carolina Press 2007).

David Nord, Communities of Journalism: A History of American Newspapers and Their Readers (University of Illinois Press 2001).

Dotan Oliar & Christopher Sprigman, *There's No Free Laugh (Anymore): The Emergence of Intellectual Property Norms and the Transformation of Stand-Up Comedy*, 94 Virginia L. Rev. 1787 (2008).

Jeffrey L. Pasley, "The Tyranny of Printers": Newspaper Politics in the Early American Republic (University Press of Virginia 2001).

William Patry, The Fair Use Privilege in Copyright Law (2d ed. Washington, D.C.: BNA Books 1985).

Kal Raustiala & Christopher Sprigman, *The Piracy Paradox: Innovation and Intellectual Property in Fashion Design*, 92 Virginia L. Rev. 1687 (2006).

Kal Raustiala & Christopher Sprigman, *The Piracy Paradox Revisited*, 61 Stanford L. Rev. 1201 (2009).

Victor Rosewater, History of Cooperative News-Gathering in the United States (New York: Appleton 1930).

Will Slauter, *Toward a History of Copyright for Periodical Writings: Examples from Nineteenth-century America, in* From Text(s) to Book(s): Studies in the Production and Editorial Process (Monica Latham & David Ten Eyck eds., Nancy: Editions universitaires de Lorraine 2014).

Melville E. Stone, Fifty Years a Journalist (Garden City, NY: Doubleday, Page & Company 1921).

12 How War Creates Commons: General McNaughton and the National Research Council, 1914–1939

S. Tina Piper*

I. Introduction

Many familiar aspects of present-day commons strategies were implemented during World War I and World War II to channel collective invention and quickly disseminate innovations. The exigencies of war, the collectivism it inspired, and the training that it afforded men in the military all contributed how the "public interest" was imagined and satisfied through creative techniques of intellectual property management in the Allied countries. This chapter explores four interrelated themes in the early twentieth century: first, how and why the metaphor of war and the practical realities of World War I inspired the creation of commons-like intellectual property (IP) mechanisms; second, how the structure of the military and its professional mores fostered commons-based approaches to IP in the 1910s, '20s, and '30s, which became early models for many contemporary commons-based approaches; third, the commons-commitments evident in the career of General Andrew McNaughton, a prolific inventor and decorated military man, as he moved from the military to become second president of the (Canadian) National Research Council (NRC); fourth, how the reality of war and the norms and practices

---

* S. Tina Piper is an Assistant Professor at McGill University's Faculty of Law and member of its Centre for Intellectual Property Policy. She is co-author, with Laura J. Murray and Kirsty Robertson, of *Putting Intellectual Property in Its Place: Rights Discourses, Creative Labor, and the Everyday* (Oxford University Press 2014).

of the military embodied by McNaughton all influenced the adoption of commons-like mechanisms in licensing practices at the NRC and created Canada's first major technology transfer institution. I focus on Canada but raise examples where appropriate from the United States and the United Kingdom and their major cultural and political influences.

The chapter brings together diverse fields and trends, in particular legal historiography, the history of military technology, and scholarship theorizing commons in intellectual and IP resources. It builds on a recent historiography of military technology that has supplemented civilian-oriented accounts of scientific and technological development with a realistic assessment of the immense role of the military from World War I to World War II (Edgerton 2008: ch. 8). This renewed focus on the power and influence of the military on science, technology, and industry reprises an approach common since antiquity that sees military institutions as essential to the state, but which has experienced a marked decline since World War I.[1] Writing out the military's influence on science, technology, and industry promoted a liberal internationalist, technologically determinist account of history that espoused values of "science, order, progress, internationalism, aeroplanes, steel, concrete, hygiene" and suppressed the other side of "war, nationalism, religion, monarchy peasants, Greek professors, poets, horses" (Edgerton 2006: 319; quoting Orwell 1941: 169). Historians of military technology, science and technology scholars, and others are increasingly studying how the military has shaped many basic elements of the state, from education (Hacker 1993) to corporate organization (Cherns & Clark 1976; Mangum & Ball 1987), social assistance and citizenship (Cowan 2005), the structure of nonprofits and most aspects of the industrial economy.[2] This chapter aims to help bring the horses back. I trace how the roots of institutionalized technology transfer lie in World War I, preparation for World War II, and the expertise of a talented military officer.

Throughout this chapter I ask four types of questions of IP scholarship on commons governance. First, I consider the narrative or metaphorical use of the concept of war and how it inspired or created commons: how is the idea of war a metaphor useful for thinking about commons? Do commons require a common enemy? Second, what mechanisms and which institutions actually created commons during war? What specific features, for example nonexclusive licensing, created commons-like conditions? How did the commons of technology transfer and its institutions mediate between the scientific norms of researchers and those of business wishing to commercialize innovation (693)? What was the relationship between commons and government? How does the concept of the "public interest" relate to the use of commons-based approaches? Third, how do professions constitute commons? What norms, enforcement measures, membership criteria, and practices make them commons-like? Fourth, how is the legal subjectivity of any profession

---

[1] Hacker (1993) goes as far to argue that the idea of the state itself is "best understood in terms of military institutions" (20).

[2] For a comprehensive review of the literature, see Hacker (1994).

embodied by its members? From a critical legal pluralist perspective, how do individuals practice commons in their daily lives (Kleinhans & Macdonald 1997)? How do individual members of professions go beyond existing normative frameworks to create and interpret norms of commons engagement? What can the study of individual commons-commitment contribute to the broader, systematic, study of the commons? Madison, Frischmann, and Strandburg's (2010) model for structured inquiry into constructed commons provides the framework for understanding the nature of the resources, the communities implicated, and the management and governance tools enrolled in the service of bringing scientific knowledge to practical application in the public interest in Canada.

II. Theme 1: War and Commons: Practices, Mechanisms, and Institutions

The early twentieth century saw a robust discussion and implementation of commons-type initiatives by scientific research institutions. This was a time of social, organizational, and technological change in the way science was pursued in Canada, the United States, and the United Kingdom. The late nineteenth century had seen the development of the university into an institution with both teaching *and* research functions (Etzkowitz & Leydesdorff n.d.; Madison, Frischmann, & Strandburg 2009), although laboratory research in Canadian universities was still embryonic by the early twentieth century (Li 2003: 87). Government increasingly regarded universities as providing scientifically trained workers for industrial laboratories (Etzkowitz & Leydesdorff n.d.). This period saw the emergence of major industrial research laboratories like General Electric and Bell, which relied heavily on the strategic use of patents to protect their inventions (Khan & Sokoloff 2001: 242; Hughes 1989: xvi). At the same time, there was a decline of the "independent inventor" (MacLeod 2007: 329), growing use of the patent system and media that encouraged or promoted its use (for example, *Scientific American*) (Jenkins 1987: 43), and an increasing role for the state in all aspects of life but particularly in supporting military, industrial, and scientific research before, during, and after World War I (Hughes 1989: xvi). To achieve this latter end, Anglo-American governments "gave way, under the stress of war" and created agencies pursuing public science like the Canadian National Research Council (NRC, founded 1916), the U.S. National Research Council (founded 1916), and the U.K. Department for Industrial and Scientific Research (DSIR, founded 1915) (Millard 2005: 307). Each of these institutions had an explicit mandate to produce inventions and supplies to support the military (Currie & Graham 1966). During peacetime they were to bridge theoretical, inquiry-based research and research directly useful to national industries through systems of fellowships and grants to university, independent, and industrial researchers.

At the Canadian NRC's first meeting in December 1916, with no inventions yet to speak of, the minutes record that "the results of any research supported by the Government should be national" and profits from any inventions should go back to supporting research; in other words "patenting in the public interest."[3] The NRC had been created in 1916 under Prime Minister Borden and officially constituted in 1924 as a result of nudging from the British government after the creation of its DSIR (Eggleston 1978: 2). The NRC's eventual contribution to both wars was substantial and included, among other inventions, radar, the proximity fuse, atomic energy, dried eggs, Canadian bacon, and the fantastic but doomed Pykrete, a floating ice aircraft carrier made out of sawdust and water for landing planes (Eggleston 1950). I focus on the NRC particularly because it laid the foundation for institutionalized technology transfer across Canadian scientific agencies and universities. In the 1960s it spun off a technology transfer agency called Canadian Patents Development Limited that commercialized technologies developed in Canadian research institutions.

In its early years, the NRC actively modeled its commercialization policies on similar institutions in other countries, such as the U.K.'s DSIR,[4] and the U.S. Mellon Institute[5] and Bureau of Standards.[6] These peer organizations had adopted different methods of disseminating the inventions they developed, many of which drew on commons-style approaches. The "commons-i-ness" of the model each adopted depended on the extent to which the organization saw itself as serving a governmental or public interest, or private partners. The U.S.-based Mellon Institute, for example, although nonprofit and affiliated with the University of Pittsburgh, styled itself as a research group serving companies, composed of fellows funded by a particular industry. All discoveries belonged to the "the Donor" (the company or industry that funded a particular research group) who could decide whether or not to patent the inventions developed by that group (United States 1947a: 4). The U.S. National Bureau of Standards had a more arms-length relationship with industry. Established in 1901 as a subdivision of the Department of Commerce, its main function was to conduct research for other government branches as well as in collaboration with private industry. It was almost entirely federally funded and charged no fees except to cover the costs of private research (United States 1947b:79). While the Bureau did not have a formal policy regarding inventions, in 1922 it encouraged any patents obtained by its employees to "be dedicated for free unrestricted use by the public" (83) a policy that, it found a year later, was not being followed (the majority of employees were patenting in their own names) (80). The Bureau stopped encouraging public dedication shortly thereafter in the late 1920s (106) as it was being blocked from research by third-party patents assigned

---

[3] First Meeting at Ottawa, 4–6 Dec. 1916, Morning session 6 Dec, Library and Archives Canada, Ottawa (LAC) RG 77 v. 94.

[4] Ibid.

[5] Third Meeting at Ottawa, 15 Feb. 1917, LAC RG 77 v. 94. "Letter to Hume Cronyn from H.M. Tory," Edmonton, September 26, 1927 (quoted in Thistle 1966: 240).

[6] "If we were able to combine the features of the Mellon Institute and the Bureau of Standards in National Research Laboratories, we will have secured a piece of unified effort on a finer scale than is done anywhere else, so far as I know." Ibid. In fact, Tory referred to the permanent establishment of the NRC as a "Bureau of Standards" (Eggleston 1978: 11).

by its employees over their on-the-job innovations (108). A third model institution, the United Kingdom's DSIR set up in 1916, had an industry collaboration model much like the NRC (United States 1947c: 99). The DSIR adopted a defensive patent policy, requiring employees to assign all rights to inventions made in the course of their duties to ensure that the DSIR was not blocked from conducting research on modifications and improvements (100). These patents were held by the Imperial Trust and licensed on a nonexclusive basis at a low royalty rate (101).[7] Overall, those institutions serving a "public interest" were most likely to encourage or require employee assignments, nonexclusive licensing or dedication. Using these commons-based IP strategies, in contrast to relying on public domain policies or market-actor commercialization approaches, government agencies managed development and commercialization for collective benefit and public use, although (as nonexclusive licensing shows) private benefit may not have been prohibited.

War created important conditions for fostering commons-based IP approaches such as these for two reasons. First was the nationalism and collectivism that fighting a war encouraged. The Crimean War (United Kingdom), the U.S. Civil War, and then World War I led to a surge of "voluntarism" in the United States, the United Kingdom, and Canada, attributed to the shared purposes and identities constructed by raising volunteer armies (Skocpol et al. 2002). The roles of the voluntary, membership-based associations that resulted were then increasingly adopted by the state after World War I (Finlayson 1990), acting in the name of a broader public interest (Skocpol et al. 2002). In particular, Canada emerged from World War I with an awakened national consciousness, which inspired publications and organizations dedicated to expressing a Canadian identity and viewpoint. The story of Canada's war effort was a powerful unifying and mobilizing force that was used to inspire individuals and organizations to act in the public good (Vance 1997: 229). The military man himself was seen as an ideal conciliator, as by virtue of his military experience he had "the ability to judge a situation on its merits, regardless of any personal interests that may be at play" (232). He was ideally suited to act in the service of the public interest that these new public organizations were tasked with pursuing. The NRC was no exception.

Second, World War I allowed the metaphorical to coexist with practical realities: since technology could win a war, technology and nationhood were intertwined. Andrews and MacLeod characterize World War I as "a struggle of invention" (1971: 4), the "engineer's war," and the "chemist's war" (MacLeod 1999). In particular, the war against Germany was both physical and economic; before World War I, Germany had used patents and state support strategically to put itself in a position of dominance in the chemical, electrical, and glassware industries, leading to great shortages of those products among the Allies during World War I when supplies were cut off (Liebenau 1988; Millard 2005: 300). Germany's success was attributed to the institutions and procedures it had developed, which had encouraged the application of science to industry (Millard

---

[7] On rare occasions they were licensed exclusively.

2005: 300). Germany had also used the patent system as a "weapon" throughout the late nineteenth and early twentieth centuries, taking out large numbers of foreign patents and building seemingly impenetrable blocks of related patents (Liebenau 1988: 14, 147; Steen 2001: 97). Thus, defeating Germany meant overcoming it militarily but also economically and scientifically, which the Allies attempted through sharing information and relaxing proprietary claims to knowledge in pursuit of a collective goal. War generated a sense of shared mission that brought about an unprecedented exchange of top-secret commercial information in the interests of an Allied victory (Eggleston 1950: 15).

Additional evidence of that shared mission leading to commons-like IP strategies is evident from a brief survey of novel IP mechanisms developed during World War I, built on during World War II, and continued by universities, businesses, and research organizations throughout the twentieth century. These mechanisms enabled sharing and pooling of proprietary rights in discoveries through several means. Collective invention boards were set up in the United Kingdom (MacLeod & Andrews 1971: 6) and the United States (Hughes 1989, 119) during World War I that invited, considered, and pooled citizen inventions. Assessments made with the benefit of hindsight, however, have concluded that these boards were little more than public relations strategies as "very little that was important for the prosecution of the war came out of this cloud of inventions" (MacLeod & Andrews 1971: 39). Patent pools were developed such as the Manufacturers Aircraft Association, which included almost all aircraft manufacturers in the United States. It was created to allow patents held by the Wright Company and Curtiss Company to be cross-licensed on reasonable terms to pool members. This pool enabled new airplane manufacture as the United States planned to enter World War I (Dykman 1964: 648). Mechanisms were also established to pool trade secrets between corporations and government. In particular, the U.S. NRC created the Research Information Service to ensure that "the secrets of allied science were, at least, to be shared among friends" (MacLeod 1999: 223). This exchange fostered what MacLeod has referred to as a model of "reciprocal generosity" (232). Meanwhile, the U.K. Trading with the Enemy Act of 1914[8] and the U.S. Alien Property Custodian created in 1917 as a patent trustee appropriated and confiscated enemy patents. In 1918 the Alien Property Custodian was given the authority to sell enemy-held (i.e., German) patents, with profits held in trust for distribution after the war. These actions were credited with stimulating the U.S. synthetic organic chemical industry through the creation of the Chemical Foundation Inc., a prototype technology transfer organization (Steen 2001). Governments were not only appropriating enemy patents, they also expropriated those of their citizens, offering compensation only after the fact.[9] For example, the U.K. Royal Commission on Awards to Inventors (RCAI)

---

[8] 4 and 5 Geo. 5, c. 87.

[9] Notably in Canada, Section 21 of the 1869 *Act Respecting Patents for Invention* 32–33 Vic., c. 11 held that "[t]he Government of Canada may always use any patented invention or discovery by paying to the patentee such sum as the Commissioner may report to be a reasonable compensation for the use thereof."

struck in 1919 after World War I, assessed claims from British inventors to technologies used during that war.[10]

While it is beyond the scope of this chapter to explicitly trace the links between war-time mobilization and broader Anglo-American patenting strategies, I do suggest that the world wars and the conditions of voluntarism and a commitment to the "public interest" created a valuable moment to experiment with innovative IP commons mechanisms. In fact, some mechanisms had been initiated before World War I (Marier & Piper 2010). This experimentation percolated through business and scientific endeavors before and after World War I as men moved back and forth from wartime activities to civilian life. For example, in Canada, Banting, co-developer of the innovative insulin commercialization model, was in the World War I medical corps; the Chemical Foundation Inc. was modeled on F. G. Cottrell's 1912 Research Corporation (Steen 2001: 100); and the Board of Invention and Research, one of the United Kingdom's collective invention boards, was later used as a prototype for the development of a public research organization, the Medical Research Council (MacLeod & Andrews 1971: 7). Necessity was the mother of invention of ways to invent. War created circumstances for experimentation, risk-taking, and collaboration that were rare in peacetime.

The period just after World War I saw extensive debate about the ethics and merits of patenting valuable discoveries, particularly in medicine and food (for example, Fishbein 1937). These debates likely arose because war, its deprivations (particularly of German goods), and a growing awareness of the role patents could play in enabling access to inventions, among other structural influences, had catalyzed important discoveries, encouraged laboratory organization of science, increased government spending on research, and generated an awareness of the importance of effective university-industry collaboration, as had been practiced in Germany. University and independent researchers were discovering life-saving advances, such as insulin and synthetic vitamin D, leading to debates about whether patents were the best way of manufacturing and distributing these advances.

It was also a time when public and quasi-public institutions experimented with commons patent models. From this period of vigorous discussion emerged a range of institutional for-profit and nonprofit patent or invention management mechanisms that I have surveyed in detail elsewhere (Marier & Piper 2010). These included independent, nonprofit foundations that carried out the business of commercialization for single or multiple institutions; effectively, nascent technology transfer organizations. A further option was to create a patent management committee, which would manage commercialization in the public interest, as happened in the case of the discovery of insulin (Bliss 2007). Other models included dedicating an invention to the public (without a patent) or obtaining a patent and dedicating that to the public. Particularly interesting were the informal networks of knowledge and information sharing about best practices,

---

[10] *Royal Commission on Awards to Inventors*, 158 NATURE 443 (Sept. 28, 1946), doi:10.1038/158443d0 (hereinafter, RCAI 1946).

as institutions and individuals tried to figure out a patent management scheme that fit their ethical, practical, and institutional priorities (see Marier & Piper 2010). Overall, novel patent strategies arose when there was some sort of complicating factor implicating the public good or a public interest. The most common of these seem to have been (1) a university researcher was involved or the institution involved was a university; (2) one of the institutions involved used significant public funds; (3) the institution identified itself as having a "public interest" mandate (other than a university); (4) the invention was perceived to be unusually important (e.g., insulin and vaccines); or (5) there was some sort of market failure that made the invention hard to market or commercialize in the conventional fashion.

The conditions of war, the collectivism it inspired, and other conditions prevailing at the time created an environment during and between World War I and World War II for enhanced appreciation of a "public interest." After World War I a new (or renewed) vision of that public interest was imagined and satisfied through creative techniques of intellectual property management in the Allied countries to channel and quickly disseminate inventions, using commons-style models pioneered or tested during wartime collaborations. Military men were particularly suited to acting in these boundary roles between government, the military, industry, and educational institutions.

III. Theme 2: Patenting in the Military

The military itself both embraced and abjured IP law and inventiveness; at times, it also adopted strategies that reflected commons-based IP approaches. Twentieth-century accounts of innovation often subscribe to a view that the military mind is inherently uninventive.[11] The poor reputation of military inventiveness obscures how military men were particularly suited to act as technology transferors. Innovation was key to military success, but it was generally impractical to consider patenting an invention in the field. As a memo in the McNaughton collection at Library and Archives Canada makes clear, inventors in the field could not readily provide detailed and accurate descriptions of their inventions.[12] Unsurprisingly then, military men in World War I patented in low numbers. Only eight patents were granted in 1926 among 215,000 men in the U.S. Army and Navy; men, who by virtue of their age, training, and experience, would have been at the peak of their inventive capacities. The total population of U.S. military men averaged

---

[11] A popular quotation was Aldous Huxley's: "If you look up 'Intelligence' in the new volumes of the Encyclopedia Britannica, you'll find it classified under the following three heads: Intelligence, Human; Intelligence, Animal; Intelligence, Military." Another, Lewis Mumford's, went: "Fortunately for mankind, the army has usually been the refuge of third-rate minds… Hence the paradox in modern technics: war stimulates invention, but the army resists it!" Both are quoted in Edgerton (2006: 309).

[12] "Memorandum of Proposed Procedure for Dealing with the Inventions of Officers and Soldiers of the Canadian Army Overseas," n.d., LAC MG 30-E133 Series III v. 143.

twenty-seven patents per year from 1910 to 1926 (encompassing World War I). Although I have only been able to find figures for the United States, figures could be even lower for countries like Canada and the United Kingdom given the historically higher prevalence of patenting in the United States (Khan & Sokoloff 2001: 239). However, the "intellectual commonplace" of the conservative, uninventive soldier contrasted with the creative civilian is an unhelpful stereotype (Edgerton 2006: ch. 8). A more plausible explanation for the general lack of military patents is that innovation filtered from enlisted men to broader use along paths other than the patent system (Rossman 1931: 415). A study of innovation in the Canadian Corps during World War I suggests that much influential invention generally happened on the ground. Trial on the battlefield determined whether a new technology would remain "in service" (Rawling 1992: 134). Innovators learned from experience, mistakes, and successes (175). Canadian soldiers "were less sheep led to the slaughter than thinking people who set their minds to the challenges of survival," and innovated accordingly (223). McNaughton confirmed this perception when he opined that better methods of fighting in battle came "not from the top, but from the lowest levels. It sprang, if you like, from man's instinct for self-preservation" (quoted in Swettenham 1968: 58).

Histories of technology in the army, navy, and military around World War I and in the interwar period among Allied forces show the contradictions created by technological innovation in the services (MacLeod & Andrews 1971). A common theme in studies of military innovation is the importance of balancing the order, discipline, and continuity required to be an effective fighting force with the need to adopt new technologies that might help against the enemy. Morison's (2004) classic case study documenting the introduction of continuous-aim firing in the U.S. Navy in 1902 observes that the Navy was a "precisely organized society … more rigidly structured, more highly integrated than most communities but still [a society]" (135). Innovating "allowed men to improve [their] own profession" within the Navy. The Navy, however, had to balance introducing new inventions with a concern that these new technologies would spread "disorder throughout a service with heavy commitments to formal organization." Morison also observes that a change in weapons or technologies portended changes in a military man's society. If not managed properly, these changes could jeopardize the military man's daily routines, habits of mind, social organization, rituals, and allegiances (136). Morison's account is echoed by Van Creveld (1989), who adds that excessively rapid technological change could lead "either to a badly trained army or to one that was well-trained but heterogeneous," and to a loss of institutional memory and cohesion (231). New technologies might also undermine training in basic skills and lead to overdependence (Rawling 1992). Since Canadian officers were not career military officers, but rather volunteers or militia officers, they were perhaps more willing to listen to advice and innovation from the ranks. General McNaughton was considered exemplary in this regard (Finan & Hurley 1997). Nonetheless, when innovation on the ground occurred, the military was most concerned with managing its potential disruptiveness.

Sparsely documented official policies toward invention during World War I in the Canadian Forces reinforce these accounts of innovation in active service. The King's Regulations and Orders for the Canadian Militia, 1917, stipulate that officers could not authorize "the trial of any invention without first obtaining the sanction of Minister in Militia Council."[13] Another provision required that "all inventions suggesting new patterns of military stores, or alterations to them are in the first instance to be referred to Militia Headquarters."[14] Thus, innovation was handled carefully in rigid military society, and in some cases rejected altogether. Useful invention, however, could also provide the basis of promotion and advancement, and likely had other internal rewards (Morison 2004; Swettenham 1968). McNaughton's biography confirms that technological innovation was a double-edged sword. Early in his time in the armed forces, in 1915, he was disciplined for using an improved gun that was longer than standard issue. He showed his innovation to his senior officers and merited "a very sharp rebuke. I was given a matter of an hour or two to get those rifles out of sight and the other ones back on. And no reason given at all" (quoted in Swettenham 42). In contrast, McNaughton's technique of spotting flashes from enemy guns to detect their position accurately so they could be taken out merited great praise from his superiors and likely aided his promotion (52).

Patenting military innovation was similarly fraught. Patents had the potential to disrupt chains of command, discipline, and order through an external system of reward and remuneration. In other professions, like medicine, this fact was sufficient for professional associations to discourage patenting among their members (Piper 2010). The potential conflict lies in the fact that the military has a defined hierarchy, entrance requirements, competence tests, and members who owe allegiance to a higher order than themselves (a "public interest").[15] As a profession, the military is characterized by responsibility and corporatism (Huntington 1957: 7). In contrast, the patent system is liberal, individual, and accessible to all; while some may argue that patent disclosure is in the public interest, the inventor generally owes allegiance primarily to herself. Its individualist, market values could threaten a professional body seeking to establish a corporate identity and its own systems of reward and recognition. The military and the patent system shared some characteristics, however. Patenting embraced a structure and respect for legal procedure that was commensurate with the military focus on order and rules. Military inventions were frequently and unproblematically patented by military suppliers (MacLeod &

---

[13] CANADA, MINISTER OF MILITIA AND DEFENCE, THE KING'S REGULATIONS AND ORDERS FOR THE CANADIAN MILITIA 1917 (Ottawa: Canadian Expeditionary Force Study Group, 1917), regulation 1252. http://archive.org/details/KRO1917, accessed Sept. 13, 2012 (hereinafter, Regulations 1917).

[14] CANADA, DEPARTMENT OF NATIONAL DEFENCE, THE KING'S REGULATIONS AND ORDERS FOR THE ROYAL CANADIAN AIR FORCE 1924 (Ottawa: King's Printer 1941), regulation 1379 (hereinafter, Regulations 1924). See also CANADA, DEPARTMENT OF NATIONAL DEFENCE, THE KING'S REGULATIONS AND ORDERS FOR THE CANADIAN MILITIA 1939 (Ottawa: JO Patenaude, ISO, Printer to the King 1939) (hereinafter, Regulations 1939).

[15] See Osiel (1999) for a critical perspective on this issue.

Andrews 1971: 4). Military men were allowed to patent, and the military merely regulated the process through legislation. In Canada, after World War I, patents obtained by military members were governed by s. 24 of the *Patent Act 1923*. This legislative provision was drafted by the NRC and passed with little debate.[16] It held that federal government employees could patent inventions relating to their employment at their own expense. The Commissioner of Patents might grant a license to a third party, but the patent holder was entitled to at least 50 percent of the royalties if royalties were to be shared with the government: a type of shared commons governance. The inventor retained all foreign patent rights. The Office of the Judge Advocate General (JAG) would resolve any disputes that arose under the employee patenting provisions. JAG files show only three decisions under the Act before 1942; the only one of significance, relating to McNaughton's radar patent in 1924, will be discussed below.[17]

The patent system does not seem to have threatened military order and chains of command, although if more military men had patented that relationship might have been tested more thoroughly. Its provisions were integrated through legislative and regulatory revisions. There was not a pure dichotomy between "patents" on the one hand and "the military" (read: the public domain, embodied by the government) on the other hand. Rather, military innovation was managed through a shared system guided by the terms of the Patent Act, 1923. The patent system was not threatening because its technique of granting rights over invention cohered with the law-abiding, process-oriented mode of military life. (Unstructured invention in the field is another story.) Legal structures governed military life as evidenced by the role of the JAG, the system of court martial, and the detailed regulations and procedures that governed every aspect of military life (even practical jokes[18]). The organization and priorities of the military and legal professions are markedly similar. Through their training, military men are imbued with a deep appreciation for the rule of law, a concomitant obedience to authority, and a reliance on precedent or historical example to develop principles to be used in the future (Huntington 1957: 64). Legislation that specified ownership and granted patents was likely regarded as one small part of the legal machinery governing military life rather than an incursion of the state into professional self-regulation.

There is some evidence to suggest that while patents by military men were not considered objectionable, there was a potential for conflicts of interest to arise. While the employee patenting provisions just discussed were aimed in part at addressing this concern, issues could still arise where a military man held a patent in which the military

---

[16] Dr. A. B. Macallum, *Policy re Patents Government Employees in Memorandum to the Hon. A.K. Maclean, Acting Minister of Trade and Commerce, Ottawa*, 3 Jan. 1919, LAC RG121 v. 110 L14-0-10. The Kings Regulations were revised that same year to specify that military men could only apply for patents under the provisions of the Act (Regulations 1924, regulation 1378).

[17] Judge Advocate General, LAC RG24 6645.

[18] See, for example, Regulations 1939, regulation 34, concerning practical jokes: "[The Commanding Officers of Units] will check any tendency among them to practical jokes."

might be interested (particularly if it related to supplies that he might be responsible for ordering). This concern animates the only substantive question the JAG received on patents in the interwar period: McNaughton's letter asking for advice about his early patent on radar. While this potential conflict did not otherwise arise in Canada, it did repeatedly in the United States. In the late nineteenth century, in *Kelton v. United States*, the court found that Colonel Kelton "could not, at one and the same time, be the adjutant general of a military department, determining the number of sights which should be manufactured for issue and use, and the inventor claiming a royalty for the device" (32 Ct. Cl. 314, 349 (1897)).[19] In a decision in 1913, the U.S. JAG refused to sanction disciplinary action where a military member claimed the government had infringed on his rights when it exercised its nonexclusive license to a technology (United States 1947d: 415–16). It is interesting that disciplinary action was even contemplated. The U.S. Army wished to encourage gifts and dedication of patent rights by members for military use, although in many cases this did not happen. McNaughton, for his part, attempted to gift his radar patent to the Canadian government, but was rebuffed until he became second president of the NRC and was in a position to accept his own gift.

To conclude, military men were likely not as uninventive as the patent numbers and popular reputation suggest, but were limited from filing claims by the exigencies of service. Innovation by military men was often inspired by necessity rather than profit. Military officers controlled and limited testing and adoption of inventions to minimize disruption to military society. There is some evidence that successful innovation could help a man to advance within the military, although the opposite is also the case. Military men might be in a conflict of interest if they held a patent, so gifts and dedications of patents were encouraged. Instruments and equipment were routinely patented, often by military suppliers, but battlefield techniques and innovations seem to have been patented less often, although evidence in this case is necessarily anecdotal. The Canadian government, directed by the NRC, passed legislation that treated members of the military as government employees, although the JAG considered only one patent (McNaughton's) under this legislation in the relevant period.

These features suggest that a commons perspective may explain innovation within the military profession. In earlier research, I documented how the U.K. medical profession in the late nineteenth and early twentieth centuries forbade its members from patenting, thus creating patent-free commons, first informally and then formally by lobbying for a legislative exception (Piper 2010). The stated justification for excluding certain medical methods of treatment from patentability was to ensure physicians were not hampered in their life-saving work by patents. The military profession was a similar sort of professional commons that seems to have preferred informal mechanisms for managing technology collectively while willingly submitting to formal IP laws. "Battlefield techniques," like medical methods, remain in a commons, in part because of the exigencies of their creation,

---

[19] See also Gill v. United States, 25 Ct. Cl. 415 (1890).

but also because of the necessity that they be shared in the heat of battle. In contrast to physicians, however, military men did not have to lobby for exclusions from patentability or special professional status in the *Patent Act*. The military did not need exclusions from patentability to help them function because their activities were so enmeshed with economic and political power structures. For all practical purposes the military *was* the patent system. The government compulsorily licensed inventions for the military's purposes; employee patent provisions protected military inventors; collective invention boards, patent pools, sharing of trade secrets, and confidential patent applications were all mechanisms that ensured that patents did not prevent members of the military from using a helpful technology. The highest levels of government fostered a commons to protect military practice; no legislative carve-out or norm-shaping through codes of conduct was required to effect technological adoption for the public good. Military men trained to be responsible to a higher interest and in the importance of collective action were likely to implement commons-type mechanisms in their practices. The implications of this conclusion are profound: the patent system in this context is quite consistent with commons, rather than an alternative to it, because the military was a well-recognized and compulsory system of sharing innovation. I now consider the commons-commitments of a particular military man to examine how these themes played out in practice.

IV. Theme 3: McNaughton the Military Man, Inventor, and Administrator

Commons techniques of IP management were adopted in the broader context of war as part of the collectivism, voluntarism, and shared objectives of the time. Many of these techniques were disseminated through the movement of military men into and out of civilian life. As they adopted different roles, military men brought tools, techniques and ideologies that inevitably shaped the organizations of which they became a part. Military men, it seems, are particularly suited to be legal boundary agents or translators: typically, they believe in the rule of law, accept the nation state as the highest form of political organization, and serve in the public interest with a strong belief in authority and precedent. General McNaughton was both an exceptional and typical military man: he held the second patent assigned to the NRC, the first patent under s. 24 employee patenting provisions of the Patent Act, 1923, was Chief of the General Staff (effectively the commander of the army), a prolific inventor, a trained engineer, and second president of the Canadian National Research Council (from 1935 to 1939).[20] In this last role he was the guiding mind in developing technology transfer mechanisms that provided templates for Canadian institutions that prevailed until the 1980s. In particular, he articulated and implemented a powerful vision of so-called "public interest" patenting that shaped the NRC's licensing practices throughout the twentieth century.

---

[20] He left the NRC on the outbreak of World War II to lead the First Canadian Infantry Division.

McNaughton had trained as an engineer at McGill University, obtained his MSc in 1912 and enlisted in the Canadian militia in 1909. His scientific advances in artillery technology are credited with helping the Canadians win at Vimy Ridge in World War I and contributed to his promotion to Lieutenant Colonel of the Canadian Corps artillery. During World War I he was responsible for a number of inventions including a range card to allow an 18-pound field gun to fire with greater accuracy on moving targets and a more effective type of shell (Swettenham 1968, 47), and even an improvised brazier to warm the troops when a manufactured one broke down (59). When he returned to Canada in 1920 he enlisted in the regular army and was appointed Chief of the General Staff in 1929. Despite the considerable talents of the first president of the NRC, H. M. Tory, his successor, McNaughton, created a technology transfer organization. McNaughton's personal documents suggest that he avidly read British and American scientific and invention literatures, and had close ties with British military men and scientists. Surviving documents evidence McNaughton's own patenting behavior and help us understand how his commitments to the public interest might have influenced the development of technology transfer at the NRC.

McNaughton was one of the first people to use s. 24 of the newly minted Patent Act. He was no exception to the military's appreciation for the rule of law, as evident in his description of a mentor's influence. "[Major J. J. Creelman] was an expert in military law and administration and I owe him a great deal for the thorough training he gave me in these matters" (quoted in Swettenham 1968: 21). The second patent ever assigned to the NRC was issued on June 30, 1925, to McNaughton and (Lieutenant-Colonel) William Arthur Steel for a "Cathode Ray Radio Compass" (Canadian Patent 251024). McNaughton recounts that the cathode ray direction finder (CRDF) was conceived in a train on the way back to Ottawa after launching the first Vickers Vedette aircraft in Montreal in July 1923 (Swettenham 1968: 220). He was inspired by the navigation demands of flying in remote parts of Canada, including the Northwest Territories. Magnetic compasses would not work efficiently so close to the North Pole, but radio promised to be an effective navigation tool.[21] His navigation instrument used a cathode ray oscilloscope to allow planes to visually determine the direction of radio beacons and their distance from those beacons. A transmitted signal from a radio beacon would invade the receiving system and trip the point of light so that it traced a stroke pointing to the transmitted signal. This was achieved by a beam of electrons streaming from the cathode to the screen, which was coated with fluorescent chemicals.

While aware of the commercial potential of his invention, in these early days McNaughton was most interested in how it might be deployed for military purposes. In a confidential memorandum dated July 14, 1924, McNaughton wrote to the Deputy Minister of National Defence that even though the JAG had held that the invention

---

[21] Andrew George Latta McNaughton, Letter to the Royal Commission, September 5, 1951, McNaughton Collection, LAC MG30-E133 v. 303, 4 (hereinafter, McNaughton Account 1951).

did not strictly relate to the nature of his employment, McNaughton and Steel wished to proceed under s. 24 of the Act as neither "wish[ed] to be placed in a position where our good faith in the performance of our duties could be questioned."[22] The Deputy Minister replied that the Department did not wish to have its own patent under s. 24, and McNaughton and Steel could go ahead and patent in their personal capacities, which they did.[23] Later in 1936, as NRC president, McNaughton formally assigned the patent to the NRC.[24] As in 1924, McNaughton reported that he wished to do so because he felt "embarrassed,"[25] and that "it would not be proper for me to press [the development of a prototype CRDF by the NRC's Radio Committee] so long as I had even any remote financial interest in the matter apart from my capacity as President of the Council."[26] McNaughton also hoped that the transfer would allow the NRC to work on radar without fearing demands of heavy royalties from third parties (i.e., the patent could be used defensively).[27] Steel communicated in turn that he only wanted "due recognition" and had no financial interest in the patent.[28] The transfer was effected on March 22, 1937, and a prototype CRDF was eventually developed in late 1938 by staff scientist J. T. Henderson, although by that stage it had already been preempted by the British invention and development of radar. This exchange shows McNaughton patenting an invention whose importance he recognized (even if the government did not) early in his career. He was preoccupied with the possibility of a conflict of interest, despite the fact that his supervisors were not so concerned, and he was familiar with patent management strategies. That McNaughton even thought to patent in 1924 suggests that as an engineer, soldier, and inventor, he was well informed about the merits and uses of the patent system well prior to his term as president of the NRC.

While McNaughton never benefited financially from his patent, a final footnote to the story suggests that he was more interested in recognition as inventor and in the development of Canadian technological capacity. In 1951, six years after the end of World War II, when McNaughton had returned to civilian life as Chairman of the International Joint Commission, he received a letter from the Principal Patents and Awards Officer at the U.K. Ministry of Supply asking to what extent "any of the user … flowed from the McNaughton and Steel direction finder" rather than from those of Sir Robert Watson-Watt and his group of colleagues.[29] The user referred to was that of radar or the CRDF; Watson-Watt

---

[22] McNaughton, Memorandum, July 14, 1924, LAC MG30 E133 v. 303.

[23] Assignment 2, LAC MG30 E133 v. 303.

[24] McNaughton to Lieut. Colonel E.L.M. Burns, Geographical Section, General Staff, Department of National Defence, December 8, 1936; and to the Secretary-Treasurer, December 12, 1936. LAC MG30-E133 v. 303.

[25] McNaughton to Steel, January 25, 1937, LAC MG30-E133 v. 303.

[26] McNaughton, Memorandum, December 8, 1936, LAC MG30-E133 v. 303. For more, see Middleton 1981.

[27] McNaughton to Mr. V.I. Smart, Deputy Minister, Department of Transport, Ottawa, December 28, 1936, MG30-E133 v. 303.

[28] McNaughton, Memorandum, December 8, 1936.

[29] Ibid.

was a recently knighted British scientist generally credited as the inventor of "radar" (Jones 2004), the American acronym for "radio detection and ranging." The United Kingdom had formed a Royal Commission on Awards to Inventors (RCAI) to compensate inventors whose "inventions, drawings or processes have been used by Government Departments and Allied Governments during the War."[30] In October 1951 the RCAI was in the process of validating twenty-five claims by Watson-Watt and a group of researchers who had worked with him.[31] The decision to award £50,000 ($150,000 Canadian at the time) to Watson-Watt in December 1951[32] recognized that he was "the indisputable creator of radar, that miraculous electronic eye" whose "…magic echo…guided the RAF to victory in the Battle of Britain in 1940."[33] Commentators at the time argued that this was "crumbs" compared to what Watson-Watt would have earned had he exploited the invention under "normal commercial conditions" (5). While Watson-Watt claimed that he had not obtained patents during the war because of the need for secrecy in developing the technology, he had obtained at least three radar-related patents with priority dates of 1926 or later.[34]

A man well known for his turns of phrase, Watson-Watt included in his claim to the RCAI that McNaughton had earlier "generously volunteered the statement that Watson-Watt had the idea and made it work, McNaughton and Steel had the idea and did not make it work."[35] McNaughton's account, however, did not square with Watson-Watt's. In his letter to the Commission, McNaughton detailed how he had, in fact, made it work[36] and expressed disbelief that given his and Steel's U.K. filing dates Watson-Watt was able to obtain a patent at all.[37] McNaughton explained the range of Canadian implementations of radar-type technologies: CRDF weather recorders at Ottawa and in Eastern Canada (early 1930s); as an aid to sea navigation (1935); antisubmarine location (early 1940s); and CRDF sets for all Canadian war-related intelligence operations (1943). McNaughton concluded his letter: "I cannot understand the statement which you quote Watson Watt as having made. I made no such observation."[38] McNaughton remained preoccupied with ensuring recognition of the Canadian contribution to radar, and perhaps more saliently,

---

[30] "Royal Commission on Awards to Inventors," 443.

[31] Principal Patents and Awards Officer to McNaughton, August 14, 1951, LAC MG30-E133 v. 303.

[32] Lord L.L. Cohen, Royal Commission on Awards to Inventors. Third report. Session: 1952–53. Cmd. 8743. His Majesty's Stationery Office.

[33] Mackenzie Porter, *Canada Recruits the 'Man Who Won the War,' MACLEAN'S MAGAZINE* (Aug. 1, 1952), 5.

[34] Canadian Patent no. 275623, 1927-11-22; French Patent no. 607249(A), 1926-06-28; German Patent no. 373327(c), 1927-04-04.

[35] Principal Patents and Awards Officer to Dr. C.J. MacKenzie, August 14, 1951, LAC MG30 E133 v. 303.

[36] McNaughton Account 1951.

[37] McNaughton Account 1951, 4. In fact, McNaughton and Steel never got a U.K. patent because of "an oversight on the part of the patent attorney," who had not followed up on the application within the proper time limit. C.J. MacKenzie to Sir Edward Appleton, January 9, 1945, LAC MG30-E133 v. 303.

[38] McNaughton Account 1951, 5–6.

his own contribution. His personal files contain a trove of underlined clippings indicating where he is mentioned or where the article failed to acknowledge his role.[39]

McNaughton's own activities as an inventor suggest that he had some awareness and confidence in the role of patents in securing and commercializing invention; he understood the need to balance complicated ethical issues; he saw the potential use of patents and patented technologies in the service of a broader public interest; and he had a strong commitment to nationalist technological interests. In demanding recognition for his work on radar, McNaughton perhaps demonstrated his faith in following procedure and the rule of law in appropriately allocating recognition. As the second president of Canada's only public science organization McNaughton was tasked with developing a program of scientific research that would be useful for applied (often military) purposes. Those inventions would be subsequently transferred through licensing, dedication, or otherwise to manufacturers and others who could commercialize and disseminate those inventions. Given the public nature of the NRC and the inventions it created, transfer was expected to occur in the "public interest."

I turn now to examining what McNaughton actually did as NRC president to lend meaning to the concept of patenting in the public interest and to the relationship between that practice and commons.

V. Theme 4: McNaughton and Technology Transfer

One of McNaughton's key contributions at the NRC was the development of its technology transfer operations. This he did by drawing on his expertise in the military and patenting and from the literatures he read. McNaughton took over the NRC helm in 1935 after his stint as Chief of the General Staff. In fact, he was only seconded (or loaned) by the army to run the NRC, in case a military "emergency" arose, as it did a few years later when war broke out. McNaughton saw his scientific leadership at the NRC as critical to developing Canadian industrial and inventive capacity should Canada go to war. As he cryptically put it, "there was a lot more reason in my going to the National Research Council than perhaps they [the NRC] or the general public knew" (quoted in Swettenham 1968: 321). The reason he alludes to was that Prime Minister Bennett had decided by 1935 that war with Hitler was inevitable and that "when we went to war, the National Research Council should be put in shape by association with the Armed Forces, [and] by industrial mobilization." McNaughton concluded from his discussions with the prime minister that he should "rehabilitate" the NRC to mobilize industry and improve the

---

[39] For example, *Radar Began By Tracking the Weather*, OTTAWA JOURNAL (June 1960), in LAC MG30-E133 v. 303; and Porter, *Canada Recruits the 'Man Who Won the War.'* McNaughton's biographer, Swettenham (1968), notes that McNaughton had a habit of underlining things, which was known to be his "stamp of approval" (304).

efficiency of the armed forces (324). This would not be an easy task. Prior to his appointment, McNaughton had sent a memo to the prime minister detailing that reserves of ammunition and equipment were nonexistent, the coast defense armament was obsolete, and there was not one modern antiaircraft gun in Canada (316). McNaughton's appointment was unpopular with NRC staff even though he had collaborated extensively with the NRC in the past. He was perceived to be more a military man than a scientist who wanted to make the Council "ready for war," an objective McNaughton felt he could not share openly with NRC staff (325–26). I have more thoroughly documented commercialization efforts at the NRC under McNaughton elsewhere, and what follows is a summary of these focusing on the commons-aspects of McNaughton's decisions (Murray, Piper, & Robertson, 2013).

When McNaughton started at the NRC, a number of patents had already been obtained, but the system of technology transfer operated on an ad hoc basis under the supervision of the Associate Committee on Patents and Awards, which met rarely, if ever.[40] Patent correspondence was disorganized, and files were not kept up to date.[41] One of McNaughton's first priorities was to fix this patent disarray and implement some "method of handling them here."[42] Soon after he began on June 1, 1935, he was taking stock of the existing patent operations, "the whole question of handling patents here and the assistance which MacRae [their patent counsel] can render us" as well as "the future work of the Associate Committee on Patents and Awards."[43] In a note to file, McNaughton writes that he had decided "that for the moment it is advisable to deal with particular [projects] rather than to try to establish a general policy in regards patents."[44] From the beginning, McNaughton's changes de-emphasized policy management by the central Associate Committee and focused on enabling action at the departmental level. McNaughton generated rigorous internal procedures for establishing and maintaining contacts with industrial partners, using his experience bridging military and scientific cultures to connect businessmen and NRC scientists. He organized files to track commercialization efforts by particular technologies as opposed to filing everything in a general "patents" folder.

The procedure McNaughton instituted for out-licensing invention was unvarying in form, although he and the patents officer adapted it to suit the technology and industry in question. The steps were first, to survey relevant markets, which included considering the patent landscape, especially whether other patents existed on the particular technology; second, to compile a list of the key industries in target jurisdictions and to assess the likelihood that the particular technology would be of use there; third, to assemble a list

[40] Lathe to Newton, March 18, 1934, LAC RG77 1988-89049 Box 7 file 4-P4-7.

[41] Lathe to Tory, January 10, 1934, LAC RG77 1988-89049 Box 7 file 4-P4-7.

[42] Lathe to McNaughton, October 21,1935, LAC MG 30-E133 Series II v. 125.

[43] Lathe to McNaughton, October 21, 1935, LAC MG 30-E133 Series II v. 125.

[44] McNaughton, note to file, n.d., LAC MG 30-E133 Series II v. 125.

of individual contacts at major companies; fourth, to solicit licensing offers through an initial invitation from the NRC president and a description of the invention written by one of the scientists involved; fifth, to follow up on any expressions of interest. Or, if no response had been received, McNaughton would send an update on the commercialization situation of a particular technology, particularly if the NRC had engaged in negotiations with a third party. McNaughton and the patents officer were aided in devising this procedure by the NRC's patent counsel, who himself was influenced by the wealth of inventor self-help manuals developed at the time.[45] These manuals advised adopting almost precisely these methods to generate interest in technologies.

In fourteen years of active patenting from when the NRC was established to when McNaughton left, the NRC applied for and obtained 227 patents, from a low of zero patents until 1921 to a high of fifty-five in 1938 (Figure 12.1). McNaughton was personally involved in licensing inventions, meeting with the patent lawyer, authoring and correcting many of the solicitations to industrial interests, and pursuing research and commercialization of technologies that he believed would be vital to winning a war. Patent applications rose dramatically during his tenure, and the bulk of these were for inventions of strategic military interest to Canada, in particular patents on magnesite; plant hormones (to be used in chemical warfare); atomic energy; and food storage and preparation for transport to the Allies and their citizens. McNaughton's military experience helped him act as a boundary agent between the scientific culture of the NRC and the world of business. As a military man he understood the importance of managing the process of technology adoption and translation carefully. McNaughton's actions and assertiveness with commercial partners suggest that he was able to think strategically, reflectively and over the long term. He was committed to following procedures and respecting existing

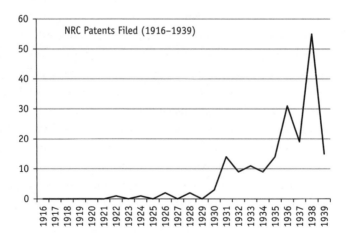

FIGURE 12.1 NRC Patents Filed 1916–1939.

---

[45] For example, Ridout (1872); Riches (1895); Fetherstonhaugh (1909); and Linton (1919).

legal rights (patents) in transferring technologies. And McNaughton appreciated that scientists who invented should be rewarded, negotiating bonuses for them.[46] He wrote and received extensive notes and memoranda updating progress. Rawling (1992) has observed that writing notes was a key communication strategy adopted by the Canadian Corps in World War I, one that it seems McNaughton adapted to the NRC's activities.

McNaughton thus encouraged the adoption of commons-creating licensing provisions and actions. He insisted on licensing inventions developed by NRC scientists in the "public interest." McNaughton's decisions as NRC president developed the contours of the public interest mandate that his predecessor, H. M. Tory, had established with optimism and that the NRC had adopted from its beginnings as a governing principle. The most coherent formulation of this public interest policy is found in a 1939 letter from Eagleson, the clerk in charge of patents, who wrote that "under the provisions of the Research Council Act these patent rights are vested in the Council and are made available to the public under conditions determined by the Council."[47] These conditions seem to have been determined on a case-by-case basis. Although the NRC repeatedly specified that inventions were licensed nonexclusively in Canada to Canadian companies and could be licensed exclusively elsewhere, actual practice shows that this policy was not followed uncompromisingly. Sometimes Canadian rights were licensed to Canadian companies under exclusive licenses, particularly in situations where the NRC felt that the "public interest" so demanded. Exclusive licensing was pursued in Canada when development of the particular technology was "sensitive," when the technology would not be developed otherwise, or when there was a threat that Canadians would be shut out of important markets for products that they had developed (Murray, Piper, & Robertson, 2013). These conditions mirror the public interest considerations adopted by early technology transfer of valuable food and medical technologies, discussed above in connection with theme one. The NRC's standard out-license included a working clause which required that the licensee use best efforts with due diligence to exploit the invention. The NRC was the sole judge as to what constituted diligent best efforts and could impose a cancellation penalty if it believed this was not done,[48] although it never did so in the period considered here.[49] The "public interest" also sometimes warranted taking offensive action, and in these instances McNaughton demonstrated himself to be a wily and strategic advocate, who also knew when he was beaten. For example, he authorized NRC scientists to file affidavits in support of infringement lawsuits over patents that threatened Canadian interests;[50] he strictly controlled sharing information about patent filings with perceived competitors; he encouraged informal negotiations with the Canadian Patent Office to bring evidence of nonobviousness and anticipation to light on patents filed

[46] Whitby to Crocker, May 14, 1937, LAC RG121 v. 109 L14-0-9 v.1-2.

[47] Eagleson to Pitt, September 7, 1939, LAC RG121 v. 110 L14-0-13 v. 2.

[48] Middleton to the NRC, August 17, 1942, LAC RG121 v. 110 L14-0-11.

[49] W.H. Courtise to Ellis Middleton, August 20, 1942, LAC RG121 v. 110 L14-0-11.

[50] McNaughton to Crocker, August 26, 1937, LAC RG121 v. 109 L14-0-9 v.1-2.

by foreign parties that threatened NRC technologies; he advocated defensive patenting strategies including filing broad blocking patents on NRC technologies; and he agreed to a royalty-free nonexclusive license to a patent when it was clear that a lawsuit would find it to be anticipated.[51] As a military man who had dedicated his own technologies to the public interest, McNaughton was uniquely equipped to articulate and manage the public interest institutionally.

McNaughton's technology transfer operation can be considered a constructed commons as it "mediate[d] among communities with different default norms" (Madison, Frischmann, & Strandburg 2010). This notion of "mediating" expresses how structured sharing was implemented institutionally. The framework developed by Madison, Frischmann, and Strandburg exposes the critical features of this structured sharing. McNaughton sought to share the NRC's scientific research results, sometimes commodified as IP, sometimes left as tacit knowledge (the "resources"), with a broader community of industries seeking to develop markets in Canada. That community was not necessarily exclusively Canadian, but rather seemed to be defined largely by the extent to which it committed to protecting and developing Canadian industry, boundaried by the research results of the NRC. The community may have included the Canadian public and similarly situated scientific research institutes in the United States and United Kingdom, and it most certainly included the staff of the NRC. The management structure of this constructed commons ranged from mundane administrative reforms and prodigious note-taking to more adventurous uses of licensing provisions, lobbying, negotiation, subterfuge, and alliance building. The governance structure of this constructed commons was framed by legislation, prime ministerial direction, and interactions between McNaughton, patent lawyers, and the NRC's scientists. It was, as a result, perhaps less self-governing than other types of constructed commons. The goal of the constructed commons—to mediate between the world of scientific research and industrial application—was shaped by the objective of serving the "public interest."

The public interest that McNaughton and NRC staff invoked constitutes the narrative of this constructed commons (Madison, Frischmann, & Strandburg 2010: 699).To McNaughton it could merely have been nationalism: what he perceived to be good for Canadian industry and the military was in the public interest. The fact that McNaughton had to appeal to the public interest suggests that the behaviors expected of those patenting in that interest were unclear. By invoking the "public interest" he was doing discursive work that served to create and form a collective interest and guide the operation of commons strategies (Warmer 2002). He was also creating a space for the state in invention and industrially applied research, which up until World War I had been the preserve of independent inventors and foreign patent-holders. He carved out a place for government applied science and formal technology transfer using patent rights, each an instantiation

---

[51] Eagleson to Middleton, February 15, 1943, LAC RG121 v. 110 L14-0-16.

of commons. He was creating a public interest in how inventions were patented and commercialized.

The impact of McNaughton's technology transfer structure was profound: the system he established continued largely unaltered, but for the addition of professional staff, throughout the 1940s and 1950s. In the 1960s the NRC was so successful that the Canadian government turned its patent arm into a Crown corporation called Canadian Patent Development Limited, which undertook technology transfer for government, most Canadian universities, and other institutions upon request. It served as the key technology transfer agency in Canada until the 1980s. The practices McNaughton introduced to the organization were the template for Canadian technology transfer organizations through much of the twentieth century.

VI. Conclusions

War provides a powerful metaphor for thinking about commons. War encompasses both the need for a shared enemy but also a common cause. It is in pursuit of this common cause that allies may come together and relax individual interests to pursue a shared objective. The metaphor of war threads through contemporary commons discourses: Lessig (2008), founder of Creative Commons, relies on "metaphoric" copyright wars to explain the appeal of commons-based licensing approaches; patent pools have been created to "fight" neglected tropical diseases.[52] A common "enemy" may help bring a public together, leading to unusual experimentation and risk-taking. This chapter has explored this claim by highlighting how many familiar commons approaches were tested and developed during an actual war, particularly during and after World War I. I explored the extent to which commons experimentation was a feature of the military profession. Innovation within the military profession had many commons features, particularly in preferring informal mechanisms for managing technology collectively with internal rewards and repercussions for violating norms, although the military willingly submitted to formal IP laws. The military never sought special exclusion from patent law, I argue, because it did not need to do so. The Patent Act, Patent Office procedures, and government agencies were adapted to meet the requirements of the military for innovative technologies. The military thus poses an interesting example of an environment of structured sharing that was not otherwise politically or legally marginal, but that manifested shared and proprietary forms of IP regulation.

Military men who moved between civilian life and military service translated IP mechanisms developed during war into civil society institutions. The ideal boundary

---

[52] *Pool for Open Innovation against Neglected Tropical Diseases*, Results for Development Institute Centre for Global Health R&D Policy Assessment, http://healthresearchpolicy.org/content/pool-open-innovation-against-neglected-tropical-diseases, accessed March 31, 2014.

agent considered in this chapter, General McNaughton, brought to his public role a strong commitment to developing technology in the "public interest" to prepare Canada for war. In exploring McNaughton's commons commitments, I considered his actions as an inventor in first obtaining a patent and then seeking to gift it back to the Canadian government. I also analyzed his actions as second president of the NRC in developing procedures and policies concerning nonexclusive licensing that bridged scientific and commercial cultures, while protecting the public interest. Individuals, their biographies, and commitments are important in exploring the creation and function of commons. Adopting a biographical approach to consider the individuals who create commons has the potential to deepen humanist approaches to commons scholarship, particularly when considering the community, management, governance, goals, and objectives of a constructed commons in Madison, Frischmann, and Strandburg's (2010) model. In considering the commons that McNaughton constructed in light of his biography, I implicitly argue that McNaughton was not merely law-obeying but law-creating, improvising his legal subjectivity and creating an internally consistent legal order within which technology transfer occurred at the NRC. That legal order is a form of commons.

Acknowledgments

I would like to thank Nick Kennedy and Amy Macdonald for their invaluable research assistance and Tim Pearson for his editorial assistance. I would also like to thank colleagues at the McGill Faculty Seminar Series, the Convening Cultural Commons workshop, NYU School of Law, September 23–24 2011, and the ISHTIP workshop at the London School of Economics, June 25– 26, 2012, for their helpful comments. In particular I am indebted to Lionel Bently, Robert Leckey, Desmond Manderson, Laura Murray, and Pamela Samuelson for their insights on earlier drafts, and Michael Madison for his thoughtful comments during the editing process.

References

MICHAEL BLISS, THE DISCOVERY OF INSULIN (University of Chicago Press 2007).

A. B. Cherns & P. A. Clark, *Task and Organization: Military and Civilian, in* TASK AND ORGANIZATION 151–72 (Eric J. Miller ed., London: Wiley 1976).

DEBORAH COWEN, MILITARY WORKFARE: THE SOLDIER AND SOCIAL CITIZENSHIP IN CANADA (University of Toronto Press 2005).

GEORGE CURRIE & JOHN GRAHAM, THE ORIGINS OF CSIRO: SCIENCE AND THE COMMONWEALTH GOVERNMENT, 1901–1926 (Melbourne: Commonwealth Scientific and Industrial Research Organisation 1966).

Harry T. Dykman, *Patent Licensing within The Manufacturer's Aircraft Association (MAA)*, 46 J. PATENT OFFICE SOCIETY 646 (1964).

David Edgerton, Warfare State: Britain, 1920–1970 (Cambridge University Press 2006).

Wilfrid Eggleston, National Research in Canada: The NRC, 1916–1966 (Toronto: Irwin Clarke 1978).

Wilfrid Eggleston, Scientists at War (Oxford University Press 1950).

Henry Etzkowitz & Loet Leydesdorff, *The Triple Helix: University—Industry—Government Relations*, EASST Review (n.d.), http://dare.uva.nl/document/41280 (accessed Sept. 13, 2012).

E. J. Fetherstonhaugh, The Prospective Patentee (Montreal: Fetherstonhaugh, Dennison & Co. 1909).

J. S. Finan & W. J. Hurley, *McNaughton and Canadian Operational Research at Vimy*, 48 J. Operational Research Soc'y 10 (1997).

Geoffrey Finlayson, *A Moving Frontier: Voluntarism and the State in British Social Welfare 1911–1949*, 1 Twentieth Century British History 183 (1990).

Morris Fishbein, *Are Patents on Medicinal Discoveries and on Foods in the Public Interest?*, 29 Industrial and Engineering Chemistry 1315 (1937).

Barton C. Hacker, *Engineering a New Order: Military Institutions, Technical Education, and the Rise of the Industrial State*, 34 Technology & Culture 1 (1993).

Barton C. Hacker, *Military Institutions, Weapons, and Social Change: Toward a New History of Military Technology*, 35 Technology & Culture 768 (1994).

Thomas P. Hughes, American Genesis: A Century of Invention and Technological Enthusiasm, 1870–1970 (New York: Viking 1989).

Samuel P. Huntington, The Soldier and the State: The Theory and Politics of Civil-Military Relations (Belknap-Harvard University Press 1957).

Reese V. Jenkins, *Words, Images, Artifacts and Sound: Documents for the History of Technology*, 20 British J. for the History of Science 39 (1987).

R. V. Jones, *Watt, Sir Robert Alexander Watson (1892–1973)*, in Oxford Dictionary of National Biography (H. C. G. Matthew & Brian Harrison eds., Oxford University Press 2004), http://www.oxforddnb.com/view/article/31811 (accessed June 16, 2010).

B. Zorina Khan & Kenneth L. Sokoloff, *History Lessons: The Early Development of Intellectual Property Institutions in the United States*, 15 J. Economic Perspectives 233 (2001).

Martha-Marie Kleinhans & Roderick A. Macdonald, *What Is a Critical Legal Pluralism?*, 12 Canadian J. Law & Soc'y 25 (1997).

Lawrence Lessig, Remix: Making Art and Commerce Thrive in the Hybrid Economy (New York: Penguin Press 2008).

Alison Li, J. B. Collip and the Development of Medical Research in Canada: Extracts and Enterprise (Montreal: McGill-Queen's University Press 2003).

Jonathan Liebenau (Ed.), The Challenge of New Technology: Innovation in British Business Since 1950 (Aldershot: Gower Press 1988).

William C. Linton, The Inventor's Adviser and Manufacturer's Handbook to Patents, Trade Marks, Designs, Copyrights, Prints and Labels (Montreal: W.C. Linton 1919).

Christine MacLeod, Heroes of Invention: Technology, Liberalism and British Identity, 1750–1914 (Cambridge University Press 2007).

Roy MacLeod, *Secrets among Friends: The Research Information Service and the 'Special Relationship' in Allied Scientific Information and Intelligence, 1916–1918*, 37 MINERVA 201 (1999).

Roy M. MacLeod & E. Kay Andrews, *Scientific Advice in the War at Sea, 1915–1917: The Board of Invention and Research*, 6 J. CONTEMPORARY HISTORY 3 (1971).

Michael J. Madison, Brett M. Frischmann, & Katherine J. Strandburg, *The University as Constructed Cultural Commons*, 30 WASHINGTON UNIVERSITY J. LAW & POLICY 365 (2009).

Michael J. Madison, Brett M. Frischmann, & Katherine J. Strandburg, *Constructing Commons in the Cultural Environment*, 95 CORNELL L. REV. 657 (2010).

Stephen L. Mangum & David E. Ball, *Military Skill Training: Some Evidence of Transferability*, 13 ARMED FORCES & SOC'Y 425 (1987).

Virginie Marier & Tina Piper, *Early Twentieth Century Canadian Medical Patent Law in Practice: James Bertram Collip and the Discovery of Emmenin*, 60 U. TORONTO L.J. 855 (2010).

W. E. KNOWLES MIDDLETON, RADAR DEVELOPMENT IN CANADA: THE RADIO BRANCH OF THE NATIONAL RESEARCH COUNCIL OF CANADA 1939–1946 (Waterloo: Wilfrid Laurier University Press 1981).

Rod Millard, *The Crusade for Science: Science and Technology on the Home Front, in* CANADA AND THE FIRST WORLD WAR: ESSAYS IN HONOUR OF ROBERT CRAIG BROWN 300 (David MacKenzie ed., University of Toronto Press 2005).

Elting Morison, *Gunfire at Sea: A Case Study of Innovation, in* MANAGING STRATEGIC INNOVATION AND CHANGE: A COLLECTION OF READINGS 59 (2d ed. Michael L. Tushman & Philip Anderson eds., Oxford University Press 2004).

LAURA J. MURRAY, S. TINA PIPER, & KIRSTY ROBERTSON, PUTTING INTELLECTUAL PROPERTY IN ITS PLACE: RIGHTS DISCOURSES, CREATIVE LABOR, AND THE EVERYDAY (Oxford University Press 2014).

George Orwell, *Wells, Hitler and the World State*, HORIZON (August 1941), *reprinted in* COLLECTED ESSAYS, JOURNALISM AND LETTERS OF GEORGE ORWELL II (Sonia Orwell & Ian Angus eds., 4 vols. Harmondsworth: Penguin 1970).

MARK J. OSIEL, OBEYING ORDERS: ATROCITY, MILITARY DISCIPLINE & THE LAW OF WAR (New Brunswick, NJ: Transaction Publishers 1999).

Tina Piper, *A Common Law Prescription for a Medical Malaise, in* THE COMMON LAW OF INTELLECTUAL PROPERTY: ESSAYS IN HONOUR OF PROFESSOR DAVID VAVER 143 (Catherine W. Ng, Lionel Bently, & Giuseppa D'Agostino eds., Oxford: Hart Publishing 2010).

BILL RAWLING, SURVIVING TRENCH WARFARE: TECHNOLOGY AND THE CANADIAN CORPS, 1914–1918 (University of Toronto Press 1992).

CHARLES H. RICHES, HAND BOOK ON PATENT AND TRADE MARK LAW OF CANADA AND THE UNITED STATES (Toronto: C. H. Riches 1895).

D. C. RIDOUT, THE INVENTOR'S POCKET COMPANION (Ottawa: I. B. Taylor 1872).

Joseph Rossman, *War and Invention*, 36 AM. J. OF SOCIOLOGY 625 (1931), *reproduced in* 14 J. PATENT OFFICE SOC'Y 409 (1932).

Theda Skocpol, Ziad Muson, Andrew Karch, & Bayliss Camp, *Patriotic Partnerships: Why Great Wars Nourished American Civic Voluntarism, in* SHAPED BY WAR AND TRADE: INTERNATIONAL INFLUENCES ON AMERICAN POLITICAL DEVELOPMENT 134 (Ira Katznelson & Martin Shefter eds., Princeton University Press 2002).

Kathryn Steen, *Patents, Patriotism, and "Skilled in the Art": USA v. The Chemical Foundation, Inc., 1923–1926*, 92 Isis 91 (2001).

John Alexander Swettenham, McNaughton, vol. 1. (3 vols. Toronto: Ryerson 1968–1969).

Mel W. Thistle, The Inner Ring: the Early History of the National Research Council of Canada (University of Toronto Press 1966).

United States Department of Justice, *Patent Policies and Practices of Educational and Other Nonprofit Organizations*, Investigation of Patent Practices and Policies—Report and Recommendations of the Attorney General to the President 3 (Washington, D.C.: U.S. Government Printing Office 1947a.).

United States Department of Justice, *Patent Policies and Practices of the Department of Commerce Concerning Inventions of Its Employees and Contractors, in* Investigation of Patent Practices and Policies—Report and Recommendations of the Attorney General to the President 75 (Washington, D.C.: U.S. Government Printing Office 1947b).

United States Department of Justice, *Patent Policies and Practices of Foreign Governments Concerning Inventions of Their Employees and Contractors, in* Investigation of Patent Practices and Policies—Report and Recommendations of the Attorney General to the President 79 (Washington, D.C.: U.S. Government Printing Office 1947c).

United States Department of Justice, *Patent Policies and Practices of the War Department Concerning Inventions of Its Employees and Contractors, in* Investigation of Patent Practices and Policies—Report and Recommendations of the Attorney General to the President 403 (Washington, D.C.: U.S. Government Printing Office 1947d).

Jonathan F. Vance, Death So Noble: Memory, Meaning, and the First World War (University of British Columbia Press 1997).

Martin Van Creveld, Technology and War: From 2000 B.C. to the Present (New York: Free Press 1989).

Michael Warner, *Publics and Counterpublics (abbreviated version)*, 88 Quarterly J. Speech 413 (2002).

13 Labor and/as Love: Exploring the Commons of Roller Derby

David Fagundes*

I. Introduction

My contribution to this volume on knowledge commons is about roller derby. It is about how and why people create and draw from the shared body of knowledge and close-knit community that make up the heart of roller derby. It is also about what their compulsion to engage in that creation on a largely share-alike, volunteer basis means for our understanding of commons and about production of cultural artifacts in the absence of pecuniary motivation more generally. I cannot begin exploring these issues, though, without saying a few descriptive words about what roller derby is, in order to familiarize the uninitiated.

Roller derby is an American-born sport in which two teams of competitors on quad skates careen counterclockwise around a (banked or flat) oval track.[1] Derby was first developed in the 1930s, and enjoyed brief but always temporary bursts of popularity

---

* David Fagundes is Professor of Law at Southwestern Law School, Los Angeles, California, USA.

[1] The rules of derby are complex enough that it is often difficult for first-time observers to understand game action and strategy. Here are some basics: In most current styles of derby, two teams of five skaters each compete. The teams consist of one jammer and four blockers. Points are scored when a jammer laps (passes twice) one of the opposing team's blockers. The bouts are broken down into four quarters of varying lengths, and the units of play are "jams" of sixty or more seconds. Full contact is legal subject to hockey-style rules (e.g., lateral hits are allowed but tripping, elbowing, or pushing from the rear are not). This brief description is a mere incomplete sketch of the game's rules, which vary more than a little among regions, leagues, and surfaces (e.g., banked versus flat track).

throughout the twentieth century. In the past ten-odd years, though, the sport has undergone a reinvention as an edgy subcultural phenomenon. As initially reconceived in Austin, Texas, back in 2001, the new derby combines compelling (and real[2]) athletic competition as well as a performance spectacle tinged with equal parts punk and camp. Skaters are serious athletes, but they also sport fishnets, tattoos, and names like Tara Armov, Raven Seaward,[3] and Gori Spelling. Skaters are almost all women,[4] and they (in combination with the many men and women who do not skate but are crucial to making derby happen) have created something extraordinary: not only a series of entertaining bouts for public consumption but also a distinctive countercultural community that provides a sense of belonging and identity for those who are part of it.[5]

This case study seeks to add to the growing discussion about commons governance strategies by focusing on the world of roller derby itself, rather than the bouts that are exhibited for the public.[6] In 2001, the contemporary roller derby world was born spontaneously and without any overriding pecuniary motivation. The main motivation appears to have been a desire for stardom and community rather than profit. At one of the first gatherings at which the contemporary version of roller derby was hatched, the event's organizer observed, "There's gonna be live music, midgets, fire breathers, and multimedia presentations, all sponsored by bars, that will battle it out through roller derby. We're all gonna be superstars!" (Barbee & Cohen 2010). Just over a decade later, roller derby continues to thrive thanks to the ongoing collaborative efforts of the thousands of people who devote themselves to derby without any expectation of financial reward. This case study discusses not only how this particular commons is constructed and governed. It also provides an opportunity to think more generally about why such commons arise in the first place, and about what the emergence of such commons means for our understanding of what motivates creative goods as well as what motivates the choice of the property regimes that govern them.

---

[2] I add this note because many people wrongly believe roller derby to be a "fake" sport like pro wrestling. It is not. The outcomes of bouts are unplanned, and the action is unscripted.

[3] Get it? See Caroline on Crack, *5 Tips for How to Create Your Derby Name*, http://carolineoncrack. com/2010/07/13/tips-on-how-create-your-roller-derby-name/ (quoting Raven as saying, "Granted, not everybody understands the true genius of this name the first time they read it, but the look on people's faces when it finally comes together is priceless.").

[4] But see http://www.mensderbycoalition.com/ (providing an overview of MRDA, the Men's Roller Derby Association). There are sixteen men's roller derby leagues nationally, as opposed to hundreds of women's roller derby leagues.

[5] This paragraph is of necessity a very brief and incomplete sketch of the sport. I provide a longer (several-page) description and history of roller derby in a related paper (Fagundes 2012a). Two great books that recount in detail the development, culture, and play of contemporary roller derby are Barbee & Cohen (2010) and Mabe (2007).

[6] As I explain in more detail below, derby bouts are not commons from the perspective of the consuming public. Rather, they are standard private entertainment goods, like movies or baseball games, to which access is limited and parceled out on a for-pay basis.

The ensuing discussion proceeds in three parts. In Part I, I reflect on the meaning of commons in light of both property theory as well as Madison, Frischmann, and Strandburg's knowledge commons framework (Madison, Frischmann, & Strandburg 2010). In Part II, I pose and answer three descriptive questions that frame an examination of roller derby through the lens of a knowledge-commons analysis: What resources related to roller derby are governed as commons, how are those resources governed, and who has access to those resources? In Part III, I turn to questions that are immanent in the preceding discussion: What causes roller derby people to devote themselves so passionately to their sport on an entirely volunteer basis, and how is this related to the decision to regulate many of roller derby's cultural resources as commons? Roller derby adds yet another case to the growing litany of examples illustrating the flaws in the traditional assumption of much property and intellectual property law that financial incentives are the key to more and better creative production. The emergence and continued thriving of roller derby further illustrates linkage between the status of an information good as a labor of love and the choice of a commons to govern it.

II. Of Commons and Commonsiness

In this part, I explore the notion of commons, with the aim of providing a framework for assessing how and whether it makes sense to think of roller derby in these terms. I begin by exploring the more formal meanings of commons that have predominated in the physical property literature, and then move on to consider Madison, Frischmann, and Strandburg's more flexible definition of the term used in their treatment of knowledge commons. The notion of commons is familiar in popular usage. Despite this familiarity, though, the term is used in divergent and often confusing ways (Eggertsson 2000).[7] In particular, two conflations have obscured understanding of this term. The first is that the word "commons" is often used to refer to both a physical place as well as the property law strategy used to govern that place. Consider Hardin's classic example, the English village green. In one colloquial usage, this space itself was referred to as "the commons." This usage persists to date and has also crossed the Atlantic. Denizens of Boston know that "let's go to the Common" means "let's go to our city's central public park." The plots of land popularly identified as "commons" are also typically regulated by governance schemes understood in property law as "commons" governance schemes (although, as I explain in the next paragraph, the term "commons" is used to refer to several different governance schemes). So it may be accurate to say that "Boston Common is governed as a commons," and it is not a coincidence that place and the legal strategy used to govern it share the same name. But this overlap illustrates the challenges of negotiating the meaning of "commons."

---

[7] Cited in Dagan & Heller (2001).

The second conflation relates to the meaning of the commons property-law governance strategy itself. The legal literature deploys the term "commons" to refer to at least three different property governance schemes. One such usage refers to a strategy whereby no public or private entity holds title to a resource, so that any individual can access the resource under virtually any conditions. Examples include the air we breathe, the high seas, and works of authorship that have fallen out of copyright protection and into the public domain. No one can exercise a right to exclude others from accessing these resources, and few if any regulations restrict their use.[8] Frank Michelman has referred to such resources as "commons" in the sense that "there are never any exclusionary rights. All is privilege. People are legally free to do as they wish, and are able to do, with whatever objects… are in the [commons]" (Michelman 1982).

A second regime sometimes referred to as a form of "commons" governance strategy arises where title in a resource is held by some entity (a private owner or the state[9]), but the title holder decides to make the resource broadly available to the public with no or few conditions on its use. A municipal park fits this bill. The state owns the land and could exercise its authority to close it off to the public, but instead chooses to allow general access conditioned only on compliance with basic, generally applicable rules (evening curfews, bans on alcohol or fires). Copyrighted works of authorship shared pursuant to Creative Commons licenses falls into this category as well. Copyright owners could keep their work secret or only release copies of it for sale, but many owners choose to share them with the public via some variation of a Creative Commons license. This "commons," though, arises at the discretion of the work's owner and is not limitless. Rather, it is subject to at least one of four use conditions: that users attribute the author, that they make the work available on a share-alike basis, that they make it available noncommercially, and/or that they not make any derivative works.[10]

In still a third variation of property governance that is often described as a "commons," a demarcated and relatively limited number of people are freely entitled to use a resource and cannot exclude other group members from doing so (Dagan & Heller 2001). Yet nonmembers of the group may not access the resource, and group members have the right to exclude nonmembers. Many historical examples of English village greens adhere to this definition: All villagers had the right to use the commons, but outsiders did not and were subject to villagers' rights to exclude. Consider also modern condominium

---

[8] International waters are governed by the United Nations Convention on the Law of the Sea (UNCLOS), but this agreement confirms the basic proposition that "the high seas are open to all states, whether coastal or landlocked." UNCLOS Art. 87(1).

[9] Public and private entities may warrant a further distinction within this category. The state's decision to render its property open to the public flows from its obligations vis-à-vis the public, especially insofar as the state is often regarded as owning land in trust for the public. By contrast, a private actor's choice to make its property freely available is a discretionary choice that is not a product of any quasi-fiduciary obligation, and so could be revoked at any time.

[10] See About the Licenses, http://creativecommons.org/licenses/.

developments, where residents have equal (albeit regulated) access to the development's shared spaces such as pools or hallways (often called "common areas"). Nonresidents, by contrast, have no rights of access to these areas, and residents can kick out any unauthorized outsiders found in the community pool or gym. Rose has characterized this latter form of governance as "commons on the inside, private property on the outside" (Rose 1998: 155). Many, perhaps most, of the "commons" governance strategies detailed in Elinor Ostrom's *Governing the Commons* fall into this third category, rather than being governed on an the more open-access bases of the first two categories (Ostrom 1990).

This disconsensus about the precise meaning of "commons" does not suggest that the term lacks coherence. Rather, it may indicate that it is more useful to think of commons as occupying some territory along a continuum of property governance schemes (Smith 2002). Madison, Frischmann, and Strandburg draw from Ostrom's multivalent account of commons in inviting us to consider what it means to govern cultural rather than physical resources as commons. The authors define commons broadly as "environments for developing and distributing cultural and scientific knowledge through institutions that support pooling and sharing that knowledge in a managed way" (Madison, Frischmann, & Strandburg 2010). The authors have construed the term capaciously by design, seeking to invite discussion about different governance strategies rather than focusing on the formal definition of the term (Madison, Frischmann, & Strandburg 2009). Their approach thus does not regard information goods in terms of whether they are or are not governed as commons in a binary sense, but rather in terms of which aspects of a commons governance strategy they possess—that is, their "commonsiness."[11]

Madison, Frischmann, and Strandburg (again, drawing from Ostrom) have identified numerous drivers that may make a governance strategy more or less commonsy for cultural resources. One of those drivers is the extent to which those entitled to extract from the commons are regulated in doing so (Madison, Frischmann, & Strandburg 2009). One approach could say that all villagers are allowed to graze livestock on the commons, without limit, raising the likelihood of the "tragic" outcomes that are a constituent feature of natural resources commons. A more moderate strategy would be to restrict the extraction rights of those entitled to access the commons, in order to avoid such tragedies (Ostrom 1990). Another driver of commonsiness looks to the constitution of the group that is entitled to use the resource (Madison, Frischmann, & Strandburg 2009). In some cases—the public domain, the high seas—this group will be without limit. Other commons—a homeowners' association or the denizens of a small village—will have a much smaller community entitled to use it. This general approach of defining commons in terms of a series of different drivers that create degrees of commonsiness rather than identifying the silver-bullet feature that characterizes all commons helps us understand

---

[11] While this is a reference to Steven Colbert's zeitgeisty term "truthiness," I should stress that by "commonsiness," I mean some feature that actually is like a commons, rather than something that is seems true but is actually not (Fagundes 2012a).

how different property governance schemes such as the ones described above may all coherently be regarded as commons.

Madison, Frischmann, and Strandburg regard as commons resources as disparate as patent pools, universities, and Wikipedia. Each of these resources exhibit various features of commons governance, though the particular strategies used to regulate them differ. Patent pools are reminiscent of the third formal category discussed above, "commons on the inside, private property on the outside." They allow a defined and relatively small number of entities access to share in the exclusive rights of patentees, but are available to others only on standard licensing terms. Universities produce and make available (usually for free) knowledge resources. Some of these resources, like libraries, are accessible only to the broad class of university members (so that it is more like the third category discussed above), while other resources, like academic articles, tend to be made available to anyone without limit (and are thereby more like the second category of commons discussed above—proprietary material held open to the public by choice of the owner). Finally, the information organized and presented on Wikipedia falls more into the first formal category discussed above, at least from the perspective of the consuming public. Wikipedia presents mostly factual information in the public domain and is made available to the public on an open-access basis. Anyone can access the online encyclopedia, free of charge, without need for a password and regardless of whether you are a devoted Wikipedian or just someone who wants to know who scored the most goals for the German national soccer team.[12]

My discussion has sought to contrast the formal/conceptual approach to defining commons that predominates in some physical property literature with the more functional/flexible understanding of the term that Madison, Frischmann, and Strandburg use in their work. This discussion provides an outline for the ensuing exploration of roller derby as a commons. Part II will consider what aspects of roller derby are governed in a commonsy way, and how they are so governed, both in terms of who is entitled to access the resource and what the terms of that access are. And as the following discussion will make clear, roller derby appears to fit uncomfortably into the notion of commons, but the apparent discomfort makes it more rather than less promising as a subject of study. The peculiar project of figuring out just how roller derby does and does not make sense as a commons may do more to tell us about the promise and meaning of commons than more obviously apt examples.

III. The Commons of Roller Derby

This part examines roller derby as a commons. The operational definition of commons developed in the foregoing part indicates three different questions to which this inquiry

---

[12] It's Gerd Mueller, with an amazing 68 goals in 62 games for Die Nationalmannschaft.

invites answers. The first question starts with *what*. What is the subject matter related to roller derby that is governed with a commons strategy? Before considering how a commons is governed, it is obviously necessary to specify what resource is subject to that form of governance. The second question starts with *how*. How is the roller derby's commons governed? This discussion focuses on the rules of extraction that limit the extent to which people can exploit roller derby's commons. In particular, it examines the extent to which this resource is being increasingly monetized. The final question starts with *who*. Who is permitted to exploit resources from roller derby's commons? This question reflects on the nexus of community and commons, leading into the broader discussion of this issue in Part III.

A. WHAT ASPECTS OF ROLLER DERBY ARE GOVERNED AS COMMONS?

Roller derby has much in common with many of the cultural phenomena that over the last couple of decades have come to epitomize a new form of production that is inspired more by sharing and passion than selfishness and pecuniary gain (Benkler 2004). Like Wikipedia or Linux, roller derby is not a project conceived with financial gain in mind. Rather, it arose and persists thanks to the innumerable incremental, voluntary, widely distributed contributions of the tens of thousands of people who share a passion for the sport. And many of derby's participants find the share-alike ethic personally inspiring. Ivanna S. Pankin, one of the founders of roller derby's contemporary renaissance, expressed her familiarity with the notion of Creative Commons, saying, "I'm really into that concept and I think it's awesome."[13] *DerbyLife* emphasized the importance of this ethic to the creation and maintenance of the sport: "The growth of roller derby owed much of its success to throngs of committed volunteers all sharing their best tips, tricks, and innovations with each other, freely."[14] And Derby News Network (DNN) is just one of many roller derby resources that boasts a crowdsourcing approach to production, reporting that "[o]ver the course of each year, many hundreds of modern derby enthusiasts contribute their Cognitive Surplus to further DNN's mission."[15]

Even though there is a general consonance between derby's ethic and the notion of commons, it remains important to specify particular aspects of roller derby that may be so governed. What features of roller derby include cultural or informational resources

---

[13] Telephone interview with Ivanna S. Pankin (Oct. 4, 2012) (digital sound recording on file with author) (hereinafter "Ivanna S. Pankin interview"). (This name, like the names of all roller derby participants quoted in this chapter, is a roller derby pseudonym.) She continued, "I like the idea of sharing," and observed that by freely providing other derby people with "building blocks that can be figured out by anyone with the time or inclination."

[14] DerbyLife, *Excellent Derby Open Source Tool Is Updated!*, DerbyLife.com (Feb. 8, 2012), http://www.derbylife.com/articles/2012/02/excellent_derby_open_source_tool_updated.

[15] Http://www.derbynewsnetwork.com/about_dnn. In a footnote that illustrates the point that roller derby is copacetic with the notion of commons in a highly general sense, this DNN page goes on to cite Wired, TED, and Wikipedia for its use of "cognitive surplus."

that are made available on a shared basis to a closed group of people? At least two candidates might fit this definition. The first is knowledge. The sport and culture of roller derby depend on information and wisdom to create and maintain the sport. At a high level of generality, there is a demand for information about what roller derby is and possibly also how to get involved. Beyond that level of knowledge, an aspirant derby girl ("fresh meat" in subcultural parlance) will need at least some, and possibly a lot of, instruction about everything from basic skating skills to the rules of the sport to the strategy used by competitors during bouts. Even experienced skaters produce and exchange knowledge about how to refine and advance their skill sets. Nascent leagues also require basic information about how to recruit members, stage a bout, build a track, and do the countless other far from obvious tasks necessary to start a new league. Here, too, there is an ongoing need for knowledge about how to address the continued challenges of league management and governance.

A second, and less obvious, feature of roller derby may be regarded as commonsy: the social world of roller derby itself. People who are part of the derby world can freely take part in the sport's distinctive camp/punk subculture, in the form of events like dances or group dinners, or simply through the informal interactions that thrive among and characterize this especially close-knit group. A significant source of roller derby's appeal is that it provides a unique[16] countercultural milieu in which participants can find a sense of belonging and identity. Indeed, for many derby people, this sense of belonging and identity provide the primary impetus for their participation in the sport.[17]

Thinking about community as a resource governed by a commons management strategy may seem puzzling. A natural resource like timber or an intangible one like information may be made available freely or for a price. But while fellowship is something we may desire and seek, we think of it as operating outside the world of acquisition and certainly of monetary exchange. Yet community seems to fit the rough contours of commons as I have defined them in this chapter: It is an incorporeal resource in which a defined group of people can participate freely.[18] In the spirit of the broadly conceived commons project, I seek to entertain the notion that the fellowship of roller derby can be studied as a commons in order to explore and refine the contours of that term.

Before moving on, I stress that roller derby is commonsy only from the perspective of the insiders who may seek to use its knowledge or community resources (Rose

---

[16] Truly: there is nothing like the derby subculture in the world, at least not to my knowledge.

[17] See telephone interview with Fighty Almighty (Apr. 15, 2012) (digital sound recording on file with author) (hereinafter "Fighty Almighty interview") (estimating that community is a major source of interest in participating in roller derby for at least 90% of derby girls). This assertion is obviously a broad and imperfect generalization. Obviously derby girls have a variety of motives for wanting to participate in the sport. Some people may be exclusively interested in the athletic competition aspects of roller derby and may not be compelled at all by the opportunity it provides to be part of a distinctive social group.

[18] One of the features of physical commons is their facilitating the kinds of social bonds that link communities together. People still gather on town greens to celebrate the Fourth of July, for example (Rose 1986). And other work has considered the relationship between community and forms of property governance (Madison 2008).

1998). To the viewing public who attend roller derby matches, by contrast, it is just a garden-variety private good (Solum 2010). Those who want to see a derby bout have to buy a limited-supply ticket just like those who want to see other forms of live entertainment, such as a music show or a baseball game. One rare but interesting exception to this private property model of roller derby bears noting. While most leagues seek to recoup their operating costs to a large extent by staging bouts for which they charge admission, a handful of other leagues seek to cover those costs with sponsorships and dues. These leagues typically do not charge for admission to their bouts, or charge very little, since their goal is primarily to compete and excel at the sport itself (including and especially in the context of Women's Flat Track Derby Association (WFTDA)-sanctioned tournaments), rather than to provide entertainment for fans.[19] To the extent that these leagues charge little or nothing to attend bouts, they are more like an open-access commons than a private entertainment good, since anyone who wants to come by is free to do so.

B. HOW IS ROLLER DERBY'S COMMONS GOVERNED?

The question that frames this subpart could be answered in a number of ways. Ostrom's case studies on, inter alia, Turkish fisheries and Japanese mountain forests typically analyze the rules governing how members can extract from the shared resource (Ostrom 1990). I will focus here on a particular iteration of the question of governance: the extent to which the aspects of roller derby purportedly governed as commons—knowledge, community—are actually parceled out. This includes the question whether these resources are available at some cost or for free, and touches on other means that may be used to regulate and limit access to them. As explained below, some of roller derby's resources are governed as commons in a variety of ways, while others are treated as regular private information goods and put up for sale.

Let's start with knowledge. The majority of the information of interest to people who want to start a league, or to start skating in a league, is available for free or for a nominal charge. You do, however, have to know where to look and to whom to talk. If you want to know how to become a sanctioned league, there is an extensive guide at the home page of the Women's Flat Track Derby Association (WFTDA). The WFTDA site explains the process for becoming an "apprentice" league, which requires compliance with WFTDA's rules for league operation (e.g., quad skating only, women skating only, governance by "democratic principles and practices").[20] Numerous resources provide freely available information for starting a league from the ground up. The most obvious is the Yahoo! Roller_Girls discussion board, which serves as a clearinghouse for all manner of

---

[19] Ivanna S. Pankin interview (distinguishing leagues such as SoCal Derby and Sin City Derby, which charge little or nothing to attend bouts because they eschew the "entertainment model" of other leagues and are thus relatively indifferent to cultivating a fan following).

[20] Http://wftda.com/apprentice-program.

questions about roller derby, from music licensing at bouts to the best helmet to use to why your name has not been registered on the centralized register of roller derby pseudonyms known as the Master Roster (Fagundes 2012a). Like most largely public information bazaars, Roller_Girls is sprawling, often disorganized, and lightly moderated, but if you want to start a league, and you dig around enough, you will find all manner of relevant and helpful information.[21]

How to go about starting a league that is sufficient to meet the threshold requirements of WFTDA's apprentice program is a different matter, and one that entails more regulation and formality. WFTDA requires that, even to be admitted to the apprentice program, nascent leagues must have already established some membership (minimum fourteen skaters practicing at least twice a week) and have already engaged in some competition (at least one bout against a WFTDA-sanctioned team, and at least one public bout in the team's hometown).[22] Less formal guidance is therefore necessary. And even if the apprenticeship requirements are met, it is not entirely free—both in the sense of "costless" as well as in the sense of "unfettered"—to become a WFTDA member. In addition to various procedural hurdles (e.g., submission of league bylaws, mission statement), applying leagues must pay a $300 application fee.[23] Most leagues find it advisable to register with the appropriate business entity with their respective secretaries of state.[24] Finally, WFTDA allows its leagues may be privately owned, subject to the proviso that participating leagues must be at least 51 percent owned by league skaters.[25]

Individual skaters seek knowledge about how to skate and what's going on in the derby world (especially scores from major tournaments). Here, too, countless resources provide both tips for starting to skate and for refining preexisting derby skills. Roller_Girls provides a useful if messy resource on all manner of issues, ranging from discussions about the best brands of bearings for skate wheels[26] to the distinction between the "pornstar" and "superman" techniques for falling while minimizing the risk of injury.[27] Numerous other open-access resources assist skaters in acquiring information about practice and skill development. Ivanna S. Pankin, for example, has posted on her public Facebook fan page complete and extremely detailed guides for running derby practice sessions.[28] News related to the roller derby world can be gleaned from any number of websites, typically

---

[21] E.g., post of Nameless Whorror, Montreal Roller Derby League, Re: new league question (Feb. 7, 2011), http://sports.dir.groups.yahoo.com/group/roller_girls/message/41635 (discussing leadership issues in newly formed leagues).

[22] Http://wftda.com/apprentice-program.

[23] Ibid.

[24] Ibid.

[25] Ibid.

[26] E.g., post of msbluemouse, Re: Bearings (Mar. 26, 2012), http://sports.dir.groups.yahoo.com/group/roller_girls/message/43912.

[27] E.g., post of estrogeenadavis (Dec. 31, 2009), http://sports.dir.groups.yahoo.com/group/roller_girls/message/37986.

[28] Https://www.facebook.com/ivannaspankin22.

free of charge. Derby News Network (DNN), for example, provides comprehensive score updates about and recaps of recent bouts,[29] with all content provided by a national network of volunteers.[30] The site also provides free webcasts of many roller derby bouts, including regional tournaments, to its viewers free of charge.[31]

Beyond digital resources, informal interpersonal networks generate and communicate knowledge about skating skills to perhaps a greater extent than any other source. As the handwritten notes that Ivanna S. Pankin has posted to her Facebook fan page illustrate, practices are usually run by experienced league members who organize, drill, and critique participants. Indeed, during the early days of derby, skaters learned through collaboration, sharing, and trial by error. Rat City Rollergirl Fighty Almighty began competing with the San Diego Derby Dolls in 2004, the early dawn of contemporary roller derby's renaissance. "Very few people knew anything back then," she observed, "So the idea was, 'Take everyone and we'll all learn together.' "[32]

The story of the Carolina Scoreboard[33] (so called for its association with the Carolina Roller Girls) provides a specific illustration of the general principle that derby's knowledge resources are governed pursuant to share-alike principles. The Scoreboard is a computer program that allows operators to project the score of derby bouts from a laptop computer onto a screen so that observers can see the teams, score, period, jam clock, and time outs remaining. The Scoreboard was written in Java by Mr. Temper, husband of Carolina Roller Girl Shirley Temper, and has become the gold standard for derby scoreboards. Derby insiders have rated the Scoreboard "one of the greatest resources ever provided to the derby community,"[34] and a "huge, massive" contribution to the sport.[35] Nor was it a simple undertaking. Mr. Temper estimated that the program included about 9000 lines of source code, totaling somewhat less than two "person years" of work.[36]

---

[29] Http://www.derbynewsnetwork.com/.

[30] Telephone interview with Hurt Reynolds (Oct. 20, 2012) (hereinafter "Hurt Reynolds interview") (digital sound recording on file with author).

[31] Http://www.derbynewsnetwork.com/live/archive. Other bouts, including many of the major WFTDA-sanctioned tournaments, are webcast—typically for a fee—by Blaze Media Productions, a for-profit web production company that (unlike DNN) was not started by roller derby insiders. Hurt Reynolds interview. This illustrates the subsequent point that not all roller derby's cultural production happens on a purely volunteer, share-alike basis, or is made available for free.

[32] Interview with Fighty Almighty. Now, by contrast, skaters are usually expected to begin with basic equipment and at least a rudimentary skill set. Ibid.

[33] Http://derbyscoreboard.sourceforge.net/.

[34] DerbyLife, *Excellent Derby Open Source Tool Is Updated!*, DerbyLife.com (Feb. 8, 2012), http://www.derbylife.com/articles/2012/02/excellent_derby_open_source_tool_updated.

[35] Ivanna S. Pankin interview.

[36] Chick Dastardly, *Bout Scoring Ain't Just Counting Fingers* (Jan. 27, 2012), http://chickdastardly.co.uk/rollerderby/bout-scoring-aint-just-counting-fingers/ (interviewing Mr. Temper about his work on the Scoreboard).

Despite the scale of this undertaking, Mr. Temper created the Scoreboard without remuneration[37] and made the resulting code available on an open-source basis.[38]

By way of some contrast, consider Rinxter, a computer program for tracking statistics in real time during bouts. This program was "built using a variety of open source technologies"[39] and is made available for free, albeit in theory only to derby leagues.[40] The Rinxter team does offer paid services like support and customization, but does so chiefly to recoup the costs of development and is seeking sponsorship to cover the rest of those costs.[41] Like Mr. Temper, Rinxter's creators are volunteers whose inspiration was their passion for roller derby, and their desire "to advance the game to the next level,"[42] rather than paid employees or businesspeople primarily concerned about turning substantial profits. In contrast to the Carolina Scoreboard, though, Rinxter is not distributed on an open-source basis but remains proprietary to its owners.[43]

As the Rinxter example indicates, it would be far too simple to conclude that all of derby's knowledge resources are governed on a share-alike basis. Increasingly, derby insiders are converting their expertise into for-pay services. The most prominent example is the trainer for hire. While most training, such as league practices, is done for free by league members, skaters—especially well-known and accomplished ones—are offering to train leagues for a limited time and, in a growing number of instances, a fee. The idea of paying an elite skater to come train your league is not new. Start-up leagues have had well-known derby girls come out to work with them for years. These early arrangements, though, were simply for cost. Ivanna S. Pankin and Trish the Dish often flew around the country to conduct training sessions for new leagues, but did so mainly for fun not profit, and asked only that the league cover the cost of their flight and provide a couch to sleep on.[44]

More recently, though, emergent trainers are seeking fees in addition to travel expenses. Nemesis on Wheels (N.O.W.) Roller Derby, for example, charges $1000/day for training services, in addition to transportation and lodging costs.[45] Other coaching services with

---

[37] He did ask that those seeking to express appreciation for his work give donations either to Derby News Network or to the Free Software Foundation. Chick Dastardly, *Bout Scoring Ain't Just Counting Fingers* (Jan. 27, 2012), http://chickdastardly.co.uk/rollerderby/bout-scoring-aint-just-counting-fingers/.

[38] The latest version of the Scoreboard is available at http://sourceforge.net/projects/derbyscoreboard/. It is subject to GNU General Public License, version 3 (June 27, 2007) (on file with author).

[39] Http://rinxter.com/www/about.php.

[40] Http://rinxter.com/www/?page_id=83. The site asks about league affiliation on the page where it makes the software available, but this is only a formality and not strictly enforced as a prerequisite for download.

[41] Http://rinxter.com/www/?page_id=79 ("We intend to keep the basic Rinxter software package free of charge to all derby leagues. We are currently working with a number of national and local sponsors to secure funding to support all future development. Rinxter is also offering special paid services, such as support and customization.").

[42] Http://rinxter.com/www/about.php.

[43] Hurt Reynolds interview. See also e-mail from Hurt Reynolds (Oct. 23, 2012) (on file with author) (confirming this via recent exchange with Rinxter creator).

[44] Ivanna S. Pankin interview. Indeed, Ivanna and Trish declined even the modest fees (about $100) that people offered to pay them for their time because "we like[d] doing [it] for its own sake." Ibid.

[45] Http://www.facebook.com/notes/now-roller-derby/now-derby-bootcamp-fees-2012/453965217954188.

similar fee structures include Fast Girl University[46] and Certifiable Derby Training.[47] And along somewhat similar lines, while DNN gets its content for free, it also seeks to earn money as well, both from ads on its site and through voluntary donations. This income does not, though, make DNN a highly profitable concern. Rather, DNN cofounder Hurt Reynolds reports that what money DNN brings in allows him to "pay the electricity"[48] and continue to pursue what is a passion project, fully "harmoniz[ed] with the DIY [do-it-yourself] ethos underlying the sport."[49] This latter point is likely true of most for-profit derby coaching as well. Any fees the coaches seek simply allow them to focus their lives entirely on training skaters, relieving them of the need to have a day job, rather than allowing them to live in "houses made of gold-plated Lamborghinis."[50]

The question about how derby's knowledge resources are governed is thus not a straightforward question about whether they are or are not a commons. Rather, they are commonsy. In many, perhaps most respects, derby people make their knowledge—whether how to skate or how to start a league—available on a free, share-alike basis to anyone interested. But increasingly, savvy derby insiders have sensed the chance to earn money from their considerable skill sets and have sought to use those skill sets as the bases for profitable business ventures. To the extent that some derby knowledge is made available only for a price, it is simply a private good rather than a commons-governed resource, even by the expansive definition used by Madison, Frischmann, and Strandburg. The emergence of for-profit endeavors in an otherwise share-alike culture raises a concern identified by numerous psychologists that the presence of self-interested motivations will crowd out other-oriented conduct (Ariely et al. 2009; Titmuss 1970). If some people are getting paid handsomely to do something you are doing for free, you may refuse to do it any longer, because you feel like a "sap" or a sucker (Gordon 2010).

Indeed, there is some sense of resistance to the increasing monetization of derby's knowledge resources. Upon learning that one coach charged $250 a day for her services, in addition to requiring provision of a hotel room and vegan meals, Ivanna S. Pankin observed, "This is the opposite of the roller derby I know. This is not how we collaborate and share in this community." And when a derby-related start-up, RDNation, attempted to get a foothold in the derby world with a purportedly improved version of the Carolina Scoreboard, they received a barrage of criticism, including the suggestion they had attempted to profit personally from their work on the modified scoreboard.[51] Yet despite some objections, the emergence of

---

[46] Http://www.facebook.com/pages/Fast-Girl-University/184075778281486.

[47] Http://www.certifiablederbytraining.com.

[48] Hurt Reynolds interview.

[49] Http://www.derbynewsnetwork.com/about_dnn.

[50] Hurt Reynolds interview (invoking sarcastic Lamborghini example to dismiss the possibility that anyone makes a massive income thanks to derby); Ivanna S. Pankin interview (explaining that the desire to seek a fee in addition to travel costs simply allows most for-profit coaches to do work that would otherwise be impossible with a full-time day job).

[51] See *New Scoreboard for Roller Derby*, forum discussion on ZebraHuddle.com, http://www.zebrahuddle.com/index.php?topic=2616.0 (stating derisively, "[just s]o we're crystal clear, this is a commercial venture. Per [the software co-creator's] personal blog: 'We personally think it has the ability to make big money.'").

some for-profit conduct in the otherwise sharing-oriented derby world does not appear to have dampened the incentives of the vast majority of derby participants, who continue to happily produce and supply knowledge for free. Ivanna S. Pankin's posting coaching information on her Facebook fan page, for example, occurred well after many other coaches began to parcel out their knowledge for a fee.[52]

Roller derby does not appear to have been affected by the crowding out phenomenon observed in other contexts, where the emergence of profit motivations tended to undermine altruistic motivations. Why might this be the case? There are at least two possible explanations. First, the difference between for-profit and share-alike knowledge provision may not be as stark as it initially seems. The coaches who have started businesses are all devoted, long-time derby competitors who are trying to blend their love for the sport with a way to make a living (as opposed to, say, outsiders seeking primarily to make a quick buck on the derby trend).[53] In some cases, the businesses did not emerge from a profit-seeking plan, but just happened.[54] In others, it might be seen as the ultimate expression of sincere derby love: wanting to make a living at the thing that is your life's passion.[55] Second, crowding out typically occurs when the presence of profit reduces your incentives to act altruistically. For example, if everyone assumes your blood donation is for money, this dampens any incentive to do it in order to express your goodwill (Titmuss 1970). But in derby, the presence of for-profit knowledge provision does not appear to crowd out entirely other motivations. Coaches who continue to travel and offer training for cost still get what they want out of the experience: a fun trip and the chance to meet and work with women who share a common love.[56] If you do not care about earning a living at coaching, and you find it rewarding on its own terms, this would likely diminish any "sap" effect. Finally, it bears noting that there has been no observed crowding-out *yet*. The emergence of for-profit derby knowledge provision is of relatively recent vintage and remains the exception to the rule. Over time, it is possible that derby—in this and other respects—may become more fully commercialized,[57] and that when some threshold is crossed, a crowding-out effect will kick in.

---

[52] See Ivanna S. Pankin interview (explaining that the emergence of for-profit coaching has not reduced her inclination to offer coaching services and resources for cost or even free of charge).

[53] Fighty Almighty interview (observing that most of the women who coach professionally have distinguished derby pedigrees and are deeply devoted to the sport).

[54] Ivanna S. Pankin interview (observing facetiously that Sin City Skates grew successful as a business selling derby gear "despite," not because of, her and her partner, Trish the Dish).

[55] Ivanna S. Pankin interview (discussing this motivation for starting derby-related businesses).

[56] Ivanna S. Pankin interview (describing a trip to train skaters in New Orleans as "not a job but a privilege" for which basic travel reimbursement was sufficient remuneration). The objection to the nascent derby-coaching industry seems as much or more about quality control than about base profit motivation. Ibid. (expressing concern about lack of any established coaching standards or certification in roller derby).

[57] All the interviewees I spoke to shared the opinion that, for better or worse, roller derby is becoming more commercial, and that it will get only more so. Ivanna S. Pankin, Fighty Almighty, and Hurt Reynolds interviews (all echoing this point).

Before concluding this subpart, I offer a quick word about the other aspect of roller derby that might be regarded as governed by a commons strategy: the social world of roller derby itself. The reason that this aspect of roller derby merits only a brief mention in the context of a discussion about open-access versus for-profit approaches to resource access is that the descriptive point is so straightforward. Those entitled to access the community elements of roller derby do so freely (save for marginal issues like having to pay for tickets to some parties, like the LA Derby Dolls' yearly "prom"). The reason for this unanimity is equally straightforward. The value of this community depends on its being freely available, as is true of most fellowship. Even if it made sense to parcel access to the derby community on a for-pay basis, that would undermine the quality of sincere exchange on which meaningful social exchange depends.[58] Investigating *who* can access this resource, by contrast, yields more complex answers.

C. WHO IS PERMITTED TO EXPLOIT ROLLER DERBY'S COMMONS?

The third and final question relates to the second constitutive feature of commons as I have defined the term for the purposes of this chapter. Commons resources tend to be freely (although not necessarily limitlessly) available to some group. This use of free, it should be noted, means "not for a price" rather than "without any limits." As the ensuing discussion illustrates, a resource may be made available for free, but this does not mean it is subject to unfettered access by any user. By contrast, just as Creative Commons licenses enable unpaid use of works of authorship, commons may condition access on a variety of rules. This subpart considers the extent to which (if at all) there are limits on who can access the knowledge or community that make up roller derby's commons.

Derby's informational resources tend not to be subject to meaningful limits on who can access them. Ivanna S. Pankin's coaching notes are free and accessible to anyone who wants to access them, simply by visiting her Facebook fan page. WFTDA's tips for how to start a league are also freely available online. DNN offers derby information and live webcasts to anyone who types in the right URL. The rich, if chaotic, trove of information available on the Yahoo! Roller_Girls forum is available to anyone whom the moderators allow to access it. In theory this could serve as a way to limit membership only to derby insiders, but in practice it is used only to make sure that those requesting access are real people, not spam bots. In this respect, they are governed more as fully open resources than by a commons management strategy.

The computer programs discussed above are subject to relatively more limits. Mr. Temper distributes the Carolina Scoreboard freely to anyone who wants to download it from SourceForge, but keeps a copyright in the material in order to enable his use of the

---

[58] At the very least, when community or fellowship are monetized, they take on very different forms. Monetary exchange turns sexual community into illegal prostitution. Monetary exchange turns sympathetic conversation into psychotherapy.

GNU General Public License (GPL). This does not limit the group that can access his program, of course, but rather limits what users can do with it. In this respect, the GPL operates like rules governing public physical property, such as a state beach. Anyone can go there, but that access is subject to use conditions (no open fires, closing hours, etc.). Rinxter's governance strategy, by contrast, seems less open and therefore less commonsy. The software is made available freely, but its developers seek to do so only to members of the roller derby community. This limit is not taken that seriously, though, since one need only provide any name of a derby league and their website in order to download the executable file containing the program.[59]

This lack of any limits on derby information may seem puzzling. After all, despite its growth over the past decade, the roller derby world remains so close-knit as to be insular (Fagundes 2012a). Why wouldn't this lead those who produce derby knowledge to guard it more jealously? There are at least two reasons, though, that this open-access governance strategy for roller derby's information resources makes sense. First, this resource—like most cultural resources—is inexhaustible and therefore not subject to tragedies of the commons. DNN bout recaps are not diminished when they are widely read, and Ivanna S. Pankin's ability to hold practices is not constrained when others use her coaching notes. Second, and perhaps more importantly, this open-access approach to roller derby knowledge not only fails to diminish the resource itself, but it furthers the goal of roller derby's participants: to encourage and facilitate the spread of the sport.[60] Here, the freer the resource, the better the outcome for derby enthusiasts. More people reading freely available coaching notes or watching freely available live bout streams helps skaters improve and helps the sport gain ever-greater exposure.[61] In the absence of concerns about exhaustible resources or personal profit, efficient use of derby's information commons is optimized by an open-access governance strategy.[62] Indeed, such use may enhance and help to constitute the roller derby world itself.

The preceding subpart showed that roller derby's knowledge resources tend to be governed by strong open-access principles. Most (though not all) of those resources are available to anyone who wants them. But a somewhat different story prevails with respect to the other aspect of roller derby that might be regarded as a commons: its community. Here, access to the intangible resource—whether termed fellowship, sisterhood, or derby love—is relatively strictly limited to members of the derby world itself. If you are an active

---

[59] Http://rinxter.com/www/?page_id=83.

[60] See http://www.derbynewsnetwork.com/mission_vision (explicitly linking DNN's mission to the continued growth of roller derby); Ivanna S. Pankin interview (explaining that her motivation for posting coaching notes on Facebook was to facilitate coaching and encourage better drills and practices).

[61] The growth of roller derby is explicitly part of DNN's mission statement. See http://www.derbynewsnetwork.com/mission_vision ("We believe the organic, DIY growth mode of modern roller derby has no limit.").

[62] This is where Rinxter provides an interesting contrast. Clearly the developers' goal was to provide a service for derby, and they have done just that, and for free. But their desire to limit access to Rinxter and to keep the code proprietary suggests that their motivations are somewhat different from the creators of the open-access information resources discussed above.

skater, referee, or record-keeper, or just one of many other kinds of devoted volunteers who help to maintain the sport, you will likely be enveloped in the derby community. This means the option to attend formally organized events (the LA Derby Dolls, for example, have a "prom" every January to which insiders can purchase tickets for a nominal fee designed mainly to cover costs), as well as informal ones (teams or groups of volunteers may have dinners or host loosely organized events like gatherings at a local bar). And it means that (for skaters, anyway) you will likely be paired with another woman in your entering fresh meat cohort who will be your "derby wife" (Barbee & Cohen 2010). But these opportunities are not available to the public at large, and so unlike derby's knowledge resources, its community lies open only to the relatively limited group of roller derby insiders.

Like most other informal social groups, of course, being part of the roller derby world does not entail membership lists, explicit requirements, or bright-line distinctions.[63] There appears to be only one (unwritten) rule for who is and is not a member of the roller derby community: You have to do your part to contribute to the sport (Barbee & Cohen 2010; Mabe 2007). Skaters get a lot of glory during bouts, but league membership almost invariably also requires engaging in a host of far less glamorous obligations: serving on committees, staffing the ticket booth, selling merchandise, and even mopping up the venue after bouts. And not everyone can skate,[64] or wants to, but this is not a bar to being part of the derby world. Non-skaters may serve as referees or record-keepers, help with venue lighting and construction, and chronicle bouts via photos or writing.[65] The result of these volunteer efforts may well be informal absorption into roller derby's community.[66] One's status in the derby world is obviously mainly linked to the quality of their skating, but can derive also from the perceived volume of their volunteerist efforts, especially when those tasks are particularly unappealing or tedious (Fagundes 2012b). People who do particularly onerous tasks for particularly extended times tend to receive the most plaudits (Fagundes 2012a). On the flip side are social sanctions for undermining roller derby's community-oriented ethic. The ubiquitous "douchebag rule" states—unsurprisingly—"don't be a douchebag." It is simple and crude, but is taken very seriously, and one way it is understood is as enforcing the sport's core principle of reciprocal contribution (Fagundes 2012a). People are expected to give back and be team players in the roller derby world. Failure to do your share may result in social sanctions, such as

---

[63] There are a few formal thresholds relating to one's status in the roller derby world. Derby girls must wait for some fixed period—three to six months, usually, depending on the league—before they can register their skate name on the Master Roster (Fagundes 2012a).

[64] Some aspirants cannot skate due to physical or skill limitations. Others, like men, are not allowed to participate due to WFTDA rules. Despite this gender limitation, men often become part of the roller derby world by virtue of their devotion to the sport in other capacities.

[65] E.g., http://ratcityrollergirls.com/teams/support-team/non-skating-officials/ (Rat City Rollergirls' non-skating officials, the "Lightning Fists of Science").

[66] Fighty Almighty interview (discussing how ancillary helpers, women and men alike, may find an "in" to the derby world through their volunteerism).

being delegated the more unappealing league responsibilities, and ultimately exclusion from the derby world itself.

The open-access governance of roller derby's information resources contrasts with its more limited-access (and hence more commonsy) governance of its community. Three reasons may help us understand this difference in resource management. First, in contrast to knowledge, which is classically nonrivalrous, community may be diminished as more people take part in it. Part of this is due to crowding effects. If the goal is to have a close-knit group of like-minded folks, this end may be undermined as the group becomes sprawling and overly populous, losing the intimacy that made it valuable when smaller (Solum 2010). Second, roller derby's community may differ for the related reason that as the group of derby insiders becomes too large, it loses any cachet. There is a certain *au courant* coolness to being part of the derby world linked to its strong countercultural overtones. But just as Harley-Davidson lost its street cred when it became the brand of choice for aging yuppies,[67] the exclusivity of the roller derby community would be diluted if just anyone could call herself a member.[68] Finally, the limit on who is a derby insider serves a valuable incentive and sorting function. To be part of the derby world, you have to show your commitment through meaningful volunteer work. This both encourages the kind of community-focused effort that is key to keep the derby world going, but also excludes hangers-on who are drawn to the subculture for trivial reasons without being deeply invested in it.

IV. Roller Derby as a Labor of Love

The previous two parts explored the notion of commons and applied that notion to roller derby. But merely analyzing a resource—knowledge, culture or something else—as a commons leaves us with one last question. Ostrom herself observed that the "problem of supply" hovers over case studies illustrating the emergence and efficacy of commons governance systems (Ostrom 1990). The puzzle is that even if commons governance maximizes the welfare of all members of the relevant group, rational choice cannot to explain why any private actor would bear the disproportionate, and widely distributed, costs of creating and maintaining the governance system in the first place. In other work, I have suggested that roller derby provides a promising site for investigating solutions to the problem of supply (Fagundes 2012b). Along similar lines, I suggest in this part that the motivations that underlie the creation of cultural goods are largely the same as those

---

[67] See Richard Webb, *Born to Be Mild: The Changing Significance of the Harley-Davidson Motorcycle*, http://www.roguecom.com/roguescholar/RWebb.html, accessed Mar. 28, 2014.

[68] It bears noting that predictions based on these general points about crowding effects and club goods have yet to materialize in the roller derby context. As the sport grows in terms of participants and visibility, its countercultural cachet has remained strong. This may be because its growth has not resulted in its dilution due to mainstream influences.

that underlie the creation of schemes regulating those goods. I further argue that these motivations are the sorts of labors of love that may be helpfully illuminated by recent work in positive psychology.

Samuel Johnson once observed, "No man but a blockhead ever wrote, but for money" (Boswell 1791). Casual empiricism shows that either Johnson was dead wrong, or that the world is chock full of blockheads. It is blindingly obvious that people produce, and especially that they produce cultural artifacts, for a variety of motives far more mysterious and complex than the desire for a buck. The institution of gift-giving furnishes a ready example of the pervasive presence of altruism in human behavior (Titmuss 1970). And we have been surrounded for centuries by institutions that generate and share knowledge freely rather than for profit, such as universities (Madison, Frischmann, & Strandburg 2009). Perhaps less obviously, humans continue to spend enormous financial and personal resources on having children, even though studies increasingly show that raising children tends to decrease parental happiness.[69]

Cultural production in the absence of pecuniary motivation has become increasingly pervasive given the advent of digital media. Distributed, collaborative production has not only increased in frequency as a modality of production (Benkler 2004). It has proven particularly efficient in creating open source software for both operating systems and applications,[70] producing massive and astonishingly complete online encyclopedias, and helping to scan the galaxy for signs of extraterrestrial life.[71] The peculiarity of Johnson's "blockhead" observation is not only its assumption that only cold, hard cash can inspire creative production. This notion—which I will refer to as "Johnson's fallacy"—not only misdescribes the range of human motivation, but it may get motivation exactly backward. Recent work suggests that while financial incentives are indeed effective at causing people to engage in menial or mechanical tasks, they are comparatively ineffective, and possibly counterproductive, as motivators of inventive or creative work (Pink 2010; Quiggin & Hunter 2008).

Thinking about roller derby—or any plausible subject matter—as a commons necessarily engages the problem of supply as well. The descriptive question raised by this and other works in this collection is typically cast as one of structure: What does it mean for a resource to be managed as a commons? This, in turn, raises a question about social welfare. How does this management structure optimize, or at least enhance, production? But implicit in these structural questions is a core motivational one. Especially in the context of noncommercial cultural production like roller derby (or Apache,[72] or SETI@home, or

---

[69] See Jennifer Senior, *All Joy and No Fun: Why Parents Hate Parenting*, New York Magazine (July 4, 2010), http://nymag.com/news/features/67024/ ("Most people assume that having children will make them happier. Yet a wide variety of academic research shows that parents are not happier than their childless peers, and in many cases are less so. This finding is surprisingly consistent, showing up across a range of disciplines.").

[70] Http://www.linux.org/article/view/what-is-linux.

[71] Http://setiathome.berkeley.edu/sah_about.php.

[72] Http://www.apache.org.

Wikipedia), we must understand what motivates people to contribute in order to explain why commons governance strategies even arise, and why, at least some of the time, they outperform traditional private-property strategies. In earlier work, I suggested that may be understood as something separate and apart from traditional motivation, as labors of love (Fagundes 2012b). This chapter offers far too little space in which to assay a complete discussion of what this emergent category of productive motivation means. Instead, the ensuing discussion seeks simply to suggest briefly how positive social psychology may help to explain the emergence of commons property governance system, and perhaps also other labors of love (Hoffman & Mehra 2009).

Johnson's fallacy—that the exclusive motivating factor for creative production is pecuniary reward—is so easily dismissed that it warrants no additional discussion here. Clearly a broad range of motivations causes us to create. So perhaps the flaw in Johnson's fallacy is that money is not the only benefit to include when engaging in cost-benefit analysis. People may also be motivated by hedonic pleasure—pure intrinsic joy in the task itself— while others may be motivated by sociopsychological factors such as a desire for fame in the public eye, or status within a cultural subgroup (Benkler 2002). A Wikipedian, for example, might edit entries in her spare time because she really enjoys the act of refining other people's language, or because she seeks status among other Wikipedians, and knows that long hours of diligent labor are key to earning their esteem. And of course, since motives are often mixed, it could be some combination of the two.

Understanding cultural production in roller derby—or any context—as a labor of love complicates the traditional rational choice story that actors engage in conduct pursuant to a welfare-maximizing cost-benefit scheme. Consider two reasons. The first is that money and other rewards are incommensurable. Wealth, whether measured in dollars or euros or Israeli shekels, is a relatively easy kind of value-measurement to comprehend, with a shared understanding of its measurement scale, which works well for telling us how much an employer values us (salary) or how much a cup of coffee costs (too damned much these days). Other values lack this quality. Constitutional law scholars often speak of the importance of free speech or human dignity, for example, in terms that do not easily translate into dollar terms (Sunstein 1994). This explains why, for example, there are many people who will not do certain things even when they might be wealth- or even welfare-enhancing (Thaler 1988). These noncommensurable values lie somewhat at odds with traditional welfare analysis because they simply cannot be scaled together, any more than it would make sense to express love for another person in terms of dollars.[73]

At the very least, the incommensurability problem precludes concluding with certainty that we can explain, say, a Wikipedian's motives by stating that their desire for fame overbore the tedium of editing a given entry. That these two values cannot be scaled together means that we will, at best, be relegated to guessing whether it is true that one won out over the other in a formal utility calculus. But the problem may be more acute than just

---

[73] But cf. the practice of giving pricey engagement rings.

indeterminacy. Research increasingly shows that altruistic and financial motives operate at cross-purposes for individual decision makers. Giving people money to donate blood cancels out the availability of an altruistic motivation, and means that those with other-regarding rather than self-regarding desires for blood donation may be less likely to give (Titmuss 1970). More recent work has illustrated that money is a good motivator when the task at hand is menial, like sorting white marbles from black ones. But these same studies indicate that when it comes to encouraging creative thinking, money not only fails to inspire better thought processes, but it actually produces worse results (Pink 2010).

The incommensurability of monetary and other motivations suggests a second concern reason that labors of love complicate the traditional social welfare calculus. A constitutive feature of labors of love may be that they simply do not correspond with the traditional notion of cost-benefit calculus altogether. The elemental story of labor is pretty simple. Work sucks, so the story goes. It's either back-breaking like moving furniture, or tedious like entering data in a soul-crushing cubicle all day long. No one in their right mind would do such a thing but for a cash payoff sufficient to make them put up with the drudgery. So conceived, cost-benefit analysis makes sense. My costs are a sore back from moving furniture or carpal tunnel syndrome from data entry, and they have to be overborne by a salary or I'll quit. The benefit side of the ledger could, of course, be expanded to include hedonic pleasure or sociopsychological rewards, and that just makes it a cost-benefit analysis with a few more variables at play.

This simple cost-benefit model of labor assumes that work is a means to an end. But for labors of love, this assumption does not work, because the means *is* the end. Labor is not a bitter pill to be swallowed in order to earn some just compensation to make the whole project worth it. Comparing the drudgery of work and the boon of compensation along a cost-benefit metric makes no sense if there is no distinction between work and compensation. This notion is encapsulated in the tired-but-true cliché (that was also the title Steve Jobs approved for his mid-life biography) that the journey is the reward. Shakespeare put it more eloquently, though: "Joy's soul lies in the doing."[74] Hence the claim, for example, that hedonic pleasure in a task itself belongs on the plus side of a cost-benefit ledger simply makes no sense. For labors of love, there is no accounting at all because there does not need to be. Roller derby, or Wikipedia, or Linux were not created in a calculated manner at all.[75] They emerged out of people's passions, suddenly and spontaneously.

The term "labor of love" is, admittedly, elusive. How might we know when a given cultural artifact or phenomenon is the product of a labor of love? In the context of roller derby, at least, I suggest three indicia that may help further refine this notion. The first lies in the

---

[74] Troilus and Cressida, I.ii.287.

[75] Similarly, the kernel that grew into contemporary roller derby in Austin started when a few organizers had a rowdy meeting about their crazy idea (Barbee & Cohen 2010). On a slightly different note, Ivanna S. Pankin's business, Sin City Skates, emerged not from a strategic plan to corner the market in derby gear but developed path-dependently from her desire to provide a service for friends and teammates who had a hard time finding reasonably priced skates. See Ivanna S. Pankin interview.

hostility shown toward those who appear to be interested in cashing in on roller derby for a lucrative, personal payday. Roller derby people remain very suspicious of selling out and to those who seek to use the sport as a source of profit and personal gain.[76] This derives in part from the contemporary derby subculture's punk rock roots, but likely also (and relatedly) because this represents the ultimate means/ends calculus rather than investment in derby for love of the sport. On a related note, those who started derby-related businesses have typically sought to extract only enough profit to keep the business alive (often barely), but this does not prevent rumors from emerging that those businesses are actually raking in loads of cash.[77] These rumors are false, and usually readily dispelled, but they suggest a real antipathy for profit motivation in derby. This could be for personal reasons: A for-profit derby simply may not be a sport in which you want to participate, since it would have a different atmospheric than the one you prefer. But it also seems to derive as well from a sense that if a person is into roller derby to make a buck is doing it for the "wrong" reasons, which is objectionable even if that person is providing a useful service for the sport.

Second, in many instances, roller derby is something insiders do because they love it, but like many things (and people) we love, it is often far from a simple and easy presence in their lives. Skaters and derby helpers devote themselves to the sport in a way that seems to cause them frustration and annoyance, or at least that loads them down with work to a crushing extent. This renders cost/benefit explanations for the production and governance of such cultural resources difficult. If you are having a great time with an extracurricular activity, it makes sense that you would remain devoted to it, but if it is making you miserable or exhausted, then if you are a reasonable person, you should quit. Yet derby people stick to the sport in ways that appear inexplicable from this perspective. The women who run the Master Roster, roller derby's name-registration system, often spend up to twenty extracurricular hours a week entering data and fending off angry e-mails from skaters who are mad about the registration backlog (Fagundes 2012b). One DNN volunteer spends an equal amount of time per week inputting scores into the website's database.[78] These tasks may be intrinsically enjoyable to some extent, but to a greater extent they are the kinds of things people do despite their unpleasantness because they are part of a greater purpose, like a parent who stays up all night caring for a sick child despite sleeplessness and risk of infection.

The third and final reason to suspect that roller derby is a labor of love is that when you ask roller derby girls (and guys) to explain their devotion to the sport, they tend to

---

[76] E-mail to Dave Fagundes from Sniperella (Oct. 10, 2012) (on file with author).

[77] Hurt Reynolds interview (describing the initial skepticism with which DNN was met, including (inaccurate) rumors that the site was earning far more money than necessary to cover its production and operating costs). This ambivalence likely has its roots in the countercultural origins of contemporary roller derby, which are punk rock and hence deeply antimaterialist. See Hurt Reynolds interview; cf. Ivanna S. Pankin interview ("I was raised in the Bay Area punk rock community where you're never allowed to make money and if you do, you're a sellout asshole.... Now I'm a successful businessperson and I realize the world's not that simple.").

[78] Hurt Reynolds interview.

explain their motivations in those terms. The answer to the question why someone would spend so much of their free time invested in a sport that not only pays nothing, but that *requires you to pay* (both in terms of league dues an in terms of countless external obligations) tends to be given immediately and in the same uniform manner: It's for the love of the game.[79] This, too, is a cliché, but that does not mean it is untrue. The love derby people have for their sport emerges most convincingly from the stories they tell about why they do it, and in turn their distaste for monetization of the activity. Consider, by way of just one example, this story from Ivanna S. Pankin, explaining her ambivalence about the marketing of roller derby as a public entertainment:

> I don't think we should be charging people to come see amateur roller derby.... In that respect I wish we were more like other sports, like soccer, where at any given moment there's a soccer field with a bunch of guys on it kicking ass at soccer and nobody gives a shit at all. We should all get better at our sport, and then the very best of the best of the best should be the ones that people go pay to see. And I'll just play in a dirty shirt in a parking lot with the rest of my friends and maybe one day I'll be good enough to play with the great team.[80]

The foregoing rubric helps us identify what labors of love are. But it does not explain their internal mechanics, and what compels us to engage in them. This matters for law, especially, because we need to understand motivation to design laws that are most likely to encourage prosocial behavior. A full exploration of how labors of love operate lies beyond the scope of this chapter, but below I seek to briefly sketch the contours of a possible answer that looks to positive social psychology.

Psychology provides a fruitful place to look for illumination of the notion of labors of love because it has long sought to understand motivations for work without invoking a cost-benefit framework. Accounts for motivations that inspire work vary, as do the motivations they describe, but there are at least three that have emerged as particularly salient. The first is autonomy. People are more likely to work, and work well, where they believe that their effort is a result of choice rather than coercion (Pink 2010). The second is effectance. Work that allows people to have a sense of efficacy in, and especially mastery over, some aspect of the world—however narrow—brings a satisfaction that leads to diligence and effectiveness in tasks (Haidt 2005). The third is purpose. Work that causes us to feel connected to a greater goal, particularly one that we believe in, is more likely to engage us regardless of salary or other pecuniary reward (Haidt 2005).

This triad of metrics helps to understand the motivation for participation in roller derby. In terms of autonomy, roller derby's constituents—skaters, referees, statisticians,

---

79 See Fighty Almighty interview, Ivanna S. Pankin interview (using the term "love" to explain their involvement in the sport).

80 Ivanna S. Pankin interview.

writers, and countless others—all choose to devote themselves to the sport as an extra-curricular activity. Derby provides a sharp contrast to the nine-to-five grind, where work is often a product of obligation to earn a living. The extraordinary demands the sport puts on its participants serves to emphasize the autonomy that they derive from it. Derby is so all-consuming that its participants are constantly reminded of their choice to make it part of their lives. In terms of effectance, roller derby provides its participants—from athletes themselves to the technicians who support the sport's infrastructure—an opportunity to contribute to the creation and maintenance of a truly distinctive subculture. Indeed, it is a prerequisite for inclusion in the derby community that one helps to effect at least some small part of the sport's continued existence. And roller derby provides a sense of purpose in two ways. First, it creates a rich network of interpersonal relationships among its participants. And second, it allows participants to live out beliefs (countercultural self-expression, female empowerment) that lie close to their hearts.

Now that we have come to the end of this chapter's final part, it is possible to look back at commons through the lens of the notion of labors of love to see what the latter can tell us about the former. The first connection is that understanding work as a labor of love helps resolve the problem of supply that hovers over all the literature on commons, physical and cultural alike. The problem of supply seems to be a problem because it is hard to explain why anyone would engage in the effort of creating and governing a commons that benefits a widely distributed group when they internalize only a fraction of the benefit created by the commons. But as roller derby illustrates, the work associated with developing and maintaining commons may not be regarded as a drudgery that must be justified by some benefits it accrues, but as an act of service that is a source of joy. This is especially true when the work of governing a commons like roller derby also tends to sustain and perpetuate a community that is deeply related to its participants' identities. And second, the notion of labors of love helps us understand why commons arise in relation to some artifacts and not others. People do not do derby—or take part in SETI@home, or create open source software—for the promise of a fat paycheck or any other largely self-regarding reward. Rather, their inspiration is to carve out a space within which they possess autonomy, can control the course of something they care about, and in so doing have a sense of purpose. It would obviously seem discordant to sell for a profit the fruits of cultural production that happens due to these nonpecuniary motivations. Hence it may be possible to say that where cultural production is a labor of love, commons governance schemes are more likely to arise and to be sustainable.

V. Conclusion

It intuitively seems plausible to speak of roller derby as a commons. The subjects I interviewed for this project all immediately sensed that there was a connection between the notion of commons and their sport.[81] This may be because the ethic that dominates derby stresses many features typically associated with noncommercial approaches to creative production. Derby News Network, which exists thanks only to the countless contributions of volunteers who populate the site with content,[82] explains that the site is "built … on the same principles that guide the sport's community: do-it-yourself, collaborative, passion-driven, crowdsourced. Many hands make light work."[83] Ivanna S. Pankin expressed similar familiarity with and enthusiasm for the notion of sharing as a modality of production. Explaining her decision to make her coaching notes available on an open-access basis, she observed, "Our whole [roller derby] community was founded on a sense of like, 'Well I know something so let me share it with you because when it comes to this other thing you know about, you can help me figure it out.'"[84] And consider how Mr. Temper explained his enormous investment of time in creating the Carolina Scoreboard:

> I don't mind at all about lack of credit or anything like that. It's not about me, it's about improving derby, and hopefully the scoreboard has been useful to leagues around the world. I enjoy working on it, and hearing about its usefulness to others is much more rewarding to me than anyone knowing who I am.[85]

The pervasiveness of a share-alike ethic in the roller derby community is evident also in the suspicion of, and to some extent animosity toward, those who start businesses related to roller derby.[86]

Roller derby does share forms of production with other institutions mentioned in the same breath with knowledge or creative commons. A completely precise account of whether a given resource is a commons remains elusive, due in part to significant variation in the usage of this term. So in this chapter, I have analyzed roller derby's information resources from the perspective of Madison, Frischmann, and Strandburg's flexible approach to commons. Along those lines, I stressed that this account of commons represents a spectrum rather than a binary, so that we might be able to speak of "commonsy" features of a resource's governance strategy. Two particular aspects of roller derby—knowledge and community—may be regarded as subject to a commons regulation scheme.

Considered through this lens, roller derby's knowledge and community resources are commonsy in some ways (albeit differently so) and not in others. Information about roller derby is often made available on a share-alike, or even entirely free, basis, which suggests a

---

[81] E.g., Ivanna S. Pankin interview (expressing knowledge of and enthusiasm for the notion of commons).

[82] See Hurt Reynolds interview (acknowledging that the site could not exist without volunteers producing content for it).

[83] Http://www.derbynewsnetwork.com/mission_vision.

[84] Ivanna S. Pankin interview.

[85] E-mail from Mr. Temper (on file with author).

[86] Hurt Reynolds interview; Ivanna S. Pankin interview.

resource more commonsy than commercial. Increasingly, though, some derby folks seek to extract money from the knowledge resources they produce, rendering those resources more like private goods than commons. The almost total lack of meaningful limits on who can access most of derby's knowledge resources indicates that along the spectrum of commons governance, this is a fully open resource, closer to copyright's public domain than to a limited-access commons. Roller derby's community, by contrast, seems commonsy as well, albeit subject to more access limits. Access to the fellowship that provides a major amenity that its participants seek from the sport is, of necessity, freely given, though only to those insiders who have proved their derby bona fides through volunteer contributions to the betterment of the sport (and who have avoided ostracism through violating the douchebag rule).

There is no simple, straightforward answer to the question whether roller derby is a commons. Indeed, the very premise of this question may be flawed. It makes more sense to investigate the extent to which roller derby is commonsy, which allows us to calibrate the inquiry by evaluating roller derby (or any other subject matter) along different commons-related metrics. But the difficulty of squaring roller derby with the notion of commons is a source of promise, rather than just a terminological morass. After all, this project and the others in this collection were not conceived simply to engage formal questions about the meaning of the term "commons" in the incorporeal, as opposed to physical, setting. Rather, it was a broad invitation to think about how work on commons strategies for natural resources may help us understand how to deploy similar strategies to optimize use of cultural resources.

My investigation of roller derby as a commons provides just one illustration of the great potential of this approach. Thinking about roller derby (or other subject matter) as a commons first prompts us to think about which commonsy governance strategies— open-access versus limited access, for example—maximize cultural production, especially insofar as different management strategies are likely be differently effective with respect to tangible and intangible resources. And second, it prompts us to broaden our traditional assumptions about the motivations for creative production, and the reason why people create those modalities in the first instance. This inquiry is especially salient in contexts like roller derby and so many other passion projects, where love, not money, provides the most compelling inspiration.

Acknowledgments

Thanks for comments on earlier drafts to Danni Hart, Art McEvoy, Gowri Ramachandran, and participants at the Convening Cultural Commons workshop at NYU School of Law in September 2011. Thanks also, of course, to my good friends in the roller derby world, especially Ivanna S. Pankin, Fighty Almighty, and Hurt Reynolds, whose insights helped make this chapter possible, and whose passion for their labors of love inspires me to pursue mine.

References

Dan Ariely, Anat Bracha, & Stephan Meier, *Doing Good or Doing Well? Image Motivation and Monetary Incentives in Behaving Prosocially*, 99 AM. ECONOMIC REV. 544 (2009).

JENNIFER BARBEE & ALEX COHEN, DOWN AND DERBY: THE INSIDER'S GUIDE TO ROLLER DERBY (Berkeley, CA: Soft Skull Press 2010).

Yochai Benkler, *Coase's Penguin, or Linux and the Nature of the Firm*, 112 YALE L.J. 369 (2002).

Yochai Benkler, *Sharing Nicely: On Shareable Goods and the Emergence of Sharing as a Modality of Production*, 124 YALE L.J. 273 (2004).

JAMES BOSWELL, THE LIFE OF SAMUEL JOHNSON, LL.D. (1791).

Hanoch Dagan & Michael Heller, *The Liberal Commons*, 110 YALE L.J. 549 (2001).

Thráinn Eggertsson, *Open Access Versus Common Property* 8–9 (2000) (unpublished manuscript, on file with the YALE LAW JOURNAL).

Daveid Fagundes, *Talk Derby to Me: Emergent Intellectual Property Norms Governing Roller Derby Pseudonyms*, 90 TEXAS L. REV. 1093 (2012a).

David Fagundes, *The Varieties of Motivation and the Problem of Supply: A Reply to Professor Ellickson*, 90 TEXAS L. REV. SEE ALSO 311 (2012b).

Wendy J. Gordon, *Response: Discipline and Nourish: On Constructing Commons*, 95 CORNELL L. REV. 733 (2010).

JONATHAN HAIDT, THE HAPPINESS HYPOTHESIS: FINDING MODERN TRUTH IN ANCIENT WISDOM (New York: Basic Books 2005).

David A. Hoffman & Salil K. Mehra, *Wikitruth Through Wikiorder*, 59 EMORY L.J. 151 (2009).

CATHERINE MABE, ROLLER DERBY: THE HISTORY AND ALL-GIRL REVIVAL OF THE GREATEST SPORT ON WHEELS (Speck Press 2007).

Michael J. Madison, *Intellectual Property and Americana, or Why IP Gets the Blues*, 18 FORDHAM INTELL. PROP. MEDIA & ENT. L.J. 677 (2008).

Michael J. Madison, Brett M. Frischmann, & Katherine J. Strandburg, *The University as Constructed Cultural Commons*, 30 WASHINGTON UNIVERSITY J.L. & POLICY 365 (2009).

Michael J. Madison, Brett M. Frischmann, & Katherine J. Strandburg, *Constructing Commons in the Cultural Environment*, 95 CORNELL L. REV. 657 (2010).

Frank I. Michelman, *Ethics, Economics, and the Law of Property*, in NOMOS XXIV: ETHICS, ECONOMICS, AND THE LAW 3 (J. Roland Pennock & John W. Chapman eds., New York University Press 1982).

ELINOR OSTROM, GOVERNING THE COMMONS: THE EVOLUTION OF INSTITUTIONS FOR COLLECTIVE ACTION (Cambridge University Press 1990).

DANIEL PINK, DRIVE: THE SURPRISING TRUTH ABOUT WHAT MOTIVATES US (New York: Riverhead Books 2010).

John Quiggin & Dan Hunter, *Money Ruins Everything*, 30 HASTINGS COMM. & ENT. L.J. 203 (2008).

Carol Rose, *The Comedy of the Commons: Custom, Commerce, and Inherently Public Property*, 53 UNIVERSITY OF CHICAGO L. REV. 711 (1986).

Carol M. Rose, *The Several Futures of Property: Of Cyberspace and Folk Tales, Emission Trades and Ecosystems*, 83 MINNESOTA L. REV. 129 (1998).

Henry E. Smith, *Exclusion Versus Governance: Two Strategies for Delineating Property Rights*, 31 J. LEGAL STUDIES 453 (2002).

Lawrence B. Solum, *Questioning Cultural Commons*, 95 CORNELL L. REV. 817 (2010).

Cass Sunstein, *Incommensurability and Valuation in Law*, 92 MICHIGAN L. REV. 779 (1994).

Richard H. Thaler, *Anomalies: The Ultimatum Game*, 2 J. ECONOMIC PERSPECTIVES 195 (1988).

RICHARD M. TITMUSS, THE GIFT RELATIONSHIP: FROM HUMAN BLOOD TO SOCIAL POLICY (New York: Pantheon Books 1970).

14 Legispedia
Brigham Daniels*

I. Introduction

This chapter will use the knowledge commons lens to examine how the U.S. Congress makes legislation. Specifically, it provides a case of cultural commons that relies upon Madison, Frischmann, and Strandburg's modified version of Elinor Ostrom's Institutional Analysis and Development framework ("the Framework") to explore the cultural community that creates and passes legislation in the United States. As the Framework suggests, the chapter looks at the background environment (in Part II of this chapter), the nature of the community and the resources it creates (in Part III), and the outcomes of community interactions (in Part IV). In creating their framework, Madison, Frischmann, and Strandburg suggested that case study research might result in refinements to their Framework (Madison, Frischmann, & Strandburg 2010: 707). In the spirit of furthering their larger project, along the way, this chapter identifies challenges in exploring this case with the Framework and, where possible, suggests modifications to the Framework.

---

* Brigham Daniels is Associate Professor of Law at Brigham Young University Law School, Provo, Utah, USA.

II. Background Environment

Given the nuanced weave of culture's tapestry, it is not surprising that the task of identifying the natural cultural background of a constructed community is a difficult one. This seems particularly true of communities with long histories, which in turn grow out of multiple cultural contexts. This is the situation surrounding Congress. As such, applying this aspect of the Framework proves quite awkward.

Following what is admittedly a failed attempt to subject legislation making to this aspect of the Framework, this part provides some suggestions about how the Framework could be modified to improve identifying background environments.

A. ATTEMPT TO APPLY THIS ASPECT OF THE FRAMEWORK

What are the relevant resources? To simplify matters, I focus on legislation in this chapter, even though there are other cultural resources Congress creates, shares, and distributes.

The Framework first asks researchers to identify the background environment from which cultural resources emerge (Madison, Frischmann, & Strandburg 2010: 683–84). It should come as no surprise that when discussing culture it is difficult to draw lines as to when one aspect of culture ends and another begins. It seems equally challenging to meaningfully separate the different building blocks that make up a culture.

In trying to provide researchers some clarity in this area, the Framework separates cultural resources into two groups: those that are typically governed by patent and copyright law and those that are not (Madison, Frischmann, & Strandburg 2010: 683–88). Congress acts as a community that uses, shares, and generates intellectual resources that are more or less in the public domain. In other words, Congress specifically opts out of intellectual property protections governed by copyright law. As such, we think about the primary resources created by Congress—including legislation—as falling into the latter category. Given that, the Framework suggests that "the most appropriate choice for the 'natural environment' is a cultural environment unmediated by rights of exclusion or other regulation" (Madison, Frischmann, & Strandburg 2010: 684).

So, does the Framework mean that we should ask whether producing legislation is unmediated by rights of exclusion or other regulation? At least within this context, this question seems quite abstract. How far would we have to reach back to draw the line for the absence of legislation? Ancient Greece? The Magna Carta? The establishment of legislative bodies on the American content? The Articles of Confederation? The Constitutional Convention? Somewhere else? Even more frustrating, the Framework suggests we also incorporate Julie Cohen's argument that the natural cultural environment "encompasses all that we inherit and experience" (Madison, Frischmann, & Strandburg 2010: 685; Cohen 2006: 135–37). All of today's citizens have inherited a world with Congress in it. This is true not only for this generation but for several others as well.

In short, it is very difficult to identify the background environment that harmonizes with the approach found in the Framework.

B. SUGGESTED REVISION TO THE FRAMEWORK

In hopes of finding further guidance, I returned to Ostrom's commons IAD framework (Ostrom 2005: 22–24), which Madison, Frischmann, and Strandburg used as a template for the Framework. The corollary question in the IAD framework asks us to identify how traits of the biophysical and material world influence the resource at issue (Ostrom 2005: 22).

Given that, it might make sense to ask, "What aspects of culture are beyond the control of the constructed cultural community and yet shape participation in that community?" Instead of trying to figure out what the world would be like absent a patent pool, an open source community, or a legislature, researchers instead would try to sort out factors other than the communities and resources themselves that influence people to want to participate or refuse to participate in cultural communities.

This line of thinking would point researchers in a very different direction from the background environment sought for currently in the Framework. For a patent pool, for example, a background factor might be that without such a pool one has to appease numerous intellectual property ownership interests and wade through an excessive bureaucracy in order to access intellectual property rights. For an open source software community, one might highlight the roles of networking, résumé building, and socializing opportunities that could be facilitated by the community. For legislation making, one might highlight the independent demand for one legislator to advance her political agenda, build political coalitions, facilitate campaign fundraising, or make good on rent seeking. In short, changing the Framework in this way would highlight factors largely outside of the control of those participating in cultural communities to impact the robustness and vulnerabilities of these communities.

This line of questioning seems less abstract and focuses on those factors that, while out of the control of the group, are often still within the control of the broader public. Understanding these factors might not only help us understand why cooperation in a particular context came into being, was difficult, or ultimately succeeded or failed, but also would instruct policy makers and others with influence how to better facilitate the creation and sustenance of such communities.[1]

---

[1] Some of this occurs in other aspects of the Framework already. One could equally argue that the analysis called for—assuming it seemed relevant—could be incorporated into the Framework's analysis of costs and benefits. This revised line of thinking also seems to harmonize with Ostrom's IAD framework.

III. Basic Characteristics of the Legislation-Making Commons

The Framework next asks researchers to identify characteristics of cultural communities and resources. Specifically, the Framework calls for discussion of cultural resources and communities, the goals and objectives associated with cultural communities, the extent to which the cultural resources and the community are open to users, and the rules that govern the cultural commons (Madison, Frischmann, & Strandburg 2010: 689). Below is a discussion of each of these in turn.

A. RESOURCES AND COMMUNITY IN THE LEGISLATION-MAKING CULTURAL COMMONS

1. Resources

From the outset, one of the reasons that Madison, Frischmann, and Strandburg were drawn to cultural communities and knowledge commons was their interest in the sorts of resources open communities were managing, sharing, and creating in modern society that challenged traditional intellectual property notions.

I now consider in more detail the resources created by the legislation-making community. After doing this, I consider an assumption in the Framework about cultural resources: that these resources are nonrivalrous.

a. Identifying Resources

When it comes to resources, the Framework asks researchers to think carefully about the sorts of resources shared, created, and used by the community (Madison, Frischmann, & Strandburg 2010: 689). However, before sifting through the specific details, I begin with the general. Examples found in the Framework include "patents in a patent pool, news items for a news service, recordings for a music database, or recipes shared within a community of French chefs" (Madison, Frischmann, & Strandburg 2010: 689). Painted with a broad brush, the most obvious resource created within the legislation-making community, not surprisingly, is legislation.

The authors of the Framework, however, ask researchers to look beyond the most obvious resources. They write: "It may take some consideration to identify the most salient description of the relevant resources" (Madison, Frischmann, & Strandburg 2010: 689). The Framework's authors provide examples of this by asking, "What resources are pooled and shared in an open source software community? Ideas? Code? Coding expertise? Debugging opportunities?" (Madison, Frischmann, & Strandburg 2010: 689). They go on to note that often "multiple types of resources are being shared within the community" (Madison, Frischmann, & Strandburg 2010: 689).

Playing off these questions, what are the implications of this framing within the legislation-making community? How do the concepts of "ideas" and "code" within the open source software communities translate in the world of legislation? Both of these questions prompt researchers to disaggregate the products shared and created by cultural communities. Embedded in most legislation are likely a number of things, including but not limited to a collection of ideas, language, reports, transcribed histories, and analysis relating to policy, budgeting, and law. The strategies used to influence legislations, while often conceived as self-motivated, could easily be cast as sharing ideas, language, arguments, and the like.

Moving on, what about the example in an open source software community of "coding expertise"? In this example, the focus shifts from the community's output to the pooled attributes of the community drawn upon in the creation of the output. Thinking along these lines, there are a large number of attributes of the legislation-making community that are drawn upon regularly. For example, Congress often draws upon experts within a particular field when drafting legislation. One could go on to list a number of community traits that are pooled in legislation making, including creativity, expertise, ability to leverage and create opportunities for political advantage, ability to negotiate, effort, ability to pressure and inspire others, and ability to filter large amounts of information.

The key word in the example of "debugging opportunities" seems to be *opportunities*. What opportunities are pooled in the creation and dissemination of legislation? At a simplistic level, there is a spectrum of stereotypical narratives about the opportunities provided to those with influence in the legislation-making process. On one end of that spectrum one might find the impressions that members of Congress strive to create during the election process, which often highlight such things as a candidate's desire to have the opportunity to make a difference, express her patriotism, and serve the community. On the other end of the spectrum, one finds views that what happens in Congress can be explained by understanding how members of Congress seek to satisfy their own interests, which might include something as simple as increasing their odds of reelection but also even more less flattering and obscure motives like gaining power or even receiving payoffs under the table.

While this discussion of legislation barely begins to skim the surface, clearly there are multiple resources shared within and created by the legislation-making community.

b. Questioning the Framework's Assumption about Nonrivalry of Resources

Madison, Frischmann, and Strandburg take the position that "the 'output' of … information, expression, invention, innovation, research, ideas, or otherwise … is naturally nonrivalrous" (Madison, Frischmann, & Strandburg 2010: 666). As illustrated in the examples above, intellectual output is only one of three categories of resources pooled by constructed cultural commons communities. Other pooled resources within the congressional cultural commons include community attributes (e.g., policy expertise) and community members' opportunities (e.g., making inroads with interest groups). These pooled goods are rivalrous resources. In fact, several scholars have applied insights from the commons literature (which assumes rivalry) to different resources related to making legislation, including the federal budget (Crain & Muris 1995: 313–14; Wilson 1986: 752), and political credit-taking among constituents (Maloney et al. 1984).

This point seems to play out similarly in knowledge commons or cultural commons more generally. To illustrate the point, take the example of coding expertise. Ask any expert if she can give expertise on an unlimited basis or if her time and energies are endless, and the answer will of course be "no." As for debugging opportunities, if these were nonrivalrous, it would be strange to call them *opportunities*.

At least some dimensions of the output of the legislation-making community—legislation—even call into question the assumption that intellectual output resources themselves are nonrivalrous. Before taking issue with that framing of output resources, note that the position that intellectual outputs are nonrivalrous is consistent with the position often taken within discussions about intellectual property (Smith 2007: 1751–52; Yoo 2007: 645–46; Lemley & O'Brien 1997: 268–69). The assumption of nonrivalry can even be traced to Thomas Jefferson:

> He who receives an idea from me, receives instructions himself without lessening mine; as he who lights his taper at mine, receives light without darkening me. That ideas should freely spread from one to another over the globe, for the moral and mutual instruction of man, and improvement of his condition, seems to have been peculiarly and benevolently designed by nature, when she made them, like fire, expansible over all space, without lessening their density in any point, and like the air in which we breathe, move and have our physical being, incapable of confinement or exclusive appropriation (Jefferson 1813: 333–34).

Supreme Court opinions have likewise used this framing.[2]

While it is difficult to argue that simply understanding the law is a limited resource, what about other uses of the law? Some of the most obvious dimensions of law are limited. Think about litigation aimed at challenging the constitutionality of a law. While the words on the page may still be accessible, many uses of the law cannot survive if a court invalidates it based on the Constitution. That outcome means that legislation may be a rivalrous resource, because one person's pursuing her own interests in invalidating the law negates the prospect that others can pursue their interests in enforcing the law. We could tell similar stories about litigation attempting to interpret the meaning of legislation, about one Congress revising the legislation of another Congress, or about an agency refusing to enforce a particular provision of a statute.[3]

---

[2] See, e.g., Int'l News Serv. v. Associated Press, 248 U.S. 215, 250 (1918) (Brandeis, J., dissenting) ("The general rule of law is, that the noblest of human productions—knowledge, truths ascertained, conceptions, and ideas—become, after voluntary communication to others, free as the air to common use."); Twentieth Century Music Corp. v. Aiken, 422 U.S. 151, 156 (1975) ("Creative work is to be encouraged and rewarded, but private motivation must ultimately serve the cause of promoting broad public availability of literature, music, and the other arts.").

[3] For a more detailed discussion of how constitutional interpretation applies to knowledge commons, see Daniels & Hudson (forthcoming).

This argument, that the resources entwined with cultural commons often have dimensions plagued by rivalry, seemingly applies to intellectual and cultural resources more generally. In fact, not long ago, Hess and Ostrom took a close look at a category of resources that they called knowledge commons (Hess & Ostrom 2007). Not surprisingly, much of what they considered knowledge commons would probably meet Madison, Frischmann, and Strandburg's definition of constructed cultural commons. However, when Hess and Ostrom discussed knowledge commons, they were not talking about nonrivalrous resources but rather commons resources subject to rivalry. According to Hess and Ostrom,

> The introduction of new technologies can play a huge role in the robustness or vulnerability of a commons. New technologies can enable the capture of what were once free and open public goods. This has been the case with the development of most "global commons," such as the deep seas, the atmosphere, the electromagnetic spectrum, and space, for example. The ability to capture the resource, with the resource being converted from a nonrivalrous, non-exclusionary public good into a common-pool resource that needs to be managed, monitored, and protected, to ensure sustainability and preservation (Hess & Ostrom 2007: 10).

Hess and Ostrom write about technology transforming public goods into commons resources. If nothing else, the story they tell shows that technology and circumstances can manifest the rivalrous dimensions of these cultural and intellectual resources. Hess and Ostrom illustrate this in the example of journal publications with worldwide distribution in print, which were later published only in an online form. When the publisher disbanded the journal, it vanished altogether. Similarly, online publications created by the U.S. government that provided a wide array of useful data and information vanished after 9/11 (Hess & Ostrom 2007: 14–15). In these cases, and others like them, we did not recognize that this knowledge was linked to an infrastructure that made it easy to corral and take out of the hands of so many. What had been thought of as a nonrivalrous good suddenly faced extinction.

Consider a simple example of a fried chicken recipe to illustrate the point. On one level, such a recipe is not rivalrous: sharing the recipe with another does not diminish the recipe owner's ability to possess the recipe. While it may be technically true that telling the recipe to another person does not change the original owner's ability to recall the recipe for himself, some of the uses that one might want to make of the recipe might be compromised by doing so. Like most intellectual resources, owners of desirable recipes can derive some sorts of value by making sure the recipe is not made freely available. While it is a bit ridiculous, consider the example of the potential value of the fried chicken recipe at the heart of a memorable speech delivered by one of Mike Myers' characters in the film *So I Married an Axe Murderer*. The character could hardly contain his scorn as he explained at Kentucky Fried Chicken that the Colonel "puts addictive chemicals in his chicken, making you crave it fortnightly" (So I Married an Axe Murderer 1993).[4] Had the Colonel blabbed the recipe far and wide, then getting out the fryer would be an alternative to paying a visit to the Colonel when those cravings kick in. In reality of course, addictive chemical or not, KFC goes to great lengths to keep the "Colonel's Secret Recipe" a secret, hiding away the recipe in a vault protected by various motion detectors and surrounded by concrete (Schreiner 2009). If the recipe were to get out, every potential customer who opted not to buy his chicken would illustrate for the Colonel the sting of rivalry.[5]

The fight about what purposes that the various resources identified as cultural commons should serve is as much about interests as it is about vision. It is a controversy that sits at the heart of intellectual property law, something the Framework recognizes: "At the core of IP law, as traditionally conceived, is the right to exclude, without which it is assumed that some producers would abandon their efforts for fear of free riding (unlicensed sharing) by competitors" (Madison, Frischmann, & Strandburg 2010: 667).

So, as we look closely, we find that at least along some dimensions, resources that transmit knowledge and enhance culture face rivalry. As laid out in further detail below, I argue that understanding the ways that rivalry rears its head is central to understanding cultural commons. For now, however, I return to applying the Framework to legislation making.

2. Community

According to the Framework, the next step is to identify the members of the constructed community (Madison, Frischmann, & Strandburg 2010: 690). With the legislation-making community, the obvious place to start is with the members of Congress. After all, it is the collective vote of these members that creates legislation. With the signature of the president, or a two-thirds vote after a presidential veto, mere proposals transform into law. Even though public approval of Congress currently hovers at an

---

[4] Another amusing example along these lines comes from the "Soup Nazi" episode of the *Seinfeld* television series. The gist of the Soup Nazi storyline is that an iron-fisted restaurateur prepares and serves delicious soup but does so only the way he wants to prepare it—no exceptions and no protests, or else, "No soup for you!" Elaine, one of the lead characters, knows the rules but flaunts them. The Soup Nazi bans Elaine from his restaurant for a year. Due to serendipity rarely seen in life but frequently seen on *Seinfeld*, Elaine ends up acquiring the Soup Nazi's armoire, which turns out to include his soup recipes in a drawer. She then proceeds to blissfully expose the Soup Nazi's recipes to the public, drying up demand for his soup and forcing him to close his business.

[5] One of the editors (Frischmann) notes: "The rivalry described in the text is different sort of rivalry than the Framework distinguishes. The intellectual resource here (the recipe) is nonrivalrously consumed. That is what stings the Colonel. All of his customers may possess and use the resource without depleting the resource itself; the customers in possession of the recipe no longer need to obtain it from him each time they would like chicken cooked using the recipe. One might say that there is a kind of rivalry between the Colonel and consumers who are no longer customers and instead are behaving more like competitors. But that competition is a consequence of the nonrivalrous nature of the intellectual resource and the high costs of excluding others from using the resource once it is in their possession."

all-time low, membership in Congress is still highly sought after, with campaign spending in recent years hitting all-time highs. In addition to campaign spending, observant citizens can easily see a great deal of effort, time, and resources of political parties and interest groups attempting to influence congressional races.

Because those in Congress have it in their power to move the country in one direction or another, it is noteworthy, and yet not surprising, that some of the most contentious controversies in American political history had to do with the composition of Congress. Consider a few examples. In what is known as the Constitutional Convention's Great Compromise, the esteemed delegates of the Convention struck a balance in 1787 between the interests of small states and the interests of large states. The content of that bargain had to do with state claims to representation in the Senate and the House of Representatives. Similarly, the Missouri Compromise was a deal brokered in 1820 between pro-slavery and anti-slavery factions, and in large part had to do with preserving the political balance of slave and non-slave states in Congress, particularly within the Senate. Moreover, one of the reasons (perhaps the main reason) that efforts to extend voting rights were so heated during the twentieth century was due to the political calculus of how new voting rights might alter political races, including congressional elections. More recently, we have seen similar themes reverberate in political controversies surrounding things like campaign finance laws, legal opinions like *Citizens United v. Federal Election Commission*,[6] and redistricting tainted by alleged gerrymandering.

Of course, even though Congress's votes pass legislation, many hands other than those of Congress's members often shape the legislation and even the political incentives at play when members cast their votes. While the true political winds might take into account the perceptions of even the most disinterested potential citizens, it makes sense to identify a few of the most important categories of those likely to influence Congress as they create legislation.

First, we begin with congressional staffers. While crafting legislation is not the only role played by congressional staff, it is a major one. Within each congressional office, we find staff members with titles like Legislative Director, Senior Legislative Assistant, and Legislative Coordinator. In addition, Congress employs staff members to assist committees and subcommittees in evaluating and drafting legislation, not to mention those employed by the Congressional Research Service, the Congressional Budget Office, and the General Accounting Office. In significant part, all of these federal employees are paid to help Congress shape legislation.

Additionally, Congress often relies on outside constituencies for their expertise and input. Even if Congress does not formally seek input, there will be many angling, if not clamoring, for Congress's attention. Obviously, interest groups, political action committees, lobbyists, and activists are often found within the halls of Congress and congressional offices. These entities go to great lengths to influence legislation, sometimes in broad

---

[6] 558 U.S. 50 (2010).

and visible ways and sometimes in narrow and largely undetectable ways. These groups not only seek to influence members of Congress directly but also seek to influence other players on Capitol Hill, including congressional staffers.

There are other constituencies that could be addressed as well. Those that immediately come to mind include the executive, the judiciary, those employed by the federal bureaucracy, the press, and concerned citizens acting on their own volition. Of course, those who influence legislation change with time, context, and political currents. Additionally, the methods used to participate in this community are many, ranging from drafting legislation to signing a petition.

B. IDENTIFYING GOALS AND OBJECTIVES IN THE LEGISLATION-MAKING CULTURAL COMMONS

Next, the Framework seeks "to identify the particular problem or problems that a given commons is constructed to address" (Madison, Frischmann, & Strandburg 2010: 691). In this aspect of the Framework, Madison, Frischmann, and Strandburg contrast what is going on within the cultural commons with that of other commons resources. They argue correctly that within the commons, the overarching goal generally boils down to managing "the risk that a common-pool resource will be exhausted by uncoordinated self-interested activity" (Madison, Frischmann, & Strandburg 2010: 691). This is necessary because of the rivalrous nature of commons resources.

On the other hand, they argue that cultural resources are "public goods" and "not rivalrously consumed" (Madison, Frischmann, & Strandburg 2010: 691). Given this chapter's previous argument that these resources are rivalrous at least along some dimensions, I suggest an additional revision to the Framework. Before detailing this revision, however, I first attempt to fit the goals and objectives of legislation making into the Framework as it currently stands.

The Framework provides,

> [T]he various problems that cultural commons institutions solve are not merely, or even primarily, problems of overuse. The problems addressed by cultural commons include the production of intellectual goods to be shared, the overcoming of transaction costs leading to bargaining breakdown among different actors interested in exploiting intellectual resource, the production of commonly useful platforms for further creativity, and so forth (Madison, Frischmann, & Strandburg 2010: 691).

In thinking about the problems for which Congress was created, we immediately think of the Founders. At a very simplistic level, the Constitution provides the Congress "all legislative powers"[7] and the power to "make all laws which shall be necessary and proper."[8]

---

[7] U.S. CONST. Art. I, § 1.
[8] U.S. CONST. Art. I, § 8.

As such, it seems that for the community that created Congress, the most fundamental purpose of Congress was to formulate, debate, write, and pass bills.

There are some other additional themes that might be attributed to the Founders. Without trying to make an exhaustive list, consider three other goals that might be associated with the creation of a Congress. First, at least to some extent, the Founders empowered Congress in order to create some uniformity of law among the states. For example, the desire to have uniformity is the genesis of the Commerce Clause. As noted by Justice Cardozo,

> [A] chief occasion of the commerce clauses was "the mutual jealousies and aggressions of the States, taking form in customs barriers and other economic retaliation." If New York, in order to promote the economic welfare of her farmers, may guard them against competition with the cheaper prices of Vermont, the door has been opened to rivalries and reprisals that were meant to be averted by subjecting commerce between the states to the power of the nation.[9]

This view of the Commerce Clause echoes the pleas of Alexander Hamilton, in his *Federalist No. 22*: "It is indeed evident, on the most superficial view, that there is no object, either as it respects the interests of trade or finance, that more strongly demands a federal superintendence" (Hamilton 1966: 55).

Second, it seems fair to say that the Founders made Congress accountable to the various states in order to create a sophisticated governing body that provides citizens a conduit to the federal government. James Madison explained the benefits of this sort of government by comparing it to a direct democracy in *Federalist No. 10*:

> The effect of the first difference [between republics and direct democracy] is, on the one hand, to refine and enlarge the public views, by passing them through the medium of a chosen body of citizens, whose wisdom may best discern the true interest of their country, and whose patriotism and love of justice will be least likely to sacrifice it to temporary or partial considerations (Madison 1966: 22).

Third, the legislative branch was seen as a check against the sorts of problems the colonies had experienced under English rule, particularly problems that might arise from a powerful executive branch of government. Because of this, it gave Congress a number of ways to safeguard the country from the executive branch, such as vesting with Congress the power to write the law, to declare war, and to tax, to name a few.

---

[9] Baldwin v. G.A.F. Seelig, Inc., 294 U.S. 511 (1935).

1. Adding to the Framework the Goals of Those Sustaining the Community

The Founders' motivations, while both relevant and interesting, are distant from the political life of Congress in the twenty-first century. So, what is motivating those who today sustain the legislation-making community? This is an important line of inquiry because a cultural community must not only be invented but also sustained. Even though the Framework does not seem to call for such evaluation, it makes sense not only to evaluate the goals and objectives of those who first invented the community but also those who reinvent the community, particularly as the interests and membership of such communities change.

Cultural communities, of course, are made up of many interests and individuals. As is often noted in this context, Congress is a "they" and not an "it" (Shepsle 1992). As such, it seems that drawing out the various motivations of subgroups (and perhaps some key individuals) within a community may prove worthwhile. To determine what fuels the process of reinventing a cultural community, even though the Framework does not formally require it, it makes sense to supplement the Framework with exploration of the goals of those within community as it currently exists as well as the goals of those who first created the community.

As an illustrative example, consider some of the goals of the subgroups identified above in discussing the communities involved in making legislation. What are the goals of the members of Congress? Of course, the full answer to this question is extremely complicated. But assumptions of what motivates members of Congress are in no way new and arise out of multiple schools of thought. Some of the themes that arise in such discussions include the notion that members of Congress attempt to mirror the majority of their electorate, to promote their own best judgment, to act as agents to political principals such as voters or interest groups, to maximize personal benefit, or to balance a variety of these interests, among many others.

Consider a few other cursory examples. For some staff members, the motivation might be as mundane as earning a livelihood, but could also include affecting policy or seeking power. Those associated with interest groups, political parties, lobbying firms, and political action committees might hope to achieve certain policy ends through the legislative process, to gain clients or a political constituency, or to make money.

Admittedly, each of these players is likely to be vastly more complex than such a simple results-oriented view would suggest. However, understanding what is sustaining interest in a community—even in very basic terms—seems essential in understanding it.

2. Another Pitch for Highlighting Rivalry into the Framework

Quickly reviewing the goals and objectives of those who sustain cultural commons communities, it is clear that rivalry plays an important role in the legislative process. While it is a defensible—though I think losing—argument that legislative output (i.e., legislation) is nonrivalrous, the same cannot be said of most of what drives people to this cultural community.

When the Speaker of the House says, "The ayes have it," the nays do not. The same goes for each of the community members with a preference regarding the legislation. When facing controversial decisions, everyone cannot be a winner. Winning for some precludes winning for others: that is rivalry. A job or a promotion of a congressional staffer or a federal bureaucrat precludes somebody else filling that same job. Again, rivalry. One interest group's access to a member of Congress leaves others scavenging the halls of Congress. Rivalry.

This discussion about goals and objectives is an important one to have if one is to understand the legislative process for a few reasons. First, it often helps us understand why people participate in communities that create cultural and knowledge resources. Where we find rivalry, we often find what sustains a community's attention. By definition, rivalry means scarcity of resources. Participation is often explained by the desire to partake of the resources being created, distributed, and consumed. This understanding is clearly imperative for those hoping to foster and sustain cultural commons endeavors.

Second, such an understanding may help us better predict what a community's end product will look like. Understanding, for example, that Wall Street generally opposes a piece of legislation and that certain members of Congress are sensitive to Wall Street's concerns might help us predict how particular members of Congress might also view that legislation.

Finally, understanding the things that motivate members of a cultural community might help us identify areas where institutional reform would be helpful. In fact, Madison, Frischmann, and Strandburg hit upon this topic in discussing goals and objectives associated with cultural commons, even though they do not associate it with rivalry. They write,

> Pooling arrangements also may exist for less socially salutary reasons. Most obvious is the case of members colluding to restrict competition, and it is certainly within the purview of our approach that commons should be evaluated in part by reference to the possibility of anticompetitive behavior and other possible costs (Madison, Frischmann, & Strandburg 2010: 693).

An analysis that explicitly tries to expose where rivalry exists may be the first step in documenting and even limiting aspects of a community that are problematic. It is not surprising that many of the reform efforts aimed at the legislative process have occurred where we find rivalry. Examples include voter fraud laws,[10] campaign finance laws,[11] political

---

[10] See, e.g., Help America Vote Act of 2002, Pub. L. 107-252, 116 Stat. 1666.
[11] See, e.g., Bipartisan Campaign Reform Act of 2002, Pub. L. 107-155, 116 Stat. 81.

protection of federal employees,[12] and ethics rules associated with gift-giving to members of Congress and their staff.[13]

It is important to stress that this sort of discussion could be had across many constructed cultural commons and knowledge commons. To illustrate the point, answer the question: What is it that brings Wikipedians back to edit and tend the wiki? Certainly, some Wikipedians have stayed true to what one might assume were the motives of the creators of Wikipedia. However, what should be made of the controversy regarding Wikipedia's decision to block the Church of Scientology from making self-promoting edits? What about the Wikipedians who began changing the story of Paul Revere after Sarah Palin flubbed it on the campaign trail? While the creators of Wikipedia may not have self-promotion and political public relations in mind when they founded the wiki, doesn't understanding this provide important information about how to manage the community and its output resource?

What about open source software? What should we make of the army of coders that are employed by private businesses? Is the way they are shaping the software only related to their employers' business interests or is it more complicated than this? Does it depend on the employer? Similarly, does coding help give volunteer coders credibility in the job market? While Linux may not have been created to provide job security for some and job opportunities for others, understanding the answers to these questions might be important in shaping, sustaining, and even tempering the community.

It seems that if we are ever going to better understand cultural commons, we need to have a more fine-grained understanding of what brings people to commons and whether (and how) to promote or discourage particular users from using cultural commons in particular ways.

C. OPENNESS AND CONTROL

The cultural commons framework identifies two sorts of openness, one that relates to openness as applied to cultural commons resources and a second that focuses on it as applied to cultural commons communities (Madison, Frischmann, & Strandburg 2010: 695–98). I will take each in turn.

1. Openness Applied to the Resource

The Framework looks at openness of resources. When it comes to resources, "openness describes the extent to which there are barriers to possession or use" (Madison, Frischmann, & Strandburg 2010: 695).

---

[12] See, e.g., Hatch Act of 1939, 52 Stat. 1147.

[13] See, e.g., Honest Leadership and Open Government Act of 2007, Pub. L. No. 110-81, 121 Stat. 735.

With legislation-making, the openness of the law as a resource depends on how one intends to use it. On the spectrum of open and closed resources, when use means accessing the law, it is extremely open. The government has made the entirety of the U.S. Code available online and free of charge.[14] In addition, the government has created more than 1000 Federal Depository Libraries where the general public can access the U.S. Code and other federal materials.[15] It does not appear that the government is attempting to exercise any intellectual property rights over the U.S. Code, and it can be found in full on several websites[16] and in part on many others. Public access to what the law is only seems limited by the public's ability to grasp legislative language.

The law can be used in other ways as well, and some of these are not as open. For example, if one wants to use the law as the basis of a lawsuit, one might be limited by whether a statute creates a cause of action or whether an individual has standing to bring a claim. And, whereas reading a statute is virtually free, even when a cause of action is available, bringing lawsuits in many instances will prove cost prohibitive.

2. Openness as Applied to the Community

The Framework next asks us to look at openness of community. In this context, openness refers to "our capacity to relate to that community as a contributor or user of resources that comprise in part the cultural commons. Thus, openness describes the extent to which there are criteria for or barriers to membership or participation in the creative or innovative processes that the cultural commons is intended to support" (Madison, Frischmann, & Strandburg 2010: 696).

How open is the legislation-making cultural commons?

Certain aspects of the community are finely filtered. While constitutionally membership of Congress is open to any U.S. citizen who meets certain age requirements,[17] getting one's name on the ballot is much different from winning an election. The difficulty of winning a race for the House or the Senate is further complicated by the fact that it is often extremely difficult to beat an incumbent (Ansolabehere & Snyder 2000: 609–10). Even when the chances of victory are small, however, the two major parties in the United States tend to field impressive candidates, almost all of whom are elites in society.

However, participation in other communities within the legislation-making cultural commons is much more accessible, though the most meaningful participation is less so. For example, an army of college students are allowed to play minor roles in these offices as interns. However, getting a job as a staffer, particularly a leadership role, is much more

---

[14] See U.S. Government Printing Office, Federal Digital System, http://www.gpo.gov/fdsys/.

[15] See U.S. Government Printing Office, Welcome to the Federal Depository Library Directory, http://catalog. gpo.gov/fdlpdir/FDLPdir.jsp.

[16] See Legal Information Institute, U.S. Code Main Page, http://www.law.cornell.edu/uscode/; Wikipedia, United States Code, http://en.wikipedia.org/wiki/United_States_Code.

[17] One must be more than 25 years old to run for House seat and more than 30 years old to run for the Senate. U.S. CONST. Art. I, § 2, cl. 2, U.S. CONST. Art. I, § 3, cl. 3.

difficult. The same is true of the many interests that descend upon Washington, D.C. to lobby Congress. If one is looking for a relatively short-term experience, the people who lobby Congress are not so much unlike average people in American life. High school students, senior citizens, people involved in different trades, and political activists of different stripes commonly find their way to Washington, D.C. to lobby congressional offices for a day. In fact, anyone who cares enough to spend a few minutes writing a letter or an e-mail can send it to a member of Congress. Yet there is very little doubt that some people are much more capable of influencing the legislative process than others. There is a major barrier to obtaining access to the powerful, particularly if one believes the conventional wisdom that much of the most influential lobbying opportunities occur in places most people cannot go: in back rooms, at parties with Washington socialites, or within the offices of members of Congress. Frustration stemming from this reality is reflected on bumper stickers with mottos like, "Invest in America, Buy a Congressman." Of course, others may win attention and access as the result of having orchestrated events to generate publicity or by mobilizing constituents to increase pressure on politicians. Succeeding in such ventures is not easy, however, and requires significant expenditures of time and energy and, more often than not, money. Similar stories can be told by other communities as well, including the press and the federal bureaucracy.

There is no doubt that one could dredge up exceptions to the rule, but the rule seems to be that those with influence in American society are by and large those who have the most of it within the community that creates legislation.

D. GOVERNANCE OR "RULES-IN-USE"

Much has been and could be said about the formal and informal rules that govern the legislation-making community. As the Framework instructs (Madison, Frischmann, & Strandburg 2010: 698), I briefly discuss a number of factors relevant to the rules of how the game is played. To do this, I first look at the history and narrative about how the cultural community and its resources come into being. Following this, I look at the various entitlements surrounding shaping and accessing community resources. Next, I briefly address the institutional setting in which the legislation-making community finds itself and the legal structures that affect it. Last, I discuss the various mechanisms found to make and enforce the rules of the game.

1. History and Narrative

We now turn to history and narrative. According to the Framework, "[a]ny given knowledge pool depends in an important sense on its creation narrative" (Madison, Frischmann, & Strandburg 2010: 698). The narrative need not be static and is in fact suspected to evolve over time: "Explicitly giving attention to creation narratives also encourages attention to evolutionary processes. Changes in the narrative over time, or conflicts embedded within a narrative, can illustrate debates over purpose, which can illuminate the normative foundations of commons and highlight points of conflict" (Madison, Frischmann, & Strandburg 2010: 699).

Indeed, the narratives surrounding Congress are both diverse and in many ways inconsistent. On one level, the work of creating Congress at the Constitutional Convention is much celebrated, if not revered. The nation, and particularly our statehouses and government buildings, often take time to pay homage to the delegates that drafted our Constitution through celebratory artworks and monuments. This episode in American history has been referred to, even in scholarly circles, as a miracle (Bowen 1966). Some even would go as far as seeing the hand of God working through these delegates, including the likes of the saucy—but still much admired—Ben Franklin.

Another narrative, one more contemporary, looks at legislation making through the lens of a mechanical civics lesson. As the children's television *Schoolhouse Rock* segment "I'm Just a Bill" illustrates, the passage of legislation is a process. Narratives, like this one, are central components of education about government in the United States.

Sometimes we find narratives about how the "little guy" somehow ends up making a difference in Congress. Whether this comes in the form of fictional Hollywood accounts like *Mr. Smith Goes to Washington* or *Legally Blonde 2* or the stories of the civil rights advocates who persevered and ultimately succeeded in winning Congress over, the notion is that people can make a difference. Admonitions like "write your member of Congress" reflect an optimism that ordinary people can make an extraordinary difference in this context.

More and more frequently, however, we seem to hear the exact opposite narrative. We hear stories of corruption, backroom deals, improprieties, and undue influence. Sometimes such stories attract much attention, such as the narrative the government presented in the criminal prosecutions of Randy "Duke" Cunningham and Jack Abramoff. We also see it in less covered stories of members of Congress getting perks from those whom Congress is supposedly regulating. Seemingly, the public's very negative perception of Congress in part grows out of this view of those in Congress.

2. Entitlement Structures and Resource Provisions

While there is no entitlement to the passage of legislation, a number of institutional factors are at work that change the likelihood of passage occurring. First, I consider what those factors are and then move on to the implications of this discussion on the Framework.

a. Factors

Some of the factors of entitlements related to resource provision are formal and others informal. From a formal perspective, the organizational design of Congress immediately comes to mind. For example, members of Congress play different roles within the leadership of the institution (e.g., Speaker of the House). Those who occupy these leadership positions often have the ability to serve as gatekeepers of legislative proposals: the higher the position, the more likely it is that one will have the chance to affect legislative proposals. Additionally, within particular policy areas, there are committees where legislative proposals often germinate and are vetted. While serving on a committee does not bring with it a guarantee that one will pass legislation in that committee's policy purview, not serving on such a committee almost guarantees that one won't, at least without some help from those on the relevant committee. Which members of Congress and staffers serve in leadership roles or on different policy areas is dynamic. Change in this area is a function of attrition, the political prominence and clout of the actors involved, and interests and assignments. The most important catalyst for change on committees is that of elections, which bring new faces to Congress and also often accompany opportunities for new committee assignments.

Next, Congress also has internal rules that govern legislation making. These rules often play a powerful, but nuanced, role in determining legislative outcomes and are often particularly important when it comes to stifling legislation proposals. Because members of Congress often find novel ways to employ these rules, and in fact use them as tactics to reach different legislative outcomes, it is often hard to predict the way the rules will play out at the outset. Additionally, it is important to note that Congress always has the option of changing rules as the drama unfolds, and even though major changes to the rules are rare, this factor certainly complicates the picture.

In addition to organizational design and internal rules, we also find that the Constitution limits what Congress may and may not do.[18] Changes to the Constitution, of course, can be made by amendment[19] and also through judicial interpretation of constitutional language.[20] Changes by amendment occur, but are rare. Changes in judicial opinions are more frequent. Both of these factors, particularly judicial opinions, are in most ways beyond the control of those who have a hand in making legislation. Changes in this realm are often incremental but are not necessarily so.

Informally, there are a many tools that might change the probability of a particular piece of legislation passing, and these tools are available to a much broader subset of the community. Consider a handful of ways that one might secure influence over the legislative process: lobbying; using the press strategically to create public pressure or concern; staging campaigns to influence public opinion; mobilizing interest groups; donating to political candidates or other political entities; leveraging the power of other branches of government (e.g., the judiciary, the executive, or administrative agencies); leveraging the power of other levels of government (e.g., foreign countries, states, and local government); gaining the favor of members of Congress and their staffers; finding ways to

---

[18] U.S. CONST. Art. I, § 8.

[19] U.S. CONST. Art V.

[20] See Marbury v. Madison, 5 U.S. 137 (1803).

facilitate compromise or friction; logrolling; and grandstanding. In almost any effort to pass legislation, we will find a myriad of these informal tools employed by a host of political players, and the way that a given political situation unfolds is likely to cause many players to change the way that they use these tools—and even the sort of tools they use. This is highly dynamic, making it nearly impossible to predict and very often even hard to understand in a meaningful way. These complex interactions make up the essence of legislative politics.

b. Implications of This Conversation for the Framework

Briefly, because the chapter has covered this point already extensively, note how much of this conversation suggests paying close attention to the role of rivalry within these cultural communities. The very notion that members of the community might have special access to create cultural resources suggests that rivalry is creeping into the picture somewhere: if there was not, why create institutions to limit provisioning of these resources at all? There is no reason to believe either that legislation is special in this respect. In fact, such limits sit at the heart of traditional intellectual property relationships, where limits (e.g., exclusivity) are in place to reward (e.g., via increased profits) the creators of culturally important goods.

3. Institutional Setting

In analyzing an institutional setting, the Framework instructs that we examine how a community relates with other organizational structures (Madison, Frischmann, & Strandburg 2010: 701).

This aspect of the Framework prompts us to note the interactions that occur among the branches of government, with those in Congress making laws, the executive enforcing them, and the judiciary interpreting legislative language. Of course, this characterization is only made more complicated by the robust role of administrative agencies, which often overlaps with all three branches of government, but particularly with the executive.

Additionally, the legislation-making community often incorporates a myriad of organizations—many of which are cultural communities in their own right—into the legislation-making process and also into other endeavors that legislation makers would often find appealing. We see coalitions of businesses, advocacy groups, labor unions, political parties, and concerned citizens sometimes banding together, sometimes opposing each other, and sometimes even breaking ranks internally. In addition, we see social structures like the press and lobbyists who also derive important benefits from their participation in the process (e.g., readership and clients). The setting in which the legislative community is nested is highly dynamic. In fact, it is particularly complex because what goes on with the legislation-making community alters the incentives of the organization that surrounds it (and therefore the setting) and vice versa.

4. Legal Structures that Affect the Pool Itself

The Framework asks researchers next to identify "legal structures that affect the pool" at issue (Madison, Frischmann, & Strandburg 2010: 702). In the context of making legislation, this is both particularly important and, because the Framework seems to assume that researchers are not exploring legal structures themselves, at the same time somewhat awkward.

On one hand, Congress has the power not only to create rules but also to pass laws relating to legislation making, and particularly interactions within the legislation-making community. These can range from policy judgments regarding campaign funding and gift-giving by lobbyists to waiving sovereign immunity in a particular context.

Of course, there is much more to law than legislation. Decisions by judges, actions by agencies, and interpretations of law by the executive all play into that which makes up the law, and all of this can—and often does—reverberate through the legislation-making process. Additionally, since the federal government is a government of limited jurisdiction, constitutional text serves as an important legal limit to Congress's power to create certain sorts of legislation. This is true even in light of the fact that many within the judiciary believe that legal interpretation can bend somewhat as the time demands.

5. Governance Mechanisms

A number of governance mechanisms might be employed to enforce the governance decisions surrounding the legislation-making community. Some decisions are handled purely internally within Congress. For example, when members behave badly, they might be formally sanctioned by their colleagues. These include a range of sanctions, such as public reprimand, fines, loss of committee status, and even expulsion. Members of Congress might also employ informal mechanisms of sanction. These can also range from the minor (e.g., decisions surrounding whether to include a colleague within a particular meeting or social function) to the major (e.g., endorsing a colleague's intraparty challenger).

The world of public relations also provides an outlet to congressional governance, and this mechanism is not only available to those in Congress but also those outside it. When a legislator feels particularly aggrieved or feels that her colleagues are mistaken in their decision to pursue a certain policy, a member might hold a press conference, talk to a media outlet, or even write a tweet. Interest groups and even individuals may do the same. While this form of sanction is often brushed aside as mere partisan bickering, the fact that what happens in Washington ends up in the *Washington Post* or on a local news channel serves as a very effective sanction for politicians worried about their reputations.

Judicial review of congressional actions sometimes provides yet another enforcement mechanism. While courts are often careful before involving themselves in congressional disputes,[21] some sorts of disputes (e.g., constitutional or congressional interpretation) routinely result in litigation. While very often courts express the desire to defer to congressional action, some judicial decisions have significant implications for Congress's power. We might see courts go as far as striking down legislation that runs contrary to the Constitution or even imprisoning a member of Congress for breaking one of the country's criminal laws.[22]

IV. Patterns and Outcomes Emanating from Legislation Making

Below, I discuss the last two aspects of the Framework, beginning with patterns of interactions and then moving on to outcomes.

A. PATTERNS OF INTERACTION

The Framework next looks at patterns of interaction and assumes that these patterns of interactions and outcomes (discussed next) have a dynamic and iterative relationship (Madison, Frischmann, & Strandburg 2010: 680). Uncovering this relationship stands as one of the Framework's most significant contributions and modifications to Ostrom's original IAD framework: community interactions affect outcomes and vice versa.

Over time, we have seen varying degrees of friction and civility among those who make legislation. During the past decade, the pattern of interaction we see in legislative community is often characterized by a great deal of partisanship. In fact, a number of members of Congress who were often recognized for their ability to work across the aisle have retired and have even been defeated by challengers (generally in intraparty races). Partisanship, obviously, does a great deal to stifle outcomes within Congress, even as some members of Congress may benefit politically as they become less cooperative. Moreover, over the past few years, we have seen this taken to an extreme as members of Congress have even participated in a form of political brinksmanship, where a faction of Congress risks an extreme result (such as the United States defaulting on its obligations) to gain leverage over political opponents anxious to counteract such a risk. Of course, our time is not unique in its tendency to highlight factions. This state of being has been the rule rather than exception. Still, the extent to which partisanship has dominated for the past decade still represents an important development.

In different eras, and still in some policy areas, cooperation with the legislative community is more common. Certain events have brought the country generally and those making legislation specifically to the table to cooperate. We can note particular policies,

---

[21] See, e.g., Baker v. Carr, 369 U.S. 186, 217 (1962) (providing the framework for analyzing the political question doctrine and justiciability).

[22] One example, out of many, is Representative William Jefferson, a former representative of Louisiana's Second District. Jefferson was convicted of corruption charges after the FBI found $90,000 in cash in his freezer.

like the first passage of the U.S.A. Patriot Act and the Clean Air Act, where Congress voted on major provisions almost unanimously and did so with very little criticism from other players within the legislation-making community.

We also see cooperation emerge in smaller ways. For example, even though it is rarely publicized much, we find instances where members of Congress trade votes (sometimes called logrolling) in order to allow for members representing different areas to all get a little of what they want. The ability to negotiate and find middle ground is often highly valued, not only among members of Congress but also by other participants in the legislation-making process. It is worth noting, of course, that the fruits of cooperation are not always desirable. However, this is really a discussion to have when evaluating legislative outcomes.

B. OUTCOMES

The Framework next asks what costs and benefits, along with what solutions and risks, do we see arising from the creation of a community-governed resource.

Determining the costs and benefits arising from legislation making is not easily done. On the microlevel, we find a good deal of discontent. People in the United States often voice frustration that Congress is not better at addressing the nation's problems. Yet, when it comes down to it, what those solutions are is often difficult to discern. To the extent that one claims to see a solution, that judgment often boils down to political aesthetics. In other words, if one likes the political makeup of a particular Congress, generally speaking, legislation making is seen as a good thing. If one does not, stagnation within the community might be preferred.

Additionally, while most Americans have a dim view of Congress, they tend to like their individual members enough that they generally reelect them. Granted, it is apparent that incumbents often have a great advantage over challengers. Many have argued that incumbent retention is a real problem and warrants our attention. Potential fixes to this challenge have been packaged in reforms such as limiting gerrymandering through things such as nonpartisan redistricting commissions, pursuing campaign finance reform, and implementing term limits.

From a macrolevel, the picture of Congress, though often clouded, seems to be seen as a net-positive. Even though Congress is one of the nation's most disliked institutions, and while many feel hostile toward Congress, one would be hard pressed to find Americans who think it ought to be disbanded. It is "Vote the bums out!" not "Abolish the bum institution!" So while Congress is far from perfect, it is still valuable.

To address the ills that plague the institution, there are many potential forms of medicine. Many of these seem to relate back to the importance of putting a focus on the dimensions of the legislation-making process where rivalry is present and where interests clash. For example, concerns about corruption within the system in many ways relate back to the notion that members of Congress, staffers, lobbyists, and other interests are competing for scarce resources, such as campaign donations, job opportunities, or clients. Again, this highlights the need for the Framework to better account for the role of rivalry. Of course, this is unlikely to be simple. The legislation community is complex and difficult to monitor, and legislation often results in unintended consequences that can also be difficult to detect and understand. Yet, it seems that if one were searching for the source of many of Congress's problems, the rock to look under would often be found where we find rivalry.

V. Conclusion and Implications

Is drafting legislation sort of like editing Wikipedia? At first blush the question may seem silly. The silliness of the question fades as one comes to recognize the characteristics the two share. Using the Framework developed by Madison, Frischmann, and Strandburg to evaluate cultural commons and knowledge commons, this chapter demonstrates that the Framework is robust enough to evaluate legislation making in the same way that one might evaluate things like Wikipedia, open source software, and patent pools. Legislation is a community-constructed resource, albeit an unusual one. Using the Framework in this context shows the robustness of the Framework. Much of what one would determine important about the workings of Congress finds itself highlighted as it is sifted through the Framework's lens. It causes us to focus upon much that is remarkable about Congress along with its vulnerabilities.

Still, looking at Congress through the Framework's lens also highlights several modifications that might be helpful in improving the Framework. The most important of these is the need for the lens to focus more on areas within these communities where rivalry and competition arises. As the Framework stands now, omitting rivalry causes us to overlook a great deal that not only explains the motivation of those within the legislation-making community but also the source of many of the problems that plague our legislative system.

References

Stephen Ansolabehere & James M. Snyder, *Soft Money, Hard Money, Strong Parties*, 100 COLUMBIA L. REV. 598 (2000).

CATHERINE DRINKER BOWEN, MIRACLE AT PHILADELPHIA: THE STORY OF THE CONSTITUTIONAL CONVENTION MAY TO SEPTEMBER 1787 (Little, Brown 1966).

Julie E. Cohen, *Copyright, Commodification, and Culture: Locating the Public Domain, in* THE FUTURE OF THE PUBLIC DOMAIN: IDENTIFYING THE COMMONS IN INFORMATION LAW 121 (Lucie Guibault & P. Bernt Hugenholtz eds., Kluwer Law International 2006).

W. Mark Crain & Timothy J. Muris, *Legislative Organization of Fiscal Policy*, 38 J. LAW & ECONOMICS 311 (1995).

Brigham Daniels & Blake Hudson, *Our Constitutional Commons*, 49 GEORGETOWN L. REV. ____ (forthcoming).

Alexander Hamilton, *Federalist No. 22*, in THE FEDERALIST PAPERS (Roy P. Fairchild ed., Garden City, NJ: Anchor Books 1966) (originally published 1787).

Charlotte Hess & Elinor Ostrom, *Introduction: An Overview of the Knowledge Commons*, in UNDERSTANDING KNOWLEDGE AS A COMMONS: FROM THEORY TO PRACTICE 3 (Charlotte Hess & Elinor Ostrom eds., MIT Press 2007).

Thomas Jefferson, *Letter to I. McPherson, 13 Aug. 1813*, in WRITINGS OF THOMAS JEFFERSON 13 (Andrew Linscomb ed., n.p.: 1904).

Mark A. Lemley & David W. O'Brien, *Encouraging Software Reuse*, 49 STANFORD L. REV. 255 (1997).

James Madison, *The Federalist No. 10*, in THE FEDERALIST PAPERS (Roy P. Fairchild ed., Garden City, NJ: Anchor Books 1966) (originally published 1787).

Michael J. Madison, Brett M. Frischmann, & Katherine J. Strandburg, *Constructing Commons in the Cultural Environment*, 95 CORNELL L. REV. 657 (2010).

Michael T. Maloney, Robert E. McCormick, & Robert D. Tollison, *Economic Regulation, Competitive Governments, and Specialized Resources*, 27 J. LAW & ECONOMICS 329 (1984).

ELINOR OSTROM, UNDERSTANDING INSTITUTIONAL DIVERSITY (Princeton University Press 2005).

Bruce Schreiner, *KFC Stores Colonel's Secret Recipe in New, Safer Vault*, HUFFINGTONPOST (Feb. 2, 2009), http://www.huffingtonpost.com/2009/02/10/kfc-stores-colonels-secre_n_165630.html.

Kenneth A. Shepsle, *Congress Is a "They," Not an "It": Legislative Intent as Oxymoron*, 12 INT'L REV. OF LAW & ECONOMICS 239 (1992).

Henry E. Smith, *Intellectual Property as Property: Delineating Entitlements in Information*, 116 YALE L.J. 116 1742 (2007).

SO I MARRIED AN AXE MURDERER (TriStar Pictures 1993).

Rick K. Wilson, *An Empirical Test of Preferences for the Political Pork Barrel: District Level Appropriations for River and Harbor Legislation, 1889–1913*, 30 AM. J. POLITICAL SCIENCE 729 (1986).

Christopher S. Yoo, *Copyright and Public Good Economics: A Misunderstood Relation*, 155 U. PENNSYLVANIA L. REV. 635 (2007).

15 Conclusion
Brett M. Frischmann, Michael J. Madison, and
Katherine J. Strandburg*

KNOWLEDGE AND INNOVATION, on the one hand, and openness and commons, on the other hand, have captured imaginations and investments in both public and private sectors over the last couple of decades, leading to considerable enthusiasm for *knowledge commons*. That enthusiasm has yet to translate into well-grounded principles for the design and deployment of commons governance in knowledge and innovation settings. Building a foundation for such principles is the primary goal of this book and of the research that we hope will come next. In this concluding chapter, we set the first part of that foundation in place by describing the substantive lessons and themes that we derive from the research shared here.

Understanding how knowledge commons are and should be organized and managed is critical both to the design of effective commons approaches and to effective innovation law and public policies. We suspect that knowledge commons governance can and does play a role at least as important as intellectual property law in overcoming the social

* Brett M. Frischmann is Professor of Law and Director of the Intellectual Property and Information Law Program at the Benjamin N. Cardozo School of Law, Yeshiva University, New York, New York, USA. Michael J. Madison is Professor of Law and Faculty Director of the Innovation Practice Institute at the University of Pittsburgh School of Law, Pittsburgh, Pennsylvania, USA. Katherine J. Strandburg is the Alfred B. Engelberg Professor of Law and a Faculty Director of the Engelberg Center for Innovation Law and Policy at the New York University School of Law, New York, New York, USA. Each is also a member of the Affiliated Faculty of the Vincent and Elinor Ostrom Workshop in Political Theory and Policy Analysis.

dilemmas that can impede innovation, creative work, and the productive development, distribution, and uses of knowledge. The primary challenge to proving, disproving, or refining that hypothesis is the paucity of systematic empirical work directed to it. What factors contribute to knowledge commons durability and effectiveness?

Answering that question requires detailed analysis and comparison of many different knowledge commons cases. To derive general insights from those cases, the empirical approach must balance structured inquiry with interpretive flexibility. The framework approach applied in this book recognizes the complexity of the interplay among the characteristics of particular resources, various communities and groups, and the social, political, economic, and institutional attributes of governance. It helps researchers to walk the difficult line between overly simplistic theoretical models and a fragmented collection of diverse, one-off studies. It imposes methodological structure and produces findings that can be used in conjunction with and interpreted using theoretical perspectives from a variety of disciplines, including law, economics, sociology, political science, and history.

As discussed in detail in Chapter 1, we pursue this balance by adapting the Institutional Analysis and Development (IAD) research framework, which was used originally to structure case studies of natural resource commons (Ostrom 2005). The IAD framework ensures that each study collects information about a common set of variables, including the biophysical characteristics of the resources involved, the attributes and roles of participants, and the effective "rules-in-use" of the commons regime. The IAD framework permitted data from a large number of case studies to be aggregated systematically and used to derive generally applicable "design principles" for natural resource commons governance.

Our knowledge commons case study framework accounts for significant differences between the natural resource and knowledge contexts. The resources are different, and the obstacles that must be overcome to produce sustainable sharing are different. Knowledge commons generally manage production and integration of new knowledge in addition to managing the use of existing knowledge resources. As a result, knowledge commons address a more varied array of social dilemmas than natural resource commons do. Participation in a knowledge commons may be driven by a variety of self-interested, altruistic, personal, and social motivations. Even the legal delineation of intellectual and knowledge resources is complex. For example, copyright law's definition of what constitutes the "expression" in the copyrightable work governed by open source software licenses is not straightforward. Knowledge commons may confront complicated resource boundary and corresponding resource management issues with respect to what resources are governed by formal legal rights and what resources are part of the public domain.

Chapter 1 (building on Madison, Frischmann, & Strandburg 2010) analyzes these and other differences and explains why they require a framework specifically tailored to knowledge commons. Developing an effective research framework for knowledge commons case studies is, like knowledge governance itself, an unavoidably iterative process. Though structured methodology is crucial to cross-case-study comparison, it is also important, particularly at this early stage of knowledge commons study, to adapt and revise the framework in response to experience in applying it to a variety of cases.

This book is an early step toward a systematic, framework-driven study of knowledge commons governance. It is much too early to derive design principles from the eleven cases presented here or to suggest general lessons about commons governance. More study is needed. These cases illustrate the potential of the structured case study approach. They also suggest refinements and improvements to the research framework. Despite the diversity of the cases, we identify several key themes common to many of them. Readers may observe different themes. As further studies accumulate, we hope that these observations will develop into more specific hypotheses and, eventually, into useful principles.

I. Emerging Themes

I. KNOWLEDGE COMMONS MAY CONFRONT DIVERSE OBSTACLES OR SOCIAL DILEMMAS, MANY OF WHICH ARE NOT WELL DESCRIBED OR REDUCIBLE TO THE SIMPLE FREE RIDER DILEMMA

Probing the "goals and objectives" of a commons often began with a general notion of cooperation to solve some generic collective action problem, but closer analysis of relevant obstacles tended to reveal multiple dilemmas that shaped action arenas and created demand for governance institutions. Almost all of the knowledge commons described in this book responded to needs both to manage existing knowledge resources and to sustain production of and contribution to a shared knowledge pool. But to stop there would be to miss the forest (or worse, the complex ecosystem) for the trees. Most of the case studies faced multiple additional social dilemmas, including:

- *Dilemmas attributable to the nature of the research and/or the research problem.* In the Urea Cycle Disorders Consortium (UCDC) case study, Strandburg, Frischmann, and Cui (Chapter 5) concluded that special problems associated with rare diseases (distributed population of patients and researchers; small numbers and the need for shared protocols; scarce inputs such as funding, time, and credit; and recruiting researchers; among others) played a more important role in shaping action arenas and corresponding governance institutions than the more basic public goods framing of "sharing knowledge" would suggest. Similarly, in the case of Galaxy Zoo, Madison (Chapter 6) noted that special problems associated with processing massive amounts of astronomical data and the fact that classifying galaxies was difficult for computers but relatively easy for human beings played a more important role in shaping action arenas and corresponding governance institutions than the public good nature of the classifications or the database of classifications.

- *Dilemmas arising from the interdependence among different constituencies of the knowledge commons.* For example, Strandburg, Frischmann, and Cui (Chapter 5) demonstrated special problems associated with managing multiple communities in connection with the UCDC. Researchers, healthcare professionals, patients and families, government officials, and pharmaceutical companies brought different backgrounds, capacities, expectations, and interests to the collaboration, and as a result, successful cooperation depended, among other things, on governance institutions that enabled trust to be built and maintained. As Contreras (Chapter 4) described, sustaining the genomic data commons depends significantly on reconciling the (sometimes conflicting) interests of multiple stakeholders, including government officials (National Institutes of Health [NIH]), funders, data generators, data users, scientific leaders, data intermediaries, data subjects, and the public.

- *Dilemmas arising from the need to manage rivalrous resources that are necessary inputs into production and use of the shared knowledge resources.* For example, in the UCDC case study, Strandburg, Frischmann, and Cui (Chapter 5) identified various rivalrous resources that gave rise to governance challenges, including funding; attention, time, and labor; and attribution and authorship credit. Daniels (Chapter 14) emphasized throughout his study of Congress the ways in which management of rivalrous resources was critical to the functioning of the commons. He noted that litigation over the meaning of laws created by Congress involved rivalry of interests that could, in a sense, render the law rivalrous. He made a similar argument in discussing the goals and objectives of those involved in the legislative process, suggesting again that both rivalry among interests and competition over rivalrous resources necessary for law making were driving factors.

- *Dilemmas arising from (or mitigated by) the broader systems within which a knowledge commons is nested.* Piper (Chapter 12) provided a detailed account of war as the driving force behind various "commons-based IP approaches" in Canada and the United States. War shaped political, cultural, and economic systems more broadly—for example, by encouraging nationalism and collectivism—and at the same time the practical realities of war set conditions in which sharing various knowledge resources was a necessity or, at least, was perceived to be necessary. " 'Battlefield techniques,' such as medical methods, remain in a commons, in part because of the exigencies of their creation, but also because of the necessity that they be shared in the heat of battle." Free rider and related dilemmas faded in importance, overshadowed by the demands of war. As Piper put it, "Patents had the potential to disrupt chains of command, discipline and order through an external system of reward and remuneration," Commons-based approaches overcame that dilemma.

2. COMPLEX RELATIONSHIPS OFTEN EXIST BETWEEN KNOWLEDGE COMMONS AND THE SYSTEMS WITHIN WHICH THEY OPERATE AND/ OR ARE NESTED

Chapter 1's outline of the framework anticipated the importance of describing the background environments that shape the knowledge commons under study. The framework suggested a primary focus on the background legal rights associated with commons resources. We did not anticipate fully how broader background contexts would influence the shape of commons governance and/or interact with other framework inquiries. In some cases, the background contexts seemed to act as external constraints much as the biophysical characteristics of the resource do in the natural resource context. In others, background contexts shaped goals and objectives, participants' roles, and action arenas in much more dynamic ways. For example:

- Strandburg, Frischmann, and Cui (Chapter 5) described the UCDC as broadly situated within a context of relatively inflexible "external" constraints consisting of "the biological realities of urea cycle disorders, the cultural contexts of medicine and academic research and the more specific contexts of rare disease research and NIH research funding." The consortium also had a complex relationship with the Rare Disease Clinical Research Network program, since UCDC researchers had important input into the design of that program, within which the UCDC was nested.
- Contreras (Chapter 4) discussed the complex relationships between the NIH and data intermediaries situated between science and industry in the context of the Human Genome Project (HGP). He emphasized how the background context and norms of the scientific community strongly influenced the governance of the HGP and the genomic data commons that have since emerged.
- Shah and Mody (Chapter 9) described the critical and interactive role that knowledge commons play in determining the formation and direction of new industries and in enabling an environment for and complementing market-based entrepreneurship.
- Murray (Chapter 11) described mid-nineteenth-century journalism as a constructed knowledge commons that was part of, rather than antithetical to or subversive of, the market. According to Murray, "Behaviors and priorities associated with commercial markets were actually imbricated with commons."
- Daniels (Chapter 14), who found our call for a discussion of the relevant background environment "very difficult" in his study of Congress as a knowledge commons, explained how Congress is situated within a political environment with significant rivalries and adjacent to a judicial system within which litigation tested and applied the legislation (outputs) from Congress. He also situated Congress within our constitutional framework and historical tradition.

- Piper (Chapter 12) explored the complex relationships between the military, industry, and scientific communities and the role of the NRC technology transfer operations in mediating those relationships and communities.
- Madison (Chapter 6) described Galaxy Zoo as a commons that both extended the norms of the astronomical research community and explicated, drew upon, and reproduced them.

3. KNOWLEDGE COMMONS OFTEN DEPEND ON SHARED INFRASTRUCTURE

Shared infrastructure often appeared to be central to the success of the knowledge commons studied here. In some cases, technical infrastructure appeared to substitute for formal rule-based governance and discipline, easing, though perhaps also obfuscating, decision-making processes.

- Fuster Morell (Chapter 8), in her study of online creation communities, provided the most extensive analysis of the role of shared infrastructure. She suggested that governance of online creation communities can be understood only by paying attention to the infrastructure for collective action. "Infrastructure provision involves [both] the provision of the platform of participation and…control over [various governance institutions]." Based on an empirical study of fifty online creation communities, she reported a correlation between community involvement in infrastructure provision and "a community having a decision-making mechanism, a role in conflict resolution at the community level, deciding its formal rules, a free license that also grants that the community owns the common-pool resource, and net-enabler conditions (including the right to fork)." Critically, Morell's study showed how ownership and/or control of the infrastructure that supports online creation communities (OCCs) may have significant impact on knowledge commons governance.
- Strandburg, Frischmann, and Cui (Chapter 5) emphasized the importance of the Data Management Coordination Center (DMCC) and various research and data management protocols in facilitating knowledge sharing among different clinical research sites. These shared infrastructures lower the costs of participation, collaboration, and research. In addition, the longitudinal study at the heart of the UCDC research agenda serves as a shared infrastructure that forms the community and brings members together and at the same time serves as a platform for other clinical research projects and activities outside of the consortia, including, for example, drug development by pharmaceutical companies.
- Madison (Chapter 6) described the importance of the design of the online interface and access to source image data in making it possible for non-scientists to participate in scientific research and in facilitating the formation of the Galaxy Zoo community. The Galaxy Zoo website, the database of galaxy classifications submitted as "votes" by volunteer classifiers and further analyzed by professional

astronomers, and the Galaxy Zoo forum that sprang up to facilitate supplemental dialogue within the Galaxy Zoo community are three related levels of technical infrastructure that enable cooperation within the volunteer community, within the professional astronomer community, and within the broader group that included both professionals and volunteers.

- Schweik (Chapter 7) noted that the project hosting site, SourceForge.net, provides a free web-based platform that allows open source software developers to store and manage their code and projects. Widely known in the software field, the site also serves as a hub where users and programmers can find open source software projects. Schweik & English (2012: 130–32) explain further how SourceForge serves as an important shared infrastructure for hundreds of thousands of open source projects. Schweik also noted that rules coded into the online systems used for collaboration often served a governance role.

- Meyer (Chapter 10), in his study of the development of the airplane, explained how a few central figures used the production of infrastructure in the form of bibliographies to turn a globally dispersed population of aviation enthusiasts into a knowledge-sharing community.

- Contreras (Chapter 4) noted the importance of various types of shared infrastructure in sustaining the genomic commons, including most importantly scientific journals and genomic databases. He also identified an important social dilemma in the provision of database infrastructure, given that work in producing and maintaining databases does not receive the traditional reputational rewards associated with scientific publication.

4. INFORMAL GOVERNANCE INSTITUTIONS, AND ESPECIALLY TRUSTED LEADERSHIP, OFTEN PLAY KEY ROLES IN KNOWLEDGE COMMONS GOVERNANCE

Informal governance, especially involving trusted leaders or decision makers, complemented and at times substituted for formal institutions in many of the cases studied here. Reliance on informal governance often seemed to grow out of relationships or norms predating the emergence of commons governance. In some cases, governance evolved toward greater formality over time. Future work should pay particular attention to the dynamic interactions between informal and formal governance institutions.

- Strandburg, Frischmann, and Cui (Chapter 5) showed that despite an array of formal governance mechanisms "on the books," the UCDC appeared to rely heavily in practice on informal governance and trusted leadership. This pattern may be a remnant of the informal collaboration among a small, close-knit community that preceded the UCDC and its formal governance regime. It also may be a function of the needs of the communities involved, including the need to accommodate different constituencies as well as the need to remain inclusive to facilitate growth. The

NIH grant process also vests ultimate responsibility for administering the consortium grant in a small group of consortium principal investigators, which may bolster the authority of those individuals, especially if they are widely respected and trusted.

- Contreras (Chapter 4) noted that in the case of the genome commons, "the formal rules established at the outset of the HGP were strongly influenced by the norms of the scientific community at the time." He traced the impact of those norms as the formal governance regimes evolved. Over time, as the communities have grown and as intellectual property rights and commercial motivations have taken on greater importance, various genomic commons projects have developed complex systems of formal rules dealing with issues such as the timing of data contribution, data use rights, and publication credit.

- Schweik (Chapter 7) also found significant reliance on informal governance (often, social norms) and trusted leaders for open source projects. He noted that significant effort on behalf of the project leader was among the most important determinants of a project's success and that most of the projects he studied (some of which were quite small) appeared to have a "benevolent dictator" model of leadership. Governance of these projects relied primarily on "very informal" social norms or on rules that were coded into the online collaborative systems used to coordinate work. Formal governance in the traditional sense was viewed negatively, though Schweik reported "some indications—as we expected—that institutions evolve and become more formalized as projects grow in numbers of developers."

- Madison (Chapter 6) described the almost-total reliance on informal governance norms within Galaxy Zoo, including substantial deference to strong informal and entrepreneurial leadership by the professional astronomers who launched the project and heavy reliance on informal social norms to moderate activity within the large community of volunteers. Even production of scholarly papers based on the Galaxy Zoo classification data was influenced heavily by a collaborative attribution norm that emerged informally within the project.

5. COMMONS GOVERNANCE OFTEN EVOLVES OVER TIME, AND COMMONS SEEMS TO PLAY AN ESPECIALLY IMPORTANT ROLE IN THE EARLY STAGES OF SOME INDUSTRIES

Several cases illustrated the proposition that commons governance may evolve as the number of participants grows or as innovation affects the nature of the shared knowledge or the balance between competition and cooperation within the group. For example:

- Schweik (Chapter 7) posed the following questions: "In moving toward a systematic study of these larger [open source] projects, key questions that we must ask are: [1] How do we systematically document the institutional designs of larger collaborations or collaborations between organizations? and, [2] How do we study the evolution of open source-like commons systematically?"

- Contreras (Chapter 4) framed the action arena for the genome commons study in terms of the *evolution of rules and norms*. He identified "a feedback loop [], in which policy-level decisions affect interactions within the action arena and cause participants to seek policy-level changes in subsequent iterations of policy making. These patterns emerge in the successive genomics projects that followed the HGP, whether publicly or privately funded."
- Murray (Chapter 11) described the evolution of mid-nineteenth-century journalism, based largely on informal commons governance through professional norms among newspaper editors, to mid-twentieth-century journalism based on more formal commons governance through a news agency, the Associated Press.
- Meyer (Chapter 10), in his study of the invention of the airplane, observed an evolution in three stages involving different social dilemmas: (1) an early period in which the creation of knowledge was motivated almost entirely intrinsically and the social dilemmas revolved around providing infrastructure for sharing that knowledge; (2) a period after successful invention in which commercial competition essentially destroyed the commons for knowledge about building airplanes, while a commons of flying practice remained intact in flying clubs; and (3) a wartime period during which sharing was effectuated through a government-facilitated industrial patent pool.
- Shah and Mody (Chapter 9) described the various paths along which user innovation may evolve into entrepreneurship, each involving different knowledge sharing structures.

6. KNOWLEDGE COMMONS GOVERNANCE OFTEN DOES NOT DEPEND ON ONE STRONG TYPE OR SOURCE OF INDIVIDUAL MOTIVATION FOR COOPERATION

Knowledge commons entail cooperation in the building, sharing, and preservation of knowledge resources, but the reasons individuals cooperated in particular knowledge commons varied. Not only did different individuals cooperate for different reasons, but sometimes a single individual had multiple motivations for cooperating, partly intrinsic and partly social. Participants often had both competitive and cooperative motives and the balance between the two often varied between individuals or changed over time. Motivations often varied according to participants' roles as creators, maintainers, and/or users of shared knowledge resources. Yet the overall contrast to the traditional free rider story, in which individuals are assumed to compete for resources as a result of self-interest, is striking. This variety of motives is partially responsible for the variety of social dilemmas that arise in governing knowledge commons. For example:

- Intrinsic, noncompetitive motivations for creating and sharing knowledge were common. According to Strandburg, Frischmann, and Cui (Chapter 5), UCDC researchers were motivated by their commitment to patient care (most were pediatricians) and their commitment to the close-knit researcher community. Contreras (Chapter 4) pointed out that genomic researchers were driven by their interest in the science. Fagundes (Chapter 13) grounded his case study of roller derby on this observation that derby participants are motivated by their love of the sport. Madison (Chapter 6) concluded that Galaxy Zoo volunteers were motivated by their desire to contribute to scientific progress and their interest in astronomy. Meyer (Chapter 10) showed that early aviation enthusiasts were motivated entirely by their fascination with the dream of flight.

- The opportunity and ability to use shared knowledge was frequently a motivation for those who created and contributed knowledge to a commons. Schweik (Chapter 7) noted that use was a major motivation for open source software programmers. Both Madison (Chapter 6) and Contreras (Chapter 4) showed that scientific researchers employ shared knowledge resources in their own research. Norms among nineteenth-century newspaper editors described by Murray (Chapter 11) permitted widespread copying of news, essentially creating a pool of information that each paper could use in producing its own local paper. Use was obviously an extremely important motivation in the wartime innovation commons described by Piper (Chapter 12).

- Shah and Mody (Chapter 9) suggested that the motives of user innovators may change over time. Where knowledge sharing may be motivated for an initial period by a desire to use pooled improvements and modifications, user innovators may turn to entrepreneurship (and may then limit knowledge sharing) when participation in the community becomes less satisfying for some reason, when there is an opportunity to turn a hobby into a career or when a market opens up outside of the dedicated user community.

- Intrinsic motivations to pool knowledge resources often coexisted with competitive motivations, raising challenges for commons governance. According to Strandburg, Frischmann, and Cui (Chapter 5) and Contreras (Chapter 4), rare disease and genomics researchers balance their intrinsic motivations to cooperate with their desire to succeed as academic researchers (measured in part by securing funding and publications). Madison (Chapter 6) detected a related balance among Galaxy Zoo researchers, who delayed publication of the Galaxy Zoo classification data until initial academic papers were published. Fagundes (Chapter 13) acknowledged that roller derby participants compete in the rink while cooperating in many other respects. Meyer (Chapter 10) noted that cooperation among aviation enthusiasts fell victim to commercial competition once a practical airplane was invented. Competition between newspapers grew heavier in the balance as communication became faster and circulation areas grew, yet Murray (Chapter 11) observed that sharing practices have reemerged in different form in the blogosphere.

II. Reflections on the Framework

The case studies in this volume were the first to employ the modified IAD framework described in Chapter 1. Experience with these case studies not only confirms the usefulness of the framework approach but also suggests additional nuances and ways to refine and improve it.

1. APPLYING THE FRAMEWORK TO SOME INSTITUTIONS THAT ARE NOT CORE EXAMPLES OF "KNOWLEDGE COMMONS"

The case studies presented here support our intuition that researchers should cast a wide net in defining proper subjects for study. Because the framework is primarily methodological rather than normative, it proved useful in guiding study of a broad range of cases, some that were closer to what many researchers would identify as "core" or "typical" institutionalized knowledge sharing regimes (research consortia, OCCs) and others that may seem, at first glance, to be unusual subjects for a study of knowledge commons (Congress, roller derby). We continue to believe that a broad invitation is warranted. Collecting data about a wide range of what Fagundes called "commonsy" institutions will help in eventually determining the properties that distinguish knowledge commons from other governance regimes, and that distinguish successful, effective commons regimes from less effective or unsuccessful regimes.

2. TAKING A BROAD APPROACH TO IDENTIFYING RELEVANT RESOURCES AND PARTICIPANTS

The framework helps researchers to avoid tunnel vision in identifying relevant resources and participants merely by prompting researchers to ask explicitly "What are the resources?" "Who are the participants?" Several case studies reported on a broader range of resources and participants than one might associate with a typical (or stereotypical) "knowledge commons":

- Strandburg, Frischmann, and Cui (Chapter 5) reported on over a dozen different types of resources shared within the UCDC community (and outside of the community) and recognized by the community members as relevant and important. They also reported on the importance of many different actors, ranging from principal investigators, researchers, and site coordinators to pediatricians, neuropsychologists, dieticians, and other healthcare professionals to NIH officials to pharmaceutical companies to patients, families, and the patient advocacy group.
- Contreras (Chapter 4) and Van Overwalle (Chapter 4B) discussed the many different types of data captured by the phrase "genomic data." Specifically, Van

Overwalle noted that "'genomic data' may refer to raw DNA sequence data (encompassing genomic sequences of individual humans, micro-organisms residing within the human body, and other organisms), to physiological data (e.g., data relating to the association between particular genetic markers and disease risk) and to phenotypic data (including elements such as de-identified subject age, ethnicity, weight, demographics, exposure, disease state, and behavioral factors)." Contreras reported that the "principal stakeholder communities" include funding agencies, data generators, data users, data intermediaries, data subjects and the public. Van Overwalle usefully differentiated among participants, "distinguish[ing] between the community per se which actually produces and shares the commons (including the data generators, data users, and data intermediaries) and the larger community, or social environment, in which the community per se is nested and which facilitates and empowers the construction of the commons. This social environment includes funding agencies and members of the public, especially as represented by patient advocacy and disease interest groups."

- Daniels's study of Congress as commons (Chapter 14) showed how legislators depend heavily on a legislative knowledge commons that involves staffers, technical experts, news media, other branches of government, and industry/lobbyists. Daniels emphasized the importance of identifying the rivalrous resources that were also relevant to the knowledge commons.

- Fagundes (Chapter 13) identified a variety of shared resources in roller derby, a counterintuitive example of knowledge commons. Shared resources include knowledge about the roller derby sport ranging from skating skills and rules to techniques for recruiting members and information about roller derby's countercultural social milieu. He also identified participant roles that would not spring immediately to mind, including trainers, referees, record keepers, and other volunteer non-skaters whose involvement brings them within the community.

3. ACCOUNTING MORE EXPLICITLY FOR EVOLUTION OF KNOWLEDGE COMMONS GOVERNANCE OVER TIME

As discussed in Chapter 1 and illustrated in Figure 1.2, we expected knowledge commons to change over time as the exogenous variables (resources, communities, rule-in-use) evolve through the decisions and actions of actors in the various action arenas. We also noted the importance of narrative and history in determining knowledge commons governance, features that are inevitably dynamic, at least to a degree. We did not anticipate fully how dramatically the character and stability of some knowledge commons would be affected by changing interactions with the background environment or changes in the knowledge resources themselves. The important changes over time observed in some of the case studies in this volume raise a broader methodological issue that remains to be addressed: *how to study the evolution of knowledge commons*. Schweik (Chapter 7) posed the following questions: "In moving toward a systematic study of these larger [open source] projects, key questions that we must ask are: [1] How do we systematically document the institutional designs of larger collaborations or collaborations between organizations? and, [2] How do we study the evolution of open source-like commons systematically?"

4. BEGINNING WITH GOALS AND OBJECTIVES AND IDENTIFYING ACTION ARENAS

Our initial discussion of the knowledge commons research framework did not fully anticipate the potential complexity in defining action arenas for knowledge commons. In the natural resource context, the primary operational action arena for a commons regime generally is the use of a specified natural resource by a community defined by geographic proximity. (Other action arenas operate at a rule-making or governance level.) Because knowledge resources are intangible and often are created by a self-selected group of commons participants, knowledge commons often form around particular goals and objectives rather than around preexisting resources tied to particular communities or particular geographies. When that is the case, there may be several primary action arenas at the operational level, and the most important action arenas may not be immediately evident at the outset of research.

To analyze a knowledge commons regime it may be most sound analytically to begin with goals and objectives, rather than resources, then to identify action arenas related to those goals and objectives, and then to identify resources, participants, rules, and so forth associated with each action arena. In practice, use of the framework is likely to be an iterative process, in which collecting data about particular knowledge resources may lead to the identification of additional goals and objectives, which may lead to the identification of additional participants or additional shared resources and so on. The UCDC case study (Chapter 5) proceeded in just this way, with study focused initially on the pooling of medical knowledge among researchers and later broadening to identify and study goals and objectives such as creating a pool of research subjects and patient data and associated action arenas such as the longitudinal study. The Galaxy Zoo case study (Chapter 6) likewise focused initially on the pooling of galaxy classifications and later broadened to examine related goals, including the production of publishable research and creation and maintenance of the volunteer forum and teaching resources for schoolteachers. The expanded scope of the inquiry and prioritizing goals and objectives helped to sharpen the contrast between Galaxy Zoo as knowledge commons and the nominally similar Nearby Supernova Factory, which was characterized instead as a kind of hierarchical firm.

The framework was critically important in ferreting out the various action arenas and resources involved in the UCDC study and in Galaxy Zoo. But we now believe that our initial conception of the framework did not put sufficient emphasis on the identification of action arenas using an iterative approach to goals and objectives, resources, and participants. This point is reflected, in part, in a question about the relationship between action arenas and goals and objectives that we added to the description of the framework in the box, "Knowledge Commons Framework and Representative Research Questions," in Chapter 1.

5. IDENTIFYING SOCIAL DILEMMAS

As we have already discussed, knowledge commons governance presents a wide variety of social dilemmas in addition to the traditional free rider problem. To analyze an action arena and understand its rules-in-use, it is helpful to identify the social dilemmas faced by participants. We have added the identification of relevant dilemmas to the set of questions under "Goals and Objectives" in the framework as described in the box, "Knowledge Commons Framework and Representative Research Questions," in Chapter 1. To understand the social dilemmas faced by a group of commons participants, it is also useful to study their motivations, especially since a theme common to the case studies presented here is diversity of participant motivation.

6. IDENTIFYING SHARED INFRASTRUCTURE

Experience with the case studies in this volume suggests that shared infrastructure may be particularly important for constructing, maintaining, and governing knowledge commons. We suggest that future case studies focus specifically on identifying infrastructural resources created or used by the commons. In some cases, such as open source software, it will be important to include infrastructural constraints in the analysis of an action arena's "rules-in-use" in order to get a complete picture of commons governance. These points are reflected in questions about infrastructure added to the framework as described in the box, "Knowledge Commons Framework and Representative Research Questions," in Chapter 1.

7. IDENTIFYING BOTH NONRIVALROUS AND RIVALROUS RESOURCES

Although the study of knowledge commons focuses on the sharing of intangible, nonrivalrous resources, it is important to identify any rivalrous resources that are important to a particular action arena. As noted above, and emphasized by Daniels (Chapter 14), social dilemmas for knowledge commons governance can and do arise from competition or conflict over the allocation of nonrivalrous resources. We now emphasize the importance of identifying both rival and nonrival resources in the representative research questions in the box, "Knowledge Commons Framework and Representative Research Questions," in Chapter 1.

8. IDENTIFYING DILEMMAS AND ACTION ARENAS ASSOCIATED WITH BOUNDARY MANAGEMENT

As emphasized in Chapter 1, knowledge commons may have different types and degrees of "openness." In particular, because knowledge resources are nonrivalrous, knowledge commons are likely to have to deal with multiple constituencies, including as users, creators, managers, or curators, and, in cases such as UCDC, subjects of the knowledge resources. These different constituencies may make different and sometimes conflicting demands on commons resources. It is important when identifying goals and objectives and action arenas to be aware of the possibility that important action arenas may be devoted to managing boundary conflicts among different participants. This point is now addressed by the questions about goals and objectives and governance in the box, "Knowledge Commons Framework and Representative Research Questions," in Chapter 1.

III. Looking Ahead

In her landmark book, *Governing the Commons,* Elinor Ostrom (1990) analyzed eighty-six case studies of natural resource commons from different sectors and geographic locations. She reported on decades of systematic scientific research that included empirical investigation and the development and testing of theories and models and identified eight design principles for stable commons management of natural resources. Ostrom inspired us, as she did thousands of others. Our book is intended as a tribute to hers. But ours is not the culmination of thirty years of research; rather it is a first step on what we hope will be a long, enlightening path.

We envision a three-part knowledge commons research agenda:

- Theoretical and empirical work using case study and other approaches focusing on various dimensions of knowledge commons and the social dilemmas confronting them (e.g., free-ridership, motivations and incentives, norms of behavior, and the design and evolution of governance).
- Building a library of knowledge commons case studies and corresponding structured database of case study information to enable identification and analysis of commonalities and differences among knowledge commons, to inform both theory and practice, and generally to support further qualitative and quantitative comparative research.
- Growing a collaborative research network of scholars from a variety of relevant disciplines to investigate the functionality and dynamics of knowledge commons and create infrastructure to facilitate its growth.[1]

The last part of the agenda is crucial. Serious progress on an empirically-based understanding of knowledge commons will require shared effort. We hope that others will

---

[1] An example of the type of long-term collaborative research network we envision is the International Forest Resources and Institutions network (http://www.ifriresearch.net/).

adopt and apply the modified IAD framework and help to refine it further. We are working to provide infrastructure for that effort, in the form of conferences, workshops, a website containing links to various useful resources, and, eventually a case study database. We also recognize, as did Ostrom herself, that there are no methodological panaceas and anticipate cooperating and collaborating with researchers taking other approaches to knowledge commons research. Accordingly, we end this book by extending an invitation to future collaborators and fellow travelers to get in touch with comments, questions, critiques, and results of your own research. Help us to create a knowledge commons for the study of knowledge commons!

References

Michael J. Madison, Brett M. Frischmann, & Katherine J. Strandburg, *Constructing Commons in the Cultural Environment*, 95 CORNELL L. REV. 657 (2010).

ELINOR OSTROM, GOVERNING THE COMMONS: THE EVOLUTION OF INSTITUTIONS FOR COLLECTIVE ACTION (Cambridge University Press 1990).

ELINOR OSTROM, UNDERSTANDING INSTITUTIONAL DIVERSITY (Princeton University Press 2005).

CHARLES M. SCHWEIK & ROBERT C. ENGLISH, INTERNET SUCCESS: A STUDY OF OPEN-SOURCE SOFTWARE COMMONS (MIT Press 2012).

Index

mission, 289
motives of Wikipedians, 436, 437, 458
output of, 36
public domain and, 93
software license, 240–41, 243
Wilson, James, 171*n*12
Windsurfer, 322–23, 323
Women's Flat Track Derby Association
(WFTDA), 425–26
Workshop in Political Theory and Policy, 50–51,
51*n*12, 63

World War I, airplane patents during, 3, 32
Wright airplane patents, 348, 359–60, 361
Wright brothers, 347, 349, 353, 353–54, 355,
356–57, 359–60
Wright Company, 3, 396
Wright-Martin Company, 361

Yahoo!, 299, 300, 308

Zooniverse, 210, 210*n*1, 214, 214*nn*6–7, 221